THE
SALE OF GOODS

This book is due for return not later than the
last date stamped below, unless recalled sooner.

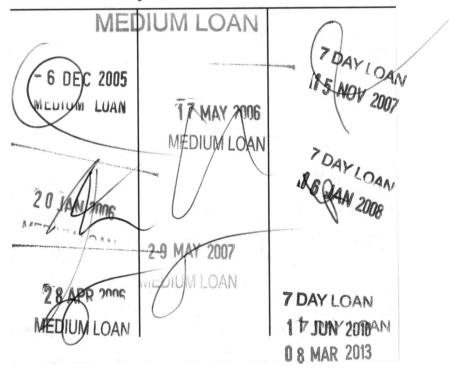

PEARSON
Education

We work with leading authors to develop the strongest
educational materials in law, bringing cutting-edge thinking
and best learning practice to a global market.

Under a range of well-known imprints, including
Longman, we craft high quality print and electronic publications
which help readers to understand and apply their content,
whether studying or at work.

To find out more about the complete range of our
publishing, please visit us on the World Wide Web at:

www.pearsoned.co.uk

THE
SALE OF GOODS

P S Atiyah QC, DCL, FBA

of the Inner Temple, Barrister
Formerly Professor of English Law,
University of Oxford

ELEVENTH EDITION

John N Adams LLB

of the Inner Temple, Barrister
Professor of Intellectual Property,
University of Sheffield

With sections on Scots law by
Hector MacQueen LLB, PHD, FRSE

Professor of Private Law
University of Edinburgh

PEARSON
Longman

Harlow, England • London • New York • Boston • San Francisco • Toronto
Sydney • Tokyo • Singapore • Hong Kong • Seoul • Taipei • New Delhi
Cape Town • Madrid • Mexico City • Amsterdam • Munich • Paris • Milan

Pearson Education Limited
Edinburgh Gate
Harlow
Essex CM20 2JE
England

and Associated Companies throughout the world

Visit us on the World Wide Web at:
www.pearsoned.co.uk

First published under the Pitman imprint in Great Britain in 1957
Second edition published in 1963
Third edition published in 1968
Fourth edition published in 1971
Fifth edition published in 1975
Sixth edition published in 1980
Seventh edition published in 1985
Eighth edition published in 1990
Ninth edition published in 1995
Tenth edition published in 2001
Eleventh edition published in 2005

ISBN 0582 894085

British Library Cataloguing-in-Publication Data
A catalogue record for this book is available from the British Library

Library of Congress Cataloging-in-Publication Data
Atiyah, P. S.
   Sale of goods / P. S. Atiyah. — 11th ed. / John N. Adams; with sections on Scottish
law by Hector MacQueen.
      p. cm.
   Includes bibiographical references and index.
   ISBN 0-582-89408-5 (alk. paper)
   1. Sales—England. 2. Sales—Wales. 3. Sales—Scotland. I. Adams, J. N. II.
MacQueen, Hector L. III. Title.
KD1650.A96 2005
346.4007'2—dc22

10 9 8 7 6 5 4 3 2 1
09 08 07 06 05

Typeset in 10/12 pt, Sabon, Roman by 69
Printed in Great Britain by Henry Ling Ltd.,
at the Dorset Press, Dorchester, Dorset

The publisher's policy is to use paper manufactured from sustainable forests.

CONTENTS

Part I
NATURE AND FORMATION OF THE CONTRACT OF SALE

Part II
THE DUTIES OF THE SELLER

Part V
EXPORT SALES

Part VI
THE REMEDIES OF THE SELLER

Part VII
THE REMEDIES OF THE BUYER

PREFACE TO THE ELEVENTH EDITION

The focus of this book is the domestic law of sale of goods. For many years this largely involved an examination of the Sale of Goods Act 1893, a statute which with minor variations was copied around the common law world, so that a great deal of cross-fertilization between jurisdictions took place. This was even true of the United States, where a substantially re-written version of the Act, Article 2 of the Uniform Commercial Code, was generally adopted by state legislatures after the Second World War in place of a model law which closely followed the 1893 Act. It is now becoming apparent, however, that domestic law is drifting away from the family to which it gave birth. One reason for this is the increasing impact of European legislation, but another is that some domestic legislation, notably the Sale and Supply of Goods Act 1994, has pushed in the same direction. The ninth edition of this book dealt with the vacuous changes to the quality warranties made by this Act, but now further modification of these may be necessitated by the Sale of Consumer Goods and Associated Guarantees Directive, which in the name of consumer protection perversely adopts a version of the Vienna Convention on international sales – a Convention drafted to deal with sales between businesses. This Directive is now implemented by the Sale and Supply of Goods to Consumers Regulations 2002. This topic has now grown to the extent that it has been felt necessary to insert a new chapter dealing with it (Chapter 16).

Not only are rifts appearing at an international level, the homogeneity of the law in this area within the United Kingdom is beginning to break up. There were features of the original Act which did not sit comfortably with Scots law. These disjunctures have largely been attended to, and there are now sufficiently significant differences between the law of England and Wales, and Scotland to justify Scots law receiving specific attention from a Scottish lawyer. I am again grateful to Professor Hector MacQueen for agreeing to revise the relevant sections.

A further development is increasingly apparent: the 1893 Act was largely a codification of decisions in cases between merchants. Although the present legislation, with its various amendments, is still recognizably a descendant of that Act, as I suggested in the ninth edition, it is becoming increasingly apparent that the domestic law of sales is developing along two routes, consumer law and mercantile law. This again is the result both of domestic and European legislation, but it is also a result of the way in which the courts now tend to approach the legislation. It could well be that in the next edition a fairly radical departure from the present scheme of the book will be required.

Another development in the consumer law area is the impact of the Civil Procedure Rules 1998. If these achieve their objective of speeding up and lowering the costs of litigation (and like previous civil procedure reforms going as far back as the Hilary Rules of 1834 it is by no means clear that they have), there is likely to be a significant reduction in the already small number of decisions reported in consumer cases. This trend is likely to be furthered by the cutting back of legal aid. If this is the effect, the result will be that we will have to learn to live with unclear legislative provisions, and perhaps adopt a more Continental 'teleological' approach to our legislation.

Against these tendencies must be set a phenomenon which has the potential to create international homogeneity of the law of sales. This is the growth of e-commerce. The chapter dealing with this topic which was added to the last edition has been extensively revised. It will be apparent from that chapter that the challenges thrown up by this development are such that neither domestic nor European legislation is capable of meeting them. What is the benefit of the raft of consumer legislation which has been built up in Europe if consumers increasingly purchase goods from sellers outside the European Economic Area who are able to take advantage of jurisdictions with a very low, or non-existent, level of consumer protection? On the other hand, as was suggested in the Preface to the tenth edition, a high level of consumer complaints could stifle growth of e-commerce, and it may be that responsible e-traders themselves will take steps to deal with the problem and ensure consumer satisfaction. In this case, it was suggested in the last edition that it was quite likely that the present anarchy of the Internet could give way to a market dominated by a few responsible players identified to consumers by their 'well-known' trade marks (this is a term of art derived from Article *6bis* of the Paris Convention for the Protection of Industrial Property). This indeed seems to have happened to some extent.

Although the focus of the book is the domestic law of sale of goods, this law is of relevance to export transactions, and Part V which deals with these has been retained. It is unlikely that the United Kingdom will adhere to the Vienna Convention on Contracts for the International Sale of Goods ('CISG') in the near future. Another consultation exercise is in progress, and a proper treatment of that convention would take us far beyond the Sale of Goods Act which is the principal focus of this work, and would result in a considerable lengthening of what has already become a substantial tome. Accordingly, treatment of CISG has been deemed inappropriate for this edition.

As with the previous edition, I would like to thank my colleagues Robert Bradgate, Christian Twigg-Flesner, and Geraint Howells for their assistance. Last but by no means least, I would like to thank Hector MacQueen for adding the sections dealing with Scots law. These are, I believe, instructive to non-Scottish lawyers. It seems to me that in certain areas the Scottish rules are better. Needless to say, responsibility for any remaining errors and omissions is mine.

John N Adams
Sheffield

In this edition, with the encouragement of John Adams, I have attempted to deepen the treatment of Scots law without undue disturbance of the balance of the text.

Hector MacQueen
Edinburgh

TABLE OF STATUTES

===

(Page numbers in bold type indicate that the section referred to or a part of it is set out verbatim in the text)

TABLE OF TREATIES

TABLE OF EUROPEAN DIRECTIVES

TABLE OF CASES

Part I

NATURE AND FORMATION OF THE CONTRACT OF SALE

1

SOURCES OF THE LAW OF SALE OF GOODS

THE SALE OF GOODS ACT 1979

The focus of this book is the domestic law of sale of goods. The domestic law of sale of goods is to be found in four main sources. The first, and still by far the most important, is the Sale of Goods Act 1979, which consolidates (with some additional amendments) the original Sale of Goods Act of 1893 and amendments to it made prior to 1979. That Act has in turn been amended by the Sale and Supply of Goods Act 1994, the Sale of Goods (Amendment) Act 1994 and the Sale of Goods (Amendment) Act 1995. Recently, European Directives, in particular that on sale of consumer goods and associated guarantees,[1] and that on distance contracts,[2] have required further amendments to the Sale of Goods Act and subordinate legislation. Secondly, there are a number of other statutory provisions, of varying importance, some of which pre-date the Act of 1893 (such as the Factors Act 1889), but others of more recent origin, such as the Unfair Contract Terms Act 1977 and the Unfair Contract Terms Regulations 1999. Thirdly, there is a considerable mass of case law interpreting the Act of 1893, much of which remains relevant to the interpretation of the Act of 1979 and, of course, there is now case law on the 1979 Act itself. Additionally there are some decisions of the European Court of Justice interpreting the various Directives and Conventions in the field. This jurisprudence is likely to grow in the future. Indeed, the present law of sale of goods is somewhat patchwork, especially that relating to consumers – there is a case now for consolidating statutes which deal separately with commercial[3] and consumer matters. Fourthly, there is still a certain amount of relevant case law which pre-dates the Act of 1893. The importance of the old case law on points actually dealt with by the Act has, however, been declining for many years. The Act of 1893 was a codifying statute, and the proper method of interpreting such a statute was laid down by Lord Herschell in *Bank of England* v *Vagliano Bros.*[4]

> I think the proper course is in the first instance to examine the language of the statute and to ask what is its natural meaning, uninfluenced by any considerations derived from the previous state of the law, and not to start with inquiring how the law previously stood, and

---

1 99/44/EC, OJ L171, 7/7/99 implemented by SI 2002/3045.
2 97/7/EC, OJ L144, 4/6/97 implemented by SI 2000/2334.
3 The Sale of Goods Act is still of international importance in commercial sales and has a close family relationship to laws in force around the Commonwealth, as well as to Article 2 of the Uniform Commercial Code in force in all US jurisdictions except Louisiana.
4 [1891] AC 107, 144–5. These observations were made with reference to the Bills of Exchange Act 1882, but they apply to all codifying statutes alike.

then, assuming that it was probably intended to leave it unaltered, to see if the words of the enactment will bear an interpretation in conformity with this view. If a statute, intended to embody in a code a particular branch of the law, is to be treated in this fashion, it appears to me that its utility will be almost entirely destroyed, and the very object with which it was enacted will be frustrated. The purpose of such a statute surely was that on any point specifically dealt with by it, the law should be ascertained by interpreting the language used instead of, as before, by roaming over a vast number of authorities in order to discover what the law was, extracting it by a minute critical examination of the prior decisions.

Lord Herschell then went on to observe that in exceptional cases, reference to earlier decisions may still be permissible. Firstly, where the provisions of the Act are ambiguous, earlier cases may help to resolve the ambiguity; and secondly, where a term has acquired a technical meaning, previous cases may be cited to illustrate this meaning. It is scarcely necessary to add that where a point is not covered by the Act, older decisions are still binding and must be followed.

Despite this warning and its subsequent repetition in later cases, it cannot be said that it has always been taken to heart by courts or writers. Indeed, there are indications in the speeches in the House of Lords in *Ashington Piggeries Ltd* v *Christopher Hill Ltd*[5] that Lord Herschell's remarks may now need qualification. In particular, in the interpretation of provisions of the Act relating to implied terms, Lord Diplock said that the Act 'ought not to be construed so narrowly as to force on parties to contracts for the sale of goods promises and consequences different from what they must reasonably have intended'.[6] More generally, it may be said that the courts have tended to treat the provisions of the Act as though they were part of the common law, and have not generally treated cases under the Act as though they were ordinary exercises in statutory interpretation.

The application of Lord Herschell's approach in some areas is, however, more controversial. For example, in the case of the former implied condition that the goods were to be of 'merchantable quality' the 1979 Act (unlike the original Act) professed to define the term 'merchantable quality',[7] but the definition appeared merely to provide a framework or skeleton in which the normal processes of case law development might continue; thus it might have been thought that the meaning of the term 'merchantable quality' would continue to be found in the case law and there were indeed many cases which proceeded on this basis. But (as we shall see) the Court of Appeal in *Rogers* v *Parish (Scarborough) Ltd*[8] insisted that this mass of case law should be jettisoned, and the words of the 1979 Act alone looked to in the decision of cases on the meaning of the term 'merchantable quality'. The merchantable quality warranty has now been replaced by a new requirement that goods are to be of 'satisfactory quality',[9] but the same issue will no doubt arise in relation

---

5 [1972] AC 441.
6 At p. 501.
7 The relevant provisions first appeared in the Supply of Goods (Implied Terms) Act 1973.
8 [1987] QB 933 see below, p. 165. See also *Harlington & Leinster Enterprises Ltd* v *Christopher Hull Fine Art Ltd* [1991] 1 QB 564. Compare the remarks of Lloyd LJ in *M/S Aswan Engineering Establishment Co* v *Lupdine Ltd* [1987] 1 WLR 1, 6 – see below, p. 165.
9 Sale and Supply of Goods Act 1994.

to the new provisions. For reasons given later, an approach which ignores the previous case law whether on the old merchantable quality provisions or on other parts of the Act is likely to produce arbitrary and unpredictable decisions, and any attempt to apply Lord Herschell's approach literally must at least take account of the variety of reasons which may inspire the legislature to codify different provisions of the common law.[10]

Another problem arising from Lord Herschell's approach is that this method of interpretation is not sufficiently adaptable to be used in the interpretation of legislation which clearly departs from general common law principles. This means that every statutory amendment of the law of sale of goods either opens up a wedge between the law of sale and the law applicable to closely analogous contracts, or it has to be followed by or accompanied by parallel legislation applicable to these other contracts. But if, when this new legislation is proposed, there are second thoughts about the earlier legislation amending the law of sale, the result is likely to be yet further amendments to the law of sale. The result is that the law of sale and the law of similar contracts are engaged in a sort of leap-frog exercise which sometimes makes it troublesome to identify the precise effect of modern legislation at any given moment. And it also means that arbitrary distinctions sometimes have to be drawn between cases according to the precise type of contract involved – sale of goods contracts sometimes being affected by legislation which does not apply to other closely similar transactions.

In addition to the law of sale of goods in the strict sense, there is, of course, the general body of the law against which a codifying statute has to be understood and, in particular, the general law of contract. The Sale of Goods Act makes no attempt to codify the general principles of contract law. Indeed, it expressly leaves them untouched, for s. 62(2) enacts that:

> The rules of the common law, including the law merchant except in so far as they are inconsistent with the provisions of this Act and in particular the rules relating to the law of principal and agent and the effect of fraud, misrepresentation, duress or coercion, mistake, or other invalidating cause, apply to contracts for the sale of goods.

Despite this section, no exposition of this subject would be complete without some account of the general rules of the law of contract insofar as they have some special bearing on the law of sale of goods.

The Sale of Goods Act was made applicable to Scotland in 1893 as a result of pressure in some commercial and legal quarters for the creation of a more uniform law of sale in the United Kingdom.[11] This was achieved with the addition of only a very few sections to the English codification statute as originally drafted. The Act is thus not a codification in any sense of the pre-existing Scots common law, but was rather a very significant change, given the Roman law roots of that law. This was particularly the

---

10 These different approaches were thoroughly canvassed in the Law Commission Working Paper No. 85, *Sale and Supply of Goods* (1983) which explored various proposals for altering the definition of 'merchantable quality'. The Final Report of the Law Commissions, *Sale and Supply of Goods* (Law Com No. 160, Scot Law Com No. 104, 1987, Cm. 137), appeared to retreat somewhat from the position arrived at in the Working Paper.

11 See Rodger (1992) 108 LQR 570. For the law pre-1893, see Gordon, in Reid and Zimmermann (eds), *History of Private Law in Scotland*, vol 2 (2000).

case in respect of the transfer of property and, albeit to a less fundamental extent, the duties of the seller and the remedies of the buyer.[12] The Act's English terminology also caused difficulties in Scotland, although these have mostly been removed by the reforms of the Sale and Supply of Goods Act 1994, in which the Scottish Law Commission played a large part. A distinguished Scottish commentator once argued that 'the task of the Scots courts is . . . to bring the statutory provisions into harmony with the principles of our common law'[13]; but this has not been the approach of the judges or of other writers in Scotland, who have preferred generally to start with the text of the statute, imperfect and sometimes difficult to understand though it may be from the perspective of Scots law.

As will appear during the course of this book, the Sale of Goods Act has not proved one of the more successful pieces of codification undertaken by Parliament towards the end of the nineteenth century.[14] The principal reason for this may well be that there has been a change in the type of sale of goods cases coming before the courts, and the types of cases, more generally, coming to legal attention. The nineteenth-century cases on which the Act was based were, in the main, sales between businessmen or organizations, i.e. sales by manufacturers and suppliers. Since the 1893 Act was passed, however, a larger proportion of the cases coming before the courts appear to have been sales by retailers to the consuming public. And even though there is still relatively little litigation arising out of many consumer transactions, because their value does not generally warrant litigation,[15] consumers and consumer organizations today are more vociferous in demanding recognition of their rights. This was one major reason why the term 'merchantable quality', which was of prime importance in defining the duties of the seller, appeared to be inappropriate to many lawyers, and why the 1994 Sale and Supply of Goods Act amends and redefines the law on this point.[16]

More generally, the very different social and economic nature of commercial and consumer transactions, both of which are in law contracts of sale of goods, means that it is not surprising that an Act devised principally for the one has not always worked satisfactorily for the other. It is now noticeable that one of the principal trends of modern legislative change is to discriminate between consumer and non-consumer transactions.

---

12 See Smith, *Property Problems in Sale* (1978); Sutherland, 1987 JR 24.

13 Gow, *The Mercantile and Industrial Law of Scotland* (1964), 76. Gow supported his approach by reference to what is now s. 62(2) of the Sale of Goods Act 1979 (see above).

14 Save in terms of its widespread adoption in the jurisdictions of the Commonwealth, and in the United States whose Uniform Sales Act (now replaced by Article 2 of the Uniform Commercial Code) closely followed it.

15 An effect of the Civil Procedure Rules 1998 may be to reduce still further the trickle of reported cases.

16 See Chapter 13, where this question is more fully dealt with.

2

DEFINITION AND NATURE OF THE CONTRACT OF SALE

DEFINITION

Section 2(1) of the Act defines a contract of sale of goods as:

> a contract by which the seller transfers or agrees to transfer the property in goods to the buyer for a money consideration, called the price.

Subsections (3) and (4) give different names to two transactions:

> (3) Where under a contract of sale the property in the goods is transferred from the seller to the buyer the contract is called a sale.
> (4) Where under a contract of sale the transfer of the property in the goods is to take place at a future time or subject to some condition later to be fulfilled the contract is called an agreement to sell.

SALE DISTINGUISHED FROM OTHER CONTRACTS

A contract of sale of goods must be distinguished from several other transactions which are normally quite different from a sale of goods but which, in particular circumstances, may closely resemble such a contract,[1] namely (1) a contract of barter or exchange, (2) a gift, (3) a contract of bailment, (4) a contract of hire-purchase, (5) a contract of loan on the security of goods, (6) a contract for the supply of services, (7) a contract of agency, and (8) licences of intellectual property such as 'sales' of computer software.[2] These distinctions were at one time of importance mainly in connection with s. 4 of the 1893 Act. This section, which was originally part of s. 17 of the Statute of Frauds 1677 and was not applicable in Scotland, required contracts of sale of goods of the value of £10 and upwards to be evidenced in writing, whereas for the other types of contract listed above there was no such requirement. Since the repeal of s. 4 by the Law Reform (Enforcement of Contracts) Act 1954, this particular point has ceased to

---

1 In early editions of this book, a contract for the transfer of a possessory interest in a chattel was also distinguished from a sale of goods. As a result of amendments first made by the Supply of Goods (Implied Terms) Act 1973, such a contract should be treated as a sale of goods – see below, p. 118.
2 Which are usually licences of the copyright in the software and are independent of the media in which the software is embedded – see below, p. 77. The distinction between sales and licences of intellectual property, such as computer software, is dealt with in Chapter 6.

be of importance in relation to domestic sales of goods,[3] because no written formalities are now required in general for any of the above kinds of contracts.[4] But it may still be necessary to decide whether a contract is a contract of sale of goods for one of a number of other reasons. In particular, of course, the provisions of the Sale of Goods Act apply only to such contracts. Given that the original Act of 1893 was largely a codifying Act, however, and given the tendency to construe the Act as though it were a part of the common law, it will often be immaterial whether a particular contract is labelled a contract of sale or a contract of a different character. In particular, when a question of implication of terms arises, the law may well be the same whether or not the Act applies. Indeed, there has been a noticeable tendency, first for the courts and then for Parliament, to model the common law contracts on the Sale of Goods Act and, in particular, to imply terms in these contracts very similar to those implied by the Act.[5]

In *Young & Marten Ltd* v *McManus Childs Ltd*,[6] the House of Lords expressed strong views on the undesirability of drawing unnecessary distinctions between different classes of contract. But the legislative structure of the law sometimes makes this an inescapable result; for instance (as we shall see later[7]) there are a number of provisions in the Sale of Goods Act (originating in the Factors Act 1889) enabling a person, subject to various conditions, to pass a good title to goods even if he does not own them, provided that he has agreed to buy them. This legislative formula clearly excludes cases in which the contract involves the acquisition of the goods without an agreement to buy. And we shall see recent examples of cases in which this distinction is critical to the result of a legal dispute.

Moreover, as noted above, even the new legislation applicable to sales and other contracts is not always, at any given moment, identical, because sometimes the law applicable to one type of contract (usually sale) is amended first and the others at a later date. Since the changes made by these Acts and subordinate legislation are clearly not declaratory, it is difficult to see how the courts could modify the law relating to these other contracts to keep them in line with contracts of sale. On the other hand, care has been taken in the most recent legislative changes to treat contracts of sale of goods and other similar transactions in the same way, subject only to necessary modifications. It is, therefore, probable that the distinction between the different types of contract will only be of practical importance in relatively unusual circumstances.

In cases under s. 4 it was necessary to draw a firm line between contracts of sale and other types of contract, but for other purposes there seems no reason why it

---

3 An equivalent provision is still to be found in many of the Commonwealth statutes based on the 1893 Act, however, as well as in the Uniform Commercial Code Article 2–201. When it exists, this requirement presents a problem when contracts are effected by e-mail – see Chapter 5. The Vienna Convention 1980, Arts 12 and 96 permit a state to require formalities where any party has his place of business in such a state.

4 Assignments, though not licences, of copyright, e.g., in software, must, however, be evidenced in writing – Copyright, Designs and Patents Act 1988 s. 90(3) (and the same is true for registered intellectual property rights). Hire-purchase contracts must comply with the statutory formalities now to be found in the Consumer Credit Act 1974 and its subordinate legislation.

5 See, e.g., *G H Myers & Co* v *Brent Cross Service Co* [1934] 1 KB 46; *Samuels* v *Davis* [1943] KB 526; *Stewart* v *Reavell's Garage* [1952] 2 QB 545; *Ingham* v *Emes* [1955] 2 QB 366. See now the Supply of Goods and Services Act 1982, below, p. 23.

6 [1969] 1 AC 454.

7 See below, Chapter 21.

should not sometimes be possible to hold that a contract is partly a contract of sale and partly something else.[8] Thus a contract for the provision of a meal in a hotel is apparently a contract of sale,[9] and so is a contract for the construction of machinery.[10] Yet such contracts in some sense also involve the provision of services, and it seems clear that the law relating to the goods and the law relating to the services aspects of such a contract may differ. For instance, under the Supply of Goods and Services Act 1982 the supplier's duties as regards any goods supplied under the contract will normally be strict (that is, it will be liable for defects in the goods even if it has not been negligent) whereas its liability in respect of services may be a liability, in effect, for negligence only. As will be seen later, this problem of distinguishing between sales and supplies of goods on the one hand, and supplies of services on the other, gives rise to considerable difficulties in relation to contracts for the provision of computer software,[11] and there are problems relating to contracts for the supply and installation of goods in relation to the sale of consumer goods and associated guarantees directive.[12]

Before considering the distinction between contracts of sale and the other types of contract mentioned above, one preliminary point needs emphasis. A contract of sale is first and foremost a contract, i.e. a consensual transaction based on an agreement to buy and an agreement to sell. So where an out-patient at a hospital obtains drugs at the hospital dispensary, even on payment of a statutory prescription charge, this is not a contract of sale at all. The patient has a statutory right to receive the drug and the hospital a statutory obligation to supply it.[13] It seems the position is the same with respect to drugs and other medical appliances supplied by a pharmacist under the National Health Service.[14] Since the transaction is not a sale of goods, the Sale of Goods Act cannot apply; and since it is not a contract at all, it presumably follows that the Supply of Goods and Services Act 1982 also does not apply.[15] But it is possible that the courts might still be willing to imply terms as to quality and fitness in such a transaction,[16] though this could open up an anomalous result. It would mean that an out-patient who is supplied with a drug, like a patient who obtains a National Health Service drug from a pharmacist, would be able to sue if the drug was defective even if the supplier was not guilty of negligence. On the other hand, an in-patient who is supplied with a drug as an incident to the hospital's supply of

---

8 See, e.g., *Hyundai Heavy Industries Co Ltd* v *Papadopoulos* [1980] 1 WLR 1129, discussed below, p. 483, where this possibility is clearly recognized by the House of Lords (contract for manufacture of ship may be both contract of sale of goods and contract for services). See also *Watson* v *Buckley* [1940] 1 All ER 174.

9 *Lockett* v *A & M Charles Ltd* [1938] 4 All ER 170. By contrast, trade mark practice treats such a supply as one of services, but a take-away meal as a supply of goods. In *Martin & Thomson Tour Operators* Current Law, August 1999, it was held that the duty of a tour operator to a consumer poisoned by food supplied under the contract was merely to exercise reasonable care and skill. This decision is almost certainly wrong, because a contract for a package holiday including meals, is surely a contract for the transfer of goods within Supply of Goods and Services Act 1982 s. 4? As to the liability of an agent where the identity of the principal is not disclosed (as will usually be the case in package holiday contracts) see 2(1) Halsbury's Laws of England (2003) para. 183 *et seq.*

10 *Cammell Laird & Co Ltd* v *Manganese Bronze & Brass Co Ltd* [1934] AC 402.

11 See p. 77 *et seq.* below.

12 See p. 297.

13 *Pfizer Corpn* v *Minister of Health* [1965] AC 512.

14 *Appleby* v *Sleep* [1968] 1 WLR 948, 954.

15 See also p. 24 below.

16 See, e.g., *Read* v *Croydon Corpn* [1938] 4 All ER 631.

services (whether a paying patient or a NHS patient) might not be able to sue in the absence of negligence. It must be noted, however, that an injured patient might well have a remedy in such cases under the Consumer Protection Act 1987.[17]

Sale and exchange

The fact that the consideration must be in money, and that the term 'goods' is defined by s. 61 so as to exclude money, serves to distinguish a sale from a contract of barter or exchange in the ordinary case. But a coin which is a collector's item may be 'goods' even though it is legal tender, and there may be a sale of such a coin. In such an event, the coin does not possess the usual negotiable qualities of money, and if the sale is by a thief he cannot pass a good title to it.[18]

The position is less clear where goods on the one hand are exchanged for goods plus money on the other, as is commonly the case when a used car is traded in part exchange for a new one. Is this a contract of sale or of exchange? In *Aldridge* v *Johnson*[19] a contract for the exchange of 52 bullocks with 100 quarters of barley, the difference in value to be made up in money, was treated without argument as a contract of sale, but the case was fought on an entirely different point.[20] One view is that the answer depends upon whether the money or the goods is the substantial consideration. The decision in *Robinson* v *Graves*[21] lays down an elastic test of this nature for distinguishing contracts of sale from contracts for skill and labour, and a similar approach may sometimes be justified here. It should be noted, however, that in relation to the implied warranties,[22] Part I of the Supply of Goods and Services Act 1982 (applied to Scotland under the Sale and Supply of Goods Act 1994) renders the distinction largely of academic importance,[23] and there is an alternative to barter as a way of analysing the used car trade-in type of transaction.[24]

However, the proper characterization of a contract depends, in the last resort, on the intention of the parties so long only as they do not include provisions manifestly inconsistent with the intended nature of the transaction.[25] So, it may well be that, if the parties envisage the transaction as a sale and use terminology more appropriate to a sale, the contract would be held to be such even if the substantial consideration is supplied in goods rather than money. In the motor trade it is, of course, a common occurrence for a person to 'trade in' an old car in part-exchange for a new one and, if the transaction relating to the new car is treated by the parties as a sale, it is

---

17 See below, p. 273.
18 *Moss* v *Hancock* [1899] 2 QB 111. But it has been held that the chips given in exchange for money in a gaming club are not 'bought' – *Lipkin Gorman* v *Karpanle* [1991] 2 AC 548. See also Chapter [21.]
19 (1857) 7 E & B 885.
20 In *Connell Estate Agents* v *Begej* (1993) 39 EG 123 the part-exchange of a house was treated as a 'sale' so that the estate agent was entitled to commission.
21 [1935] 1 KB 579.
22 Though not necessarily in relation to other matters regulated by the Sale of Goods Act, so that, for example, the remedies applicable may be different.
23 See below, p. 23.
24 See below.
25 See *Street* v *Mountford* [1985] AC 809 and *A G Securities* v *Vaughan* [1988] 3 All ER 1058 where the House of Lords settled the approach to be adopted in the analogous case of an agreement designed to be a lease but dressed up to look like a licence.

improbable that the courts would treat it as anything else, even if the dealer's 'allowance' for the traded-in car does not fall far short of the price of the new one.[26] It seems that the transaction relating to the old car would also amount to a sale even though no money actually passes if, as is usual, the parties fix a notional price which is set off against the price of the new car. But it has been held in the Republic of Ireland that if no price is allocated to the old car, the whole transaction is one of barter, or exchange, and not sale.[27]

As noted above, a contract of exchange of goods for goods (or even of goods for some other consideration such as shares or land) is a contract for the transfer of goods within the Supply of Goods and Services Act 1982.[28] This Act incorporates into such a contract terms almost identical to those applying to a contract of sale; so if the question is one concerning the quality or fitness of goods supplied, it will in future be of very little importance whether the goods are supplied under a contract of sale or a contract of exchange.

Sale and gift

In the ordinary way, there is no difficulty in distinguishing between a sale and a gift. A gift is a transfer of property without any consideration and as such it is, of course, not binding while it remains executory unless made by deed.[29] But difficulty may sometimes arise with regard to transactions in which a 'free' gift is offered on the condition of entering into some other transaction. In *Esso Petroleum Ltd* v *Commissioners of Customs & Excise*,[30] garages selling petrol advertised a 'free' gift of a coin (bearing a likeness of a footballer) to anyone buying four gallons. It was held by the House of Lords that, although the transaction was not a gift, inasmuch as the garage was contractually bound to supply the coin to anyone buying four gallons of petrol, it was not a sale of goods either. The transaction was characterized by Lord Simon and Lord Wilberforce as one in which the garage promised to supply a coin in consideration of a customer buying the petrol. It was thus, in substance, a collateral contract existing alongside the contract for the sale of the petrol.[31] On this analysis it would presumably be a contract for the transfer of goods within the Supply of Goods and Services Act 1982, which is dealt with later.

An unsolicited offer to sell goods, accompanied by a delivery of those goods to the offeree, may be treated as a gift in the circumstances laid down in the Unsolicited

---

26 See *Sneddon* v *Durant* 1982 SLT (Sh Ct) 39, commented upon by Forte (1984) 101 SALJ 691. See also Smith (1974) 48 Tulane LR 1029.

27 *Flynn* v *Mackin* [1974] IR 101, criticized in a note in (1976) 39 MLR 589. The reason why the distinction was of practical importance in this case was that it was assumed that the property passes at different times in the two transactions. But if the contract is so close to the border between two classes of contract, it would seem absurd if such consequences were held to depend on the label attached to the contract, though sometimes this may be inevitable.

28 See below, p. 23. For examples of contracts of barter, see *Widenmeyer* v *Burn Stewart & Co* 1967 SC 85 and *Ballantyne* v *Durant* 1983 SLT (Sh Ct) 38.

29 In Scots law, donation is also a contract (*Laws of Scotland: Stair Memorial Encyclopaedia*, vol. 8 (qv)) and a promise to give is binding if in formal writing (Requirements of Writing (Scotland) Act 1995, s. 1).

30 [1976] 1 All ER 117, criticized in a note in (1976) 39 MLR 335. See also *GUS Merchandise* v *Customs & Excise Commissioners* [1981] 1 WLR 1309.

31 Lord Russell and Viscount Dilhorne held, however, that there was no intention to create legal relations. Lord Fraser held that there was a sale, however.

Goods and Services Act 1971. This deemed gift now takes place immediately and the rights of the sender are extinguished.[32]

Sale and bailment

A bailment is a transaction under which goods are delivered by one party (the bailor) to another (the bailee) on terms which normally require the bailee to hold the goods and ultimately to redeliver them to the bailor or in accordance with his directions. The property in the goods is not intended to and does not pass on delivery, though it may sometimes be the intention of the parties that it should pass in due course, as in the case of the ordinary hire-purchase contract. But where goods are delivered to another on terms which indicate that the property is to pass at once, the contract must be one of sale and not bailment. In *Chapman Bros v Verco Bros & Co Ltd*[33] farmers delivered bags of wheat to a company carrying on business as millers and wheat merchants. The wheat was delivered in unidentified bags which were identical to those in which other farmers delivered wheat to the company. The terms of the transaction required the company to buy and pay for the wheat on request by the farmer or failing such a request, on a specified date, to return an equal quantity of wheat of the same type; but there was no obligation to return the identical bags. Although the contract referred to the company as 'storers', it was held by the Australian High Court that this transaction was necessarily one of sale as the property passed to the company on delivery.

Similarly, if the nature of the transaction is such that the property must pass (even if not at once) the transaction seems inconsistent with the possibility of a bailment. It will be an 'agreement to sell' within s. 2(5) of the Act. If the goods are delivered to the buyer before the property passes he will be a 'buyer in possession' rather than a mere bailee.

Scots law does not know the terminology of bailment but speaks rather of the contract of deposit, under which the owner of an item places it in the custody of another, imposing on that other obligations to provide a secure place of custody and to exercise due care to prevent the loss of or damage to the property. Deposit is usually contrasted with hire and loan, under which the possessor has the use of the article hired or lent, and not just custody.

In modern times the distinction between a sale and a bailment has gained renewed importance as a result of the widespread use of *Romalpa*[34] (or retention of title) clauses in contracts for the supply of goods. These clauses take a variety of forms, but their purpose is always to allow a seller of goods to treat the goods as his property even after they have been delivered, as a sort of security for the payment of the price. In substance these are contracts of sale in which, however, the seller claims that the delivery of the goods is, in the first instance, by way of bailment only. In some cases, the clauses go further and provide that even though the 'buyer' may deal with the

---

32 Consumer Protection (Distance Selling) Regulations 2000/2334 Regulation 24 replacing with amendments S.1, 1971 Act.

33 (1933) 49 CLR 306; see also *South Australian Insurance Co v Randell* (1869) LR 3 PC 101. Distinguished in *Coleman v Harvey* [1989] 1 NZLR 723.

34 See the *Romalpa* case [1976] 1 WLR 676, below, p. 470 *et seq.*

goods (for instance, by using them in a process of manufacture, or by reselling them), the original supplier is to be entitled to (or to a charge upon) any goods manufactured with the goods supplied, or to (or to a charge on) the proceeds of resale when received by the 'buyer'. These clauses give rise to much legal difficulty and are considered at greater length later.[35] Here it is enough to say that any bailment will be limited to the actual goods delivered. An attempt to extend the seller's security interest into goods manufactured using the goods delivered is liable to give rise to a charge registrable under the Companies Act 1985,[36] as where resin was supplied for use in the manufacture of chipboard.[37] The result of this is that, prima facie at least, the seller can have no right to trace the goods supplied when they have once been used or resold. On the other hand, if the contract involves a true bailment,[38] the seller probably has rights over any goods made with the goods supplied, or over the proceeds of the sale, where they have been resold, although even this is not entirely free from doubt.[39]

A contract of hire is one species of bailment[40]; such contracts are readily distinguishable from sales since there is no intention that property should pass in a hiring contract. The Supply of Goods and Services Act 1982 contains implied terms applicable to a contract of hire which are similar to, though not identical with, those in a contract of sale; it is also possible to exclude these terms by contrary agreement so long as they comply with the 'reasonableness' requirement under the Unfair Contracts Terms Act 1977, although this is not always possible in contracts of sale.[41]

Sale and hire-purchase

Contracts of hire-purchase resemble contracts of sale very closely and, indeed, in practically all cases of hire-purchase the ultimate sale of the goods is (in a popular sense) the real object of the transaction. Nonetheless, for present purposes, the legal distinction is clear and important, though its importance has greatly diminished since the Sale of Goods (Implied Terms) Act 1973,[42] and the Consumer Credit Act 1974. A sale is a contract whereby the seller 'transfers or agrees to transfer' the property in goods to the buyer; that is to say, as soon as the contract is made the ultimate destination of the goods is determined even though the property is not to pass for some considerable time, for example until all the instalments of the price have been paid. A contract of hire-purchase, on the other hand, is a bailment of the goods coupled with an option to purchase them which may or may not be exercised. Only if and when the option is exercised will there be a contract of sale.

The similarity between the two transactions is accentuated by the artificial nature of most hire-purchase agreements. This is brought out by consideration of three

35 See below, p. 470 *et seq.*
36 See p. 476.
37 *Borden (UK) Ltd v Scottish Timber Products Ltd* [1981] Ch 25.
38 That is, not merely the use of a form to create a security interest – see p. 476.
39 See p. 476 *et seq.*
40 But note that in Scots law hire is distinguished from deposit.
41 See below, p. 236 and p. 243.
42 Up to the Hire-Purchase Act 1964 there had been significant differences between the warranties in hire-purchase contracts and those in sales of goods. The relevant provisions of this Act were replaced by the Hire-Purchase Act 1965 which in turn was replaced by the 1973 Act (as amended by the Consumer Credit Act 1974, Sch. 4 and the Sale and Supply of Goods Act 1994) and see p. 18 below.

points. First, as already observed, the real object of a contract of hire-purchase is almost invariably the ultimate sale of the goods to the hirer. Secondly, the amount which the hirer is bound to pay under the contract is usually far in excess of that which he would have had to pay if he were really hiring the goods[43]. And thirdly, the legal purchase price for which the hirer has the option to buy the goods is frequently nominal only and, in fact, is sometimes not exacted in practice. Moreover, for the purposes of the hirer claiming capital allowances, hire-purchase transactions in respect of machinery or plant are treated in the same way as outright purchases.[44]

There is a further practical complication about hire-purchase contracts which often makes them different from contracts of sale. A transaction under which a person 'buys' goods on hire-purchase is often and, in the motor trade is usually, a complex transaction involving three and not two parties. Many retailers have no wish to act as financiers themselves supplying credit to consumers. So a hire-purchase transaction often involves, first, a sale, under which the retailer sells the goods to a finance company, and then, secondly, a hire-purchase contract, under which the finance company lets the goods on hire-purchase terms to the 'buyer'. It follows that the 'buyer' has no contractual relations with the seller and this sometimes has important legal consequences, although the reality is that 'the identity or even existence of the finance company is a matter (to customers) of indifference; they look to the dealer, or his representative, as the person who fixes the payment terms and makes all the necessary arrangements'.[45] Nevertheless, it means, for instance, that the seller cannot be sued on the terms implied by the Sale of Goods Act, which create liability even in the absence of negligence,[46] although he may sometimes be liable in tort if negligence can be proved against him.[47] And if the seller gives an express warranty to the 'buyer', in consideration of which the latter enters into the contract of hire-purchase with the finance company to which the seller has sold the goods, then the seller can be held liable on this separate contract of guarantee.[48] The finance company may also be liable on the terms implied by the Supply of Goods Act 1973. Since the Consumer Credit Act 1974, it would be more correct to refer to the hirer as the debtor and to the seller as the supplier, but the principles themselves are not changed.[49]

Hire-purchase contracts were developed in England and Wales towards the end of the nineteenth century, and it is impossible to understand why they came into existence without an appreciation of the legal context which already existed. There was

---

43 Because the capital cost of the goods plus interest needs to be amortised over the term. True hire, by contrast, is time-share of an asset e.g., short-term hire of a car.

44 Capital Allowances Act 1990, s. 60.

45 *Branwhite* v *Worcester Works Finance Ltd* [1969] 1 AC 552 per Lord Wilberforce, foll'd *J D Williams & Co (t/a Williams Leasing)* v *McCauley, Parsons & Jones* [1994] CCLR 78 (CA); *Woodchester Equipment (Leasing)* v *British Association of Canned and Preserved Foods Importers and Distributors* [1995] CCLR 51.

46 *Drury* v *Victor Buckland Ltd* [1941] 1 All ER 269. Nor, presumably, can the buyer sue the dealer under the implied terms in the Supply of Goods and Services Act 1982 (see below, p. 23, as to this Act) because if there is no contract at all between buyer and dealer, the relationship between them can hardly amount to a 'contract for the transfer of goods' within s. 1(1) of that Act.

47 *Herschtal* v *Stewart & Ardern Ltd* [1940] 1 KB 155.

48 *Brown* v *Sheen & Richmond Car Sales Ltd* [1950] 1 All ER 1102.

49 The effect of s. 56 of the Consumer Credit Act 1974 is that in regulated agreements the supplier is the agent of the finance house for all purposes connected with the transaction.

clearly a need for a form of contract of sale of goods on credit, under which the seller could reserve some security right to the goods. Consumers wanted to buy on credit, and financiers who were willing to supply the credit wanted security. Two obstacles existed to achieving this desired end through the most obvious legal methods. One obvious method would have been for the seller simply to sell and deliver the goods on credit while expressly stipulating that the property in the goods should remain his until the buyer had paid the price. This is a conditional sale, and it does give the seller some security: it protects him against the possibility of the buyer's insolvency. But it does not protect him against the possibility that the buyer may sell the goods to a third party before he has paid the whole price. Even though the seller has reserved the property in the goods, s. 25(1) of the Sale of Goods Act enables a person who has 'bought or agreed to buy goods' to pass a good title to a third party. In *Lee* v *Butler*,[50] the Court of Appeal held that the equivalent of this provision[51] clearly applied where the buyer was in possession of the goods under an agreement to buy the goods and pay the price in instalments. So this obvious method of selling goods on credit failed to give the seller adequate security.

A second obvious method of achieving the desired result was for the seller to sell and deliver the goods outright to the buyer but to require the buyer to grant him a mortgage, or charge, or a right to repossess the goods in the event of the buyer's failure to pay the instalments. At common law, it was possible to create a charge of this nature on goods which would be binding even on third parties. Most probably, a legal arrangement of this nature would still have been caught by s. 25 of the Sale of Goods Act, but there was a more fundamental objection to this device. The whole essence of this scheme is that one person, the buyer (A), should have the possession of goods and be entitled to the use of them as though he were the owner, while another person, the financier (B), should actually have a charge or mortgage on the goods. Now this kind of transaction is one which is frowned upon by the law because third parties may be induced to do business with, or give credit to, A in the belief that he is the unencumbered owner of the goods in question. And if A becomes insolvent, they will then find that B has a prior claim to the goods. It is generally thought to be unfair that B should be able to do this unless he has in some way publicized his transaction with A. Accordingly, in England the Bills of Sale Acts of 1878 and 1882 require a transaction of this kind to be made by a written instrument, called a bill of sale, which is required to be registered under the Acts.

The Bills of Sale Acts had two great disadvantages. First, they required some degree of publicity – that was their whole purpose, of course – and many borrowers disliked this requirement. But secondly, they rapidly attracted a body of extremely technical case law, and it became easy to fall foul of the Acts by accident so that the security granted (and in some cases the right to interest also) might become void.[52]

The result of these difficulties was a search for a legal form of sale which enabled the seller to retain security in the goods without falling foul of the Bills of Sale Acts

---

50 [1893] 2 QB 318.
51 Section 25(2) – see below, p. 401.
52 The Crowther Committee 1971 (Cmnd. 4596) recommended their abolition, along with the Hire-Purchase Acts and other measures, and replacement by a Lending and Security Act – see below, p. 17.

and which also gave protection against bona fide purchasers from the buyer. The contract of hire-purchase was the answer, and its efficacy was upheld by the House of Lords in two cases in 1895. In *Helby* v *Matthews*,[53] it was held that a person in possession of goods under a hire-purchase agreement had not 'bought or agreed to buy' them within the meaning of s. 25(2) (now s. 25(1)) of the Sale of Goods Act. This meant that the buyer, or the 'hirer' as it now became more correct to call him, could not dispose of the goods to a third party in contravention of the agreement, and the seller's (or 'owner's') security was thus fully protected. And in *McEntire* v *Crossley Bros*[54] it was also held that a hire-purchase contract did not fall within the Bills of Sale Acts; those Acts, it was held, applied only where an owner of goods granted a charge, or right to seize the goods, to another party, while in the hire-purchase contract the hirer was not owner at the time he granted the right to seize the goods.

With the blessing of the House of Lords to the legal arrangements, the way was paved for the great commercial expansion of the use of hire-purchase contracts. For the next 40 years the use of the contract spread throughout the entire field of consumer purchasing of goods, other than purely consumable or perishable goods; and it also began to be used in some commercial situations.

As time went on, it became increasingly obvious that the contract of hire-purchase was being used as a form (in effect) of secured sale. Instead of borrowing the money to buy the goods and mortgaging the goods to the lender as a security, the consumer entered into a hire-purchase contract with the financier. While this achieved similar results from the financier's point of view, at least in the sense that it gave it the security it wanted, it created a good deal of difficulty because the legal form of the transaction did not reflect the fact that, as a sort of mortgagor (though not, of course, in strict law), the hirer had an 'equity' in the goods. In land law it has for centuries been recognized that a mortgage is a security device (no matter what its form) and that the mortgagor has an 'equity' in the land mortgaged. This 'equity' means that for most purposes the mortgagor is treated as owner of the land and the mortgagee's interests are confined to using the land as a security for repayment of the loan. So long as the mortgagee obtains repayment, plus interest, the mortgagor is always entitled to the residuary 'equity'. These familiar principles of the land law were never recognized as applicable to hire-purchase contracts; and so long as total freedom of contract prevailed, much hardship to the consumer resulted. For example, if the hirer paid nine-tenths of the price and defaulted in payment of the final instalment, the finance company might seize the goods and resell them, retaining the proceeds for itself.

Abuses of this kind led to the gradual legislative recognition of the hirer's equity, though not by that term, nor by the same methods as equity had brought to bear on mortgages of land. These reforms began with the Hire-Purchase Act 1938, and were greatly extended and strengthened in the Hire-Purchase Acts of 1964 and 1965. But these reforms did not touch one basic problem, that the form of the hire-purchase

---

53 [1895] AC 471.
54 [1895] AC 457.

contract was recognized as creating a sharp difference between a hire-purchase and a sale of goods. The law distinguished between the legal rights and duties of a consumer who borrowed money to buy goods, and one who bought them on credit, or acquired them under a hire-purchase contract.

A movement for reform began to attract support under which hire-purchase contracts, as a separate legal contract, would be abolished. If a person wanted to buy goods by instalments he would, in law, buy those goods under a contract of sale of goods; if he did not have the cash to pay the full price down, he could borrow the money from a third party (such as a finance company or a bank) or, alternatively, he could buy on credit from the actual seller. If necessary, the law could then provide some simple process to enable the buyer to 'mortgage' the goods to the lender by way of security. This movement for reform began to grow after the general adoption throughout the United States of the Uniform Commercial Code, Article 9 of which proceeded along these lines. Then in 1971 the Crowther Committee on Consumer Credit examined this problem at length as part of a general inquiry into the whole field of consumer credit.[55] This Committee proposed the abolition of hire-purchase contracts and the enactment of legislation along lines similar to those of the American Uniform Commercial Code. This recommendation was not wholly accepted by the government. Partly because there was some disagreement with the idea that a hire-purchase agreement was always based on a 'fiction', and partly because the public and the trade were familiar with the concept, it was felt to be going too far to abolish the contract altogether. Consequently, the Consumer Credit Act 1974 retained the hire-purchase contract.

It is, however, very important to appreciate that, although the name and form of hire-purchase as a distinct contract have been retained, the substance of the matter is very different. The Hire-Purchase Acts have been almost entirely repealed by the Consumer Credit Act, and the rights and duties of the parties involved in a hire-purchase contract now differ hardly at all from those of parties to a sale of goods in which the consumer has obtained credit, whether from the seller or a third party. The principal remaining differences are those noted at the beginning of this section.[56]

The Crowther Committee's recommendations as to the law relating to the use of chattels as security have never been implemented, though further examination by the government did take place.[57] In the meantime, a contract of hire-purchase (or of conditional sale) remains the principal method by which a financier or seller can reserve a security interest in the goods sold; a sale on credit, without any reservation of property, means that the seller retains no security rights in the goods.

Under the provisions of the Consumer Credit Act 1974 (provisions first enacted by the Hire-Purchase Act 1965), a conditional sale agreement in which the price is payable by instalments[58] is, for most purposes, assimilated to a hire-purchase

---

55 Cmnd. 4596.
56 See p. 13 *et seq.*
57 See A. L. Diamond, *A Review of Security Interests in Property* (DTI, 1989) HMSO. Reform has been proposed in Scotland but as yet there has been no legislation – see DTI Consultation Paper 'Security over Moveable Property in Scotland', November 1994. See also p. 470, n. 94.
58 But not a sale where title is reserved against payment of the price in one instalment – Consumer Credit Act 1974 Sch. 4 para. 4 – see below.

agreement, with the result that a 'sale' of goods in which the price is payable by instalments can now take only one of two forms.

1 The contract may be a genuine contract of sale in which the buyer is bound to buy and to pay the whole price, and the seller is bound to sell. The property in the goods will pass at once with a purely personal obligation to pay the price in instalments. In this case, there is an absolute contract of sale, and obviously the buyer can pass a good title to a third party; and, should he go bankrupt, the seller has no claim to the goods. The seller has no security right to the goods themselves.

2 Alternatively, the passing of the property may be made conditional on the payment of a number of instalments. Under the Hire-Purchase Act 1965, it made virtually no difference whether this transaction was drafted as a sale or in the traditional form of a contract of hire, together with an option to purchase. Since the Supply of Goods (Implied Terms) Act 1973, this has no longer been wholly true. Today the sections in the 1979 Act dealing with sales, and not those in the 1973[59] Act dealing with hire-purchase, apply to conditional sales. But this is of little moment because the wording of the two sets of provisions is virtually identical. It therefore remains true to say that for most purposes there is now no distinction between a conditional sale and a hire-purchase contract. In either event, the agreement takes effect as a hire-purchase agreement and the 'buyer' is unable to pass a good title to the goods should he purport to sell them before the property has vested in him. The exception for motor vehicles also applies in both cases.[60] Again, in either event, the property remains in the seller (in the one case, until the condition is satisfied; in the other, till the option is exercised) and the seller would be able to claim the goods should the buyer become bankrupt before the property has vested in him.

As mentioned above, it is now quite common to find reservation of title clauses in sales made to commercial bodies (as distinct from consumer sales) and these clauses are, in some respects, similar (at least in general purpose though not in legal form) to hire-purchase contracts. They are similar in that their purpose is to give the seller some security where the goods are delivered before the price has been paid; this security is not as extensive as that obtained by a hire-purchase contract because it only protects the seller against the risk of the buyer's insolvency. As seen above, it does not protect the seller against the risk that the buyer may resell the goods without authority. Reservation of title clauses also differ from hire-purchase agreements in that the latter do contemplate some sort of hiring arrangement under which the hirer will be allowed to *use* the goods. Reservation of title clauses do not involve any element of hiring, though they do often contemplate that the buyer may use the goods in a different sense, that is, may use them in the course of manufacture, for example may use leather to make handbags or may use resin to make chipboard.[61]

---

59 In fact the relevant sections derive from Sch. 4 to the Consumer Credit Act 1974, which amends the 1973 Act, and further amendments effected by the Sale and Supply of Goods Act 1994.
60 See below, p. 410.
61 See further on these reservation of title clauses, p. 470 *et seq.* below.

Sale and loan on security

Parties sometimes enter into, or go through the motions of entering into, a contract to sell goods with the intention of using the goods as a security for a loan of money. If the owner of goods (A) wishes to borrow money on the security of the goods, he may charge or mortgage them to B on the understanding that (1) A will retain possession of the goods, (2) A will repay B what he or she has borrowed together with interest, and (3) B will have a right to take the goods from A if and only if A fails to repay the loan or interest at the agreed time. Such a transaction differs from a hire-purchase contract which is designed to enable a person to acquire goods on credit. A loan on security is designed to enable someone who already owns goods to *borrow money* on the security of the goods.

Partly in order to evade the Bills of Sale Acts, but partly for other reasons, parties sometimes enter into this kind of transaction in the form of a sale – thus A can 'sell' his or her goods to B, though retaining possession of them and only giving B the right to seize them in certain events. In modern times, this kind of transaction is almost invariably reinforced with a hire-purchase agreement, or (in commercial transactions) a 'leaseback'. A 'sells' the goods (usually a motor vehicle) to B for a cash price and then B lets the same vehicle back to A under a hire-purchase contract. Or a manufacturing company may 'sell' plant or machinery to a finance company which then 'leases' the goods back to the manufacturers. Under s. 62(4) of the Sale of Goods Act:

> The provisions of this Act about contracts of sale do not apply to a transaction in the form of a contract of sale which is intended to operate by way of mortgage, pledge, charge or other security.

In analysing a transaction of this nature the courts have always insisted that the substance of the transaction and not merely its form must be examined. If the transaction is 'really' a loan on the security of the goods the Bills of Sale Acts will apply, and if it is unregistered (as it nearly always is) the contract is void and the chargee will be unable to seize the goods or even to recover the agreed interest, though the actual loan itself will be recoverable in a restitutionary claim, formerly known as the action for money had and received.[62] If, on the other hand, the parties 'really' intend the transaction to be a genuine 'sale' followed by a genuine hire-purchase or leaseback contract, the transaction will be valid and the two contracts will take effect according to their terms. For instance, in *Kingsley v Sterling Industrial Securities Ltd*,[63] Winn LJ said:

> In my definite view the sole or entirely dominant question upon that part of the appeal to which I have so far adverted is whether in reality and upon a true analysis of the transactions and each of them, and having regard in particular to the intention of the parties, they constituted loans or sales. It is clear upon the authorities that if a transaction is in reality a loan of money intended to be secured by, for example, a sale and hiring agreement, the document or documents embodying the arrangement will be within the Bills of Sale Acts; it is equally clear that each case must be determined according to the proper inference to be drawn from the facts and whatever the form the transaction may take the court will decide according to its real substance.

---

62 *North Central Wagon Finance Co Ltd v Brailsford* [1962] 1 WLR 1288.
63 [1967] 2 QB 747, 780.

It might have been thought that such an approach would usually lead to the transaction being struck down since in most such cases the parties do not 'really' intend the goods to be 'sold'.[64] This is borne out by the fact that the sale price will rarely be fixed by the market price of the goods but will depend on the amount of the loan the seller wishes to raise, though doubtless the market price will normally represent at least the maximum which the buyer will pay or lend. Moreover, there is never any intention in such transactions for the possession of the goods to be given unless the seller defaults in payment of the hire-purchase rental; hence the implied conditions under the Sale of Goods Act would be absurdly inappropriate. Nevertheless, the modern tendency has been to uphold the genuineness of these transactions, though judicial disagreements have been frequent.[65] The difficulty is to formulate any criterion by which the 'real intention' of the parties may be judged. In practice there is rarely any problem about commercial sales and leasebacks, but more difficulty has often arisen with sales followed by hire-purchase contracts.

In Scots law, where the Bills of Sale Acts do not apply, the interpretation of s. 62(4) has caused some difficulties against the background of the general principle that the creation of a security in moveables requires that the creditor be in possession of the security subjects. Thus the 'buyer' in the transaction has no security. The disapplication of the Sale of Goods Act also means that the pre-1893 rules on transfer of property apply, with the effect that the 'buyer' in the transaction cannot be the owner of the goods unless there has been delivery. As in England, the Scottish courts have emphasised the need to investigate the substance of the transaction and the true intention of the parties.[66] If the evidence shows that the aim of the transaction was to raise finance by means of a security, then there is no sale.[67]

The courts tend to take at their face value the intention of the parties as expressed in the written documents which they have executed. The argument that these documents are 'shams' because they do not express the 'real intention' of the parties has been rejected unless it is shown that both parties do not intend the documents to operate according to their terms. Thus in *Snook v London and West Riding Investments Ltd*, Diplock LJ said:

> As regards the contention of the plaintiff that the transactions between himself, Auto Finance and the defendants were a 'sham', it is, I think, necessary to consider what, if any, legal concept is involved in the use of this popular and pejorative word. I apprehend that, if it has any meaning in law, it means acts done or documents executed by the parties to the 'sham' which are intended by them to give to third parties or to the court the appearance of creating between the parties legal rights and obligations different from the actual legal rights and obligations (if any) which the parties intend to create. But one thing, I think, is clear in legal principle, morality and the authorities (see *Yorkshire Railway Wagon Co v Maclure*[68] and *Stoneleigh Finance Ltd v Phillips*[69]), that for acts or documents to be a

---

64 See Fitzpatrick [1969] J Bus Law 211.
65 See *Stoneleigh Finance Ltd v Phillips* [1965] 2 QB 537; *Kingsley v Sterling Industrial Securities Ltd*, above; *Snook v London and West Riding Investments Ltd* [1967] 2 QB 786.
66 *Scottish Transit Trust Ltd v Scottish Land Cultivators Ltd* 1955 SC 254.
67 See, e.g., *G and C Finance Corp v Brown* 1961 SLT 408; *Ladbroke Leasing Ltd v Reekie Plant Ltd* 1983 SLT 155. The section does not apply to retention of title clauses (*Armour v Thyssen Edelstahlwerke AG* 1990 SLT 891 (HL)).
68 (1882) 21 Ch D 309.
69 [1965] 2 QB 537.

'sham', with whatever legal consequences follow from this, all the parties thereto must have a common intention that the acts or documents are not to create the legal rights and obligations which they give the appearance of creating. No unexpressed intentions of a 'shammer' affect the rights of a party whom he deceived. There is an express finding in this case that the defendants were not parties to the alleged 'sham'. So this contention fails.[70]

These refinancing transactions are not prohibited by the Consumer Credit Act 1974, although that Act has the result of conferring upon the 'seller' the protection of the general provisions relating to the provision of credit. It is possible, however, that the Unfair Contract Terms Act 1977 may indirectly affect the situation. Because of the restrictions on the right of the parties to contract out of the terms as to quality and fitness imposed by that Act[71] financiers may become more reluctant to enter into a transaction of this nature. What is more, absurd consequences could follow if the 'seller' was held entitled to complain of defects in the very goods he has himself sold and taken back on hire-purchase. So the courts may be more inclined now to hold that such transactions are not genuine sales, but fall within the Bills of Sale Acts.

The question has also arisen as to whether an arrangement under which the supplier of goods to a customer acts as agent of a finance house to sell goods to the customer, and then to resell them to the finance house, creates a charge over the supplier company's assets.[72] It has been held that it does not.[73]

Sale of goods and supply of services

Traditionally the law has distinguished between contracts for sale of goods and contracts for the supply of services. In older law, contracts for the supply of services were often subdivided, for instance, into contracts for skill and labour, or contracts for labour and materials, according to whether the supplier was providing services only, or materials as well. It was, however, generally assumed that in a contract for services the law applicable was not the law of sale of goods even though some goods might incidentally be supplied. For example, it was always said that a contract for the services of a solicitor was a contract for services, even though the solicitor might be expected to draft some document and deliver it to the client so that it would become the client's property.[74]

The first question that needs to be asked is when does it matter whether a contract is for the sale of goods or for supply of services? In many cases it will not matter at all; the applicable law will be the same. But there are some cases in which it has mattered in the past, and yet others in which it may still matter. First, as we have seen,

---

70 [1967] 2 QB 786, 802. See also *Street* v *Mountford* [1985] AC 809 and *AG Securities* v *Vaughan* [1988] 3 All ER 1058, above, n. 25, and *Re Curtain Dream plc* [1990] BCLC 925.
71 There were, of course, similar restrictions in the previous Hire-Purchase Acts. But the new Act makes no specific provision, as the old one did, for second-hand goods. It is, therefore, more likely that a refinancing transaction could involve the finance company in liability for the quality and fitness of the goods if transactions are held valid according to their terms.
72 Which would be registrable, or void in the event of the company's insolvency – see p. 476 *et seq.*
73 See *Welsh Development Agency* v *Export Finance* [1992] BCLC 148.
74 See Blackburn J in *Lee* v *Griffin* (1861) 1 B & S 272, 277–8.

in England until 1954 the law required that contracts for the sale of goods of the value of £10 or more should be evidenced in writing. No such requirement applied to contracts for the supply of services. This difference between the two kinds of contract disappeared with the repeal of the requirement of writing, but older authorities on the distinction which may still be cited today were often concerned with this requirement. Secondly, a contract in which a person is to manufacture goods and then supply them, or in which a person is to supply and install materials in a house or other building, may also differ from a simple contract of sale of goods in some important respects. For example, the time at which the property in the goods is to pass from the supplier to the buyer or client may differ in the two cases.[75] Thirdly, in the case of goods to be manufactured by the seller, there may sometimes be a difference between a contract under which the seller simply contracts for a result, and cases in which he actually contracts to manufacture and deliver the goods. In the former case, the contract is one of sale and nothing else, while in the latter case the contract is both for services and for the sale of goods. Important results may sometimes turn upon whether the contract falls into one class or the other. For example, a buyer who pays part of the price in advance, and then defaults, may be entitled to recover his advance payment (subject of course to the seller's claim for damages for the default) if the contract is a pure contract of sale,[76] while it seems that he cannot recover any such advance payment if the contract is one for *manufacture and sale*.[77]

The reason for this apparently arbitrary distinction is that if the contract is a pure sale, the whole consideration for the buyer's price is the transfer of the property in the goods to the buyer: hence it is inconsistent for the seller at one and the same time to claim that he need no longer transfer the goods to the buyer because of the buyer's default, and yet that he may retain the buyer's advance payment, which is simply the consideration for that transfer of the goods. On the other hand, where the contract is for the manufacture and supply of the goods, the manufacture of the goods is itself part of the consideration for the price; if the seller has devoted time and money to making the goods, any advance payment can be considered as a payment towards the manufacture as much as a payment towards the actual transfer of the goods. Hence, the mere fact that as a result of the buyer's default the goods will no longer be transferred to him at all does not mean that the consideration for the advance payment has wholly failed. However, despite this element of logicality, the result is far from satisfactory, and the law remains in a somewhat uncertain state.[78]

A more general reason why it may be necessary to distinguish between a contract of sale of goods and a contract for services is simply that the provisions of the Sale of Goods Act do not in general apply to contracts for services. And although in

---

75 See *Pritchett and Gold and Electrical Power Storage Co v Currie* [1916] 2 Ch 515 – see below, p. 336.

76 *Dies v British & International etc Mining Corpn* [1939] 1 KB 724 – see below, p. 555.

77 *Hyundai Heavy Industries Co Ltd v Papadopoulos* [1980] 1 WLR 1129 – see below, p. 483. Cf. the *Fibrosa* case [1943] AC 32, where nobody seems to have had any doubt that there was a total failure of consideration when a contract to manufacture machinery was frustrated before any of it was delivered. The effect of the developing law of restitution in this area should be noted, however. In *British Steel Corp v Cleveland Bridge Engineering* [1984] 1 All ER 504, the defendants were held liable to pay a reasonable sum to the plaintiffs for work done at their request, though no contract had been entered into. See also Jaffey [1998] NILQ 107. It is not clear that Scots law would draw these distinctions. See further, below, p. 558.

78 See below, p. 558.

some situations there is corresponding legislation governing contracts of services – in particular, the Supply of Goods and Services Act 1982 – there are other situations in which no corresponding legislation applies. In particular situations this may make a critical difference to the outcome of a case.[79] In the case of consumer transactions the legal position with regard to goods to be manufactured or produced, or sold and installed, is now in principle affected by the sale of consumer goods and associated guarantees directive,[80] but implementation of these provisions is problematic as will be seen later.[81]

Another reason why it may be important to distinguish between a contract of sale of goods and a contract for the supply of services concerns the implied duties of the seller or supplier as to the quality and fitness of the goods or services supplied. Until the enactment of the Supply of Goods and Services Act 1982, the position was, roughly speaking, as follows:

1 If the contract was a sale of goods, the implied duties under the Sale of Goods Act were incorporated in the contract, and these duties were, and remain, prima facie duties of strict liability, that is to say the seller is responsible for defects in the goods, even in the absence of negligence.

2 If the contract was for the supply of services, then, insofar as the services themselves were concerned, the supplier's duties were generally duties of due care only; but where goods were supplied incidentally as a part of such a contract, it was generally held that the supplier's duties as regards the goods so supplied were strict, at any rate in a transaction for commercial (as opposed to professional) services.[82] Although the implied terms in the Sale of Goods Act did not apply to goods supplied in the course of a contract for services the courts tended to imply terms at common law which were more or less identical with those implied under the Act.

The Supply of Goods and Services Act 1982 in effect enacts the position as set out in paragraph 2 above. Under this Act, implied conditions as to quality and fitness, almost identical to those implied under the Sale of Goods Act, are incorporated in all contracts for the 'transfer of goods' other than contracts of sale and hire-purchase which are already covered by other statutes.[83] So, also, restrictions on contracting out of these implied conditions are imposed, closely analogous to those governing contracts of sale of goods.[84] A contract for the transfer of goods which thus falls within the 1982 Act is defined by s. 1(1) of that Act as a contract under which 'one person transfers or agrees to transfer to another the property in goods' (other than the

---

79 See, e.g., *Hanson (W) (Harrow) v Rapid Civil Engineering & Usborne Depts Ltd* (1987) 38 Build LR 106, below, p. 400.
80 Articles 1(4) and 2(5).
81 See p. 525 *et seq.*
82 See, e.g., *Myers v Brent Cross Service Co* [1934] 1 KB 46; *Watson v Buckley* [1940] 1 All ER 174.
83 There are a number of other exceptions of minor importance, e.g. a gift (even if made by deed) is not covered: s. 1(1)(d) of the 1982 Act. The Law Commissions' Final Report on *Sale and Supply of Goods*, which is discussed in Chapter 13, proposed a number of important amendments to the law of sale which are also applied to other contracts for the supply of goods by the Sale and Supply of Goods Act 1994. This Act also applies to Scotland the provisions of the 1982 Act about contracts for the transfer of goods.
84 See s. 7 of the Unfair Contract Terms Act 1977, as amended by the 1982 Act, below, p. 234.

excepted contracts which are covered elsewhere) and s. 1(3) makes it clear that these contracts fall within the 1982 Act even if services are also provided under the contract. Then ss. 12–16 of the 1982 Act deal with contracts for the supply of services, and it is made clear that these sections apply even if goods are also to be transferred under the contract.[85] The implied terms under these sections, however, only impose a requirement to carry out the services with reasonable care and skill (s. 13) and do not impose strict liability;[86] furthermore, the restrictions on contracting out are not the very severe restrictions governing implied conditions in (consumer) contracts of sale of goods or contracts for the transfer of goods, but the more lenient restriction that any exclusion must comply with the 'reasonableness' requirement of ss. 2(2) and 3 of the Unfair Contract Terms Act 1977.[87]

Thus, the 1982 Act appears to simplify and clarify the law. Where a contract might be classified as a contract of sale of goods or a contract for the supply of services, the new Act will often make it quite immaterial how the contract is classified. Insofar as goods are supplied under the contract, the seller's (or supplier's) duties will normally be strict and excludable only in the limited circumstances provided for contracts for sale or supply of goods, while insofar as the contract concerns services, the supplier's duties will be duties of care, which will be excludable subject to the reasonableness requirement of the Unfair Contract Terms Act 1977. Unfortunately, the 1982 Act does not wholly succeed in separating out duties regarding goods and duties regarding services. Although the position prior to the Act was (as stated above) that normally the supplier was strictly liable as regards the goods, and only liable for negligence as regards services, there were many exceptions to this position. On the one hand, there were some cases in which goods were supplied as an incident to a contract for services in which the seller's or supplier's duties were not strict, but only duties of care; and on the other hand, there were also a number of cases (rather more in this situation than the previous one) in which the supplier's duties as regards the services were held to be strict and not just duties of care.

The first group of cases concerns contracts for professional services. These are plainly contracts for services, but in the course of some transactions of this general nature materials of a certain kind may be supplied which would perhaps not be thought of as 'goods' in the ordinary way. For instance, it has never been suggested in England that a doctor or hospital which supplied drugs to a patient (even a paying patient) could be held liable if the drugs, despite all reasonable care, turned out to be unfit for their purpose; nor has it ever been suggested that a patient inoculated with some contaminated vaccine could sue for breach of an implied warranty of fitness, as opposed to suing for negligence.[88] Similarly, it has never been suggested that a patient who receives a transfusion of contaminated blood could sue the

---

85 But these provisions do not apply in Scotland, where the supplier of services still has only the common law duty of care.
86 Though under Arts 1(4) and 2(5) of the sale of consumer goods and associated guarantees directive they may do so – see p. 525 *et seq.*
87 Section 16 of the 1982 Act. Liability for death or personal injury cannot, however, be excluded – 1977 Act s. 2(1). As to the requirement of 'reasonableness', see below, p. 243. Again this could, in principle, be affected by the sale of consumer goods and associated guarantees directive – see p. 529.
88 See, e.g., *Roe v Minister of Health* [1954] 2 QB 66.

supplier (even if he is a paying patient and a contract can be established) on the basis of implied warranties. In America, this possibility was specifically rejected by the decision of the New York Court of Appeals in *Perlmutter* v *Beth David Hospital*[89] in which the plaintiff was given a blood transfusion in the defendants' hospital. The blood was contaminated with jaundice viruses which, according to the expert evidence, were not detectable by any scientific tests at the time, and the plaintiff suffered injury in consequence. The plaintiff was a paying patient at the hospital and in the account rendered to him he was charged a separate sum for the cost of the blood itself. The plaintiff claimed that the blood had been 'sold' to him and that the defendants were therefore liable for 'defects' on the basis of implied warranties.[90] But the majority of the court held that the transaction was one of services only and that the supply of the blood was merely incidental to those services, and an English court would almost certainly concur with this decision.[91]

On the other hand, in *Dodd* v *Wilson*,[92] the plaintiff contracted with a veterinary surgeon to inoculate his cattle with a serum, which the surgeon did, using vaccine which he had himself bought from suppliers of vaccine. It was held that this was not a contract of sale but that, nevertheless, the surgeon impliedly warranted the vaccine to be fit for the purpose for which it was supplied. Hence he was liable, despite the fact that he was not himself guilty of any negligence.

It is by no means easy to distinguish these cases. Perhaps what underlies the distinction is that human blood for transfusion is not ordinarily thought of as the subject of commerce which is bought and sold,[93] whereas cattle serum clearly is ordinarily the subject of contracts of sale. And although in *Dodd* v *Wilson* the contract between the plaintiff and the surgeon was not one of sale, the judge evidently did not wish to deprive the plaintiff of the remedy which he would undoubtedly have had if he had himself bought the serum and merely obtained the services of the defendant to inoculate his cattle with the serum. In fact, the surgeon brought in his suppliers as third parties to the case and they brought in the manufacturers as fourth parties. Since the transactions between these parties, and between the surgeon and his suppliers, were clearly contracts of sale, the liability was passed down the line to the manufacturers.

The effect of the 1982 Act on these problems is unclear.[94] A literal approach would suggest that strict duties as to the quality and fitness of the goods would now apply in all these cases on the ground that they involve the transfer of goods even as an incident to a contract for services, but a court might still strive to avoid this result by holding (for instance) that human blood for transfusion is not 'goods' at all.[95] The case would be even stronger with organ transplants[96] but, on the other hand, manufactured objects which are implanted in a body (such as heart pacemak-

---

89 123 NE 2d 792 (1955). Not all US states follow this approach, but in most states where warranty liability has been recognized at common law, the result has been reversed by statute.
90 See below, p. 206.
91 An alternative approach is suggested at pp. 278 *et seq.*
92 [1946] 2 All ER 691.
93 See Titmuss, *The Gift Relationship*, Harmondsworth, 1973.
94 It appears to have been outside the terms of reference of the Law Commission inquiry, *Law of Contract: Implied Terms in Contracts for the Supply of Services* (Law Com. No. 156, Cmnd. 9773, 1986).
95 See pp. 276 *et seq.*
96 For some arguably relevant dicta, see *Browne* v *Norwich Crematorium Ltd* [1967] 1 WLR 691, 695.

ers or artificial heart valves or hip joints) would presumably be 'goods' and so could attract the strict duties of quality and fitness.[97] Similarly, the contract in *Dodd* v *Wilson* would now seem clearly to fall within the 1982 Act.

A similar problem arises with other goods transferred as a minor incident to a contract for services. Reference has been made above to the case of a contract with a solicitor for the drafting of a legal document which is thereupon supplied to the client and plainly becomes his property. Again, literal construction of the 1982 Act would suggest that the solicitor might now become strictly liable if the document fails of its purpose, even if the solicitor has taken all due care; again, it does not seem likely that this result was actually intended by the Act, and a court would presumably strive to avoid it.[98] A possible distinction which might be made is between the legal document as goods, i.e. as paper and ink, and the legal effect it is intended to produce which is entirely dependent on the legal framework within which it operates.[99] An analogous distinction is between the medium upon which a painting is painted, which becomes the property of the purchaser, and the copyright in the painting, which remains vested in the artist until he assigns it. A related problem arises in relation to computer software which is specially written for a customer. This question is dealt with in Chapter 6.

The second main problem raised by the 1982 Act's attempt to separate out the legal treatment of implied conditions regarding goods on the one hand and services on the other is, in a sense, the converse of the first. Prior to the Act there were some circumstances in which services were supplied as an incident to a contract for the sale (or transfer) of goods and in which the seller, or supplier, was held to the strict standard appropriate for the quality and fitness of goods, both for the goods and the services themselves. This would normally have been the case (whatever the nature of the contract) if the seller or supplier contracted to produce a result. For instance, a seller who contracted to make and deliver a machine would not normally have been able to escape liability for the machine's failure to meet the specified (or implied) quality or fitness required under the contract by pleading that he took all due care and that the resulting failure was not because the goods (or parts) were in any way defective, but because they had been defectively put together in some way not due to his negligence. Similarly, a repairer who subcontracted part of the work to competent subcontractors

---

97 It seems that at one time it was intended that items implanted under the NHS should remain the property of the NHS, but this suggestion was vetoed by Ministers (see former Health Minister Edwina Currie in *The Sunday Times*, 22 October 1989, p. C2), so it must be assumed that the property in an implanted object is intended to pass to the patient. Problems may well arise in relation to implants under the Consumer Protection Act 1987 – see below, p. 276 *et seq*. Of course, the transaction under which these articles were implanted would have to be a consensual one, which might create an indefensible distinction between private and NHS patients – see p. 9.

98 But *quaere* the proper application of the sale of consumer goods and associated guarantees directive 99/44/EC, OJ L171, 7/7/1999 in such cases – see p. 529 *et seq*.

99 In *Winter* v *G P Putnam's Sons* 938 F 2d 1033, 9th Cir. (1991) the plaintiffs, relying on erroneous information in a reference book, ate poisonous mushrooms and suffered serious physical injury. The court refused to hold the publishers liable on products liability theory, on the ground that the expressions and ideas contained in the book were intangible, and products liability theory is concerned with tangibles. It must be borne in mind, however, that American courts are concerned not to place restrictions on the unfettered exchange of ideas, which might run into problems with the First Amendment to the Constitution. The court distinguished the case of *Fluor Corp* v *Jeppesen & Co* 216 Cal Rptr 68 (Cal Ct of App 1985) in which the defendants were held liable on products liability theory in respect of a defective aeronautical chart. For a discussion of the question of the liability of sellers of books containing erroneous information see Lloyd [1993] JBL 48 – and see p. 276 *et seq*. below.

might have been liable for the negligence of the subcontractors on the ground that he impliedly warranted that the work under the contract would be fit for the purpose required – not just that he would do the work with due care.[100] Although the 1982 Act only implies a duty of reasonable care with regard to services (whether or not they are supplied under a contract which also involves a transfer of goods), it seems probable that the same result would still be arrived at because of s. 16(3) of the 1982 Act. This section leaves open the possibility of a court implying terms which are stricter than those of due care, so that, in effect, the implied duty that services are to be performed with reasonable care must be taken as a minimum legal requirement (subject to the possibility of valid exclusion), and not as excluding the possibility of a higher duty.

It is thus clear that the distinction between goods and services will often remain of some importance in the law, and it will still occasionally be necessary to distinguish between a contract of sale of goods and a contract for the supply of services. The test for deciding whether a contract falls into the one category or the other is to ask what is 'the substance' of the contract.[101] If the substance of the contract is the skill and labour of the supplier, then the contract is one for services, whereas if the real substance of the contract is the ultimate result – the goods to be provided – then the contract is one of sale of goods. Hence a contract for the painting of a picture is a contract for services – the skill of the artist is clearly more important than the incidental fact that the property in the completed picture (though not the copyright in it) will pass to the client.[102] A fortiori, on this test a contract with a professional person such as a lawyer or an accountant is a contract for services even though documents may be prepared and passed to the client so as to become his property.[103] On the other hand, a contract for the construction of two ships' propellers was held by the House of Lords in *Cammell Laird & Co Ltd* v *Manganese Bronze and Brass Co Ltd*[104] to be unquestionably a contract for the sale of goods. Similarly, a contract for the manufacture of a ship is a contract of sale of goods, but it is not necessarily a pure contract of sale:[105] if the process of manufacture itself forms part of the contract, the contract in effect consists of two sub-parts, (1) a contract under which the supplier is to make the ship – which is a contract for services – and (2) a contract under which the supplier agrees to sell the completed ship – in effect, a contract of sale of goods. A contract for the supply of a meal in a restaurant, as previously noted, seems to be a contract of sale of goods.[106]

Sale and agency

It may, at first sight, seem a little odd that it is thought necessary to distinguish a contract of sale of goods from a contract of agency, but in a certain type of case the

---

100 See, e.g., *Stewart* v *Reavell's Garage* [1953] 2 QB 545.
101 *Robinson* v *Graves* [1935] 1 KB 579.
102 Ibid.
103 Though in the old case of *Lee* v *Griffin* (1861) 1 B & S 272 a contract to manufacture false teeth was held to be a contract for the sale of goods – an outcome perhaps indicative of the regard in which dentists were held in the mid-nineteenth century! *Quaere* the proper application of the sale of consumer goods and associated guarantees directive 99/44/EC, OJ L171, 7/7/99, to such cases – see p. 529 *et seq.*
104 [1934] AC 402.
105 *Hyundai Heavy Industries Co Ltd* v *Papadopoulos* [1980] 1 WLR 1129 – see below, p. 483.
106 *Lockett* v *A & M Charles Ltd* [1938] 4 All ER 170.

distinction may well be a fine one by no means easy to draw. Where, for example, A asks B, a commission agent, to obtain goods for him from a supplier or from any other source, and B complies by sending the goods to A, it may well be a fine point whether this is a contract under which B sells the goods to A, or is a contract under which B acts as A's agent to obtain the required goods from other sources.

It is important to distinguish between the two transactions for a number of reasons. In the first place, the Commercial Agency Regulations[107] apply to many agency contracts,[108] and regulate the rights and duties of the parties in certain respects. Furthermore, if the transaction is an agency contract there may be privity of contract between the buyer and the agent's supplier which will enable action to be brought between them.[109] On the other hand, if it is a sale, there will be no privity between the buyer and the seller's own supplier. Other reasons for distinguishing the relationship of agent and seller may be that the duties of a commission agent are less stringent than those of a seller and, in the event of a breach of contract, the measure of damages may also be different. Thus if a seller delivers less than he is bound to under the contract, the buyer can reject the whole;[110] but if, despite his best endeavours, a commission agent delivers less than his principal has ordered he has committed no breach of contract and the principal is bound to accept whatever is delivered.[111] Again, should the commission agent deliver goods of the wrong quality he will only have to pay as damages the actual loss suffered by the buyer.[112] On the other hand, should a seller be guilty of such a breach he may have to pay as damages the buyer's probable loss of profit. So, also, an agent who merely introduces a seller to a buyer is not necessarily warranting the seller's title to sell, whereas if he is himself buying and reselling, such a warranty is invariably implied.[113]

In *Esso Petroleum Co Ltd* v *Addison*[114] Moore-Bick J left open whether petrol station franchisees who provided customers with 'gifts'[115] in return for tokens, furnished the gifts as agents for Esso or on their own account.[116]

Where one person contracts to manufacture goods for another out of materials to be supplied by that other, it may again be doubtful whether the manufacturer is a seller or an agent.[117]

---

107 SI 1993/3053 which implements EC Directive number 86/653 of 18 December 1986.

108 They apply in general contracts between self-employed agents and their principals – reg. 2(1), but there are certain exclusions.

109 *Teheran-Europe Corpn Ltd* v *Belton Ltd* [1968] 2 QB 545.

110 Section 30(1) – see below, p. 139.

111 *Ireland* v *Livingston* (1872) LR 5 HL 395. Similarly, in the case of late shipment: *Anglo-African Shipping Co* v *J Mortner Ltd* [1962] 1 Lloyd's Rep 610.

112 *Cassaboglou* v *Gibb* (1883) 11 QBD 797.

113 See *Warming Used Cars Ltd* v *Tucker* [1956] SASR 249, where it was held that the defendant did not warrant title although the transaction was a sale; but it seems that the defendant might more properly have been treated as a mere agent.

114 [2003] EWHC 173.

115 As to whether such transactions are really gifts or sales see *Esso Petroleum* v *Commissioners of Customs & Excise* [1976] 1 All ER 117 – discussed at p. 11 above.

116 Id. para. 54.

117 Cf *Dixon* v *London Small Arms Co Ltd* (1876) 1 App Cas 633; *Hill & Sons* v *Edwin Showell* (1918) 87 LJKB 1106. But where consumer goods are concerned the possible effect of the consumer goods and associated guarantees directive 99/44/EC, OJ L171, 7/7/99 needs to be considered – see pp. 525–6.

In the converse position, where a person contracts to dispose of the goods of another, it is again necessary to decide whether the relationship between the parties is that of buyer and seller or principal and agent. In the latter case, the agent is not in precisely the same position as a buyer and, for instance, cannot pass a good title to a third party without the principal's actual or apparent authority.[118] Again, where a person contracts to dispose of another's goods, it may be important to decide whether he is a buyer or an agent if he receives any payment from a third party as a result of disposing of the goods. If he is a buyer, such payment will discharge the third party, wholly or *pro tanto*. But if he is an agent and he fails to account to his principal for the money, the third party will only be discharged if the agent was authorized to receive the money.[119] The relationship between the principal and the agent depends, of course, on the terms, express or implied, of the contract between them; but in some cases where goods have been delivered to an agent for sale, the agent will have the goods on 'sale or return' or similar terms, in which case, although the transaction is not strictly a sale, some provisions of the Sale of Goods Act may apply.[120]

NUMBER OF PARTIES

It has been decided that the requirement that the property be transferred from one party to another means that there must be two distinct parties to a contract of sale. In *Graff* v *Evans*,[121] decided in 1882, 11 years before the original Act was passed, it was held that the transfer of intoxicating liquor by the manager of an unincorporated club to a member for money was not a 'sale' within the Licensing Act, but merely a transfer of special property. The basis of the decision was that the member was himself a part owner of the liquor and that consequently the transaction was a release of the rights of the other members to the 'purchaser'. It might have been thought, therefore, that when s. 1(1) (now s. 2(2)) of the Act specifically enacted that:

There may be a contract of sale between one part owner and another

the basis of *Graff* v *Evans* had been swept away. But in *Davies* v *Burnett*,[122] a divisional court followed the earlier case and the Sale of Goods Act was not even referred to. This view of the law has now been accepted for so long that it is unlikely to be upset by a higher court.[123] Scots law appears also to accept this position in principle.[124]

---

118 *Edwards* v *Vaughan* (1910) 26 TLR 545.
119 See, e.g., *Sorrell* v *Finch* [1977] AC 728 (estate agent).
120 Section 18, Rule 4 – see below, p. 329.
121 (1882) 8 QBD 373.
122 [1902] 1 KB 666.
123 In any event, the particular difficulty in question has been met by legislation: see Part II of the Licensing Act 1964, which regulates the 'supply' of liquor in clubs. See also *Carlton Lodge Club* v *Customs & Excise Commissioners* [1974] 3 All ER 798. But see the discussion at p. 343 *et seq.*; otherwise it is questionable whether the Supply of Goods and Services Act 1982 applies to such a transaction, or whether the buyer can have any remedy in respect of defective goods under that Act or otherwise.
124 *Laws of Scotland: Stair Memorial Encyclopaedia*, vol. 2, para. 803. For Scottish licensing law in relation to the sale and supply of alcoholic liquor in unincorporated clubs, see the Licensing (Scotland) Act 1976, Part VII. The Act is under review at the time of writing (April 2004).

Although the Act contemplates two distinct parties to the contract, namely a buyer and a seller, it does not follow that the buyer cannot already be the owner of the goods, for the seller may be a person having legal authority to sell them, for example a sheriff acting in execution of a writ of execution.[125] However, if a person contracts to buy his own goods from someone else under the mistaken impression that the goods belong to the seller, it seems clear that he can recover any price paid on the ground of total failure of consideration. A fortiori if he has not yet paid the price, the seller cannot sue him for it. This does not mean that such a contract is necessarily void, though it may be in some circumstances.[126]

THE PRICE

Section 8 of the Act is as follows:

(1) The price in a contract of sale may be fixed by the contract, or may be left to be fixed in a manner agreed by the contract, or may be determined by the course of dealing between the parties.

(2) Where the price is not determined as mentioned in subsection (1) above the buyer must pay a reasonable price.

(3) What is a reasonable price is a question of fact dependent on the circumstances of each particular case.

We have already seen that the consideration must be paid in money and that, strictly speaking, the contract will not be a contract of sale of goods if the consideration is in some other form.[127]

Section 8 has given rise to more difficulty than might have been thought. The section assumes that a contract has been made by the parties and then proceeds to explain the methods by which the price can be ascertained. But the first point which must be considered in an action on the sale is whether a contract has in fact been finally agreed upon by the parties, and the absence of an agreement as to the price (or even as to the mode in which the price is to be paid[128]) may show that the parties have not yet reached a concluded contract.

Another problem concerns the question whether the parties can make a binding contract in which they agree to fix the price at some future date. When s. 8 says that the price can be 'left to be fixed in a manner agreed', does this exclude the possibility that 'the manner' may simply require the parties to agree on the price? One view is that the parties simply cannot make a binding contract for the sale of goods at prices 'to be agreed', and that s. 8 does not apply to such a case, because under that section the buyer would have to pay a reasonable price, that is a price

---

125 But an argument can be made that this is not a sale at all, but a contract to release a lien – see *Hain SS Co Ltd v Tate & Lyle Ltd* [1936] 2 All ER 597.

126 In *Cooper v Phibbs* (1867) LR 2 HL 149 the House of Lords held that a contract for the lease of a fishery which turned out already to belong to the lessee was voidable. It is probable, however, that it should have been held void – see *Bell v Lever Bros* [1932] AC 161, 218.

127 There are dicta in *Koppel v Koppel* [1966] 1 WLR 802, 811, indicating that a contract to transfer goods in return for services is a sale of goods, but these seem to have been per incuriam.

128 See *Ingram v Little* [1961] 1 QB 31, 49, per Sellers LJ. Cf., however, *R & J Dempster Ltd v Motherwell Bridge & Engineering Co. Ltd* 1964 SC 308; *Glynwed Distribution Ltd v S Koronka & Co* 1977 SC 1.

fixed by a judge (or arbitrator) which is not the same thing as a price agreed between the parties.

There is undoubtedly some support for this view in the difficult case of *May & Butcher* v *The King*.[129] The House of Lords here held that an agreement for the sale of goods at a price to be later fixed by the parties was not, in the circumstances of the case, a concluded contract; but the later case of *Hillas & Co Ltd* v *Arcos Ltd*[130] shows that we cannot regard the earlier case as laying down any general rule and that that case is best regarded as one where the parties had not in the circumstances arrived at a concluded agreement.[131] In *Foley* v *Classique Coaches Ltd*,[132] the Court of Appeal held that an agreement to supply petrol 'at a price to be agreed by the parties' was a binding contract as the parties had clearly evinced an intention to be bound, and the contract contained an arbitration clause under which a reasonable price could be fixed in the event of disagreement.

On the other hand, it must be admitted that in a number of modern decisions the courts have reiterated the old (but not strictly accurate) learning that the law does not recognize 'an agreement to agree' as a binding contract. So in *Courtney & Fairbairn Ltd* v *Tolaini Bros (Hotels) Ltd* the Court of Appeal refused recognition of a contract at a price 'to be agreed'.[133] Of course, an arbitration clause to determine the price or the relevant terms would alter the case.[134] In the Australian High Court, suggestions have also been made that s. 8 is 'anomalous' and is not to be extended,[135] and it has also been suggested in the same case that the section only applies where the goods have been delivered and accepted, and that it has no application to a purely executory contract.[136] These dicta have not been followed, even in Australia,[137] but there does seem to be good sense in distinguishing between executed and executory contracts for this purpose. If the parties have already begun to carry out the contract, it is more troublesome as well as more unjust to declare the transaction void altogether.[138]

In *Sudbrook Trading Estate Ltd* v *Eggleton*[139] the House of Lords reviewed some similar problems which have arisen in contracts for the sale of land which are, of course, governed by common law and equitable rules and not by the Sale of Goods Act. The case did not involve anything in the nature of an 'agreement to agree' although it did involve an option to a lessee to buy the freehold of the leased premises

---

129 [1934] 2 KB 17n.
130 [1932] All ER Rep 494. The facts of this case illustrate the principle that parties who have had a previous course of dealings will be taken to intend the unexpressed terms of their new dealing to be those of the previous course of dealings unless a particular term is inapplicable or inappropriate to the new dealing – *Banque Paribas* v *Cargill* [1992] 1 Lloyd's Rep 96.
131 See *Smith* v *Morgan* [1971] 2 All ER 1500; *Brown* v *Gould* [1972] Ch 53. Compare *King's Motors* v *Lax (Oxford) Ltd* [1970] 1 WLR 426.
132 [1934] 2 KB 1.
133 [1975] 1 WLR. Terms 'to be negotiated' would be open to the same objections.
134 See s. 9 below, p. 32.
135 *Hall* v *Busst* (1960) 104 CLR 206.
136 Ibid., at 234.
137 *Wenning* v *Robinson* (1964) 64 SR (NSW) 157.
138 See *F & G Sykes (Wessex) Ltd* v *Fine Fare* [1967] 2 Lloyd's Rep 52, 57–8; *Avintair Ltd* v *Ryder Airline Services Ltd* 1994 SC 270.
139 [1983] 1 AC 444.

at a price to be fixed by valuers appointed by the two parties or in default of agreement by the valuers, at a price to be fixed by an umpire appointed by the valuers. It was held that the failure of the lessor to appoint a valuer could not be allowed to deprive the lessee of his right to a decree of specific performance once he had exercised his option to buy. The court could direct an inquiry to ascertain the reasonable price to be paid as the lessor had waived his right to appoint a valuer. The decision does not strictly have anything to do with s. 8 of the Sale of Goods Act, but there are dicta indicating that where an agreement has been partly performed, the court will strain to find some way of enforcing the intended arrangements even in the absence of agreement on a term which might have been fatal if the whole agreement had remained executory. It seems possible, therefore, that where parties agree on a sale of goods at prices to be agreed in the future, and the goods are actually delivered and accepted, or the agreement is otherwise partly performed, the courts may now be more willing to treat this as a binding contract to sell at reasonable prices, and to provide machinery for the ascertainment of such reasonable prices, even in the absence of a provision such as an arbitration clause by which this could be done under the contract itself.

This is perhaps borne out by two Court of Appeal decisions (though these did not involve price terms) in which it was stressed that in commercial cases, it is the intention of the parties which is decisive.[140] A failure to agree even on relatively important terms is not necessarily fatal; indeed, it cannot even be said that a failure to agree on the 'essential' terms is fatal. Provided that the parties intend to be bound, and that the agreement is sufficiently complete to be enforced as a contract, it is immaterial that they have failed to agree on some term which might appear, objectively speaking, to be important or even essential.[141]

The most recent authority in this area is the important House of Lords decision in *Walford v Miles*.[142] Again, this was not a sale of goods case, but the principles are applicable. The plaintiffs who were negotiating to buy a photographic processing business from the defendant entered into what allegedly amounted to a 'lock out' agreement according to which the defendant agreed to terminate negotiations with third parties and not to consider alternative offers. The agreement did not specify for how long the defendant was bound, but the plaintiffs asserted that it provided the parties with an exclusive opportunity to try to come to terms with the defendant. The defendant sold to a third party, and the plaintiff sued for breach. It was argued that the agreement implied a duty to negotiate in good faith with the plaintiffs, and that it should endure for a reasonable time, which was such time as was necessary to permit good faith negotiations either to come to fruition, or to fail. However, the House of Lords, following *Courtney v Fairbairn Tolaini*, held that an agreement to negotiate was not enforceable, and was not persuaded that the argument was improved by glossing a bare agreement to negotiate with a duty to negotiate in good faith.[143] In Lord Ackner's view, the plaintiff's argument was fundamentally at odds

---

140　*Pagnan SpA v Feed Products* [1987] 2 Lloyd's Rep 601; *Pagnan SpA v Granaria* [1986] 2 Lloyd's Rep 547.
141　*Pagnan SpA v Feed Products* [1987] 2 Lloyd's Rep at 619 per Lloyd LJ.
142　[1992] 2 AC 128.
143　The House of Lords rejected the view that a duty to use 'best endeavours' and to negotiate in good faith amount to the same thing, but how they differ is not clear.

with the adversarial ethic of contract law. Although this appears to have settled the matter in England and Wales for the time being, it must be noted that the experience of other jurisdictions suggests that *Walford* v *Miles* is unlikely to be the last word on the subject.[144] It must also be noted that Lord Ackner expressly recognized the possibility of a valid 'lock out' agreement.[145] Such an agreement does not lock the parties *into* negotiations; what the agreement achieves is to 'lock out' one party from negotiations with third parties for a certain period,[146] in order to give the other party an opportunity to try to come to terms.[147]

Section 9 runs as follows:

(1) Where there is an agreement to sell goods on the terms that the price is to be fixed by the valuation of a third party, and he cannot or does not make the valuation, the agreement is avoided; but if the goods or any part of them have been delivered to and appropriated by the buyer he must pay a reasonable price for them.

(2) Where the third party is prevented from making the valuation by the fault of the seller or buyer, the party not at fault may maintain an action for damages against the party at fault.

An agreement for the sale of goods at a valuation to be made by a third party must be distinguished from an agreement for sale at a valuation without naming any third party who is to make the valuation. In the former event, s. 9 applies, and if the third party does not make the valuation the contract is avoided, subject to the effect of s. 9(2). But in the latter event (for example, a sale of stock 'at valuation'), the agreement is in effect an agreement for sale at a reasonable price and, if no valuer is agreed and the parties otherwise fail to come to some arrangement for valuation, the contract will stand as a contract for sale at a reasonable price under s. 8.[148]

The sort of situation which is probably envisaged by s. 9(2) is, for example, a refusal by the seller to allow the valuer access to the goods, thereby preventing him obtaining the necessary material for making his valuation. It is a little difficult to imagine circumstances in which the buyer could prevent the valuer making his valuation, but no doubt this was inserted *ex abundanti cautela* to meet all possible contingencies. It is, perhaps, not entirely clear whether s. 9(2) envisages a sort of action for breach of a duty of good faith, or whether it envisages that in the circumstances postulated there would be an actual contract of sale. The measure of damages could perhaps differ according to the correct answer to that question.

144 See Farnsworth (1987) 87 Col LR 217. See also the Australian case of *Coal Cliff Collieries Pty Ltd* v *Sijehama Pty Ltd* (1991) 24 NSWLR 1. For comment from a Scottish perspective, see MacQueen in Forte (ed.), *Good Faith in Contract and Property* (1999), and note also *McCall's Entertainments (Ayr) Ltd* v *South Ayrshire Council (No. 1)* 1998 SLT 1403, in which *Walford* v *Miles* was cited, but not discussed.

145 At p. 139.

146 It is difficult to understand why the specification of a time seems to have been considered so important. Since the object of the contract is to give the parties time to reach a valuation, there seems to be no good reason why a contract giving a reasonable time for the parties to effect that object should not be upheld.

147 See *Pitt* v *PHH Asset Management* [1993] 4 All ER 961.

148 *F & G Sykes (Wessex) Ltd* v *Fine Fare*, n. 138 above. But it may be that as a result of the *Sudbrook Trading Estate* case, p. 31 above, even the failure of a named third party to make a valuation will only avoid the contract if his identity was essential to the arrangements. Otherwise it may be held that the contract is really for sale at a reasonable price, and the naming of the third party is simply machinery which can be replaced by the court.

Where a sale at a valuation is agreed upon and a valuation is subsequently made, it cannot be upset merely on the ground that the valuer has been negligent or has set about the valuation in an incorrect manner. As Lord Denning MR said in *Campbell v Edwards*:[149]

> It is simply the law of contract. If two persons agree that the price of property should be fixed by a valuer on whom they agree, and he gives that valuation honestly, they are bound by it. If there were fraud or collusion, of course, it would be very different.

It is now clear, however, that the valuer himself will normally be liable for negligence if it can be shown that he has adopted a wholly incorrect basis for his valuation.[150] As Lord Denning made clear in the above-cited passage, the valuation can be upset if there has been fraud or collusion. There are also some first-instance decisions holding that a valuation which sets out the basis on which it is arrived at may be open to challenge on the ground that the method disclosed is unsound in law.[151] But it cannot be assumed that the party aggrieved will always have a remedy if the valuation is made on an incorrect basis, because if the basis for the valuation is not disclosed and it was made in accordance with a permissible (though wrong) professional judgment, the valuation will stand and the valuer will not be liable for negligence.

CONVEYANCING EFFECT OF THE CONTRACT

Some comment must be made here on the words 'A contract of sale of goods is a contract by which the seller transfers . . . the property in goods' in s. 2(1). As is clearly apparent from these words, the actual contract may suffice to transfer the property in the goods, that is to say it may operate both as a conveyance and a contract. Attention is frequently drawn to this as though it were a remarkable rule, and a contrast is often made with the corresponding provisions of Roman law in which a sharp line was drawn between the contract and the conveyance. There is some point in this contrast, which is important in Scotland,[152] but a note of caution should be sounded against pursuing it too far, for remarkably few results follow in English law from the transfer of property by the mere agreement, which would not in any event follow from the transfer of property by delivery. This topic will be more fully examined later.[153]

It is possible that these words in s. 2(1) may also have the effect of bringing a transaction within the scope of a contract of sale even though it would be difficult to say that the object of the transaction was the transfer of the property in any goods. For example, if a person organizes a party, for which he sells tickets entitling a purchaser to help himself to drinks, it seems that a sale takes place when this

---

149 [1976] 1 WLR 403, 407; *Baber v Kenwood* [1978] 1 Lloyd's Rep 175.
150 *Arenson v Casson Beckman Rutley & Co* [1977] AC 405; *Arenson v Arenson* [1977] AC 747.
151 See *Wright v Frodoor* [1967] 1 WLR 506; *Burgess v Purchase & Sons (Farms) Ltd* [1983] Ch 216. Compare *Jones v Sherwood Computer Services* [1992] 2 All ER 170.
152 See Reid, *The Law of Property in Scotland* (1996), paras 606–18.
153 See p. 315 *et seq.*

happens, although it would be difficult to say that there was a contract of sale of goods arising from the mere sale of the ticket.[154] On the other hand, the courts have shown little inclination to make use of this analysis in civil cases. Thus in the case of a contract for work and materials, the courts have not said that there is a contract of sale within the Act when property in the materials eventually passes to the party ordering the work and materials.[155] And since the passing of the Supply of Goods and Services Act 1982, a court is perhaps more likely to hold that such a transaction is a contract for the transfer of goods rather than a contract for the sale of goods. But it would only be a matter of practical importance in very special circumstances.

154 See *Doak v Bedford* [1964] 2 QB 587, 596 per Paull J; but cf. Lord Parker CJ at 594. An entry ticket in such cases confers a licence to enter the premises concerned – *Hurst v Picture Theatres Ltd* [1915] 1 KB 1 (CA).
155 See *Young & Marten Ltd v McManus Childs Ltd* [1969] 1 AC 454.

3

FORMATION OF THE CONTRACT

OFFER AND ACCEPTANCE

Though Part II of the Act is entitled 'Formation of the Contract', it is somewhat para-doxical that there is nothing in it which regulates the actual formation of the contract of sale of goods. The only section which deals with this subject is s. 57 in Part VII governing the sale of goods by auction.

We are left to infer from s. 62(2) that a contract of sale of goods is formed accord-ing to the ordinary principles of the common law of England and Scotland, that is to say by offer and acceptance. As there is nothing in these rules of special significance in the law of sale of goods, this subject need not be enlarged upon here.

Apart from the Act's (and some other) provisions on auction sales, only two other matters relating to formation need be dealt with here, namely the doctrine of mistake in offer and acceptance, and the special provisions relating to contracts concluded away from business premises, i.e. the provisions designed to safeguard consumers against the consequences of 'doorstep selling'.

AUCTION SALES

The first two subsections of s. 57 are as follows:

(1) Where the goods are put up for sale by auction in lots, each lot is prima facie deemed to be the subject of a separate contract of sale.
(2) A sale by auction is complete when the auctioneer announces its completion by the fall of the hammer, or in other customary manner, and until the announcement is made any bidder may retract his bid.

These two subsections restate the common law rules governing auction sales.[1] Under these rules it is quite clear that the bidder is the offeror, that the auctioneer is entitled to accept or to refuse any bid,[2] and that the contract is made on the fall of the hammer. As each bidder may retract, the offeree may withdraw the article from sale even after bidding has commenced.[3] But, in practice, many auction sales are con-ducted under special 'Conditions of Sale' and these may sometimes affect the application of s. 57. For example, a condition justifying the auctioneer in re-opening

---

1 But in Scotland the common law may be that a bid cannot be retracted unless it is refused or a higher bid is made: *Cree v Durie*, 1 December 1810 (FC).
2 See, e.g., *British Car Auctions v Wright* [1972] 3 All ER 462.
3 *Fenwick v Macdonald Fraser & Co* (1904) 6 F 850.

the bidding in the event of a dispute has been applied even where the auctioneer intended to knock the goods down to the person who intended to buy them.[4]

The next four subsections give rise to more difficulty:

(3) A sale by auction may be notified to be subject to a reserve or upset price, and a right to bid may also be reserved expressly by or on behalf of the seller.

(4) Where a sale by auction is not notified to be subject to a right to bid on behalf of the seller, it is not lawful for the seller to bid himself or to employ any person to bid at the sale, or for the auctioneer knowingly to take any bid from the seller or any such person.

(5) A sale contravening subsection (4) above may be treated as fraudulent by the buyer.

(6) Where, in respect of a sale by auction, a right to bid is expressly reserved (but not otherwise) the seller, or any one person on his behalf, may bid at the auction.

The effect of these subsections may be considered under three heads.

Auction sale expressly subject to reserve price or right to bid

First, where the auction is expressly advertised subject to a reserve price or to the right of the seller to bid, subss. (3) and (6) preserve the seller's right not to sell below the reserve price, or to bid himself or to employ one (but not more than one) person to bid on his behalf, as the case may be. But as we have seen, subs. (2) preserves the common law rule that no contract of sale comes into existence until the seller accepts a bid. Subsection (3) therefore has independent force only where the auctioneer knocks the goods down below the reserve price by mistake. The effect of such a mistake was discussed in *McManus* v *Fortescue*.[5] In that case, the printed catalogue at an auction sale stated that each lot was subject to a reserve price, but the auctioneer knocked the goods down to the plaintiff for less than the reserve price by mistake. Recollecting the reserve price, the auctioneer then refused to sign a memorandum of sale.[6] It was held by the Court of Appeal that an action against the auctioneer must fail. Since the sale was expressly subject to a reserve price, the auctioneer could not be made liable for breach of warranty of authority. An action against the owner would presumably also have failed as the auctioneer's authority was known to be limited and was in fact exceeded. It is a fair inference that had the sale not been notified to the public as being subject to a reserve price, the seller would have been liable as the buyer would have been able to rely upon the auctioneer's apparent authority.

Auction sale with no express statement as to reserve price or right to bid

Where nothing is said about any reserve price or right of the owner to bid, a distinction must be drawn between the two cases. In the former case, the effect of s. 57(2) is that the auctioneer is still entitled to decline to accept any bid. In the latter case, however, subs. (4) applies and the buyer may set the contract aside, or presumably may sue for damages. Even where a reserve price is notified, the owner is still not entitled to bid unless this right also is expressly reserved; and if he does so

---

4 *Richards* v *Phillips* [1968] 2 All ER 859.
5 [1907] 2 KB 1.
6 If he had signed, it seems he would have been liable – see *Fay* v *Miller* [1941] 2 All ER 18.

bid and the reserve price is reached, the contract may be treated as fraudulent by the buyer. If the reserve price is not reached, however, although the seller may have wrongly bid himself, no one will have suffered damage so as to entitle him to sue the seller.

Auction sale expressly advertised without reserve

The effect of an express notification that the sale will be without reserve is left obscure by the Act. It is at any rate clear that s. 57(2) prevents any contract of sale coming into existence if the auctioneer refuses to accept a bid. There remains the possibility that the auctioneer may be held liable on the basis that he has contracted to sell the goods to the highest bidder, a device sanctioned by the Court of Exchequer Chamber in *Warlow* v *Harrison*.[7] The difficulties of this case have been explored by two learned writers.[8] Put briefly, these are (a) the fact that the highest bidder cannot be identified until the hammer has fallen, and we are postulating a case where the auctioneer has not accepted any bid; and (b) the apparent lack of consideration for the auctioneer's promise. Neither of these seems to be a fatal objection, for the person who had made the highest bid when the goods were withdrawn should prima facie be able to claim that he was the highest bidder, and a rather generous approach to the requirement of consideration is a feature common to most cases of breach of warranty of authority by an agent, as for example in *Collen* v *Wright*.[9] In Scotland consideration is not required in any event. Moreover, the decision in *Warlow* v *Harrison* has been affirmed by the Court of Appeal in *Barry* v *Heathcote Ball & Co (Commercial Auctions) Ltd*.[10]

Bidding agreements

Certain undesirable auction practices by buyers are dealt with by the Auctions (Bidding Agreements) Act 1969. The purpose of this Act (and the earlier Act of 1927 of the same name) is to prevent dealers from agreeing to abstain from bidding at a sale so that goods may be purchased at less than their true value if no other party is interested in bidding. Section 3 of the 1969 Act provides that where such an agreement is made the seller may avoid the contract and recover the goods or, in default, any loss he has suffered (namely the difference between the sale price and the true or fair price) from any party to the agreement. It is, however, difficult in practice to control these bidders' 'rings' because of problems of proof. Moreover, the Act does not prohibit a genuine agreement to buy the goods on joint account and, in practice, it may well be difficult to distinguish such an agreement from one whereby one dealer agrees not to bid for one item and another dealer agrees not to bid for another item.

---

7 (1859) 1 E & B 309.
8 Slade (1952) 68 LQR 238; ibid., 457; and Gower (1953) 69 LQR 21.
9 (1857) 8 E & B 647. See also *Starkey* v *Bank of England* [1903] AC 114 and *Sheffield Corpn* v *Barclay* [1905] AC 392, in both of which it was assumed by the House of Lords virtually without discussion that action in reliance could be treated as consideration in such cases. See also *Blackpool and Fylde Aero Club* v *Blackpool Borough Council* [1990] 3 All ER 25, discussed by Adams and Brownsword (1991) 54 MLR 281.
10 [2001] 1 All ER 944.

Mock auctions

Certain types of fraudulent 'mock auctions' are the subject of criminal penalties under the Mock Auctions Act 1961. Under the Enterprise Act 2002 notice of intended prosecution must be given to the Office of Fair Trading.[11] A 'mock auction' is defined by s. 1(3) of the 1961 Act as a sale of goods by way of competitive bidding if the goods are sold at less than the highest bid, or part of the price is repaid to the bidder, or the right to bid is restricted to persons who have bought or agreed to buy other goods, or any articles are given away or offered as gifts. The Act has given rise to a number of intricate questions of interpretation.[12]

MISTAKE IN THE OFFER OR ACCEPTANCE

English law

Certain kinds of mistake, although traditionally treated as part of the generic subject 'mistake' (as they were in the first edition of this book), are today often treated as part of the law of offer and acceptance. These cases, usually referred to nowadays as cases of 'mutual' and 'unilateral' mistake, involve a denial by one of the parties that an agreement has ever been reached on the ground that the intentions of the parties, judged objectively or subjectively as the case may be, never coincided. However, the expressions 'mutual mistake' and 'unilateral mistake' are somewhat misleading. The important question is not whether a mistake is one-sided or two-sided, but whether or not the mistake has prevented an agreement from coming into existence. In deciding whether the parties have in fact agreed, or must be taken in law to have agreed, the first thing to determine is whether it is a case where the parties' intentions are to be judged objectively or subjectively, for until this is done it is obviously impossible to say whether the intentions are the same, and hence whether the parties have agreed.

Where neither party is aware of the other party's real intentions, the law is clear that the offeree is entitled to judge the offerer's intentions objectively. If, so judged, the intentions coincide, then there is an agreement, and if the other requirements of the law are satisfied, a contract. For example, in *Tamplin* v *James*,[13] the defendant agreed to buy a public house under a mistaken impression that a certain field was included in the sale. There was nothing in the sale which should have led the buyer to make this mistake, and the seller was unaware of it. Applying the objective, reasonable man test, the Court of Appeal held that the buyer was liable on the contract for the sale of the public house without the field. The objective test in these cases means no more than that the parties are bound by what a reasonable man would have regarded as their intentions.

It may happen that even on the application of the objective test it is still not possible to spell out any definite contractual agreement between the parties and in such a case there is no contract. For example, in *Raffles* v *Wichelhaus*,[14] the

---

11 Section 230 – SI 2003/1376.
12 See, e.g., *R* v *Ingram* (1976) 64 Cr App Rep 119; *Clements* v *Rydeheard* [1978] 3 All ER 658; *Allen* v *Simmons* [1978] 1 WLR 79.
13 (1880) 15 Ch D 215.
14 (1864) 2 H & C 906.

plaintiff agreed to sell and the defendant agreed to buy a consignment of cotton *ex Peerless* from Bombay. In fact, there were two ships of that name, one leaving Bombay in October and the other in December. The plaintiff shipped by the one leaving in December. It was pleaded by the defendant that the ship mentioned in the agreement and intended by the defendant was the one which sailed in October. The plaintiff demurred to this plea, thereby admitting the ambiguity as to which ship was intended by the agreement, and the court held that the buyer was not liable for refusing to accept the consignment arriving in the later ship.

In such circumstances the main practical reason for holding that there is no contract is that the 'agreement' is incapable of being enforced by the courts because its meaning is not sufficiently certain. The requirement of certainty, while it may for reasons of convenience be treated independently, is really no more than a requirement that an offer must be certain in order to be capable of being converted into a contract by acceptance.[15]

It only remains to add that cases in which the contract will be held void on these grounds are necessarily rare for the application of the objective test will usually produce a definite result. The contract will nearly always be held binding on the terms intended by one party or the other. This is not always a wholly reasonable or fair result because, in the case of a genuine misunderstanding, there is something to be said for compromising on the terms intended by the parties.[16] But the courts rarely regard themselves free to achieve such results.[17]

Where, on the other hand, one party is aware, or ought reasonably to be aware, that the other party's intentions are not the same as his own, the mistaken party's intentions cannot be judged objectively and the party who is not mistaken cannot hold the other to a contract on the terms intended by him. There is no justification for permitting a person to assume that the other meant what he said where the former *knows* that the latter did *not* mean what he said. Thus in the famous case of *Smith* v *Hughes*,[18] the defendant bought some oats from the plaintiff but refused to take delivery on the grounds that the oats were not old, as he had thought, but new oats. The judge left to the jury the question as to whether the plaintiff had believed the defendant to believe that he was contracting for old oats, and directed them that if they answered that question affirmatively, they should find for the defendant.[19] In ordering a new trial on the ground of misdirection, the court drew a distinction between these two possibilities:

---

15 In *Scriven* v *Hindley* [1913] 3 KB 564, another case of sale of goods, hemp and tow was sold at an auction by the plaintiffs in bales bearing identical markings. The defendants bid an extravagant price for a lot of tow, believing it was hemp. It was held that the supposed sale could not be enforced against them.

16 See, e.g., *Butler Machine Tool Co* v *Ex-Cell-O Corpn* [1979] 1 WLR 401, the 'battle of the forms' case – p. 227.

17 But see, for some special cases, Ball (1983) 99 LQR 572.

18 (1871) LR 6 QB 597. See also at p. 217.

19 This complicated question is really only a reflection of the proposition that promises should be enforced in the sense in which the promisor understands the promisee to take them – Paley's *Moral Philosophy*, 1809 edn, p. 126 *et seq.* Paley cites the case of the tyrant Temores, who, having promised the inhabitants of Sebastia that if they surrendered to him no blood would be shed, buried them alive.

1   If the defendant mistakenly thought that the goods were old then, in the absence of warranty by the plaintiff, the defendant would be bound by the contract even though the plaintiff was aware of the mistake.
2   On the other hand, if the defendant mistakenly thought that the plaintiff was offering to sell him the oats *as old oats*, and the plaintiff was aware of the mistake, then the defendant would not be liable for refusing to accept the oats.

Precisely why he would not have been liable is more difficult to say. One explanation would be that, in this event, there would have been a binding contract to sell old oats and, the oats not being old, the defendant would have been entitled to reject them. But another possibility is that in this event the agreement really would have been void.

Similar uncertainty surrounds the decision in *Hartog* v *Colin & Shields*[20] where the plaintiff snapped up an offer to sell hare skins at so much *per pound* when he must have known that the offeror really meant to offer to sell at that price *per piece*. It was held that the plaintiff could not sue on a contract at the per pound price, but it is not certain what would have happened if the offeror had tried to sue on a contract at the per piece price. The answer would presumably depend on whether the offeror had reasonably understood the offeree to be accepting his intended offer, as opposed to the erroneous offer actually stated, or written.

The principle to be applied in cases of mistake as to the person is exactly the same, although the application of this principle in this case is more likely to make the contract void. First, a person cannot accept an offer which he knows is not intended for him, but for some third person.[21] And, secondly, a person cannot hold another to an acceptance when he knows that that other was intending to accept an offer not made by him, but by some third person.[22] Knowledge of the mistake by the one party is essential if the contract is to be held void. It cannot be said that one party is simply unable to accept an offer not intended for him, for a person can accept an offer not intended for him if he reasonably thinks it was so intended.[23]

It is also essential that there should be some identifiable third person for whom the offer or acceptance was intended if the contract is to be held void.[24] For if there is no such third person, the usual analysis is that the mistaken party does intend to contract with the other party although he is mistaken as to his attributes.[25]

These principles all go back to the late nineteenth century, if not earlier, and are well illustrated by two leading cases from that period which have caused trouble ever

---

20 [1939] 3 All ER 566.
21 *Boulton* v *Jones* (1857) 27 LJ Ex 117. It must be inferred that the plaintiff knew that the defendant intended to contract with Brocklehurst, and with him alone, otherwise the decision could not be supported today.
22 *Cundy* v *Lindsay* (1878) 3 App Cas 459.
23 *Upton RDC* v *Powell* [1942] 1 All ER 220; cf. Blackburn J in *Smith* v *Hughes* (1871) LR 6 QB 597, 607.
24 *King's Norton Metal Co* v *Edridge* (1897) 14 TLR 98. On this point see the classic analysis of Glanville Williams in (1945) 23 Can Bar Rev 271. See also the House of Lords decision in *Shogun Finance Ltd* v *Hudson* [2003] UKHL 62 discussed below.
25 See Unger (1955) 18 MLR 259 replying to Wilson (1954) 17 MLR 515.

since. In *Cundy* v *Lindsay*,[26] a swindler named Blenkarn ordered some goods from the plaintiffs in a letter in which he signed his name so as to resemble that of Blenkiron & Co, a firm known to the plaintiffs. Although the address of Blenkarn was not the same as that of Blenkiron & Co, they were both in the same street. The plaintiffs, without noticing the discrepancy in the street number, despatched the goods to Blenkarn, who promptly disposed of them to the defendants, who bought in good faith and for value. It was held by the House of Lords that no contract existed between the plaintiffs and Blenkarn, and the case had to be decided as though Blenkarn had stolen the goods; at no stage had the plaintiffs voluntarily decided to entrust the possession of their goods to Blenkarn. On the other hand, in *King's Norton Metal Co* v *Edridge*,[27] a swindler ordered goods under a false name, which was not that of any identified third party, and the plaintiffs despatched these goods on credit on the strength of the order. Once again the swindler disposed of the goods to the defendants. The Court of Appeal rejected the plaintiffs' claim on the ground that this was a simple case of a contract voidable for fraud and not a contract wholly void. And it is, of course, old and well-established law that goods obtained under a voidable title and resold to a bona fide purchaser cannot be claimed back by the original owner. The bona fide purchaser obtains a good title, and the original owner is left to pursue his remedy against the fraudulent party, for what that is worth – which is usually very little. The distinction between these two famous cases was considered by the House of Lords in *Shogun Finance Ltd* v *Hudson*,[28] discussed below.

The application of these cases to situations where parties have dealt with each other face to face has proved particularly troublesome. In *Phillips* v *Brooks*,[29] a swindler bought some jewellery in a shop by representing himself to be 'Sir George Bullough', a real third person known by name, but not personally, to the jeweller. It was held that there was a voidable contract. On the other hand, in *Ingram* v *Little*,[30] a different result was arrived at. Here, a swindler (H) representing himself to be a certain PGMH of Caterham, a real person not known personally to the plaintiffs, bought a car from them. The Court of Appeal (Devlin LJ dissenting) held that there was no contract at all between the plaintiffs and H. Sellers LJ summarized the views of the learned judge below, with which he agreed, as follows:

> The judge, treating the plaintiffs as the offerors and the rogue H as the offeree, found that the plaintiffs, in making their offer to sell the car not for cash but for a cheque . . . were under the belief that they were dealing with, and therefore making their offer to, the honest Mr PGMH of Caterham, who they had reason to believe was a man of substance and standing. H, the offeree, knew precisely what was in the minds of the two ladies [i.e. the plaintiffs] for he had put it there, and he knew that their offer was intended for Mr PGMH of Caterham, and that they were making no offer to, and had no intention to contract with

---

26 Above, n. 22.
27 (1897) 14 TLR 98.
28 [2003] UKHL 62.
29 [1919] 2 KB 243.
30 [1961] 1 QB 31.

him, as he was. There was no offer which he, H, could accept, and therefore there was no contract.[31]

However, in *Lewis v Averay*,[32] yet another case of a similar nature in which a swindler bought a car in return for a cheque by representing himself to be a well-known television star, the Court of Appeal threw doubt on *Ingram v Little*. In this case the court emphasized that where parties are dealing with each other face to face, there is a strong presumption that there is a contract between them. But only Lord Denning MR suggested that *Ingram v Little* was wrongly decided. It was also said to be surprising if the result of such cases was to turn, as suggested by Sellers LJ in *Ingram v Little*, on the swindler's state of mind.

The distinctions drawn in some of these cases are very fine ones; for instance, *Ingram v Little* is scarcely distinguishable from *Phillips v Brooks* and *Lewis v Averay*. So too, *Cundy v Lindsay* is barely distinguishable from *King's Norton Metal Co v Edridge*. Of course, fine distinctions do not necessarily mean that the distinctions are inherently unsound. It is the business of the law to draw distinctions and fine distinctions are often a necessary consequence. But these cases involve fine distinctions which are based on abstract concepts rather than on real social or commercial distinctions. It is, of course, clear that the only purpose of drawing these distinctions is to decide whether the contract is void or voidable and hence whether or not a bona fide purchaser should be protected. But whether or not the bona fide purchaser should be protected should depend on more substantial considerations than those which decide these cases. It is true that distinctions can be drawn between these cases which to some degree are more real than those which the courts drew. For instance, in *Phillips v Brooks*, the plaintiff was a shopkeeper who dealt in jewellery, whereas in *Ingram v Little*, the plaintiffs were two private sellers. Plainly, a shopkeeper who sells goods on credit to someone not known to him by sight and accepts a cheque in return is, in many respects, in a very different situation from a private seller. On the other hand, the plaintiff in *Lewis v Averay* was also a private seller and yet he was held not protected. Equally, in comparing *Cundy v Lindsay* with the *King's Norton* case, it is clear that the sellers in the latter case consciously took a much greater commercial risk than the sellers in the former case. In the *King's Norton* case, the sellers fulfilled an order by delivering goods on credit to a company of whom they had never heard and without any attempt to secure payment in advance. In *Cundy v Lindsay*, the sellers did at least think they were dealing with buyers known to them by repute. These distinctions may well be valid and they may even have influenced the actual decisions, but they are not the distinctions drawn by the courts.[33]

These cases were reviewed by the House of Lords in *Shogun Finance Ltd v Hudson*,[34] in which the authority of *Cundy v Lindsay* [35] was affirmed in a majority

---

31 At p. 49.

32 [1971] 3 All ER 907. See also *Whittaker v Campbell* [1983] 3 All ER 582. In Scotland, compare *Morrisson v Robertson* 1908 SC 332 with *MacLeod v Kerr* 1965 SC 253.

33 The HL decision in *Shogun Finance v Hudson* n. 28 above has scarcely improved matters. Though it does seem that *Lewis v Averay* may have been wrongly decided as *Cundy v Lindsay* (a HL decision) was not cited.

34 [2003] UKHL 62.

35 (1878) 3 App Cas 459.

decision. In that case, a rogue, who had stolen the identity of a real person, a Mr Patel, purported to enter into a hire-purchase agreement in Mr Patel's name to finance the purchase of a motor car, with the claimant finance company. The claimants carried out the usual credit status checks on Mr Patel, and accepted the purported proposal of Mr Patel. The dealer then allowed the rogue to take possession of the vehicle, and the rogue sold it to the defendant, who bought it in good faith and without notice. It was held by the majority that there was no contract between the rogue and the finance company; the only agreement that could have been in existence was the purported one between the finance company and Mr Patel. Accordingly, the defendant could not acquire title under s. 27 of the Hire-Purchase Act 1964.[36] Lord Nicholls and Lord Millett delivered strong dissenting speeches, and considered the decisions in *Phillips* v *Brooks Ltd* and *Lewis* v *Averay* preferable to that in *Cundy* v *Lindsay*. Lord Millett would have been prepared to overrule *Cundy* v *Lindsay, Ingram* v *Little* and the rather unsatisfactory decision in *Hector* v *Lyons*.[37] The result of the majority holding is that the law of mistake in England and Wales requires a distinction to be drawn between dealings in writing, and face-to-face dealings.

Proposals were made to abolish the distinction between void and voidable contracts, and to protect the bona fide purchaser in both cases alike.[38] But these proposals were not implemented, and even if they had been, it is not clear that they would wholly dispose of the difficulties. So long as a person from whom goods are *stolen* is to be entitled to recover his goods even from a bona fide purchaser to whom the thief may resell them, it will be necessary to distinguish between cases where the goods have been so stolen and cases where the original owner has been deprived of the goods by fraud or deception of some kind. Frauds and deceptions take a very large variety of forms, and it will almost certainly remain necessary to draw fine distinctions between fraud which does not, and fraud which does, totally negative the owner's consent to parting with the goods. It is true that the line between the cases could be drawn a little beyond where it is now drawn; it could (for instance) be so drawn that a bona fide purchaser obtains title where the owner has *voluntarily entrusted* the goods to the swindler, or where he has *voluntarily parted with the possession* of them. The second formulation would probably be wide enough to protect the third party in a *Cundy* v *Lindsay* situation, though the first might not. But it will remain necessary to distinguish cases of voluntary parting with possession from cases of fraud or deception so great that the owner is deprived of his possession without really consenting at all. Thus fine distinctions will almost inevitably remain here unless the law is so drastically reformed that even a bona fide purchaser from an actual thief is allowed protection, and that raises many doubts. It has never been proposed as a serious suggestion here.[39]

36 As to which see p. 410.
37 Unsatisfactory, because the facts were unclear. The best explanation for the decision would have been the maxim 'He who comes to equity must come with clean hands' as the plaintiff, who was seeking specific performance of a contract for the purchase of a house, had forged his son's signature – see *Shogun Finance Ltd* v *Hudson* n. 33 above per Lord Walker at [192].
38 See the Twelfth Report of the Law Reform Committee, discussed below, p. 413.
39 But see criticism of the Sale of Goods (Amendment) Act 1994, p. 393, and there is something to be said for the clarity provided by Uniform Commercial Code Art 2-403 (1) (a) discussed in *Shogun Finance* v *Hudson* (above) by Lord Millett at [84].

Scots law

As with the law in England and Wales, the objective approach to questions of agreement limits the scope for pleas of error in Scots law, so that, for example, when parties differed over whether a contract for the supply of a piano was one of sale or hire-purchase, it was held to be the former, applying an objective approach to the words used, rather than to be void for dissensus. Lord President Dunedin let fall a famous dictum: 'Commercial contracts cannot be arranged by what people think in their inmost minds. Commercial contracts are made according to what people say.'[40] But at common law error and fraud are grounds of invalidity for any contract entered into as a result of either. On one view, fraud has been subsumed in error as a ground for invalidating a contract.[41] Conventional wisdom, however, sees fraud as a ground making a contract annullable (or voidable).[42] The effect of error is one of the great unresolved controversies of Scots law. Mutual error is recognised: so where in a sale of coping stone where the price was 1s. 9d 'per foot', and the seller believed this to require measurement by superficial foot, while the buyer thought it meant lineal foot, the court held that there was no contract.[43]

Unilateral error has been more difficult. The conventional view is that error induced by another party's misrepresentation causing the first party to enter the contract, generally makes the resultant contract annullable (or voidable), but that where the error is 'essential' or 'in the substantials' – for example, an error as to the identity of the party with whom one is contracting where that identity is of the essence of the contract – it is absolutely null (or void).[44] Where a party enters a contract under such essential error induced by fraud, the contract may be absolutely null (or void).[45] But the late T. B. Smith propounded the view that even essential error in this sense did not necessarily render the contract null or void, but only annullable or voidable.[46]

Uninduced or unilateral error in general does not give rise to any invalidity: 'there must be "error plus", that is error with some other factor' (e.g. misrepresentation by the other party, innocent or fraudulent).[47] However, there is some authority that, if a negotiating party knows that the other is in error and takes advantage of that to procure a better bargain for himself, then the contract is reducible.[48] The limits on this, which must exist,[49] may perhaps be found in concepts of the risks accepted by reasonable persons in the circumstances, or of good and bad faith.[50] The classic example is the second-hand book which is much more valuable than the seller's price. The buyer is

---

40 *Muirhead and Turnbull v Dickson* (1905) 7 F 686, 694.
41 MacQueen & Thomson, *Contract Law in Scotland* (2000), para. 4.27.
42 McBryde, *Law of Contract in Scotland* (2nd edn, 2001), ch. 14, especially paras 14.63, 14.67–14.71.
43 *Stuart & Co v Kennedy* (1885) 13 R 221.
44 McBryde, *Contract*, ch. 15. Other 'essentials' may include subject-matter of the contract, price, quality of the thing supplied if expressly or tacitly essential, and the nature of the transaction (*Stewart v Kennedy* (1890) 17 R (HL) 25), but these all have their difficulties, discussion of which may be left to specialist works on contract law.
45 Ibid, paras 14.70, 15.90.
46 *Short Commentary on the Laws of Scotland* (1962), pp. 808–835.
47 McBryde, *Contract*, para. 15.23.
48 *Steuart's Trs v Hart* (1875) 3 R 192; *Angus v Bryden* 1992 SLT 884; McBryde, *Contract*, paras 15.31–15.34. See also *Sword v Sinclair* 1771 Mor 14241.
49 See Gloag, *Contract*, p. 438; Scot. Law Com. Memo. No. 42, para. 1.28.
50 McBryde, *Contract*, para. 15.34.

entitled to the book at the marked price because the loss is one of the risks of the second-hand book trade falling squarely on the seller; in using superior knowledge, the buyer is not in bad faith.

Another view is that uninduced error only has effect if it is *in transaction,* that is, relates to the provisions of the contract or to the context which has produced the contract.[51] Thus, if a contract for the sale of a painting provides that the seller-artist is Picasso, and he is not, so that at least one of the parties must be in error on the matter, that party can have the contract annulled.[52] But if one party simply bought in the belief that the seller-artist was Picasso, without that having been the subject of negotiation between the parties or a term of the contract, then the contract is valid despite the buyer's error, which is merely *in motive* and thus requires misrepresentation by the other to have effect. Again, if party A knows from negotiations that B will not sell her painting for under £10,000, and B by slip of the pen offers to sell for £1,000, the latter can reduce or annul the contract produced by A's acceptance of that offer; whereas if A offered £1,000, knowing, as B did not, that the painting was worth £10,000, the contract would stand.[53] Similarly, if B offered her painting for sale at £1,000, and A knew it was worth £10,000, B could not subsequently challenge the sale at the former figure; A is entitled in the circumstances to assume that B would sell at that price.

Error as to identity and fraud have become important in practice again as a result of the growth of buying on the Internet, where, famously, you can be the person you want to be and nobody knows you are a dog.[54] Since the success of e-commerce is probably even more dependent than its real-time, hard-copy counterpart on mutual trust and confidence between the contracting parties, the freedom of identity in cyberspace presents significant difficulties.

How would *Shogun Finance* v *Hudson* be decided under the doctrines of fraud and error in the Scots law of contract? As we have seen, while fraud generally makes a contract annullable or voidable, many think it capable of making a contract null or void if it gives rise to error in the essentials or substantials of the contract, which may include the identity of the other party to the contract. The classic case is *Morrisson* v *Robertson,*[55] where the rogue Telford represented to Morrisson, the seller of cows, that he (T) was the son of Wilson of Bonnyrigg, a credit-worthy figure, and wished to buy the cows on Wilson's behalf. Having obtained possession of the cows on credit, T sold and delivered them to Robertson, who was in good faith. It was held in a case between M and R that the contract between M and T was void for error of identity and that accordingly R had no title to retain the cows against M.

Morrisson v *Robertson* is however controversial and has never been followed. It was approved, but distinguished, in *MacLeod* v *Kerr,*[56] which in some ways is equivalent to the English cases such as *Ingram* v *Little* and *Lewis* v *Averay.* Kerr sold his car to a rogue who paid with a bouncing cheque. By the time Kerr discovered the fraud, the

---

51 See MacQueen and Thomson, *Contract Law in Scotland,* paras 4.45–4.56.
52 There may of course also be a claim in the alternative for breach of contract (Sale of Goods Act 1979, s. 13).
53 MacQueen & Thomson, *Contract Law in Scotland,* paras 4.45–4.56.
54 See Larry Lessig, *Code and Other Laws of Cyberspace* (1999), pp. 30–34, 64–68; and Peter Steiner's famous cartoon in *The New Yorker* for 5 July 1993, "On the Internet, nobody knows you're a dog".
55 1908 SC 332.
56 1965 SC 253.

rogue had sold the car to a good-faith third party. Here the contract between the seller and the rogue was held to be merely voidable, and the third party acquired good title under section 23 of the Sale of Goods Act. Where in *Morrisson* the real identity of the rogue had been material to the contract (no sale would have taken place had the true identity been known), in *MacLeod* the seller intended to sell to whoever was in front of him, and the actual identity was not material. The distinction is somewhat thin, and the court was clearly moved by a preference for the third party as against the seller; although both were innocents suffering for the wrongdoing of another, the seller had allowed the situation to arise when he could have prevented it by delaying delivery of the car until clearance of the cheque.

T.B. Smith launched a fundamental re-analysis of *Morrisson* v *Robertson,* in order to remove it as an obstacle to his contention that essential error generally made a contract annullable or voidable, rather than null or void. In Smith's argument, M got his cows back, not because his contract with T was void, but because he had never ceased to be owner of them. He had intended to make Wilson of Bonnyrigg the owner, and T was therefore no more than a thief, having been an agent for their delivery to W.[57] Since the cows in T's hands were stolen goods, a *vitium reale* attached to them and prevented T transferring ownership to R. The result was to be explained by the law of property rather than the law of contract. Smith developed a further argument, fundamentally distinguishing between the validity of a contract of sale and and the validity of a transfer of property under or following the contract. Unlike English law, the nullity of the underlying contract did not automatically entail the nullity of a conveyance of ownership. Thus property might be transferred despite the nullity or voidness of the underlying contract, because the transferee as possessor even if the contract is null is presumed to be the owner. *Traditionibus non nudis pactis dominia rerum transferuntur.*[58] It should be noted, however, that not all have been persuaded by this argument.[59]

Applying these analyses to the facts of *Shogun* v *Hudson,* or e-commerce cases where a rogue uses the identity of another to obtain goods on credit, the transaction between the supplier and the rogue is at least annullable for fraud and perhaps error, and may even be null if the error as to identity is found to be essential or in the substantials. Possibly which of these is the outcome matters less if we can, as Smith and others have argued, separate the validity of the transfer between the rogue and the third party from the validity of the contract between the rogue and his supplier. At least in *Shogun* Lord Hobhouse thought the rogue was a thief; certainly he had appropriated goods which he knew the owner intended to transfer to someone else. Many Scots lawyers, however, would have greater sympathy with the dissenting positions of Lords Nicholls and Millett on the invalidity of the contract, and think Scots law closer to the lax continental systems excoriated by Lord Hobhouse than to English law. In the particular context this would have meant that the rogue *was* the debtor under the Hire-Purchase Act 1964, and, presumably, someone who could

---

57 Smith was able to prove that T had been convicted of theft (see (1967) 12 JLSS 206), thus refuting Lord President Clyde in *MacLeod* v *Kerr* when he criticised the argument that T was a thief.

58 Smith, *Short Commentary,* 539–40; D. L. Carey Miller, *Corporeal Moveables in Scots Law* (1991), pp. 106–114; K. G. C. Reid, *The Law of Property in Scotland* (1996), paras 607–612.

59 See e.g. McBryde, *Contract,* ch. 13.

transfer the creditor's title to the goods to a good faith private purchaser. If more generally the validity of contract and conveyance are interdependent in Scots law, then the general policy of favouring the good faith third party over the deceived seller seems preferable, if only to promote the flow of commerce. It is worth noting that the German law praised by Lord Millett reaches his preferred result by separating contract from transfer of ownership; that is, as he notes, the problem is solved in property rather than contract law. But it must be admitted that if an electronic seller takes all possible electronic steps to check that a prospective electronic purchaser is creditworthy, it has more equities in its favour than many of the sellers in the old case law, whose few checks on their buyers were really inadequate, even given the difficulties of a pre-computer age.

DOORSTEP SELLING

In 1985 the EC promulgated a Directive to protect consumers in respect of contracts negotiated away from business premises.[60] This Directive is implemented by the Consumer Protection (Cancellation of Contracts Concluded Away from Business Premises) Regulations 1987.[61] The Regulations apply, subject to the exceptions set out below, to contracts under which a trader supplies goods and services to a consumer, and which are concluded during an unsolicited visit by the trader to the consumer's home or to the home of another person, or to the consumer's place of work. They also apply to contracts concluded during a visit made at the request of the consumer which are for the supply of goods and services other than those in respect of which the visit was requested. In the latter case, however, the Regulations only apply if the consumer did not know, or could not reasonably have known, that the relevant goods or services formed part of the trader's business activities. In addition, they apply to contracts in respect of which an offer was made by the consumer under similar conditions, and to contracts concluded during excursions organized by traders away from the premises where they are carrying on business.

Where the Regulations apply, they provide for a 'cooling off' period of seven days during which time the consumer may give notice of cancellation. The consumer must be given written notice of this right, and failure to give this notice will render the contract unenforceable against the consumer.

The exceptions to the Regulations applying are as follows:

1 contracts relating to land,[62] but not contracts for the supply of goods and their incorporation into land, or contracts for improving or repairing buildings;
2 contracts for the supply of food, drink and other goods intended for current consumption in the household and supplied by regular roundsmen (such as milk);
3 certain contracts concluded on the basis of a trader's catalogue;
4 insurance contracts;

---

60 85/577/EEC.
61 SI 1987/2117.
62 But the Directive *does* apply to a loan secured on land and entered into at the consumer's home – *Georg Heininger and Helga Heininger* v *Bayerische Hypo- und Vereinsbank AG*, Case C-481/99, 13.12.01.

5 investment agreements;
6 contracts not falling within (7) below, which do not require the consumer to make total payments exceeding £35;
7 any contract under which credit is provided not exceeding £35.

Upon cancellation, payments made for the relevant goods and services become repayable, and any goods received are returnable. Any credit transaction is also cancelled.

4

FORMALITIES

REPEAL OF FORMAL REQUIREMENTS

In 1954, the Law Reform (Enforcement of Contracts) Act repealed s. 4 of the 1893 Act which had been law since the enactment of the Statute of Frauds 1677, with the result that nearly all contracts for the sale of goods can now be made by word of mouth, irrespective of the value of the goods sold. In this way English law was brought into line with Scots law, which since the seventeenth century at latest has treated sale of goods as an entirely consensual contract, not requiring any writing or other formality to have validity.

Section 4 of the Sale of Goods Act 1979 enacts:

(1) Subject to this and any other Act, a contract of sale may be made in writing (either with or without seal), or by word of mouth, or partly in writing and partly by word of mouth, or may be implied from the conduct of the parties.

(2) Nothing in this section affects the law relating to corporations.

Since the repeal of the old s. 4, the opening words of the above section have been deprived of their meaning since there are no other provisions in the Act relating to formalities. The only exceptions which need to be noted to the general effect of s. 4 are contracts of hire-purchase or credit-sale, which come within the provisions of the Consumer Credit Act 1974, and contracts for the purchase of a British ship or of a share therein which come within s. 16 of and Sch. 1 para. 2 to the Merchant Shipping Act 1995.[1]

It is possible that a contract for the sale of goods may sometimes also be a contract for the sale of an interest in land within the meaning of s. 2 of the Law of Property (Miscellaneous Provisions) Act 1989 (which has now replaced s. 40 of the Law of Property Act 1925), or of s. 1 of the Requirements of Writing (Scotland) Act 1995, and may therefore be void if it is not in writing. This possibility arises from the fact that the definition given to 'goods' by s. 61 of the Sale of Goods Act includes 'emblements, industrial growing crops, and things attached to or forming part of the land which are agreed to be severed before sale or under the contract of sale'. There can be little doubt that this definition embraces certain goods, what used to be called *fructus naturales*, at any rate in some cases, which at common law were regarded as being an interest in land. The fact that since 1893 these are 'goods' within the meaning of the Sale of Goods Act does not rule out the possibility that they may at the same time be land within the meaning of the Law of

---

1 Section 16 and Sch. 1 para. 2 (1).

Property (Miscellaneous) Provisions) Act or of the Requirements of Writing (Scotland) Act.[2]

BILLS OF SALE

A further word needs to be said on bills of sale within the Bills of Sale Acts to which reference has already been made in distinguishing contracts of sale from loans on the security of goods.[3] Strictly speaking, these Acts do not require a contract of sale to which they apply to be in writing or in any particular form. There is nothing to prevent a person buying goods under an oral contract and allowing the seller of them to remain in possession of them, so far as the Bills of Sale Acts are concerned. But in practice a buyer who does not obtain possession of the goods would almost invariably wish to have some written evidence of the sale and if the sale is in writing, or is evidenced in writing (even by a mere receipt), the Acts will apply.

Under the Act of 1878, a sale of goods which is evidenced in writing, and under which the seller remains in possession, is void against trustees in bankruptcy and persons seizing goods in judicial execution, unless the sale is made by a written instrument called a bill of sale and registered in accordance with the Act.[4] No particular form is required for a bill of sale under the Act of 1878. But a breach of this Act does not affect the validity of a sale as between the immediate parties to it; the sale itself remains completely valid between the parties.

The above provisions only apply if the first transaction is a genuine sale. If it only takes the form of a sale but is intended to operate as a security, the Sale of Goods Act does not apply at all by reason of s. 62(4). Such a transaction is covered by s. 8 of the Bills of Sale Act 1882, which makes the transaction completely void, even as between the immediate parties, unless it is made by a registered bill of sale.[5] Moreover, a bill of sale by way of security must be made in the form prescribed in the Schedule to the Act of 1882 and failure to comply again renders the bill wholly void.

The two Acts were designed for quite different purposes. The 1878 Act was designed to protect third parties, while the second Act was an early sort of consumer protection measure intended to protect needy borrowers who gave charges over household possessions and such like in the late Victorian period, often on terribly harsh terms. So the 1882 Act was a major interference with freedom of contract which forced lenders to use the statutory form of bill of sale and so prevented them from inserting into the contract their own contractual clauses.

But one thing the two Acts have in common is that they have not worked well, and both are largely obsolete in practice. This is because the two Acts were found excessively technical in application, so that alternative legal methods were devised of

---

2 See Hudson, 'Goods or Land?' (1982) 22 Conv 137. But the title of this article is somewhat misleading, because the question is not, 'goods or land?', but rather, 'goods only, or goods *and* land?' The replacement of the relevant 1925 Act provisions by the 1989 Act makes no difference to this question. In Scotland see *Paul v Cuthbertson* (1840) 2 D 1286, *Morison v Lockhart* 1912 SC 1017, and *Munro v Liquidator of Balnagown Estates Co* 1949 SC 49.

3 See above, pp. 19–21. Note that the Bills of Sale Acts have never applied in Scots law.

4 Bills of Sale Act 1878, s. 8 of which is still in force as regards sales, despite its apparent repeal by s. 15 of the Act of 1882.

5 Nevertheless, sums actually advanced on an unregistered bill of sale are apparently recoverable in a restitutionary claim for money had and received: *North Central Wagon Finance Co Ltd v Brailsford* [1962] 1 WLR 1288.

achieving the objects of the parties through transactions which did not come within either of the Acts. In particular, the invention of the hire-purchase contract very soon rendered both Acts largely obsolete. In modern times the Acts rarely apply except by accident, that is to say, parties rarely knowingly enter into a transaction intending it to be governed by the Acts, but technical infringements of the Acts remain a common legal problem.

The two purposes of the Acts – the protection of third parties, and consumer protection – were somewhat confused in these Acts by the fact that the first Act applied to outright sales, and the second to sales which were designed to be security for loans. In fact third parties require protection in both cases – indeed more often in the second than in the first. An owner of goods who grants a charge or mortgage over them, while retaining possession, has been put in a position in which he can easily mislead third parties as to his assets, and if he becomes insolvent, it is often unfair that the third parties may receive nothing, while the chargee simply claims all the goods by virtue of some secret document. Because the Acts are so easily evaded, this part of the law remains a serious problem and requires reform, as we shall see later. Thus the 1878 Act really needs to be replaced by more up-to-date legislation.

The second main purpose of the Acts – consumer protection of small borrowers and credit users – was also largely a failure, and the Acts were superseded, first by the Moneylenders Acts, and now by the Consumer Credit Act 1974. So far as this purpose is concerned, therefore, the Acts could now safely be repealed.

5

DISTANCE SELLING, INCLUDING E-COMMERCE

INTRODUCTION

Mail order sales have been with us since the nineteenth century, and most readers will be familiar with at least the possibility now of purchasing goods via the internet. This latter form of trade is part of what is commonly styled 'e-commerce'. There is no agreed definition of this term,[1] but for present purposes we are concerned only with the buying and selling of *products* over the internet. The term 'products' is used in this chapter to include products which can be delivered by electronic means such as software and music, as well as goods.[2] By using mail order or the internet, products can easily be purchased either from sellers within the buyer's jurisdiction, or from sellers in other jurisdictions. Sales of products within a single jurisdiction of the UK using the internet raise few problems which are not present in domestic sales by mail order. It is the problems which arise when a buyer within one of the UK jurisdictions purchases goods from a seller in another UK jurisdiction, or from a seller situated abroad, which require special consideration. As we will see, where the parties to the transaction are within the European Economic Area some of the most difficult problems have been addressed by legislation. The real problems lie where the seller is outside the European Economic Area.

Although e-commerce has been a fashionable topic for some years, as the House of Commons Select Committee on Trade and Industry warned[3]:

> Policy makers must be careful not to be carried away by the hyperbole and exaggeration which has, at times, come to characterise the debate on the future development of electronic commerce.

These words proved to be prescient, in that the collapse of many e-commerce businesses followed shortly after they were published. Since then, things appear to have settled down, and e-commerce is now an established alternative to mail order. It is unlikely, however, that mail order will entirely lose its market to the more convenient electronic form. The reason for this is that a large part of traditional mail order business involves credit sales to the poorer part of the population, and arranging small

---

1 See House of Commons Trade and Industry Committee Tenth Report 'Electronic Commerce' HC 648 1999 para. 11.
2 For a discussion of whether products delivered electronically are 'goods' for the purposes of the Sale of Goods Act, see p. 66 *et seq*.
3 See House of Commons Trade and Industry Committee Tenth Report (n. 1 above) para. 10.

consumer finance across frontiers is not at present really practical, even between the UK and other EEA states (though this may change). E-commerce is thus confined to those who have credit cards and access to computers (though with the ready availability of internet cafés most of the UK population who want it can afford access to the internet). Moreover, to the extent that it involves supplies of goods (using this term in its traditional sense of tangible objects), it is dependent on existing delivery systems to get the goods to the buyer. In *this* respect it has no advantages over mail order.

Given the growth of distance selling in its various forms, it is necessary that this book should deal with the problems to which these transactions give rise. Goods have been traded around the known world since prehistoric times of course, and legal forms have been developed over the centuries to facilitate this.[4] But these legal forms developed in the context of sales between *merchants*. What is different at the present day is the increasing participation of consumers in cross-border sales. As a World Trade Organisation report puts it:[5]

> These modern technologies [*computer, telecommunications and information technology*] are being combined, especially through the Internet, to link millions of people in every corner of the world. Communications are increasingly unburdened from the constraints of geography and time. Information spreads more widely and more rapidly than ever before. Deals are struck, transactions completed, and decisions taken in a time-frame that would have seemed inconceivable a few years ago.
>
> [W]ith the Internet all elements of a commercial transaction can be conducted on an interactive basis with one or many people, unconstrained by time and space, in a multimedia environment with sound, image and text transmission, and at a relatively low (and still declining) cost.[6]

For low-value goods purchased in cross-border transactions from outside the EEA, the consumer is largely dependent on the goodwill and reputation of the supplier to provide redress if goods fail to arrive or prove to be defective. However, given that the credit card is virtually the universal mode of payment over the internet, UK consumers have a remedy against the card company, as explained below, which in practice is more valuable than any theoretical legal remedy which may exist against the supplier.[7] Within the EEA, European legislation, as implemented in member states, has supplemented this by giving the consumer remedies against the supplier additional to those conferred by pre-existing domestic laws. In the UK these supplement those originally existing under the Sale of Goods Act 1979.[8] For *commercial* transactions involving distance selling, the situation is largely as it was under the unamended Sale of Goods Act 1979, however. Moreover, in these cases the Consumer Credit Act 1974 s. 75 discussed below,[9] will not usually be applicable, because the cardholder will not be an individual, so that even if the amount of the credit

---

4 See Chapter 22.
5 *Electronic Commerce and the Role of the WTO* (1998).
6 Ibid. p. 5.
7 See p. 55 *et seq.*
8 See p. 525 *et seq.*
9 See p. 55 *et seq.*

transaction falls within the limits for a 'regulated agreement' under the Act,[10] the Act is not applicable.

Discussion of the problems with which we are concerned in this chapter are principally grouped under the two following headings: 1. Consumer sales (where consumer protection measures are of paramount concern); 2. Commercial distance transactions (and consumer transactions where cross-border litigation is viable, though it should be noted that the sections on 'Formation of the contract' of sale are of relevance where consumers have mistakenly been 'offered' goods at a ridiculously low price).[11] We then go on to deal with a number of matters that affect all kinds of distance contract involving the importation of goods into the United Kingdom: possible infringements of intellectual property; payment of the price and security (other than in international business transactions dealt with in Chapter 24); and, risk of loss or damage in transit.

CONSUMER SALES

The Consumer Credit Act 1974

As noted above, the credit card is the main method of payment over the internet. For UK buyers this leads to a useful source of redress against the credit card company where the goods supplied are defective.[12] The key provision is s. 75(1). This provides –

> If the debtor under a debtor-creditor-supplier agreement falling within section 12(b) or (c) has, in relation to a transaction financed by the agreement, any claim against the supplier in respect of a misrepresentation or breach of contract, he shall have a like claim against the creditor, who, with the supplier, shall accordingly be jointly and severally liable to the debtor.

Subsections 12(b) and (c) respectively define 'debtor-creditor-supplier agreements' which are 'restricted' and 'unrestricted-use' credit agreements. The exact details of these definitions do not concern us here. The key to them is the definition of 'consumer credit agreement'. Under s. 8(2) this is –

> ... a personal credit agreement by which the creditor provides the debtor with credit not exceeding [£25,000].[13]

Since almost all distance selling transactions involving consumers will fall within these financial limits, most potentially fall within s. 75(1). Where the seller is within the UK or outside the UK but within another member state of the EEA, the consumer will have the remedies against the seller set out below and in other sections of this

---

10 Section 8 (as amended). The current financial limit for the application of the Act is credit provided by the creditor not exceeding £25,000 (SI 1989/996). Section 75(3)(b)(as amended) has the further limitation that the cash price of the goods must not be less than £100 nor more than £30,000.
11 See p. 40 *et seq.*
12 For the position where the goods are not defective, but the consumer nevertheless wishes to cancel the transaction, see p. 59.
13 As amended by SI 1998/996. As noted above, s. 75(3)(a) further limits its application by requiring the value of the goods to exceed £100 and not to exceed £30,000.

book cross-referred to, and in consequence will potentially have a remedy against the credit card company under s. 75(1). However, two restrictions on this need to be noted. First of all, some cards which in popular parlance are referred to as credit cards, are not credit cards for the purposes of the Act. Whilst Visa and Mastercard offer the option of paying off the monthly debt in full, or partially, and are therefore true credit cards, American Express and Diners Club do not offer this option, but require the monthly debt to be paid off in full. Therefore they are not credit cards within the meaning of the Act, and are not, therefore, subject to s. 75. On the other hand, the credit limits imposed by both Visa and Mastercard on individual card-holders mean that almost all agreements with these companies will be 'personal credit agreements' within the meaning of the Act.

Problems could arise where the seller is outside the EEA. For example, if as is often the case, the seller is in the United States, Article 2 of the Uniform Commercial Code, will usually be applicable.[14] Although Article 2 of the Uniform Commercial Code, which is in force in all states except Louisiana, provides warranties similar to those contained in s. 13–14 of the unamended Sale of Goods Act 1979, it is relatively easy to excluded those warranties under §2-316 and to modify the remedies available to the consumer under §2-719. Although these modifications are subject to the overriding requirement of conscionability in §2-302,[15] given the sums of money involved in most consumer transactions, it will simply not be worthwhile litigating this unless the goods have caused serious personal injury.[16] In practice therefore, were the card company to take the point that the consumer had no remedy against the supplier because the supplier had excluded its liability, the consumer would, in principle, have no remedy for the supply of defective goods under s. 75.[17] Under the Unfair Contract Terms Act 1977 ss. 6 and 20, liability for breach of the Sale of Goods Act warranties cannot be excluded as against a person dealing as consumer.[18] However, as against a seller outside the UK there are difficulties with the application of the Unfair Contract Terms Act. Although s. 27(2) provides that the Act has effect where a consumer is habitually resident in the UK, this only applies if the essential steps necessary for making the contract were taken in the UK.[19] As we will see, the steps for making distance contracts by e-mail usually result in the contract being formed in the seller's place of business.[20] Furthermore, the Act does not apply to international supply contracts, which are sales of goods in which the parties' places of business are in different states (other than the parts of the UK, the Channel Islands and the Isle of Man).[21] Although a business can deal as consumer,[22] the effect of this would appear to be that a business so dealing in a contract that fell

---

14 Under the choice of law rules set out below – see p. 69 *et seq.*

15 And the conscionability requirement set out in §2-719(3) mentioned in the following footnote.

16 See §2-719(3) – limitation of liability for consequential damages for injury to the person in the case of consumer goods is *prima facie* unconscionable. In cases of personal injury (or damage to property in most jurisdictions other than pure economic loss) there may additionally be a remedy under §402A Restatement 2d.

17 There might be a remedy for a total failure to deliver on the basis of the liability of the seller for a consideration that has wholly failed.

18 See p. 241 *et seq.*

19 Section 27(2)(b).

20 See p. 69.

21 s. 26.

22 *R & B Customs Brokers* v *United Dominions Trust* [1988] 1 All ER 847 – see p. 237.

within the definition of 'international supply contract' could not claim the benefit of the Act.

There are also difficulties in arguing that the terms of the Unfair Terms in Consumer Contracts Regulations[23] are mandatory. Regulation 7 provides –

> These Regulations shall apply notwithstanding any contract term which applies or purports to apply the law of a non member State, if the contract has a close connection with the territory of the member States.

But, as we will see, the default rule of private international law is that it is generally the law of the seller's place of business that applies.[24] The reference to 'the contract' would seem to preclude the possibility of arguing that the place of the consumer's residence is a relevant consideration.

A separate possibility might be to argue that European consumer protection legislation is mandatory,[25] and so the exclusion of warranty liability under Article 2 is ineffective.[26] Under domestic UK law, the argument that this is so could be made under the principle laid down in *The Hollandia*,[27] and the terms of the Rome Convention Article 5.[28] However, there are some difficulties with this. The situation envisaged here has the obvious difference that the choice of law rule that results in the law of a United States jurisdiction applying is the default rule in conflict of laws that normally the law of the seller's jurisdiction governs.[29] Moreover, given that the constitutional legitimacy of EEA legislation depends on the fact that it contributes to the achievement of the internal market, it is not easy to see how making it applicable to suppliers outside the EEA can further this objective. The cases on commercial agents can be distinguished, as the constitutional authority for the Commercial Agents Directive largely derives from what is now Article 136 of the Treaty of Amsterdam which requires member states to promote the improvement of working conditions. This clearly has no applicability in the case of sales of goods. Subject to this, is seems clear that it will be UK law that will govern the contract between the card company and the consumer.[30]

Sections 2–7 and 16–21 of the Act are also disapplied where the proper law of the contract is that of a part of the UK only by reason of a choice of law clause.[31]

---

23 SI 1999/2083 – see p. 234 *et seq.*

24 See p. 69 *et seq.*

25 As we will see, however, the Distance Selling Regulations 2000, SI 2000/2334 do not have an equivalent of Art. 12 of Directive 97/7/EC which establishes the binding nature of the provisions of the Directive – see p. 61 *et seq.*

26 In *Ingmar GB Ltd v Eaton Leonard Technologies* Case C-381/98 [2001] All ER (Comm) 329 it was held by the ECJ that the Commercial Agents Directive (86/653/EEC) applied to a contract between a commercial agent within the community and a principal outside, even though a choice of law clause made the contract subject to the law of a non-member state. See also *Pace Airline Services v Aerotrans Luftfahrtagentur GmbH Case* C-64/99.

27 [1983] 1 AC 565. See also discussion of Contracts (Applicable Law) Act 1990 and Rome Convention Art. 5 below.

28 Implemented in the UK by the Contracts (Applicable Law) Act 1990 – see p. 71.

29 See p. 69 *et seq.* By contrast, in *The Hollandia* there was an express choice of law clause which, if given effect to, would have overridden the mandatory provisions of English law. Similarly, in *Ingmar* (n. 26 above) the express choice of law clause would have overridden the mandatory provisions of EEA law.

30 *Jarrett & anor v Barclays Bank* [1997] 2 All ER 471 – misrepresentation by vendor concerning timeshare properties in Portugal.

31 Section 27(1).

Directive of the European Parliament on the protection of consumers in respect of distance contracts[32] and the Consumer Protection (Distance Selling) Regulations

This Directive, which is implemented in the UK by the Consumer Protection (Distance Selling) Regulations,[33] has as its object the approximation of the laws of member states concerning distance contracts between consumers and suppliers. The Regulations apply to 'distance contracts'. A 'distance contract' is –

> ... any contract concerning goods or services concluded between a supplier and a consumer under an organised distance sales or service provision scheme run by the supplier who, for the purpose of the contract, makes exclusive use of one or more means of distance communication up to and including the moment at which the contract is concluded.[34]

The Regulations therefore apply, *inter alia*, to sales of goods effected through the internet,[35] though where the seller is located outside the EEA, the problems alluded to above, and further dealt with below, exist as to their application.[36] There are certain exemptions, the most important of which for present purposes are auction sales,[37] which would appear to include internet auctions.[38] There is also partial exemption for contracts for the supply of food, beverages or other goods intended for everyday consumption supplied to the consumer's residence or to his workplace by regular roundsmen.[39] The exemption is from the application of many of the Regulations, including reg. 7 dealt with below.[40]

Regulation 7 requires the consumer to be provided with the following information prior to the conclusion of the contract:

(i) the identity of the supplier and, where the contract requires payment in advance, the supplier's address;

(ii) a description of the main characteristics of the goods or services;

(iii) the price of the goods or services including all taxes;

(iv) delivery costs where appropriate;

(v) the arrangements for payment, delivery or performance;

(vi) the existence of a right of cancellation except in the cases referred to in regulation 13;

(vii) the cost of using the means of distance communication where it is calculated other than at the basic rate;

(viii) the period for which the offer or the price remains valid; and

(ix) where appropriate, the minimum duration of the contract, in the case of contracts for the supply of goods or services to be performed permanently or recurrently.

---

32 97/7/EC OJ 1997 L144.

33 SI 2000/2334.

34 Ibid. reg. 3(1).

35 Article 2(4) and Annex 1 provide the Directive covers telephone means of communication with or without human intervention and e-mail.

36 See p. 56 above.

37 Ibid. reg. 5(1)(f).

38 But note that s. 12(2) Unfair Contract Terms Act 1977 has been amended so that the buyer on a sale by auction is not to be regarded as dealing as consumer if the goods are second hand, or if the buyer is not an individual, the goods are sold by auction or by competitive tender and the buyer has the *opportunity* to attend in person – Sale and Supply of Goods to Consumers Regulations 2002, SI 2002/3045, reg. 14 – see p. 236 *et seq.*

39 Regulation 6(2)(a) exempts such contracts from the application of regs. 7–19(1).

40 Ibid. reg. 6(2)(a).

The Directive requires timely, written confirmation in a durable medium of the matters referred to in (i)–(vi) above to be received by the consumer, and in any event not later than at the time of delivery.[41] The Regulations are more comprehensive.

> The supplier shall ensure that the information required by paragraph (1) is provided in a clear and comprehensible manner appropriate to the means of distance communication used, with due regard in particular to the principles of good faith in commercial transactions and the principles governing the protection of those who are unable to give their consent such as minors.[42]

The supplier must provide in addition –

- written information on the conditions and procedures for exercising the right to cancel;[43]
- the geographical address of the place of business of the supplier to which the consumer may address any complaints;[44]
- information on after-sales services and guarantees which exist;[45]
- the conditions for cancelling the contract, where it is of unspecified duration or a duration exceeding one year.[46]

Compliance with these requirements is likely to cause serious problems for certain retail sectors such as those selling *via* mobile telephones.

Cancellation

The consumer is given a minimum of seven working days beginning with the day after he or she receives the goods to cancel the contract without penalty, and without giving any reason.[47] The mode of cancellation is set out in reg. 10(4) which provides –

> A notice of cancellation given under this regulation by a consumer to a supplier or other person is to be treated as having been properly given if the consumer –
>
> (a) leaves it at the address last known to the consumer and addressed to the supplier or other person by name (in which case it is to be taken to have been given on the day on which it was left);
>
> (b) sends it by post to the address last known to the consumer and addressed to the supplier or other person by name (in which case, it is to be taken to have been given on the day on which it was posted);
>
> (c) sends it by facsimile to the business facsimile number last known to the consumer (in which case it is to be taken to have been given on the day on which it is sent); or
>
> (d) sends it by electronic mail, to the business electronic mail address last known to the consumer (in which case it is to be taken to have been given on the day on which it is sent).[48]

Where the consumer, instead of serving notice of cancellation complying with the above provisions, chooses instead to pursue any remedy he or she may have under

---

41 Ibid. Art. 5.
42 Ibid. reg. 7(2).
43 Ibid. reg. 8(2)(b).
44 Ibid. reg. 8(2)(c).
45 Ibid. reg. 8(2)(d), and see Sale and Supply of Goods to Consumers Regulations 2002, reg. 15(3).
46 Ibid. reg. 8(2)(e).
47 Ibid. regs. 10(1) and (2).
48 Note that there is already consultation taking place on amendment to these Regulations.

s. 75 of the Consumer Credit Act 1974 against the card company first,[49] there would appear, strictly speaking, to be a problem. Section 75, as we have seen, is contingent on the consumer having a remedy against the supplier. If the consumer has failed to give notice of cancellation within the cancellation period set out in the Regulations, the supplier's liability under the above provisions cannot arise. In this case, the card company's contingent liability would have to derive from the supplier's liability under the Sale of Goods Act 1979 (as amended) or equivalent legislation, and this in turn would depend on the supplier having committed a breach of contract, and in the case of overseas sellers, this could give rise to the difficulties discussed above.[50] By contrast, the rights under the Regulations are not dependent on this.

Following cancellation, the consumer has a duty to retain the goods and to take reasonable care of them.[51] He or she is under a duty to restore the goods to the supplier,[52] but has no duty to *deliver* the goods except at his or her own premises.[53] If the supplier asks for the goods to be returned, the consumer must take reasonable care to ensure that they are received by the supplier, and not damaged in transit; apart from this, his or her obligations cease.[54] Because the consumer's duty is only to deliver the goods at his or her own premises, presumably the consumer can insist that the supplier bear the cost of post or carriage, and packing.

If the obligations laid down in reg. 8 have not been complied with, the period for withdrawal is three months and seven working days from receipt of the goods.[55] If during the three-month period the reg. 8 information is supplied, the seven-day withdrawal period starts to run from the time of such supply.[56] Within 30 days of the exercise of the right of withdrawal, the supplier must reimburse all sums paid by the consumer free of charge.[57]

There are certain exclusions from the right of withdrawal the most important of which for present purposes are in relation to products customised for the consumer, audio and video recordings and software where *the packaging* has been unsealed by the consumer,[58] and contracts for the supply of newspapers, periodicals, and magazines.[59]

Any credit arrangements made in connection with the supply must be cancelled without penalty.[60]

---

49 See p. 55 *et seq.*
50 See p. 56.
51 Ibid. reg. 17(2).
52 Ibid. reg. 17(3).
53 Ibid. reg. 17(4).
54 Ibid. reg. 17(6).
55 Ibid. reg. 11(4).
56 Ibid. reg. 11(3).
57 Ibid. reg. 14(3).
58 The italicised words do not appear in reg. 13(1)(d), but presumably this exclusion is limited to software etc. delivered in the form of a CD or similar, and not delivered online. The word 'unsealed' would be inappropriate to any online transaction.
59 Ibid. reg. 13(1)(d).
60 Ibid. reg. 15(1). The definition of 'related credit agreement' in reg. 15(5) confines these to 'fixed sum' credit agreements within the meaning of Consumer Credit Act 1974 s.10. A credit card agreement is a facility under which the debtor is able to receive credit up to a credit limit, and would therefore appear to be running-account credit within the meaning of Consumer Consumer Credit Act 1974 s. 10(1)(a), and is therefore outwith these provisions, which therefore bite only on a relevant hire-purchase transaction and the like. The credit card company would, however, be obliged to recredit the consumer's account following effective cancellation under the normal contractual provisions governing the relations between the consumer and the card company.

A particular problem with some mail order houses has been that they have got themselves over difficult periods by taking the consumer's money, and delaying delivery of the products thereby improving their cash flow. A similar problem could arise in relation to transactions effected through the internet. Accordingly, under reg. 19(1) suppliers are required to execute orders within 30 days. If they are not, the consumer is entitled to a refund as soon as possible, and in any case within 30 days.[61]

The Regulations cover other matters such as inertia selling, but the above are the most important provisions for present purposes.[62]

The Regulations came into effect on 31 October 2000. There is currently a DTI consultation on them.[63] In the light of representations, particularly from the vehicle rental and leasing sector, the DTI has been considering the scope to amend parts of the Regulations which may be unclear, impracticable or unduly costly for suppliers. The key proposals are:

- explicitly to require the information to be provided to the consumer prior to contract to cover the existence *or absence* of a right to cancel and, in the case of services whose performance is to start within seven days, information that the right to cancel will expire once performance begins (reg. 7);
- to require consumers to be given, during the performance of a service, information (in writing or another durable form) about the loss of cancellation rights once performance begins. At present this information must be provided prior to contract (reg. 8);
- to allow consumers to cancel contracts by phone (reg. 10).

The DTI consultation closed on 23 April 2004, and amendment of the Regulations (which of course must remain within the scope of the Directive) may follow: a report is expected soon. Further, however, the European Commission will publish a report on the Distance Selling Directive by the end of 2004. If this leads to change in the Directive, then there will of course have to be corresponding change in the UK Regulations.[64]

Contracting out

These provisions are clearly mandatory so far as buyers and sellers in the European Economic Area are concerned. The Directive provides in Article 12(2):

> Member states shall take measures needed to ensure that the consumer does not lose the protection granted by this Directive by virtue of the choice of law of a non-member country as the law applicable to the contract if the latter has a close connection with the territory of one or more member state.

---

61 Ibid. reg. 19(2) and (4).
62 Ibid. reg. 24 replacing with amendments Unsolicited Goods and Services Act 1971 s. 1 – see p. 12.
63 See World Wide Web at website page http://www.dti.gov.uk/ccp/topics1/ecomm.htm.
64 The Office of Fair Trading has published IT Consumer Contracts at a Distance (OFT 672: October 2003), which is a consultation (closed end January 2004) on a draft guidance on the Distance Selling and Unfair Terms in Consumer Contracts Regulations; and in February 2004 it published Cars and Other Vehicles Sold by Distance Means (OFT 689), a Consultation Paper on guidance for motor traders who sell cars and other vehicles to consumers by distance means – such as online, by mail order or by telephone. These can be accessed at the OFT website: http://www.oft.gov.uk/News/Publications/Leaflet+Ordering.htm.

Regulation 25(1) implements this as follows –

> A term contained in any contract to which these Regulations apply is void if, and to the extent that, it is inconsistent with a provision for the protection of the consumer contained in these Regulations.

Regulation 4 provides that the Regulations apply to 'distance contracts' other than excepted contracts. The definition of 'distance contract' was given at the beginning of this section.[65] Whatever difficulties may exist in relation to the application of UCTA and the Unfair Terms in Consumer Contracts Regulations, and in relation to treating *European* law as mandatory, vis-à-vis sellers outside the EEA, it certainly seems that this Regulation is mandatory *domestic* law. Thus, since the Directive is based on a 'home state' principle, UK companies selling online around the EEA can specify that the law of England and Wales, or Scotland applies. But, as noted below,[66] under Article 5 of the Rome Convention, where the object of the contract is to provide goods or services to a consumer, a choice of law made by the parties cannot deprive a consumer of the protection afforded to him by the mandatory rules of the country where he has his habitual residence, so that if a sale is to a consumer in another member state of that Convention, the seller could find itself bound by a law of that member state. Furthermore, the provisions as choice of jurisdiction set out in Regulation 44/2001 are effectively mandatory in this context.[67] These are dealt with below.[68] Where one of the contracting parties is outside the EEA, the view that the Brussels Convention (and the Regulation) is not intended to regulate disputes on jurisdiction between contracting and non-contracting states, would appear to be correct.[69] So, if the supplier is in the United States, it would appear that the law of the state in which the supplier is situated will apply together with any applicable Federal law.[70] Whilst there are practical problems with treating the information requirements as mandatory for the reasons dealt with below, there would appear to be no good reason not to treat the cancellation provisions as mandatory. Unfortunately, since payment will almost certainly have been made by credit card,[71] under reg. 15 notice of cancellation will not have the effect of cancelling the credit card debt as a 'related credit agreement'. This is because the latter term is defined by reg. 15(5) as –

> ... an agreement under which fixed sum credit which fully or partly covers the price under a contract cancelled under regulation 10 is granted –
>
> (a) by the supplier, or
> (b) by another person, under an arrangement between that person and the supplier.

---

65 See p. 58.
66 See p. 72.
67 Article 17 of the Brussels Convention, which is the subject of the Regulation (see p. 68, provides that choice of jurisdiction clauses shall be in writing or evidenced in writing and shall be *'in a form which accords with practices in that trade or commerce of which the parties are or ought to have been aware'* (emphasis supplied). It is the italicised words which are likely to create serious problems for the efficacy of choice of law clauses in consumer contracts.
68 See p. 68 *et seq.*
69 See Tritton *Intellectual Property in Europe*, 2nd edn, Sweet & Maxwell, 2002, §13-005.
70 E.g. the Magnuson-Moss Act.
71 As to the meaning of 'credit card' see pp. 55–56.

Since a credit card is a credit facility which fluctuates from time to time, it is 'running account' credit within the meaning of s. 10(1)(a) Consumer Credit Act 1974, not 'fixed sum credit' so that it would appear that cancellation of the sale with the overseas seller does not automatically cancel the credit card debt. However, it does appear that in practice the credit card companies will take up such matters with sellers on behalf of their debtors, and try to ensure that the purchase price is refunded to the cardholder's account.

The normal mechanism to ensure compliance with these Regulations is an injunction issued on the application of the Director General of Fair Trading,[72] and injunctions being orders *in personam* that are generally enforceable only against defendants within the jurisdiction.[73] Whilst it might be argued that the enforcement mechanism chosen by the regulations is equally ineffective so far as *any* suppliers outside the jurisdictions of the UK courts are concerned, so that they are equally ineffective against suppliers within the EEA as they are against suppliers outside it, this is not particularly helpful to consumers and suggests the Directive has been improperly implemented.

Other possible measures

The Federal Trade Commission of the USA issued a Notice on Consumer Protection in the Global Electronic Marketplace, inviting comments. In its response to this of 21 April 1999 the European Commission pointed out that in the European Union a body of law and policy on consumer protection already exists that facilitates cross-border trade in products and services, which is generally applicable to electronic commerce and covers all stages of the business-to-consumer commercial relationship, including advertising, promotion and marketing, pre-contractual information and disclosures, contract formation, payment, delivery, guarantees and after-sales services and ultimately redress.[74] It pointed out that the core elements of consumer protection must be co-ordinated at an international level. Accordingly, it welcomed the work in this area being done by WTO, OECD and UNCITRAL.

Where, therefore, e-commerce takes place between buyers and sellers *within* the European Economic Area there is already a raft of legislation which will regulate the transactions.

COMMERCIAL DISTANCE TRANSACTIONS (AND CONSUMER TRANSACTIONS WHERE CROSS-BORDER LITIGATION IS VIABLE)

Introduction

The special rules applicable to international business transactions are dealt with in Chapter 22. Here we are concerned with the rules that regulate the choice of jurisdiction where suits are litigated, and the choice of law applicable.

---

72 Ibid. reg. 27.
73 Because equity operates *in personam*.
74 Ibid. paras 7 and 8.

It is usual and necessary to separate issues of which court has jurisdiction from issues of what law the court with jurisdiction should apply. It should be noted, however, that the distinction between rules determining jurisdiction and choice of law rules, is not always as clear-cut as this dichotomy might suggest.[75]

This section focuses on distance sales involving sellers situated outside the UK, as well as sellers situated in a jurisdiction of the UK different from that of the buyer. Accordingly, the following matters are relevant: the rules governing the jurisdiction of the English and Welsh, Scottish and Northern Irish courts over these transactions; the applicable law assuming the courts of one of these countries has jurisdiction; intellectual property;[76] payment and security; risk of products in transit to the buyer; regulation (including taxation); and cryptography. The last two problem areas, regulation and cryptography, do not concern us here. Furthermore, as stated above, we are concerned only with the situation where products are ordered by a buyer in England and Wales, Scotland or Northern Ireland, from a seller in another UK jurisdiction, or elsewhere. In relation to the latter, purchases from sellers outside the European Economic Area must be distinguished from those from sellers within that area, since within the European Economic area some of the problems are dealt with by treaty and European legislation.

Where the contract contains a choice of jurisdiction clause, this will in general be given effect to, unless this has the effect of contracting out of mandatory domestic laws.[77] The rules set out below are the default rules.

Jurisdiction of the English and Welsh, Scottish and Northern Irish courts over distance contracts

For the purposes of exposition, it is convenient to start with the rules to be applied where the buyer and the seller are both in different member states adhering to either the Brussels or Lugano Conventions.

Transactions within the European Economic Area: Council Regulation (EC) No 44/2001 of 22 December 2000 the Brussels and Lugano Conventions[78]

The provisions of the Brussels and Lugano Conventions are now enacted with certain changes[79] in Regulation 44/2001. Since the provisions for present purposes are virtually the same, and because the present case law and jurisprudence is on the Conventions rather than the Regulation, it is proposed for convenience to refer to the Conventions. It should be noted that the numbering of the provisions of the articles of the Regulation is identical to those provisions of the Conventions with which we

---

75   This was classically the case with the old 'double actionability' rule in *Phillips* v *Eyre* (1870) LR 6 QB 1, abolished by the Private International Law (Miscellaneous Provisions) Act 1995 s. 10.

76   This of course in theory ought to concern consumer buyers, but in practice, as explained below, they are unlikely to be affected save in the case of the unauthorised downloading of software and MP3 files – see p. 74.

77   See p. 57.

78   Note that amendments to these Conventions are being proposed. The commentary below is based on the existing text as implemented by the Civil Jurisdiction and Judgments Act 1982 in Great Britain and Northern Ireland.

79   The most important differences are: (1) the definition of 'domicile' is changed most especially in relation to the domicile of legal persons; and (2) there is now a detailed definition of when a court is seized of an action for the purpose of the *lis pendens* rule in Article 21.

are concerned here. The Regulation does not apply to Denmark, in relation to which only the Conventions are applicable. Where the buyer and the seller are within different member states of the Brussels and Lugano Conventions[80] a standard set of jurisdictional rules is laid down. They do not, however, regulate relations with non-member states.[81] These Conventions are separate from the European Union Treaties, but the Brussels Convention provides that the European Court of Justice has jurisdiction to interpret it.[82] They are given effect to within the UK by the Civil Judgments and Judgments Act 1982 which applies a similar set of rules between the jurisdictions which make up the UK.[83] Since the Brussels and Lugano Conventions are for present purposes identical, it is proposed throughout to refer only to the former.

Choice of jurisdiction clauses have only limited efficacy under the Regulation. Article 17 of the Brussels Convention provides that they must be in writing, or evidenced by writing, and must be in a form which accords with practices in their trade or commerce of which the parties are or ought to have been aware. It is these last words which will severely limit the efficacy of choice of jurisdiction clauses in the case of consumer contracts, and also in many commercial contracts. Accordingly, the rules on jurisdiction set out below, will in many cases effectively be mandatory.

(i) The basic rule The basic rule on choice of jurisdiction, under the Brussels Convention, is set out in Article 2. The claimant[84] *must* sue the defendant in the courts of the defendant's domicile[85] and no other court, *unless* one of the exceptions set out in the Conventions apply. The important ones for present purposes are set out below.

(ii) Article 5(1) Article 5 provides –

A person domiciled in a Contracting State may, in another Contracting State be sued:

(1) in matters relating to a contract, in the courts for the place of performance of the obligation in question ...

This provision was considered in *Viskase Ltd and another* v *Paul Kiefel GmbH*.[86] The defendant company which was domiciled in Germany, supplied eight machines to the plaintiffs for use in their factory in England. Delivery took place at the defendant's factory in Germany as required by the contract. The machines were installed in the plaintiff's factory in England, but the plaintiffs contended that they were not fit for their purpose, and sued in the High Court in England, relying on Article 5(1).

---

80 Membership of these Conventions corresponds to the states which constitute the European Economic Area.

81 Collins (1990) 106 LQR 538. This opinion was endorsed in *Re Harrods (Buenos Aires)* [1992] Ch 72.

82 1971 Protocol Art. 3(1). The Protocol does not, of course, apply to non-member states of the European Union. In practice, the courts of non-member EEA states are likely to follow the interpretation provided by the European Court of Justice.

83 I.e. Great Britain and Northern Ireland. 'Great Britain' means England, Scotland and Wales – Union with Scotland Act 1706 Preamble Art. 1.

84 The term for 'plaintiff' introduced by the Civil Procedure Rules 1999 for England and Wales. The equivalent Scottish term is 'pursuer'.

85 Under Article 52 domicile is determined by the internal law of the Contracting State whose courts are seised of the matter. Article 53 provides that in the case of companies, the seat of a company shall be treated as its domicile. However, in order to determine that seat, the court shall apply its rules of private international law.

86 [1999] 3 All ER 362. See also *MBM Fabri-Clad Ltd* v *Eisen und Huttenwerke Thale AG* 3 November 1999 (unreported).

It was held that where a party had an obligation to supply a machine which was reasonably fit for its purposes, that obligation was performed at the time and place of supply, i.e. Germany. Accordingly, the English courts had no jurisdiction.

If this rule applies to consumer sales of products, the effect of the above decision, which seems right in principle, is that the buyer must sue in the courts of the seller's jurisdiction in member states of the Brussels Convention, because products will be mailed, or delivered to a carrier for transmission to the buyer, at the seller's place of business.[87]

(iii) Article 5(3) If the buyer is able to sue in tort, as may often be the case,[88] he or she may optionally be able to sue in his or her home jurisdiction by virtue of Article 5(3). Under this provision, in matters relating to tort, delict or quasi-delict, the defendant may be sued in the courts of the place where the harmful event occurred. As construed by the European Court of Justice, under this provision the plaintiff can choose either the courts of the defendant's domicile *or* the courts of the place where 'the harmful event occurred'. In *Handelskwekerij GJ Bier BV and Stichting Reinwater* v *Mines de Potasse d'Alsace SA*[89] the ECJ ruled that the expression 'place where the harmful event occurred' in Article 5(3) must be interpreted in such a way as to acknowledge that the plaintiff has an option to commence proceedings either at the place where the causative event giving rise to the damage occurred[90] *or* in the jurisdiction where the damage occurred. Clearly, the causative event where products are at the seller's risk[91] occurs where the events giving rise to the defect in the products occur. For the sake of simplicity, we will assume for the present that it is the seller's factory. Which is the jurisdiction where the damage occurs? If the products cause damage to person or property within the buyer's jurisdiction due to a latent defect clearly that is the place where the damage occurs. What is the situation, however, if the goods are merely defective?[92] Where the Sale of Goods Act applies, the buyer has the remedies set out in that Act, so that it could be argued that the jurisdiction where the damage occurs is the place where the buyer examines the goods. But the Act will only apply where the the relevant jurisdiction in England and Wales, Scotland or Northern Ireland determines that it applies under the choice of law rules set out in the Rome Convention,[93] and we can only know if these apply if the relevant jurisdiction in England and Wales, Scotland or Northern Ireland, is properly seised of the matter. The way out of this circle might be to argue that the damage occurs where it is first discovered, and that will

---

87 Where the Sale of Goods Act 1979 applies, this is the point at which unconditional appropriation of the products to the contract will take place under s. 18 r. 5(2) – see p. 334. This point would appear to be unaffected by the Sale and Supply of Goods Regulations 2002, SI 2002/3045 discussed at p. 359 below, as these merely affect the passing of risk.
88 The most likely causes of action are negligence, or under the Products Liability Directive as implemented in the various member states of the EEA – see p. 264 *et seq*.
89 Case 21/76 [1977] 1 CMLR 284.
90 The first plaintiffs in this case were nursery gardeners in Holland. The defendants were alleged to discharge more than 10,000 tonnes of chlorides into the Rhine each day in Alsace, thereby increasing the salinity of the water reaching Holland, which caused damage to the plaintiffs' seed beds.
91 The risk in products after they leave the seller's place of business is dealt with at p. 75 *et seq* and Chapter 22.
92 It should be noted that under the Sale of Goods Act, when it applies, property can pass in defective goods unconditionally appropriated to the contract, so that such goods will be at the buyer's risk in transit – see p. 356.
93 See p. 71.

be where the goods are first examined which will occur after they have been delivered to the buyer.

In *Verein für Konsumenteninformation* v *Henkel*[94] the European Court of Justice held that this provision conferred on an Austrian Consumers' Association (VKI) the status to take preventive action under the Austrian equivalent of the Unfair Contract Terms Act to prevent a trader from using unfair contract terms, because the concept of 'harmful event' was wide enough to cover the undermining of legal stability by the use of unfair contract terms which it was the task of consumers' organisations to prevent.

(iv) Other exceptions There are other exceptions to the basic rule contained in Article 2, but it is beyond the scope of this work to deal with them.

Sellers and buyers domiciled or situated in England and Wales, Scotland or Northern Ireland

For an English or Welsh buyer wishing to sue a seller in Scotland or Northern Ireland, or a Scottish or Northern Irish buyer wishing to sue a seller in England and Wales, the Civil Jurisdiction and Judgments Act 1982 applies a similar set of rules domestically to those applying when the defendant or defender is in another member state of the Brussels Convention.[95] It also applies, of course, to litigation between buyers and sellers in Scotland and Northern Ireland.

Seller outside the European Economic Area

(i)   England and Wales: leave to serve out of the jurisdiction For an English buyer to sue a seller in another jurisdiction, other than Scotland or Northern Ireland or a member state of either the Brussels or Lugano Conventions,[96] leave to serve the claim (writ) outside the jurisdiction must be obtained pursuant to the Civil Procedure Rules 1998 r. 6.20(5). It is beyond the scope of this book to deal in detail with the rules applied under this Order. Broadly, claims in contract may be brought with leave of the court, if the contract:

- (i)   was made within the jurisdiction; or
- (ii) was made by or through an agent trading or residing within the jurisdiction on behalf of a principal trading or residing out of the jurisdiction; or
- (iii) is by its terms, or implication, governed by English law; or
- (iv) contains a term to the effect that the High Court shall have jurisdiction to hear and determine any claim in respect of the contract.

In *Brinkibon* v *Stalig Stahl und Stahlwarenhandelsgesellschaft MBH*[97] the issue was whether the contract had been made within the jurisdiction. An English company

---

94 Case C-167/00 1 October 2002.
95 See id. Schedule 4 Title II.
96 In relation to which the situation is regulated by the Civil Judgments and Judgments Act 1982.
97 [1983] 2 AC 34. See Wightman 'Does Acceptance Matter' in Adams (ed.) *Essays for Clive Schmitthoff*. Professional Books, 1983, p. 145.

sought leave under the above Rules, to serve an Austrian company for breach of contract. The contract had been made by telex with the buyer in London accepting a counter-offer made by the seller situated in Vienna. It was held that the contract was made in Vienna, where the acceptance had been received. It is clear from this case, however, that this rule might be displaced if this appeared to be the intention of the parties. The question of jurisdiction raised in this case would now be resolved by reference to the Brussels Convention to which both Austria and the UK adhere.

Where a seller has sought to avoid liability to a consumer buyer by a choice of law clause this might be taken into account by an English or Welsh court in exercising its discretion (where the requirements of Ord.11 set out above are otherwise satisfied) on the question of jurisdiction, under the principle of *The Hollandia*,[98] and the Rome Convention Article 5.[99]

Where the claim is founded on a tort, and the damage was sustained, or resulted from an act committed within the jurisdiction, the English or Welsh courts may again give leave for service out of the jurisdiction under RSC Order 11.[100]

(ii)   Scotland When a Scottish buyer wishes to sue a seller from another jurisdiction, other than England and Wales or Northern Ireland, or a member state of either the Brussels or Lugano Conventions, Schedule 8 to the Civil Jurisdiction and Judgments Act 1982 applies a regime similar to that for jurisdiction within Scotland as between Scotland and Brussels and the Lugano countries.[101] The procedure for execution of service furth of the United Kingdom is set out in Chapter 16.2 of the Rules of the Court of Session 1994 and Chapter 5.5 of the Sheriff Court Ordinary Cause Rules 1993.[102]

(iii)   Northern Ireland Order 11 of the Rules of the Supreme Court (Northern Ireland) 1980 is immaterially different from Order 11 above. Accordingly, the position with regard to service out of the jurisdiction is essentially the same as for England and Wales.

The Draft Convention on International Jurisdiction and the Effects of Foreign Judgments in Civil and Commercial Matters

The Hague Conference on Private International Law has produced a draft treaty[103] which in essence is intended to apply a similar set of principles to the Brussels and Lugano Conventions on a global scale. At the moment, however, there seems to be little likelihood of this reaching a final draft, much less entering into force.

---

98   [1983] AC 565. It should be noted that this case came before the English court as a result of an action *in rem* against *The Hollandia* which was a sister ship belonging to the defendants to the one involved in the damage complained of.

99   See p. 71 below.

100   Civil Procedure Rules 1998 Sch 1.

101   See especially rr. 2.2 and 2.3, and as regards consumer contracts r. 3.

102   For which see the *Parliament House Book* (Greens).

103   The current draft is that of June 1999.

Assuming the courts of England and Wales, Scotland or Northern Ireland have jurisdiction, what law should they apply?

Introduction

Except as regards jurisdictions in relation to which the Rome Convention harmonises the law of all signatory states,[104] we must again distinguish (but for different reasons) the situation where the seller is in England and Wales, Scotland or Northern Ireland, to a buyer in another one of those jurisdictions from the situation where the seller is in another member state of the European Economic Area. We must also distinguish the situation where the seller is outside the European Economic Area and the buyer is in England and Wales, Scotland or Northern Ireland.

Formation of the contract of sale: present rules for sellers and buyers in England and Wales, Scotland or Northern Ireland

Many websites through which products may be purchased are set up to resemble ordinary stores, where the purchaser selects products and takes them to a till where they are paid for. England and Wales, Scotland and Northern Ireland apply the rules as to formation set out in Chapter 3. Accordingly, the contract would be formed when the seller accepts the buyer's offer to purchase the products (which is made by taking them to the 'till'), and the contract would be formed in the jurisdiction where the buyer is situated. The reason for this is that in principle, the contract is formed at the point in time, and place, at which the message of acceptance is received (not sent).[105]

This would not be satisfactory for sellers who may find themselves dealing with buyers in many different countries, and sellers who are properly advised usually set up their sites differently. A common set-up is as follows. The buyer having selected the products submits particulars of the products, his identity and credit card details to the seller. The seller then signifies order confirmation to the buyer by e-mail, and asks for the buyer to click the purchase button, which when done completes the formation of the contract. The effect of the above rule on place of acceptance would accordingly be that the place of acceptance would be the seller's[106] so far as a buyer in England, Scotland or Northern Ireland, is concerned.

---

104   This too may soon be supplemented by a Regulation. There may also be 'Rome II' in respect of the law applicable to non-contractual obligations.

105   *Entores v Miles Far Eastern Corporation* [1955] 2 QB 327; *Brinkibon v Stalig Stahl und Stahlwarenhandelsgesellschaft MBH* [1983] 2 AC 34. Unlike contracts effected by post – see *Adams v Lindsell* (1818) 1 B & Ald 681. The impact of the proposed European Parliament and Council Directive on this question is discussed below.

106   In a well-publicised incident some years ago, Argos by mistake offered for sale on their Website £300 television sets for £3. Argos, it was reported, refused to supply those who purported to purchase their television sets for £3. At least one customer was said to be willing to sue, but this seems to have come to nothing (see (1999) 1 (9). *Electronic Business Law* 9). More recently, in March 2003 the Amazon website mis-priced an iPaq Pocket PC which was advertised for sale at £7.32 on the site, compared to a normal retail price of about £287 including VAT. Customers were also able to order an iPaq H5450 – normally priced at more than £500 – for £26.27. After the products had become within a day the best-selling products on the Amazon website, the company pulled the advertisements, and subsequently refused delivery to customers who had made orders, relying on a condition of use imposed upon its customers: "No contract will subsist between you and Amazon.co.uk for the sale by it to you of any product unless and until Amazon.co.uk accepts your order by email confirming that it has dispatched your product." Again, there seems to have been no *further activity from customers.* Leaving aside the line of argument taken by Amazon based on offer and acceptance, there would be the possibility of arguing that there was a mistake preventing any contract coming into existence, as in *Hartog v Colin and Shields* [1939] 3 All ER 566. Although it is possible that advertisements, which a website is equivalent to, are offers, as in the well-known case of *Carlill v Carbolic Smoke Ball Co* [1892] 2 QB 484, something more is required than a mere advertisement – id. and *Lefkowitz v Great Minneapolis Surplus Stores* 251 Minn 188 (1957).

Formation of the contract of sale, sellers and buyers in member states of the European Economic Area: European Parliament and Council Directive on certain legal aspects of electronic commerce in the internal market[107]

Under Article 9 of this Directive, member states must ensure that their legislation allows contracts to be concluded electronically. English law almost certainly permitted this,[108] as did the laws of Scotland and Northern Ireland.[109] However, the Electronic Communications Act 2000 contains power for the Secretary of State by statutory instrument to modify 'in such manner as he may think fit for the purpose of authorising or facilitating the use of electronic communications or electronic storage' to make modifications, *inter alia*, to any existing primary or secondary legislation. In 2001 the Law Commission were asked to conduct a review of existing formal requirements. Their advice appeared later in the same year.[110] The Commission concluded that the requirements for 'writing' or 'signature' would generally be satisfied by electronic means.

The formation of contracts by electronic means is governed by the Electronic Commerce (EC Directive) Regulations.[111] Regulation 11 applies to contracts made by technological means. Where the customer's order constitutes the contractual offer, the service provider must make available 'appropriate, effective and accessible means allowing him to identify and correct input errors prior to the placing of the order.'[112] The effect of this is to require some system such as a double-click system (as described above) to be put in place before an effective order is placed. Presumably, therefore, a customer will not be bound by an on-screen response until asked to confirm the order and has indicated that it is in fact what he or she requires. Non-compliance with this requirement renders the contract voidable at the instance of the customer, unless a court orders otherwise.[113] In addition, the internet service provider must acknowledge receipt of the order by electronic means 'without undue delay'.[114] The effect is that even though the customer's order is in ordinary contractual terms an acceptance of the supplier's offer, the acceptance must be acknowledged. Contracting out of these provisions is permitted in the case of non-consumer buyers, but not consumer buyers.[115] These requirements do not apply to contracts concluded exclusively by e-mail or equivalent individual communication.[116]

The Directive implemented by these Regulations, as usual, by its terms seeks to ensure the proper functioning of the internal market between member states.[117]

---

107   2000/31/EC,OJ L178, 17/7/2000.
108   See *Entores v Miles Far Eastern Corporation* [1955] 2 QB 327, *Brinkibon v Stalig Stahl und Stahlwarenhandelgesellschaft MBH* [1983] 2 AC 34.
109   See also *Clipper Maritime Ltd v Shirlstar Container Ltd* [1987] 1 Lloyd's Rep 546 – document produced by fax held to be a writing.
110   'Electronic Commerce: Formal Requirements in Commercial Transactions: Advice from the Law Commission' December 2001.
111   SI 2002/2013 implementing various articles of the Electronic Commerce Directive 2000/31/EC, OJ 2000 L178, 17/7/2000.
112   Ibid. reg. 11(1)(b).
113   Ibid. reg. 15.
114   Ibid. reg. 11(1)(a).
115   Ibid. reg. 11(1). Accordingly, it would appear that this must be treated as a mandatory principle of domestic law under the principle laid down in *The Hollandia* [1983] AC 565 and Article 5 of the Rome Convention implemented by the Contracts (Applicable Law) Act 1990.
116   Ibid. reg 11(3) – the latter words would presumably cover telephone text messaging for example.
117   Article 1(1).

Member states are to ensure compliance by service providers within their territory.[118] As implemented by the Regulations, application is limited to service providers in the UK or another member state of the EEA.[119]

Law applicable to the contract itself in litigation within the EEA between sellers and buyers wherever situated: the EEC Convention on the Law Applicable to Contractual Obligations (the Rome Convention)[120]

This Convention[121] is given effect to in the UK by the Contracts (Applicable Law) Act 1990. Although the object of the Convention was to facilitate the free movement of goods within the member states of the then EEC, its operation is not confined to disputes between litigants from member states. Article 1(1) provides:

> The rules of this Convention shall apply to contractual obligations in any situation involving a choice between the laws of different countries.

Article 2 provides:

> Any law specified by this Convention shall be applied whether or not it is the law of a contracting state.

In the House of Lords, during the passage of the Bill to implement this Convention, Lord Goff and others expressed disquiet at this. Lord Goff suggested that customers of the English Commercial Court will ask 'Why England of all countries should apply a European test to contracts between parties, both of whom come from outside Europe'.[122] Although optional, the Convention has been implemented so that it will apply to transactions between buyers in England and Wales, Scotland and Northern Ireland and sellers in another of those jurisdictions.[123]

The general rule is that a contract is, in the first place, to be governed by the law chosen by the parties.[124] In the absence of choice, Article 4 provides that a contract will be governed by the law of the country (jurisdiction)[125] with which it is most closely connected. It is presumed that the country (jurisdiction) with which the contract is most closely connected is that where the party who is to effect the performance which is characteristic of the contract has at the time of conclusion of the contract his habitual residence, or in the case of a corporation, its central administration.[126] This would appear to lead to the conclusion which had been reached at common law that it is the law of the seller's place of business which will be the applicable law.[127]

---

118 Article 3(1).
119 SI 2002/2013 reg. 4(1).
120 OJ 1980 L266. This may soon be supplemented by a Regulation.
121 80/934/EEC, OJ 1980 L266.
122 Hansard, House of Lords vol. 515 col. 1482 (1990).
123 1990 Act ss. 2 and 8.
124 Article 3.
125 See *Whitworth Street Estates* v *James Miller and Partners* [1970] AC 583.
126 Article 4(1) and (2).
127 See *Iran Continental Shelf Oil Co & ors* v *IRI International Corp* Queen's Bench Division, 5 December 2001 (unreported).

Article 5 contains special rules for consumer contracts. It provides that where the object of the contract is to provide goods or services to a consumer,[128] a choice of law made by the parties shall not have the result of depriving the consumer of the protection afforded to him by the mandatory rules of the country in which he has his habitual residence,

  – if in that country conclusion of the contract was preceded by a specific invitation addressed to him or by advertising, and he had taken in that country all the steps necessary on his part for the conclusion of the contract, or
  – if the other party or his agent received the consumer's order in that country ...

It goes on to provide that in the absence of choice in accordance with Article 3, the contract is to be governed by the law of the country where the consumer has his habitual residence, if the contract is entered into in the circumstances set out above. If these circumstances are not present, the applicable law, in the absence of a choice of law clause, will be governed by reference to Article 4. Article 5 does not answer the question as to whether e.g. the Sale of Goods Act warranties and the provisions of the Unfair Contract Terms Act which restrict their exclusion are to be regarded as mandatory.[129]

INTELLECTUAL PROPERTY

We will see[130] that a sale by a seller of goods which infringe intellectual property rights will amount to a breach of section 12 of the Act. With the exception of European trade marks, designs[131] and plant breeders' rights, all intellectual property rights are national. In consequence, products may legitimately be produced in a country where no relevant rights exist, but as soon as they are exported to a jurisdiction where those rights do exist there will, in principle, be an infringement. What is the position of a buyer of products over the internet which infringe UK intellectual property rights? The relevant rights for these purposes are patents, trade marks, copyrights and designs.[132] Let us take some examples.

Example 1

A buyer who seeks to take advantage of the lower cost of new right-hand steering wheel cars in Japan and some Commonwealth countries, orders one through the internet. Is the car liable to be seized by the UK Customs?

---

128 I.e. the object of the contract is the supply of goods or services to a person which can be regarded as outside his trade or profession – Art. 5(1).
129 Article 16 of the Convention also provides that the application of a rule of foreign law, which by virtue of the Convention would apply, may be refused if such application is manifestly incompatible with the *ordre public* of the forum.
130 At p. 122.
131 Granted by the Office for the Harmonisation of the Internal Market in Alicante.
132 Measures prohibiting the release for free circulation, export, re-export, or entry of counterfeit and pirated goods are contained in the Goods Infringing Intellectual Property Rights (Customs) Regulations 1999 SI 1999/1601 and SI 1995/751 (in relation to counterfeit and pirated goods) and SI 1999/654 (in relation to goods infringing a patent and goods infringing a supplementary protection certificate).

It is necessary to take each form of intellectual property right separately.

Trade marks – the maker's badge

The Trade Marks Directive[133] as interpreted in *Silhouette*,[134] applies a doctrine of exhaustion of trade mark rights only in relation to goods first marketed within the European Economic area. The result is that even perfectly genuine goods exported by the manufacturer in question to the particular country from which the purchase is made, in principle infringe the manufacturer's trade mark rights when they are reimported into the EEA without the manufacturer's consent.[135] Section 10(4)(c) of the UK Trade Marks Act 1994 provides that a person uses a sign (i.e. for present purposes a trade mark) if he imports goods under the sign. However, the governing section is 10(1) which requires use to be in the course of a trade, so that an importer for private and personal use would not infringe. Consequently, the goods are not infringing goods and are not liable to seizure by the Customs and Excise.[136]

The 'designer' aspects of the car

Some 'designer' aspects of a car's design can enjoy copyright protection or protection through registered designs, and the functional aspects 'design right', which is a quasi-copyright form of protection, so that the importation of the car could, in principle, infringe all of these rights. But, the Copyright, Designs and Patents Act 1988 s. 22, which deals with secondary infringement by importation, excepts importation by a person for private and domestic use, and similarly the provisions which allow the Customs and Excise to seize infringing copies exclude articles imported for private and domestic use.[137] Similarly, s. 7(1) of the Registered Designs Act 1949 (as amended) requires importation to be in the course of a trade.

Patented parts of the car

For those parts of the car which are patented, we need to turn to s. 60(1) of the Patents Act 1977 which includes importation of patented goods amongst infringing acts. Section 60(5), however, provides that acts which apart from this subsection would

---

133 89/104/EEC, OJ 1989 L40, implemented in the UK by the Trade Marks Act 1994.
134 Case C-355/96 [1998] 2 CMLR 953. See also the Advocate-General's opinion in *Sebago* 25 March 1999, which has now been accepted by the European Court of Justice. The prohibition of the importation of 'grey area' goods, i.e. genuine goods of a trade mark proprietor, from outside the European Economic Area, was condemned by the House of Commons Select Committee on Trade and Industry in its Report on this question – HC 380, 1999.
135 An alternative approach based on consent, which would have permitted such 'parallel importing', was taken by Laddie J in *Zino Davidoff SA* v *A & G Imports Limited* [1999] RPC 631, but this was rejected by the European Court of Justice, which in effect held that such consent must be express, and cannot be implied save where the circumstances unequivocally demonstrate that the proprietor is renouncing his right to oppose placing the goods on the market within the EEA – Case C-414/99 [2002] RPC 403 (joined with *Levi Strauss* v *Tesco*). A further argument in favour of parallel importers has been advanced on the basis of Article 10 of the European Convention on Human Rights. This Article guarantees the right to freedom of expression which includes the freedom to impart information, including commercial information. A person who sells genuine goods as such in the European Economic Area is making a statement which is true, and the right to make that statement is guaranteed by this Article.
136 Under Trade Marks Act 1994 s. 89.
137 Copyright, Designs and Patents Act 1988 s. 111(3) – because by virtue of s. 22 the copy is not an infringing copy. This follows from the Whitford Committee's recommendation (Cmnd. 6732 para. 725).

constitute infringement shall not do so if they are done privately for purposes which are not commercial.

Example 2

A buyer orders infringing copyright works, such as sound recordings in hard copy,[138] from a seller in another jurisdiction.

The analysis set out in Example 1 above applies in this case also. It follows from the above that the domestic buyer of goods is safe from an action for infringement being taken by the proprietor of intellectual property rights, and from the liability to have goods seized by the Customs and Excise. However, the problem of the widespread importation of infringing goods, such as copies of records made in jurisdictions with little or no copyright protection by parallel importers,[139] is unlikely to be ignored by rights owners.[140] Pending international legislation to deal with this problem, rights owners will no doubt wish to try to use local law to deal with the problem. An argument might be developed from the authorities reviewed by the US Supreme Court in *Burger King Corp* v *Rudzewicz*.[141] In *Worldwide Volkswagen Corp* v *Woodsen*,[142] cited with approval in that case, the court said 'the forum State does not exceed its powers under the Due Process Clause[143] if it asserts personal jurisdiction over a corporation that delivers its products into the stream of commerce in the expectation that they will be purchased by customers in the forum state'. On this analogy, it could be argued that electronic contracts 'purposefully directed' at persons in a particular jurisdiction, are in fact *de facto* importations of goods, so that the 'exporter' is in fact an importer. If this argument is accepted, the goods would be liable to seizure by the Customs and Excise. The buyer's remedy in this case would be under s. 12 of the Sale of Goods Act,[144] assuming the Act applied to the contract;[145] alternatively, the buyer would appear to have a remedy against his or her credit card company, something of importance given that this is the normal mode of payment in e-commerce.[146]

PAYMENT OF THE PRICE AND SECURITY[147]

As noted above, no satisfactory method has yet been devised for setting up consumer credit transactions between buyers and sellers in different jurisdictions. No doubt an

---

138 If the recording is delivered online the issues are quite different. The downloading of e.g. MP3 files without the consent of the copyright owner is infringement of copyright – Copyright, Designs and Patents Act 1988 ss. 16(1)(a) and 17(2).

139 As to the meaning of 'importer' see below. A parallel importer is someone who buys goods in low-cost markets and resells them in markets where a high price can be achieved.

140 In the case of genuine goods, a likely reason for the availability of goods for parallel importation is the manufacturer itself which has offloaded surplus capacity. This seems to be a reason why action is seldom taken against those who engage in parallel importation as a business activity – see Report of the House of Commons Trade and Industry Committee 1999 HC 380.

141 471 US 462 (1985).

142 444 US 286, 297–8 (1980).

143 *14th Amendment*

144 See p. 112 *et seq.*

145 See p. 69 *et seq.*

146 See p. 55 *et seq.*

147 The payment mechanisms in the international business transactions dealt with in Chapter 24 are not the concern of this section.

international registry along the lines of those which exist in the United States for the purposes of Article 9 of the Uniform Commercial Code would be desirable, but it would require a treaty to establish it, and such a possibility must be regarded as remote. Accordingly, the invariable method of payment over the Internet is the credit card.[148] The guidance given in *Re Charge Card Services*[149] on such transactions, is relevant in the present context also, at least where the applicable law is that of England and Wales, Scotland or Northern Ireland.

A problem not infrequently encountered with internet purchases is that the price quoted is without tax. If the goods are sold by a seller in the USA, there will be local sales tax to be paid, and on their importation into the UK, VAT will be payable. The cost of the goods can thus end up considerably greater than the apparent bargain the buyer thought he was getting. Under domestic law, misleading pricing is an offence under Part III of the Consumer Protection Act 1987,[150] but a seller in a jurisdiction outside those to which that Act applies, can scarcely be held liable because someone in this country has accessed the information about what the seller has for sale from the seller's website, and ordered goods accordingly. The seller cannot know the tax laws of every jurisdiction in the world, and thus there would seem to be a legitimate reason for quoting prices without tax, though it is perhaps less legitimate to quote them without taking account of a relevant *local* sales tax which will *have* to be paid. Certainly, in contracts governed by the Distance Selling Directive dealt with above the price plus tax must be given.[151] This problem exists in relation to mail order, of course, but it will grow acute if the volume of international consumer sales grows because of e-commerce.

This is a problem which might be taken up by the proposed UK E-Envoy.[152] One of the roles of the E-Envoy will be to act as a public figurehead for the Government on electronic commerce issues in international discussions.

AT WHOSE RISK ARE GOODS DISPATCHED BY THE SELLER TO THE BUYER?

Under the rules discussed below[153] the normal rule was that goods will be unconditionally appropriated to the contract when they are posted to the buyer, or delivered to an independent carrier to be transported to the buyer, and are thenceforth at the buyer's risk. This rule is now amended in cases where the buyer deals as consumer, by the Sale and Supply of Goods Regulations, which add a new s. 20(4) as follows.[154]

---

148 In the USA this is overwhelmingly the method of payment. Other methods are insignificant though there is evidence that many consumers would prefer e-cash, a checking [US spelling] account or payment by ATM/debit card – survey by Jupiter Communications reproduced in *The Economist* 19 February 2000. Attempts to develop digital currencies have so far proved a disappointment.
149 [1987] Ch 150 – see p. 308.
150 See p. 58.
151 See p. 264.
152 See Tenth Report of the House of Commons Trade and Industry Committee para. 32.
153 At p. 332 *et seq.*
154 SI 2002/3045 reg. 4.

In a case where the buyer deals as consumer or, in Scotland, where there is a consumer contract in which the buyer is a consumer, subsections (1) to (3) above must be ignored and the goods remain at the seller's risk until they are delivered to the consumer.

Section 32 (which deals with delivery to a carrier) is modified accordingly. Section 32(4) provides –

In a case where the buyer deals as consumer or, in Scotland, where there is a consumer contract in which the buyer is a consumer, subsections (1) to (3) above must be ignored, but if in pursuance of a contract of sale the seller is authorised or required to send the goods to the buyer, delivery of the goods to the carrier is not delivery of the goods to the buyer.

Accordingly, in consumer sales subject to the Sale of Goods Act 1979 (as amended),[155] goods travel at the seller's risk, and the seller must insure.[156]

In non-consumer sales which are not subject to the rules set out in Chapter 20, goods in transit are generally at the buyer's risk, and should be insured by the buyer. [157] The buyer can reject only for defects which arose before the risk passed. Claims against the mail authorities will be a matter for the national laws of the country concerned. Any claim against a private carrier will have to be framed in negligence as there will usually be no contractual nexus between the carrier and the consumer.[158] There may be a possibility of the seller suing and recovering on behalf of the consumer under the principles laid down in *Dunlop* v *Lambert*[159] and *The Albazero*,[160] but the value of the goods would have to be considerable for this to be worthwhile. The Contracts (Rights of Third Parties) Act does not confer rights on third party consignees in the case of contracts for the carriage of goods by road, rail or air which are subject to the appropriate international convention.[161] However, it is possible that the Act would apply in relation to domestic carriage of goods where delivery is by courier which is not covered by any specific legislation. In Scotland, consignees in general might well have enforceable rights under the common law doctrine of *jus quaesitum tertio*, although the issue has never been thoroughly canvassed in the courts.[162]

---

155 In order to determine whether or not the Sale of Goods Act is applicable, the rules set out at p. 7 *et seq.* must be applied.

156 Moreover, the buyer is not deemed to have accepted the goods until he or she has had a reasonable opportunity of examining them under s. 34 Sale of Goods Act 1979. The result would appear to be that where, as often happens, the carrier fails to deliver the goods because the buyer is not at home, the goods remain at the seller's risk – see *Ron Mead TV & Appliance* v *Legendary Homes Inc.* 746 P 2d 1163 (OKI. App. 1987) appliances left in garage not delivered to buyer.

157 Because delivering the goods to the mails, carrier etc. will generally amount to an unconditional appropriation within s. 18 r. 5(1) of the Sale of Goods Act 1979, and cause property to pass – see p. 332 *et seq.*

158 Unless a sea carrier is involved, when the Carriage of Goods by Sea Act 1992 applies – see p. 318.

159 (1839) 6 Cl & Fin 600.

160 [1977] AC 774.

161 Section 6(5) – see p. 221 *et seq.*

162 See *Laws of Scotland: Stair Memorial Encyclopaedia*, vol. 15, para. 846.

6

SUBJECT-MATTER OF THE CONTRACT

MEANING OF 'GOODS'

The term 'goods' is defined by s. 61 as including 'all personal chattels other than things in action and money', or, for Scots law, 'all corporeal moveables except money'. The term includes 'emblements, industrial growing crops, and things attached to or forming part of the land which are agreed to be severed before sale or under the contract of sale'.[1]

This definition is fairly extensive – indeed, virtually all-embracing[2] – but there are nevertheless some 'things' which do not, or may not fall within this definition. First, the definition clearly excludes non-physical items, such as company shares, which are technically 'things in action' or incorporeal moveables and so are excluded by the plain words of the definition. Similarly, items of 'intellectual property' such as copyrights, patents and trade marks are not 'personal chattels' or corporeal moveables and so fall outside the definition, although of course goods may exist which embody these intellectual property rights.[3]

In modern times an important point, not yet wholly resolved, is whether computer software may constitute 'goods' within the meaning of the Act.[4] Software is normally embedded in some physical form, such as disks, or as part of a package in which it is sold along with computer hardware, that is computers or computer parts. It is protected as a literary work by the law of copyright.[5] Usually only the medium in which the software is embedded, e.g., a disk, is sold. The copyright in the software remains in the software house which developed it. The software house licenses the user to make working copies of the disks and to load the

---

1 Emblements were growing crops sown by a tenant for life which his personal representatives had the right to take. They were personal property.

2 The difficult question as to whether forms of energy such as gas and electricity are goods has not come before a court in the UK. In *Singer Co, Link Simulation Systems Div* v *Baltimore Gas and Electricity Company* 558 A 2d 419 it was held that electricity in an electricity company's distribution system was not a 'good' within §2-105 of the Uniform Commercial Code (so that the company were not liable under the Sales Article for electrical failures), and this corresponds to similar decisions in other states. Given that the definition of 'goods' in the above section is if anything broader than that in the Sale of Goods Act, it could well be that a court in the UK would come to a similar conclusion. However, electricity is a 'good' for the purposes of product liability. This is dealt with elsewhere – p. 276.

3 By contrast, for the purposes of the Law of Property Act 1925 'property' is defined so as to include intellectual property – s. 205(1)(xx).

4 See Rowland [1993] Cambrian LR 78.

5 The level of copyright protection afforded to computer software is governed by the Copyright (Computer Programs) Regulations 1992, SI 1992/3233 which implement the Software Directive 91/250 OJ 1991 L122/42, 17/5/91, and, *inter alia*, make certain amendments to the Copyright, Designs and Patents Act 1988. The Directive has as its object the harmonization of the level of protection afforded to software by the laws of the Member States of the EU.

software into a computer, acts which otherwise would be infringements of copyright.[6] Software can also, of course, be delivered online subject to licensing terms.

The question as to whether or not a supply of computer software is a sale of goods, has had to be answered both by the Outer House of the Court of Session and by the Court of Appeal. In *Beta Computers (Europe) Ltd* v *Adobe Systems (Europe) Ltd*,[7] the defender had ordered from the pursuer by telephone a standard computer package to upgrade its existing software. The software was delivered in a package which bore the words 'Opening the Informix S.I. software package indicates your acceptance of these terms and conditions'. These were the terms and conditions of Informix's copyright licence, Informix being the proprietor of the software. The defender did not open the package but attempted to return it. The pursuer refused to accept its return, and sued for payment of the price. The pursuer argued that it had supplied exactly what was ordered, and that it was not concerned with the terms of the licence imposed by the authors of the software. The defender argued that acceptance of the licence conditions was an implied condition suspensive of its agreement with the pursuer. Lord Penrose held that the supply of proprietary software for a price was a single contract *sui generis* though it contained elements of contracts such as sales of goods and the grant of a licence. It was an essential feature of such a contract that the supplier undertook to make available to the purchaser *both* the medium on which the program was recorded *and* the right to access and use the software. There could be no *consensus ad idem* until the conditions of use stipulated by the copyright owner were produced and accepted by the parties, which could not occur earlier than the tender of those conditions to the purchaser. Furthermore, whether the tender of software subject to conditions for use was regarded as a breach of a previously unconditional contract, or as being subject to a suspensive condition entitling the purchasers to reject if the conditions for use were unacceptable, or as made when there was no concluded contract, the defender was entitled to reject.[8]

In *St Albans City and District Council* v *International Computers Ltd*,[9] the facts of which are given later,[10] both Scott Baker J at first instance and Sir Iain Glidewell in the Court of Appeal expressed the view that a computer disk is within the definition of 'goods' contained in s. 61 of the Sale of Goods Act 1979 and s. 18 of the Supply of Goods and Services Act 1982. A computer program on the other hand is not goods. However, when a defective program is encoded and sold or hired on a disk, the seller or hirer of the disk will be in breach of the terms as to quality and fitness implied by s. 14 of the Sale of Goods Act or s. 9 of the Supply of Goods and Services Act. Accordingly, both judges were of the view that a supply of a disk carrying software is either a sale or a supply of goods. In this they were at variance with the views expressed by Lord Penrose. Who is right? Or are both approaches mistaken? It will be argued that it is less important to worry about how we should slot

---

6 See Copyright, Designs and Patents Act 1988, s. 17(1) and (2).
7 1996 SLT 604.
8 We deal further with this aspect of the case later – see p. 226.
9 [1996] 4 All ER 481.
10 See p. 252.

software into existing legal categories, than what we think the respective liabilities of the software house or of any intermediary supplier to the purchaser should be.[11] Once the latter is decided, other questions are relatively straightforward. We return to this below.[12]

In a crucial passage[13] Lord Penrose criticized both the views expressed by Christopher Reed,[14] to the effect that where software is supplied on a physical medium it should be regarded as physical property like a book or a record, and the views expressed by Steyn J in *Eurodynamics Systems plc v General Automation Ltd*,[15] that the transfer of software is a transfer of a product. Lord Penrose said:

> This reasoning appears to me to be unattractive, at least in the context with which this case is concerned. It appears to emphasise the role of the physical medium, and to relate the transaction in the medium to sale or hire of goods. It would have the somewhat odd result that the dominant characteristic of the complex product, in terms of value or of the significant interests of parties, would be subordinated to the medium by which it was transmitted to the user in analysing the true nature and effect of the contract. If one obtained computer programs by telephone, they might be introduced into one's own hardware and used as effectively as if the medium were a disk or CD or magnetic tape.

The basic argument that the rights of the parties should not depend upon the medium of supply must be right. But the point has to be made that there is the possibility that *any* original copyright work can, at the present stage of technological development, be delivered either on a physical medium or online. Does the fact that the contents of a book can be delivered online, or the image of a painting, mean that sales of books and paintings must now be treated as *sui generis* and thus outwith the Sale of Goods Act? Surely not: it is a characteristic of many supplies of information in the modern world that they can either be carried out using goods media, or supplied directly online. But, in the case of books, we distinguish the liability of the author from that of the shop and publisher. If a book has missing pages, or falls to pieces just after it is bought, the shop is clearly liable under the Sale of Goods Act quality warranties, and so is the publisher who sold it to the shop. On the other hand, neither is likely to be held liable in respect of erroneous information in a reference book.[16] This is a useful starting point in considering the liability of the various undertakings in the distribution chain for software. First of all, however, it may be useful to explore where the analogy between books and software breaks down.

Clearly, in one respect a disk is analogous to a book, and if it is physically defective the seller should be liable in the same way as the seller of a physically defective

---

11 Even before the Supply of Goods and Services Act 1982 the courts tended to treat contracts analogous to sales of goods in the same way as sales of goods so far as the implied warranties were concerned – see *Young & Marten Ltd v McManus Childs Ltd* [1969] 1 AC 454.

12 See p. 81.

13 At pp. 608–9.

14 *Computer Law*, 2nd edn, p. 44.

15 6 September 1988 (unreported). He does not appear to have had other English authorities cited to him.

16 See *Winter v G P Putnam's Sons* 938 F 2d 1033, 9th Cir. (1991), where the plaintiffs suffered serious physical injury after eating poisonous mushrooms relying on a reference work. The court distinguished *Fluor Corporation v Jeppesen & Co* 216 Cal Rptr 68 (liability of products liability theory in respect of a defective aeronautical chart). See also *Cardozo v True* 342 So 2d 1053. For a discussion of the liability of the sellers of books containing erroneous information, see Lloyd [1993] JBL 48.

book. But there is an important difference when we consider the contents. However defective the content of a book, it is unlikely to harm its physical environment.[17] Software, on the other hand, may cause harm, and the probability of this occurring (although small) is not insignificant. Defective software containing, say, a virus can do considerable damage.[18] It has been suggested that an analogy can be drawn between a reference work, such as a DIY manual, and software, since software is commonly described as a 'set of instructions to a computer'.[19] The analogy is false, however. A computer cannot 'understand' in any epistemological sense: it is a machine, and simply follows instructions.[20] It would be a very stupid person who followed an instruction in a receipt for a fish dish to 'cook under the gill', but a computer would do exactly that. This would argue for a more 'mechanical' finding of liability in the case of defective software.

Much software is sold over the counter in stores in the same way as books and records. For some sorts of defect in the software, the consumer would expect to have a remedy against the store in much the same way as if a television set proved to be defective. Equally, it is probable that most stores would expect their liability to be the same in both cases. To what sort of defect in software would these expectations apply, however? Two types of defect come to mind. First of all, software infected with a virus ought to be considered defective, and the supplier should incur liability equivalent to that laid down in the quality warranties of the Sale of Goods Act. Secondly, the content of the disk may simply be corrupt, just as a book with faulty printing is considered defective, e.g., the ink has come right through the page so that it cannot be read.[21] Defects in the way the program itself performs, however, are more analogous to defects in the contents of a book, and liability should, in principle, be similar.

Should the liability be different if the consumer were to choose to acquire the software directly online from the software house rather than purchase it in a store? The answer to this must surely be, no! Liability for defective software should not in principle depend upon the carrier medium, but upon whether what is involved is mass-produced 'off-the-shelf' software, or customized software specially written for a client. It is helpful as a starting point to take an example. Suppose an accounting package for small businesses had a defect in its program which caused certain items to be under-recorded so that a false picture of the profitability of the business emerged over a period of time. Would the software house which wrote the program be liable? It might be. We might make it liable on one of two bases: negligence in writing the program; or, in the absence of negligence, loss spreading. If we adhere to the view that the software house is liable in negligence, we might want to make the shop (if any) which sold the software liable as a conduit for passing liability back up

---

17 Though a book infested with bookworm could obviously do so.
18 Though contrary to popular belief this is rarely serious. The damage done by the vast majority of viruses can be made good in a fairly short time.
19 MacDonald [1995] MLR 585, 590.
20 In any event, the leading case on misleading instructions, *Wormell v R H M Agriculture (East) Ltd* [1987] 1 WLR 109 is not satisfactory, especially when applied to software.
21 Ironically, the first print run of the second edition of a well-known book on intellectual property suffered from this defect. The defective copies were replaced.

the line, and achieve this by saying there is a breach of the quality warranties of the Sale of Goods Act; but we must be clear that this is what we are doing, and that the store's liability is no greater than the ultimate liability of the supplier. We are not doing it *simply* because, if the program was off-the-shelf software, we think off-the-shelf software is goods. On the other hand, if we adopt a loss-spreading approach, we might make the store liable as the best loss spreader in the distribution chain, by making it liable under the Sale of Goods Act, but *strictly speaking* on this approach we might not want to make the software house liable at all, for the same sort of reasons that we do not make the author of a defective cookery book liable if a receipt is wrong.[22] In the United States, where these issues have been discussed openly by the courts, there is authority for this approach.[23] This approach to the problem of product liability is probably more open than any European court would be able to stomach. They are likely to opt either for a fudge, or for what essentially boils down to negligence liability, as a basis for awarding damages.

Having regard to the above, it is useful in this context to examine whether there are rational policy reasons for the liability imposed on suppliers of services such as the writing of customized software being less strict than the liability imposed on the supplier of mass-produced goods. It can be argued that there are. In the first place, the distinction can be justified in terms of a risk-spreading approach. Suppliers of expert services to individual customers in the nature of things do not have the high volumes necessary to spread the risk amongst a large number of customers, whereas producers of off-the-shelf software are more likely to.[24] Secondly, the customers usually deal directly with the providers of the services, and are therefore in a better position to prove negligence than is the consumer injured by a defective product.[25] Thirdly, the provider of the services and the customer are in a position to bargain for the level of liability to be undertaken. If nothing is said, the supplier's duty is only to exercise reasonable care and skill, but if a higher level of liability is accepted, as in *Saphena Computing Ltd v Allied Collection Agencies Ltd*,[26] then so be it. Lastly, the provider of a service which is essentially a 'one-off' is not in a position to test the software in the way in which the manufacturer of a mass-produced product is.

Conversely, the imposition of a 'strict' standard of liability on a supplier for the sort of defects in respect of which it was suggested above that a supplier of software ought to be liable in much the same way as a bookseller, would seem to be justified by precisely the considerations which apply in contracts for the sale of goods generally. Making the supplier liable is a convenient mechanism for passing liability back up the line to the person ultimately responsible for the defect, the manufacturer. But whether the manufacturer's *ultimate* liability for defects is in fact different from negligence liability in the Learned Hand sense, is questionable. In *US v Carroll Towing Co*,[27] which we will return to later,[28] Justice Learned Hand suggested that the duty of care

---

22 See n. 16 above.
23 *Goldberg* v *Kollsman Instrument Corp* 191 NE 2d 81 (1963) – see p. 284.
24 See *La Rossa* v *Scientific Design Co* 402 F 2d 937, 942, 3d Cir (1968).
25 See, for example, *Daniels* v *R W White & Sons and Tabard* [1938] 4 All ER 258.
26 3 May 1989 (unreported).
27 159 F 2d 169 (1947).
28 See p. 279 *et seq.*

in negligence is a function of three variables: (1) the probability of harm; (2) the gravity of the resulting injury; and (3) the burden of adequate precautions. If we build into (3) opportunity costs, we have a fairly good, workable formula for understanding the nature of so-called 'strict' product liability. Thus software sold in 2000 will have technical improvements (including 'safety' features such as locks) not present in equivalent packages sold in 1995, yet the 1995 packages are not defective even though they might have had the 2000 features had the programmers worked at it longer and the software house delayed marketing for this purpose. Little software would appear on the market if this were not the case, and the opportunity costs of doing without admittedly less than perfect software would be great.

In other words, the key to the conundrum is not to get lost in metaphysical questions as to whether or not software is goods, but to focus on who is being sued in respect of what sort of defect, and to be clear as to the basis on which liability is being imposed. The imposition of liability on the basis of loss spreading is different from the imposition of liability on the basis of negligence in the special sense in which it was used above. In Europe generally, liability in this special sense (negligence) is arguably what is accepted under the Product Liability Directive,[29] and, as suggested above, a shop's liability for defects ought not in principle to be greater than that of the ultimate manufacturer.

The question as to the warranties to be implied in software supply contracts has been explored in a number of recent cases. In *Watford Electronics Ltd v Sanderson*[30] Judge Thornton QC held that the Sale of Goods Act was not applicable, as the software had not been sold, but merely licensed (as is usually the case). However, he held that quality warranties could be implied from two sources: there was a contract of bailment within s. 6(1) of the Supply of Goods and Services Act 1982 because the definition of 'software' in the contract meant that goods were being supplied. Possession, not ownership, of the software was being transferred subject to a use payment. This meant that the terms implied by the 1982 Act,[31] which are identical to those in sales of goods could be implied. Given that what was being acquired was not a medium, but the software itself, this argument is somewhat difficult to follow. However, he also held that similar terms to those implied by this Act, and the Sale of Goods Act, could be implied at common law. In the light of the views expressed in *Young & Marten Ltd v McManus Childs Ltd*[32] this must be correct.[33] This issue was not pursued further in the Court of Appeal.

The seller's assertions about the performance of the software will often be crucial. These representations may themselves, of course, give rise to a claim for damages for material misrepresentation.[34]

---

29 See p. 273 *et seq.*
30 [2001] 1 All ER (Comm) 696.
31 See 1982 Act, s. 9.
32 [1969] 1 AC 454 – see p. 8.
33 *Watford Electronics* was discussed at length in the later case of *SAM Business Systems Ltd v Hedley & Co* [2002] EWHC 2733 (TCC) but only in relation to the application of the Unfair Contract Terms Act 1977 – see p. 234 *et seq.* See also on this latter point *Horace Holman Group Ltd v Sherwood International Group Ltd* (TCC) 12 April 2000 (unreported.)
34 See *Eurodynamics Systems plc v General Automation Ltd*, 6 September 1988 (unreported) – statement by the sellers that their system supported ANSI Cobol 74 programming language. As to material misrepresentations which give rise to a claim for damages see p. 98 *et seq.*

Another modern area of doubt as to the scope of the definition of 'goods' has previously been noted.[35] It is not wholly clear whether the term 'goods' would cover human blood for transfusion or other similar items not ordinarily thought to be the subject of commerce.

A further point which requires comment has previously been referred to briefly, but remains to be dealt with here. This point concerns the meaning of the latter part of the statutory definition. Since the products of the soil must always be sold with a view to their ultimate severance 'under the contract of sale', it appears that, whether or not they are also land within the meaning of s. 2 of the Law of Property (Miscellaneous Provisions) Act 1989 or s. 1 of the Requirements of Writing (Scotland) Act 1995, they are now always goods within the meaning of the Sale of Goods Act. It is, however, still necessary to distinguish the products of the soil or 'things attached to or forming part of the land' on the one hand, from the actual land itself, or interests therein, on the other. The sale of sand from a quarry, for example, is not a sale of things attached to or forming part of the land, but a sale of an interest in the land itself. Thus, in *Morgan v Russell*,[36] it was held that the sale of cinders and slag, which were not definite or detached heaps resting on the ground, was not a sale of goods but a sale of an interest in land and, therefore, the Sale of Goods Act did not apply. Similarly, in the Australian case of *Mills v Stockman*,[37] a quantity of slate which had been quarried and then left on some land as waste material for many years was held to be part of the land, and not goods. The slate was 'unwanted dross cast on one side with the intention that it should remain on the land indefinitely, and, by implication, that it should form part of the land'.[38] In Scotland, a contract with the owner of ground under which the other party gains for a period a right to quarry in the ground and remove material found therein, such as rock or sand, is conventionally described as a 'mineral lease' of the ground rather than as a sale of the excavated materials.[39] Although this usage has been criticized judicially as inapt, because the tenant is not merely occupying or using the ground, but consuming or taking away part of it,[40] it remains in use in practice.

DIFFERENT TYPES OF GOODS

Section 5 of the Act is as follows:

(1) The goods which form the subject of a contract of sale may be either existing goods, owned or possessed by the seller, or goods to be manufactured or acquired by him after the making of the contract of sale, in this Act called 'future goods'.
(2) There may be a contract for the sale of goods, the acquisition of which by the seller depends upon a contingency which may or may not happen.
(3) Where by a contract of sale the seller purports to effect a present sale of future goods, the contract operates as an agreement to sell the goods.

---

35 Above, p. 24.
36 [1909] 1 KB 357.
37 (1966–67) 116 CLR 61.
38 Per Barwick CJ at 71.
39 *Gowans v Christie* (1873) 11 M (HL) 1.
40 *Nugent v Nugent's Trustees* (1899) 2 F (HL) 21 at 22.

The subject-matter of the contract of sale may be either existing goods owned or possessed by the seller, or future goods, or (a possibility not mentioned by the Act) a *spes*, or chance.

Existing goods

Little need be said here except to point out that existing goods may be either specific or unascertained, and that important consequences follow from this distinction, for example in relation to the application of s. 6 and in connection with the passing of the property. These will be discussed later.[41]

Future goods

Future goods include goods not yet in existence, and goods in existence but not yet acquired by the seller. It is probably safe to say that future goods can never be specific goods within the meaning of the Act. This certainly seems to be true of those parts of the Act dealing with the passing of property. There remains some doubt about a number of other sections, such as ss. 6 and 7, which apply to contracts for the sale of specific goods. In cases under s. 7 of the Act, future goods, if sufficiently identified, may be specific goods in the limited sense that their destruction may frustrate the contract. In *Howell* v *Coupland*,[42] a sale of 200 tons of potatoes to be grown on a particular piece of land was held to be a sale of specific goods, despite the fact that they were not existing goods, for the purpose of the common law rules of frustration. Failure of the crop was thus held to avoid the contract. Since the Act was passed, it is largely immaterial whether this result is arrived at by application of s. 7 or not, because the same result may be arrived at by holding the contract to be a sale within s. 5(2) dependent upon a contingency.[43]

The most important question in connection with future goods, the passing of the property, will be dealt with later.[44]

A *spes*

The sale of a *spes* – a chance – must be distinguished from the contingent sale of future goods, though the distinction is not so much as to the subject-matter of the contract but as to its construction. Thus it is possible for a person to agree to buy future goods from a particular source and to take the chance (or, in language appropriate to the sale of goods, the risk) of the goods never coming into existence. For example, a person may agree to buy whatever crop is produced from a particular field at a fixed price. Such a transaction comes perilously close to a gamble but, as the

---

41 Pages 108 and 332 below.
42 (1876) 1 QBD 258. Similarly, in *Goldsborough Mort & Co Ltd* v *Carter* (1914) 19 CLR 429, the Australian High Court held (before the enactment of the Sale of Goods Act in New South Wales) that a sale of 'about' 4,000 sheep pastured on certain lands was a sale of specific goods although the sheep were not then individually identified.
43 *Re Wait* [1927] 1 Ch 606, 631 per Atkin LJ; *H R & S Sainsbury* v *Street* [1972] 1 WLR 834.
44 See below, p. 332.

seller stands to gain the same amount in any event, it appears that the sale cannot be a wager within s. 18 of the Gaming Act 1845 or be subject to the doctrine of sponsiones ludicrae in Scotland.[45]

A transaction such as that in *Howell* v *Coupland* is thus open to at least[46] three possible constructions:

1 It may be a contingent sale of goods within s. 5(2), in which case if the crop does not come into existence the contract will not become operative at all and neither party is bound.
2 Alternatively, it may be an unconditional sale, that is the seller may absolutely undertake to deliver the goods, so that in effect he warrants that there will be a crop, in which case, if there is no crop, he will be liable for non-delivery.
3 Thirdly, it may be a sale of a mere chance, that is the buyer may take the risk of the crop failing completely, in which case the price is still payable.

Despite the fact that s. 5, which expressly deals with the subject-matter of the contract, classifies the types of subject-matter as either existing or future goods, there is in fact a much more important classification which cuts right across this one. This is the distinction between specific and unascertained goods, which is of the greatest importance in connection with the passing of the property and risk in the contract of sale. Specific goods are goods 'identified and agreed on at the time a contract of sale is made',[47] for example this particular car or this particular load of wheat. Unascertained goods are not defined by the Act, but they seem to fall into three main categories:

1 Goods to be manufactured or grown by the seller, which are necessarily future goods.
2 Purely generic goods, for example 1,000 tonnes of wheat, or the like, which must also be future goods, at least where the seller does not already own sufficient goods of the description in question which can be appropriated to the contract. Where the seller does own such a quantity of the goods, but the sale is not expressed to be of those particular goods but for goods of that generic kind, it is not easy to apply the 'future goods'/'existing goods' distinction. In one sense, the goods appear to fall within the definition of 'existing goods' in s. 5(1) but, on the other hand, until the goods are appropriated to the contract, the mere fact that the seller has sufficient goods for that purpose seems irrelevant. In either event it seems that nothing turns on the distinction.
3 An unidentified part of a specified whole, for example 1,000 tonnes out of a particular load of 2,000 tonnes of wheat; these may be either future or existing goods within the meaning of s. 5.

It will be seen that the distinction between the third type of unascertained goods and specific goods is only a matter of degree, and in a particular case it may be slight

---

45 See *Ellesmere* v *Wallace* [1929] Ch 1; McBryde, *Contract*, 2nd edn, para 19.50 *et seq.*
46 At least three, because it is now clear that, where part only of the crop has perished, yet other possibilities are available – see *H R & S Sainsbury* v *Street*, above, discussed in more detail below, p. 109.
47 So defined by s. 61.

indeed. Thus if A agrees to sell to B 9,000 tonnes of the wheat on a certain ship which is carrying 10,000 tonnes in all, this is a sale of unascertained goods because they are not identified, but it is obvious that such a transaction has more affinities with a sale of specific goods than with a sale of purely generic goods. It is also true, although less obviously, that the distinction between the second and third kinds of unascertained goods is only a matter of degree. The more detailed is the description of the genus, the more it comes to resemble a sale from a specified bulk or stock. It will be seen later that the failure of the Act to draw these distinctions has led to unfortunate results. In particular, the classification of the third of the above three types as unascertained has led to difficulties in connection with the passing of property and risk,[48] and also in connection with the doctrine of frustration.

48 See Chapter 20.

7

THE TYPES OF OBLIGATION CREATED

FUNDAMENTAL TERMS

At the time when the old Sale of Goods Act was passed, contractual obligations in England and Wales[1] were generally thought to fall into two principal classes, namely conditions and warranties. In addition, there existed a body of equitable rules governing mere misrepresentations, that is statements inducing a party to enter into a contract which were not subsequently incorporated into the contract itself. In the 1950s and 1960s, it came to be suggested in a number of decisions that the distinction between a condition and a warranty was not exhaustive. This development took two forms. On the one hand, it came to be said that there were terms more important even than conditions – fundamental terms. On the other hand, it also came to be said that there was a category of terms mid-way between the condition and the warranty – innominate, or intermediate terms. Innominate terms are considered further below;[2] here we consider fundamental terms.

For most practical purposes, it mattered little whether a term was called a condition or a fundamental term. In either event, a breach of the term, however minor in itself, justified the innocent party in repudiating his own obligations under the contract, and treating it as discharged. But the doctrine of the fundamental term was devised principally to deal with the growing menace of the unfair and unreasonable exemption clause. It was held in a large number of decisions that an exemption clause, no matter how sweeping and no matter how broadly drafted its language, could not protect a guilty party from liability for breach of a fundamental term of the contract.

In 1967, the House of Lords cut down this doctrine in the *Suisse Atlantique* case.[3] It was held here that the doctrine of the fundamental term was nothing more than a rule of construction; an exemption clause was not to be assumed to be drafted so as to justify one party in breaking the fundamental terms of the contract. The rule of construction was, no doubt, a strong one; that is, even though the words of an exemption clause might appear to be wide enough to cover the events which had occurred, the rule would normally be applied, and the words of the exemption clause interpreted so as to cover only less drastic breaches. Nevertheless, however strong the rule of construction, the logical result of refusing to recognize it as a rule of law was

---

1 As to the position in Scotland see below p. 99.
2 See below, p. 91.
3 *Suisse Atlantique Société D'Armement Maritime SA v Rotterdamsche Kolen Centrale* [1967] 1 AC 361.

that, in the last resort, the parties must be free to make their own contract, however unfair or unpalatable the terms might be. So long only as it was absolutely clear that the words of the exemption clause were designed to cover the circumstances that had occurred, no matter how fundamental, the courts were obliged to apply the clause.

Some inroads were made on this doctrine by subsequent decisions, but it was clear that legislative intervention was called for. In due course this was forthcoming and, first, the Supply of Goods (Implied Terms) Act 1973 and, later, the Unfair Contract Terms Act 1977 and Unfair Terms in Consumer Contracts Regulations[4] have given the courts a substantial degree of control over unfair exemption clauses. The result of these developments is likely to be that the distinction between fundamental terms and conditions will cease to be of much significance. Clauses which are unreasonable can usually be struck down, and it will be less necessary for parties to try to persuade the courts to construe the exemption clause in a strict way so that it does not cover the breach of a fundamental term. However, it cannot be said that the distinction will never be of any importance. Given the way lawyers tend to argue cases, it is likely that (unless severely discouraged by the courts) they will still usually try to persuade a court that (1) a clause ought not to be construed to cover the breach of a fundamental term, and that (2) even if it does cover such a breach, it should be held to be unreasonable under the 1977 Act or unfair under the Regulations.[5] Moreover, as noted above, a purchase of computer software is both a sale of the disks etc. and a licence of the software. The Unfair Contract Terms Act does not apply to contracts so far as they relate to the creation or transfer of a right or interest, *inter alia*, in a copyright.[6] Control of exemption clauses in such contracts, therefore, depends on common law. It can be argued, however, that this does not prevent the Act from applying to a licence which is simply a permission[7] and does not create or transfer any interest.[8]

George Mitchell (Chesterhall) Ltd v *Finney Lock Seeds Ltd*[9] was the first case to reach the House of Lords on the reasonableness requirement. In this case, plaintiff farmers ordered from the defendants, who were seed merchants, a quantity of 'Finney's Late Dutch Special Cabbage' seeds but were unfortunately supplied instead with an inferior type of seed which was, indeed, not a 'Late' seed at all, and proved quite unsuitable to the plaintiffs' needs. A clause limiting the defendants' liability was held unreasonable for reasons which are discussed later.[10] But it was also argued that the clause should not be construed to apply to the breach which had occurred

---

4 SI 1999/2083 – see p. 257 *et seq.*

5 It must be noted, however, that in *Fastframe Ltd* v *Lohinski*, 3 March 1993 (unreported – discussed by Adams (1994) 57 MLR 960), the Court of Appeal expressed strong disapproval of this approach. That case, however, involved the construction of a 'no set-off' clause, and, as noted below, the approach may retain some life where it is arguable that the wrong goods have been supplied.

6 Schedule I, para 1(c). There is no equivalent provision in the Scottish Part of the Act, however, although intellectual property licences are not included in the list of those contracts to which the Part applies (s. 15, as amended by the Law Reform (Miscellaneous Provisions) (Scotland) Act 1990, ss. 68 and 74 and Sch. 9).

7 *Federal Commissioners of Taxation* v *United Aircraft Corp* (1943) 68 CLR 525.

8 In *Fastframe Ltd* v *Lohinski*, n. 5 above, the Court of Appeal applied the Act to a franchise contract, which licensed, *inter alia*, a trade name, without commenting on this point, which was raised in the appellant's skeleton arguments. See also p. 252 *et seq.*

9 [1983] 2 AC 803.

10 Below, p. 248 *et seq.*

because the suppliers had delivered something quite different from what had been ordered. The House of Lords rejected this argument, but in terms suggesting that if indeed the goods supplied had been of a totally different character (as where beans instead of peas are supplied) it would have been accepted.

It seems, then, that the concept of the fundamental term retains a small residuary significance.[11] Where such a term is breached a limitation clause will not be construed to cover the breach unless this is almost unavoidable. The strong rule of construction which also continues to apply to total exclusion clauses (as opposed to limitation clauses)[12] thus seems also to continue to apply to limitation clauses which seek to protect against breach of a fundamental term and not merely a breach of condition. This is somewhat unfortunate because it means that the courts will continue to have to draw fine and somewhat arbitrary distinctions between the 'peas and beans' type of case, on the one hand, and less drastic departures from the contract such as that between early and late cabbage seed, or good quality and cheap quality seed. Inevitably this means that difficulties will be encountered with other cases as, for example, where a person contracts to sell cabbage seed, but supplies beetroot or carrot seed.[13] Moreover, these difficulties will be almost completely gratuitous, since drawing these distinctions will never dispose of the whole case; they will merely decide whether a rule of construction applies, and even if it does prima facie apply it may be displaced by other contrary indications, or the clause may be declared void under the 1977 Act.

In the second edition of this book, it was suggested that there could be a second type of case in which it might be important to distinguish between a fundamental term and a condition. It was there suggested that there could be no acceptance, and hence no loss of the right to reject goods, where there was a complete non-performance of the contract. In the third edition, as a result of the decision in *Charterhouse Credit Co Ltd v Tolley*,[14] this suggestion had to be modified, if not altogether rejected. In this case the Court of Appeal held that the hirer of a car under a hire-purchase agreement had affirmed the contract and accepted the goods, despite a fundamental breach by the owner in supplying a car with a defective rear axle. And it seems clear that the court contemplated the possibility of a buyer 'accepting' goods delivered by the seller even where there was a delivery of goods wholly different from those sold, for example a horse instead of a tractor.

But the decision in *Charterhouse Credit v Tolly* has now been overruled[15] and the suggestion previously made may now be put forward again. As will be seen later,[16] there are circumstances (though they will be rare) in which a buyer can be treated as having accepted goods even though he has no knowledge of defects in them, but it is

---

11   On the other hand, where beans are delivered instead of peas it could simply be said that the exemption clause is inoperative on the analogy of the *Gibaud* or 'four corners' rule – see *Gibaud* v *Great Eastern Railway* [1921] 2 KB 426.

12   See below, p. 228.

13   In the *George Mitchell* case counsel in the lower court conceded that the limitation clause would not apply in this event, but in the House of Lords the concession was withdrawn. The House did not, however, decide whether the concession was correctly withdrawn; nor was it made clear whether (and if so, why) the 'peas and beans' case differs from the 'cabbage seed' and 'beetroot or carrot seed' case.

14   [1963] 2 QB 683.

15   By *Photo Production Ltd* v *Securicor* [1980] AC 827, below, p. 227.

16   See below, p. 512 *et seq.*

arguable that in some of these cases a buyer would be held not to have accepted the goods if there has been a breach of a fundamental term, although a breach of condition would not help him. For example, suppose that A agrees to sell peas to B but sends him beans instead. If B, in ignorance of the substitution but having had an opportunity to examine the goods, resells and delivers the goods to C, it seems that B would not thereafter be precluded from rejecting the goods. In the *Suisse Atlantique* case, Lord Reid suggested that such a delivery could not properly be treated as a delivery under the original contract at all, but only as an offer to enter into a new contract.[17] On the other hand, if A had merely been guilty of a breach of condition, B would, in such circumstances, have lost his right of rejection under the law prior to 3 January 1995.[18]

Otherwise, the principal use of the expression 'fundamental term' is in written contracts where draftsmen sometimes use it in preference to 'condition' in an attempt to make it clear that *any* breach of such a term will enable the innocent party to terminate.[19]

CONDITIONS

The term condition is not defined by the Act, but s. 11(3) states that:

> Whether a stipulation in a contract of sale is a condition, the breach of which may give rise to a right to treat the contract as repudiated, or a warranty, the breach of which may give rise to a claim for damages but not to a right to reject the goods and treat the contract as repudiated, depends in each case on the construction of the contract; and a stipulation may be a condition, though called a warranty in the contract.

This subsection therefore explains the term condition by reference to its legal effect, but it does not explain how a condition is to be distinguished from a warranty. It is enough here to say that in its usual meaning a condition is a term which, without being the fundamental obligation imposed by the contract, is still of such vital importance that it goes to the root of the transaction. The importance of a condition in contracts for the sale of goods is that its breach, if committed by the seller, may give the buyer the right to reject the goods completely and to decline to pay the price, or, if he has already paid it, to recover it.[20]

No doubt this is the usual meaning of the word 'condition'. If the term is strictly a condition, this means that its full performance is a *condition* of the other party's obligations; his duties are *conditional* on the performance of conditions. For example, the seller's statutory implied obligations as to the quality and fitness of the goods, and as to their compliance with their description, are all conditions under the Sale of Goods Act, both as originally enacted and in its amended form. That means that the duties must be strictly complied with by the seller and that any breach of these conditions, however trivial, prima facie justifies the buyer in refusing to accept the goods.

---

17 [1967] 1 AC at 404.
18 See ss. 34 and 35 of the Act, as amended – see below, p. 511 *et seq.*
19 This practice has grown up since *Wickman Machine Tools Sales Ltd* v *Schuler AG* [1974] AC 235.
20 The term 'condition' is used in a large number of different senses – see Stoljar, 'The Contractual Concept of Condition' (1953) 69 LQR 485; see also Montrose [1960] CLJ 72.

Until 1962, the general opinion was that the distinction between conditions and warranties was exhaustive (at any rate leaving aside fundamental terms which were not material to this question). Thus it was assumed that all contractual terms had to fall within one class or another and that this distinction could, in principle, be drawn at the time when the contract was made. Any term whose breach *could possibly* take a serious form naturally tended to be treated as a condition as a result of this approach. Since the distinction related to the terms of the contract and not to the consequences of the breach and, indeed, had to be applied in theory as at the date when the contract was made, there was a tendency for many terms to be treated as conditions even though, in the result, their breach only caused minor inconvenience or loss, or even none at all. Only where it could be said at the outset that no breach of a term could ever have really serious consequences was it possible to classify the term as a warranty.

The consequence of this was that in the law of sale of goods, the duties of the seller were traditionally treated very strictly. Any deviation from the terms implied by the Act (as mentioned above) justified the buyer in rejecting the goods. But it was also widely assumed by lawyers that there was nothing peculiar in the law of sale or even in the Sale of Goods Act with respect to these questions. It was generally thought that (for example) the position was the same with respect to all the seller's duties, whether they were implied conditions under the Act or express conditions laid down by the contract.

It will be seen that this approach tended to shut out from consideration as irrelevant the actual consequences of a breach of contract. Some breaches, of course, are serious enough on any view to justify the other party in repudiating the contract; but many breaches have relatively trivial consequences and some have no ill consequences at all. Generally speaking, the law on this point as it was understood until 1962 paid little attention to the actual results of a breach of contract. This result possibly favoured the certainty which was – especially perhaps in the last century – regarded as a very important goal of the law. Particularly in commercial contracts, it was often necessary that a buyer should be in a position to make an instant decision as to whether he would accept goods (or shipping documents) delivered under a contract of sale. So long as he could reject the goods for any breach of contract (on the ground that it was a breach of condition), his position was relatively simple. He did not have to ask himself how serious the breach was, an inquiry which obviously might cause serious difficulty where the future results of the breach remained still unknown. But, nevertheless, this whole approach paid a high price for the certainty that was thus purchased. For the result undoubtedly was to permit termination of a contract for many breaches of no serious import at all. It began to seem increasingly unjust to lawyers that this should be permitted.

INNOMINATE TERMS

Since the early 1960s something of a legal revolution has been under way on this question. The first case in the story was *Hong Kong Fir Shipping Co Ltd* v *Kawasaki Kisen Kaisha*,[21] which was not a contract of sale of goods at all. The contract here involved a

---

21 [1962] 2 QB 26.

charterparty under which a ship was hired, or chartered, by the plaintiffs to the defendants. Now it has long been the law that a charterparty imposes obligations on the owners to take due diligence to provide a seaworthy ship. And it is clear enough that such a term may be broken in such serious respects that the charterer must be entitled to repudiate the contract altogether. If a ship is supplied which is manifestly in no fit state to go to sea at all, and if it is clear that no prospect exists of repairing the ship sufficiently to make her fit to sail, then it can hardly be doubted that the charterer must be entitled to repudiate the charterparty altogether. But seaworthiness is, on the authorities, a comprehensive standard, and a ship may be unseaworthy in the legal sense as a result of some very trifling defect which can be easily remedied. In these circumstances, it was held by the Court of Appeal that the owners' duties as to seaworthiness could not be classified at the outset as a condition or a warranty. The truth was that this was an 'innominate term' whose consequences depended on the actual outcome of breach. The law has to have regard to the nature and gravity of the breach before it becomes possible to say whether the innocent party is entitled to repudiate a contract for breach of a term of this character.

Passing over *The Mihalis Angelos*,[22] another important decision of the Court of Appeal, which has, however, now been superseded by House of Lords authority to be discussed below, the next case in this story is *Cehave NV* v *Bremer Handelsgesellschaft*,[23] which was a case of sale of goods. This contract was for the sale of citrus pulp pellets for use in animal foods, and it was a term of the contract that the goods should be shipped 'in good condition'. It was also an implied condition under the Sale of Goods Act that the goods should be of merchantable quality. The goods were somewhat damaged, though to a relatively minor degree, and in fact they were ultimately used for their intended purpose by the buyers. But the market had fallen at the time of delivery and the buyers contended that they were entitled to reject them for breach of the implied condition of merchantability[24] and also for breach of the express condition that they should be in 'good condition'. It was held that the Sale of Goods Act did not exhaustively divide all terms into conditions and warranties. Although s. 11 only talks of these two possibilities, s. 62(2) preserves the effect of common law rules save insofar as they are inconsistent with the Act. The court took the *Hong Kong Fir* case as correctly laying down the common law rules and as demonstrating the existence of the 'innominate term', breach of which may discharge the other party, but only if the nature and consequences are sufficiently serious to justify this result. The court went on to hold that such innominate terms can exist in contracts of sale of goods and that the express term that the goods had to be in good condition was a term of that character. However, the court also assumed that the terms under the Act, including the implied condition of merchantability, were (as they have always been thought to be) conditions in the strict sense, but in the result they held that this term was not broken. Although the actual decision in this case was undoubtedly fair, the reasoning leads to the very odd conclusion that an *implied* term of merchantability is an entirely different thing from an express term. If it is express, it may or may not be

---

22 [1971] 1 QB 164.
23 Also known as *The Hansa Nord* [1976] QB 44.
24 Note the modifications to the right to reject in such cases effected by the 1994 Act, and discussed at p. 499 *et seq.*

a condition in the strict sense, but if it is implied under the Act, then it must be (because the Act says it is) a condition – and it was assumed that this means a condition in the strict sense. In order to arrive at a reasonable result, the court had to conclude that the goods in this case were merchantable, but not 'in good condition', a somewhat contradictory holding.[25] Of course, because of the modifications made to the right to reject by the 1994 Sale and Supply of Goods Act, which inserted a new s. 15A into the 1979 Act modifying the non-consumer buyer's right to reject, if similar facts were to recur in the present day, a more satisfying outcome could be reached.[26]

The next stage in the history of this legal revolution is the decision of the House of Lords in *Reardon Smith Lines Ltd v Hansen Tangen*,[27] though this again was not a contract of sale of goods. In this case, a ship which was to be constructed by the plaintiffs was chartered by them to the defendants for delivery when completed. As the ship did not exist at the time when the contract was made, it was described by reference to a specification which declared that it was to be built at Yard No. 354 at Osaka Zosen. In fact, it was built at another yard, owned by another shipbuilding company to whom the plaintiffs had subcontracted the work. Now (as will be seen later) in the law of sale of goods, there is an implied condition that the goods to be delivered must correspond with their description. This has always been treated as a strict condition, so that any deviation from the contractual description has been treated as a breach of condition justifying the buyer in rejecting the goods. These cases will be examined later.[28] Here it is enough to say that the analogy of these cases was naturally much pressed on the House of Lords in the *Reardon Smith Lines* case. If the plaintiffs in this case had contracted to sell (rather than charter) the vessel in question, then there is no doubt that on the law as it then stood, the sellers would have been held guilty of a breach of the condition that the goods must comply with their description. But the argument was rejected by the House, and it is clear that some of the sale of goods cases did not find favour with their Lordships.[29] Lord Wilberforce, who delivered the principal speech in this case, indicated that some of the leading cases on the law of sale might need reconsideration in the future.[30] In the meantime, he insisted that the general law of contract had developed along more rational lines than the strict law of sale of goods on the point. It is clear that he preferred to treat the results of a breach of contract as something to be settled *after* the breach occurred. Moreover, he approved of the decision in the *Cehave* case to treat *express* contractual conditions in a contract of sale of goods as subject to the general law of contract and not to the peculiar rules laid down by the Sale of Goods Act.

---

25 But the case has been followed several times, most notably in *The Aktion* [1987] 1 Lloyd's Rep 283 (express terms on sale of ship held innominate because too severe to hold that minor mechanical or body problems which could easily be rectified were conditions). See also *The Puerto Buitrago* [1976] 1 Lloyd's Rep 250 and *Tradax International SA v Goldschmidt SA* [1977] 2 Lloyd's Rep 604.

26 See p. 499 *et seq.*

27 [1976] 1 WLR 989.

28 See below, p. 499 *et seq.*

29 See below, p. 151.

30 In the event, the modification of the right to reject effected by s. 15A (inserted by the 1994 Act) should obviate many of the difficulties created by this old case law – see p. 153 *et seq.*

The developments described above have certainly not eliminated the legal type of term known as condition. Indeed, the terms as to quality and fitness implied under the Sale of Goods Act are all conditions, and many non-statutory terms are also conditions – for instance stipulations as to time. However, as we will see, in the case of commercial contracts the consequences of a term being characterized as a 'condition' in the Sale of Goods Act etc. have been significantly modified.[31]

Stipulations as to time

There is a strong tendency to treat stipulations as to the time when some part of a contract is to be performed as conditions, breach of which is thus a repudiation which can be instantly accepted, thereby terminating the contract while leaving open a claim for damages. This tendency is noticeable especially in commercial contracts where a contractual breach may create a situation in which the innocent party needs to know at once what his rights are; he may need to know immediately whether he is entitled to make alternative arrangements, rather than wait and see what are the consequences of the breach. In *Bunge Corpn* v *Tradax*,[32] sellers sold goods for shipment from an American port in the Gulf of Mexico, and the buyers were required to name a vessel to carry the goods. Notice of the vessel's name was to be given at latest by 13 June, but in fact the buyers failed to give the notice until 17 June by which time the sellers claimed that it was too late, and that the contract was terminated by the buyers' breach. The sale in this case was one of a 'string', that is one of a whole series of sales of the same goods; it is commonplace in certain areas of business for this to happen, and strings may involve as many as 50 or more sales. In this event the last buyer who actually intends to have the goods shipped (rather than reselling before shipment) must give the requisite notice, and each other person in the chain or string must pass the notice upwards, or ensure that it is sent direct to the first seller who is actually going to deliver the goods for shipment. It was held by the House of Lords that in cases of this nature, terms as to the time of performance of various contractual duties must be treated as conditions. It is essential that such notices be given on time, in order that they can be passed on, and so that the ultimate seller can himself comply with his own contractual duties as regards delivering the goods to the necessary port for shipment and so on.

In deciding that the term in question was a condition in this case the House of Lords stressed a number of points which will no doubt be invoked in future cases where it is unclear whether a contractual term is or is not a condition. First, it was said that a term as to time can only be broken in one way (namely by delayed performance) and that such terms differ therefore from other terms which can be broken in a variety of ways, some more and some less serious. However, this is not entirely convincing, because delays in performance can vary from the trivial and technical to the inordinate and substantial and, indeed, it is already established by other House of Lords' decisions that a failure to perform a contractual duty on time does not always amount to a breach of condition. For example, in *Bremer Handelsgesellschaft*

---

31 Page 499 *et seq.*
32 [1981] 1 WLR 711.

v *Vanden Avenne-Izegem*[33] sellers were freed from liability for non-delivery by a contractual clause concerning governmental prohibitions of export, but they were required to notify the buyers of any such prohibition 'without delay'. It was held by the House of Lords that a failure to give the notice within such a time did not prevent the sellers relying on the clause in question.

On the other hand, other points stressed by the House of Lords in *Bunge Corpn* v *Tradax* may be more critical. These include such questions as: does the performance by the innocent party of his duties under the contract depend on receipt of notices in the required time? Is the contract likely to be one of a string so that many other commercial parties will be affected by delays? Would it be difficult to assess damages for breach if the term is not construed as a condition? Taking the decision as a whole, it seems reasonably clear that in ordinary commercial contracts for the sale of goods, terms as to the time of shipment, delivery, payment and the like, as well as terms as to documents to be presented and other incidental matters to be performed by either party, will still usually fall to be treated as conditions, any breach of which will justify the other party in repudiating the whole contract. These duties have always been strictly treated as conditions in the past and it seems clear from *Bunge Corpn* v *Tradax* that more recent case law cannot be taken to throw any doubt on the continuation of this traditional position.[34] However, 'It remains true', Lord Wilberforce insisted, 'that the courts should not be too ready to interpret contractual clauses as conditions'.[35]

But these cautionary words do not appear to be having much effect so far as concern stipulations as to time. In one subsequent case, for instance, it was held that evidence of a 'more relaxed' attitude to punctuality in the trade was not enough to displace the presumption that a clause requiring the buyer to nominate the port of shipment 'at latest Monday 14 November' was a condition.[36] And in another case it has been held that a long course of dealing between the parties in which goods were sold under terms requiring payment by a letter of credit did not affect the rule that the time for opening the credit is a condition, even though on many previous occasions one or other party had been late in opening the credit.[37]

There are, indeed, grounds for thinking that it is commercial lawyers, rather than commercial men themselves, who believe that certainty is so important in commercial transactions that these time stipulations should nearly always be treated as conditions. The truth is that reasonable commercial people rarely respond to a breach of a time stipulation by immediately throwing up the whole contract and claiming damages. Usually some attempt is made at an accommodation, some inquiry is made to find out if the other party can still perform within a reasonable period. Moreover, the law itself recognizes that this is reasonable behaviour, and indeed occasionally insists upon it, even where the

---

33 [1978] 2 Lloyd's Rep 109. See also *United Scientific Holdings* v *Burnley BC* [1978] AC 904 as to the effect of delay in the exercise of contractual rights.

34 See also *Toepfer* v *Lenersan-Poortman NV* [1980] 1 Lloyd's Rep 143.

35 [1981] 1 WLR at 715.

36 *Gill & Duffus SA* v *Société Pour L'Exportation des Sucres* [1986] 1 Lloyd's Rep 322; see also *Warde (Michael I)* v *Feedex International* [1985] 2 Lloyd's Rep 289.

37 *Nichimen Corpn* v *Gatoil Overseas Inc* [1987] 2 Lloyd's Rep 46.

term broken was a condition, by penalizing a party who has failed to mitigate the damage.

Although prima facie the innocent party is entitled to treat a contract as terminated instantly on a breach of condition, the rules as to mitigation will in some, perhaps many, cases undercut the treatment of stipulations as to time as conditions. The mitigation rules require the innocent party to take reasonable steps to mitigate or minimize the damage or loss likely to flow from the other party's breach. A contracting party who fails to perform in due time but tenders, or offers to perform, very shortly after will often be able to argue that this offer ought to be accepted as it is likely that the damage done by the delay will thereby be minimized.[38] Of course, there may be answers to this: the innocent party may say that it is already too late; that, having cancelled the contract as a result of the delay, steps have been taken to obtain (or dispose of) the goods elsewhere which are by this stage irrevocable; or he may say – with more or less plausibility depending on the facts – that he was not confident enough that the guilty party, who had already breached once, would perform as he now promised to do.

But if the mitigation rules do not help the guilty party the present law is undoubtedly very severe in its consequences. Not only is the innocent party entitled to treat a breach of condition as the equivalent of a repudiation, justifying him in instant termination of the contract, it is also immaterial why the innocent party wants to behave in this way. He is not required to act reasonably, or in good faith, in exercising his rights. Indeed, usually it seems that technical breaches of condition (such as very short delays) are only treated as grounds for termination where the innocent party is seeking a way out of the contract because market conditions have changed, or for some equally irrelevant reason. In practice it is probably quite rare that technical breaches of condition are themselves the motive (as well as the legal justification) for a claim that the contract must be treated as terminated.

Sale and Supply of Goods Act 1994

As indicated earlier, the modern developments discussed above do not fit easily into the framework of the Sale of Goods Act itself. In particular, all the implied terms as to quality and fitness of the goods under the Act are conditions, and there is no room for treating any of these terms as innominate terms.[39] It seems clear, as the Law Commissions suggested, that if the Sale of Goods Act had not been drafted in this form, modern courts would not have arrived at this result.[40]

After a lengthy inquiry the Law Commissions published proposals for change in the law relating to conditions,[41] and the government accepted these in principle.

---

38 See below, p. 541. Note especially *The Solholt* [1983] 1 Lloyd's Rep 605.

39 The new Act in its body uses the word 'term' instead of 'condition' but provides in Sch. 2 that in England and Wales and Northern Ireland the implied terms are conditions (save in the case of subss. 12(2), (4) and (5)). In other words, no change of substance is made to the former provisions in this regard.

40 Law Com. Working Paper No. 85, *Sale and Supply of Goods*, para 2.30. The subsequent Final Report, *Sale and Supply of Goods* (Law Com. No. 160, Cm. 137, 1987) as to which see below, was markedly more conservative in tone than the Working Paper, and appeared to accept unreservedly the current structure of the law and the classification of contractual terms.

41 See last note for the Final Report, *Sale and Supply of Goods*.

They are given effect to by the Sale and Supply of Goods Act 1994. This is dealt with in detail later.[42] For present purposes it is sufficient to note that it does not affect the law applicable where the buyer deals as consumer, because the Law Commissions eventually concluded (after much consultation and discussion) that consumers should continue to be allowed to reject goods for breach of any condition.[43] In non-consumer sales, the law has been amended for contracts entered into after 3 January 1995 so that the buyer no longer has the right to reject for any breach of the implied terms if the consequences and nature of the breach are so slight that rejection would be unreasonable.

Some regret may be expressed here that none of the changes so far effected will mean an end to the process of classifying terms. The 1994 Act does not reclassify the implied terms in the Act as innominate terms. The terms remain conditions, but in non-consumer sales the remedy for breach of condition is limited. Moreover, the changes do not affect any conditions except those implied under ss. 13, 14 and 15 of the Act, and s. 30, as to delivery of the correct quantity, so that (for instance) breach of a condition as to time is not affected. This is a regrettable result of the fact that the terms of reference of the Law Commissions' inquiry were limited. A more rational change would surely have extended to all breaches of condition.

WARRANTIES

The term warranty is defined by s. 61 as an:

> . . . agreement with reference to goods which are the subject of a contract of sale, but collateral to the main purpose of such contract, the breach of which gives rise to a claim for damages but not to a right to reject the goods and treat the contract as repudiated.

This definition thus explains both the meaning and the legal effect of a warranty. The term 'collateral', though hallowed by usage, is not very happily chosen, for it may give the impression that a warranty is a term which is somehow outside the contract, whereas it is in fact a term of the contract.[44] In practice, very few terms are ever classified as warranties in this narrow technical sense. It is clearly rare that one can say, at the outset, that no breach of a term can ever have such serious consequences as would justify treating the whole contract as at an end; this is (as seen above) why the courts generally classify terms as conditions. It is even doubtful whether many pure warranties ever exist as a matter of strict law, and the Law Commissions at one time appeared inclined to suggest that the whole category of warranties should be abolished.[45] But their final recommendations contained no proposals to change the situation, and the terms in contracts of sale of goods are still divided into conditions, innominate terms and warranties.

---

42 See p. 499.
43 This right is not affected by the additional remedies provided to consumers under the Sale and Supply of Goods to Consumers Regulations 2002, SI 2002/3045 – see p. 499 *et seq*.
44 See Stoljar (1952) 15 MLR 425, 430–2.
45 Law Com. Working Paper No. 85, para 2.32. But there are statutory implied warranties in s. 12(2) of the Act. The older use of the word 'warranty' and 'to warrant' is also still often found, especially where the question is whether a statement is a contractual term or a representation. In this context the word simply means 'contractual term'. This usage is followed in this book because there is simply no alternative to the verb, 'to warrant'.

REPRESENTATIONS

From terms of the contract it is necessary to distinguish mere statements or representations, which are not part of the contract but may have serious consequences nonetheless. On the details of this topic, reference should be made to the standard works on the law of contract.[46] It is, however, necessary to say a few words on the distinction between a term and a misrepresentation, because (it will be suggested later) despite the use sometimes made by the courts of s. 13,[47] the Act does in truth leave intact the age-old distinction between a contract term and a representation.

Whether a statement is or is not a part of the contract is said to depend upon the intention of the parties, but this most elusive criterion is often of little use in this connection.[48] This has become especially so since the courts have been prepared to hold that an oral statement may override the written terms of a contract. It is probably true to say that the courts are now much readier to interpret a statement as a term of the contract than they were a hundred years ago. This tendency may be illustrated by contrasting the two cases of *Hopkins v Tanqueray*[49] and *Couchman v Hill*.[50] In the former case, the defendant, who was offering his horse for sale by auction, gave an assurance to the plaintiff on the day before the sale that the horse was perfectly sound. It was held that this statement was a mere representation and not a term of the contract. In the second case, the defendant was offering his heifer for sale by auction. In reliance on an assurance given by the defendant and also by the auctioneer that the heifer was unserved, the plaintiff bid for and bought the animal. This statement was held to be a term of the contract. In a strictly technical sense there is no conflict between these cases because questions of intention must depend upon all the circumstances of the case, and superficial similarities may hide underlying differences.[51] It would be more realistic, however, to admit this general change of attitude on the part of the courts. It is in fact uncommon, and becoming increasingly so, for a court to hold that a material statement made by one of the parties to a contract is only a misrepresentation.[52] This is particularly true of statements made by a seller in a contract for the sale of goods.

The tendency these days frequently appears to be for the courts to hold a statement to be a term of the contract when they think it reasonable to impose liability in damages on the person making the statement, and vice versa. Thus to attempt to decide

---

46 See Atiyah, *Introduction to the Law of Contract*, 5th edn, 1995, Ch. 10; Cheshire, Fifoot and Furmston, *Law of Contract*, 14th edn, pp. 139–145; Treitel, *Law of Contract*, 11th edn, pp. 330–335.

47 See *Beale v Taylor* [1967] 1 WLR 1193, discussed below, p. 150 – and see discussion p. 151 *et seq.*

48 Except of course where the contract in terms states that the truth of a statement is warranted by the party making it, as, e.g., in *Liverpool & County Discount Co Ltd v A B Motor Co (Kilburn) Ltd* [1963] 1 WLR 611.

49 (1854) 15 CB 130. Another possible explanation of this case is given in n. 51 below.

50 [1947] KB 554.

51 The earlier case was not cited in *Couchman v Hill*, and in an editorial note in [1947] 1 All ER 103 it was suggested that the decision in the later case might otherwise have been different. But in *Harling v Eddy* [1951] 2 KB 739 the CA held the two cases to be distinguishable, though on what grounds it is not wholly clear. The correct explanation of *Hopkins v Tanqueray* may well be that the auction was held at Tattersalls where, by custom (as everyone knew – though not the parties it would seem), all sales were without warranty – see Greig (1971) 87 LQR 179, 183–4. See also *Schawel v Reade* [1913] 2 Ir R 81, a somewhat neglected authority.

52 See also *J Evans & Son v Andrea Merzario* [1967] 1 WLR 1078; *Brikon Investments Ltd v Carr* [1979] QB 467. Some of the judgments in these cases proceed on the basis of a 'collateral contract' and some on the basis of estoppel, but these tend to be mere devices. The results are uniform.

whether a statement is a term of the contract or a mere representation without reference to the result is, in many cases, to put the cart before the horse. On the one hand, a statement as to the quality or state of the goods by a seller will almost invariably be held to be a term of the contract if the seller is a dealer in the goods. So in *Dick Bentley (Productions) Ltd v Harold Smith (Motors) Ltd*,[53] where a dealer, in selling a car, told the buyer that it had done only 20,000 miles, this was held by the Court of Appeal to be a term of the contract and not a mere representation. On the other hand, in *Oscar Chess Ltd v Williams*,[54] where a person selling a second-hand car in part-exchange for another innocently misrepresented the age of the car (relying on the log book, which was in fact forged), the Court of Appeal held the statement to be a mere representation. It seems from these cases that, in the absence of a clear intention one way or the other, a statement is a term of the contract where the person making it had, or could reasonably have obtained, the information necessary to show whether the statement was true.

It is unnecessary in a work of this nature to make more than a brief reference to the possibility of a claim for negligent misrepresentation at the suit of a buyer, whether or not he is able to establish that the representation amounts to a term of the contract. Although it is now clear that a claim for negligent misrepresentation will lie in some circumstances even at common law,[55] it will not often be possible for a buyer to pray in aid this cause of action in a case where the representation is not a term of the contract.[56] But this is now of little importance for, under s. 2(1) of the Misrepresentation Act 1967, a contracting party is given a statutory cause of action for misrepresentation against the other contracting party. Since the onus is placed on the representor to show that he had reasonable grounds to believe, and did believe up to the time the contract was made, that the facts represented were true, it seems probable that claims based on misrepresentation will in future frequently be joined with claims for damages for breach of condition or warranty.[57] But damages under the Misrepresentation Act may not be assessed in the same way as damages for breach of a term of the contract, so the distinction may still be important in some cases.[58]

SCOTS LAW

Much of what has been said in this chapter is, at best, interesting background information for the Scots lawyer. The distinction of contractual terms into conditions and warranties is unknown in Scots law, although its deployment to categorize the terms implied under the Sale of Goods Act did cause some confusion until the passage of the Sale and Supply of Goods Act 1994. But as the implied terms are now defined in

---

53 [1965] 2 All ER 65.
54 [1957] 1 WLR 370; see also *Routledge v McKay* [1954] 1 WLR 615; *Hummingbird Motors Ltd v Hobbs* [1986] RTR 276; *Harlingdon & Leinster Enterprises Ltd v Christopher Hull Fine Art Ltd* [1991] 1 QB 564 – see below, p. 150 *et seq.*
55 *Hedley Byrne & Co Ltd v Heller & Partners Ltd* [1964] AC 465.
56 But this did happen in *Esso Petroleum Ltd v Mardon* [1976] QB 801. See also *Howard Marine & Dredging Co Ltd v A Ogden & Sons (Excavations) Ltd* [1978] QB 574.
57 But it is important that the claimant clearly puts his case on the grounds of negligence, at common law, or under the statute, namely that the defendant had no reasonable grounds for his belief in the facts stated, otherwise a claim based purely on non-fraudulent misrepresentation is still liable to fail: see *Hummingbird Motors Ltd v Hobbs* [1986] RTR 276.
58 See below, p. 554.

Scotland without use of the words 'condition' or 'warranty',[59] this difficulty has ceased to cause trouble. The Scottish approach to the customer's right to terminate a contract for the supply of goods following breach of an implied term by the supplier is now the same as it would be for any other contract, namely, to ask whether the breach is sufficiently 'material' to justify the remedy.[60] Scots lawyers do, however, refer to contractual terms as warranties, usually when the term is an undertaking as to a state of fact, such as the condition of goods; but it does not follow from this that the only remedy for breach is damages. Termination will be possible if the breach is material.

The distinction between a contract term and a representation is well established in Scots law, and the tests used in this regard in England are also applied in Scotland.[61] Negligent and fraudulent misrepresentations are delicts, giving rise to claims for damages. There may be recovery for a pre-contractual negligent misrepresentation under s. 10 of the Law Reform (Miscellaneous Provisions) (Scotland) Act 1985.

---

59 Sale of Goods Act 1979 ss. 12–15, as amended by Sale and Supply of Goods Act 1994 s. 1.
60 Sale of Goods Act 1979 s. 15B, as amended by Sale and Supply of Goods Act 1994 s. 5. See further, p. 500.
61 See MacQueen and Thomson, *Contract Law in Scotland* (2000), paras 3.14–3.19.

Part II

THE DUTIES OF THE SELLER

8

THE EXISTENCE OF THE GOODS

NO IMPLIED CONDITION THAT THE GOODS EXIST

It might have been thought that in a sale of specific goods there would be an implied condition on the part of the seller that the goods were in existence at the time when the contract was made. Since the seller warrants, as we shall see shortly, that he has a right to sell the goods, and since he is in many cases responsible for defects in the quality of the goods, it might seem that *a fortiori* he should be liable if he has sold non-existent goods. Nevertheless, this is not generally so, for s. 6 enacts that:

> Where there is a contract for the sale of specific goods, and the goods without the knowledge of the seller have perished at the time when the contract is made, the contract is void.

This section has been commonly understood to confirm the decision of the House of Lords in *Couturier* v *Hastie*.[1] The defendant in that case was a *del credere* agent who sold, on behalf of the plaintiffs, a cargo of corn shipped from Salonika. Before the date of the sale, the cargo had been lawfully sold by the master of the ship, so that there was no corn available for delivery to the buyer; instead, the sellers tendered the usual shipping documents. These documents included an insurance policy but since the goods had been lost before the buyer had any interest in them he would (presumably) have been unable to claim under the policy, even assuming it covered the loss. Possibly the buyer could, if he had been compelled to pay the price, have required the seller to claim under the policy and hand over the proceeds. But the buyer obviously wanted corn, not the proceeds of an insurance policy, and he refused to accept or pay for the documents. The sellers thereupon sued the agent, whose liability depended on whether the buyer would have been liable. It was held that the agent was not liable.

It was for many years thought that the case was decided in this way on the ground that the contract was void for mistake. It is, however, now widely accepted that the decision turned simply on the construction of the contract,[2] or perhaps (though this is probably saying the same thing in a different way) that the decision does no more than illustrate the well-known principle that if the seller cannot deliver the goods the buyer is (anyhow prima facie) not bound to pay the price, a rule affirmed by s. 28 of the Act.[3] If the buyer had brought an action for non-delivery, then the court would have had to decide a very different question. This might have been whether the con-

---

1 (1856) 5 HLC 673.
2 See Atiyah (1957) 73 LQR 349.
3 Slade (1954) 70 LQR at 396–7.

tract was void for mistake, but a better approach would have been to regard it as a question of construction. In other words, the question to be decided would have been, did the defendant contract that the goods existed, or was there an implied condition that if there were no goods there would be no contract? This apparently was the view of Lord Atkin in *Bell* v *Lever Bros Ltd*,[4] for in the course of his speech in that case he said:

> This brings the discussion to the alternative mode of expressing the result of a mutual mistake . . . The proposition does not amount to more than this, that if the contract expressly or impliedly contains a term that a particular assumption is a condition of the contract, the contract is avoided if the assumption is not true.

Looking at the problem as one of interpretation, the facts of *Couturier* v *Hastie* were open to at least three possible constructions:

1 There might have been an implied condition precedent (or, in Scotland, a resolutive condition) that the goods were in existence, in which case, if they were not, neither party would be bound; or,
2 the seller might have contracted, or warranted, that the goods were in existence, in which case he would be liable for non-delivery, and the buyer would not be liable for non-acceptance; or,
3 the buyer might have taken the risk of the goods having perished, in which case he would be liable for the price even in the absence of delivery, and the seller would not, of course, be liable for non-delivery.

In *Couturier* v *Hastie*,[5] the House of Lords merely decided that the contract could not be construed in the third of the above three ways, but the House did not decide, as it was not called upon to decide, whether the proper interpretation was of the first or second types above. A decision between these two possibilities would only have been necessary if the buyer had sued for damages for non-delivery. Such a decision was necessary in *McRae* v *Commonwealth Disposals Commission*,[6] where the defendants contracted to sell to the plaintiffs a shipwrecked tanker on a certain reef. After the plaintiffs had incurred considerable expenditure in preparing a salvage expedition, it was discovered that not only was there not and had never been any tanker, but also that the reef was non-existent. The High Court of Australia approached the case on the basis that the defendants were liable for breach of contract unless they could establish that there was an implied condition precedent that the ship was in existence. Manifestly, on the facts of the case, no such condition could be implied. On the contrary, the court concluded that:

> The only proper construction of the contract is that it included a promise by the Commission that there was a tanker in the position specified. The Commission contracted that there was a tanker there.[7]

---

4 [1932] AC 161, at 224–5.
5 (1856) 5 HLC 673.
6 (1951) 84 CLR 377.
7 At p. 380. The plaintiffs could presumably have recovered the same damages on the basis of negligence since they did not claim their loss of profits, but only their reliance expenses.

In this connection, the earlier decision of the same court in *Goldsborough, Mort & Co Ltd v Carter*[8] is also of some interest, although this case (like *Couturier v Hastie*) was decided at common law. In this case, the defendant agreed to sell 'about' 4,000 sheep pastured on certain lands at a price per head. It was agreed to muster and count the sheep on a certain date and the contract also stated that if it should be found that there were less than 4,000 sheep, the buyer would take and pay for the actual number delivered. In fact, there had been conditions of severe drought in the area and these were followed by cold winter rains, with the result that, on muster, only 890 acceptable sheep were found. The buyer claimed damages for the short delivery, but his claim was rejected. Griffith CJ treated the contract as one for the sale of specific goods, and said:

> It is an implied condition of such a contract that at the time of making the contract or before the time of performance the chattels are or will be in existence (*Couturier v Hastie*), and, further, that they shall still be existing when the time comes for performance (*Howell v Coupland*).

But the majority of the court held that this principle was displaced in the particular circumstances of the case on the true construction of the contract. Since the seller did not know how many sheep there were and since the buyer was aware of the possibility of shortage and had agreed to take what number were delivered, it was held that the contract was only for the sale of such sheep as existed and could be delivered on muster.

A case resembling the *McRae* case in some respects more recently came before the English courts. In *Associated Japanese Bank v Crédit du Nord SA*[9] one JB entered into a sale and leaseback transaction with the plaintiffs, under which he sold four large machines to them for over one million pounds, and they leased the machines back to him. Such a sale and leaseback transaction is simply a way of raising money on the security of goods, and is not unusual in practice; but what was unusual about this case was that the machines did not exist at all, and the whole scheme was a fraud by JB. The validity of the contract between JB and the plaintiffs did not directly arise in the action, because JB was of course not worth suing, and the action was actually brought to enforce a guarantee of the transaction given by the defendants. The action failed because Steyn J held that the guarantee contract was void either for mistake or for failure of an implied condition that the goods existed. But if the plaintiffs had sued JB on the contract itself it seems hardly credible that he could have defended the action by claiming that the contract was void because the goods did not exist – a conclusion not rendered more plausible merely because in any event JB could plainly have been sued for fraud. Obviously, the only possible construction of the sale and leaseback contract, like that in the *McRae* case, was that the seller was guaranteeing the existence of the goods.

So it seems clear that in appropriate circumstances a seller of non-existent goods may be held liable on the basis that he has impliedly or even expressly warranted that the goods do exist. The impact of s. 6 of the Act on the problem must next be

---

8 (1914) 19 CLR 429.
9 [1988] 3 All ER 902.

considered. In terms, the section clearly contemplates a case where the goods have existed at one time, but have perished before the contract was made, so that the sales in the *McRae* case and the *Associated Japanese Bank* case would not come within it at all (in the latter case *a fortiori* because the seller *knew* the goods did not exist). Consequently the common law position would remain and the result should be that already suggested – the seller should be liable for breach of contract, as indeed was held in the former case by the High Court of Australia. But this does not answer the question where the goods have in fact existed but have perished before the contract was made. In such a case, it appears at first sight that the contract must be held void under s. 6, but it is difficult to believe that this can be right. If a seller, in effect, contracts that the goods are in existence, is he entitled to avoid all liability on the ground that s. 6 applies and the contract is void? This extraordinary result can, it is submitted, best be avoided by giving a liberal interpretation to s. 55(1) of the Act which now runs:

> Where any right, duty, or liability would arise under a contract of sale of goods by impli-
> cation of law, it may (subject to the Unfair Contract Terms Act 1977) be negatived or varied
> by express agreement or by the course of dealing between the parties, or by such usage as
> binds both parties to the contract.

Read literally, it might appear that this section would not prevent the operation of s. 6 in a case such as that being considered, for the whole effect of the section is to prevent any right, duty or liability arising; moreover, literally construed, s. 6 prevents any contract of sale of goods coming into existence to which s. 55(1) can apply at all. But in preventing the principal obligations from arising, s. 6 may give rise to other rights and duties, for example as to the return of the price,[10] and perhaps the reference to 'a contract of sale of goods' could generously be read as including a reference to a contract which is void under s. 6 (which does, after all, itself refer to 'a contract for the sale of goods'). In any case, the clear object of the section does seem to be to enable the parties to vary, by agreement, all those provisions of the Act which do not affect third parties.

Of course, it is clear that anomalous results would follow if s. 6 were held to be a rule of law to be applied irrespective of the intention of the parties. Since the section is limited in various ways (for example, in that it only applies to a sale of specific goods, and only applies also where the goods perish) closely parallel cases may fall just within or just outside the section. Those outside will be settled at common law according to the true construction of the contract. It would be unfortunate if those just on the other side of the line had to be determined by a rigid application of s. 6. It is submitted, therefore, that if, on the true construction of the contract, it appears that the seller is contracting that the goods do exist, s. 6 will not apply and the seller will be liable for non-delivery.[11] If the seller has been negligent in not discovering that

---

10 Professor Atiyah noted in earlier editions that a learned reviewer first drew his attention to this argument (see (1959) 75 LQR 417), but he had come to feel that there were difficulties with it. Cf. Treitel, *Law of Contract*, 11th edn, pp. 296–297.

11 In *Joseph Constantine SS Ltd* v *Imperial Smelting Corpn* [1942] AC 154, 184–6, there are dicta by Lord Wright clearly showing that he at least thought that ss. 6 and 7 of the Act merely embody common law rules of construc-tion. See also *Christopher Hill Ltd* v *Ashington Piggeries* [1972] AC 441, 501, where Lord Diplock says that the Act should not 'be construed so narrowly as to force on parties to contracts for the sale of goods promises and conse-quences different from what they must reasonably have intended'.

the goods have perished, it may be that the better solution would often be to hold that there is no such implied exclusion of s. 6, but that the seller should be held liable for misrepresentation. In that event the buyer could obtain damages for some of his actual ('reliance') losses, but not for his expectation losses.[12]

The only effect of s. 6 is thus to give rise to a presumption, in the cases to which it applies, that the seller is not contracting that the goods exist. In effect, the section gives rise to a rule of construction rather than a rigid rule of law. Where, on the other hand, as in *McRae*, the goods have never existed at all, s. 6 cannot apply, and the presumption may be that the seller is contracting that the goods exist.

Although this problem may appear to be of greater academic than practical importance, it is perhaps unfortunate that s. 6 was written into the Act at all in its present form. It should, of course, be remembered that *Couturier* v *Hastie* was decided before the invention of modern methods of communication and on the facts of that case, in the year 1856, it might well have been reasonable to hold that the seller was not contracting that the goods were in existence. If the identical facts were to recur today, however, it is in the highest degree improbable that the seller would not be aware of the sale of the cargo even before it occurred, and if he were not it would most probably be due to his own negligence. Such a possibility could today give rise to a claim for negligent misrepresentation at common law or under s. 2(1) of the Misrepresentation Act 1967 or under s. 10 of the Law Reform (Miscellaneous Provisions) (Scotland) Act 1985. No doubt in some circumstances this may seem a better solution than an action for breach of contract, for example, if it seems unreasonable to award damages for loss of bargain against the seller.

The sort of facts to which s. 6 may be applied today may well differ considerably from the *Couturier* v *Hastie* situation. For example, in *Barrow, Lane & Ballard Ltd* v *Phillip Phillips & Co Ltd*,[13] the plaintiffs contracted to sell to the defendants 700 bags of nuts which were believed to be lying in certain warehouses. In fact, 109 of the bags had disappeared, presumably by theft, at the time when the contract was made, and after 150 bags had been delivered about two months later, it was eventually discovered that no further bags remained. On the face of it, one would have thought this was a plain case. The sellers had sold a specific parcel of 700 bags of nuts when in fact there were only 591 to deliver. This would seem, therefore, to have been a simple case of breach of contract by the sellers. But that was not the result.

The actual claim in this case was on two bills of exchange which had been given in payment of the price of the whole of the 700 bags. In fact, the buyers obtained delivery of the 150 bags which were available when delivery was required, and they admitted their liability to pay for these bags, though, it seems, not under the contract itself. The buyers, however, refused to honour the bills of exchange, on the ground that the sellers were in breach of an implied term that the goods were in existence. This is hardly surprising because the buyers' loss was probably not covered by their insurance, while it may well have been covered by the sellers' insurance. Wright J appears to have preferred the view that the contract was void under s. 6, rather

---

12 For the difference between expectation and reliance damages, see Atiyah, *Introduction to the Law of Contract*, 5th edn, pp. 444–9 (1995).
13 [1929] 1 KB 574.

than that the sellers were in breach.[14] But it is unsatisfactory to say that the whole contract here was void when the buyers in fact obtained delivery of 150 of the bags, and admitted their liability to pay for them. If the contract was indeed void, then some strange results would have ensued. First, the terms governing the delivery of the 150 bags would not have been the terms agreed upon by the parties, and the buyers would only have been liable for a reasonable price in a restitutionary claim. This would also have ruled out any claim for breach of the statutory implied terms as to quality and fitness which seems an extraordinary result. And thirdly, it would also have meant, presumably, that the sellers could have refused to deliver the 150 bags if the facts had been discovered before delivery had been required. For reasons given below this also seems wrong.

Section 6 gives rise to three other difficulties which are considered in the next three sections.

Meaning of 'specific goods'

'Specific goods' are defined by s. 62 as 'goods identified and agreed upon at the time a contract of sale is made'. In most cases this is clear enough, and serves to distinguish such cases from contracts of sale of future or generic goods. Thus, if A contracts to deliver 1,000 tonnes of wheat to B, this is not a sale of specific goods and A's obligations are unaffected by the fact that he had a particular 1,000 tonnes in mind which have, unknown to him, perished before the date of the contract. Some cases, however, are not so clear. What of a contract to sell 200 tonnes of potatoes to be grown on a particular piece of land? In *Howell* v *Coupland*[15] (a case dealing with subsequent destruction, now covered by s. 7 of the Act)[16] it was held that this was a sale of specific goods for the purpose of the common law rules of frustration. However, the modern tendency appears to be to confine the meaning of 'specific goods' under the Act to cases of existing goods which have actually been identified or agreed upon. Thus in *Re Wait*,[17] a case to be considered at length later,[18] it was held that a sale of 5,000 tons out of a cargo of 10,000 tons of wheat on a particular ship was not a sale of specific or ascertained goods within the meaning of s. 52 of which specific performance could be ordered. Similarly, in *H R & S Sainsbury* v *Street*,[19] it was held that a sale of 275 tons of barley to be grown on a particular farm was not a sale of specific goods. The effect of the perishing of the goods in such circumstances must, therefore, be a matter for the common law rather than s. 6 of the Act.

Effect of part of goods perishing

Where there is a sale of specific goods, part of which have perished before the date of the sale, the effect of s. 6 is now somewhat obscure. In *Barrow, Lane & Ballard*

---

14 At p. 582.
15 (1876) 1 QBD 258.
16 See below, p. 360.
17 [1927] 1 Ch 606
18 See below, p. 351
19 [1972] 1 WLR 834.

Ltd v *Phillip Phillips & Co Ltd*, the facts of which have been given above, Wright J, emphasizing that he regarded the 700 bags of nuts as an indivisible parcel of goods, held that the contract was avoided by s. 6, even though only 109 bags had apparently disappeared by the time the contract was made. It has been pointed out above that this decision entails some strange results. Amongst others, it would mean that if the sellers had refused to deliver the 150 bags which were actually available when delivery was demanded, they would not have been liable to the buyers. That conclusion would seem particularly suspect in the light of *H R & S Sainsbury* v *Street*.[20] In this case the defendant agreed to sell a crop of about 275 tons of barley to be grown by him on his farm. In fact, owing to general crop failure, only some 140 tons were produced, which the defendant sold and delivered to a third party at a substantially higher price. McKenna J held that, although the contract was frustrated as to that part of the crop which failed, this did not exonerate the defendant from offering the crop actually produced to the plaintiffs. Somewhat puzzlingly, he did not seem to regard the plaintiffs as being obliged to take the 140 tons,[21] which suggests that the seller but not the buyer was bound by the contract in the events which actually occurred. What is at any rate clear is that, treating the problem purely as a common law question of construction, there are three additional possible constructions of the contract to be added to those dealing with total perishing of the goods.[22] These are that if part of the goods perish:

4　the seller may be obliged to deliver the balance and the buyer may be bound to take it; or

5　the seller may be obliged to tender delivery of the balance to the buyer who is not bound to take it; or

6　the seller is not bound to tender delivery to the buyer, but if he does so, the buyer is bound to take it.

Which of these is the correct construction of any particular contract must depend, as usual, on the terms of the contract and all the circumstances of the case.

Although *H R & S Sainsbury* v *Street* was decided at common law, it would seem very odd if, on parallel facts falling within s. 6, a different result had to be arrived at. It would seem, therefore, that the buyers in the *Barrow Lane & Ballard* case may have been entitled to insist on delivery of the 150 bags of nuts remaining, notwithstanding s. 6, which is not easy to reconcile with the idea that the contract there was actually void.

Meaning of 'perish'

Barrow, Lane & Ballard Ltd v *Phillip Phillips & Co Ltd*[23] is also material on the next point, namely the meaning of the word 'perished'. Read literally, this might be thought to cover only physical destruction, but in fact it is submitted that it should

---

20　Ibid.
21　Perhaps because of s. 30(1) – see below, p. 139 (which says that if the seller delivers less than he contracted to sell the buyer may reject the goods). This provision is now modified in the case of commercial buyers – see below p. 142 *et seq*.
22　See above, p. 103–4.
23　[1929] 1 KB 574.

be construed to cover also perishing in a commercial sense. Although this point was not argued in this case, the actual result supports this contention. There are no other English cases precisely in point under s. 6,[24] but several cases on freight and insurance law deal with a very similar question, that is whether there has been a total loss of goods. On this topic one cannot do better than quote the pungent observations of Lord Esher MR in *Asfar & Co Ltd* v *Blundell*:[25]

> The first point taken on behalf of the defendants, the under-writers, is that there has been no total loss of the dates . . . The ingenuity of the argument might commend itself to a body of chemists, but not to business men. We are dealing with dates as a subject matter of commerce; and it is contended that, although these dates were under water for two days, and when brought up were simply a mass of pulpy matter impregnated with sewage and in a state of fermentation, there had been no change in their nature, and they still were dates. There is a perfectly well known test which has for many years been applied to such cases as the present – that test is whether, as a matter of business, the nature of the thing has been altered.

Mutatis mutandis these remarks could apply equally to the meaning of the word 'perish' in s. 6. The only case which is inconsistent with this view is *Horn* v *Minister of Food*,[26] which was a case under s. 7 of the Act. Morris J here held that potatoes which had so rotted as to be worthless had not perished within the meaning of s. 7 because they were still potatoes, but in any event he held that the section did not apply because the risk in the goods had already passed to the buyer, and the section is excluded in such a case. His remarks on this point are therefore obiter and it is submitted that they cannot be supported.

If a wide meaning is given to the word 'perish' it becomes all the more important that s. 6 of the Act be treated only as a rule of construction. For (as will be seen later) a seller is usually under stringent obligations as to the quality and fitness of the goods to be supplied under the contract. So, for example, a seller who contracts to sell a specific load of potatoes will be liable for breach of his implied obligations if he delivers unmerchantable potatoes, and it will be immaterial whether they were unmerchantable before the contract was made. But if he can plead s. 6 of the Act he will escape all liability. Such a result was arrived at in the New Zealand case of *Turnbull* v *Rendell*[27] where the seller agreed to sell 75 tons of 'table potatoes' from a specific crop, some of which were still undug. At the time of the contract, the potatoes were so badly affected with secondary growth that they no longer answered the description 'table potatoes'. Prima facie one would have thought, therefore, that there was a breach of s. 13 of the Act (that the goods must answer their description)[28] but, in fact, the buyer's claim for damages was rejected. The court held that the potatoes had 'perished' within the meaning of s. 6 of the Act and the contract was therefore void. It may seem strange that the seller's position is improved in such a case

---

24 [1896] 1 QB 123, 127.
25 There is the New Zealand decision, however, in *Oldfield Asphalts Ltd* v *Grovedale Coolstores (1994) Ltd* [1998] 3 NZLR 479, which supports the views expressed in the text below. The court in that case also rejected the argument that the operation of s. 6 was confined to perishable goods such as foodstuffs.
26 [1948] 2 All ER 1036.
27 (1908) 27 NZLR 1067.
28 See below, p. 149.

where the potatoes are so rotten as to be no longer describable as 'potatoes' so that he can rely on s. 6 of the Act. But the result can be justified on the ground that in such a case the event which has occurred is so far outside the contemplation of the parties that it would be unfair to place the risk of its occurrence on either party alone. In effect, this is the justification for the doctrines of mistake and frustration, and of course s. 6 is a part of the former doctrine. Still, it is important that sufficient flexibility is retained in the operation of s. 6 so that it is not available as an excuse to a seller who ought plainly to be treated as warranting the quality of the goods.

At all events there seems no inclination to extend the meaning of 'perish' by analogy to cases where the seller is clearly responsible for the unavailability of the goods. Thus it has been held no defence for a seller who is sued for non-delivery to prove that, after agreeing to sell the goods to the plaintiff, he sold and delivered the goods to another buyer.[29]

Even granting that s. 6 covers perishing in a commercial sense, a difficulty still exists in the case of goods lost by theft. Suppose, for example, that A sells his car to B, which unknown to them both has just been stolen. It may be a long time before the police give up all hope of tracing the car, and until this happens the vehicle can hardly be said to have perished even in a commercial sense, but what is to happen in the meantime? The validity of the contract can hardly depend upon the activities of the police. The insurance cases are not of much assistance here because a theft can clearly be a commercial loss and, of course, this is often the whole object of the insurance, while it is not so clear that a stolen car can be said to have perished even commercially. *Barrow, Lane & Ballard Ltd* v *Phillip Phillips & Co Ltd*[30] is distinguishable from such a case because there the nuts had in all probability been dispersed by sale after the theft and, indeed, some or all of them might well have been consumed by the ultimate purchasers. Whether, and if so at what stage, a stolen article can be said to have perished, therefore, is a question which is still open and awaits solution by the courts. Perhaps the answer is to treat the question as one of fact and degree. If, as a practical matter, there is no realistic prospect of recovering the goods, they should be treated as having perished within the meaning of s. 6.

---

29 *Goodey* v *Garriock* [1972] 2 Lloyd's Rep 369, 372.
30 [1929] 1 KB 574.

9

THE DUTY TO PASS A GOOD TITLE

THE SELLER'S RIGHT TO SELL THE GOODS

Among the most important terms implied by the Act in a contract of sale of goods are those relating to the seller's duty to pass a good title to the goods. Section 12(1) of the 1979 Act, incorporating amendments made by the Supply of Goods (Implied Terms) Act 1973, is as follows:

> In a contract of sale, other than one to which subsection (3) below applies, there is an implied condition on the part of the seller that in the case of a sale, he has a right to sell the goods, and in the case of an agreement to sell, he will have such a right at the time when the property is to pass.

It is clear that the main purpose and effect of the section is to require the seller to transfer the property or title to the goods to the buyer. Plainly, if the seller is himself the owner, and nobody else has any claims to the goods, the seller's property in the goods will pass to the buyer under the contract and s. 12(1) will be satisfied. But the section does not require that the seller should himself be owner, or even that he should acquire a title to the goods before transferring them. 'A contract of sale can perfectly well be performed by a seller who never has title at any time, by causing a third party to transfer it directly to the buyer.'[1]

Section 12(1) is not, however, drafted in terms of 'property' nor of 'title';[2] what it requires is that the seller has, or should have, a 'right to sell', and this causes problems because of the inevitable ambiguity of the word 'right'. The question whether the seller has a right to sell the goods cannot be answered until it is known precisely what it is which the seller must transfer to the buyer. The Act itself does not provide a very clear answer to this problem. All we have is the statement in s. 2(1) that 'a contract for the sale of goods is a contract by which the seller transfers or agrees to transfer the property in goods to the buyer', and the definition of the term 'property' in s. 61 as 'the general property in goods and not merely a special property'. In other words, unless the seller has a right to pass the general property to the buyer, he will be in breach of s. 12(1). But what is meant by a 'right' to sell the goods? The natural and primary meaning of the word 'right' in s. 12(1) seems to be 'power'; in other words, the seller must have the *power* to vest the general property in the goods in the buyer.

---

1 *Karlshamns Oljefabriker* v *Eastport Navigation Corp* [1982] 1 All ER 208, 215, per Mustill J.
2 Compare Uniform Commercial Code Art. 2-312(1) which imposes an obligation on the seller to pass a good 'title'.

In most cases, of course, the 'power' to confer a title and the 'right' to sell the goods will go together. But there are some exceptional cases in which they may be separated, and it may then be significant that the section is not drafted in terms of a 'power'. First, there are some rare cases in which a seller may have a 'right' to sell the goods, and yet may have no power to confer a good title on the buyer. For example, a debtor who sells goods which have already been seized (but not physically removed) by the sheriff under a writ of execution has a right to sell them (at least until they are sold by the sheriff) but he sells them subject to the sheriff's rights.[3] He is thus unable to confer a good title on the buyer free from the sheriff's claims. No action lies under s. 12(1) in such a case, though (as noted later) there is a remedy under s. 12(2).

The second type of exceptional case concerns the reverse situation – that is, where the seller has the power to confer a good title on the buyer, but yet no 'right to sell the goods'. It appears, for instance, from the decision in *Niblett* v *Confectioners' Materials Co*[4] that the seller may in some circumstances be guilty of a breach of s. 12(1) although he had the power to transfer the property in the goods. The facts of this case were as follows: the defendants, an American company, sold 3,000 tins of preserved milk to the plaintiffs, but when the goods arrived in England they were detained by the customs authorities on the ground that their labels infringed the trade mark of a well-known English company. It was held that as this company could have obtained an injunction to restrain the sale of the goods, the sellers had no right to sell them.[5]

This was a very unusual case. But there are many other cases, which will be fully examined later,[6] in which a person who is not the owner of goods and who sells them without the owner's authority is enabled by the Act (or by other statutes) to pass a good title to the buyer. In such cases, it seems that there is a breach of the condition implied by s. 12(1), but the buyer has in fact suffered no damage from the breach and cannot therefore maintain an action against the seller.[7] It is true that in *Niblett* v *Confectioners' Materials Co Ltd*[8] Atkin LJ thought that in such a case the condition would not be broken at all, but it is submitted that the solution given here is better because there may be circumstances in which the buyer may justifiably wish to reject the goods, even though he has acquired a good legal title. For example, it seems that the legal title which is obtained under Part III of the Hire-Purchase Act 1964, where a private purchaser buys a motor vehicle which is the subject of a hire-purchase agreement, is not in practice always a very satisfactory one. The reason for this is that if the buyer later wishes to sell or trade in the vehicle to a motor dealer, the dealer will in all probability discover the outstanding hire-purchase agreement and may well refuse to buy it. It seems, therefore, that the buyer should

---

3 See *Lloyds & Scottish Finance Ltd* v *Modern Cars & Caravans (Kingston) Ltd* [1966] 1 QB 764.
4 [1921] 3 KB 387.
5 Cf. *Sumner Permain & Co Ltd* v *Webb & Co Ltd* [1922] KB 55, the facts of which are given at p. 177, where no question was raised as to the application of s. 12(1).
6 Chapter 21 below.
7 See the Report of the Crowther Committee on Consumer Credit (Cmnd. 4596), para 5.7.32.
8 [1921] 3 KB 387, 401; and it was so held in *Anderson* v *Ryan* [1967] IR 34, though apparently without argument on this point.

be entitled to reject the goods in such a case.[9] And such a result would be justifiable because even though in these cases the seller has the power to confer a title on the buyer, he does not have what the Act specifically requires him to have, namely a 'right to sell the goods'.

The effect of a breach of s. 12(1)

The normal remedies open to the innocent party where there is a breach of condition are (a) repudiation of the contract, and/or (b) a claim for damages, while in Scotland he may terminate the contract, if the breach is material, and/or claim damages. In addition, there are in England and Wales common law remedies of a restitutionary character, formerly known as quasi-contractual rights, such as the right to recover money paid when there is a total failure of consideration.[10] Section 54 preserves these common law rights by enacting that:

> Nothing in this Act affects the right of the buyer . . . to recover money paid where the consideration for the payment of it has failed.

In the usual case the buyer will not stand to gain financially from choosing to repudiate the contract rather than sue for damages. The reason is that he cannot retain any benefit under the contract if he wishes to repudiate it, nor does the restitutionary remedy preserved by s. 54 usually help because *ex hypothesi* there must have been a total failure of consideration, and the buyer cannot therefore have obtained any benefit under the contract. A fair summary of the normal position, therefore, would be that the buyer cannot both have his cake and eat it.

In the case of a breach of the condition implied by s. 12(1), however, it appears that the buyer can do just this. The leading case is *Rowland v Divall*.[11] The plaintiff bought a car from the defendant for £334 and resold it for £400 to a sub-buyer who used it for four months. He then discovered that the car had never belonged to the defendant, who had bought it in good faith from someone without title. The car having been claimed by the original owner, the plaintiff paid off the sub-buyer by refunding him the £400 and claimed to recover, in turn, the £334 which he had paid the defendant. It was held by the Court of Appeal that the buyer was entitled to recover the whole purchase price and that the seller was not entitled to set off anything for the four months' use of the car which the sub-buyer had enjoyed.[12] Atkin LJ observed:[13]

---

9 See the interesting American case of *Jeanneret v Vichey* 693 F 2d 259, US Ct of Appeals, Second Circ. (1982) – purchase of a painting which the purchaser later discovered was suspected of having been exported illegally from Italy thereby destroying its resale value.

10 Scots law does not have the doctrine of total failure of consideration, and analogies with its enrichment remedy *condictio causa data causa non secuta* are not helpful. See *Connelly v Simpson* 1993 SC 391 and discussion thereof in MacQueen 1994 JR 137.

11 [1923] 2 KB 500.

12 It is not clear whether Scots law would reach the same result. In the only Scottish case on breach of s. 12(1) the buyer recovered the full price paid, but as damages rather than restitution (*Spink & Co v McColl* 1992 SLT 471). Thus in principle recovery should be based upon what the buyer has lost through the breach, which, being normally the value of the goods *at the date of eviction*, may be more, less, or the same as the original price. However, the seller appears to have no claim against the buyer, since the latter's enrichment through the use of the goods has been at the expense of the true owner, *not* of the seller.

13 At p. 507.

The buyer has not received any part of that which he contracted to receive – namely, the property and right to possession – and, that being so, there has been a total failure of consideration.[14]

The full implications of this decision are shown by two later cases. In *Karflex Ltd v Poole*[15] the plaintiffs were hire-purchase dealers who bought a car from one K and hired it to the defendant with the usual option to purchase on payment of all the instalments. The defendant paid the deposit and took possession of the car, but he defaulted on the first instalment and the plaintiffs commenced proceedings against him. It then transpired that K had never been the owner of the car at all, but the plaintiffs paid off the true owner and proceeded with their action against the defendant. It was held by a Divisional Court that the action failed because the plaintiffs were in breach of an implied condition that they had a right to sell the goods, since at the date of the delivery of the car they had no such right. The defendant, therefore, who had defaulted in payment of the very first instalment was held entitled to repudiate the contract and, indeed, to recover his deposit despite the fact that he had not been evicted by the true owner, and that by the time the case came on for trial there was no possibility of eviction because the original owners had been paid off. This was not actually a case of sale, but of hire-purchase, but the court regarded the principles applicable as the same. Since then, the implied condition as to title in s. 12(1) of the Sale of Goods Act has been extended, with only essential alterations in the wording, to hire-purchase contracts,[16] so at least it seems clear that the same principle must apply in the two cases.[17]

The second case is *Butterworth v Kingsway Motors Ltd*,[18] where A took delivery of a car under a contract of hire-purchase. Mistakenly thinking that she had a right to sell it subject to her continuing to pay the instalments, she purported to sell it to B. B sold it to C, who sold it to the defendant, and the defendant sold it to the plaintiff. After the plaintiff had had the use of the car for no less than eleven and a half months, he received a notification from the original hire-purchase dealers, who were of course still the owners of the car, claiming the delivery up to them of the vehicle. Seeing the opportunities which presented themselves, the plaintiff lost no time in writing to the defendants, claiming the return of the entire purchase price which he had paid. Within one week of this, A paid off the balance of the hire-purchase price to the original owners. The defendant might have been forgiven for thinking that this payment removed all difficulties and closed the transaction, because the payment vested the title to the car in A and this title

---

14 He also observed that 'there can be no sale . . . of goods which the seller has no right to sell' (at p. 506), a view criticized by Ho (1997) 56 CLJ 571, at pp. 582 *et seq*. The merits of the case are somewhat complicated by the fact that, in the end, the buyer was able to get the car back on payment of £260. His claim for the full £334 which he paid thus seems to have been somewhat unfair, apart altogether from the fact that no account was taken of the use made of the car by the sub-buyer. Cf. Treitel, *Law of Contract*, 11th edn, p. 1053 *et seq*.

15 [1933] 2 KB 251.

16 See ss. 8–11 of the Supply of Goods (Implied Terms) Act 1973, re-enacted with minor alterations in Sch. 4 to the Consumer Credit Act 1974.

17 As well as to an express term – see *Barber v NSW Bank plc* [1996] 1 All ER 906. The same implied condition now applies, *mutatis mutandis*, in other contracts for the transfer of goods by virtue of the Supply of Goods and Services Act 1982, ss. 2 and 7. The latter section applies to cases of hire where, however, it would seem even more troublesome to apply the decision in *Rowland v Divall*.

18 [1954] 1 WLR 1286.

'went to feed' the defective titles of the subsequent purchasers. It was held, however, that the plaintiff was entitled to recover the full purchase price of £1,275 as the defendant had been guilty of a breach of s. 12(1). As the market had dropped in the meantime, the car was worth only about £800 at the date when the plaintiff repudiated the contract. Consequently, the Act enabled him to make a handsome profit of £475, a fact which no doubt explains the learned judge's view that 'the plaintiff's position was somewhat lacking in merits'.[19]

It is indeed possible to imagine circumstances, by no means unrealistic, which are far more extreme than those in the above cases. For example, suppose that A buys a crate of whisky from B. Suppose further that after consuming the whisky, A discovers that it never belonged to B but that B had bought it in good faith from a thief. Is it to be said that A can recover the full purchase price on the ground that there has been a total failure of consideration? This suggestion is perhaps not quite so ridiculous as might appear at first sight because the consumption of the whisky lays the consumer open to an action of conversion by the true owner. There would be nothing absurd about a rule which enabled the buyer to recover the full price from the seller if he were compelled to pay the value of the goods to the true owner. But the difficulty about *Rowland* v *Divall* is that the right of the buyer to recover the full price is not made dependent on a claim by the real owner. It is quite possible, especially where stolen goods have changed hands several times, that the real owner may never be traced at all. Again, it is quite possible that the real owner may choose to sue the seller rather than the buyer for conversion. Indeed, he will probably sue the first solvent person in the chain because the damages will probably be higher. If such were to happen in the hypothetical case above, the remarkable result would seem to follow that B would have to pay the whole price back to A, on the one hand, and the whole value again to the true owner, while A, on the other hand, will have had a free crate of whisky.

One possible way of avoiding this result might be as follows. Normally, a party who claims to repudiate a contract must return any benefits received. In *Rowland* v *Divall*, it was pointed out that the defendant could not complain that the car had not been returned to him for it was his very breach of condition that made this impossible. In the hypothetical case above, however, it might be argued that the plaintiff's inability to return the goods is due to the fact that he has consumed the whisky. This does not dispose of all difficulty, however, for if the plaintiff is to be met by this argument the injustice may well be on the other side. The true owner may yet turn up and choose to sue the buyer for conversion.[20] In this case the buyer, having failed to recover his price from the seller, may then have to pay the value of the goods to the true owner. But the solution to this difficulty in England and Wales may be to recognize the buyer's right to seek contribution or indemnity from the seller under the Civil Liability (Contribution) Act 1978.

---

19 At p. 1291. Pearson J here left open the question whether the plaintiff would have succeeded had he not claimed the return of his money before A paid off the owners. In New South Wales it has been held that if the seller obtains title (for example, by paying off the true owner) before the buyer seeks to repudiate the contract, it will then be too late for the buyer to recover his price: *Patten* v *Thomas Motors Pty Ltd* [1965] NSWR 1457.

20 Again, a doctrine to which there is no equivalent in Scots law. It would appear, however, that the true owner might have a recompense (unjustified enrichment) claim in these circumstances.

It may thus be possible to deal with the case discussed above so as to achieve substantial justice in the end. But this does not eliminate the serious injustice of such cases as *Butterworth* v *Kingsway Motors Ltd*. Nor does it dispose of the main objection to *Rowland* v *Divall*, which is that the decision rests basically on a fallacy. The object of a contract of sale is surely to transfer to the buyer the use and enjoyment of the goods free from any adverse third-party claims. If the buyer has such use and enjoyment and no third-party claim is made against him, it seems unrealistic to talk of a total failure of consideration.

These problems have been examined by law reform agencies over a period of several years. In 1966 the Law Reform Committee recommended in their Twelfth Report[21] that the buyer should not be allowed to recover the price in full in a *Rowland* v *Divall* situation with no allowance for the use he has had of the goods.[22] Since then the Law Commission has re-examined the problem on several different occasions. At first the Law Commission, while agreeing in principle with this recommendation, pointed out a number of practical difficulties in the proposal.[23] They concluded that no satisfactory amendment of s. 12 could be proposed until a study had been made of the rules relating to the law of restitution and the 1973 Supply of Goods (Implied Terms) Act did not, therefore, deal with this question. Since then two other Law Commission papers continued to take the view that the rule in *Rowland* v *Divall* ought to be abolished, and the buyer victim of a breach of s. 12(1) should only be entitled to damages rather than the return of his whole price.[24]

But in 1987, after still further consideration, the Law Commission finally abandoned all attempts to deal with *Rowland* v *Divall*.[25] The reasons for this change of front appear to have been twofold. First, the Commission is not now satisfied that justice requires that a buyer from a seller without title should have to pay him for the use he has had of the goods. Why, asks the Commission rhetorically, should the buyer have to pay the seller for the use of someone else's goods? But the second reason appears the dominant one, and that is the sheer complexity of trying to work out a set of rules which copes adequately with the intricate relationship between s. 12(1) of the Act and the law of conversion. It is undoubtedly true that this interrelationship makes any detailed solution very hard, but the answer may well lie, not in abandoning all attempt at reform, but rather in abandoning the attempt to reform the law by working out the detailed rules in advance. After all, this has never been the common law's preferred methodology, and it would surely have been possible to give the court a little discretion to adjust the normal rules as to damages under s. 12(1). It does seem lamentable to tolerate the injustice which arose in *Butterworth* v *Kingsway Motors Ltd* (and this, surely, was gross injustice, despite the Law Commission's

---

21 1966 Cmnd. 2958, para 36.

22 See also Treitel (1967) 30 MLR at 146–9.

23 Law Commission and Scottish Law Commission, *Exemption Clauses in Contracts, First Report: Amendments to the Sale of Goods Act 1893* (Law Com. No. 24 and Scot Law Com. No. 12), paras 15–16, hereafter cited as Law Commission, *Exemption Clauses, First Report*.

24 See Law Com. No. 121, *Pecuniary Restitution on Breach of Contract* (1983) and their Working Paper No. 85, *Sale and Supply of Goods*, p. 109.

25 Law Commissions, Final Report, *Sale and Supply of Goods*, paras 6.1–6.5. Under these recommendations no substantial change at all is to be made to s. 12, though there are trivial changes in the terminology of the section.

rhetorical question) merely because the problem seems too complex to permit of a detailed legislative solution in terms of rules.

This particular problem does not seem to have arisen in other contexts. It is, however, possible that a similar situation could occur where goods are rejected for breach of one of the terms as to quality or fitness. In practice, this has not hitherto been a serious problem in such cases because the buyer is usually treated as having accepted the goods after a very short period of use.[26] However, problems with title can occur after a considerable lapse of time. In the United States, the majority response to this problem seems to be to award the plaintiff the value of the goods at the time dispossession occurred, plus any incidental damages that can be proved, on the principle that the plaintiff should be compensated for what has been lost, and surely this is the value at the time of dispossession?[27]

The 1979 Act (following the 1973 amendments) has cleared up one other problem. The opening words of s. 12(1) of the 1893 Act[28] originally contemplated the possibility of the parties contracting out of the implied conditions as to title. In exceptional circumstances a person may agree to buy goods from a bona fide possessor expressly subject to all defects in title. Goods seized and sold under a distress warrant, for instance, are sold without any warranty of title.[29] In such a case it is usual to sell merely the 'title and interest' of the debtor, whatever that may be. This means, for example, that the buyer takes the risk that the goods may not belong to the tenant, but may be held by him under a hire-purchase agreement. Under the new s. 12(3) and (4), the possibility of a sale of a limited interest is spelt out more clearly. The position now is that, where the parties intend only to transfer such title as the seller (or a third party) may have, there is an implied warranty that all charges or encumbrances known to the seller and not known to the buyer have been disclosed to the buyer before the contract is made. Moreover, under ss. 6(1) and 20 of the Unfair Contract Terms Act 1977 the seller cannot contract out of this liability.[30]

In general, this simplifies and clarifies the law, though one slightly odd result of these provisions seems to be that the seller cannot now contract out of s. 12(1) even to the extent that this goes beyond the implication of title. In *Niblett* v *Confectioners' Materials Co*,[31] for example (the facts of which have already been given), it appears to have been assumed by all the members of the court that the seller would not have been liable had there been a contrary intention which negatived the implication that the sale of the tins would not constitute an infringement of a trade mark. This would seem no longer possible. Given the uncertain ambit of the rights conferred by many forms of intellectual property, especially patents, this seems unjustifiable. The only practical

---

26 See below, p. 518.
27 See e.g. *Metalcraft Inc* v *Pratt* 65 Md. App. 281, 500 A 2d 329 (1985).
28 'Unless the circumstances of the contract are such as to show a different intention.' See on this Hudson (1957) 20 MLR 237 and (1961) 24 MLR 690; see also Reynolds (1963) 79 LQR at p. 542.
29 See *Payne* v *Elsden* (1900) 17 TLR 161, *Bogestad* v *Anderson* 143 Minn. 336, 173 NW 674 (1919) and Hudson, loc. cit. See also *Warming Used Cars Ltd* v *Tucker* [1956] SASR 249, where it was held that in the particular circumstances of the case the condition in s. 12 was negatived by implication. It seems, however, that the 'seller' in this case was more properly a mere agent.
30 See below, p. 234 *et seq.*, for the effect of these provisions.
31 [1921] 3 KB 387.

solution where the parties are prepared to deal on the basis that it is uncertain whether or not intellectual property rights are infringed, would appear to be insurance.

One final problem arising out of *Rowland v Divall* concerns the relationship between the condition implied by s. 12(1) and s. 11(4). This latter clause, which has enough difficulties of its own, will be fully discussed later,[32] but something must be said about it here. This clause states that when the buyer has accepted the goods he is no longer entitled to reject them for breach of condition but is relegated to a claim for damages. In *Rowland v Divall*,[33] it was contended that this clause precluded the buyer from recovering his full price, and compelled him to sue for damages, but the court rejected this argument apparently on the ground that there can be no sale at all where the seller has no right to sell the goods. This involves saying that s. 11(4) has no application at all to breaches of s. 12(1) and Atkin LJ went to the length of saying precisely that. It is, however, difficult to find any warrant for this view in the Act itself.[34]

WARRANTY OF FREEDOM FROM ENCUMBRANCES AND OF QUIET POSSESSION

The new s. 12(2), which amalgamates, with amendments, the original ss. 12(2) and (3), provides that (except where a limited interest is sold) there is an implied warranty that:

(a) the goods are free, and will remain free until the time when the property is to pass, from any charge or encumbrance not disclosed or known to the buyer before the contract is made, and

(b) the buyer will enjoy quiet possession of the goods except so far as it may be disturbed by the owner or other person entitled to the benefit of any charge or encumbrance so disclosed or known.

In *Rubicon Computer Systems Ltd v United Paints Ltd*,[35] a dispute arose between the parties to a contract to install a computer system. The supplier, who had access to the system after installation, wrongfully attached a time-lock to it, which when activated denied the defendants access to their system. It was held that the claimants were in breach of s. 12(2)(b). Other than in cases such as this, it is not easy to see what additional rights this confers on the buyer over and above those conferred by s. 12(1) (especially s. 12(2)(a)). At first sight it might appear that s. 12(1) was intended to give the buyer a right to recover no more than the price of the goods, whereas a breach of s. 12(2) might entitle the buyer to recover additional damages. But this explanation is untenable for, as Singleton LJ pointed out in *Mason v Burningham*:[36]

---

32 See below, p. 506.

33 [1923] 2 KB 500.

34 Moreover, it has been said that if the buyer is aware of the seller's lack of title there can be an acceptance within s. 11(4) (formerly s. 11(1)(c)): see per Devlin J in *Kwei Tek Chao v British Traders & Shippers Ltd* [1954] 2 WLR 365, 372, where he also points out that the contract in *Rowland v Divall* was voidable and not void. These remarks are omitted from the report at [1954] 2 QB 459. As to this, see the note in (1955) 18 MLR 496.

35 (2000) 2 TCLR 454.

36 [1949] 2 KB 545. And see *Stock v Urey* [1954] NI 71, where the buyer of a car which was seized by the customs authorities was held entitled to recover what he had to pay to secure the release of the car, although this was more than the purchase price. Cf. *Darbishire v Warran* [1963] 1 WLR 1067, a case in tort.

> In any event if there was a breach of the implied condition the plaintiff was entitled to treat that as a breach of warranty.

In this case the plaintiff recovered damages under the old s. 12(2) covering the cost of repairs done to a typewriter, in addition to the price, when it appeared that the seller was not the true owner.[37]

The scope of s. 12(2) is not entirely clear. A 'charge or encumbrance' presumably means a proprietary or possibly a possessory right, and does not extend to a mere contractual right.[38] It seems that s. 12(2) would protect the buyer against a wrongful disturbance of his possession by the seller himself;[39] in this situation the remedy under s. 12(2) would overlap with a right of action in tort. Where the disturbance of the buyer's possession is by a third party, the buyer may be entitled to treat this disturbance as the responsibility of the seller if, as a result of any acts or defaults of the seller, some third party with whom the seller is in contractual relations asserts an encumbrance or lien on the goods.[40]

But if the third party acts independently, the buyer can probably only rely on the subsection where the third party's act was a lawful act.[41] A seller can hardly be taken to warrant that no third party will ever tortiously interfere with the buyer's possession in the future.[42] The analogous covenant for quiet possession on a sale of land did not protect a buyer in England when he was evicted by title paramount (i.e. by a party with a title superior to the seller's), but that was because of the peculiar rule that a vendor of land did not warrant that he had a good title.[43] Accordingly this qualification was thought not to apply to the old subs. (2)[44] and this seems clearly to be confirmed by the present version of the implied warranty in s. 12(2).

Even where the third party's act is a lawful one, it will not amount to a breach of s. 12(2) unless it is based on rights to the goods which subsisted at the time when they were sold to the buyer. In *The Barenbels*[45] the sale of a ship was expressly guaranteed 'free from all encumbrances and maritime liens', but this express term (which obviously closely resembles the implied term in s. 12(2)) was held not broken where the ship was seized by a foreign court as a way of compelling the seller to pay debts to a creditor previously incurred in connection with the ship. Although the debts themselves pre-existed the contract of sale here, the creditor's actual rights in the ship itself only came from the foreign court order, and they did not pre-date the sale. So the creditor had no proprietary or even possessory rights in the ship at the time

---

37 On such facts it would now be a serious question whether the cost of the repairs would be recoverable from the seller. Under s. 6 of the Torts (Interference with Goods) Act 1977, the claimant should be able to keep the typewriter, merely paying its unimproved value to the owner as damages.

38 *The Barenbels* [1985] 1 Lloyd's Rep 528.

39 *Healing (Sales) Pty Ltd v Inglis Electrix Pty Ltd* (1968) 121 CLR 584; *Industria Azucarera Nacional SA v Exportadora de Azucar* (1982) Com LR 171.

40 *The Rio Sun* [1985] 1 Lloyd's Rep 350, 361.

41 *Niblett v Confectioners' Materials Co Ltd* [1921] 3 KB 387, 403.

42 See *Stephen v Lord Advocate* (1878) 6 R 282; *Dougall v Dunfermline Magistrates* 1908 SC 151.

43 *Bain v Fothergill* (1874) LR 7 HL 158. This case has, in any event, now been overturned by the Law of Property (Miscellaneous Provisions) Act 1989, s. 3.

44 *Mason v Burningham* [1949] 2 KB 545, 563.

45 [1985] 1 Lloyd's Rep 528.

of the contract of sale, and the creditor's rights were therefore held not to be encumbrances within the express terms of the contract.[46] At first sight, it may seem difficult to distinguish this case from *Rubicon Computer Systems Ltd* v *United Paints Ltd.*[47] The difference is that the supplier of the computer system was a party to the original contract, and was performing under it when it wrongfully attached the time lock. In *The Barenbells* what was involved was third-party rights, and no third-party rights to the goods existed until the court orders were made, which was after the contract containing the above warranty was made. A more difficult decision to reconcile this case with is *Microbeads AG* v *Vinhurst Roadmarkings Ltd* dealt with below.

There are two other possible distinctions between the effects of subss. (1) and (2); first, time under the Prescription and Limitation Acts would run against the buyer from the moment of sale under subs. (1), while under subs. (2) it is now clear that there is a continuing warranty of quiet possession. Consequently, time will only run against the buyer under (2) from the time his possession is disturbed. Secondly, as we have already seen, there are some rare circumstances in which a person may have a 'right to sell' goods and yet may not be able to sell them free from some third party's rights. In such a case a buyer would have a remedy under s. 12(2) but not under s. 12(1). We have already noted the example of a debtor who sells goods which have already been 'seized' (but not physically removed) by the sheriff under a writ of execution. The debtor has a right to sell the goods (at least until they are sold by the sheriff) but he sells them subject to the sheriff's rights. If, then, the buyer has to surrender the goods, he has an action for breach of s. 12(2).[48]

The practical operation of that part of s. 12(1)(b) dealing with freedom from encumbrances is limited because the law does not generally recognize real encumbrances over chattels by a person not in possession, and even equity only does so subject to the rights of the bona fide purchaser without notice. If, therefore, the third party is not in possession of the goods, he can rarely have an encumbrance which will be binding on the purchaser; on the other hand, if he is in possession the buyer has no need to rely on this subsection because the seller will simply be unable to make delivery. The buyer, therefore, will not be bound to pay the price or, if he has already paid it, will be entitled to recover it.[49]

But there are important exceptions to this general position. In particular, charges or encumbrances on ships (and aircraft) are common, and these may be valid and binding on a subsequent owner. So a buyer of a ship may be affected by such charges or encumbrances previously created, and for this reason these are usually the subject of express terms in a contract for the sale of a ship. But even in the absence of an express term, s. 12(2) would protect a buyer. Another exceptional type of case where s. 12(2) may be useful would arise if, for example, a person pledged goods but obtained delivery from the pledgee for some limited purpose. An unauthorized sale by the pledgor would enable the buyer to invoke this part of s. 12(2) against him,

---

46 But the buyers succeeded on a different ground, namely that the sellers had also given the buyers an indemnity which was wide enough to cover the events which had occurred.
47 At n. 35 above.
48 *Lloyds & Scottish Finance Ltd* v *Modern Cars & Caravans (Kingston) Ltd* [1966] 1 QB 764.
49 Section 28, which makes payment and delivery concurrent conditions – see below, p. 125.

although he could not allege a breach of s. 12(1) because the seller had a right to sell the goods, though subject to the rights of the pledgee.[50] Another, very exceptional, case is illustrated by the decision in *Microbeads A C v Vinhurst Road Markings Ltd*,[51] where the Court of Appeal awarded damages to a buyer under the old s. 12(2). In this case, the buyer's quiet possession had been disturbed by a patentee whose patent was only granted after the sale in question, so that there had been no breach of s. 12(1) at the time of the sale.[52] This decision is difficult to reconcile with *The Barenbells* dealt with above. The difference may be this. The causal events which led to the grant of the patent were in train at the time the contract was made, though until publication of the specification neither party could know this. By contrast, the seizure of the ship was one of a number of options no doubt open to the foreign court as a way of compelling the payment of the debts in question; there was nothing at the time the contract was made which inevitably led to the seizure of the ship. However, it should be noted that the decision in *Microbeads* has been criticized.[53]

---

50 See the cases cited below, p. 374, n. 11.
51 [1975] 1 All ER 529.
52 A patentee's rights accrue from the date of publication of the specification, but he can only sue in respect of infringe-ments of them from the grant of the patent – Patents Act 1977 s. 69. In the case of trade marks the relevant date is the date of application – *Denny* v *United Biscuits* [1981] FSR 114; Trade Marks Act 1994 s. 9(3). In the case of reg-istered designs, rights commence on registration – Registered Designs Act 1949 s. 7, and the same is true of plant breeders' rights – Plant Varieties and Seeds Act 1964 (as amended) s. 4.
53 See Law Reform Commission, New South Wales, *Working Paper on the Sale of Goods*, paras 12.5 (1975).

10

THE DUTY TO DELIVER THE GOODS

THE DUTY TO DELIVER

Under s. 27 of the Act:

> It is the duty of the seller to deliver the goods, and of the buyer to accept and pay for them, in accordance with the terms of the contract of sale.

The duty of the seller to deliver the goods is a somewhat ambiguous concept, for (leaving aside the fact that it is not generally the duty of the seller to 'deliver' them in the popular sense, but the duty of the buyer to take them) it covers three entirely different possibilities.

In the first place, there may be a duty to deliver to the buyer goods in which the property has already passed. Here the duty is specific and, subject to the question of payment, it is a duty which will be broken should the seller fail to deliver those particular goods. If the property has already passed, there can be no question of the seller substituting some other goods without the consent of the buyer. He must deliver those particular goods and no others will do.

In the second place, the seller's duty to deliver may be a duty to procure and supply to the buyer goods in accordance with the contract, but without any particular goods being designated to which the duty of delivery attaches. Thus a contract for the sale of purely generic goods does in one sense put upon the seller the duty of delivering 'the goods', but there is no duty to deliver any particular lot of goods. Until such a duty arises, therefore, the seller is perfectly free to deliver any particular quantity of goods answering the contract description. If, for example, the seller should procure goods answering the contract description, intending to use those in performance of the contract, but later changes his mind and sells them to someone else, the buyer cannot complain that the seller has broken his duty to deliver.[1] Nor can the buyer obtain a decree of specific performance in such a case.[2]

But there is a third possibility mid-way between the first two. It may be that the seller is under a personal duty to deliver a particular lot of goods although the property has not yet passed to the buyer. This is always so in the case of an agreement to sell specific goods, and clearly the seller cannot resell those goods without being guilty of a breach of contract. Even in the sale of unascertained goods it is possible

---

1 See *Carlos Federspiel & Co SA* v *Charles Twigg & Co Ltd* [1957] 1 Lloyd's Rep 255–6 per Pearson J. The relevant passage is cited below, pp. 337–8.
2 Because such a decree can only be granted where the goods are 'specific or ascertained' – see below, p. 560. Specific implement in Scotland may be different – see below, p. 560, n. 4.

for the seller's duty to deliver to attach to a particular lot of goods before the property passes. This, for example, is the effect of a notice of appropriation in a c.i.f. contract which does not pass the property, but fixes the goods to be delivered. Similarly in a f.o.b. contract where the seller ships goods but retains the bill of lading as security, the seller will come under an obligation to deliver to the buyer the actual goods shipped, though the property remains in the seller for the moment.[3] So these three possibilities are not mutually exclusive, but are rather three stages in the performance of the contract. Thus the duty to deliver may start by being unattached to any particular goods, may then become so attached and, finally, the property may pass. On the other hand, the three stages may be merged in one, as in the sale of specific goods, or two of them may be so merged, as where goods are appropriated to a contract fixing the duty to deliver and passing the property at the same time.

It should next be noted that the legal meaning of 'delivery' is very different from the popular meaning. In law, delivery means the 'voluntary transfer of possession', which is a different thing from the dispatch of the goods. There is, indeed, no general rule requiring the seller to dispatch the goods to the buyer, for under s. 29:

(1) Whether it is for the buyer to take possession of the goods or for the seller to send them to the buyer is a question depending in each case on the contract, express or implied, between the parties.

(2) Apart from any such contract, express or implied, the place of delivery is the seller's place of business, if he has one, and if not, his residence; except that, if the contract is for the sale of specific goods, which to the knowledge of the parties when the contract is made are in some other place, then that place is the place of delivery.

This section, therefore, does two things. First, it creates a presumption that in a sale of specific goods the place of delivery is the place where the goods are known to be at the time of the contract. Secondly, it lays down that in all other cases, in the absence of any special agreement, the place of delivery is the seller's place of business and, failing that, his residence. Thus in the absence of a contrary intention, it is the duty of the buyer to collect the goods, and not of the seller to send them. But in modern conditions of business, a contrary intention will frequently be inferred from the circumstances of the case. For example, where a buyer ordered certain goods from the seller in the form 'Please supply us with the following goods', an Australian court held that it was the seller's duty to send the goods to the buyer.[4] As the court said:

Purchasers who intend to purchase goods from people whose business it is to sell them do not as a rule send in advance an order for these goods to be supplied, if their intention is to go to the shop or warehouse of the sellers and there purchase them.[5]

Despite the general rule laid down in s. 29 that it is not for the seller to send the goods to the buyer, it is his responsibility to see that the goods are in a 'deliverable

---

3 See *Wait v Baker* (1848) 2 Ex 1, 8–9; and see s. 19(1) and (2). C.i.f. and f.o.b. contracts are described below, pp. 420 and 426.
4 *Wiskin v Terdich Bros Pty Ltd* [1928] Arg LR 242.
5 At pp. 242–3.

state'. Thus s. 29(6) enacts that:

> Unless otherwise agreed, the expenses of and incidental to putting the goods into a deliverable state must be borne by the seller.

The meaning of this phrase is considered later.[6]

Where the seller is, properly speaking, under a duty to dispatch the goods to the buyer, then this duty is absolute in the absence of frustrating circumstances; that is to say, the seller cannot plead that he was unable to dispatch the goods through no fault of his own, or that he had taken all reasonable care in dispatching them. But a duty to deliver the goods at the buyer's premises is discharged by delivery to a respectable-looking person at these premises even though it should prove that he was not authorized to take delivery on behalf of the buyer.[7]

PAYMENT AND DELIVERY CONCURRENT CONDITIONS

Under s. 28 of the Act:

> Unless otherwise agreed, delivery of the goods and payment of the price are concurrent conditions, that is to say, the seller must be ready and willing to give possession of the goods to the buyer in exchange for the price, and the buyer must be ready and willing to pay the price in exchange for possession of the goods.

It is not necessary for the seller actually to tender delivery before being entitled to sue for the price or for damages if it is clear that the buyer would have refused to accept the goods, but it is enough that he (the seller) was ready and willing to do so.[8] And, similarly, a buyer need not formally tender the price before becoming entitled to sue for non-delivery provided that he was ready and willing to do so.

But although the seller does not have to make a formal tender of delivery, he must have 'not only the disposition but the capacity to perform the contract'.[9] Moreover, a party is not precluded from relying upon one ground for repudiation merely because at the time he gave another and unjustifiable reason for repudiating. So if the buyer repudiates the contract in advance, and shows that he will not accept the goods if delivered or tendered, the mere fact that he gave an unjustified reason for this will not prevent him afterwards proving that the seller could not in fact have performed the contract. This rule, however, must be reconciled with another established proposition, namely that if the buyer wrongfully repudiates the contract, the seller can accept the buyer's repudiation and then maintain an action even though it is shown that he did not have the capacity to perform the contract when the buyer repudiated it. If the buyer meets the seller's claim for damages by pleading that, notwithstanding that he previously gave an unjustified reason for repudiating, the seller was himself in breach in failing to deliver at the appointed time (or, in the case of a repudiation by the buyer before the time for delivery, that the seller would not

---

6 See below, p. 324.
7 *Galbraith & Grant Ltd* v *Block* [1922] 2 KB 155; but cf. *Linden Tricotagefabrik* v *Wheat & Meacham* [1975] 1 Lloyd's Rep 384.
8 *Levey & Co Ltd* v *Goldberg* [1922] 1 KB 688, 692.
9 Per Lord Abinger in *De Medina* v *Norman* (1842) 9 M & W 820, 827, cited by Lord Atkinson in *British & Bennington Ltd* v *N W Cachar Tea Co Ltd* [1923] AC 48, 63.

have been able to deliver at the appointed time), these two principles appear, at first sight, to conflict.

Fortunately, the difficulty in stating the law was cleared up by the House of Lords in *Fercometal SARL v Mediterranean Shipping Co SA*,[10] although difficulties in the application of the law may continue. In the *Fercometal* case charterers of a vessel were informed by the owners that the vessel would not arrive in time to load in accordance with the terms of the charterparty. The charterers then purported to cancel the charter, which they had no right to do, as there was at that time no right of cancellation under the charter. But the owners in any event refused to accept this repudiation and insisted that the vessel would, after all, be ready to load on time. These assurances were false, however, and the vessel never was ready to load on time. The charterers having persisted in their refusal to load, the owners eventually sued them for damages for breach of the charterparty, and the charterers responded by pleading that the owners were never in a position to perform the contract. This defence was upheld. The House of Lords insisted that an anticipatory repudiation must either be accepted or refused. If accepted, the contract is then terminated, and the innocent party is freed from his duty of performance. But if the repudiation is rejected, the innocent party keeps the contract alive for all purposes. His own duty to perform is kept alive, together with the duty of the guilty party. So he then must be able to perform the contract when performance is due. There is no third alternative, by which the innocent party can keep the contract alive, while himself being absolved from performance.

The first possibility – that the seller's duty to deliver has been terminated by acceptance of the buyer's repudiation – is illustrated by another decision of the House of Lords, namely *Gill & Duffus SA v Berger & Co Inc*.[11] In this case the sellers contracted to sell 500 tons of Argentina Bolita beans and undertook to provide a certificate of quality. The goods were delivered in two loads; the first of 445 tons was covered by a certificate but the buyers wrongly rejected the certificate, and repudiated the contract. The sellers as a result failed to tender a certificate for the other 55 tons, and in the Court of Appeal it was held that this failure was fatal to the sellers' claim. But the House of Lords reversed this decision, holding that the buyer's repudiation had been accepted by the sellers before the certificate for the second load of goods was required to be presented, and that that duty accordingly never arose at all. (It does not seem to have been argued by the buyers that the failure to deliver the whole 500 tons in one load was itself a breach of contract by the sellers.)[12]

Although the *Fercometal* case was not a case on the law of sale of goods, it is clear that the principles discussed there are of general application. Indeed, one of the earlier cases, much discussed in the *Fercometal* case, was also a case of sale of goods. This was *Braithwaite v Foreign Hardwood Co Ltd*[13] where the plaintiff had agreed to sell to the defendant 100 tons of Honduras rosewood, delivery in two instalments.

---

10 [1989] AC 788.
11 [1984] AC 382.
12 See p. 139.
13 [1905] 2 KB 543; and see also *Taylor v Oakes Roncoroni & Co* (1922) 38 TLR 349, 547.

The plaintiff shipped about 63 tons, but the defendant then heard that the plaintiff had shipped 468 tons to another buyer, and he regarded this as a breach of a collateral oral contract. He therefore repudiated the contract, but the seller insisted that the goods were already at sea, and he was ready to deliver the bill of lading. The defendant refused to take it, and the seller eventually resold elsewhere. The defendant later discovered that part of the timber anyhow did not conform to the contract, and when sued for damages for non-acceptance, he pleaded that the sellers could not have performed for this reason. The buyer's defence was rejected by the Court of Appeal, and for many years the basis of this decision was controverted; but the House of Lords in the *Fercometal* case has now explained this decision as resting on the fact that, although the seller first refused to accept the buyer's repudiation, he did eventually accept it. That ultimate acceptance, therefore, terminated the contract, and with it the seller's duty to deliver conforming goods. Hence the buyers were no longer entitled to raise this point.

The *Fercometal* case thus clarifies the law, but to some degree the clarification of the law itself was only achieved by leaving open for solution in particular cases certain difficulties of application. Whenever a buyer wrongfully repudiates in advance, and indicates that he will not take delivery, and the seller at first refuses to accept this as terminating the contract, some uncertainty will remain as to the resultant outcome if the contract remains unperformed. When the seller eventually realizes that the buyer remains obdurate, clearly he is likely to take certain steps such as not appropriating goods to the contract, or arranging for their delivery, or alternatively, disposing of the goods elsewhere. Unless he can show that he did ultimately accept the repudiation he may then have to face the accusation that he did not have the capacity to perform at the time when delivery was due. This result would often seem quite unreasonable, and the House of Lords in the *Fercometal* case approved an alternative route by which the seller may succeed in such a case.

This alternative route is to hold that the seller was freed from his duty to deliver, not by the termination of the contract (that is, by the acceptance of the repudiation) but by an estoppel or waiver. So far as the former possibility is concerned, if the buyer has clearly represented to the seller that there is no point in his attempting to deliver the goods because, come what may, he will not take them, and if the seller acts upon that representation (for instance by not arranging for delivery or by disposing of the goods elsewhere) then the buyer will be estopped from complaining that the seller has after all failed in his duty to deliver. Thus here (as in many other areas of contract law) a representation, followed by action in reliance, is in effect treated as an alternative ground for achieving results normally achieved by offer and acceptance, or (as here) by repudiation and acceptance.

All this is admirably clear in theory and legal principle. But it seems probable that it will in practice cause difficulties of application because it will often be difficult to say whether a repeated repudiation which is first rejected has ultimately been accepted, or whether it gives rise to an estoppel, or whether the seller's duty to deliver remains alive. A further complicating factor, which did not arise in the *Fercometal* case, but which could often arise in contracts of sale, is that a resale of the goods by the seller, following a repudiation by the buyer, may rescind the contract under s. 48(3) or (4), whatever the general common law rules as to acceptance of a repudiation may be.[14]

Yet another complicating possibility is that the seller may occasionally be able to rely on the doctrine of waiver. Under this doctrine one party may waive performance of an act which would otherwise be a condition precedent to the performance of his own obligations. In this event, the other party is entitled to sue for breach of contract even though he could not have fulfilled his own contractual duties as a result of non-performance of that condition. Clearly the doctrines of waiver and estoppel largely overlap here, as they so often do, and it is not even certain that they are really distinct doctrines.[15] In *Peter Turnbull & Co Ltd* v *Mundas Trading Co (Australasia) Ltd*,[16] the defendants contracted to sell a quantity of oats to the plaintiffs f.o.b. Sydney, to be loaded on a ship nominated by the buyers in January or February 1951, the buyers to give 14 days' notice of nomination. The plaintiffs informally told the defendants that they would want delivery about 14 February and intimated that they would nominate the *Afric*. The sellers later told the buyers that they could not deliver f.o.b. Sydney, but offered delivery f.o.b. Melbourne instead. Negotiations followed in which the buyers sought to persuade sub-buyers to accept delivery f.o.b. Melbourne, but without success. On 23 February, the buyers told the sellers that they would insist on delivery f.o.b. Sydney, the sellers stated flatly that they could not make such delivery and the buyers thereupon bought in the market at an increased price. The *Afric* did not in fact arrive in Sydney till March. In an action by the buyers for damages for non-delivery, the sellers pleaded that they were excused from non-delivery because the buyers had not made the required nomination and that owing to the late arrival of the *Afric* the buyers could not have taken delivery f.o.b. Sydney during the contract period. The Australian High Court held for the buyers because the sellers had 'clearly intimated to the plaintiffs that it was useless to pursue the conditions of the contract applicable to shipment in Sydney and that the plaintiffs need not do so'.[17] This was held to amount to a waiver of the buyer's duty to take delivery in Sydney; but equally it seems the decision could have been based on estoppel, according to the requirements of that doctrine as laid down in the *Fercometal* case.

Although the seller must normally be ready and willing to deliver before he can claim that the buyer is in breach, it must be remembered that delivery has its usual legal meaning of transfer of possession in law. The meaning of this will be examined shortly, but it should be said here that where goods are shipped the shipping documents represent the goods, and transfer of these transfers possession of the goods. It follows that when the seller is ready and willing to deliver the shipping documents, he is prima facie entitled to demand payment of the price. A mere provision that payment shall only be due on delivery does not alter the position because delivery of the documents *is* equivalent to delivery of the goods. This was clearly laid down in the

---

14 See below, p. 467.
15 See, however, Adams (1972) 26 Conv (NS) 245 for an analysis of the possible conceptual bases of the common law doctrine of waiver. In Scotland, waiver is distinguished from personal bar, and English authorities should be treated with caution here: *Armia* v *Daejan Developments Ltd* 1979 SC (HL) 56, at p. 72 (Lord Keith); *James Howden & Co Ltd* v *Taylor Woodrow Property Co Ltd* 1998 SCLR 903; *Moodiesburn House Hotel Ltd* v *Norwich Union Insurance Ltd* 2002 SLT 1069. The subject is treated in detail in Blackie and Reid, *Personal Bar and Waiver* (2005).
16 (1954) 90 CLR 235. See also *Cerealmangini SpA* v *Alfred C Toepfer* [1981] 3 All ER 533 – see below, p. 135.
17 Per Dixon CJ at 246.

dissenting judgment of Kennedy LJ in *Biddell Bros Ltd* v *E Clemens Horst & Co Ltd*,[18] which was upheld in the House of Lords.[19]

It must also be borne in mind that if the goods have perished after the risk has passed to the buyer, the seller's right to receive payment ceases to depend upon his willingness to deliver the goods.[20] It is odd that s. 28 says nothing of this possibility.

One final point needs to be made about s. 28 which could otherwise be a source of confusion. The effect of the section is that, in the absence of a contrary agreement, the seller is entitled to *demand payment* when he is ready and willing to deliver. But it does not follow, if the buyer refuses to pay, and refuses to accept the proffered delivery, that the seller can sue for the price. To be entitled to demand payment of the price and to be entitled to *sue for the price* are two different things.[21] If the buyer refuses to accept a good tender of delivery, the seller can in general sue for damages for non-acceptance only. His right to sue for the price normally arises only when the buyer actually accepts the delivery of the goods and the property passes to him. The point is discussed more fully at a later stage.[22]

THE MEANING OF DELIVERY

Section 61 defines delivery as a 'voluntary transfer of possession' but it would be beyond the scope of this work to examine what exactly is a voluntary transfer of possession. Suffice it to say that for present purposes delivery may take one of the following forms.

In the first place, there may be a physical transfer of the actual goods themselves. This is the most obvious case, and although difficult questions of law may arise in deciding whether the physical transfer is enough to transfer legal possession, we need not go into these here.

Secondly, the seller may transfer possession to the buyer by handing over to him the means of control over the goods, for example the keys to the warehouse in which they are situated.[23]

Thirdly, s. 29(4) provides that:

> Where the goods at the time of sale are in the possession of a third person, there is no delivery by seller to buyer unless and until the third person acknowledges to the buyer that he holds the goods on his behalf; but nothing in this section affects the operation of the issue or transfer of any document of title to goods.

This acknowledgment is called 'attornment' in English law and is of special importance where the goods are in the custody of warehousemen. Where the seller gives the buyer a delivery order or warrant for goods stored in a warehouse, this does

---

18 [1911] 1 KB 934.

19 [1912] AC 18.

20 See, e.g., *McPherson, Thorn, Kettle & Co* v *Dench Bros* [1921] VLR 437, 445: 'non-delivery was here excused by the loss of the goods which at this time were at the purchaser's risk'.

21 The majority of the CA seems to have been guilty of confusing these two things in *Damon Cia Naviera* v *Hapag-Lloyd* [1985] 1 All ER 475 – see below, pp. 556–7.

22 See below, p. 481.

23 *Hilton* v *Tucker* (1888) 39 Ch D 669; *Dublin City Distillery Ltd* v *Doherty* [1914] AC 823; *Wrightson* v *Macarthur* [1921] 2 KB 807; *Macdougall* v *Whitelaw* (1840) 2 D 500; *Moore* v *Gledden* (1869) 7 M 1016; *Thomson* v *Scoular* (1882) 9 R 430; *West Lothian Oil Co* v *Mair* (1892) 20 R 64.

not transfer possession or property until the warehousekeeper attorns by accepting the order or warrant.[24] Mere receipt of the delivery order without any comment does not, without more, amount to an attornment.[25] In Scots law, s. 29(4) appears to narrow slightly the common law rule that where the thing to be transferred is in the hands of a third party, holding subject to the transferor's instructions, delivery can be made and completed by the giving and acceptance of such instructions.[26]

Fourthly, the goods may be delivered by the delivery of documents of title thereto. A document of title is defined by s. 1(4) of the Factors Act 1889 (extended to Scotland by the Factors (Scotland) Act 1890) as:

> Any bill of lading, dock warrant, warehousekeeper's certificate, and warrant or order for the delivery of goods, and any other document used in the ordinary course of business as proof of the possession or control of goods, or authorising or purporting to authorise, either by endorsement or by delivery, the possessor of the documents to transfer or receive goods thereby represented.

This definition, which is rather vague, appears to cover any document showing that the holder is entitled to claim the property specified in it.[27] The peculiar feature of documents of title is that the mere transfer or endorsement of the document, if accompanied by the necessary intention, suffices to transfer the possession and the property in the goods, even without attornment. By far the most important type of document of title is the bill of lading. When goods are shipped, the shipowner or his agent delivers to the shipper a bill of lading, and this document 'in law and in fact represents the goods. Possession of the bill of lading places the goods at the disposal of the purchaser.'[28] There seem to be few other kinds of documents of title in British commercial practice today, presumably because it is not customary for warehousekeepers' receipts and similar documents to authorize or to purport to authorize the holder to claim the goods by mere endorsement or delivery of the receipt without attornment by the warehousekeeper.[29] But it has been held that a delivery order may in certain circumstances be a document of title,[30] as also may railway receipts if suitably worded.[31] Moreover, under some private Acts of Parliament, certain warehousekeepers' delivery warrants are specially made documents of title and, indeed, in some cases they are fully negotiable instruments, so

---

24 *Sterns Ltd v Vickers Ltd* [1923] 1 KB 78; *Wardar's (Import and Export) Co Ltd v W Norwood & Sons Ltd* [1968] 2 QB 663. Even after attornment no actual property passes if the goods are not physically segregated or otherwise ascertained, though the attornment may be enough to raise an estoppel against the warehouseman: *In re London Wine Co (Shippers) Ltd* (1986) PCC 121. See below, p. 345, as to this case.

25 *Laurie & Morewood v John Dudin & Sons* [1926] 1 KB 223; *D F Mount Ltd v Jay & Jay (Provisions) Co Ltd* [1960] 1 QB 159.

26 Reid, *Law of Property in Scotland*, para. 620.

27 Reid, *Law of Property in Scotland*, para. 621 (n. 10).

28 *Biddell Bros Ltd v E Clemens Horst & Co Ltd* [1911] 1 KB 934, 956–7 per Kennedy LJ. As to the time at which a bill of lading ceases to be a document of title, see *Barclays Bank Ltd v Commissioners of Customs & Excise* [1963] 1 Lloyd's Rep 81.

29 A vehicle registration document is not a document of title, because it merely identifies a 'keeper' (*Joblin v Watkins and Roseveare (Motors) Ltd* [1949] 1 All ER 47; *Central Newbury Car Auctions Ltd v Unity Finance Ltd* [1957] 1 QB 371, CA).

30 *Ant. Jurgens v Margarinefabrieken v Louis Dreyfus & Co Ltd* [1914] 3 KB 40.

31 *Official Assignee of Madras v Mercantile Bank of India* [1935] AC 53.

that an innocent transferee obtains a good title despite the transferor's lack of title.[32] Bills of lading are not, of course, fully negotiable in this sense.

Fifthly, the parties may agree that the seller should hold the goods as the buyer's agent or bailee. This suffices to transfer possession of the goods for present purposes, that is to say, in the absence of a contrary intention, it entitles the seller to demand payment of the price, although in other cases it is a question of the greatest difficulty whether or not the bailor with an immediate right to take the goods can be said to have legal possession of them.

Sixthly, delivery of the goods to the buyer's agent transfers possession to the buyer himself. Moreover, delivery to a carrier is prima facie deemed to be delivery to the buyer. Section 32(1) of the Act says:

> Where, in pursuance of a contract of sale, the seller is authorized or required to send the goods to the buyer, delivery of the goods to a carrier (whether named by the buyer or not) for the purpose of transmission to the buyer is prima facie deemed to be a delivery of the goods to the buyer.[33]

But where the carrier is an agent or servant of the seller himself, delivery to him cannot constitute delivery to the buyer, for it is merely a delivery to the seller's *alter ego*.[34]

---

32 For example, Port of London Act 1968 s. 146(4).
33 This provision does not apply where the buyer deals as consumer, or in Scotland, where there is a consumer contract – s. 32(4) added by SI 2002/3045 reg. 4 – see p. 359 *et seq*.
34 *Galbraith & Grant Ltd* v *Block* [1922] 2 KB 155, 156; *Badische Anilin und Soda Fabrik* v *Basle Chemical Works* [1898] AC 200.

11

THE DUTY TO SUPPLY THE GOODS
AT THE RIGHT TIME

THE TIME OF DELIVERY

Section 10, after laying down in subs. (1) that the time of payment is prima facie not of the essence, goes on to state in subs. (2) that:

> Whether any other stipulation as to time is of the essence of the contract or not depends on the terms of the contract.

Although the Act thus declines to lay down any general rules, the courts have done so, and it is well settled that 'In ordinary commercial contracts for the sale of goods the rule clearly is that time is prima facie of the essence with respect to delivery.'[1] If the time for delivery is fixed by the contract, then failure to deliver at that time will thus be a breach of condition or a material breach, which justifies the buyer in refusing to take the goods. This rule applies to the time of delivery in the strict legal sense, and thus operates not only when the seller is under an obligation to dispatch the goods to the buyer but also when the buyer is bound to collect the goods from the seller. As we have previously seen, the House of Lords has affirmed that this rule applies in most commercial contracts, not merely with respect to the time of delivery but also with regard to the time for the performance of many other contractual obligations, such as the giving of notices.[2] It also applies to many duties of the buyer, especially where they are interwoven with the seller's duties, such as often occurs in cases of international trade.[3] And although, strictly speaking, this chapter is concerned with the duties of the seller, some cases relating to the duties of the buyer as to the time of delivery are also dealt with here.

Where goods are to be shipped by the seller before a fixed date or within a stipulated period, it is also well established that time is of the essence, so that any deviation from the stipulations of the contract justifies the other party in treating the whole contract as at an end.[4] If, as is commonly the case in commercial contracts, the seller is allowed a period within which to deliver or ship (for example, delivery 'during March', or 'shipment January/February'), the seller has the whole

---

1 Per McCardie J in *Hartley v Hymans* [1920] 3 KB 475, 484.
2 *Bunge Corpn v Tradax SA* [1981] 1 WLR 711 – see above, p. 94.
3 See for example *Gill & Duffus SA v Société Pour L'Exportation des Sucres* [1986] 1 Lloyd's Rep 322.
4 *Bowes v Shand* (1877) 2 App Cas 455. As this case makes clear, early shipment is just as much a breach as late shipment. See below, p. 133, for the facts.

period in which to deliver or ship, as the case may be.[5] He is not in default until the period has expired.

Where the contract provides that the seller will use his best endeavours to deliver the goods by a certain date but, despite his best endeavours, he is unable to do so, he must still deliver the goods within a reasonable time after that date.[6]

Where no time has been fixed by the contract, it is provided by s. 29(3) that:

> Where under the contract of sale the seller is bound to send the goods to the buyer, but no time for sending them is fixed, the seller is bound to send them within a reasonable time.

Presumably the position is the same where the seller is not bound to send the goods but is only bound to have them ready for collection. Reference should also be made here to s. 29(5):

> Demand or tender of delivery may be treated as ineffectual unless made at a reasonable hour; and what is a reasonable hour is a question of fact.

Failure to deliver within a reasonable time (like failure to deliver within a specified time) may amount to a breach of condition by the seller.[7]

A formula sometimes encountered is that delivery will be 'as required'. This means that the buyer must give notice of his requirements to the seller, and the seller must then presumably be allowed sufficient time to make delivery (though that time may be very short in appropriate circumstances). This formula also means that the buyer must require delivery within a reasonable time – he cannot in effect abandon the contract, or spin things out indefinitely simply by not requiring delivery.[8] But it is perhaps not entirely clear whether failure to require delivery within a reasonable time is by itself enough to justify the seller in treating the contract as repudiated, or whether he in turn must give some appropriate notice or warning to that effect to the buyer.[9]

It is important to observe that since the failure of the seller to deliver on time is a breach of condition, the buyer may reject the goods although he has suffered no damage as a result of the breach. Thus in the well-known case of *Bowes v Shand*,[10] the sellers agreed to ship a quantity of Madras rice during the months of March and/or April. In fact, the bulk of the rice was shipped at the end of February and only about one-eighth was shipped during March. It was held by the House of Lords that the buyers were entitled to reject the goods, although it was conceded that there was no difference between the rice actually shipped and any rice which might have been shipped in March.

It will be appreciated that the reason why the buyer rejects in such cases will very often not be that he is really aggrieved by the early (or even late) shipment but that

---

5 But if the last day is a non-working day (for example, a bank holiday) the seller will not have an extension of time to the next day: *Jacobson Van Den Berg & Co v Biba Ltd* (1977) 121 Sol Jo 333.

6 *McDougall v Aeromarine of Emsworth Ltd* [1958] 1 WLR 1126.

7 *Thomas Borthwick (Glasgow) Ltd v Bunge & Co Ltd* [1969] 1 Lloyd's Rep 17, 28.

8 *Jones v Gibbons* (1853) 8 Ex 920. See the discussion of this case in *Pearl Mill Co Ltd v Ivy Tannery Co Ltd* [1919] 1 KB 78 and *Allied Marine Transport Ltd v Vale do Rio Doce Navegaçao SA (The Leonidas D)* [1985] 2 All ER at 806–7, superseding the use made of the *Pearl Mill* case in *The Splendid Sun* [1981] QB 694.

9 Ibid.

10 (1877) 2 App Cas 455.

the market has fallen, and the buyer wants to escape from a bad bargain. This will not, however, necessarily be the case where the buyer complains of the failure to give notices on time or other similar breaches. Opinions may differ as to the desirability of retaining these rules. On the one hand, it may be objected that they permit an innocent party to escape from a bad bargain as a result of a highly technical breach of contract; on the other hand, there are serious problems about allowing a party to litigation to raise issues about the motives which have led the other party to act in a certain way. Examination of such motives often leads to very serious and difficult factual disputes. There are no current proposals for amendment of the law on this question. The Law Commission's Final Report, *Sale and Supply of Goods*, which proposed modification of the right to reject where it would be 'unreasonable' and the consequent amendments effected by the Sale and Supply of Goods Act 1994 (which is discussed further later[11]) do not affect breaches of stipulations as to the time of delivery or other aspects of performance. These changes only affect breaches of the implied conditions as to quality and fitness in ss. 13 to 15 of the Act, and breaches of the seller's duties as to the quantity under s. 30.

WAIVER OF CONDITIONS AS TO DELIVERY TIME[12]

Although time is thus prima facie of the essence with respect to delivery, buyers do not usually refuse to accept delivery merely because it is late. Actual acceptance of a late delivery is clearly binding on the buyer; so also even an agreement to accept late delivery will normally be binding whether made with or without consideration. It seems immaterial whether such waiver or estoppel is regarded as binding at common law[13] or by virtue of s. 11(2) of the Act which states:

> Where a contract of sale is subject to any condition to be fulfilled by the seller, the buyer may waive the condition . . .

McCardie J in *Hartley* v *Hymans*[14] rested his decision on s. 11(2), while Denning LJ in *Charles Rickards Ltd* v *Oppenhaim*[15] preferred to base it on the doctrine of promissory estoppel. In modern decisions, no clear distinction appears to be drawn between waiver and estoppel in such cases,[16] even though differences can be found between the conceptual bases of the two doctrines.[17]

In commercial transactions, some of the most difficult questions that commonly arise are those concerning pleas of waiver and estoppel and the like. The difficulty often arises from the fact that when a breach is committed or threatened (for example, where the seller informs the buyer that he cannot ship or deliver in time) it is rare that the buyer instantly breaks off negotiations and treats the contract as repu-

---

11 See below, p. 499 et seq.
12 These provisions are not applicable to Scotland. For Scotland, see above, p. 128, n. 15.
13 Either under the common law doctrine of waiver (as to which see Adams (1972) 36 Conv (NS) 246), or in equity under the rule in *Hughes* v *Metropolitan Railway Co* (now usually known as promissory estoppel).
14 [1920] 3 KB 475.
15 [1950] 1 KB 616.
16 See, e.g., *Finagrain SA Geneva* v *P Kruse* [1976] 2 Lloyd's Rep 508.
17 See Adams (1972) 36 Conv (NS) 245.

diated.[18] More commonly, messages pass between the parties as some attempt at accommodation is sought; sometimes, too, a buyer may get in touch with his sub-buyers because his own attitude to delay may be governed by their attitude. During this time, the seller may still be doing his best to arrange delivery as soon as possible. If, finally, negotiations break down, or more extensive delays ensue, it may be very difficult to say whether the buyer has waived the delay or any part of it. Although issues of waiver and estoppel can arise with regard to other matters besides stipulations as to time, these are so commonly the source of such questions that they can most conveniently be dealt with here.

The principles to be applied in these cases can be summarized as follows. First, there must be a promise or a clear and unequivocal representation that the innocent party will not insist on strict performance of the original contract according to its terms. This does not mean that the promise or waiver needs to be expressly made. As Lord Salmon said in *Bremer* v *Vanden Avenne-Izegem*,[19] a case concerned with a notice which the sellers were entitled to give extending the date for delivery, but which was given late, 'To make an unequivocal representation or waiver, it is not necessary for the buyers to say – "We hereby waive it". It is quite enough if they behave or write in such a way that reasonable sellers would be led to believe that the buyers were waiving any defect there might be in the notice and were accepting it as effectively extending the date for delivery.'

A difficult and controversial question concerns the possibility of a waiver or estoppel arising if the party against whom waiver or estoppel is pleaded did not know all the facts at the relevant time. Prima facie, at least, it still seems to be the general opinion that a party cannot be taken to have waived rights which he did not know he had, because (for instance) he was ignorant of the breach of contract in question.[20] And similarly, a person cannot very well be held to have represented that he will not enforce his rights unless he knew what rights he had. At the same time, it is clear that there can sometimes be waiver or estoppel (or some legal equivalent) even without full knowledge of all the facts. In particular, it seems from the Court of Appeal's latest pronouncement that a representation (express or implied from words or conduct) may found a promissory estoppel if the representation carries a strong implication that the representor did have full knowledge of the facts.[21] Furthermore, on principle, there seems no reason to doubt that a party could make it clear by his words or conduct that he does not care what the relevant facts are, but is prepared to condone a breach if there has been one.

As with the cases dealt with in the last chapter (such as the *Fercometal* case[22]) there is often a conflict here between two sets of principles. On the one hand, the mere fact

---

18 All this applies also to breaches by the buyer, e.g. of an obligation to open a letter of credit for payment. Here, too, breach will often justify immediate repudiation in law, but the seller is more likely to respond by demanding to know why the letter of credit has not yet been opened, and perhaps to allow some extension of time.

19 [1978] 2 Lloyd's Rep 109, 126.

20 The leading case is now *Procter & Gamble Philippine Manufacturing Corpn* v *Peter Cremer GmbH & Co (The Manila)* [1988] 3 All ER 843; see also *Panchaud Frères SA* v *Établissements General Grain Co* [1970] 1 Lloyd's Rep 53 (where, however, the judgment of Denning LJ can no longer be wholly relied upon); *Bremer* v *Mackprang* [1979] 1 Lloyd's Rep 220; *Cerealmangini SpA* v *Alfred C Toepfer* [1981] 3 All ER 533.

21 See the *Procter & Gamble* case, above, n. 20.

22 [1989] AC 788; see above, p. 126.

that the buyer does not at once complain of late delivery does not necessarily prevent him raising this later. A party is entitled, when sued, to set up any justification for his previous conduct, even though he did not give that justification at the time. It has also been stressed that waiver of one contractual term does not necessarily preclude the innocent party insisting on other related terms. Thus where a seller was bound to deliver goods shipped in June and give a notice of appropriation by 10 July, a waiver of the latter requirement was held not to involve a waiver of the former. It was still possible for the seller to find a June shipment to supply to the buyer, and the buyer had not waived his right to a June shipment.[23]

On the other hand, a buyer who does not complain of the relevant breach at the time when it is committed, but who at that stage appears to be willing to continue with the contract, may be held bound by waiver or estoppel so as to preclude his raising that breach at a later date. The question always is whether the buyer has led the seller to believe that he does not intend to complain about the breach. So a buyer who rejects shipping documents tendered to him on the ground that they do not include a certificate of quality, or who rejects the goods on grounds of quality, but makes no complaint of the time of delivery, may find that an eventual attempt to raise the issue of delay in delivery is too late: he may be told that he has, in effect, waived the late delivery.

Parties who are victims of breach of contract sometimes attempt to have things both ways by 'reserving their rights', while at the same time showing willingness to continue with the contract despite the breach. Use of this or a similar formula does not in law rule out the possibility of waiver or estoppel if the other conditions of these doctrines are satisfied.[24] The victim of a breach of condition has alternative remedies: he can either treat the contract as terminated or affirm it, but he must choose between the two. He cannot, by claiming to 'reserve his rights', demand the right to affirm the contract while keeping in reserve the possibility of treating it as terminated. At the same time, the innocent party can, if he is well advised, achieve precisely the same result by first terminating the contract, and making it quite clear that he does so. He can then enter into new negotiations to try to sort out the consequences of that termination, and of course these new negotiations may even lead to a renewal of the contract on more advantageous terms for the innocent party. Unfortunately, businessmen often think they can proceed straight to this second stage, by 'reserving their rights', only to find that the courts hold this to be ineffective for the reasons already given.

A reservation of rights may, however, be of some legal effect up to a point. For instance, the buyer may make it clear by some such formula that he is reserving his right to seek damages, while not insisting on treating the breach as a breach of condition justifying him in terminating the contract. The recent case law does not throw any doubts on this possibility.

Another important question which is still not totally resolved is whether a waiver must be acted upon to the detriment or prejudice of the party in breach before he can rely upon it. In general, it seems that this is necessary: a bare waiver or representation

---

23 *Finagrain SA Geneva v Kruse* [1976] 2 Lloyd's Rep 508.
24 *Bremer* v *Mackprang*, above, n. 20; *Vargas Pena Apezteguia y Cia Saic* v *Peter Cremer GmbH* [1987] 1 Lloyd's Rep 394; *Nichimen Corpn* v *Gatoil Overseas Inc* [1987] 2 Lloyd's Rep 46.

which is instantly retracted before it is acted upon is unlikely to be held to be binding.[25] In *Société Italo-Belge* v *Palm & Vegetable Oils*,[26] sellers were required to make a declaration of shipment as soon as possible after the vessel sailed, but the declaration was in fact made a month later. But the buyers did not protest when they received it; indeed, they asked the sellers to pass the shipping documents straight to the sub-buyers. However, the sub-buyers rejected them because of the delay, and the buyers thereupon also claimed the right to reject them. The sellers argued that there had been an implied waiver and that they had acted upon it by delivering the documents to the sub-buyers. It was held by Robert Goff J that although these contentions were sound, it was not inequitable for the buyer to be able to retract the waiver. Although it may not be strictly necessary to show that the representee has acted on the representation or waiver to his detriment, it is necessary to show that he has acted on it so that it would be inequitable to allow the other party to insist on the contractual delivery date; and here such a short time had elapsed since the documents had been delivered to the sub-buyers (only two days, in fact) that there was nothing inequitable in permitting the buyers to reject the documents. Moreover, the buyers here had good reason for retracting their waiver.

Extension of time for delivery

The seller in a contract with a fixed delivery date sometimes indicates that he will not be able to deliver by that date, and asks for an extension of time. The buyer may respond in one of two ways (assuming he does not simply reject the request). He may either grant an extension, fixing at once a new delivery date, in which case the new date simply replaces the old one; and if time was of the essence (as it usually is) this means that the contract continues to operate, with the delivery time being of the essence, but the new time simply replaces the old time.[27]

Alternatively, the buyer may grant the seller an extension of time without actually fixing a new date or time. If this were an alteration of the original contract, supported by new consideration, the result would presumably be a contract to deliver within a reasonable time in accordance with s. 29(3). But where a delivery date is merely waived before the goods are delivered, the buyer is entitled to give the seller reasonable notice that he will not accept delivery after a certain date. In *Charles Rickards Ltd* v *Oppenhaim*,[28] the plaintiffs agreed to supply a Rolls-Royce chassis for the defendant, to be ready at the latest on 20 March 1948. It was not ready on this day, but the defendant continued to press for delivery, thereby impliedly waiving the condition as to the delivery date. By 29 June, the defendant had lost patience and wrote to the plaintiffs informing them that he would not accept delivery after 25 July. In fact, the chassis was not ready until 18 October, and the defendant refused to accept it. The Court of Appeal held that the defendant was entitled to reject the chassis as he had given the plaintiffs reasonable notice that delivery must be made by a certain

---

25 As to the circumstances in which a waiver will be binding see Adams (1972) 36 Conv (NS) 245.
26 [1982] 1 All ER 19.
27 *Buckland v Farmar & Moody* [1979] 1 WLR 221; *Nichimen Corpn v Gatoil Overseas Inc*, above, n. 24.
28 [1950] 1 KB 616.

date. If this kind of waiver is an illustration of the principle of promissory estoppel, then *Charles Rickards Ltd* v *Oppenhaim* can be regarded as an illustration of the principles discussed by the House of Lords in *Tool Metal Manufacturing Co Ltd* v *Tungsten Electric Co Ltd*[29] as to the termination of the binding effect of a promissory estoppel by reasonable notice.[30]

Where it is clear that the party to whom the indulgence has been granted could not in any event have performed the contract within a reasonable time, notice may not be necessary, and a mere intimation that the contract is regarded as cancelled may be sufficient.[31]

Although s. 11(2) only refers to a waiver of a condition by the buyer, it is clear that the principles of waiver and promissory estoppel are general principles of contract law, and apply equally to buyer and seller. So, for example, a seller who leads a buyer to suppose that a letter of credit required by the contract will not be insisted on is not thereafter entitled to plead the failure to open such a letter of credit as an answer to a claim for non-delivery.[32]

---

29 [1955] 1 WLR 761.
30 For an explanation of *Charles Rickards* v *Oppenhaim* based on the doctrine of common law waiver see Adams (1972) 36 Conv (NS) 245 at p. 251 *et seq.*
31 *Etablissements Chainbaux SARL* v *Harbormaster Ltd* [1955] 1 Lloyd's Rep 303.
32 *Panoutsas* v *Raymond Hadley Corpn of New York* [1917] 2 KB 473; *Plasticmoda Societa* v *Davidsons (Manchester) Ltd* [1952] 1 Lloyd's Rep 527.

12

THE DUTY TO SUPPLY GOODS IN THE RIGHT QUANTITY

DELIVERY OF THE RIGHT QUANTITY

The seller must deliver the correct quantity of goods. In the first place, s. 30(1) states:

> Where the seller delivers to the buyer a quantity of goods less than he contracted to sell, the buyer may reject them, but if the buyer accepts the goods so delivered he must pay for them at the contract rate.

Moreover, the seller cannot excuse a short delivery on the ground that he will deliver the remainder in due course because s. 31(1) states that:

> Unless otherwise agreed, the buyer of goods is not bound to accept delivery thereof by instalments.

There are no doubt circumstances (for example, where the goods are to be shipped) in which it can be inferred from the contract quantity and the time allowed for shipment that the sellers are entitled to ship in more than one load, and therefore entitled to deliver in separate loads.[1] But the general rule is that the seller must deliver in one load.

The operation of these subsections is illustrated by *Behrend & Co Ltd* v *Produce Brokers Co Ltd*,[2] where the sellers agreed to sell a quantity of cotton seed ex the *Port Inglis* in London. The ship discharged a small part of the cargo in London, and then left for Hull where she discharged other goods. Fourteen days later, she returned to London and discharged the remainder of the cotton seed which was the subject of the sale. It was held that the buyers were entitled to reject the later delivery while retaining the earlier one.

A similar case, but one with a surprising twist to its tail, is *Gill & Duffus SA* v *Berger & Co Inc*,[3] where sellers who had agreed to sell 500 tons of beans delivered them in two loads or shipments, the first of 445 tons and the second of 55 tons. The buyers rejected both loads on the ground that they did not conform to the contract description. This ground was held to be good as regards the second load, but bad as regards the first. It might therefore seem that the buyers were only entitled to reject the second load; but the Court of Appeal held that in the light of s. 30 of the Act, they

---

1 *Pagnan & Fratelli* v *Tradax Overseas SA* [1980] 1 Lloyd's Rep 665.
2 [1920] 3 KB 530.
3 [1983] 1 Lloyd's Rep 622.

must be held entitled to reject both loads because 'a right of rejection limited to 55 tons was not a possible conclusion in law'.[4] It seems that even if the buyers had waived any right to object to the fact of separate deliveries, their rejection of the first delivery, which was originally wrongful, was retrospectively validated by their rightful rejection of the second. Once the buyers had rejected the second delivery, it followed that the sellers were guilty of a breach of their duty to deliver 500 tons. On the facts that was not an unreasonable result, but the implication – that the buyers could have rejected the first load after rejection of the second, *even if they had originally accepted the first load* – does seem somewhat strange. This decision was reversed by the House of Lords[5] on grounds not affecting this point, namely that in fact the buyers did not have the right to reject the second load at all, because their wrongful rejection of the first load was a complete repudiation of the contract which had been accepted by the sellers, so no duty of delivery arose at all as regards the second load.[6]

Where delivery in separate instalments is permissible under the contract, the question whether a shortfall in the quantity required permits the buyer to treat the whole contract as discharged is dealt with by s. 31(2) of the Act which is discussed in more detail later.[7] Here it is enough to say that that subsection is not as strict in its requirements as s. 30(1), and that a shortfall in quantity in one instalment does not justify the buyer in treating the whole contract as discharged unless it is sufficiently serious to go to the root of the contract as a whole.[8] The result may seem curious at first sight. Leaving aside the effect of s. 30(2A), suppose a seller contracts to sell and deliver 62 suits to the buyer, but he only delivers 61. If the suits were to be delivered in one load, the buyer could reject the whole lot (unless the absence of one suit is merely *de minimis*, which it probably is not). But if the suits are to be delivered in separate instalments, the buyer's rights are regulated by s. 31(2) and on these facts it has been held that the shortfall of one suit was not sufficiently serious to justify the buyer in treating the contract as completely discharged.[9] But the result is not so odd as it seems. Where the parties do expressly contemplate instalment deliveries, serious problems would arise if a shortfall on one instalment gave a right to reject previous instalments already accepted. So it is natural that such a right should be severely limited, and each instalment treated as a separate delivery.[10]

The counterpart of the duty not to deliver too little is the duty not to deliver too much, although it is less obvious why this should be so objectionable. At first sight there seems no obvious reason why the buyer should not be required to accept that

---

4 At p. 627. This particular point is not affected by the Sale and Supply of Goods Act 1994 – see p. 499 *et seq.*
5 [1984] AC 382.
6 See above, p. 116.
7 Below, p. 501.
8 It should be noted that the Uniform Commercial Code which preserves the 'perfect tender' rule in its full rigour – see §2–601 adopts a more relaxed rule for instalment contracts – §2–612.
9 *Regent OHG Aisenstadt v Francesco of Jermyn Street* [1981] 3 All ER 327.
10 But if each instalment is a separate delivery under s. 30(1) it might seem that the buyer should at least be able to reject the whole of an instalment if there is any shortfall in it. In the *Francesco of Jermyn Street* case Mustill J did not consider whether the buyer was not entitled to reject the whole of the consignment which contained the short delivery. This would then have raised the further problem that the application of s. 31(2) might have had to be considered on the supposition that the seller was in breach in respect of one whole consignment, and not just one suit. See also below, p. 504.

part which should have been delivered, whether or not he accepts the rest. But this is not the law, for s. 30(2) lays down that:

> Where the seller delivers to the buyer a quantity of goods larger than he contracted to sell, the buyer may accept the goods included in the contract and reject the rest, or he may reject the whole.

Subsection (3) then says that if the buyer accepts all the goods delivered he must pay for them at the contract rate. This subsection does not actually say when the buyer can and when he cannot accept any excess delivered by the seller. It merely says that if the buyer does accept any excess he must pay for it at the contract rate. It may well have been assumed that the buyer can always accept any excess, and it certainly seems that he should usually be able to accept whatever is delivered, whether too much or too little, because the delivery would usually be treated as a counter-offer which the buyer accepts by accepting the goods themselves.[11]

In their Working Paper on Sale and Supply of Goods, the Law Commissions raised the question whether it is right to treat an excess delivery as always amounting to an offer to sell the surplus. While this appears reasonable in the case where the seller delivers 1,004 tons of grain instead of 1,000, it is rather different where the buyer orders one article, perhaps of a special nature, and two are mistakenly delivered.[12] The answer to this seems to be that the buyer obviously cannot accept the surplus when he knows the seller does not mean to make an offer to sell those goods. That is the effect of the common law rules as to mistake which are preserved by s. 62(2) of the Act, and s. 30(3) must be read subject to those common law rules. In their Final Report the Law Commissions ultimately decided to leave s. 30(3) unamended and unrepealed.[13] They concluded that while there are theoretical difficulties in deciding when a buyer can accept an excess delivered by the seller, the difficulties do not appear to be of serious practical importance, and in any event the mere repeal of s. 30(3) would not resolve those problems.

The *de minimis* principle

The former law was very strict in its insistence on the correct quantity. Any shortfall or any excess, no matter how small, was a breach of the section and justified rejection of all the goods. There was, and presumably still is, however, a principle of very limited application, known by the Latin phrase *de minimis non curat lex* (the law pays no attention to trifles) which could occasionally be invoked to excuse what would otherwise have been a technical breach. To illustrate the application of this principle in the present context, two cases, one on either side of the line, may be contrasted. In *Wilensko Slaski Towarzystwo Drewno v Fenwick & Co Ltd*,[14] the sellers sold timber of specified measurements to the buyers. There were certain permitted, but strictly

---

11 *Hart v Mills* (1846) 15 M & W 85.
12 Working Paper No. 85, Consultative Memorandum No. 58, para 6.32.
13 See Final Report, *Sale and Supply of Goods*, para 6.23.
14 [1938] 3 All ER 429. See also *Regent OHG Aisenstadt v Francesco of Jermyn St* [1981] 3 All ER 327, where the seller's counsel declined even to argue that a failure to deliver one, out of a contract for the delivery of 62 suits, was *de minimis*.

defined, variations from these specifications. Slightly under 1 per cent of the timber failed to comply with the contract requirements. The buyers were held entitled to reject the goods. On the other hand, in *Shipton Anderson & Co Ltd* v *Weil Bros & Co Ltd*,[15] the sellers contracted to sell to the buyers 4,500 tons of wheat or 10 per cent more or less. The sellers delivered 4,950 tons (the agreed upper limit) and 55 lb, but they did not claim payment for the 55 lb. It was held that the buyers were not entitled to reject the goods. The excess over the stipulated amount being a little over 1 lb in 100 tons, the case clearly called for the application of the maxim *de minimis*. If it had not been applied in this case the rule would have lost all commercial importance.[16]

The maxim *de minimis non curat lex* is a legal principle of general application, but its applicability to any particular case seems to be a question of fact which depends, *inter alia*, on how far precise accuracy can be obtained, or whether there are limits of accuracy which are commercially reasonable.[17] Given the new provisions restricting the right of rejection in non-consumer sales discussed in the next paragraph, the principle ought seldom to be applied to cases falling under the present provisions, for the effect of applying it is that there is no breach of warranty at all.[18] There may theoretically perhaps be occasions when it might be applied in consumer sales,[19] though having regard to the additional rights of the buyer in consumer cases added to s. 48 by the Sale and Supply of Goods to Consumers Regulations[20] it is unlikely that in practice there will be need to resort to this doctrine.

In their *Final Report* on these matters the Law Commissions recommended that the non-consumer buyer should no longer be entitled to reject the whole of the goods delivered where the shortfall or excess is so slight that it would be unreasonable to reject the whole. The buyer would remain entitled always to reject any excess; and the consumer buyer would be unaffected by these changes. Accordingly, the 1994 Act[21] inserts s. 30(2A) which provides as follows:

> (2A) A buyer who does not deal as consumer may not—
>   (a) where the seller delivers a quantity of goods less than he contracted to sell, reject the goods under subsection (1) above, or
>   (b) where the seller delivers a quantity of goods larger than he contracted to sell, reject the whole under subsection (2) above,
>
> if the shortfall or, as the case may be, excess is so slight that it would be unreasonable for him to do so.
>
> (2B) It is for the seller to show that a shortfall or excess fell within subsection (2A) above.

This amendment brings the right of rejection for breach of the quantity provisions of the Act into line with the new provisions regarding the right to reject for breach of the

---

15 [1912] 1 KB 574.
16 See also *Arcos Ltd* v *E A Ronaasen* [1933] AC 470, p. 144, below, and *Payne and Routh* v *Lillico & Son* (1920) 36 TLR 569, which was much relied on in *Rapalli* v *K L Take Ltd* [1959] 2 Lloyd's Rep 469, a case of quality rather than quantity.
17 *Margaronis Navigation Agency Ltd* v *Henry W Peabody & Co Ltd* [1965] 1 QB 300. See also below, p. 441, for the effect of the Uniform Customs and Practice for Documentary Credits on the *de minimis* rule in contracts where the price is payable by letter of credit.
18 See *Cehave* v *Bremerhandelsgesellschaft* [1976] QB 44. In that case the right of the buyer to recover damages for breach of warranty arose for breach of an express condition – see above, p. 92.
19 See *Millars of Falkirk* v *Turpie* 1976 SLT (Notes) 66 discussed at p. 187, n. 213, below.
20 SI 2002/3045 reg. 5.
21 See s. 4(2) of the Sale and Supply of Goods Act 1994.

implied terms as to quality and fitness, and it is discussed further in the chapter on the buyer's remedies.[22]

A minor point of some doubt is whether the buyer can accept only a part of what is delivered and reject the rest, except in the one case specifically covered by s. 30(2), that is where an excess is delivered and the buyer proposes simply to keep what should have been delivered. He obviously cannot do this if the delivery conforms to the contract in respect of quantity and quality. But if too much or too little is delivered, it seems that the buyer may accept a distinct part of the goods, rejecting the rest.[23]

A slightly different position was dealt with by s. 30(4) (now repealed) which dealt with the situation where the seller delivered to the buyer the goods he contracted to sell mixed with goods of a different description. It was not clear that s. 30(4) was really needed. The first two subsections of s. 30 deal with the cases where the seller delivers too little and where he delivers too much. Subsection (4) clearly overlapped largely with these two subsections. It is repealed with effect from 3 January 1995.

In the event of a breach of s. 30 by the seller, the buyer is entitled to recover a proportionate part of what he has paid as on a total failure of consideration, notwithstanding that he may have accepted and retained a part of the goods.[24]

Relationship between the seller's duties as to quality and duties as to quantity

The fact that the buyer may be entitled to reject the whole of the goods delivered in the circumstances dealt with by s. 30 means that in substance the seller in such cases is treated under English law as though he commits a breach of condition by delivering the wrong quantity. In this respect the duties of the seller are parallel to those laid down as regards sales by description. Indeed, the whole of s. 30 is merely an application of the duty to deliver goods conforming to the description imposed by s. 13, and it is one of the peculiarities of the drafting of the Act that s. 13 is dealt with under the heading 'Conditions and Warranties', while s. 30 is dealt with under 'Performance of the Contract'.

For a start, the buyer's prima facie right of rejection means that he can always convert a breach of the rules as to quality into a breach of the rules as to quantity. If the seller contracts to deliver 100 tons of wheat of a certain quality and 10 tons are not of that quality so that the buyer rejects them, then the seller will only have effectively delivered 90 tons (and the question will now be whether the shortfall is so slight that it would be unreasonable for the buyer to reject). More generally, though, the rules as to quality and the rules as to quantity are very similar in their effect, even if different in form. In particular, the close resemblance between the duties created by ss. 13 and 30 is brought out all the more when they are examined in detail. In both cases, until the right of rejection was modified by the 1994 Act, the slightest deviation

---

22 Below, p. 499 *et seq.*
23 *Hart v Mills* (1846) 15 M & W 85; *Champion v Short* (1807) 1 Camp 53; and see Hudson (1976) 92 Law QR 506.
24 *Behrend & Co Ltd v Produce Brokers Ltd* [1920] 3 KB 530; *Biggerstaff v Rowlatt's Wharf Ltd* [1896] 2 Ch 93; *Ebrahim Dawood Ltd v Heath Ltd* [1961] 2 Lloyd's Rep 512.

from the terms of the contract was (in effect) a breach of condition entitling the buyer to reject the goods. If the seller delivered goods which failed by the slightest margin to conform to the contract description, or if he delivered a fraction too much or too little, the buyer might reject the whole. The only qualification on this was that if the deviations were 'microscopic',[25] the seller might be able to plead *de minimis*. But this principle was, and presumably will continue to be, applied as rarely in cases of quality as in cases of quantity. In fact, as suggested above, given the new provisions restricting the right of rejection in non-consumer sales, it ought not to be, for the effect of applying it is that there is no breach of warranty at all.[26] So too the former s. 30(4) interrelated with s. 14(2) and (3) because, as will be seen later, the statutory implied terms under those subsections extend to all goods delivered in purported pursuance of the contract.[27]

The same close relationship between the duty to deliver the right quantity and the duty to deliver the right quality will be observed when we consider instalment contracts.[28] Here too, the buyer's right to reject is the same whether the breach consists in short delivery or delivery of the wrong quality.

For these reasons, it is undesirable for the law to distinguish between breaches of ss. 13–15 and breaches of s. 30, and in general the law does not do so. So it seems clearly right that the limitation on the right to reject in non-consumer sales introduced by the 1994 Act should apply equally to breaches of the implied terms as to quality and to breaches of s. 30.[29]

Unfortunately one distinction does now exist. The Unfair Contract Terms Act distinguishes between these two different sorts of breaches. As we shall see in Chapter 14, in consumer sales, that Act renders void any attempt to exclude or limit liability for a breach of ss. 13–15, but only an unreasonable attempt to exclude or limit any other liability. And differences also exist with respect to non-consumer sales which are dealt with further in Chapter 14. In some situations these distinctions will cause trouble because (for instance) of the difficulty of distinguishing between a breach of s. 13 and a breach of s. 30.

25 *Arcos v E A Ronaasen & Son* [1933] AC 470, 480, per Lord Atkin. But in light of the modern cases discussed above, p. 91 *et seq.*, it may be wondered whether this famous decision, though of the highest authority, is not now somewhat suspect. Cf. *Tradax International SA v Goldschmidt SA* [1977] 2 Lloyd's Rep 604. See also below, p. 152.
26 See p. 141 *et seq.* above.
27 See below, p. 173 *et seq.*
28 See s. 31(2) of the Act, discussed later, p. 501 *et seq.*
29 In this respect the Law Commissions' second thoughts were welcome. Compare Final Report, *Sale and Supply of Goods*, para 6.20 with Working Paper No. 85, Consultative Memorandum No. 58, paras 4.59 and 6.28. The Law Commissions still maintained that there was no general reason for treating breaches of duty relating to quality and quantity in the same way. But in view of the new provisions inserted by the 1994 Act, little will remain of the distinction between quality and quantity except the shape of the law and the effect of the Unfair Contract Terms Act – see text above.

13

THE DUTY TO SUPPLY GOODS OF THE RIGHT QUALITY

FROM *CAVEAT EMPTOR* TO *CAVEAT VENDITOR*?

In England, the implied terms as to quality and fitness in ss. 13–15 of the 1893 Act represented an important step in the abandonment of the original common law rule of *caveat emptor*. The common law had itself largely modified the rigours of this rule by 1893, but in several important respects the Act went further than the courts ever did before it was passed. On the other hand, in Scotland the rule until 1856 was that a fair price demanded a fair article, and the seller was therefore bound to provide goods of reasonably good quality.[1] The Mercantile Law Amendment (Scotland) Act 1856 introduced the doctrine of *caveat emptor*, before itself being replaced by the 1893 Act. But weaknesses in the drafting of the original sections gradually became apparent, and there was also growing concern at the freedom permitted to sellers to contract out of their liabilities. The Supply of Goods (Implied Terms) Act 1973 was designed to meet these objections. This Act, largely based on the Law Commissions' recommendations,[2] remodelled ss. 13–15 of the original Act and also contained major new provisions restricting the right of a seller to contract out of the implied terms through use of exclusion clauses. The control of exclusion clauses in contracts was later taken over by the broader provisions of the Unfair Contract Terms Act 1977, which is dealt with in Chapter 14. In the present chapter the discussion will concentrate on the implied terms themselves.[3]

Since the 1973 Act there have been further developments concerning implied terms, and further changes are now likely in the light of the EC's Directive on Certain Aspects of the Sale of Consumer Goods and Associated Guarantees.[4] The first of these developments was the passing of the consolidated Sale of Goods Act 1979 which incorporated the amendments made by the 1973 Act into the rest of the Sale of Goods Act with some trivial verbal alterations, but no changes of substance. The second development was that the statutory implied terms as to quality and fitness were gradually extended to other contracts for the supply of goods as well as contracts of sale. The 1973 Act itself did this for contracts of hire-purchase while the

---

1 See Sutherland 1987 JR 24.
2 See the Law Commissions' Report, *First Report on Exemption Clauses in Contracts* (1969) Law Com. No. 24, Scot Law Com. No. 12 (1968–69) HC 403.
3 (2002) 25 *Journal of Consumer Policy* is focused entirely on the regulation of product quality, and contains much useful material.
4 See p. 299 *et seq.*

Supply of Goods and Services Act 1982 did it for other contracts for the supply of goods.[5] These contracts are not further dealt with here although future authorities on the interpretation of these terms will mostly be relevant across the whole field.

In 1979 – before the new Sale of Goods Act was passed – the Law Commissions were invited by the Lord Chancellor to consider a number of further questions relating to the implied terms in contracts of sale of goods, and to certain related matters such as the remedies available for breach of these terms. After issuing a Working Paper in 1983 which contained many provisional proposals or suggestions for reform,[6] the Law Commissions published their Final Report, *Sale and Supply of Goods*, in 1987.[7] This Report contained yet further proposals for change and as these were accepted in principle by the government, legislative implementation might have been expected. Although there was considerable pressure for this from consumer organizations, many commentators were unhappy with some aspects of the proposals.[8] The Consumer Guarantees Bill 1990 would have implemented the Law Commission's proposals with certain changes. This Bill failed to become law, but the DTI issued a Consultation Document[9] which took the Law Commission's recommendations as a starting point, subject to certain amendments. Finally, in 1994 a Bill was introduced which has now passed into law as the Sale and Supply of Goods Act 1994. The principal changes effected by this Act are to modify the quality warranties, to amend the rules on acceptance and rejection, and to extend the supply of Goods and Services Act 1982 to Scotland (so far as it applies to goods). The changes which are relevant to the quality warranties dealt with in this chapter are to do with the former 'merchantable quality' warranty, and are dealt with below.[10]

The three primary terms laid down in the Act now appear in s. 13, s. 14(2) and s. 14(3), and their combined effect is to give buyers a substantial degree of protection against the risk of the goods proving to have defects of quality or fitness for purpose. Indeed, it is now unrealistic to treat the basic principle of the law as *caveat emptor* rather than *caveat venditor*.

In one sense the three main implied terms in s. 13, s. 14(2) and s. 14(3), taken in that order, lay down a series of graduated duties upon the seller. In the first place, there is the implied term that where goods are sold by description the goods must correspond with their description. This applies in far wider circumstances than those in which the two other terms apply but, on the other hand, it does not afford a great deal of protection to the buyer, especially where the description of the goods is not a detailed one. Obviously, for example, a car may be described as a car, potatoes as potatoes, a reaping machine as a reaping machine, but in all cases the goods may be seriously defective.

---

5 In a county court case the question was raised as to whether a tour operator's liability in respect of food supplied was strict (as it is under s. 4 of the 1982 Act) or to exercise reasonable care and skill (s. 13 of the 1982 Act). It was held the latter, but this is almost certainly incorrect. Liability should be strict in respect of the supply of goods – *Martin v Thomson Tour Operators* Current Law, August 1999 – see p. 9 n. 9 above.

6 Working Paper No. 85, Consultative Memorandum No. 58, *Sale and Supply of Goods*.

7 Law Com. No. 160, Scot Law Com. No. 104, Cm. 137 (1987).

8 See, e.g., Adams and Browsword (1988) 51 MLR 481.

9 *Consumer Guarantees*, DTI Consultation Document 1992.

10 At p. 162 *et seq.*

The next implied term is that the goods must be of satisfactory quality. This does not apply in all the circumstances in which the first term applies but, on the other hand, it affords the buyer a greater degree of protection, because goods that correspond with their description may not be of satisfactory quality. Even this, however, may not suffice to protect the buyer, since goods may correspond with their description and may be of satisfactory quality, and yet they may still be unsuitable for the buyer's purpose. Hence, in still more limited circumstances, the buyer may be able to rely on the third implied term, namely that the goods must be fit for the purpose for which they were sold.

The difficulties of exposition of this part of the law have unfortunately not been greatly reduced by the legislation of 1973–94, though there has been some gain in simplification. As will be seen, the sections frequently overlap in practice, and the same words appear several times in different places. The changes made since the EC Directive on certain aspects of the sale of consumer goods and associated guarantees was implemented by the Sale and Supply of Goods to Consumers Regulations[11] must also be considered, and the effect of the reform of the English privity doctrine by the Contracts (Rights of Third Parties) Act 1999. It is, therefore, impossible to deal with this topic section by section, and it is proposed to deal with it under the following nine heads:

1 Express terms;
2 Implied terms that the goods must correspond with their description;
3 Implied terms that the goods are of satisfactory quality;
4 Implied terms that the goods are fit for a particular purpose;
5 Implied terms in sales by sample;
6 Implied terms annexed by trade usage;
7 Other implied terms;
8 Mistake as to quality;
9 Reform of the English privity doctrine.

Time for compliance

There is at the outset a problem. As we will see,[12] risk generally passes with the property in the goods, so that if goods deteriorate after the property has passed to the buyer, usually the buyer will have no remedy, and *vice versa* if the goods deteriorate before that time. However, it is generally said that it is the duty of the seller to *deliver* goods of the right quality, which may occur *after* the property in them has passed to the buyer. Professor Atiyah suggested the way of resolving this apparent contradiction may be as follows. Delivery can be actual or constructive. When property passes to the buyer before actual delivery, there is a constructive delivery of the goods, and that is the point at which the conformity of the goods with the contract must be judged.[13] Thereafter, the seller is a bailee of the buyer, and the latter must take the risk of

---

11 SI 2002/3045.
12 See p. 353 *et seq.*
13 The editor, Adams, is grateful to his colleague Professor Robert Bradgate for this suggestion.

deterioration, subject to the seller's duties as bailee having been complied with.[14] Although the Act defines 'delivery' as the 'voluntary transfer of possession from one person to the other',[15] this term seems to have reference to Part III of the Act, 'Performance of the Contract', which is clearly dealing with *actual* delivery. Given the criticisms made elsewhere in this book of constructive doctrines, editor Adams thinks an alternative way of reconciling the contradiction is practical. The buyer clearly has the right to inspect the goods, and to reject them if they are defective, and this right will be exercised when the buyer takes physical delivery of the goods. If at that time they are defective, the buyer will have the right to reject them.[16] In most cases it will be difficult for the seller to show, *as a matter of evidence,* that at the time the property passed, the goods were conforming – even if sellers did, as a matter of course, focus their minds on the time of passing of the property.[17] In f.o.b. export sales there will usually be evidence of the state of the goods at the time the risk passed,[18] and thereafter goods are at the buyer's risk, and should be insured by him. But in other sales, there will usually be no evidence as to the state of the goods at the time the property passed.

1. EXPRESS TERMS

Express terms relating to the description, quality and fitness of goods sold are, of course, relatively common in commercial transactions. No doubt they are less common in consumer sales other than in the case technically complex goods such as computers and audio equipment, and goods sold through advertisements placed in news papers or other media. There is no doubt that, apart from the *de minimis* rule, it is still the law that any deviation from an express term, however trifling, is a breach of contract for which the buyer is entitled to some remedy.[19] The modern cases which have inaugurated something of a legal revolution in England by recognition of the concept of an innominate term, neither condition nor warranty,[20] have been concerned solely with the nature of the buyer's remedy, and not with the question whether he has any remedy at all. As we have seen, the position at present is that, in the absence of express provision as to the remedy for breach, an express term of the contract will often be treated as an innominate term, rather than a condition, unless the case is one where certainty is the paramount consideration. If it is an innominate term, breach of that term will not necessarily entitle the buyer to reject the goods and repudiate the contract. Where the nature and consequences of the breach are not of such gravity as to justify repudiation of the whole contract, he will be compelled to accept the goods. But there is no doubt of his right to damages.[21]

---

14 As to the duty of a bailee, see *Palmer on Bailments*, 2nd edn (1991). Presumably, the seller's duties will be those of a gratuitous bailee – see op. cit., p. 504 *et seq*. In Scots law, it is difficult to see how the seller in such circumstances can be treated as a depositary, but it is clear that the buyer does not have the risk of damage or deterioration of the goods attributable to the seller's fault (*Pommer* v *Mowat* (1906) 14 SLT 373; *Knight* v *Wilson* 1949 SLT (Sh Ct) 26 nor does the buyer being owner of the goods preclude a right of rejection for defects (*Kinnear* v *Brodie* (1901) 3F 540).
15 Section 62(1).
16 Unless in the case of commercial buyers, the defects are trivial – see p. 499.
17 Highly unlikely.
18 In the bill of lading bearing a form of words such as 'shipped in apparent good condition'.
19 See, e.g., Roskill LJ in *Cehave* v *Bremer Handelsgesellschaft (The Hansa Nord)* [1976] QB 44, 69–70; Lord Denning, ibid., at 61.
20 See above, p. 91.
21 In Scotland, see *Webster & Co* v *Cramond Iron Co* (1875) 2 R 752, at p. 754 per LP Inglis: 'It is impossible to say that a contract can be broken even in respect of time without the party being entitled to damages.'

On the other hand, the terms as to quality and fitness implied by the Act are all conditions in English law,[22] breach of which under the Act until it was modified by the 1994 Act, justified rejection of the goods, no matter how trifling both in consumer and non-consumer sales. The 1994 Act has modified the right of rejection in non-consumer sales, but it does not eliminate the distinction between conditions and warranties and innominate terms, so it must be expected that there will continue to be occasional difficulties over the need to distinguish between express and implied terms. The legal rules applicable to the two classes of terms will remain different. Although the new restrictions on the buyer's right to reject for slight defects will bring the statutory implied terms closer to innominate express terms, it will not equate the two types of term. In Scotland, however, where there is no distinction between conditions and warranties, breach of the implied terms must be material before rejection is justified, although in consumer contracts breach of any of the implied terms as to description and quality is to be deemed a material breach.

2. IMPLIED TERMS THAT THE GOODS MUST CORRESPOND WITH THEIR DESCRIPTION

Sections 13(1) and (2) are as follows:

(1) Where there is a contract for the sale of goods by description, there is an implied term that the goods correspond with the description.
(2) If the sale is by sample, as well as by description, it is not sufficient that the bulk of the goods corresponds with the sample if the goods do not also correspond with the description.

The relationship between s. 13 and the common law distinction between representations and contractual terms

The first question to be examined here is the effect of s. 13 on the traditional common law distinction between mere representations on the one hand and terms of the contract on the other hand.[23] At first blush it might seem that s. 13 does away with this distinction in the case of a sale by description since the section states that 'there is an implied term that the goods shall correspond with the description'. If the section applied only to those parts of the description which amounted to contractual terms in any event, it would seem to be performing the somewhat odd (and redundant) function of declaring that it is an implied term that the seller must comply with express terms of the contract.

However, despite this oddity, the section does not seem, in legal theory at all events, to obliterate the distinction between mere representations and contractual terms. For instance, in *T & J Harrison v Knowles and Foster*,[24] the sellers sold two ships to the buyers, each of which had been stated in particulars supplied to the buyers to have a deadweight capacity of 460 tons, but no reference was made to this

22 1994 Act Sch. 2 para 5 – this provision does not apply in Scotland.
23 See p. 98 *et seq.*
24 [1918] 1 KB 608.

in the actual memorandum of sale. In fact, the capacity of each ship was only 360 tons. In one sense these ships had been sold by description and the description certainly referred to their capacity. But the Court of Appeal held that the statements about the capacity were merely representations.[25] So also in a very careful judgment in the New Zealand case of *Taylor v Combined Buyers Ltd*[26] – which seems to be the only case in which this question has been explicitly and fully considered – Salmond J held that the section does not affect the traditional distinction between mere representations and terms of the contract. Similarly, in the well-known case of *Oscar Chess Ltd v Willams*,[27] where the seller sold a car which he described as a '1948 Morris', contrary to the facts, it does not seem to have occurred to anybody that the statement could have been treated as part of the description of the car and an action brought under s. 13, unless the buyer could first establish that the statement was a term of the contract and not a mere representation. It could, no doubt, be argued that the sale in this case was not a sale by description but a sale of a specific chattel, but it would certainly be strange if this distinction were to lead to the same statement being held a representation in one case and a condition in another. In the case of *Harlingdon & Leinster Enterprises Ltd v Christopher Hull Fine Art Ltd*[28] it was held that the sale of a painting as a 'Gabriele Münter' (a German expressionist painter) was not a sale by description. In this case it was held that the fact that a description was applied to goods either in the negotiations leading up to a contract, or in the contract itself, did not necessarily make it a sale by description for the purposes of s. 13(1). For the sale to be *by* description, the description had to be influential in the sale so as to become an essential term or condition of the contract. It was possible for a description to become a term of the contract although it was not relied on, but the court had to be able to impute to the parties a common intention that it should be a term of the contract before the sale could be said to be 'by description', and in determining what the intention of the parties was, the absence of reliance on the part of the buyer was a very relevant factor. The plaintiff dealers were specialists in German expressionist paintings, and the defendant dealers were not, and the plaintiffs had inspected the painting. Nourse LJ observed:

> For all practical purposes, I would say that there cannot be a contract for the sale of goods by description where it is not within the reasonable contemplation of the parties that the buyer is relying on the description.[29]

On the other hand, in *Beale v Taylor*,[30] the Court of Appeal appears to have come very close to disregarding the distinction between representations and contractual terms by giving a wide application to s. 13 of the Act. In this case, the defendant advertised his car for sale as a 'Herald, convertible, white, 1961' and it was bought by the plaintiff after examination. In fact, the car was made of two parts which had been

---

25 Cf. *Howard Marine & Dredging Co v Ogden (Excavations) Ltd* [1978] QB 574, where on similar facts, damages were awarded under s. 2(1) of the Misrepresentation Act 1967.
26 [1924] NZLR 627.
27 [1957] 1 WLR 370.
28 [1991] 1 QB 564.
29 At p. 574.
30 [1967] 1 WLR 1193. See also *Fordy v Harwood* 30 March 1999 (unreported).

welded together, only one of which was from a 1961 model. Although the facts bore some resemblance to those in *T & J Harrison* v *Knowles and Foster* (which was not cited), the Court of Appeal here held that the words '1961 Herald' were part of the contractual description. If this case illustrates the modern trend, it seems to suggest that, whatever the legal theory of the matter may be, in practice s. 13 makes it easier for a buyer to argue that a descriptive statement by a seller is a contractual term and not a mere representation. Although the seller in *Beale* v *Taylor* was a private and not a trade seller, so that the sale was not a consumer sale as now understood, or as defined in the Unfair Contract Terms Act,[31] the decision may well reflect a modern trend to hold that statements about the goods by sellers are to be treated as contractual terms rather than mere representations, particularly where the buyer was reasonable in relying on the statement.[32] After all, the seller in *Beale* v *Taylor* presumably obtained a price well above the fair value of the vehicle. In the *Oscar Chess* case, by way of contrast, the decisive fact may have been that the buyer, a garage, was not reasonable – or had no right – to rely on what the seller, a private person, had said.[33]

However, although this question remains tantalizingly undiscussed in the cases, it seems reasonably clear from some House of Lords decisions, and the case of *Harlingdon & Leinster Enterprises Ltd* v *Christopher Hull Fine Art Ltd*[34] that s. 13 of the Act does not automatically convert any or all descriptive words into conditions, or even terms. Some descriptive words may be inserted in the contract without having any legal force at all. For example, in the *Reardon Smith Lines* case[35] where the shipbuilders contracted to build a vessel to a certain specification at Yard No. 354 at Osaka Zosen, and the ship was in fact built at another yard, it was held that these words had no legal significance at all. They were of no substantial importance to the parties who were not concerned with where the ship was built (though it might of course have been different if that particular yard had a particular reputation among shipowners and shipbuilders); the important descriptive words were in the specification, and that specification had to be complied with. Since the words in this case described the yard where the ship was to be built and there was no suggestion that the shipbuilders had not intended to build the ship there, these words could not even have amounted to a misrepresentation. In other cases, however, descriptive words which fail to amount to an implied condition under s. 13 may simply be a misrepresentation, and may give the representee the usual remedies available for a misrepresentation.

In the *Reardon Smith Lines* case (which did not involve a contract of sale)[36] and again in *Ashington Piggeries* v *Christopher Hill Ltd* (which did),[37] the House of Lords

---

31 Below, p. 236.
32 See *Fordy* v *Harwood* 30 March 1999 (unreported).
33 In previous editions it was suggested that this was contrary to the orthodox view which holds that a statement is a contractual term if this is the intention of the parties, and that Australian cases seem to follow this orthodoxy more frequently than English ones – see, e.g., *J J Savage & Sons* v *Blakeney* (1970) 119 CLR 435. This may be true of Australian cases, but so far as the English courts are concerned, *Oscar Chess* seems to be in line with orthodox thinking – see *Harlingdon & Leinster Enterprises Ltd* v *Christopher Hull Fine Art Ltd*, n. 28 above.
34 See n. 28 above.
35 [1976] 1 WLR 989, above, p. 93.
36 For the reasons given at p. 93.
37 [1972] AC 441.

discussed another question, closely related to the one above, namely whether compliance of the goods with all parts of a description is required by the implied term in s. 13, or whether parts of the description can be treated as giving rise to liability by way of a warranty or innominate term. In both cases it seems to have been taken for granted that not all descriptive words automatically fall within s. 13; the discussion in the two cases centred round the proper test for determining which parts of the descriptive words fall within s. 13 and which do not. As regards any other words, it was stated explicitly (for example by Lord Diplock)[38] that these might still give rise to a warranty (or, it can be added, an innominate or intermediate term). It thus seems established that s. 13 does not override the traditional distinctions which need to be drawn between (a) descriptive words which are words of contractual obligation and those which are mere representations, or even without any legal effect, and also between (b) descriptive words which are words giving rise to liability by way of condition, on the one hand, or by way of warranty or innominate or intermediate term, on the other.[39]

The next question concerns the test by which it can be decided what words of description do fall within s. 13 and thereby give rise to liability if the description is not complied with. In this connection, some of the case law has adopted a tendency to overlook the above distinctions and treat all descriptive words as though they must create liability under s. 13. For example, in *Arcos Ltd* v *E A Ronaasen & Son*,[40] the buyers agreed to buy a quantity of staves which they required, as the sellers knew, for making cement barrels. The contract stated that the staves were to be half an inch thick. In fact, only about 5 per cent conformed to this requirement, but a large proportion was over half an inch, but not more than ⁹⁄₁₀ of an inch; some were larger than this but less than ⅝ inch; and a very small proportion was larger than that. It was found as a fact that the goods 'were commercially within and merchantable under the contract specification', and also that they were reasonably fit for the purpose for which they were sold. Despite these findings it was held by the House of Lords that the buyers were entitled to reject the goods for breach of s. 13.[41] Lord Atkin said:[42]

> It was contended that in all commercial contracts the question was whether there was a 'substantial' compliance with the contract: there must always be some margin: and it is for the tribunal of fact to determine whether the margin is exceeded or not. I cannot agree. If the written contract specifies conditions of weight, measurement and the like, those conditions must be complied with. A ton does not mean about a ton, or a yard about a yard. Still less when you descend to minute measurements does ½ inch mean about ½ inch. If the seller wants a margin he must and in my experience does stipulate for it . . .
>
> No doubt there may be microscopic deviations which business men and therefore lawyers will ignore . . . But apart from this consideration the right view is that the conditions of the contract must be strictly performed. If a condition is not performed the buyer has a right to reject.

---

38 [1972] AC 441 at p. 503.

39 It is surprising that in the *Reardon Smith Lines* case the leading speech of Lord Wilberforce makes no reference to the *Ashington Piggeries* case (which, indeed, seems not to have been cited, somewhat astonishingly) and his words are a trifle hesitant on this last point. But if his opinion is taken together with the speeches in the *Ashington Piggeries* case, it does seem clear that the proposition stated in the text has the support of the House of Lords.

40 [1933] AC 470. See also *Rapalli* v *K L Take* [1958] 2 Lloyd's Rep 469, a very similar case.

41 The right to reject in such a case is now modified by s. 15A inserted by the 1994 Act – see below, p. 499 *et seq.*

42 [1933] AC 470, 479–80.

Perhaps the most extreme case was *Re Moore & Co Ltd and Landauer & Co Ltd*[43] where buyers agreed to buy 3,000 tins of Australian canned fruit packed in cases of 30 tins. When the goods were delivered, it was found that about half the cases contained only 24 tins, although the correct total quantity was delivered altogether. The arbitrator found that there was no difference in value between tins packed 30 to a case and those packed 24 to a case, but despite this finding it was held by the Court of Appeal that the buyers were entitled to reject the whole consignment on the ground that there had been a breach of s. 13.[44] In the *Reardon Smith Lines* case, Lord Wilberforce (speaking for a majority of the House of Lords) expressed serious doubts as to the correctness of this decision, which he found 'excessively technical'.[45]

In the *Ashington Piggeries* case, and again in the *Reardon Smith Lines* case, the House of Lords seems to have accepted that the only descriptive words which are to be treated as the subject of s. 13 are words which identify the subject-matter of the contract. For example, in the *Ashington Piggeries* case, Lord Diplock said:[46]

> The 'description' by which unascertained goods are sold is, in my view, confined to those words in the contract which were intended by the parties to identify the kind of goods which were to be supplied. It is open to the parties to use a description as broad or as narrow as they choose. But ultimately the test is whether the buyer could fairly and reasonably refuse to accept the physical goods proffered to him on the ground that their failure to correspond with what was said about them makes them goods of a different kind from those he had agreed to buy. The key to s. 13 is identification.

The concept of words of identification is, however, more troublesome than seems to be implied. In the *Reardon Smith Lines* case it was argued for the appellants that the words in the contract requiring the ship to be built at the particular yard specified were words of identification, because it was only with the aid of these words that it was possible to identify the vessel being built at a particular yard with the vessel contemplated under the contract. This argument was rejected by the House of Lords, and Lord Wilberforce pointed out that there are two different meanings to the idea of words of 'identity' or 'identification'. It is only words whose purpose is to state or identify an essential part of the description of the goods which are words of identity in this special sense, and so attract the implied condition in s. 13. Words which merely identify the goods in the sense of pointing out where they can be found are not words of identity in this special sense. Lord Wilberforce also expressed dissatisfaction, as already noted, with the excessive technicality of some of the cases under s. 13 such as *Re Moore and Co Ltd and Landauer*,[47] and indicated that it would be better if s. 13 were confined to descriptive words which constitute a 'substantial ingredient of the "identity" of the thing sold', other words being left to give rise to liability for breach of warranty or of an intermediate or

---

43 [1921] 2 KB 519.

44 See, however, below, p. 499 *et seq.* for changes effected by the 1994 Act on the right of rejection.

45 For a defence of these decisions see Sealy and Hooley, *Commercial Law, Text, Cases and Materials*, 3rd edn, Butterworths, 2003, p. 378–9.

46 [1972] AC at pp. 503–4.

47 [1921] 1 KB 519.

innominate term. He added, however, that a different view might still be taken of contracts for the sale of unascertained future goods (for example, commodities – and he probably had *Arcos* v *E A Ronaasen* particularly in mind) where each detail of the description must be assumed to be vital.

These words of Lord Wilberforce concerning the concept of words of identification are very important. Not only do they rule out the application of s. 13 to words which merely point out the goods being sold while not actually constituting a substantial ingredient of the goods, but they also help to explain why even on a sale of specific goods, it is possible to hold that the sale is a sale by description and the descriptive words do fall within s. 13. As will be seen later it is well established that prima facie the sale of consumer manufactured goods should be treated as a sale by description if the goods are sold not as specific things, but as things answering a general description. For example, if a consumer buys a suit of clothing in a shop, and the suit is labelled 'pure wool', it seems clear that this is a sale by description, and that the words on the label are part of the contractual description. If the suit is not pure wool, there will be a clear breach of s. 13 and a buyer who deals as consumer will be entitled to reject the goods.[48] Yet it will be seen that in such a case the words cannot be said to be words of identification in the sense that they are needed to point out which are the goods which are the subject-matter of the contract. In a sale of specific goods like this, there will be no need to identify the goods in that sense: the identity of the goods is clear. But the words on the label are still plainly enough words of identification in the other sense mentioned by Lord Wilberforce – they identify a substantial ingredient of the goods. They are, in short, words which identify, not which goods are being sold, but what the goods actually are (a woollen suit, not just any suit). The actual decision in *Beale* v *Taylor*[49] could also be supported in this manner, assuming that the words in that case were indeed contractual and not just representational. The words in the advertisement, '1961 Herald', were not needed to identify which car was the subject of the sale, but they were identifying what the car was (a 1961 Herald, not just any Herald).

There are, however, a few cases, pre-dating the *Ashington Piggeries* case and the *Reardon Smith Lines* case, in which s. 13 has been applied to words which, even if they could be called words of description at all, do not appear to be words which identify a substantial (or indeed any) ingredient of the goods sold. For example, it has been held that words about the way in which the goods are packed, or even marked, may be words of description under s. 13 of the Act.[50] So also, it has been held that words describing where the goods are situated ('Afloat per *SS Morton Bay*, due London approximately June 8th') are descriptive words within the protection of s. 13.[51] Although this last case was cited without disapproval by Lord Guest in *Ashington Piggeries*, it is hard to reconcile it with Lord Wilberforce's more subtle analysis of the concept of words of identification in *Reardon Smith Lines*. The authority of decisions of this character is today somewhat doubtful.

---

48 It is assumed that, in the case of descriptive words in a consumer sale such as this, it is almost unthinkable that the words could be held to be mere representations, and not terms at all.
49 [1967] 1 WLR 1193, above, p. 150.
50 *Smith Brothers (Hull) Ltd* v *Gosta Jacobson & Co* [1961] 2 Lloyd's Rep 522.
51 *Macpherson Train & Co* v *Howard Ross & Co* [1955] 1 WLR 640.

The upshot of all this is of some complexity. It seems that the position can be summarized as follows:

1   Descriptive words must first be analysed to see whether they are contractual, or merely amount to representations. If they are misrepresentations only, then the normal common law and equitable rules apply, as modified by the Misrepresentation Act 1967 and the Law Reform (Miscellaneous Provisions) (Scotland) Act 1985 s. 10.
2   If the words are held to be contractual, it must next be seen whether there is an express term requiring compliance with the words of description. In England and Wales, such a term may be a condition or a warranty, but is most likely to be an innominate term, as in the *Cehave* case. The buyer's remedies for breach of such a term depend on the nature and consequences of the breach. In Scotland, likewise, it will be a question of the materiality of the breach.
3   If there is nothing amounting to an express term, then the next stage is to see whether the description relates to unascertained future goods like commodities. In this event (as in the *Arcos* case) the term is a condition in English law, and strict compliance is required, though a non-consumer buyer's right to reject is now modified by s. 15A inserted by the 1994 Act. In Scots law, however, materiality of breach remains the touchstone.
4   If the contract is of a different character, it must next be inquired whether any item in the description of the goods amounts to a 'substantial ingredient' in the identity of the thing sold. If it does, compliance with the item will again be a condition in English law, but a matter of the materiality of the breach in Scots law.
5   In any other case, the requirement of compliance with descriptive words is not a condition, but a bare warranty or (more probably) an intermediate or innominate term in English law; while Scots law will still operate on the basis of whether or not the breach is material.

English law as opposed to Scottish law may seem complicated, but both systems do at least avoid putting the court into a straitjacket. The courts will in effect be able to arrive at whatever decision seems appropriate in the circumstances. It will be noticed that s. 13 itself seems to have been largely forgotten in this discussion. It is almost impossible to reconcile the law as stated by Lord Wilberforce in the *Reardon Smith Lines* case with the precise words of the Act. It appears thus that s. 13 needs revision, if not outright repeal. Indeed, it is not clear that s. 13 actually does anything at all, since all it seems to say, as now interpreted, is that where the seller uses words of description which would otherwise amount to a condition, then it is an implied condition that the goods should comply with that description. This hardly seems worth saying, although, of course, in a true codification propositions may be stated which are not designed in any sense to alter the law. It is perhaps unfortunate that s. 13 appears to have been outside the terms of reference of the Law Commissions' inquiry which led to the 1994 Act.

Prior to the passing of the 1973 Act, it was important to consider the relation between s. 13 and the doctrine of the fundamental term or fundamental breach. This question is now of very little importance because the Unfair Contract Terms Act 1977 greatly restricts the power of a seller to contract out of his liability under s. 13 and the doctrine of the fundamental term and fundamental breach has essentially been killed off by *Photo Production Ltd* v *Securicor Transport Ltd*.[52] Under ss. 6 and 20 of that Act, there can be no contracting out of s. 13 at all against a person dealing as consumer.[53] In a non-consumer sale, contracting out of s. 13 is only permissible to the extent that it is 'fair and reasonable'. For example, the breach in *Arcos Ltd* v *E A Ronaasen & Son*[54] would seem on the face of it to have been one of trivial significance; and if the contract in that case had contained an exemption clause, it would have been most unreasonable to hold the seller liable for the breaches which occurred. Rules of construction, formerly widely applied to limit the operation of exemption clauses, will now be of much less importance, though doubtless they may still be used.[55] For instance, in *Robert A Munro & Co Ltd* v *Meyer*,[56] the defendant agreed to buy goods 'with all faults', but it was nonetheless held by Wright J that this clause did not shut out the overriding requirement that the goods should answer to their description, but only served to protect the sellers from the obligation to supply merchantable goods.[57] But insofar as the requirements of satisfactory (or formerly merchantable[58]) quality overlap with those regarding the description of the goods, it seems that a clause which validly excludes the condition that goods be of satisfactory quality (merchantable) must also protect against non-conformity with description.[59]

Meaning of 'sale by description'

The next question concerns the meaning of the phrase 'sale by description'. In the first place, it has been held that this phrase 'must apply to all cases where the purchaser has not seen the goods but is relying on the description alone'.[60] Hence it follows that a sale must be by description if it is of future or unascertained goods.[61] But, in addition, the term applies in many cases even where the buyer has seen the goods. Early doubts as to whether an ordinary sale in a shop could be a sale by description were soon set at rest.[62] To quote from Lord Wright in *Grant* v *Australian Knitting Mills Ltd*:

> It may also be pointed out that there is a sale by description even though the buyer is buying something displayed before him on the counter: a thing is sold by description, though it is specific, so long as it is sold not merely as the specific thing, but as a thing corresponding to a description, e.g. woollen undergarments, a hot-water bottle, a second-hand reaping machine, to select a few obvious illustrations.[63]

---

52 [1980] AC 827. The doctrine never applied in Scotland: see *Alexander Stephen (Forth) Ltd* v *J J Riley (UK) Ltd* 1976 SC 151. See now Unfair Contract Terms Act 1977 s. 22.
53 See p. 236 as to this term.
54 [1933] AC 470.
55 Though in *Fastframe Ltd* v *Lohinski* 3 March 1993 (unreported), the Court of Appeal indicated that it was not prepared to countenance arguments based on the old (artificial) rules of construction – see Adams (1994) 57 MLR 960.
56 [1930] 2 KB 312.
57 Cf. also *Pinnock Bros* v *Lewis & Peat Ltd* [1923] 1 KB 690; *Vigers Bros* v *Sanderson Bros* [1901] 1 KB 608.
58 In the case of contracts made before 3 January 1995.
59 *Toepfer* v *Continental Grain Co Ltd* [1974] 1 Lloyd's Rep 11; *Gill & Duffus SA* v *Berger & Co Inc* [1983] 1 Lloyd's Rep 622, reversed on different grounds, [1984] AC 382.
60 *Varley* v *Whipp* [1900] 1 QB 513, 516 per Channel J.
61 *Joseph Travers & Sons Ltd* v *Longel Ltd* (1947) TLR 150, 153 per Sellers J.
62 *Morelli* v *Fitch & Gibbons* [1928] 2 KB 636.
63 [1936] AC 85, 100. These are 'obvious illustrations' to a lawyer, because they are drawn from decided cases; otherwise the selection may have, for the reader, a somewhat surreal quality.

One could add to this list beer sold in a public house,[64] though this is perhaps a less obvious illustration. Moreover, it has now been made clear by s. 13(3) that the term 'sale by description' is wide enough to cover a sale even where the goods have been exposed for sale and selected by the buyer, as in a supermarket or department store:

A sale of goods is not prevented from being a sale by description by reason only that, the goods being exposed for sale or hire, are selected by the buyer.

Even prior to the 1973 Act amendments it had been held that a sale could be by description though the buyer had examined the goods with care,[65] or even where he had himself selected them from stock offered to him by the seller.[66] But a sale is not by description where the buyer makes it clear that he is buying a particular thing because of its unique qualities, and that no other will do, or where there is absolutely no reliance by the buyer on the description.[67] In fact, it is probably true to say that the *only* case of a sale not being by description occurs where the buyer makes it clear that he is buying a particular thing because of its unique qualities, and that no other will do.[68]

For this reason the sale of a manufactured item will nearly always be a sale by description (except where it is second-hand) because articles made to an identical design are not generally bought as unique goods but as goods corresponding to that design. So it has even been held in Australia that the sale of an ordinary pair of 'walking shoes' was a sale by description, although the buyer had tried on and examined the shoes and might well have been thought to be buying the particular pair as specific goods.[69] As we have seen, even the purchase of a second-hand car which was fully examined by the buyer was held in *Beale* v *Taylor*[70] to be a sale by description because the buyer had relied in part on a newspaper advertisement issued by the seller.

These cases suggest that the real question at issue in deciding whether the sale should be classified as a sale by description is whether, on the true construction of the contract, the buyer has agreed to buy a specific item exactly as it stands to the exclusion of all liability on the part of the seller. For example, the buyer may examine a second-hand car and the seller may offer it for sale in terms which amount to saying: 'There is the car; there is my offer; I guarantee nothing; take it or leave it.' In this event it is thought the sale would be held to be a sale of a specific thing and not a sale by description.

One of the consequences of the 1893 Act was that if the sale was held to be a sale by description there would often be an implied condition under s. 14 that the goods were merchantable. This consequence of holding a sale to be by description was so important that it seems that the courts in practice tended to interpret s. 13 with half an eye to s. 14. In other words, if the court thought that on the true construction of

---

64 *Wren* v *Holt* [1903] 1 KB 610.
65 *Beale* v *Taylor* [1967] 1 WLR 1193.
66 *H Beecham & Co Pty Ltd* v *Francis Howard & Co Pty Ltd* [1921] VLR 428.
67 *Harlingdon & Leinster Ltd* v *Christopher Hull Fine Art Ltd* [1991] 1 QB 564.
68 Ibid.
69 *David Jones Ltd* v *Willis* (1934) 52 CLR 110.
70 Above, n. 30.

the contract the seller should be held to warrant the merchantability of the goods, it would tend to hold the sale to be a sale by description; but after the 1973 Act the condition of merchantability was not limited to sales by description, and in previous editions it was suggested that this might possibly lead to a tendency to a narrower construction of s. 13 in the future. Although the merchantable quality warranty has been replaced by the 1994 Act, this observation still remains apposite in relation to the new section.

The application of s. 13

It is to be noted that s. 13 (unlike s. 14) applies even though the goods are not sold by a person who sells 'in the course of a business'. Thus in *Varley* v *Whipp*,[71] the defendant agreed to buy from the plaintiff a second-hand reaping machine, which was stated to have been new the previous year and hardly used at all. This was a gross misdescription, and the defendant declined to accept it or pay for it. The defendant could not rely on s. 14 (which imposes requirements as to quality and fitness for purpose) because the plaintiff was not a dealer in agricultural machinery, but as the goods did not correspond with the description it was held that there was a breach of s. 13. (Changes made by later legislation are immaterial to this point.)

The relationship between the description and the quality or fitness of the goods

As we shall see later, s. 14 deals with implied conditions as to the quality and fitness of the goods for a particular purpose. Section 13 does not on the face of it deal with quality or fitness for purpose. As we have seen from *Arcos Ltd* v *E A Ronaasen & Son*,[72] it is quite possible for goods to be of satisfactory (formerly merchantable) quality and fit for their purpose and yet not correspond with their description.

Conversely, if the goods do correspond with their description the fact that they are unsatisfactory or not fit for the purpose for which they are sold will not enable the buyer to plead a breach of s. 13. In this event he will frequently be able to rely on s. 14(2) or (3), but there are some circumstances in which a buyer may wish to use s. 13 rather than s. 14 even though his complaint may in a broad sense be said to be one of quality. First, as seen above, s. 13 applies to a sale by a private seller while s. 14 only applies to a seller who sells in the course of a business. So a person who buys from a non-business seller can only complain about quality if he can bring his case under s. 13. This explains a case like *Beale* v *Taylor*[73] where the buyer of the car obtained damages for breach of the condition implied by s. 13 – the car was wrongly described as a 1961 Herald. If the buyer had been buying from a business seller, he would probably have had a clear case for damages under s. 14 on the ground that the vehicle was not of merchantable quality (the relevant quality warranty at the time).

71 [1900] 1 QB 513. Note also *Beale* v *Taylor*, above, n. 30 (private sale of second-hand car).
72 [1933] AC 470.
73 Above, n. 30.

But secondly, the buyer may wish to rely on s. 13 because the goods are in fact of satisfactory quality in a general sense, but still do not amount to the goods he thought he was buying. In the hypothetical example given earlier, a person who buys a suit described as 'pure wool' may very well want to return it if he discovers it is not pure wool, even though it may be perfectly satisfactory, and of good quality. But he can only do that under s. 13 because there would be no breach of s. 14 on these facts.

A third type of case in which a buyer might wish to rely upon s. 13, even though his complaint is in a broad sense about quality, occurs where the contract contains a clause excluding liability for matters of quality, but not for matters of description – something which could still happen despite the Unfair Contract Terms Act.

Particular problems often arise where goods are described in general terms, but some extraneous substance is included with the goods, which does not alter the general nature of the goods but significantly affects their utility. The point is illustrated by the decision of the House of Lords in *Ashington Piggeries Ltd v Christopher Hill Ltd*[74] where herring meal contaminated with a substance which made it unsuitable for feeding to mink was sold to the buyers for use as mink food. It was held that there was no breach of s. 13 because the goods were still properly described as 'herring meal',[75] and it was pointed out that not every statement about the quality or fitness of the goods can be treated as a part of the 'description'.

On the other hand, in *Pinnock Bros v Lewis and Peat Ltd*[76] the contract was for the sale of copra cake but the goods delivered were in fact an admixture of copra cake and castor beans; it was held that the goods did not correspond with their description. As Lord Wilberforce pointed out in *Ashington Piggeries*, the question whether a substance which has added to it some extraneous material, or is contaminated by the presence of some chemical, remains in substance what it always was, though with the addition or contamination, or whether it really becomes a different substance altogether, 'may, if pressed to analysis, be a question of an Aristotelian character'. But he went on to say that the Sale of Goods Act was not intended to provoke metaphysical discussions as to the nature of what was delivered as compared with what was sold. The question whether the goods correspond with their description is intended to be a broader, more commonsense, test of a mercantile character. The question whether that is what the buyer bargained for has to be answered according to such tests as men in the market would apply, leaving more delicate questions of condition, or quality, to be determined under other clauses of the contract or sections of the Act.[77]

So where there was a contract for the sale of 500 tons of Argentina Bolita beans but the goods delivered contained a small proportion of other beans, the court referred the case back to arbitrators to find whether the goods as a whole would still be called by businessmen in the trade 'Argentina Bolita beans'.[78]

---

74 [1972] AC 441.
75 Lord Dilhorne dissented on this point – see ibid., pp. 484–5.
76 [1923] 1 KB 690.
77 [1972] AC 441, 489.
78 *Gill & Duffus* v *Berger & Co Inc* [1981] 2 Lloyd's Rep 233, and, after the resubmission, [1983] 1 Lloyd's Rep 622, reversed on different grounds [1984] AC 382.

In some cases the description may carry with it an implication of quality of a certain kind. For instance, in the New Zealand case of *Cotter* v *Luckie*[79] the buyer bought a bull described as 'a pure bred polled Angus bull' from the seller. The bull had been wanted, as the seller knew, for breeding purposes, but it turned out to have a physical abnormality which prevented it from breeding. The court held that the sale was a sale by description and that the description implied that the bull was capable of breeding. The court said:

> The question . . . for decision is whether this was or was not a sale by a description having the effect of describing the animal as a stud bull. Both parties are farmers. The respondent could have no use for the animal save for the purpose of serving his cows, and it is to be observed that it was sold not as a bull merely, but as a pure-bred polled Angus bull. The descriptive words appear to me to be meaningless unless intended to convey the impression that the animal might be used to get this class of stock.[80]

There is another type of case which may involve the relation between s. 13 and the quality or fitness of the goods. If the contract calls for goods of a certain quality, this quality may itself become part of the contract description, but it seems that statements as to quality will not usually be treated as part of the contract description.[81] On the other hand, there are some cases in which quality and description significantly overlap. To take an example once given by Lord Denning, if the goods being sold are said to be 'new-laid eggs' this goes both to quality and description.[82] However, for most purposes such cases give rise to no special problems. Breach by the seller will normally involve liability under ss. 13 and 14, and the overlap is of no particular importance. It would only be of importance where the implied condition under s. 14 is not applicable for some reason (for example, where the seller is not a dealer) and the buyer has to rely exclusively on s. 13. He may then wish to argue that the term 'new-laid eggs' implies not merely that the eggs are literally new-laid, but that they are of good quality, because that is the natural implication of the term. Conversely, if the buyer cannot complain about the quality (for example, because of a valid exclusion clause) he is not entitled to raise the same complaint under the guise of a failure to conform to description.[83]

Compliance with s. 13

Whether goods correspond with their description will normally be a simple question of fact, but it is to be stressed that the duty of the seller is very strict indeed. We have already referred to *Arcos Ltd* v *E A Ronaasen & Son* as an illustration of the extreme severity of the duties which the section can place on the seller. Although some of these older cases are (as we have seen) suspect insofar as they hold trivial breaches to be

---

79   [1918] NZLR 811.
80   At p. 813. See also some of the examples discussed by the CA in *Ashington Piggeries* [1969] 3 All ER 1496, 1512, such as the description of goods as 'oysters' which may carry the implication that they are fit for human consumption.
81   See the *Ashington Piggeries* case [1972] AC 441 and *Border Harvesters Ltd* v *Edwards Engineering (Perth) Ltd* 1985 SLT 128.
82   *Toepfer* v *Continental Grain Co Ltd* [1974] 1 Lloyd's Rep 11, 13. The common description 'free range eggs' might be a more pertinent example.
83   See the *Toepfer* case, above, n. 82, and also *Gill & Duffus SA* v *Berger & Co Inc* [1983] 1 Lloyd's Rep 622, reversed on different grounds [1984] AC 382.

breaches of conditions, that does not affect their authority as to what is a breach. It is still quite clearly the law that any non-conformity with the contract description (so long as it is a part of the description which constitutes a term of the contract[84]) is a breach of contract, subject only to the *de minimis* principle.

Reference has already been made to the fact that 'microscopic' deviations may be disregarded in relation to the quantity of goods delivered, in accordance with the maxim *de minimis*, and there seems no reason to doubt that the same is true of compliance with the contract description.[85] However, in *Moralice (London) Ltd v E D & F Man*,[86] McNair J held that where the price is payable by means of a documentary credit against shipping documents, the maxim *de minimis* has no application as between the seller and the bank: the shipping documents must comply strictly with the requirements of the letter of credit.[87] McNair J went on to suggest that in this situation it is probably a necessary inference that the *de minimis* maxim is also excluded even in the contract of sale as between buyer and seller.

In a number of more recent cases *Arcos Ltd v E A Ronaasen & Son* has been distinguished by the courts. Where goods have been sold in some such terms as 'fair average quality' or the like, it has been held that this phrase must be construed as businessmen would construe it and as referring only to such qualities as are normally observable by ordinary visual examination. Thus goods contaminated by some undetectable substance could still be of 'fair average quality'. Similarly, in *Steel & Busks Ltd v Bleecker Bik & Co Ltd*[88] it was held that goods accorded with their description – which was 'quality as previously delivered' – despite the presence of some new chemical, not present in the original deliveries, which rendered the goods unfit for the buyers' purposes. Sellers J found that 'by the standard applied and accepted in the trade they complied with the description and were of the quality called for by the contract, quality not being affected by the chemical'. This decision was approved by the House of Lords in the *Ashington Piggeries*[89] case on the ground that statements of this kind are not intended to be treated as part of the contract description of the goods. They are intended to indicate the quality desired, but not to identify the goods which the contract calls for. But this does not mean that the buyer is without remedy, for he may be able to claim damages under s. 14(2) or (3).

But if the statement is part of the contract description it must be strictly complied with, though it does not follow that a description must always be taken literally. If goods have acquired a trade description they may correspond to their description even if they are not what a literal reading of the trade description suggests they are. As Darling J said in *Lemy v Watson*,[90] 'If anybody ordered Bombay ducks and somebody

---

84 See the discussion of this point, above, p. 149 *et seq.*
85 *Arcos Ltd v E A Ronaasen & Son* [1933] AC 470, see above; *Margaronis Navigation Agency Ltd v Henry W Peabody & Co Ltd* [1965] QB 300; *Tradax International SA v Goldschmidt SA* [1977] 2 Lloyd's Rep 604.
86 [1954] 2 Lloyd's Rep 526; see also *Soproma SpA v Marine & Animal By-Products Corpn* [1966] 1 Lloyd's Rep 367, 390.
87 But in practice this kind of problem would in most cases now fall under the *Uniform Customs and Practice for Documentary Credits*, which has a built-in version of *de minimis*, less strict than the common law version – see below, p. 441.
88 [1956] 1 Lloyd's Rep 228; *F E Hookway & Co Ltd v Alfred Isaacs & Sons Ltd* [1954] 1 Lloyd's Rep 491.
89 [1972] AC 441, 471, 514.
90 [1915] 3 KB 731, 752.

supplied him with ducks from Bombay the contract to supply Bombay ducks would not be fulfilled.'[91] Usually this approach would be adopted to protect a buyer but it may sometimes protect the seller. In *Grenfell* v *E B Meyrowitz Ltd*,[92] the defendants were held not to be in breach of s. 13 when they supplied goggles of 'safety-glass' to the plaintiff which subsequently splintered in an accident, as it was proved that 'safety-glass' had acquired a technical trade meaning and the goggles in fact conformed to the normal design.[93] Similarly in *Peter Darlington Partners Ltd* v *Gosho Co Ltd*,[94] there was a contract for the sale of 50 tons of canary seed on a 'pure basis'. It was shown that there was no such thing in the trade as 100 per cent pure seed, and that the highest standard of purity was 98 per cent, and it was therefore held that the buyers were in breach in refusing to accept 98 per cent pure seed.

Knowledge by the buyer and contracting-out

It is, perhaps, slightly odd that s. 13 says nothing about the possibility that the buyer may examine the goods and come to realize that the description is not entirely accurate, or perhaps that he should have realized this. As we shall see later,[95] there are now severe limits on the extent to which a seller can contract out of liability under s. 13, so this possibility cannot be dealt with by holding that the implied condition is excluded by a contrary intention where the buyer knows that the description is inaccurate. Nevertheless, it would be very odd to hold that the seller is liable for a breach of s. 13 in such a case, and it must be expected that the courts would strive to avoid such a result, for instance by holding that the sale is not by description.[96]

3. IMPLIED TERMS THAT THE GOODS ARE OF SATISFACTORY QUALITY

There are two distinct cases where the Act implies a term that the goods supplied are of satisfactory quality, namely s. 14(2) and s. 15(2). These are as follows:

14. (2) Where the seller sells goods in the course of a business, there is an implied term that the goods supplied under the contract are of satisfactory quality.

    (2A) For the purposes of this Act, goods are of satisfactory quality if they meet the standard that a reasonable person would regard as satisfactory, taking account of any description of the goods, the price (if relevant) and all the other relevant circumstances.

---

91 The point of the dictum may be lost unless the reader is aware that a Bombay duck is in fact a small fish, the bumalo, usually eaten dried, and which does not come from Bombay.

92 [1936] 2 All ER 1313. As to the meaning in the motor trade of a 'new' car, see *Morris Motors Ltd* v *Lilley* [1959] 1 WLR 1184; *R* v *Ford Motor Co* [1974] 1 WLR 1220.

93 But this decision seems out of tune with the modern trend towards consumer protection; although trade terms may be allowed a technical meaning between businessmen, it is not so clear today that a consumer would be held bound by such a meaning unless he knew of it. Under the Trade Descriptions Act it is an offence to apply a false or misleading trade description to goods, and there would clearly be a breach of the Act if the facts of this case occurred today.

94 [1964] 1 Lloyd's Rep 149.

95 See p. 234 *et seq.*

96 See p. 149 *et seq.* and especially *Harlingdon & Leinster Ltd* v *Christopher Hull Fine Art Ltd* [1991] 1 QB 564.

(2B) For the purposes of this Act, the quality of goods includes their state and condition and the following (among other things) are in appropriate cases aspects of the quality of goods—
  (a) fitness for all the purposes for which goods of the kind in question are commonly supplied,
  (b) appearance and finish,
  (c) freedom from minor defects,
  (d) safety, and
  (e) durability.

(2C) The term implied by subsection (2) does not extend to any matter making the quality of goods unsatisfactory—
  (a) which is specifically drawn to the buyer's attention before the contract is made,
  (b) where the buyer examines the goods before the contract is made, which that examination ought to reveal, or
  (c) in the case of a contract for sale by sample, which would have been apparent on a reasonable examination of the sample.

(2D) If the buyer deals as consumer or, in Scotland, if a contract of sale is a consumer contract, the relevant circumstances mentioned in subsection (2A) above include any public statements on the specific characteristics of the goods made about them by the seller, the producer or his representative, particularly in advertising or on labelling.

(2E) A public statement is not by virtue of subsection (2D) above a relevant circumstance for the purposes of subsection (2A) above in the case of a contract of sale, if the seller shows that—
  (a) at the time the contract was made, he was not, and could not reasonably have been, aware of the statement,
  (b) before the contract was made, the statement had been withdrawn in public or, to the extent that it contained anything which was incorrect or misleading, it had been corrected in public, or
  (c) the decision to buy the goods could not have been influenced by the statement.

(2F) Subsections (2D) and (2E) above do not prevent any public statement from being a relevant circumstance for the purposes of subsection (2A) above (whether or not the buyer deals as consumer or, in Scotland, whether or not the contract of sale is a consumer contract) if the statement would have been such a circumstance apart from those subsections.[97]

Section 14(6) provides that as regards England, Wales and Northern Ireland, the terms implied by subs. (2) (and subs. (3) the fitness for purpose warranty which is dealt with below) are conditions, so that, subject to the changes noted later,[98] the effect of breach of these terms is the same as under the previous law. In Scotland, the effect of the breach depends upon its materiality.

Section 15(2) provides:

In the case of a contract for sale by sample[99] there is an implied term:
  (c) that the goods shall be free from any defect, making their quality unsatisfactory, which would not be apparent on reasonable examination of the sample.

---

97 Subsections (2D)–(2F) added by the Sale and Supply of Goods to Consumers Regulations 2002, SI 2002/3045 reg. 3. Regulation 7 inserts an equivalent set of provisions into the Supply of Goods and Services Act 1982.
98 See p. 499 *et seq*. below.
99 The meaning of this term is discussed at p. 212 below.

Again, in England, Wales and Northern Ireland this implied term is a condition.[100] In Scotland, the effect of breach again depends on its materiality.

The implied term requiring goods to be of satisfactory quality is substituted for the former condition requiring goods to be of merchantable quality by the Sale and Supply of Goods Act 1994, and is in many respects the most important part of the law of sale of goods. It is here that the seller's obligations as to the quality of the goods supplied must be found, and this is the very heart of the law of sale. So it is not surprising that there has been a great deal of case law on this subject, and that there have been several attempts to reform the law, culminating in the 1994 Act.

Under the 1893 Act no attempt to define the concept of 'merchantable quality' was made, and the matter was left entirely to case law. Probably the word 'merchantable' seemed sufficiently precise and appropriate to most lawyers and judges of the time, especially when the cases coming to their attention were mostly commercial contracts between businessmen. But to many, it appeared less appropriate in modern times when applied to consumer sales. But despite this the word did service for some 80 years without any statutory definition. A very large body of case law eventually developed, not merely in this country, but also in the many common law jurisdictions (including the USA)[101] which modelled their sales law on the 1893 Act. Not surprisingly no simple or single judicial *definition* ever emerged. The contract of sale of goods covers such an extraordinarily wide range of transactions that it seems impossible that a single standard of quality could be formulated which is appropriate to all kinds of goods, extending from consumer durables to agricultural produce, to foods and drinks, to live animals and fish, to commodities like coal or iron ore or oil sold as raw materials, to goods sold for resale as well as for use, and to goods sold to consumers as well as to commercial concerns.

There were many and repeated demands for a simple statutory statement of the standard of quality required of the seller, though lawyers were divided in their response to these demands. Some appear to have thought that a simple definition or statement of the seller's duties could be provided which would be applicable over a wide range of cases, and would simplify the law, and eliminate the need to consult a large body of cases. Others, including Professor Atiyah and the editors, thought (and continue to think) that this is a hopeless quest, that no simple statutory statement or definition of the seller's duties as regards quality could possibly cope with the wide variety of problems which the case law has illustrated, and that any attempt to avoid reference to the old case law would only lead to the new statutory term becoming itself encrusted with interpretive case law.[102] There is still plenty of scope for a judge to manoeuvre, so that the outcome of particular cases will no doubt continue to be influenced by the view the judge forms of the reasonableness of the plaintiff's behaviour.[103] Moreover, it is surely inevitable that where the application of the new warranty to new fields such as computer software has to be considered, courts will

---

100   1994 Act Sch. 2 para 5(6)(b).
101   The Uniform Commercial Code Art. 2–314(2) attempts to spell out the characteristics that goods must have to be 'merchantable', but this is not particularly helpful either.
102   Rather than attempting a comprehensive definition, the Law Commission might perhaps have been better advised to have provided non-exhaustive definitions and illustrative examples of when the warranty would (or would not) be broken.
103   See, e.g., *Millars of Falkirk Ltd* v *Turpie* 1976 SLT (Notes) 66 discussed p. 187, n. 213 and p. 182 below.

look at the case law from other common law jurisdictions, where the old merchantable quality warranty is still in force. It will not be so easy to apply that case law directly, however, because of the new wording.

The Supply of Goods (Implied Terms) Act 1973 first made some response to the demand for reform and simplification by providing a statutory definition of the term 'merchantable quality', and this, together with some minor amendments made by the same Act, was eventually incorporated in the 1979 consolidation as s. 14(6), which was as follows:

> Goods of any kind are of merchantable quality within the meaning of subsection (2) above if they are as fit for the purpose or purposes for which goods of that kind are commonly bought as it is reasonable to expect having regard to any description applied to them, the price (if relevant) and all the other relevant circumstances.

In addition it is necessary to note that under s. 61 of the Act the word 'quality' was defined[104] as including 'the state or condition of the goods'.

But this definition, which was based on the recommendations of the Law Commissions, was probably not intended to have any substantial effect on the law. The Law Commissions at that time appear to have accepted the impossibility of solving all the difficulties of application by the apparently simple process of definition.

For some years, the case law proceeded in the old way, despite the statutory definition. Former editions of this book continued to discuss the case law at some length, before even considering the statutory definition. Likewise, in *Aswan Engineering Establishment Co v Lupdine Ltd*,[105] in 1987, the Court of Appeal analysed the cases at length before proceeding to the statutory definition, and clearly thought this was the appropriate procedure. In the same year a case concerning the merchantability of a car was brought before Rougier J who was told that the motor trade was concerned at the lack of any definition of the concept in its application to vehicles.[106] Rougier J responded that it was doubtful if 'any all-embracing definition of a car of merchantable quality could ever be made',[107] and he added that the statutory definition was probably deliberately left in the widest possible terms 'in order to cater for the great variety of situations which may occur'.[108] He went on to say:

> Any attempt to forge some exhaustive, positive and specific definition of such a term, applicable in all cases, would soon be put to mockery by some new undreamt of set of circumstances.[109]

But in *Rogers v Parish (Scarborough) Ltd*[110] another panel of the Court of Appeal adopted a completely different approach to the question. The court here insisted that the then fairly recent definition in s. 14(6) was in simple language which could easily be applied to a variety of circumstances without difficulty. They deprecated the practice

104 This definition is omitted in the new provisions, and is included in the new warranty – s. 14(2B).
105 [1987] 1 WLR 1.
106 *Bernstein v Pamson Motors (Golders Green) Ltd* [1987] 2 All ER 220.
107 Ibid., at p. 222.
108 Ibid.
109 Ibid.
110 [1987] QB 933. The *Aswan Engineering* case, though decided before this case, appears to have been only reported after it, so it was apparently not cited.

of looking at the old case law, and insisted that the new definition should be applied without reference to the prior law.

At the same time that the courts were thus disagreeing on their attitude to this question, the Law Commissions were re-examining the whole issue. In their Working Paper issued in 1983, the Commissions still appeared to think, as their predecessors had done, that all attempts at simple definitions were doomed to failure.[111] At the same time they thought that there would be advantages in jettisoning the term 'merchantable' and also in clarifying the law on a number of specific points which had previously given rise to doubts and difficulties. By the time of the 1987 Final Report, however, the Law Commissions appeared to have changed their stance.[112] They now appeared to think that it was possible to lay down a simple standard of 'acceptable' quality, which, when fleshed out with some supplementary provisions, would be workable and meaningful. So the draft Sale and Supply of Goods Bill recommended by the Law Commissions contained a number of new subsections designed to replace the existing s. 14(2) and the definition of merchantable quality in s. 14(6). The 1994 Act substantially adopts these recommendations, but substitutes the words 'satisfactory quality' for the Law Commissions' 'acceptable quality'. It is not altogether easy to understand the reason for this change, as the word 'satisfactory' in many modern contexts tends to be associated with mediocrity.

While Professor Atiyah and the editors remain firmly of the opinion that resort to the old case law will still turn out to be necessary in a wide variety of situations, it is possible, though we believe it unlikely, that views equivalent to those expressed by the Court of Appeal in *Rogers v Parish (Scarborough) Ltd* will prevail and that the new provisions will be treated as making a fresh start. Presumably, relaxation of the rule prohibiting the courts from referring to parliamentary material as an aid to statutory construction which is the result of the House of Lords' decision in *Pepper (Inspector of Taxes) v Hart*[113] will mean that use may be made of the Law Commissions' Report which led to the enactment of the 1994 Act, and the views expressed there on the old cases will have some relevance to the interpretation of the new provisions. At all events, extensive treatment of the old cases may be justified, in the absence of a body of case law on the new provisions, as illustrating the wide variety of fact situations the courts may have to grapple with in applying them, and also because for some time yet cases coming before the courts will fall to be dealt with under the old provisions.[114]

But it is first necessary to start with an examination of the circumstances which give rise to the seller's obligations under s. 14(2) – whatever those obligations may be.

---

111 *Sale and Supply of Goods*, Law Com. Working Paper No. 85.

112 See Law Com. Final Report, *Sale and Supply of Goods*, paras 3.16–3.22.

113 [1993] 1 All ER 42. Compare *Aswan Engineering Establishment Company v Lupdine* [1987] 1 WLR 1 where Lloyd LJ wished to look at the earlier reports dealing with the then present statutory definition of 'merchantable quality' but both counsel objected. *Pepper v Hart* has been accepted in Scotland: *Short's Tr v Keeper of the Registers of Scotland* 1994 SC 122, aff'd 1996 SC (HL) 14.

114 The new provisions came into effect on 3 January 1995, and were not retrospective: the old law still applied to contracts made before that date – Sale and Supply of Goods Act 1994 s. 8(3).

In what circumstances does the condition apply?

Where the seller sells goods in the course of a business

The implied term of satisfactory quality in s. 14(2) only applies to goods sold by the seller in the course of a business,[115] and in this respect no change is made from the former position. The 1973 Act and the present Act affirm the construction placed on the less clear words of the original s. 14(2) by the House of Lords in the *Ashington Piggeries* case.[116] Goods sold privately by a seller, not selling in the course of business, are therefore not within the section, though, as seen above, they are within s. 13 which requires conformity with description. Thus, as previously seen, a person who sells a second-hand car privately as a '1961 Herald' impliedly promises that it is a 1961 Herald though he does not otherwise impliedly promise that it is of any particular quality. In *Stevenson and another v Rogers*,[117] it was held that having regard to the changes effected to s. 14(2) of the Sale of Goods Act 1893 by the Supply of Goods (Implied Terms) Act 1973, now to be found in s. 14(2) of the 1979 Act, habitual dealing in the type of goods sold is not required, a 'one off' sale in the course of a business sufficing. That case involved the sale of a fishing boat by a fisherman. The judge at first instance held that this was not a sale in the course of a business because it did not have any element of regularity. The Court of Appeal, however, decided that habitual dealing in the type of goods sold was not a requirement of the section; it sufficed that the sale was in the course of a business.[118]

Section 14(5), which was first enacted in the 1973 Act, deals with the problem of a private seller who sells through an agent. This provides as follows:

---

115 The original s. 14(2) required that the goods be bought by description from a seller who dealt in goods of that description. The reason for that is clear from the cases referred to by Judge Chalmers in his commentary on the section – *Sale of Goods*, 2nd edn, p. 29 (in reality the first edition after the 1893 Act). All of those cases involved unexamined goods bought by description, which explained the proviso 'provided that if the buyer has examined the goods, there shall be no implied condition as regards defects which such examination ought to have revealed'. In the case of specific goods, there would have been only two implied warranties – title and, if appropriate, fitness for purpose – and property would pass under s. 18 r. 1 when the contract was made, so that the buyer could not reject (see original s. 11(1)(c)). In the case of unexamined goods, if the seller purported to appropriate non-conforming goods, no property could pass until the buyer accepted them, either by retaining them or by doing an act inconsistent with the seller's ownership – s. 35 of the 1893 Act. On this interpretation, the provisions of the 1893 Act fitted together, and the passing of property and acceptance or rejection were linked. Problems arose when s. 14(2) was extended to other circumstances than its original sphere of application, especially in order to protect consumers. The result has been the need for ingenious reworking of the concept of 'property', as seen in *Kwei Tek Chao v British Traders & Shippers Ltd* – see p. 515. We are grateful to Professor Robert Bradgate for suggesting this line of research.
116 [1972] AC 441.
117 [1999] QB 1028.
118 In *R & B Custom Brokers Co Ltd v United Dominions Trust Ltd* [1988] 1 All ER 847 – see p. 172 – it was held that a private company which bought a car for the personal and business use of its directors, as it had done two or three times previously, dealt as consumer. The Court of Appeal reached this decision, on the basis that the same test is applicable as in the case of the Trade Descriptions Act 1968, under which the court has to decide whether a false trade description has been applied '*in the course of a business*'. Under that case law, a transaction only incidental to a business activity, rather than integral to it, is not done 'in the course of a business': a degree of regularity must be established. This same approach might be applied in the present context. It is clear from *Stevenson and another v Rogers* that the ratio of this decision is limited to the application of s. 12 of the Unfair Contract Terms Act 1977. The requirement of regularity does not mean, however, that the very first sale made by a business, or indeed its very last sale, are beyond the scope of s. 14(2) – see *Buchanan-Jardine v Hamilink* 1983 SLT 149. *Stevenson and another v Rogers* and *R & B Customs Brokers v United Dominions Trust* were discussed by the Court of Appeal in *Feldaroll Foundry plc v Hermes Leasing (London) Ltd* 12 May 2004 (as yet unreported). The Court held it was bound by the decision in the latter case.

(5) The preceding provisions of this section apply to a sale by a person who in the course of a business is acting as agent for another as they apply to a sale by a principal in the course of a business, except where that other is not selling in the course of a business and either the buyer knows that fact or reasonable steps are taken to bring it to the notice of the buyer before the contract is made.

So the implied term under s. 14(2) applies if the agent is selling in the course of business unless the principal is not acting in the course of business and the buyer is aware of this, or reasonable steps are taken to bring it to the buyer's notice. So, for instance, an auctioneer acting for a private seller can exclude these sections by making it clear that the principal is a private seller. If he does not do so, the auctioneer will be liable under this section, and the owner will also be liable unless he can bring himself within the exception. In *Boyter v Thomson*,[119] a principal, acting privately, sold a boat through an agent acting in the course of a business, but the buyer was unaware of the principal's existence at the time of the sale. The House of Lords found the principal liable to the buyer for defects in the boat under s. 14(5) and the principles of the common law of agency, whereby an undisclosed principal may be sued on any contract made on his behalf. An argument that only the agent could be liable under s. 14(5) was rejected. No change in this subsection is made by the 1994 Act.

Section 15(2)(c), which deals with sales by sample, contains no words corresponding to those in s. 14(2) discussed above. This is presumably a recognition of the fact that a person who sells goods by sample is unlikely to be a private seller, but will almost invariably be selling in the course of business.

Second-hand goods

There was nothing in the former s. 14(2) which restricted its application to new goods, and the sale of second-hand vehicles has therefore been held to be within the subsection.[120] Furthermore, the test of merchantability to be applied in the case of second-hand vehicles was held to be precisely the same statutory test as applied to new goods,[121] though it did not follow that goods must be held to be merchantable when sold new just because they would be regarded as satisfying the statutory test if sold as second-hand.[122] Also, the exceptions in the old paras (a) and (b) were much more likely to be relevant in second-hand sales.[123] No change in respect of these points is made by the 1994 Act, or was contained in the Law Commissions' recommendations.

No reliance on seller need be shown

In contrast to the implied condition as to fitness for purpose which is contained in s. 14(3) (and which is dealt with later) the implied condition in s. 14(2) normally

---

119 1995 SC (HL) 15.
120 See, e.g., under the pre-1973 law, *Bartlett v Sydney Marcus* [1965] 1 WLR 1013; and since 1973, *Lee v York Coach & Marine* [1977] RTR 35; *Business Appliances Specialists Ltd v Nationwide Credit Corpn Ltd* [1988] RTR 32. On the current provision, see *Thain v Anniesland Trade Centre* 1997 SLT (Sh Ct) 102.
121 See the *Business Appliances Specialists* case, cited in the last note.
122 Ibid.; see also *Bernstein v Pamson Motors (Golders Green) Ltd* [1987] 2 All ER 220, 226.
123 Identical in effect to subs. (2C)(a) and (b) inserted by the Sale and Supply of Goods Act 1994 set out at p. 162 *et seq.* above.

applied even though the buyer had in no way relied on the seller's skill and judgment. The implied term was a guarantee of inherent quality, and did not depend on any showing that the buyer had relied on the seller. This could lead to liability in extreme situations. For example, if a buyer ordered goods from the seller which were only made by one manufacturer so that the goods could only be obtained from that manufacturer or from someone who had bought from him, the seller would still be treated as warranting the merchantable quality of the goods.[124] In such a case it might seem that the seller had complied with his contract simply by supplying the buyer with precisely what he had asked for, but this did not exonerate the seller from liability. The reason for this rule, which might seem hard on the seller, was that in most circumstances the seller would himself be able to obtain an indemnity from the manufacturer on the ground that the contract between them also imported the implied term of merchantable quality.[125] The rule applied, however, even though the seller could not in the particular circumstances obtain such an indemnity, for example because the manufacturer was insolvent or the time under the Limitation Act had run out.[126] The 1994 Act does not alter this.

However, if the manufacturer was only willing to supply the goods subject to some limitation on his liability and the buyer knew this fact when he ordered the goods from the seller, it was held that this would normally negative the implied condition between buyer and seller.[127] The 1994 Act does not affect this, but it seems that this would now only be the case in non-consumer sales because the Unfair Contract Terms Act 1977 prevents the exclusion of s. 14(2) in consumer sales. Even in a non-consumer sale the resulting implied exclusion of s. 14(2) must satisfy the requirement of reasonableness in the Unfair Contract Terms Act 1977; but since this is an implied exclusionary term, which derives from the courts' sense of its fairness and justice, it can hardly be suggested that it would be unreasonable. If in any particular circumstances the court felt that the seller should be liable despite these facts, it would presumably refuse to imply a term excluding the application of s. 14(2) and the application of the 1977 Act just would not arise.

A similar problem would arise if the buyer ordered goods made to his own specification, and the specification was itself such that any goods made to that specification would be inherently defective or unsatisfactory. It could hardly be supposed that in such a case the buyer could sue under s. 14(2), though it is not easy to state the precise ground on which the seller could escape liability. The problem was discussed by the Court of Appeal in the *Ashington Piggeries* case[128] where a number of possible reasons were given, some of which cannot survive the House of Lords appeal in that case.[129] But one suggestion which is not inconsistent with the decision of the House of Lords is that where the essence of the contract is the making or

---

124 *Young & Marten Ltd v McManus Childs Ltd* [1969] 1 AC 454.
125 Ibid., p. 466.
126 *Ibid.*, at p. 467, per Lord Reid.
127 *Gloucestershire CC v Richardson* [1969] 1 AC 480, a decision at common law, because the contract was strictly not a sale of goods but the House of Lords regarded the applicable law as the same. See also *Helicopter Sales (Australia) Pty Ltd v Rotor-Work Pty Ltd* (1974) 132 CLR 1.
128 [1969] 3 All ER 1469 at p. 1518.
129 [1972] AC 441.

compounding of goods to someone else's order or prescription, the seller's duty may be limited to using all reasonable skill and care in selecting materials and making the goods. But this may be criticized because the seller's duties are traditionally thought of as warranties involving strict liability, and it could hardly be supposed that the seller would be free from liability in such a case if, despite all care and skill, he delivered goods not precisely in accordance with the specifications. It is thought that the best reason for denying liability in the case of goods made to the buyer's own specification would be that, in the circumstances given, the goods should not be treated as unsatisfactory. As we shall see later, merchantability was a somewhat flexible concept (despite the statutory definition introduced by the 1973 Act),[130] and it seems to have been considered that the buyer was the best judge of what he wanted. If the buyer got exactly what he had ordered, it hardly lay in his mouth to say that the goods were unmerchantable. It is reasonable to suppose that this would still be the same under the new provisions. An alternative way of dealing with the above hypothetical problem – namely of treating s. 14(2) as excluded by implication in such circumstances – might also be available in non-consumer sales, and it is perhaps unlikely that the problem would arise in a consumer sale.

Since the problems discussed in the last two paragraphs arose entirely as a matter of case law, and did not arise from the wording of the then existing Act, nor of the statutory definition of 'merchantable quality' in s. 14(6), it is not surprising that the new s. 14(2) is no clearer on these points than the former sections. There is absolutely nothing in the language of the new s. 14(2) which is directly relevant to these difficulties, so it was presumably not intended to have any effect on them. Yet it is just arguable that the change from the concept of 'merchantable quality' to that of 'satisfactory quality' may indirectly affect the result in these cases. It may, perhaps, be arguable that if the buyer gets precisely what he has ordered from the seller it would be very unreasonable of him to complain that the goods are not of 'satisfactory quality'. This point is discussed further when we come to a more detailed examination of the concepts of 'merchantable' and 'satisfactory' quality, but it can be said here that the argument appears to be misconceived. Probably the amendments have no effect on the principles applicable to these questions.

Defects drawn to the buyer's attention, and examination of the goods

The implied condition that the goods must be satisfactory is excluded in two cases (formerly covered by s. 14(2)(a) and (b) of the 1979 Act). These exclusions are now to be found in s. 14(2C)(a) and (b), but the new Act makes no substantive change in them. In addition, s. 14(2C)(c) provides that in a contract for sale by sample, the condition does not extend to any matter which would have been apparent on a reasonable examination of the sample. The first excluded case concerns defects specifically drawn to the buyer's attention before the contract is made, or after the contract is made at the time the goods are delivered.[131] No difficulty arises on this score, except that the wording of the paragraph probably does not help a seller who tries to draw the buyer's attention to defects in the goods solely by printed wording

---

130 See p. 174 *et seq.* below.
131 See *Clegg v Olle Andersson (T/A Nordic Marine)* [2003] EWCA Civ 320 discussed at p. 519 below.

in a written contract. It is hardly to be supposed that the court would regard this as sufficient to draw the buyer's attention 'specifically' to any defects.

In addition to matters specifically drawn to the buyer's attention by the seller, it is clear that a course of dealings between the parties might affect the extent of the seller's duties, if the buyer became aware of defects in the goods, but continued to order them. In such circumstances there must come a point where the buyer becomes unable to seize on the defects as a reason for rejecting the goods, or indeed for claiming damages in respect of them. An interesting illustration of this is the American case of *Royal Business Machines* v *Lorraine Corporation.*[132] The buyers in that case were dealers in Royal's photocopiers. One of the statements made by Royal about their machines was that service calls were needed only every 7,000–9,000 copies, a statement which if untrue would clearly have rendered the seller liable to the dealers at the outset. However, over an 18-month period, the dealers learned the truth about the performance of the machines, which was that they needed rather more frequent service calls. Since they had continued to purchase the machines, there must have been a point at which they had ceased to rely on the seller's assertion about service calls. After that, they could scarcely complain about the seller's breach of warranty.

The second exclusion, concerning examination of the goods, is now contained in para. (b) of s. 14(2C) and the third exclusion, in the case of a sale by sample, in s. 14(2C)(c), but the effect of these provisions is slightly different. It was clear that the old subsection (2)(b) only applied if the buyer had *actually* examined the goods, and the wording of s. 14(2) inserted by the 1973 Act[133] did not alter the effect of the 1893 Act on this point. But the subsection probably did alter the law on another point. In *Thornett & Fehr* v *Beers & Son,*[134] it was held that the proviso to the original s. 14(2) of the 1893 Act applied where the buyer, being pressed for time, examined some barrels of glue only from the outside, although the seller offered him every facility for a more complete examination. The original section in the 1893 Act had itself modified the common law rule, which was that the implied condition was excluded by the mere opportunity for examination, even if in fact the opportunity was not taken. *Thornett & Fehr* v *Beers & Son* went some way to restore the common law position and was open to criticism on the wording of the original section. The proviso formerly said that 'if the buyer has examined the goods, there shall be no implied condition as regards defects which such examination ought to have revealed'. The crucial words were 'such examination', that is, the examination actually made, not a hypothetical examination which might or ought to have been made. As there was no evidence to suggest that the defect should have been revealed by the examination actually made, the proviso should not have been relevant. This seems to have been the view taken in the Australian case of *Frank* v *Grosvenor Motor Auctions Pty Ltd*[135] and the present wording deriving from the 1973 Act specifically refers to 'that examination', which seems to have put the point beyond doubt. No change is made on this point by the 1994 Act.

---

132   633 F 2d 34, US Ct of Appeals 7th Circ (1980).
133   Consolidated in the 1979 Act.
134   [1919] 1 KB 486.
135   [1960] VR 607, 609.

A problem had arisen about s. 14(2)(b) – which could also have arisen with regard to para. (a) of the 1979 Act. (This is, perhaps, one more illustration of how new and unforeseen problems constantly arise out of the simplest statutory wording.) In *R & B Customs Brokers Co Ltd* v *United Dominions Trust*[136] a car was bought on conditional sale for the private use of a company director. The car was delivered a few days before the relevant documents were signed, and thus before the contract had legally been concluded. Before this happened the plaintiffs' director discovered that the roof was leaking, though he naturally expected that the dealers would put this right, and in fact they undertook to do so some days later. However, despite numerous attempts, the leak was never satisfactorily repaired, and eventually the plaintiffs claimed to reject the car for breach of the implied conditions as to quality and fitness. But the defendants argued that as a result of the plaintiffs' examination of the car before the contract was made, they had knowledge of the defect in question so as to exclude liability under s. 14(2)(b). The Court of Appeal felt that if this was the result of the statutory wording, it would be a trap for any buyer who took delivery of the goods before making a concluded contract, but they expressed no final opinion on the question. The sellers were held liable under s. 14(3) (the fitness for purpose warranty). The amendment effected by the 1994 Act provides that the buyer is not deemed to have accepted goods merely because he asks for or agrees to their repair,[137] but otherwise does not address the above problem.

Of course if, before the contract is made, the seller points out a defect to a buyer, or if the buyer discovers it for himself, and the seller undertakes to put it right, then it will be immaterial if the implied condition under s. 14(2A) is excluded as regards that defect, because the seller would plainly be liable on a separate, collateral contract, or for breach of a simple express term of the contract. But in the *R & B Customs Brokers* case the dealer's undertaking to repair the leak was apparently made after the contract was concluded, and no separate collateral contract or warranty was pleaded on the basis of this undertaking.[138]

In the case of a sale by sample the effect of s. 14(2C)(c)[139] is to exclude the implied condition that the goods are satisfactory if the defect would have been apparent on a reasonable examination of the sample, *whether or not* it has in fact been examined. In a sale by sample the seller is entitled to assume that the buyer will examine the sample, and the latter can hardly be heard to complain of defects which he could have discovered by the simple process of examining the sample.[140] *A fortiori* this is the case where the buyer does in fact examine the sample and discovers the defect, but decides to take the goods all the same. 'If there is a defect in the sample which renders the

---

136   [1988] 1 All ER 847.

137   Section 35(6).

138   Nevertheless, it is arguable that the dealer could be liable on such an undertaking on the basis of *Blackpool & Fylde Aero Club Ltd* v *Blackpool Borough Council* [1990] 3 All ER 25. Alternatively, consideration might be found in the buyer not exercising the right of rejection.

139   Section 15(2)(c) of the 1979 Act.

140   It has, however, been argued in relation to the former provisions that, where the implied condition of merchantable quality was excluded under s. 15(2)(c) as regards defects which examination of the sample ought to have revealed, the buyer might still be able to sue under s. 14(2) in respect of a defect which the actual examination could not have revealed. See Murdoch (1981) 44 MLR 388. Only a very literalist interpretation of the Act could justify such an absurd conclusion, and the 1994 Act makes it clear in relation to s. 14(2) as well as s. 15 that when a sample is provided, it is what a reasonable examination of the sample ought to have revealed, and not any actual examination.

goods unmerchantable and the buyer, notwithstanding and with knowledge of that defect in the sample, is content to take a delivery which corresponds with the sample and gets such a delivery, he has no ground of complaint.'[141]

It is common in the case of a consumer sale, where the goods actually supplied remain packaged in their original container and unopened throughout the transaction, for the customer to have examined an identical item displayed in the shop. If the defect is one which is present and apparent in all models of the goods, the implied condition obviously could be excluded.[142] Equally, many cases can be envisaged in which a court might be reluctant to reach this result. Either it could make the requirement that the defect be 'apparent' a stringent one, or it could hold that such cases are not sales by sample at all, on the ground that they are not intended as such.[143] They could be described as sales 'by model' perhaps.[144]

There are many illustrations in the reports in any event of defects which could not have been discovered by *any* reasonable examination, but two will suffice here. In *Wren* v *Holt*,[145] the plaintiff recovered damages for breach of the condition of merchantability of beer which was contaminated by arsenic. The proviso was clearly inapplicable as the defect was not discoverable on reasonable examination. In *Godley* v *Perry*,[146] a child's catapult which broke in ordinary use was likewise held to be suffering from a defect not discoverable on reasonable examination.

What is the extent of the seller's obligation?

Goods to which s. 14(2) extends

It was established under the former provisions, and the new provisions are no different on this point, that the subsection covers not only the goods actually bought by the buyer and passing to him, but packages or containers in which the goods are sold, even if these remain the property of the seller. In *Geddling* v *Marsh*[147] (a case under the old s. 14(1), now s. 14(3)) it was held that the seller's obligations covered not only goods which were the actual subject-matter of the sale, namely mineral waters, but also the bottles in which the waters were contained, even though these remained the property of the seller.[148] Consequently, the plaintiff was able to recover damages for injuries received when a defective bottle burst.

A similar point arose in *Wilson* v *Rickett Cockerell & Co Ltd*,[149] where the plaintiff ordered a consignment of Coalite from the defendants. Unknown to either party the Coalite contained an explosive substance which blew up in the plaintiff's fireplace, causing considerable damage. Here the plaintiff succeeded under s. 14(2) on

---

141 *Houndsditch Warehouse Co Ltd* v *Waltex Ltd* [1944] 2 All ER 518, 519.
142 'Defect' is perhaps the wrong word in this context. If the displayed goods lack a feature which would be present in more expensive goods, and this is obvious, the buyer could scarcely complain.
143 See p. 212 as to the meaning of 'sale by sample'.
144 See p. 214, thereby preserving the consumer buyer's right to repair or replacement – see p. 214 *et seq.*
145 [1903] 1 KB 610.
146 [1960] 1 WLR 9.
147 [1920] 1 KB 668.
148 Cf. *Beecham Foods Ltd* v *North Supplies (Edmonton) Ltd* [1959] 1 WLR 643.
149 [1954] 1 QB 598. For similar cases under the Food and Drugs legislation (now the Food Safety Act 1990), see *Meah* v *Roberts* [1977] 1 WLR 1187; *Barton* v *Unigate Dairies* [1987] Cr L Rev 121.

the grounds that the goods were not of merchantable quality. Referring to the words 'goods supplied under a contract of sale' (which have been replaced without significant alteration in the present sections), Lord Denning observed:

> In my opinion that means the goods delivered in purported pursuance of the contract. The section applies to all goods so delivered whether they conform to the contract or not: that is, in this case, to the whole consignment, including the offending piece, and not merely to the Coalite alone.[150]

Dealing with the defendants' argument that there was nothing wrong with the Coalite as such and that it was only the presence of the piece of explosive that made the goods dangerous, Lord Denning went on:

> Coal is not bought by the lump. It is bought by the sack or by the hundredweight or by the ton. The consignment is delivered as a whole and must be considered as a whole, not in bits. A sack of coal, which contains hidden in it a detonator, is not fit for burning and no sophistry should lead us to believe that it is fit.[151]

It might have been thought that the contrary was unarguable were it not for the decision of the Court of Session in *Duke* v *Jackson*[152] where, on the same facts, the coal merchant was held not liable on the ground that there was nothing wrong with the coal itself. The Court of Appeal, in refusing to follow this case, pointed to *Chapronière* v *Mason*,[153] where the defendant sold a bun containing a stone on which the plaintiff broke a tooth, and a verdict for the defendant was set aside by the Court of Appeal. These cases received implicit statutory confirmation in the provisions replacing them from 1973 onwards, because they expressly extended the implied conditions in these subsections to the 'goods supplied under the contract'.[154] The new s. 14(2) continues to use the same words.

The former statutory definition of merchantable quality, and its replacement by 'satisfactory quality'

The extent of the seller's duty depended largely upon the meaning to be attached to the term 'merchantable quality' and therefore after the 1973 Act on s. 14(6) which attempted a definition of that term. Section 14(6) was set out above.[155]

As we have previously noted, there were two approaches to the problems of deciding what was the meaning of 'merchantable quality'. On the one hand, there was the view that the statutory definition really had little substantive content. The basis for this view was that vague, general terms like 'merchantable' tend to be meaningless in practice – indeed, a substantial degree of flexibility is needed in applying such general terms because of the very varied transactions which come

---

150 At p. 607.

151 At p. 606.

152 1921 SC 362.

153 (1905) 21 TLR 633.

154 Presumably a buyer in a situation such as that in *Wilson* v *Rickett, Cockerell & Co Ltd* (though not in *Chapronière* v *Mason*) who discovered the foreign substance in the goods before damage was done would have been able to reject under s. 30(4) (now repealed), on the ground that the seller had 'delivered the goods he contracted to sell mixed with goods of a different description' – see p. 143 as to the former s. 30(4).

155 See p. 165.

within the law of sale of goods. The same can be said of the term 'satisfactory'. All vague statements or definitions of the standard of quality required by the law, it may be suggested, are somewhat vacuous in practice. They tend to be replaced with concepts of reasonableness which have substantial flexibility. Most such standards give little guidance as to what kind of defects or damage will render goods unsatisfactory (unmerchantable under the former provisions), and are unhelpful in the practical application of the law. All rely heavily upon the test of reasonableness: would a reasonable buyer, if he knew the condition of the goods, accept them under the contract? Would a reasonable buyer expect goods of that condition to be delivered under that sort of contract? Tests which depend so heavily upon standards of reasonableness tend to be somewhat circular in practice. What is the buyer entitled to expect under the contract? Answer – goods of satisfactory/merchantable quality. What is satisfactory/merchantable quality? Answer – goods of that quality (roughly speaking) which it is reasonable to expect. What would the buyer reasonably expect? Answer – goods suitable for reasonable use. What is reasonable use? Answer – the sort of use which a reasonable buyer would intend. And so on.

On the other hand, as we have also noted,[156] there was a Court of Appeal decision, *Rogers v Parish (Scarborough) Ltd*,[157] which suggested that the statutory definition of 'merchantable quality' provided by the 1973 Act could in most cases be applied by a fact finder without any detailed analysis of old case law. It must be suggested that the reasoning in this case was fallacious. The court assumed here that the application of the statutory definition in the old s. 14(6) was a *question of fact* but the introduction of reasonableness into the definition meant that questions of evaluation were necessarily involved. It is not possible to posit the 'reasonable man' and ask how he would behave as though that were a question of *fact*. How a reasonable man would behave in any given circumstances is not a fact, but an *evaluation*. Questions of reasonableness require the court to provide the answer from its sense of justice, but that means that detailed analysis and illustration must remain necessary unless every case is to be disposed of by an appeal to the court's idiosyncratic views on what justice demands. That would, surely, be quite unacceptable in such a large and important area of law as this. This same point can be made in relation to the new section, which provides that goods are satisfactory if they meet the standard that a reasonable person would regard as satisfactory.

The test of fitness for purpose

Section 14(6) which provided the statutory definition of merchantable quality had as its main element the requirement that the goods should be reasonably fit for the purpose or purposes for which goods of that kind were commonly bought. The present provisions provide that the quality of goods includes their state and condition and that among other things which are aspects of the quality of goods is their fitness for *all* (emphasis supplied) the purposes for which goods of the kind in question are commonly supplied. Clearly, fitness for purpose was an important – indeed, an essential – element in the concept of merchantable quality, and remains important under the

---

156 See p. 165 *et seq.*
157 [1987] QB 933.

present provisions. In this connection it must be noted that s. 14(3) is also, and more especially, concerned with fitness for purpose, but that subsection is directed more to the case where the goods are required for some particular purpose which has been made known to the seller. Section 14(2), on the other hand, concerns fitness for ordinary purposes, which do not have to be specially made known to the seller. (In fact the distinction between the two subsections has been muddied because such a wide interpretation has been given to s. 14(3) that in practice it often covers ordinary purposes as well as special purposes; so the two subsections in practice overlap significantly.)

The question arises whether the new statutory definition clears up one major ambiguity which had previously been explored in the cases. Many goods are used for a variety of purposes, and the goods supplied under the contract may be fit for some of these purposes while being unfit for others. If the buyer has not made known to the seller the particular purpose he wanted the goods for (in which case he could sue under s. 14(3)) are the goods to be treated as satisfactory/merchantable or not? In *Aswan Engineering Establishment Co v Lupdine Ltd*[158] the plaintiffs bought waterproofing compound in plastic pails for export to Kuwait from the defendants L. L had bought the pails from the second defendants, B. When the pails were unloaded on the quayside at Kuwait, they were stacked (six pails high) in intense sun (reaching a temperature of 60 to 70 degrees celsius) for some days. As a result the pails collapsed under their own weight and the waterproofing compound was lost. The plaintiffs sued L and succeeded on grounds not stated in the reports. L then in turn claimed damages from B for breach of s. 14(2) and (3), as well as in tort. Only the former claim falls to be considered here. So far as liability under s. 14(2) was concerned, the problem obviously was that the pails were perfectly fit for most purposes for which such pails would be used; they were simply unfit to be stacked six high in such intense heat. The Court of Appeal held that the goods satisfied the requirement that they should be of merchantable quality. But it must be said that the court reached this conclusion by looking at the earlier case law first, and then concluded that the statutory definition was not intended to alter the law. Section 14(6) required goods to be 'as fit for the purpose or purposes for which goods of that kind are commonly bought' as it was reasonable to expect. The present provision requires 'fitness for all the purposes for which goods of the kind in question are commonly supplied', so that if the seller knows that goods are not fit for one of the purposes for which goods of the kind are commonly supplied, he must make this known to the buyer.[159] It is unlikely, however, that if the facts of the *Aswan* case were to recur, and the case fell to be decided under the present provisions, the outcome would be any different.

It therefore seems impossible at this point to avoid looking at some of the earlier case law. The particular point under consideration here was exhaustively discussed by the House of Lords in *Henry Kendall & Sons v William Lillico & Sons Ltd*,[160] in which the plaintiffs bought for their pheasants animal feeding stuff which turned out to be contaminated with a substance contained in Brazilian ground nut extraction which was one of the ingredients of the feeding stuff. The ground nut extraction had

---

158 [1987] 1 WLR 1.
159 Law Commissions, Final Report, No. 160, para. 3.36.
160 [1969] 2 AC 31.

been bought by the sellers from G who had in turn bought it from K. The sellers paid damages to the plaintiffs, and claimed those damages in turn from G who claimed from K. G and K were held not liable under s. 14(2) on the ground that the ground nut extraction was not of unmerchantable quality. The reason for this was that the extraction was perfectly suitable to be used in making up animal feeding stuffs for use for cattle and other animals; it was only unsatisfactory for use in making feeding stuff for pheasant and partridge chicks. Apart from one further complication considered again later, this was therefore held not to make the goods of unmerchantable quality because in substance the goods were perfectly usable for one of the main purposes for which such goods were commonly bought. It was pointed out that commodities sold under a general description such as 'Brazilian ground nut extraction' may be bought by different buyers for a wide variety of uses. The House of Lords thought that it would be unreasonable to say that because the goods were unsuitable for only one of these possible uses the goods were to be treated as unmerchantable. A buyer whose complaint was that the goods were unsuitable just for the one use he had in mind must try to bring his case under s. 14(3) if he could do so (which would normally mean that he would have to show that he told the seller the particular purpose he had in mind), and could not expect to persuade the court that the goods were altogether unmerchantable. If the purposes for which the buyer requires the goods is not a common one, this will still be the case under the new provisions, but, as explained below, the actual outcome on the facts of this case might be different.

A similar case is the older decision in *Sumner Permain & Co Ltd v Webb & Co Ltd*.[161] The sellers sold Webb's Indian Tonic to the buyers, which they knew the buyers intended for resale in the Argentine. The tonic contained a quantity of salicylic acid which, unknown to both parties, made its sale illegal in the Argentine. When the tonic reached the Argentine it was seized and condemned by the authorities as unfit for human consumption. It was held that there had been no breach of s. 14(2) as the goods could not be said to be unmerchantable by reason of the provisions of Argentinian law. There was nothing wrong with the quality of the goods, which could have been resold by the buyers anywhere except in the Argentine. Goods were not unmerchantable merely because they were not fit for one particular purpose. The buyers' complaint was really that the goods were not fit for the purpose for which they were sold, but they also failed under s. 14(3) because they had ordered them under their trade name. The case again illustrates the difference between s. 14(2) and (3).[162] It is submitted that the outcome should still be the same under the new provisions. It is quite unreasonable to expect sellers to know the rules of law in operation in every country from which orders emanate, or into which a buyer wishes to export. These are matters within the knowledge of the buyer/exporter. It would be different if the seller had taken active steps to penetrate a target market so that the seller could be said to be exporting *into* that market.[163]

At this point it is necessary to consider what effect on these decisions the enactment of the present provisions may have. It is clear from their Report that the Law

161 [1922] 1 KB 55.
162 See also *Phoenix Distributors Ltd v L B Clarke* [1967] 1 Lloyd's Rep 518.
163 This point is of possible relevance in the case of e-commerce – see p. 74.

Commissions intended to reverse the decision in the first of the above three cases.[164] They took the view, though not without some doubt, that the goods should always be fit for *all* their common purposes, and that the buyer should only be compelled to fall back on s. 14(3) when his purpose is an *uncommon* one. Section 14(2B)(a) is designed to achieve this result by requiring fitness 'for all the purposes for which goods of the kind in question are commonly supplied'. On the other hand, it is clear that the judges in the above two cases thought this would be an unreasonable result, and where judges find this result unreasonable, it may still be possible in some cases for them to hold the particular purpose in question to be an uncommon one, so as to exclude liability under the new provisions. It seems likely that the judges in the *Aswan Engineering* case would have held that the particular use to which the pails were there subjected was very uncommon.

The word 'commonly' which was found in s. 14(6) and is found in s. 14(2B)(a) is of course a very difficult word to apply because all depends on the standards of comparison. Some uses, which may appear very uncommon in certain contexts, are perfectly common in a different context. To take an extreme example, the sale of wrecked cars which will not go, and are totally unroadworthy, for use as a source of spare parts is no doubt a relatively uncommon use in relation to the number of cars which are sold for ordinary use. But the sale of such cars as a source of spare parts is quite common if some different standard of comparison is used. Indeed, a thriving industry exists in which traders buy up old wrecks for this purpose, and sell spares to consumers, especially where the cars are out-of-date models. It is even more common where vintage cars are concerned.[165] But under the present law there is no doubt that a car which was only fit for use as a source of parts would not be regarded as of unsatisfactory quality if it was sold as such, either expressly or by implication. The main reason for this is that regard must be had to the price when considering the question of unsatisfactory quality. We return to this question of the price below.

But although, then, fitness for purpose is a main element in the present definition of 'unsatisfactory quality', the law does not require the goods to be *immediately usable*. Many goods are sold which are not intended to be fit for immediate use. If it is in the contemplation of the parties that something should be done to the goods before they are used, they will be satisfactory even if they may be, in some sense, defective on delivery, so long as they will be satisfactory when they have been dealt with as contemplated.[166] The Law Commissions gave a number of examples,[167] such as, for instance, furniture sold in kit form which has to be assembled by the consumer, (or less commonly these days) electrical goods sold without plugs attached, or food sold in such a condition that it needs to be cooked (or to ripen) before it is edible.

---

164 See Final Report, *Sale and Supply of Goods*, para 3.36.
165 See, e.g., the Scottish case of *MacGill v Talbot* 2002 GWD 12-382 (Sheriff G. J. Evans).
166 In *Underwood v Burgh Castle Brick and Cement Syndicate* [1922] 1 KB 343 Rowlatt J observed that the mere fact that a chattel such as a sideboard needed to be dismantled before delivery did not prevent the passing of property. This implies that he thought such goods were in a deliverable state, and thus conformed to the contract. This dictum is of relevance in relation to the many items of household furniture which are sold in 'flat packs' – see below. By contrast, in that case, it was held that a condensing engine, which required much work and expense on the part of the seller to make it ready for delivery, was not in a deliverable state – as to 'deliverable state' see p. 324.
167 Final Report, para 3.64.

There appear to be only two authorities bearing directly on this question. In *Heil* v *Hedges*[168] it was held that pork, which may be harmful if eaten when not properly cooked, is not unmerchantable if it would have been harmless when well-cooked.[169] By contrast, in *Grant* v *Australian Knitting Mills*[170] it was held that new underpants (which contained an excess of harmful chemicals) had to be fit for immediate wear, and it was no defence for the seller to show that they would have been harmless if washed before use. Clearly, the test to be applied is to ask whether it is in the reasonable contemplation of the parties that the goods will be treated in the suggested manner before they are used.[171]

Safety

There was nothing in the 1979 Act requiring goods to be safe in order that they should be held to be merchantable, but there were a number of cases, mostly dealing with motor vehicles, which made it clear that goods which could not be safely used were not merchantable.[172] Section 14(2B) specifically mentions safety in para. (d) as one of the factors to be taken into account in deciding whether goods meet the present standard of 'satisfactory quality' under s. 14(2).

Hidden defects

There remains, however, a serious problem about hidden defects which are only dangerous *because they are hidden*. One thing at any rate has never been in doubt. Even before the 1973 statutory definition it was never suggested that goods were merchantable merely because they looked all right and so were literally saleable in the market. In order to decide whether they were merchantable it had to be assumed that any hidden defects were fully known.[173] The same must be the case under the present provisions.

In most cases this is straightforward enough, but in some cases it leads to a problem. It is quite common for goods to be sold which may be dangerous if the buyer does not have some specific piece of information about the goods, but which are not at all dangerous if the facts are fully known. Many medicines and drugs, for instance, are perfectly safe if certain simple precautions are taken (such as taking them with water, or not combining them with alcohol, or not exceeding a stated dosage) but which would be potentially dangerous if these simple precautions were not observed.

---

168 [1951] 1 TLR 512.

169 The pork was infected with trichinae, a distressingly common cause of infection in America, where this question has given rise to much litigation: see *Williston on Sales*, vol. 1, 243a (revised edn, 1948 and 1949 Supplement).

170 [1936] AC 85.

171 But it is perhaps doubtful whether *Heil* v *Hedges* would be followed today; it seems to go too far to treat the failure to cook pork thoroughly as such an unusual thing as to break the causal chain and relieve the seller of responsibility: it would depend upon the extent to which, as a matter of fact, the dangers of undercooked pork were commonly known. Where more exotic foodstuffs are concerned, the duty of the seller must surely be to warn of dangers? As to the duty to warn see p. 182 below.

172 See, e.g., *Unity Finance* v *Mitford* (1965) 109 Sol Jo 70 (strictly a case of fundamental breach); *Lee* v *York Coach & Marine* [1977] RTR 35; *Bernstein* v *Pamson Motors (Golders Green) Ltd* [1987] 2 All ER 220.

173 *Grant* v *Australian Knitting Mills Ltd* [1936] AC 85, 100 per Lord Wright. Analogously, where the market value of defective goods is in issue, it must be assumed that buyer and seller know of the defects. The fact that the defects are hidden, and that a buyer in the market may therefore pay more than the goods are actually worth, does not establish that this is the fair market value: *Jackson* v *Chrysler Acceptances Ltd* [1978] RTR 474, 481.

Such drugs and medicines therefore nearly always come with adequate information printed on the container, or on some attached leaflet. Many of them, too, are only available on prescription,[174] so that the patient will get the necessary warnings from his doctor.[175] Clearly, goods supplied with the necessary information would not be unsatisfactory merely because, without it, they might be dangerous or unsafe. But equally clearly, it would seem extraordinary if such goods were not regarded as unsatisfactory if they were sold without the necessary information.[176]

The problem extends far beyond the particular case of medicines and drugs. All sorts of goods are sold which require something to be done to them to make them fit for safe use. For instance, some electrical products require to have a three-pin plug attached, which is properly wired. If the product was supplied without informing the buyer that this was the case, the goods might well have been held unmerchantable, and would now surely be held unsatisfactory – although possibly this sort of knowledge might now in particular cases be attributed to the public as a whole. Any product which is supplied in a container which states (for example): 'Warning: this product is dangerous for use unless such and such precautions are taken' would normally be regarded as satisfactory with the warning, but very likely as unsatisfactory without it. And so on.

All this seems a plain matter of common sense. But there is unfortunately a major decision in the way (at least of some) of these commonsense conclusions. In *Kendall* v *Lillico*,[177] which has already been referred to several times, the majority of the House of Lords held that the ground nut extraction involved in that case was merchantable because it was fit for its most common use, namely for compounding into animal feeding stuffs. Any feeding stuff containing the extraction was perfectly fit for use for feeding to cattle and other animals, but it was not suitable for feeding to pheasant and partridge chicks. Had the matter stopped there, the case would not have involved the particular problem under discussion. But it transpired that the animal feeding stuffs made with the ground nut extraction were not merely unsuitable for feeding to pheasant and partridge chicks – they were actually dangerous or poisonous to pheasant and partridge chicks. The buyers who bought the ground nut extraction for compounding into animal feeding stuffs would not have been injured or damaged if they had known of this fact, because they could simply have labelled the feeding stuffs produced with the extraction, 'Warning: Not Suitable for Poultry',[178] or something of that kind. But the buyers did not know of the toxic

---

174 As to whether goods supplied on prescription under the National Health Service are 'sold' see p. 9 above.

175 The warnings are standardized within the pharmaceutical trade – see *John Richardson Computers* v *Flanders and Chemtec* [1994] FSR 144. Failure to give such a standard warning would certainly amount to negligence on the part of the pharmacist.

176 This is expressly stated by Lord Pearce (though dissenting) in *Kendall* v *Lillico* [1969] 2 AC 31, 119. It is also supported by the decision in *Vacwell Engineering Co Ltd* v *BDH Chemicals* [1969] 3 All ER 1681. And see *Willis* v *FMC Machinery & Chemicals Ltd* (1976) 68 DLR (3rd) 127. See also, however, *Lem* v *Barotto Sports Ltd* (1976) 69 DLR (3rd) 276, 290. This problem could arise as a result of the activities of parallel importers of pharmaceuticals, for instances have been observed where drugs have been supplied to patients with the instructions only in a foreign language. Subject to the point made in n. 174 above as to whether goods supplied on prescription are 'sold' (see p. 209 *et seq.*), such goods would appear not to be of satisfactory quality.

177 [1969] 2 AC 31.

178 In ordinary usage 'poultry' does not include game birds, but the implication of the sixth holding in the case is that such a warning ought to have sufficed.

quality of the extraction, and so the feeding stuffs made with it were sold for general animal use, with disastrous results. A bare majority of the House of Lords held that these facts did not render the ground nut extraction of unmerchantable quality.

The ground for this decision is not entirely clear, but it seems to have been based on the following reasoning. The House applied the 'acceptability' test to decide the question of merchantability. This involved, they held, asking whether a buyer *with full knowledge of all the facts* would have accepted the goods in discharge of the contract without a substantial abatement of the price. The answer to that, they reasoned, was patently yes, because if the buyer had had *full knowledge of all the facts* he would have known that the goods were toxic to pheasant and partridge chicks, and would still have bought them, but have labelled his products as suggested above. This reasoning appears over-logical. Where the very nature of the defect in question depends on the fact that it is hidden and unknown, it seems absurd (the word is surely not too strong) to test the question of merchantability by asking whether a buyer *with full knowledge of the facts* would have accepted them. The whole problem arose from the very fact that the buyer did not know, and had no reason to know, all the facts. In circumstances like these it is precisely the fact that the condition is hidden which constitutes the danger, and therefore the defect in the goods. If this were not held to render the goods of unmerchantable quality, it would seem to have followed that a person who bought a piece of machinery (say a car) which was in a very dangerous state, but which could be rendered perfectly satisfactory merely by tightening up a nut, could not complain that the goods were unmerchantable.[179] If this was the case there was clearly something too narrow about the concept of 'merchantability' – for what renders such a car dangerous is precisely the fact that the buyer will have no reason to know or even suspect that the car is in a dangerous condition. Under the new provisions, in answering the question whether a reasonable person would regard the goods as 'unsatisfactory', it might appear that a similar approach might be adopted to that adopted by the House of Lords in *Kendall* v *Lillico*, by positing a reasonable person with full knowledge of the facts. Moreover, the specific reference to 'safety' does not assist in reaching a more sensible conclusion, because, in a fact situation like *Kendall* v *Lillico*, a buyer with full knowledge of the facts would regard the goods as safe, and therefore satisfactory. It is not clear, however, that the approach adopted by the House of Lords would be entirely inappropriate in commercial commodity contracts – again we have the problem of trying to draft a simple statutory provision which will cover all eventualities. Perhaps the solution in future in the case of commodity contracts will be to focus on the restriction of the right of rejection contained in the new s. 15A rather than to hold that no breach of s. 14(2) has occurred.

It is to be hoped, however, that this approach will not in general be adopted, and it is certainly highly unlikely that it would be in the case of unsafe consumer goods, otherwise the Law Commissions' purpose in spelling out a requirement of safety would largely be defeated.[180]

---

179 See *Bernstein* v *Pamson Motors (Golders Green) Ltd* [1987] 2 All ER 220 discussed at p. 187 below. Compare *Millars of Falkirk Ltd* v *Turpie* 1976 SLT (Notes) 66 – decided under the definition of 'merchantability' contained in the 1973 Act, later re-enacted in the 1979 Act.
180 Report para 2.16.

It was arguable that the majority decision on this point in *Kendall* v *Lillico* had been impliedly overruled by the test of merchantability in s. 14(6). But in the *Aswan Engineering* case[181] in 1986 the Court of Appeal followed the majority on this point, without specific reference to s. 14(6). Although Lloyd LJ seems to have preferred the reasoning of the minority of the House of Lords in *Kendall* v *Lillico*, the court declined to hold that the manufacturers of the pails should have warned that the pails would not be fit for stacking six high in conditions of extreme heat, on pain of their being found unmerchantable. But since the pails were held, in the event, to be fit for most of their common uses, this discussion would seem to have been *obiter*.

Since the changes to the Sale of Goods Act effected by the Sale and Supply of Goods to Consumers Regulations,[182] there would now appear to be no reason to hold that a car, or other goods, with minor defects is of satisfactory quality in consumer sales, as the buyer now has a right to require repair or replacement.[183] Moreover, in non-consumer sales, the buyer's right of rejection has been modified, so that a holding that the goods are unsatisfactory no longer gives rise to an automatic right of rejection.[184]

Knowledge, warnings, instructions, etc.

The problem discussed in the last section extends beyond questions of safety and hidden defects. Many products require to be used in a particular manner, or under specified conditions, if they are to work effectively, or at all. Garden weedkiller, for instance, may have to be applied when the weather is not wet, and garden fertilizer when it is.[185] Products of this kind which are supplied without any or without adequate instructions may be held unsatisfactory, while if they are supplied with adequate instructions they will be perfectly satisfactory.[186]

A related problem concerns minor defects which are very easily rectifiable. Many consumer goods, sometimes expensive and high quality goods, may be totally unusable because of some trifling defect which can be easily corrected once the source of the trouble is known. A car sold, for instance, with a missing battery lead would simply be unusable, and in the *Bernstein*[187] case Rougier J suggested that this would, strictly speaking, render the car unmerchantable under the statutory definition in s. 14(6).[188] Yet if the 'acceptability' test relied on by the House of Lords in *Kendall* v *Lillico* were applied in the same way as was done in that case, the answer might well have been different. More generally, Rougier J insisted that even a very minor defect which could easily be discovered and put right would often render a new car unmerchantable. This holding appears inconsistent with the reasoning of the majority in *Kendall* v *Lillico*. The specific reference to 'freedom from minor defects' in s. 14(2B)(c) really only makes sense on the basis that the new Act is in accordance with the views

---

181 [1987] 1 WLR 1.
182 SI 2002/3045, implementing Directive 1999/44/EC.
183 See discussion of *Bernstein* v *Pamson's Motors (Golders Green) Ltd* at p. 187 below.
184 Compare *Cehave NV* v *Bremer Handelsgesellschaft* [1976] QB 44 – see p. 92.
185 There are many US cases where farmers have sued the sellers of weedkillers which have failed to control the particular weed problem for which they were applied, and the result has been serious crop failure – see. p. 209.
186 See the *Wormell* case, dealt with below, p. 209; see also case cited in n. 331.
187 [1987] 2 All ER 220. See also *Lamarra* v *Capital Bank plc* 2004 GWD 40–817 (Sh Prin J C McInnes).
188 See, however, *Millars of Falkirk* v *Turpie* 1976 SLT (Notes) 66.

of Rougier J and with the Law Commissions' similar views.[189] Moreover, as noted above, the changes effected by the Sale and Supply of Goods to Consumers Regulations would seem to reinforce these. Again, however, in the case of commodity contracts, it may be that the *Kendall* v *Lillico* view makes some sense,[190] but in the case of this sort of slight defect, the limitation on the right of rejection in the new s. 15A ought to render the point academic.

Public statements

The Sale and Supply of Goods to Consumers Regulations[191] insert the new subsections (2D)–(2F) into s. 14 of the Sale of Goods Act.[192] The effect of these provisions is that public statements by a 'seller' or 'producer'[193] about the specific characteristics of goods are, in addition to the other matters discussed in this chapter, to be regarded as relevant in determining whether or not goods are of satisfactory quality. However, this will not apply where the seller was unaware of the statement, or if it had been publicly corrected, or if it could not have influenced the buyer's decision to buy the goods.[194] Regulations 11 and 13 insert an equivalent set of provisions into the contracts of hire[195] and hire-purchase.[196]

The word 'public statement' is not defined. Probably little guidance can be obtained from other bodies of law, such as copyright law where infringement can consist of performing a work in public,[197] because the issue here is not the infringement of a property right, but the likely influence of the statement on a consumer. Probably any statement which the consumer knew of, would amount to a public statement. Problems could arise where a disgruntled employee of a producer, or an employee as a practical joke, has posted statements on the Internet, which have in fact influenced a buyer's decision to buy particular goods, e.g. to the effect that the goods are suitable for uses for which they are quite unsuited. Clearly, statements transmitted over the Internet are public statements. Probably in such cases the provisions added by the 2002 Regulations will add little. The issue is whether or not the producer is bound by unauthorised acts of its employees,[198] and unless the representation was so obviously false that no reasonable claimant could have relied on it, the producer will be liable.[199]

---

189 Final Report para 3.34. Moreover, all kinds of warning notices, labels, instructions, etc., which render goods perfectly safe and satisfactory would then, apparently, cease to be necessary. The leading case on warnings is *Wormell* v *RHM Agriculture (East) Ltd* [1987] 1 WLR 1091, which was a case under s. 14(3) and is therefore dealt with at p. 209 below.

190 See *Cehave NV* v *Bremer Handelsgesellschaft* [1976] QB 44 – p. 92 above.

191 SI 2002/3045.

192 These are required by the Guarantees Directive 1999/44/EC, OJ 1999 L171/12.

193 These words are defined in s. 61(1) of the Act (as amended).

194 Section 14(2E).

195 Falling within the definition contained in the Supply of Goods and Services Act 1982 s. 6.

196 Falling within the definition contained in the Supply of Goods (Implied Terms) Act 1973 s. 15. Section 11J of the Supply of Goods and Services Act 1982 was inserted by the Sale and Supply of Goods Act 1994. The Regulations insert a new s. 11J(3A).

197 Copyright Designs and Patents Act 1988 s. 19.

198 Which depends on whether the employee was acting within the scope of authority conferred by the employer – see *Heatons Transport (St Helens) Ltd* v *Transport and General Workers Union* [1973] AC 15.

199 This follows from basic common law principles, but also from s. 14(2E)(c) Sale of Goods Act inserted by SI 2002/3045 reg. 3.

The standard of fitness for use

As we have seen, the law required that in order to be merchantable, the goods had to be fit for their use (or one of their common uses), and the 1994 Act requires fitness for all the purposes for which goods of the kind in question are commonly supplied. But standards of fitness for use are variable. The law does not require the goods to be perfectly fit for use. They are to be as fit for use as 'it is reasonable to expect' having regard to the various factors enumerated in the statutory definition. This appears to mean that goods may be satisfactory even though they are in some sense defective. For example, a second-hand car may be satisfactory, so long as it is reasonably fit for use, even though it is by no means in perfect condition.[200] But second-hand goods cause special difficulties in this connection, and they are better dealt with at a later point.

So far as other goods are concerned, it must be admitted that it goes against the current trend of opinion to suggest that defective goods can be satisfactory (unmerchantable under the former provisions). Indeed, it never seems to have been doubted under the original Sale of Goods Act that actually defective goods were unmerchantable. In the case of manufactured goods, quite trivial defects were occasionally held to render goods unmerchantable.[201] The reason for this very strict approach was quite simple. In the case of manufactured goods it was generally felt that the buyer was entitled to the goods in perfect condition. Any defect requiring any expenditure of money or time to put right naturally detracted from the buyer's purchase; moreover, it must be remembered that this was not simply something which went to the right of rejection. The buyer's remedy even in damages depended upon his right to goods of merchantable quality in many circumstances.

It seems clear that the Law Commissions intended to extend the responsibility of the seller with respect to these matters by the new test of 'satisfactory quality' in s. 14(2A) and (2B). In particular, s. 14(2B)(c) requires the goods to be free from minor defects which at first sight seems to eliminate the possibility that the seller can supply goods which are 'far from perfect'. Yet in practice this may not make much difference, because (as we shall see more fully below) the overriding test under the new section is the requirement that goods are of 'satisfactory quality' in s. 14(2A). The specific matters listed in s. 14(2B) are merely declared to be 'aspects of the quality of goods' – they are not themselves absolute requirements. So far as fitness for purpose is concerned, therefore, it cannot be said that even the new section will require the goods to be perfectly fit. Goods are of satisfactory quality if they meet the standard that a reasonable person would regard as satisfactory.

Under the old law, the court seems occasionally to have narrowed the scope of the merchantability warranty in order to prevent a buyer seizing on a minor defect as a pretext for avoiding what had turned out to be a bad bargain. In the *Cehave* case[202] the court was prepared to find the goods (citrus pulp pellets for animal feed) to be merchantable although part of the cargo had been damaged while at sea. Roskill LJ

---

200 See on previous Acts, *Bartlett v Sydney Marcus Ltd* [1965] 1 WLR 1013, *Business Appliances Specialists Ltd* v *Nationwide Credit Corpn Ltd* [1988] RTR 332; and on the present Act, *Thain v Anniesland Trade Centre* 1997 SLT (Sh Ct) 102.
201 *Jackson v Rotax Motor & Cycle Co Ltd* [1910] 2 KB 937; *Parsons (Livestock) Ltd v Uttley Ingham & Co* [1978] QB 791; *IBM v Scherban* [1925] 1 DLR 864; *Winsley v Woodfield* [1925] NZLR 480.
202 *(The Hansa Nord)* [1976] QB 44 – see p. 92 above.

admitted that the goods were 'far from perfect', but nevertheless held that they were merchantable. However, it might be dangerous to read too much into this decision; the facts were very peculiar, and the merits were all on the seller's side. Moreover, a buyer had actually bought the goods (at a much reduced price) when they were publicly sold after the original buyer had rejected them, and passed them on to the original sub-buyers who, in fact, used them without complaint for the purpose for which they were wanted, that is compounding into animal feeding stuff. In the circumstances, it may well be that even though the goods were not in perfect condition, it was legitimate to find that a reasonable buyer, acting reasonably, could have accepted the goods as of merchantable quality. Moreover, there was an express term that the goods should be of 'good quality' and this term was held to have been broken. So perhaps the existence of this term justified the court in placing an unusual significance on the more normal meaning of merchantable quality. As noted above, under the 1994 Act it would be possible for the court to attain the result it wanted in similar circumstances, i.e. to deny the buyer the right to reject, under the new s. 15A. Accordingly, if the same facts were to occur today, a court might find that s. 14(2) had been broken, but that the buyer was not entitled to reject.

It seems unlikely that new consumer goods – cars, television sets, washing machines, etc. – would be held to be of satisfactory quality if delivered in a condition which was 'far from perfect', and indeed there is now specific authority that this may be so, but because that authority deals with other aspects of the warranty than fitness for purpose, it is discussed below.

Non-functional aspects of quality

As we have seen, the former law concentrated heavily on the fitness for purpose test in asking whether the goods were merchantable, and fitness for all purposes for which goods of the kind are commonly supplied is also an aspect of the quality of the goods which must be taken into account under the new provisions. But many goods, especially consumer goods, suffer from defects which do not necessarily affect their ordinary usability, or general fitness for purpose. For example, they may be delivered scratched, dented, discoloured or dirty; they may have minor parts missing; ancillary parts may not work well, or may not be fit for their purpose even though the goods as a whole may be reasonably fit for use; and so on.

Before the 1973 statutory definition was enacted these sorts of defects were generally considered sufficient to render the goods unmerchantable because the test of merchantability applied at that time was, arguably, wider than the statutory test. In particular, the majority of the House of Lords in *Kendall* v *Lillico*[203] appears to have settled for an 'acceptability' test which was not very different from that included in the Law Commissions' original draft of s. 14(2A). This test stemmed from the definition of merchantable quality given by Farwell LJ in *Bristol Tramways Co Ltd* v *Fiat Motors Ltd*,[204] as amplified by Dixon CJ in the Australian High Court in the case of *Australian Knitting Mills Ltd* v *Grant*.[205] It was generally taken to mean that even non-functional

---

203 [1969] 2 AC 31.
204 [1910] 2 KB 831, 841.
205 (1930) 50 CLR 387, 418, affirmed in the Privy Council [1936] AC 85.

defects could be held to render the goods unmerchantable, and there was at least one specific Court of Appeal authority to this effect, in which it had been held that dented and scratched goods were unmerchantable, although they could have been put right by polishing.[206]

After the 1973 definition was enacted fears were expressed in some quarters that the old law had actually been weakened, and that a buyer could no longer complain that the goods were unmerchantable merely because they suffered from minor non-functional defects. The basis for these fears appears to have been that many complicated manufactured goods like cars must be expected to have minor teething problems and that defects of this kind did not render goods unmerchantable. If a car was broadly fit for its purpose, it was suggested, the fact that minor defects might exist did not, in the words of this definition, prevent the goods from being 'as fit for the purpose or purposes for which goods of that kind are commonly bought as it is reasonable to expect'.[207]

These fears never seemed very realistic,[208] and they were largely put to rest by the Court of Appeal decision in *Rogers v Parish (Scarborough) Ltd*.[209] In this case the buyer had bought a new Range Rover at a cost exceeding £16,000, but the vehicle had many minor defects such as deterioration of the oil seals and defects in the engine and gear box which made it excessively noisy and caused misfiring at all speeds. There were also many minor defects in the bodywork. Despite numerous attempts to repair it by the dealers, these defects remained after six months' use. It was held that the vehicle was not merchantable. It was not enough, insisted the Court of Appeal, that the vehicle could still be driven on the road. Mustill LJ brought the non-functional aspects of what the buyer was entitled to expect within the statutory definition by reading it broadly:

> Starting with the purpose for which 'goods of that kind' are commonly bought, one would include in respect of any passenger vehicle not merely the buyer's purpose of driving the car from one place to another but of doing so with the appropriate degree of comfort, ease of handling and reliability and, one may add, of pride in the vehicle's outward and interior appearance.[210]

After that, matters were taken a stage further by the Court of Appeal in *Shine v General Guarantee Corpn Ltd*[211] where a car which had been submerged in water and had been an insurance 'write-off' was held not to be merchantable, despite the fact that no specific defect or unroadworthiness was alleged. Here the mere fact of the prior accident was enough to reduce the market value of the goods very significantly (as was proved) presumably because the market judges that such an accident may have an effect on the long-run reliability and wear of the vehicle concerned. So the mere fact of such an accident having happened could render a car

---

206 *Jackson v Rotax Motor & Cycle Co Ltd* [1910] 2 KB 937.
207 Reasoning of this kind underpinned the decision of the First Division of the Court of Session in *Millars of Falkirk v Turpie* 1976 SLT (Notes) 66.
208 See the seventh edition of this book, pp. 134–5.
209 [1987] QB 933.
210 At p. 944.
211 [1988] 1 All ER 911 – and see p. 195 below.

unmerchantable, at any rate, unless the fact were disclosed sufficiently to bring into play s. 14(2)(a). What the court emphasized here was the buyer's reasonable expectations as having a bearing on merchantability. The outcome would, no doubt, be the same under the present provisions.

Another case of the purchase of a new car in which detailed consideration was given to the requirements of the former law with regard to merchantability was *Bernstein* v *Pamson Motors (Golders Green) Ltd.*[212] The plaintiff here bought a new car for just under £8,000, but the car broke down within three weeks, on a motorway, after doing only 140 miles. Investigation revealed that a very minor defect (the presence of a piece of sealant in the lubricating system) had caused the breakdown, but unfortunately this minor defect had caused extensive damage, because it had completely blocked the oil supply, causing the camshaft to seize up. Three main factors appear to have weighed with Rougier J in holding that the car was unmerchantable. First, there was the nature and consequences of the defect. Here the defect was minor, but the consequences very serious – indeed they could have been even more serious had the plaintiff not stopped in time. Secondly, the main requirements of a merchantable car were that it should be capable of being driven, and that it should be safe (though he also regarded cosmetic factors as relevant). This car was not safe.[213] A third factor was how easy it was to remedy the defect once the trouble occurred. Here the repairs took several days and cost over £700 although the makers claimed that the car was then as good as new again. Another factor which was regarded by the judge as less important was that the defect might have been easily discovered. Even missing battery leads, he suggested, would render a car unmerchantable until they were replaced.

The present s. 14(2), as we have suggested, confirms the result of these decisions, for it lists freedom from minor defects among the aspects of the quality of the goods which a court must consider in determining whether or not they are of satisfactory quality. It must be noted, however, that the present legislation appears largely to have been driven by concerns about mass-produced manufactured consumer goods. In the case of natural products such as fruit and vegetables, freedom from minor defects may be impossible to achieve. It is in such cases that the qualifying words in s. 14(2B)(c) 'in appropriate cases' will be important.[214] Moreover, this issue would be most likely to crop up in the commercial context, and the modification of the right of rejection in the new s. 15A would also be important.

The Sale and Supply of Goods Act 1994: 'reasonably satisfactory'

The Law Commissions (which began their inquiry before the decisions concerning motor cars discussed above) were concerned that the 1973 statutory definition concentrated too much on fitness for purpose and failed to take account of some of the non-functional aspects of merchantability. Hence their Report proposed to replace

---

212 [1987] 2 All ER 220.

213 See also *Lamarra* v *Capital Bank plc* 2004 GWD 40–817 (Sh Prin J C McInnes): top of range vehicle with several minor cosmetic defeats and one other not minor (defective differential) held unsatisfactory although defects remediable under warranty.

214 'The following (among other things) are in appropriate cases aspects of the quality of goods— (c) freedom from minor defects . . .'

the term 'merchantable quality' with 'acceptable quality', and in effect to adopt a test of 'reasonable acceptability' which was rather similar to the test often widely used in the cases before 1973. In addition, the list of specific matters referred to in s. 14(2B) is intended to set at rest any lingering doubts about non-functional defects. Clearly, under this provision, minor dents, scratches and other non-functional imperfections may be sufficient to render the goods of unacceptable quality under the new statutory implied condition. As noted above, the government accepted the recommendations, subject to substituting a requirement that goods should be of 'satisfactory quality' for the recommended requirement that they be of 'acceptable quality', and the 1994 Act, which was the result of a private member's Bill, adopts the government's formulation.

Nevertheless, as already suggested, the overriding test will be that of satisfactory quality laid down in s. 14(2A), and the matters listed in (2B) will only be taken account of in applying that overriding requirement. So minor defects (para. (c)) or blemishes of appearance and finish (para. (b)) will only render the goods unsatisfactory if a reasonable person would regard them as rendering them unsatisfactory, having regard to the price and other circumstances. Manifestly, in some cases, such as on the purchase of a second-hand car of some age, such blemishes are almost certain to be present, and no reasonable buyer would regard them as making the car unsatisfactory.[215]

In general it does not seem likely that the changes effected by the 1994 Act will make much difference to the law, except for a few points specifically mentioned in s. 14(2B), and dealt with separately in this section. The concept of 'satisfactory quality', it must be said, has even less genuine meaning than the concept of 'merchantable quality', and must be fleshed out by the case law in varying circumstances, and unfortunately, as previously suggested, the effect of the present provisions could be to sever this country from the useful lines of authority which have developed in other common law jurisdictions on the meaning of 'merchantability'. Worse still, for many people the word 'satisfactory' implies a fairly mediocre standard, though it is clearly intended that many minor defects in goods, both under the present law and under the matters specifically listed in s. 14(2B), will still justify rejection, even though a reasonable buyer would often accept the goods and put up with the defects – perhaps claiming damages, and perhaps often not even doing that.[216] Indeed, even the buyer in the particular case may accept the goods, and may be acting reasonably in doing so, but this only deprives him of his right to reject, not of his right to claim damages for breach of the implied term as to quality. This is why it was suggested earlier that the Act should not have any effect on the cases where it has been held that the seller is liable even though he has supplied exactly what the buyer ordered.[217] We must now look at some specific aspects of the quality of the goods which may affect the application of the new provisions.

Durability
There was some controversy as to whether the seller's duty to supply merchantable goods implied that the goods must continue to be satisfactory for any particular

---

215 See *Thain v Anniesland Trade Centre* 1997 SLT (Sh Ct) 102.
216 Note, however, the repair or replacement remedy now available to consumer buyers – see p 525 *et seq.*
217 See above, p. 169 *et seq.*

length of time. In *Mash and Murrell* v *Joseph I Emmanuel*[218] sellers in Cyprus sold potatoes c.&f. Liverpool. The potatoes, though sound when loaded, were rotten by the time the ship arrived, and it was held by Diplock J that the sellers were liable under s. 14(2) on the ground that in such a contract the goods must be loaded in 'such a state that they could endure the normal journey and be in a merchantable condition on arrival'.[219]

On the face of it this seems a reasonable decision. Indeed, it seemed inherent in the concept of merchantability that the goods would remain in a satisfactory condition for a reasonable length of time according to the circumstances of the contract and the nature of the goods. For example, if in *George Wills & Co Ltd* v *Davids Pty Ltd*,[220] discussed below, the sellers had supplied beetroot canned in vinegar with a life of only a few weeks, while the normal life of beetroot canned in vinegar was 12 months, there seems no doubt that the goods would have been unmerchantable. Despite doubts cast on Diplock J's decision in some cases,[221] the House of Lords (in a speech delivered by Lord Diplock) has since unanimously affirmed that the implied condition under s. 14(3) of reasonable fitness for purpose is a warranty that the goods will continue to be fit for a reasonable time.[222] At all events, the new provisions seem to put the matter beyond doubt, as 'durability' is specifically mentioned in s. 14(2B)(e) as one of the aspects of the quality of the goods to which regard is to be had. It must also be noted that cases such as *Mash & Murrell* involved f.o.b. and c.i.f. contracts where risk in general passes to the buyer on loading. If the bill of lading states that the goods were 'shipped in apparent good order and condition', the assumption will tend to be that the deterioration which occurred was due to the hazards of transit, the risks of which are the buyer's. This indeed was what turned out to be the case in *Mash & Murrell* itself.[223] In short, the buyer's decision to accept or reject will, as a matter of practicality, often be determined by what is said in the bill of lading. In *VAI Industries (UK) Ltd* v *Bostock & Bramley Org.*[224] where machinery was delivered f.o.b. with an express warranty, the majority of the Court of Appeal held that a breach of this warranty occurred at the time of delivery, not at the time the breach was discovered.[225]

Of course, what is a reasonable time during which the goods must remain satisfactory will be a question of fact which will depend on the nature of the goods and the circumstances of the case, including no doubt the price paid. High-quality carpets sold at a price commensurate with their quality can be expected to last longer than cheaper carpeting sold at a low price. It must also be appreciated that the seller's continuing obligation does not mean that the goods must remain of the same quality or in the same condition for any length of time, nor even that they must remain, strictly speaking, at the same standard of 'satisfactory quality' as they were at the time of

---

218 [1961] 1 All ER 485, reversed on the facts [1962] 1 All ER 77, but followed in *The Rio Sun* [1985] 1 Lloyd's Rep 350. See also *Beer* v *Walker* (1877) 46 LJQB 677 and, in Scotland, *Knutsen* v *Mauritzen* 1918 1 SLT 85, *Buchanan & Carswell* v *Eugene Ltd* 1936 SC 160, and Ervine, 1984 JR 147.
219 [1961] 1 All ER at p. 485.
220 (1956–57) 98 CLR 77 – see below, p. 196.
221 *Cordova Land Corpn* v *Victor Bros Inc* [1966] 1 WLR 793.
222 *Lambert* v *Lewis* [1982] AC 225, 276; see also *Lee* v *York Coach & Marine* [1977] RTR 35.
223 See [1962] 1 All ER 77.
224 [2003] EWCA Civ 1069.
225 For a useful discussion of this case and others on this point, see Twigg-Flesner (2004) 120 LQR 214.

delivery. Clearly, very few goods will remain in the same condition after delivery and especially after use, and many of them may rapidly cease to be of satisfactory quality in the relevant sense. Even new consumer goods will, soon after delivery, be second-hand goods, and if delivered in *that condition* would hardly be regarded as satisfactory when a new price has been paid. But what is required is that the goods, when delivered, should have the capacity to remain reasonably fit for the purpose, and retain their non-functional attributes, for a reasonable time. It must also be borne in mind that the fact that goods break down within a short time of purchase may be evidence that they were defective at the time of the sale.[226]

Relevance of the price

The price at which goods are sold is often relevant in deciding what quality the buyer is entitled to expect. This was the case under the former provisions,[227] and is the case under the 1994 Act which again expressly mentions price.[228] Clearly, goods which are commonly sold for a variety of purposes are also commonly sold at a variety of prices. And this is not just because market prices may vary, but because some uses may require goods of better quality, and goods fit for those purposes may therefore command a premium. The new provisions require fitness for all purposes for which goods of the kind in question are commonly sold. The words 'kind in question' are obviously crucial. So, in the example of the wrecked car sold as a source of spares, one would obviously expect the price to be very much lower than if the car was sold as a roadworthy vehicle for ordinary road use. Hence if the price was a normal sort of price for a roadworthy vehicle of that type, the vehicle clearly would be unsatisfactory if it was not in fact roadworthy.[229] So the price is an important indicator as to what the buyer could reasonably expect.

As the Sheriff Principal said in *Thain v Anniesland Trade Centre*,[230] where a second-hand car with 80,000 miles in the odometer developed a fault in the gearbox after two weeks' use:

> People who buy second-hand cars get them at less than their original price in a large part because second-hand cars have attached to them an increased risk of expensive repairs. The price of the Renault, £2,995, was considered reasonable because there was the risk of expensive repairs attached to the Renault.

In several large cities there are now car warehouses, selling off what is presumably ex-car-hire company stock, which has reached its 10,000-mile or six months ceiling (or whatever). These establishments offer the vehicles at significantly lower prices than the prices of equivalent vehicles sold by motor dealers. It would appear, however, that the car warehouses would be liable on the quality warranties in the same way as ordinary motor dealers, and that the price at which the goods are sold would not be

---

226 *Crowther v Shannon Motor Co* [1975] 1 WLR 30, 33 per Lord Denning MR. For a critique see Hudson (1978) 94 LQR 566.
227 Section 14(6).
228 Section 14(2A).
229 See, e.g., *Cruickshank v Specialist Cars (Aberdeen) Ltd* 2002 GWD 25-858 (Sheriff A. L. MacFadyen).
230 1997 SLT (Sh Ct) 102.

a relevant consideration. This situation is distinguishable from that in *Thain* v *Anniesland Trade Centre*[231] in that the buyer's expectations of a reasonably new, low mileage car, would be significantly different from those of a high mileage vehicle sold at a low price. Moreover, where the buyer deals as a consumer (as will usually be the case) there is no contracting out.[232] It seems that at least some of these establishments offer title and repair warranty insurance at extra cost. This is, in effect, equivalent to the extended warranty offered with some types of electrical goods.[233] Although the availability of an extended warranty was considered relevant in *Thain* v *Anniesland Trade Centre*,[234] the case is almost certainly wrong on this point.

If the transaction was characterized as being about the sale of a 'collector's car', the fact that it was unroadworthy might not render it unsatisfactory.[235] In short, in borderline cases of this sort, the way in which the court characterizes the deal will be crucial. To some extent this may appear to violate the traditional English canon that the adequacy of consideration is irrelevant, but it was plain that this principle was virtually obsolete in cases concerning merchantable quality, and the same must apply in relation to the persent provisions. The implications of the present law are that a buyer is entitled to value for money.[236] On the other hand, in *Harlingdon & Leinster Ltd* v *Christopher Hull Fine Art Ltd*, the facts of which were given above,[237] it was held that the fact that a painting was not the work of the artist by whom it appeared to have been painted did not make it unmerchantable, even though its value as a forgery was much lower than as the genuine article. The finding on the s. 13 issue was crucial to this determination. The Court of Appeal did not, however, endorse the judge's observation that the words 'merchantable quality' related to anything beyond the physical qualities of the goods sold.

It is also clear from the earlier case law, which surely remains relevant for this purpose, that a buyer cannot complain that the goods are unsatisfactory merely because he has paid slightly over the odds for them. Under the case law pre-dating the statutory definition in s. 14(6) introduced by the 1973 Act it was often said that 'merchantable' meant, in effect, 'commercially saleable' but of course goods may be commercially saleable though only at a discount off the contract price. In *Australian Knitting Mills Ltd* v *Grant*,[238] Dixon CJ had adopted a slightly different test for deciding whether goods were merchantable. According to this test, the goods:

> . . . should be in such a state that a buyer, fully acquainted with the facts . . . would buy them without abatement of the price obtainable for such goods if in reasonable sound order and condition and without special terms.

This seems to have been the first time that the price was explicitly considered as a relevant factor in deciding on merchantability, and Dixon CJ's opinion was later

---

231 1997 SLT (Sh Ct) 102.
232 See p. 234.
233 See p. 297 *et seq.*
234 See p. 195.
235 See e.g. the Scottish case of *MacGill* v *Talbot* 2002 GWD 12-382 (Sheriff G. J. Evans).
236 See *Rogers* v *Parish (Scarborough) Ltd* [1987] QB 933, 944 per Mustill LJ.
237 See p. 150.
238 (1930) 50 CLR 387, 418.

accepted, though with qualifications, by the House of Lords. In *B S Brown & Son Ltd* v *Craiks Ltd*[239] buyers ordered a quantity of cloth from the seller manufacturers. The sellers of the cloth thought it was wanted for industrial purposes but the buyers wanted it for making dresses, for which it proved unsuitable. The buyers had not made known their purpose to the sellers and thus they failed in their claim under s. 14(1) (now 14(3)). The contract price was 36.25d. per yard, which was higher than would normally have been paid for industrial cloth but not substantially higher. In fact, the sellers resold some of the cloth at 30d. per yard. The buyers' claim for damages on the ground that the cloth was unmerchantable was rejected by the House of Lords. The cloth was still commercially saleable for industrial purposes although at a slightly lower price. It was held that the reference to price in the test of merchantability stated by Dixon CJ in *Grant*'s case[240] was too rigidly put. Goods could not be said to be unmerchantable merely because they were not commercially saleable at the contract price but only at a slightly lower price. They would not be unmerchantable unless they could only be resold at a substantially lower price. In this case the buyers had resold some of the cloth (after they had found that it was unsuitable) for 15d. per yard, but it was found that they had not obtained the best market price reasonably obtainable in so doing. Some of the judges clearly thought that if this had been the real market value of the goods, then the difference in price would have been so great as to render them unmerchantable.

An Australian decision of 1921 illustrates a situation where the price difference was substantial enough to produce this result. In *H Beecham & Co Pty Ltd* v *Francis Howard & Co Pty Ltd*[241] the defendants bought spruce timber for piano-making from the plaintiffs. The defendants themselves selected the timber from the plaintiffs' stock but later much of it was found to be affected by dry rot, not observable on reasonable external examination. The sellers argued that the timber was merchantable because it was still saleable as timber for making boxes which was in fact one of the uses to which spruce timber was commonly put. But the buyer paid 80 shillings per hundred feet of timber while spruce timber for box-making was only worth 30 shillings per hundred feet. It was held that the timber was not merchantable under the contract description because 'no businessman, having a contract to buy spruce timber whether for resale or for purposes of manufacture would think for a moment of accepting this timber, its condition being known, without a very large reduction upon current market prices'.

In considering the decision in *B S Brown* v *Craiks*,[242] a word of caution may be desirable. It seems probable that this decision was not intended to apply to goods which are actually defective. Before 1973, it never seems to have been doubted that even trifling defects rendered goods unmerchantable,[243] although they may in fact still be commercially saleable at a price not much lower than the contract price. It is not thought that the House of Lords intended to cast any doubt on this proposition; and

---

239 [1970] 1 All ER 823; 1970 SC (HL) 51.
240 Above, n. 238.
241 [1921] VLR 428.
242 Above, n. 239.
243 See *Jackson* v *Rotax Motor & Cycle Co Ltd* [1910] 2 KB 937.

this may explain why in this case Lord Reid suggested that 'it is [not] possible to frame, except in the vaguest terms, a definition of merchantable quality which can apply to every kind of case'.[244] As we have seen, despite some doubts, it seemed clear that the statutory definition in s. 14(6) did not affect the law on this point. Even relatively minor matters of appearance, finish and other non-functional attributes, could render goods unmerchantable, although obviously some of them might be so minor that they would not substantially affect the price even if known to the buyer at the time of purchase. The present provisions seem to put the matter beyond doubt, and should have the effect that in a case such as *Millars of Falkirk* v *Turpie*[245] the goods would not be held to be of satisfactory quality.[246]

There are some kinds of goods in which the quality is almost infinitely variable, and in which it would seem that compliance with the requirements of merchantability, or the new requirement of satisfactory quality, may depend almost entirely on the price. For example, if a person buys minced beef from a butcher and is supplied with minced beef with a 30 per cent fat content, proof that most minced beef has a lower fat content does not necessarily mean that the goods are not of satisfactory quality. If the price is commensurate with the quality in fact supplied, the goods will be satisfactory.[247] Indeed, there would have to be a substantial disparity between the price appropriate to the quality actually supplied and the price charged before it could be said that the goods were unsatisfactory.

It must be added that the present provisions may cause some problems in this connection, which do not appear to have been anticipated by the Law Commissions. So long as the goods only had to be suitable for some of the purposes for which such goods were commonly bought, it did not matter that such goods sold for other purposes would have cost much more. But now that the new Act requires the goods to be fit for *all* the purposes for which such goods are commonly bought, the question of price will, presumably, become even more critical. Suppose, to take a hypothetical example, based on the Australian *Beecham* case discussed above, that a seller sells spruce wood for box-making at a price appropriate to that use. It would obviously be absurd for the buyer to be allowed to contend that because spruce wood is also often sold for piano-making, therefore the wood he has bought is unmerchantable unless fit for that purpose also. Clearly, the court would have to interpret the new Act in such a way as to avoid this result, and this could perhaps be done by holding that in these circumstances spruce wood for box-making and spruce wood for piano-making are simply not goods of the same kind within the meaning of the new s. 14(2B)(a).

Second-hand goods

As we have already seen, there is nothing in the statutory provisions to exclude their application to second-hand goods, and they have often been applied to such goods,

---

244 [1970] 1 All ER 823, 825; 1970 SC (HL) 51, 73.
245 1976 SLT (Notes) 66.
246 See p. 187 as to remedies available to consumers. The right of rejection might not be exercisable in non-consumer sales – see p. 499 *et seq.* below.
247 See *Goldup* v *John Manson Ltd* [1981] 3 All ER 257, a case under the Food and Drugs legislation (see now the Food Safety Act 1990).

both before and after the 1973 legislation. Again, there is nothing in the new Act to alter this result.

But although second-hand goods have to be satisfactory, no less than new goods, it is clear that nobody can expect second-hand goods at a lower price to be as good as new goods at a higher price.[248] Under the original law, and before the 1973 statutory definition was enacted, the question arose occasionally with motor vehicles, and there was a tendency then to hold that the requirement of merchantability, as it applied to second-hand vehicles, meant that the vehicle must at least be safe and roadworthy. But in *Business Appliances Specialists Ltd v Nationwide Credit Corpn Ltd*[249] the Court of Appeal rejected this approach. The requirement of merchantability extended to other matters besides safety and roadworthiness. They stressed that the statutory definition of merchantability applied also to the case of second-hand goods. Indeed, the test to be applied was precisely the same as the test to be applied for new vehicles, as discussed in *Rogers v Parish (Scarborough) Ltd*.[250] The question always was: whether the goods were as fit for their purpose as it was reasonable to expect. But, of course, it was also abundantly clear that what it was reasonable to expect would differ according to the price, and having regard to the fact that the goods were second-hand.

A few illustrations from the case law under the former provisions reveal some variation of judicial attitudes.[251] *Crowther v Shannon Motor Co*[252] is, perhaps, the most favourable decision from the buyer's point of view. In this case the buyer bought a second-hand Jaguar which had done over 82,000 miles for the (at that time) fairly modest price of £390. The engine seized up after the buyer had done a further 2,000 miles in the space of three weeks; a reconditioned engine had to be fitted to the car. It was held that a breach of s. 14 had been committed because of evidence from the former owner (who had sold it to the defendants) that the engine was 'clapped out' when he sold them the car. An award of no less than £460 in damages was upheld. The plaintiff thus, in effect, obtained a Jaguar with a clapped-out engine for nothing and, in addition, received £70 towards the price of the new engine.

In *Bartlett v Sydney Marcus Ltd*[253] the plaintiff bought a second-hand car from the defendant dealers for £950. The dealers informed the plaintiff that the clutch was defective and they offered either to put it right and sell it at £975 or to leave the buyer to put it right and sell for £950. The buyer chose the latter alternative but, when he came to have the clutch repaired, the defect was found to be more serious than expected and the repair cost him £84. The Court of Appeal held that the car was not unmerchantable merely because the defects proved more serious than expected. There were suggestions in this case that a car which would go, even though not perfectly, might still be merchantable, but it seems clear that these remarks must be confined to the case of second-hand cars. There can, it is thought, be no doubt that

---

248 See passage from the judgment in *Thain v Anniesland Trade Centre*, quoted on p. 190.
249 [1988] RTR 332. See also the helpful judgment of Carswell J in *Lutton v Saville Tractors (Belfast) Ltd* [1986] 12 NIJB 1 (second-hand car should be 'reliable and capable of giving good service and fair performance'), but see observations at p. 190 above.
250 [1987] QB 933.
251 Some of these illustrations are actually drawn from cases in which s. 14(3) was applied rather than s. 14(2) but, as already noted, there is often an overlap between these subsections, and the cases may be equally relevant to both subsections.
252 [1975] 1 All 139. Compare *Thain v Anniesland Trade Centre* 1997 SLT (Sh Ct) 102 – see p. 195.
253 [1965] 1 WLR 1013.

if a *new* car were sold with a defective clutch, the car would be properly said to be unsatisfactory (formerly, unmerchantable). But in this case the car was sold *as second-hand with a defective clutch*. Under that description, the car could not be said to be unmerchantable merely because the defect proved more serious than expected. Equally, under the present provisions, it could not be said to be unsatisfactory.

Two decisions of the Court of Appeal after the statutory definition of merchantability was enacted by the 1973 Act continue to show some variation of judicial attitude. In *Business Appliances Specialists Ltd* v *Nationwide Credit Corpn Ltd*[254] the plaintiff bought a second-hand Mercedes, which had done some 37,000 miles, for £14,850. After a few months, and only 800 miles, serious wear in the valves, valve guides and oil seals appeared, and repairs were required costing £635. Expert evidence was produced to the effect that such wear was very unusual on a Mercedes of that age and mileage. Nevertheless, it was held that there was no breach of the requirement of merchantability.[255] Second-hand cars, it was said, must be expected to have some defects, and some ordinary wear and tear. It was a matter of degree whether the defects exceeded the expectations of the reasonable buyer. Yet this was clearly a very expensive car of extremely high quality. The case is perhaps borderline.

In *Shine* v *General Guarantee Corpn Ltd*[256] the car turned out to have been submerged in water for 24 hours, and had been an insurance company 'write-off'. Although there were no specific defects alleged, and the car appeared to be generally usable, this was enough to persuade the Court of Appeal that the car was unmerchantable. Perhaps the decisive fact here was that a dealer gave evidence that if the facts had been fully known, the car would have been worth £1,000 less than the price. So clearly the buyer had hardly got 'value for money', and that was apparently enough to show a breach of the subsection.[257]

The new provisions shed no light on the rightness or wrongness of these decisions, and if the same fact situations were to fall to be decided under them, the outcomes would no doubt be the same. In *Thain* v *Anniesland Trade Centre*,[258] decided after the 1994 changes, the pursuer purchased for £2,995 a second-hand Renault 19, which was about five years old and had done about 80,000 miles. After two weeks' use, the car developed a gearbox fault which could not be sorted economically, and the car was written off. It was held to be sufficient that the car was fit for initial use, *Crowther* being distinguished on the ground that the defect existed at the time of sale, and that the purchaser assumed the risk that a defect might emerge at any time, given the age and mileage of the car. Durability was not a quality reasonably to be expected of a second-hand car.

Satisfactory quality and differing grades of quality
It is perhaps surprising how little authority there appears to have been on the relationship of the requirement of merchantability under the former provisions[259] to the

---

254 [1988] RTR 332.
255 See also *Thain v Anniesland Trade Centre* (p. 190 above), decided under the 1994 Act. See also text at n. 258 below.
256 [1988] 1 All ER 911.
257 See above, n. 211.
258 1997 SLT (Sh Ct) 102.
259 There is none under the present provisions.

possibility of different grades of quality. Obviously many goods are sold in different grades of quality, and no doubt the price is normally commensurate with the particular quality sold. And we have seen that the price may well be relevant in deciding whether the goods are of satisfactory quality in any given case. But the price is not everything, and it might seem that a requirement of 'satisfactory quality' would have some bearing on the particular grade of quality which the buyer is entitled to receive. For instance, under the American Uniform Commercial Code the requirement of merchantable quality means, in the case of fungible goods, that the buyer is entitled to receive goods at least of 'fair average quality' within the contract description.[260] But it does not seem that the Sale of Goods Act requires the goods to be of any particular grade of quality. The new provisions do not appear to have any bearing on this problem at all.

The term 'satisfactory', like its predecessor 'merchantable', does not necessarily connote that the goods are of any specific grade or quality. As was said by Salmond J in the New Zealand case of *Taylor* v *Combined Buyers Ltd*:[261]

> The term 'merchantable' does not mean of good, or fair, or average quality. Goods may be of inferior or even bad quality but yet fulfil the legal requirement of merchantable quality. For goods may be in the market in any grade, good, bad or indifferent, and yet all equally merchantable. On a sale of goods there is no implied condition that they are of any particular grade or standard. If the buyer wishes to guard himself in this respect he must expressly bargain for the particular grade or standard that he requires. If he does not do so, *caveat emptor*; and he must accept the goods, however inferior in quality, so long as they conform to the description under which they were sold and are of merchantable quality – the term 'quality' including state or condition.

Similarly, Lord Reid in *Kendall* v *Lillico*[262] pointed out that where commodities are sold in the market under some general description, of which there may be several different qualities available, it is sufficient (indeed in that case it was not disputed) that the goods comply with the lowest quality under which goods of that description can commonly be sold. But again, it may be necessary to have regard to the price, for the price paid may show clearly that the buyer was entitled to something more than the lowest quality available in the market.

Again, if the goods comply with the normal condition of goods of the quality and description under which they are sold they will not be unsatisfactory merely because they are inferior to other goods of a similar type. For instance, in the Australian case of *George Wills & Co Ltd* v *Davids Pty Ltd*,[263] the defendants manufactured and sold canned beetroot. For some time it had been customary to can beetroots in brine, but the defendants then started to can them in vinegar. Such cans had a much shorter life – about 12 months – than beetroot canned in brine, or other canned foods, which keep for at least three years, but it was held by the Australian High Court that this did not render the goods unmerchantable. The court said:

> . . . if the contract called for the supply of beetroot canned in vinegar, the parties were bound to deliver and accept goods of this description and, if the condition and quality of the goods

---

260 UCC, s. 2–314(2).
261 [1924] NZLR 627, 645.
262 [1969] 2 AC 31, 79–80.
263 (1956–57) 98 CLR 77.

were normal for goods of this description, the purchaser could have no complaint on the ground of their merchantability. It would be nothing to the point, on any such complaint, to show that beetroot canned in vinegar would not keep for as long a period as canned peas or canned beans or, indeed, beetroot canned in brine or for as long as other canned food-stuffs. Nor would it be material to show that a wholesaler, who had purchased such goods, might still have them in his store more than twelve months later. Indeed, evidence as to the keeping quality of the other goods and as to the practice in the wholesale grocery trade would not be admissible in such circumstances.[264]

As suggested above, it does not seem that the amendments in the new Act will have any effect on this question.

'Quality includes state or condition'

'Quality' was stated by s. 61 of the 1979 Act to include 'the state or condition' of the goods and certain conclusions have been drawn from this definition. In *Niblett v Confectioners' Materials Co Ltd*,[265] the facts of which have already been given, Bankes and Atkin LJJ were of the opinion that there had been a breach of s. 14(2) as well as of s. 12(1). Bankes LJ said:

> Quality includes the state or condition of the goods. The state of this condensed milk was that it was packed in tins bearing labels. The labels were as much part of the state or condition of the goods as the tins were. The state of the packing affected the merchantable quality of the goods.[266]

As this case shows, the concept of 'merchantable quality' might extend beyond matters which would ordinarily be thought of as pertaining to quality. In some contexts, this could be relevant and important with regard to goods which are supplied without proper or adequate instructions. This might also be held to be a matter going to the 'state or condition' of the goods which could involve a breach of s. 14(2) even though the goods themselves might be perfectly satisfactory. But, as we have seen above, it was often possible to arrive at the conclusion that goods were unmerchantable without resorting to these words, if adequate warnings or instructions were not given with the goods.

In the 1994 Act, the words relating to the state or condition of the goods are transferred from s. 61 of the Act to s. 14(2B) itself. This does not appear to lead to any change in the effect of the words.

Part of goods unsatisfactory

The cases which have so far been considered were concerned with goods, all of which were unmerchantable/unsatisfactory. It may happen, however, that only part of the goods are unsatisfactory and that the rest may be satisfactory. In *Jackson v Rotax Motor & Cycle Co Ltd*,[267] the plaintiff supplied motor horns to the defendant. One consignment was rejected by the defendant as unmerchantable on the ground

---

264 At pp. 89–90.
265 [1921] 3 KB 387, above, p. 113.
266 In South Australia there is specific authority holding that the goods may be unmerchantable because of bad packaging: *Gilbert Sharp & Bishop v Wills & Co* [1919] SASR 114.
267 [1910] 2 KB 937.

that about half the goods were dented and scratched owing to bad packing. The Court of Appeal held that the buyer was entitled to reject the whole consignment, as it was not possible in the circumstances of the case to invoke the *de minimis* rule. The requirement of merchantability obviously applied to all the goods, and if part of the goods were unmerchantable the buyer might reject the whole. No change on this point is made by the 1994 Act, though, as we will see, the right of rejection is modified in commercial contracts.[268]

Maintenance of spare parts and servicing facilities

In modern times an important aspect of complex manufactured goods is the commercial practice by which the manufacturer continues to manufacture spare parts for the goods, sometimes for many years after those goods have themselves been discontinued. Similarly, the manufacturer's willingness to supply servicing facilities may, in certain cases, be a matter of some importance. But in the unreported Court of Appeal decision in *L Gent & Sons v Eastman Machine Co Ltd*[269] it was held that there was no legal duty on the manufacturer to observe these practices, and goods could not be held to be unmerchantable merely because these facilities were not, or were no longer, available.[270] The matter was discussed briefly by the Law Commissions in their Final Report, and they concluded, inevitably it would seem, that it was too complex to be dealt with by legislation, and suggested instead that Codes of Practice should be settled under the auspices of the Office of Fair Trading.[271] The EU's Green Paper did not propose legislation on this issue either.[272]

Commissioning goods

In the case of complex goods such as machinery and customized software,[273] the seller may have a duty not merely to supply goods but also to commission them, ironing out in the process any 'teething problems'. In such cases the seller has a reasonable period in which to effect the commissioning before the buyer can reject for breach of either s. 14(2) or (3).[274] Presumably, where this is in the contemplation of the parties, the buyer cannot complain of losses consequential on the defects until after such a reasonable period has expired. If no time is specified, what amounts to a reasonable time will depend upon the facts of the particular case. In the *Burnley Engineering Products* case,[275] a 'high tech' welding machine was delivered in August

---

268 See p. 499 *et seq.*

269 CA 1985, cited by the Law Commissions, Final Report, *Sale and Supply of Goods*, para. 3.66.

270 There is, of course, the possibility of other manufacturers stepping in and filling the gap by manufacturing compatible spare parts. If the original manufacturer seeks to use its intellectual property rights to prevent this, it might have been answered with the 'non-derogation' principle laid down in *British Leyland Ltd v Armstrong Patents* [1986] RPC 279, but this case was criticised by the Privy Council in *Canon Kabushiki Kaisha v Green Cartridge Co (HK)* [1997] AC 728 (replacement cartridges for printers) and in *Mars UK v Teknowledge* [2000] FSR 138 Jacob J refused to apply the doctrine even to repairs (its original field of application). An exercise of intellectual property rights is not, however, of itself, an abuse of a dominant position contrary to Article 82 (former 86 of the Treaty of Rome) – see *Volvo v Veng (UK) Ltd* (Case 238/87) [1989] 4 CMLR 122; see also the Opinion of the Advocate-General in *Magill TV Guide/ITP, BBC and RTE* (1 June 1994, joined cases C–241/91P and C–242/91P) [1995] ECR I-743.

271 See Final Report, *Sale and Supply of Goods*, para. 3.66. Such codes do in fact exist for particular industries.

272 COM (93) 509, p. 80.

273 The question as to whether this is 'goods' is dealt with at p. 78 *et seq.*

274 See *Burnley Engineering Products Ltd v Cambridge Vacuum Engineering Ltd* (1994) 5 Const LR 10.

275 Above.

1991 and rejected on 25 September 1992. It was held that if the de[...] remedied by that date, the buyer would not have been entitled to rejec[...]

4. IMPLIED TERMS THAT THE GOODS ARE FIT FC PARTICULAR PURPOSE

Section 14(3), replacing the original s. 14(1) in the 1893 Act, lays down the following condition:

> Where the seller sells goods in the course of a business and the buyer, expressly or by implication, makes known—
> (a) to the seller, or
> (b) where the purchase price or part of it is payable by instalments and the goods were previously sold by a credit-broker to the seller, to that credit-broker,
> any particular purpose for which the goods are being bought, there is an implied condition that the goods supplied under the contract are reasonably fit for that purpose, whether or not that is a purpose for which such goods are commonly supplied, except where the circumstances show that the buyer does not rely, or that it is unreasonable for him to rely, on the skill or judgment of the seller or credit-broker.[276]

No change in this section is made by the 1994 Act.

In what circumstances is the condition implied?

Reliance on the seller's skill or judgment

Under the original s. 14(1), the buyer had first to satisfy the court that he had expressly or by implication made known to the seller the particular purpose for which the goods were required so as to show that he relied on the seller's skill or judgment. In consumer sales, the courts leaned heavily in favour of the buyer in this respect. For example, in *Grant* v *Australian Knitting Mills Ltd*,[277] Lord Wright said:

> The reliance will seldom be express: it will usually arise by implication from the circumstances; thus to take a case like that in question, of a purchase from a retailer the reliance will be in general inferred from the fact that a buyer goes to the shop in the confidence that the tradesman has selected his stock with skill and judgment.[278]

The trend of the cases was to hold that if the seller knew the purpose for which the buyer wanted the goods, the buyer would be taken to have relied on the seller's skill

---

276 The references to credit-brokers relate to conditional sale agreements (like hire-purchase contracts), and are designed to cover the situation in which a person who acquires goods under a consumer credit contract does not deal directly with the finance company, with whom he actually contracts, but with an ordinary dealer. Such a dealer who introduces the buyer to a finance company (for instance, by getting him to fill in the appropriate forms) is called a credit-broker in the Consumer Credit Act 1974.

277 [1936] AC 85, 99.

278 See, e.g., *Godley* v *Perry* [1960] 1 WLR 9.

judgment.[279] The present s. 14(3) largely confirms the old case law on this point, so that it is still relevant to refer to it. It is now clear that the onus on the buyer in the first instance is only to show that he has made known the purpose for which the goods are being bought. Reliance will then be presumed unless it is positively disproved, or unless the seller can show it to have been unreasonable.

Strictly speaking, of course, reliance is a question of fact, although whether reliance is unreasonable must involve an element of evaluation.[280] But a number of illustrations from typical cases may nonetheless be useful. The fact that both buyers and sellers are members of the same commodity market does not of itself show that the buyer does not rely on the seller, though it no doubt tends against the inference of such reliance.[281] But where one merchant has brought the goods to the attention of another and has recommended them to him, such reliance may be found. When the seller is also the manufacturer, the inference that the buyer has relied on him, at least in part, will rarely be rebutted.[282] The fact that the buyer proposes to analyse or inspect or test the goods on delivery does not mean that he is not relying on the seller.[283] Where the seller is selling for export from the United Kingdom to some country overseas, the mere fact that he knows that the buyer is buying for import into a foreign country does not show that the buyer relies on the seller's skill or judgment with respect to the suitability of the goods for that particular country.[284] In such a case it is the buyer who would normally be presumed to have the necessary knowledge of the conditions in the country of import and reliance may thus be disproved or, alternatively, may be held to be unreasonable.

The concept of 'unreasonable' reliance, introduced by s. 14(3), was not explicitly used before 1973, but it was in fact largely inherent in the old law. Prior to the 1973 Act a court which found that the buyer had acted unreasonably in relying on the seller could always hold that the implied condition was excluded by a contrary intention. As a result of the Unfair Contract Terms Act, this is now no longer always

---

279 See Lord Guest in the *Ashington Piggeries* case [1972] AC 441, 477, explaining some dicta of Lord Reid's in *Kendall v Lillico* [1969] 2 AC 31, 81 where Lord Reid said:
> I do not think that [*Manchester Liners v Rea* — discussed below] is any authority for the view which has sometimes been expressed that if the seller knows the purpose for which the buyer wants the goods it will be presumed that the buyer relied on his skill and judgment.

Of this dictum Lord Guest observed:
> I do not understand my noble and learned friend, Lord Reid, to be saying that the presumption can now be drawn from the mere fact that a particular purpose is made known to the seller. He emphasizes that the question is whether in the whole circumstances the reasonable inference can properly be drawn that a reasonable man in the shoes of the seller would realize that he was being relied on.

It is submitted that, despite the change of wording in the present s. 14(3) from that with which their Lordships were dealing, Lord Guest's dictum is still apposite – few of the cases discussed in the text would have been decided differently under the present provisions.

280 See *Jewson Ltd v Boyhan* [2003] EWCA Civ 1030.

281 *Kendall v Lillico* [1969] 2 AC 31, 124, per Lord Wilberforce.

282 *Kendall v Lillico* [1969] 2 AC 31, 84 (Lord Reid); *Aswan Engineering Co* case [1987] 1 WLR 1, 27 (Nicholls LJ), though cf. Lloyd LJ at pp. 18–19, who thought there was no reliance because the buyer had simply selected the goods from the maker's catalogue. This seems unsound. Selection of goods from a catalogue is no evidence that the buyer does not rely on the manufacturer's skill and judgment, any more than selection of the goods themselves.

283 *Kendall v Lillico* at p. 95 (Lord Morris).

284 *Teheran-Europe Corpn v S T Belton Ltd* [1968] 2 QB 545. This may be of some significance in the case of goods bought over the Internet. Goods which may work perfectly well in the seller's country may be quite inadequate for the conditions in the buyer's country. See Chapter 5.

possible, and it was therefore necessary to give power to the court to exclude liability where 'unreasonable reliance' was shown. It will, of course, be for the courts to decide what amounts to 'unreasonable reliance'. But a good case can be made for treating reliance as unreasonable where the seller in effect disclaims responsibility and merely proffers his advice for what it is worth.[285]

Where the buyer's complaint is that the goods do not perform as well as had been hoped rather than that they are defective in any real sense, it may be relevant that the goods have been made to a new and experimental design. In *Dixon Kerly Ltd* v *Robinson*,[286] the defendant agreed to buy a yacht in course of construction to an untried design of the plaintiffs. Although the plaintiffs knew that the defendant wanted the boat for sea-cruising and cross-channel trips, it was held that the plaintiffs gave no warranty that the yacht would be suitable for this purpose.

It is sufficient if the buyer relies only partially on the skill or judgment of the seller. In *Cammell Laird & Co Ltd* v *Manganese Bronze & Brass Co Ltd*,[287] the defendants agreed to construct two propellers for two ships for the plaintiffs. These were to be made according to certain specifications laid down by the plaintiffs, but certain matters, and in particular the thickness of the blades, were left to the defendants. One of the propellers proved useless owing to defects in matters not laid down in the specification. It was held by the House of Lords that the defendants were liable for breach of the condition implied by the old s. 14(1) as 'there was a substantial area outside the specification which was not covered by its directions and was therefore necessarily left to the skill and judgment of the seller'.[288] But where the buyer has only relied partially on the skill or judgment of the seller, 'the reliance in question must be such as to constitute a substantial and effective inducement which leads the buyer to agree to purchase the commodity'.[289] Moreover, it must be shown that the matters of which the buyer complains were matters in respect of which he relied on the seller.[290]

If, however, the buyer is well aware that the seller can only supply him with one particular brand of the goods in question, it can scarcely be said that the buyer relies on the seller's skill or judgment. Thus in *Wren* v *Holt*,[291] where the plaintiff bought beer in a public house which he knew to be tied, the Court of Appeal held that there was evidence on which the jury could find that the buyer had not relied on the seller's skill or judgment. Mere suspicion that only a certain type of goods can be supplied is not enough to exclude liability, however.

In *Manchester Liners Ltd* v *Rea*,[292] the defendants supplied coal to the plaintiffs for their ship the *Manchester Importer*. The coal was unsuitable for this ship, and the

---

285 See Law Commissions Report, *Exemption Clauses: First Report*, para. 37. No doubt the disclaimer must be properly brought home to the buyer and not just contained in small print.
286 [1965] 2 Lloyd's Rep 404.
287 [1934] AC 402. But, it must be the particular quality at issue in respect of which there is partial reliance – *Jewson Ltd* v *Boyhan* [2003] EWCA Civ 1030.
288 At p. 414, per Lord Warrington.
289 *Medway Oil & Storage Co Ltd* v *Silica Gel Corpn* (1928) 33 Com Cas 195, 196 per Lord Sumner.
290 *Christopher Hill Ltd* v *Ashington Piggeries* [1969] 3 All ER 1496, upheld on this point, [1972] AC 441.
291 [1903] 1 KB 610. But the implied condition of satisfactory quality still applies.
292 [1922] 2 AC 74 – the decision in this case has been criticized, however – notably by Lord Denning MR in *Teheran-Europe Corpn* v *S T Belton Ltd*, n. 284 above, but see n. 293 below.

sellers were held liable under the section although the buyers had good ground for suspecting that the seller might have difficulty in supplying the right type of coal owing to a railway strike.[293]

Where the buyer has invited a third party to inspect the goods on his behalf, and the third party has reported favourably to the buyer in reliance on the seller's skill and judgment, it may be a nice question whether the buyer himself can be regarded as having relied on the seller's skill and judgment or whether he has merely relied on the third party's report. If the third party is the buyer's employee acting in the course of his duty,[294] or perhaps if he actually passes on to the buyer what the seller has said, it seems that the buyer can invoke the section. But as we have seen above, the fact that the buyer proposes to have the goods inspected or tested *after* delivery does not rebut the inference that he is relying on the seller's skill or judgment.

Where sellers sold potatoes for export from Northern Ireland to Poland and it was shown that a clearance certificate was required from the Northern Ireland Ministry of Agriculture, it was held that the buyers relied on the certificate rather than on the sellers in respect of matters covered by the certificate.[295] However, this may have been a special case. In export sales it is common for buyers to demand certificates of quality from impartial third parties who are required to inspect the goods, or samples, prior to shipment. Buyers clearly rely substantially on such certificates because they often have to pay for the goods before they receive them, but this does not deprive them of their normal remedies against the sellers under the contract of sale itself.

'Particular purpose'

Although the old s. 14(1) referred to 'the particular purpose for which the goods are required' it was well settled that the word 'particular' was used in the sense of 'specified' rather than in contradistinction to 'general'.[296] The purpose may in fact be a very general purpose, for example a car to drive on the road. In *MacGill* v *Talbot*[297] a classic car collector advised a commercial car dealer that he wished to buy a Rolls Royce that was reasonably fit for the purpose of economic restoration. The dealers provided a car which it was estimated would cost about £23,500 to restore; in fact it cost £85,000 to £100,000. It was held that the buyer had made known a particular purpose, in the light of previous dealings between the parties. Moreover, the word 'particular' did not exclude cases where the goods could only be used for one purpose. In *Priest* v *Last*,[298] for example, the Court of Appeal held that a hot-water bottle was required for a particular purpose within the section although it had only one purpose in the ordinary way. To quote again from Lord Wright in *Grant* v *Australian Knitting Mills Ltd*:[299]

---

293 The actual decision in this case seems to have turned on a crucial finding of fact that the coal actually delivered was not fit for an ordinary Manchester steamer (a well-known class of vessel at the time) in the hands of average officers and crew – see *Kendall* v *Lillico* [1969] 2 AC 31, 81 per Lord Reid. Given that the seller was a coal merchant, he ought to have known that the coal was unsuitable.
294 *Ashford Shire Council* v *Dependable Motors Pty Ltd* [1961] AC 336.
295 *Phoenix Distributors Ltd* v *L B Clarke Ltd* [1967] 1 Lloyd's Rep 518.
296 *Kendall* v *Lillico* [1969] 2 AC 31, 123 per Lord Wilberforce.
297 2002 GWD 12-382 (Sheriff G. J. Evans).
298 [1903] 2 KB 148.
299 [1936] AC 85, 99.

There is no need to specify in terms the particular purpose for which the buyer requires the goods, which is nonetheless the particular purpose within the meaning of the section, because it is the only purpose for which anyone would ordinarily want the goods.

These decisions appear to be largely confirmed by the present s. 14(3), which has substituted the words 'any particular purpose' for 'the particular purpose'.

Some difficulty has arisen where the purpose for which the buyer wants the goods is made known to the seller but there is some peculiarity about the purpose of which the seller is unaware. In *Griffiths* v *Peter Conway Ltd*[300] the plaintiff contracted dermatitis from a Harris Tweed coat which she had bought from the defendants. It was found as a fact that the plaintiff had an unusually sensitive skin and that the coat would not have harmed a normal person. It was argued for the plaintiff that the case fell within the precise words of the section as the coat was not fit for the purpose for which it was required, namely her personal use. This argument was rejected by the Court of Appeal[301] on the ground that the plaintiff's sensitive skin rendered the required use so special that she had not made known to the sellers the purpose for which the coat was required in the relevant sense.[302]

In reaching this decision, the court was obliged to distinguish *Manchester Liners* v *Rea*,[303] which has been referred to above, and in which it was held that coal supplied by sellers for a particular ship was required by the section to be suitable for that ship. Lord Greene pointed out that ships differed in their types and requirements and that coal merchants knew this well enough; hence, if a merchant undertook to supply coal for a particular ship, he was bound to supply coal suitable for that ship. There was no normal or standard type of ship from which the plaintiff's ship differed. But in *Griffiths* v *Peter Conway Ltd*[304] this was the position. A normal person would have been unaffected by the coat. This does not mean that persons who are, in one sense, 'abnormal' are never protected by the subsection, because there are clearly degrees of abnormality. For instance, a drug unfit for use by pregnant women would seem clearly to be unfit for its purpose if sold for use by a woman who is in fact pregnant.

In the *Ashington Piggeries* case[305] herring meal was sold for compounding into animal feeding stuffs, but the meal was contaminated with some toxic element. This rendered the meal mildly toxic to most animals though it was only seriously dangerous to mink. It was held that the case differed from *Griffiths* v *Peter Conway Ltd*, which was a 'highly special case' because, although mink were peculiarly susceptible to the toxic element, there was evidence that this element was also harmful to other animals. Moreover, it was held that the burden of proof was on the seller to establish

---

300 [1939] 1 All ER 685.
301 See also *Ingham* v *Emes* [1955] 2 QB 366, a case of skill and labour. It is also instructive in this connection to compare *Sumner Permain & Co Ltd* v *Webb & Co Ltd* [1922] 1 KB 55 (above, p. 177) and *Mash & Murrell* v *Joseph I Emmanuel Ltd* [1961] 1 All ER 485 (above, p. 177).
302 See also *Slater and Slater and others* v *Finning Ltd* [1996] 2 Lloyd's Rep 353, 1997 SC (HL) 8 – supply of camshafts for a marine engine which suffered an abnormality which created excessive torsion resonance in the shafts. The House of Lords held that the suppliers not having been made aware of the abnormality were not in a position to exercise skill and judgment for the purpose of dealing with it.
303 [1922] 2 AC 74.
304 [1939] 1 All ER 685.
305 [1972] AC 441.

that the toxic element was harmless to other animals. Thus, in the upshot, the herring meal was held to be unfit for the purpose for which it was sold (namely compounding into animal feeding-stuff) even though it could have been safely compounded into such feeding-stuff in small quantities so long as the resultant compound was sold as not fit for use by mink. But this was largely because the dangerous element in the meal was not known. If it had been known, and the buyers had bought it all the same, then it would clearly have been fit for the purpose for which it was sold.

Resale may be a particular purpose within the meaning of the section where it is clear enough for what purposes the goods will ultimately be used. But where a buyer buys goods which have a wide variety of possible uses the responsibility placed on the seller may be heavy indeed. In *Kendall* v *Lillico*[306] (which was much discussed in the section on satisfactory quality) Brazilian ground nut extraction was sold for the purpose of compounding it into feeding-stuff for cattle and poultry, and it was held that there was a breach of the section because the extraction proved fatal to pheasant and partridge chicks, though it was not dangerous to cattle. In the *Ashington Piggeries* case (referred to above) the original suppliers were merely selling herring meal for compounding into animal feeding-stuffs and this proved fatal to mink. Again the suppliers were held liable. It will be seen that in cases of this nature, the 'particular purpose' may be very wide indeed, and although the goods may be quite satisfactory for a wide range of uses, the seller will be liable if the goods are in fact unsuitable for any one of those uses to which the buyer puts the goods.[307] The only qualification on this seems to be that it must be shown that the particular use to which the buyer put the goods was not unforeseeable or abnormal. It is unnecessary to show that this particular use was actually contemplated by the parties. Nor, under s. 14(3), is it necessary that the goods are commonly supplied for the purpose in question. Thus in the *Ashington Piggeries* case it was enough to render the ultimate suppliers liable that herring meal commonly used in feeding-stuffs for mink; it was not necessary to go further and show that this was the particular purpose for which the feeding-stuff would be likely to be used.

Status of seller is irrelevant

Since the subsection formerly stated that the seller was liable 'whether he [was] the manufacturer or not', it might have been thought that it only applied to manufactured goods, but it was well settled that it also applied to non-manufactured goods, such as foodstuffs.[308] The present s. 14(3) has dropped these words altogether.

'Where the seller sells goods in the course of a business'

The original s. 14(1) applied only where the goods were of a description 'which it is in the course of the seller's business to supply'. The 1973 Act made it clear that so

---

306 [1969] 2 AC 31.
307 But see below for the view of Nicholls LJ in the *Aswan Engineering* case [1987] 1 WLR 1, 27, which suggests that where the goods are sold for one broad purpose they will be reasonably fit for that purpose even though unfit for some unusual subdivisions within it.
308 *Frost* v *Aylesbury Dairy Co Ltd* [1905] 1 KB 608 (typhoid-infected milk); *Wallis* v *Russell* [1902] 2 IR 585 (infected crabs).

long as the seller was selling 'in the course of a business'[309] this requirement was satisfied. This provision is now reproduced in the 1979 Act.[310]

Whatever interpretation is given to these words, it is clear that they exclude from the operation of s. 14(3) all cases of private sales, for example of second-hand goods, and that, in practice, only manufacturers, wholesalers, retailers and dealers will be caught by this implied condition. Since the implied condition that the goods are satisfactory is limited in the same way, as has been seen, it follows that there is still fairly wide scope for the application of the maxim *caveat emptor* in private sales. Of course, actual reliance by a buyer in such a case may justify a finding that an express warranty was given, but there is no implied term under s. 14(2) or (3).

Onus of proof

It is for the claimant to prove, on the balance of probabilities, that the defendant's product was not fit for its purpose.[311]

The former proviso to s. 14(3)

Section 14(3) (which was formerly s. 14(1)) originally had a proviso which excluded liability where goods were sold under a 'patent or other trade name',[312] but once again the courts leaned heavily in favour of the buyer in interpreting the words of the Act. There were two leading cases on the interpretation of the proviso, *Bristol Tramway Co Ltd* v *Fiat Motors Ltd*[313] and *Baldry* v *Marshall*.[314]

The second case virtually interpreted the proviso out of existence, since it was plain that the only circumstances in which the proviso applied were those in which the buyer had not relied on the skill or judgment of the seller. The fact that goods were ordered under a patent or trade name was not enough to exclude the seller's liability unless the circumstances showed that the buyer was not relying on the seller's skill or judgment. Although normally a person who buys goods in a shop is relying impliedly on the seller's skill and judgment, it is reasonably clear that where he orders the goods under a trade name he is relying on the reputation of the maker rather than on the shopkeeper. 'If a person goes in[to a shop] and asks for a bottle of R White's lemonade, or somebody's particular brand of beer, he is not relying on the skill and judgment of the person who serves it to him.'[315] The Law Commissions felt that the proviso had ceased to serve any purpose and it disappeared in the 1973 Act.

---

309 And the discussion at p. 167 *et seq* as to what amounts to sale 'in the course of a business' in relation to s. 14(2) is pertinent here.

310 The meaning of 'in the course of a business' was discussed in *Stevenson* v *Rogers*, and *Buchanan-Jardine* v *Hamilink* considered above at p. 167.

311 *Leicester Circuits Ltd* v *Coates Brothers plc* [2003] EWCA Civ 290.

312 This archaic usage is not today sustainable. A trade name in this context is either a registered or an unregistered trade mark. It is implausible that this archaic designation was sustainable at the time the Sale of Goods Act 1893 was passed.

313 [1910] 2 KB 831.

314 [1925] 1 KB 260.

315 *Daniels* v *White* [1938] 4 All ER 258, 263 per Lewis J.

What is the extent of the seller's obligation?

The second question which arises under this subsection is: what is the extent of the seller's obligation? Several points arise here.

Goods to which s. 14(3) extends
A precisely comparable point arises under s. 14(2) and has already been dealt with above.[316] Reference should be made to this discussion.

Triviality
As in the case of the requirement of satisfactory quality, it seems clear that the condition under s. 14(3) can be violated even though the unfitness is a trivial matter, and could easily have been rectified. In *Parsons (Livestock) Ltd* v *Uttley, Ingham & Co*[317] it does not seem to have been seriously disputed that the sellers were in breach of s. 14(3) when they supplied an animal-food hopper to the plaintiffs, but left open a ventilator (which could not be seen from the ground) with ultimately disastrous results. The only thing wrong with the hopper as supplied was that the ventilator was closed, a matter which could have been easily and instantly rectified if it had been discovered.

Strictness of seller's liability
It is now beyond doubt that the defendant's obligations can extend under s. 14(3) to latent defects not discoverable by any amount of diligence or care. In *Frost* v *Aylesbury Dairy Co Ltd*[318] the argument was pressed that the buyer 'could not be said to rely on the skill or judgment of the sellers in a case in which no skill or judgment would enable them to find out the defect' in the goods supplied. The goods in question were milk infected with typhoid against which it was not at the time practical to test. The sellers were held liable, though a reason for this appears to have been that they warranted the milk 'free from germs and disease'. In a number of American cases, the 'blood bank' cases, patients were infected by diseases in blood given in transfusions. These were such that at the time it was not feasible to test for their presence. In some cases the courts refused to hold that there had been a sale.[319] In other cases, however, the courts held that a warranty was implied, and was breached.[320]

In *Kendall* v *Lillico*,[321] Lord Reid said:

> If the law were always logical one would suppose that a buyer who has obtained a right to rely on the seller's skill and judgment, would only obtain thereby an assurance that proper skill and judgment had been exercised, and would only be entitled to a remedy if a defect in the goods was due to failure to exercise such skill and judgment. But the law has always gone further than that. By getting the seller to undertake to use his skill and judgment the

---

316   See p. 173.
317   [1978] QB 791.
318   [1905] 1 KB 608.
319   *Perlmutter* v *Beth David Hospital* 123 NE 2d 792 (1955); *Balkowitsch* v *Minneapolis War Memorial Blood Bank* 132 NW 2d 805 (1965).
320   *Russell* v *Community Blood Bank* 185 So 2d 749 (1966); *Hansen* v *Mercy Hospital* 570 P 2d 1309 (1977). Compare *A* v *National Blood Authority* [2001] 3 All ER 289, a case decided under the Consumer Protection Act 1987 – see p. 278.
321   [1969] 2 AC 31, 84.

buyer gets under s. 14(1) [now 14(3)] an assurance that the goods will be reasonably fit for his purpose and that covers not only defects which the seller ought to have detected but also defects which are latent in the sense that even the utmost skill and judgment on the part of the seller would not have detected them.

It should be noted, however, that this remark appears to address the question of the liability of a seller, rather than that of the manufacturer or ultimate supplier. As suggested below,[322] the liability of the latter may be less than absolute. If we regard the holding of the seller liable to be principally a device for passing back liability 'up the line', it can be argued that the seller's liability should not be greater than that of the manufacturer or ultimate supplier, unless the seller has expressly or impliedly undertaken a greater liability. In any event, the seller's duty is only to supply goods which are 'reasonably' fit, not which are absolutely fit. This is likely to be of special importance where the relevant 'particular purpose' is very broadly stated. For if the goods are suitable for most subdivisions within a broad 'purpose', the fact that they may not be reasonably fit for some rare and improbable subdivision will not necessarily involve a breach of s. 14(3).[323] This point was discussed by Lord Pearce in *Kendall v Lillico*:[324]

> I would expect a tribunal of fact to decide that a car sold in this country was reasonably fit for touring even though it was not well adapted for conditions in a heat-wave: but not, if it could not cope adequately with rain. If, however, it developed some lethal or dangerous trick in very hot weather I would expect it to be found unfit. In deciding the question of fact the rarity of the unsuitability would be weighed against the gravity of its consequences. Again, if food was merely unpalatable or useless on rare occasions, it might well be reasonably suitable for food. But I should certainly not expect it to be held reasonably suitable if even on very rare occasions it killed the consumer. The question for the tribunal of fact is simply 'were these goods reasonably fit for the specified purpose?'

In the *Ashington Piggeries* case,[325] which has been referred to above, the sellers sold herring meal to buyers which was suitable for inclusion in foodstuffs for most animals but was contaminated with some substance which rendered it poisonous to mink. The buyers used the meal in preparing foodstuffs which were sold to mink companies; the companies used the foodstuffs as mink food and suffered serious losses in consequence. They sued the buyers, who claimed in turn against the sellers. The buyers argued that the meal was required to be reasonably fit for inclusion in animal foodstuffs generally; the sellers argued that the meal was only required to be reasonably fit for inclusion in feeding-stuffs for pigs, poultry and cattle. It was held, in effect, that the meal was required to be fit for inclusion in feeding-stuffs for any animals to which the sellers ought to have contemplated that it might be fed, and that was sufficient to impose liability on the sellers on the facts.

A slightly less stringent test was favoured in the *Aswan Engineering* case,[326] where pails bought by the plaintiffs for filling with waterproofing compound proved unfit

---

322 See p. 283.
323 See *Slater v Finning Ltd* [1996] 3 All ER 398, 1997 SC (HL) 8 – failure of camshafts on vessel due not to the camshafts themselves but to an idiosyncrasy of the appellant's vessel.
324 [1969] 2 AC 31, 115.
325 [1972] AC 441.
326 [1987] 1 WLR 1.

for stacking six high in the intense heat of a Kuwaiti dockside. The Court of Appeal rejected the buyers' claim under s. 14(3) (as well as the claim under s. 14(2)). Lloyd LJ rejected the claim because he thought the plaintiffs had not relied on the sellers; but Nicholls LJ thought that such reliance had been proved on the facts. Nevertheless, he took the view that even if the particular purpose for which the goods had been required was simply 'for export', this would not have been enough to fix liability on the sellers. Where the purpose is stated as broadly as this, it adds little to the requirements of merchantability, because it is enough to make the goods reasonably fit 'for export' that they are in fact fit for export to most parts of the world.

Fitness for purpose and unusual consequences

Where very unusual consequences follow from the use of the goods – sometimes causing unexpected accidental injury and damage and the like – it is sometimes argued that the goods were perfectly fit for all ordinary purposes, and that the unusual consequences in the particular case should not be laid at the seller's door. In *Vacwell Engineering Co Ltd v B D H Chemicals*[327] the defendants sold glass ampoules containing a chemical known as boron tribromide to the buyers, who required it for use in certain manufacturing processes. The chemical, in itself, was perfectly fit for the plaintiffs' purposes but it was liable to react with great violence on contact with water, though this was unknown to the plaintiffs. The plaintiffs' process required the labels to be washed off the ampoules and this was done with water. While this was being done one of them broke, causing a reaction which shattered all the others and as a result a very violent explosion occurred. It was held that the goods were not reasonably fit for the purpose for which they were sold and the defendants were liable because they ought to have foreseen the possibility of the chemical coming into contact with water, and they had not warned the buyers of this danger.[328] Both in this case and in the *Ashington Piggeries* case, the issue under s. 14(3) was very similar to a general argument that the damage which occurred was too remote in accordance with the ordinary principles of contract law discussed by the House of Lords in the *Heron II*.[329] In this type of situation it seems that the application of these principles is in effect identical with the question whether the goods are reasonably fit for their purpose under s. 14(3).

This appears to be borne out also by the decision of the House of Lords in *Lambert v Lewis*[330] where manufacturers had made a defective towing coupling which was sold by retailers to a farmer. The farmer continued to use the coupling after it was apparent that it was in a dangerous or unfit state, and an accident resulted which led to the farmer having to pay damages to the injured plaintiffs. The farmer sought to recover these damages in an action against the retailer for breach of s. 14(3) of the Act. There clearly was such a breach because the coupling was sold in a condition in which it was not reasonably fit for its purpose (or at least

---

327 [1969] 3 All ER 1681.
328 Three books in the defendants' own library warned of the danger.
329 [1969] 1 AC 350.
330 [1982] AC 225.

was not likely to remain so fit for a reasonable time), but the House of Lords nevertheless held that the farmer could not recover from the retailer the damages he had to pay the plaintiff. The reason for this was, in effect, that the damages were too remote. In accordance with ordinary principles of remoteness, the farmer's own negligence in continuing to use the coupling in an obviously dangerous state was sufficient to sever the causal chain and free the retailers from liability for the farmer's own negligence.

Knowledge, warnings, instructions, etc.

Just as with the implied condition that goods are of satisfactory quality (merchantable quality under the former provisions) the seller may be liable because the goods are supplied with inadequate information, warnings or instructions. The *Ashington Piggeries* case, referred to several times above, is one example of goods which were unfit for their purpose because they involved a toxic element unknown to the buyers. If the buyers (not being the ultimate users) had been warned about this element of toxicity, the goods would probably have been fit for their purpose. The *Vacwell Engineering* case, also mentioned above, is another case where the goods were probably unfit for their purpose only because the buyers had not been warned by the sellers that the chemical must on no account be allowed to come into contact with water.

More recently the Court of Appeal had to consider a case of alleged inadequate instructions for use in *Wormell v R H M Agriculture (East) Ltd*,[331] where the plaintiff, a farmer, had bought a weed-killer from the defendant sellers for spraying his crops. Detailed instructions were on the canisters in which the weed-killer was supplied, saying in large letters (among other things) that spraying was not recommended after a certain stage in the growth of the crops. But the plaintiff thought this warning was designed to avoid the risk of damage to the crops, and he was willing to take the risk of damage. Accordingly he used the spray even during the period not recommended, but it proved virtually worthless, and the plaintiff sued for the wasted price of the weed-killer. The trial judge found that the instructions were somewhat ambiguous and misleading, and the plaintiff had quite reasonably understood the warning to refer only to the risk of crop-damage. But the Court of Appeal reversed this decision. They insisted that there was nothing wrong with the weed-killer, which would have done its job if applied in the right conditions (and it was immaterial that those conditions had scarcely existed at all during the year in question because of the weather). The case was not, insisted the Court, an action for negligence or misrepresentation. The question concerned the fitness of the goods themselves, and these were (said the Court) quite fit for their use if used properly. The warning on the instructions should have been heeded. It was, however, not doubted that the instructions had to be taken into account in deciding whether the goods were fit for their purpose,[332] so it seems that the Court was (in effect) finding that the instructions were not misleading. It is, perhaps, not clear if the Court was rejecting the usual objective methods

---

331 [1987] 1 WLR 1091. The type of fact situation in this case has given rise to much litigation in the United States –
see *Durham v CIBA-Geigy* 315 NW 2d 696 (SD 1982) and citations therefor.
332 At pp. 1098, 1099–1100.

of interpreting contractual documents, because there are indications in the judgment that the sellers would not have been liable if the weed-killer had been fit for use when used as intended by the sellers, even if the buyer reasonably misunderstood their intentions because of misleading instructions. If this is the implication of the decision it is out of line with the usual principles of interpretation, and there seems no reason why these principles should not apply to warnings and instructions as much as to all other contractual documents.

Durability

The next point concerns the length of time during which the goods must remain reasonably fit for the purpose. Similar questions arise in dealing with the implied condition that the goods must be of satisfactory quality.[333] The principle is the same here and there is no reason to duplicate the above discussion. Even though the new s. 14(2B)(e) specifically covers 'durability' in the requirement that goods should be of 'satisfactory quality', and this does not extend to the implied condition under s. 14(3), there is no reason to doubt that the case law mentioned above covers this point quite adequately.

Minor defects, non-functional defects, etc.

As we have seen, the authorities on the implied condition of merchantable quality interpreted that condition so as to cover non-functional defects, such as minor blemishes, cosmetic defects and so forth.[334] They also interpreted that implied condition as extending to minor defects which were easily rectifiable, at any rate, where they were potentially dangerous, and perhaps even in other cases as when (for instance) the defects simply made the goods unusable, albeit only until the defect is put right.[335] There seems no reason why this approach should not also apply to the implied condition under s. 14(3). Even after the statutory amendment to s. 14(2) made by the Sale and Supply of Goods Act 1994, it is difficult to think of circumstances where goods not of satisfactory quality would be held fit for their purpose, and breach of both warranties is commonly pleaded.[336]

So far as new vehicles are concerned, it is arguable that they must be free from all defects and even that accessories and components must all be in proper working order. It does not seem enough to say that the purpose for which a buyer wants a vehicle is simply the purpose of driving it on the road, and that so long as it can do that, it must be reasonably fit for its purpose.[337] If that were the case, a buyer would not be able to complain under this section that (for instance) a car radio or cigarette lighter did not work. Yet a buyer is surely entitled to say that if he has bought a new car with a radio or lighter, he must have made it clear to the seller that one of the purposes for which he bought it (even if only a minor or subsidiary

---

333 See above, p. 188 *et seq.*
334 See above, p. 185 *et seq.*
335 See the example of the car with a missing battery lead given by Rougier J in *Bernstein v Pamson Motors (Golders Green) Ltd* [1987] 2 All ER 220.
336 See *Teheran-Europe Co Ltd v S. T. Belton (Tractors) Ltd* [1968] 2 QB 545, 562–3.
337 See Mustill LJ's comments in *Rogers v Parish (Scarborough) Ltd* quoted at p. 186 above.

purpose) is to be able to listen to the radio while driving, and another to be able to light a cigarette while using the car.

In practice, few cases are brought which deal solely with such minor defects, doubtless for the good reason that buyers do not normally attempt to reject cars in such circumstances.[338] But it may well be a serious question whether a buyer can reject, for a breach of this section, a car which suffers from a collection or series of very trivial defects.[339] Generally, the courts have accepted the argument that a 'congeries of defects', each of which may be relatively minor in itself, may in total render a car unfit for its purpose.[340]

Comparison between s. 13, s. 14(2) and (3) and s. 15(2)(c)

It is clear by now that the conditions implied by s. 13, s. 14(2), s. 14(3) and ss. 14(2C)(c) and 15(2)(c)[341] (which apply to sales by sample – sales by sample are discussed later)[342] must frequently overlap in practice and, in fact, it has often happened that a plaintiff has succeeded under several of the corresponding sections of the original Act. It may therefore be useful to complete this examination of these implied conditions by comparing and contrasting the provisions of the various subsections.

First, both s. 14(2) and (3) only apply where the goods are supplied by a seller who sells in the course of business,[343] and it is clear that this qualification means the same in the two cases.[344] In sales by sample, this restriction does not apply.[345] Nor does it apply to the requirements of s. 13.[346]

Secondly, in all cases, the provisions apply to manufactured and non-manufactured goods alike.

Thirdly, s. 14(3) only applies where the buyer relies on the skill or judgment of the seller,[347] whereas ss. 14(2) (and 15(2)(c)) apply even where this is not the case.[348] This distinction may be more apparent than real because the most obvious way in which the buyer can show that he is not relying on the seller is to examine the goods himself and, if he does so, s. 14(2) excludes liability for defects which ought to have been revealed by that examination. Section 15(2)(c) also excludes liability for defects discoverable by reasonable examination of a sample whether it is in fact examined or not. In one respect, however, s. 14(3) is clearly wider than the other two subsections, because a person may examine the goods and still rely partly on the seller's skill or judgment. In another respect it is narrower than the other two, because if an examination is taken to

---

338 In the case of consumer sales, because of the changes made to the Sale of Goods Act 1979 s. 48 by the Sale and Supply of Goods to Consumers Regulations 2002, SI 2002/3045, whether or not buyers are entitled to reject for minor defects is of little practical importance because most consumers will choose to require repair or replacement – see p. 525 *et seq.*

339 Again in the case of consumer sales the point made in the previous footnote is applicable.

340 *Farnworth Finance Facilities* v *Attryde* [1970] 1 WLR 1053. But cf. *Porter* v *General Guarantee Corpn Ltd* [1982] RTR 384.

341 See p. 163 for text.

342 See p. 212 below.

343 See pp. 167 and 204 *et seq.*

344 Ibid.

345 See p. 163 above.

346 See p. 158.

347 Note the onus of proof is now on the seller to show that the buyer did not rely on the skill a judgment of the seller – see p. 199 *et seq.*

348 See pp. 199 *et seq.* and 168 *et seq.*

indicate a lack of reliance on the seller's skill or judgment it will exclude s. 14(3) altogether, whereas it will only exclude liability under s. 14(2) in respect of defects which could have been discovered by the examination, and the same is true of s. 15(2)(c). There are also other situations in which it is plain that the buyer is not relying on the seller's skill and judgment (as where he orders goods only obtainable from one source) and yet s. 14(2) applies. Examination appears at first sight to be irrelevant to s. 13, and there is no doubt that the condition in s. 13 can apply even though the buyer has examined the goods.[349] But it is also clear that examination of the goods may be a relevant factor in deciding whether the sale is a sale by description or not. Moreover, it seems unlikely that a buyer could rely on non-conformity with description where he is aware of such non-conformity from his examination of the goods.

Fourthly, s. 14(3) is wider than the other subsections in that goods may be perfectly satisfactory although not fit for the purpose for which they were bought. On the other hand, the wider liability only attaches if the purpose is expressly or impliedly made known to the seller, while the condition as to satisfactory quality applies in any event. Section 13, as we have seen, deals with description and not quality or fitness, but in some circumstances the description includes matters of quality or fitness. Goods may comply with their description but be unsatisfactory or unfit for their purpose, but the converse is also true.

Fifthly, s. 14(2) and s. 14(3) apply to all sales whether by description or by sample, or in any other way, whereas s. 13 only applies to sales by description, and s. 15(2)(c) only to sales by sample.

5. IMPLIED TERMS IN SALES BY SAMPLE

The meaning of a sale by sample has been left for treatment here, where it can be most conveniently dealt with. Section 15(1) says somewhat unhelpfully:

> A contract of sale is a contract for sale by sample where there is an express or implied term to that effect in the contract.

This subsection means that the mere fact that a sample is provided for the buyer's inspection does not make the sale a sale by sample. It is only a sale by sample if there is evidence of an intention that it should be such. In this connection the parol evidence rule has given rise to some difficulty; it has been held in a number of cases[350] that, if the contract is reduced to writing, and the writing contains no reference to a sample, parol evidence is not normally admissible to show that a sample was produced to the buyer and that the sale is a sale by sample. But where the description of the goods has no common or definite trade meaning, such evidence may be admissible to identify the description with a sample. So, for instance, where sellers sold 'matchless No. 2475 39/40 white voile' under a written contract, the Australian High Court held that it was open to the buyers to identify this product by reference to a sample, though no mention of the sample was contained in the contract.[351] It has

---

349 See p. 156.
350 *Meyer* v *Everth* (1814) 4 Camp. 22; *Gardiner* v *Gray* (1815) 4 Camp. 144; *Ginner* v *King* (1890) 7 TLR 140.
351 *Cameron & Co* v *Slutzkin Pty Ltd* (1923) 32 CLR 81.

also been held in Australia that a parol collateral contract may be proved under which the goods are warranted equal to sample, even where the contract is in writing and contains no reference to a sample.[352]

The classic exposition of the effect of a sale by sample is that of Lord Macnaghten in *Drummond* v *Van Ingen*:

> The office of a sample is to present to the eye the real meaning and intention of the parties with regard to the subject matter of the contract which, owing to the imperfections of language, it may be difficult or impossible to express in words. The sample speaks for itself. But it cannot be treated as saying more than such a sample would tell a merchant of the class to which the buyer belongs, using due care and diligence, and appealing to it in the ordinary way and with the knowledge possessed by merchants of that class at the time. No doubt the sample might be made to say a great deal more. Pulled to pieces and examined by unusual tests which curiosity or suspicion might suggest, it would doubtless reveal every secret of its construction. But that is not the way in which business is done in this country.[353]

It follows from this, as was held by the House of Lords in this case and as s. 15(2)(c) of the Act lays down in requiring the goods to be free from any defect making their quality unsatisfactory,[354] that the use of a sample does not protect the seller from liability in respect of defects not reasonably discoverable on examination of the sample, although the bulk may in fact correspond perfectly with it. This is clear from s. 14(2C)(c) added by the 1994 Act.

We have already dealt with the warranty of freedom from defects rendering the quality of the goods unsatisfactory in sales by sample.[355] The other provisions of the 1979 Act in respect of sales by sample were:

> 15. (2) In the case of a contract for sale by sample there is an implied condition that—
>   (a) the bulk will correspond with the sample in quality;
>   (b) the buyer will have a reasonable opportunity of comparing the bulk with the sample;

The 1994 Act repeals subsection (b) and the equivalent provision is now to be found in s. 35(2)(b),[356] and it substitutes the word 'term' for 'condition', but goes on to provide that in England, Wales and Northern Ireland the term implied by subsection (2) is a condition so that the effect is the same as previously.[357] In Scotland, however, the test for rejection under s. 15 continues to be the materiality of the breach.

Section 15(2)(a) lays down the obvious requirement that the bulk must correspond with the sample. It has been held that 'it is no compliance with a contractual obligation for an article to be delivered which is not in accordance with the sample but which can by some simple process, no matter how simple, be turned into an

352 *L G Thorne & Co Pty Ltd v Thomas Borthwick & Sons Ltd* (1956) 56 SR (NSW) 81.
353 (1887) 12 App Cas 284, 297. See also *Godley v Perry* [1960] 1 WLR 9. But in these days of sophisticated technological products it must sometimes happen that a sample is provided which is indeed expected to be subjected to very extensive scientific testing. In such a case, of course, this dictum would be inapplicable.
354 The text of the subsection is given at p. 163 above.
355 Ibid.
356 See p. 163.
357 Section 15(3).

article which is in accordance with the sample'.[358] But where, according to the normal usages of trade, the sample is intended merely for visual examination, the buyer cannot complain that the bulk does not correspond with it so long as, on a normal visual examination, it would appear to correspond, even though there are in fact differences, perhaps material differences. The point is that, if the sample is only intended for a simple visual examination, the buyer has in no way been misled by a sample being different from the bulk if the difference could only have been discovered by microscopic examination.[359]

It is, of course, perfectly possible for a seller to sell goods without guaranteeing that they comply with some sample provided to the buyer. The seller may require the buyer to make his own examination of the bulk, leaving it to him to decide how much of the bulk he will examine, and how far he is prepared to take the risk of assuming that the rest of it corresponds with the sample. And in some cases (for example, on a sale of agricultural produce yet to be grown) the parties must know that there may be variation in the quality of the crop from year to year, and the seller is unlikely to guarantee precise correspondence of the bulk with a sample. But in such a case, the sale would not be a sale by sample within the meaning of the section.[360]

Section 35(2)(b) provides:

> Where goods are delivered to the buyer, and he has not previously examined them, he is not deemed to have accepted them . . . until he has had a reasonable opportunity of examining them for the purpose— . . .
> (b) in the case of a contract for sale by sample, of comparing the bulk with the sample.

This is, in effect, a special instance of the general right of examination conferred by s. 34.[361] The former subsection was not very happily expressed because it was difficult to see how there could be a breach of the condition which it implied without a breach of the more fundamental duty of delivering the goods. What it really meant, and what s. 35 now says, is that the buyer is not to be deemed to have accepted the goods until he has had an opportunity of examining them and comparing the bulk with the sample. The effect of the acceptance is that the buyer can no longer reject for breach of condition, but is relegated to his right to claim damages.[362]

It may finally be remarked here that in a sale by sample and by description, the combined effect of ss. 13 and 15 is that the goods must correspond with the sample and with the description, and (if the seller is selling in the course of business) be satisfactory. But s. 14(2)(c) still operates so as to exclude liability in respect of defects rendering goods unsatisfactory which should have been discovered on reasonable inspection of the sample.

The Act makes no provision for what might be called a 'sale by model'. It is an everyday occurrence for a consumer to buy some product in a shop after examining

---

358 *E & S Ruben v Faire Bros Ltd* [1949] 1 KB 254, 260, per Hilbery J.
359 *Hookway & Co v Alfred Isaacs* [1954] 1 Lloyd's Rep 491; *Steels & Busks v Bleecker Bik & Co* [1956] 1 Lloyd's Rep 228. But see also the caveat in n. 353.
360 See the helpful article by Murdoch (1981) 44 MLR 388.
361 See pp. 506–7.
362 See s. 11(4), below, p. 506. For possible differences between the right of examination under s. 15(2)(c) and s. 34, see Murdoch, above, n. 360.

an identical product. But very often he is not actually supplied with the very goods which he has examined, but with another version, still packaged, but which is believed to be identical to the one examined. This is not exactly a sale by sample (there is no 'bulk'), though it is clearly very close to a sale by sample. It seems that there should be an implied condition that the actual goods supplied will be identical with the one examined (unless any differences are expressly mentioned or brought to the buyer's attention), and no doubt such a condition can be implied as a matter of general contract law. The implied conditions under s. 14(2) and (3) are, of course, unaffected by the particular nature of such a transaction.

Having regard to what was said above, it is difficult to see what these sale by sample provisions add to ss. 13 and 14.[363]

6. IMPLIED TERMS ANNEXED BY TRADE USAGE

Section 14(4), replacing and slightly altering the original s. 14(3), lays down that:

> An implied condition or warranty about quality or fitness for a particular purpose may be annexed to a contract of sale by usage.

This subsection merely illustrates the general rule applicable to all contracts that the intention of the parties must be ascertained in the light of all the surrounding circumstances. Where the transaction is connected with a particular trade, the custom and usage of that trade must be considered as a part of the background against which the parties contracted. In the words of Parke B in a leading case:

> It has long been settled, that, in commercial transactions, extrinsic evidence of custom and usage is admissible to annex incidents to written contracts, in matters with respect to which they are silent.[364]

A simple modern illustration is provided by *Peter Darlington Partners Ltd v Gosho Co Ltd*,[365] which has already been referred to.[366] The case was concerned with a sale of canary seed and, according to the custom of the trade, the buyer was not entitled to reject the goods for impurities in the seed, but was entitled to a rebate on the price, proportionate to the percentage of admixture in the seed. It was held that the contract was governed by this trade custom.

7. OTHER IMPLIED TERMS

Section 14(1) is as follows:

> Except as provided by this section, and section 15 below and subject to any other enactment, there is no implied condition or warranty about the quality or fitness for any particular purpose of goods supplied under a contract of sale.

---

363 Article 2 of the Uniform Commercial Code has no equivalent of these provisions.
364 *Hutton v Warren* (1836) 1 M & W 466, 475.
365 [1964] 1 Lloyd's Rep 149.
366 See p. 162.

Given that the provisions of s. 14 have been overhauled by Acts starting from the Sale of Goods (Implied Terms) Act 1973, and culminating in the 1994 Sale and Supply of Goods Act, this residual exclusion of additional implied terms is unobjectionable and indeed inevitable. What is perhaps surprising is that the draftsman did not see fit to relegate this clause to the end of the section rather than leave it at the head.

8. MISTAKE AS TO QUALITY

English law

It is traditional to treat the problem of mistake as to subject-matter in general, and mistake as to quality in particular, in isolation from the conditions implied by the Sale of Goods Act,[367] but now that it is becoming increasingly accepted that a mistake of this kind is merely a relevant factor to be considered in the construction of the contract, this approach has become inappropriate. If the correct view of English law is that a mistake as to quality only renders a contract inoperative (or, as it is usually put, void) where this is the true construction of the contract, it is plain that it is impossible to consider the question of mistake without first examining the implied terms as to quality laid down in the Act.

As it has been sought to show elsewhere,[368] where there is a contract for the sale of goods which turn out to be defective, the courts are in principle faced with three possible solutions to the case. (1) It may be held that the responsibility is on the seller, because of an express or implied term or misrepresentation. (2) It may be held that the buyer has taken the risk of the goods being defective, that is that it is a case of *caveat emptor*. (3) It may be held that neither seller nor buyer has taken the risk or may reasonably be held to have taken the risk or responsibility of the goods being defective. Although lawyers frequently discuss cases of the third sort as being part of some 'doctrine' of mistake the courts have rarely adopted this approach.

Claim by buyer that contract void for mistake
In practice, a party who alleges that a contract of sale is 'void' owing to a mistake as to the quality of the goods does so for the very reason that the terms implied by the Sale of Goods Act do not protect him or, alternatively, because he wishes to reject the goods and he cannot do so for breach of condition owing to the strict limitations imposed on the right of rejection by the Act.[369] For this reason it will be found that it is nearly always a buyer, rarely a seller, who claims a contract to be 'void' on such a ground. Confusion has also arisen from some cases, because in holding that a buyer is entitled to reject goods for breach of condition, the courts have sometimes used language which is capable of being interpreted to mean that the contract is itself void.

---

367 A tradition followed in earlier editions of this book.
368 See (1961) 24 MLR 421 (P. S. Atiyah with F. A. R. Bennion).
369 See below, p. 506. Or again, a buyer may invoke mistake in order to evade the normal limitation period, though in this case he will have to rely on s. 32 of the Limitation Act 1980, rather than on an ordinary claim at common law, or in equity, because such claims are themselves subject to limitation periods. See *Peco Arts Inc v Hazlitt Galleries* [1983] 3 All ER 193.

In practice, the courts have nearly always dealt with cases of this sort by asking 'Has the seller not delivered what he contracted to sell?' (that is, 'Has there been a breach of s. 13?') and 'Has there been any express or implied condition or warranty relating to the quality of the goods?' (that is, 'Has there been a breach of s. 14(2) or (3)?'). If the answer to either of these questions is 'Yes', the buyer has his remedy, whereas if the answer to both questions is in the negative, the buyer has no remedy: it is a case of *caveat emptor*. To argue that the contract is void for mistake in such circumstances is an attempt to add new terms to those implied by the Act, or to evade the restrictions on the right of rejection imposed by ss. 11 and 35. It has already been seen that s. 14(1) prevents the implication of terms, other than those there set out, which would impose additional responsibilities on the seller in respect of the quality or fitness of the goods.[370]

Nevertheless, it is possible that s. 14(1) would not prevent the implication, in suitable cases, of genuine conditions in the offer or acceptance, subject to which the buyer is prepared to contract. Such a condition would not impose a liability on the seller, but would, if unsatisfied, prevent a contract coming into existence, or from operating where it has already come into existence. *Financings Ltd v Stimson*[371] could be regarded as an illustration of a contract 'void by mistake', but the courts simply do not adopt this analysis. In that case, where the goods, unknown to the parties, were damaged between the offer and the acceptance, the court treated the question as one of construction of the offer.

While it is not possible in a book of this nature to examine in detail all the cases on this subject, it is necessary to glance at a few of them. For many years *Smith v Hughes*[372] has been a leading, if puzzling, case on this point. In this famous case the defendant agreed to buy a specific quantity of oats from the seller after the seller had given the buyer a sample. The buyer declined to accept the goods on the ground that they were new oats and not, as he thought, old oats. In such circumstances the approach of the courts today would simply be to ask if the seller had contracted to deliver old oats or the specific parcel of oats sold, old or not. As the buyer had seen a sample of the oats, it is hard to see how the buyer could today get such a case on its feet unless he could show that the seller had described the oats as old. Any attempt to rely on mistake is simply to fudge the issue.

In *Leaf v International Galleries*[373] the plaintiff bought a painting from the defendants which was believed by both parties to be, and was stated by the defendants to be, a Constable. Some years later the plaintiff discovered that the picture was a copy, and he brought an action claiming rescission of the contract. Now it is possible that the buyer could have obtained damages for breach of condition, but he did not want damages – he wanted to rescind the contract. Unfortunately for him his claim to reject the goods for breach of condition was plainly barred by the Act, and he accordingly attempted to argue that he could rescind for innocent misrepresentation instead. This claim was rejected by the court on the ground that he was too late.

---

370 See above, p. 215 *et seq.*
371 [1962] 1 WLR 1184.
372 (1871) LR 6 QB 597; see above, p. 40.
373 [1950] 2 KB 86.

It will be seen that no suggestion was made that the contract was void for mistake, but Denning LJ discussed the possibility in his judgment and rejected it because:

> Such a mistake does not avoid the contract: there was no mistake at all about the subject matter of the sale. It was a specific picture 'Salisbury Cathedral'. The parties were agreed in the same terms on the same subject matter, and that is sufficient to make a contract.[374]

Denning LJ might also have added that if the sellers had expressly stated that the picture was a Constable, the risk of its not being a Constable was plainly on them, and accordingly any construction of the contract which would have placed the risk on neither party was ruled out. There was thus no room for any holding that the contract was void for mistake.

Another case which seems to bear out this view is *Harrison & Jones v Bunten & Lancaster*,[375] where the appellants (from arbitration) agreed to buy from the respondents a quantity of Calcutta Kapok 'Sree' brand. Both parties were under the impression that this was a brand of pure Kapok but, in fact, it contained a proportion of cotton, which rendered it unsuitable for the buyers' purposes, and they claimed to reject it. Pilcher J held that the contract was not void for mistake. He said:[376]

> When goods, whether specific or unascertained, are sold under a known trade description without misrepresentation, innocent or guilty, and without breach of warranty, the fact that both parties are unaware that goods of that known trade description lack any particular quality is, in my view, completely irrelevant; the parties are bound by their contract, and there is no room for the doctrine that the contract can be treated as a nullity on the ground of mutual mistake, even though the mistake from the point of view of the purchaser may turn out to be of a fundamental character.

It is true that elsewhere in his judgment,[377] Pilcher J said that 'there are, no doubt, many cases in which proof of a mutual mistake[378] as to a quality of a fundamental character will serve to avoid a contract of sale', but the fact remains that (except for the cases as to perished goods, dealt with in Chapter 8) there is scarcely a single modern case in our reports to illustrate such a rule with the dubious exception of *Nicholson & Venn v Smith Marriott*.[379] In this case the plaintiffs bought a set of table linen described as Caroline, whereas it was in fact discovered to be Georgian. The plaintiffs sued for and obtained damages for breach of warranty, but the learned judge went on to say that in his opinion the contract was void for mistake. His remarks on this point were therefore obiter, and they were disapproved by Denning LJ in *Solle v Butcher*.[380]

It remains to consider whether the position in equity differs from the position at law. Before the decision in *Solle v Butcher* there was no ground for thinking that

---

374 At p. 89.
375 [1953] 1 QB 646.
376 At p. 658.
377 At p. 656.
378 That is, common mistake.
379 (1947) 177 LT 189.
380 [1950] 1 KB 671, 692. The learned judge (Hallett J) did not explain how he was able to award damages for breach of warranty if, as he thought, the contract was void.

equity recognized a wider doctrine of common mistake than law. The only difference was that equity treated contracts affected by common mistakes as voidable and not void. The reason for this was that most of these cases involved title to land and, in such cases, the parties went to the Chancery because they wished to have documents delivered up for cancellation. Once within the jurisdiction of equity, they had of course to accept such terms as the court wished to impose. Hence the impression arose that such contracts were not void but voidable.

Solle v *Butcher* is not a case of sale of goods, and whatever the *ratio decidendi* of the case it would appear that the profession has not yet been convinced that there is an independent doctrine of mistake in equity which entitles a court to set aside contracts owing to a mistake as to the subject-matter of the contract.[381] Even if the views of Denning LJ are eventually accepted, it is unlikely that they will be applied to purely commercial contracts such as the sale of goods, and it would probably be unfortunate if this were ever done. The law applicable to the sale of goods is on the whole both well-known and reasonably definite. It might create considerable uncertainty in business relations if a vague and discretionary doctrine of mistake in equity were to be applied to the sale of goods. An argument based on mistake in equity was also pressed in *Harrison & Jones* v *Bunten & Lancaster*, but Pilcher J said:[382]

> In the facts of the case . . . neither party was at fault . . . I am well satisfied that it would not be right on the facts of this case to say that the contracts were voidable on equitable grounds, and I do not propose to say any more about that.

It is submitted that this dictum is applicable to all cases of sale of goods if not, indeed, to all commercial transactions, and it is proposed to follow the learned judge's example and not to 'say any more about that'.[383]

Claim by seller that contract void for mistake

We have mentioned above that a claim that a contract is void for mistake is more usually made by the buyer and not by the seller. Buyers are now well protected by the law, at least in respect of mistakes as to the quality of the goods they buy, and for this reason, it has been suggested, there has been increasing reluctance to recognize additional buyer rights by holding a contract void for mistake at the suit of a buyer.[384] The converse situation is somewhat different. There are no implied terms to protect the seller or to ensure that he receives fair value for his goods. Doubtless this difference has arisen for a variety of reasons, but the main one would seem to be that buyers are more likely to be private individuals than sellers. Of course, in the commercial sphere, where goods are bought and sold in bulk, buyers and sellers are

---

381 However, it was followed in *Grist* v *Bailey* [1967] Ch 532, and again in *Laurence* v *Lexcourt Holdings Ltd* [1978] 2 All ER 810; it appears to have been accepted as good law in *Associated Japanese Bank SA* v *Crédit du Nord SA* [1988] 3 All ER 902; it was also in substance adopted by the Australian High Court in *Taylor* v *Johnson* (1983) 151 CLR 422. In *Clarion Ltd and others* v *National Provident Institution* [2000] 2 All ER 265 (not a sale of goods case) it was held that it was ordinarily not part of equity's function to allow a party to escape from a bad bargain.

382 [1953] 1 QB 646, 654.

383 For a more general discussion of the role of equity in relation to mistake, see Atiyah, *Introduction to the Law of Contract*, 5th edn, pp. 228–9 (1995).

384 See *Clarion Ltd and others* v *National Provident Institution*, n. 381 above, the observations in which seem pertinent to sales of goods, although it was not a sale of goods case.

businessmen alike, but in the consumer sphere, the consumer is usually the buyer and less commonly the seller. However, this is not invariably the case. Individuals sometimes sell goods to dealers, for example second-hand cars, antiques or farm produce. In such situations, the law still offers no real protection to the individual seller against the danger of being over-reached. Of course, in extreme cases there may be the possibility of relying on fraud, misrepresentation or undue influence, but there are no implied terms to protect the seller.

It is in precisely this sort of case that courts may be found willing to protect a seller by invoking mistake doctrines. The most famous such case is undoubtedly the American decision in *Sherwood* v *Walker*,[385] which concerned the sale of a cow, believed by both parties to be barren, for $80. In fact the cow was with calf and her true value was between $750 and $1,000. The majority of the court held the contract to be void for mistake on the ground that the parties were mistaken as to the substance of the thing sold. There is a sense in which the goods here were *more* than fit for the purpose for which they were sold; the court's holding goes some way to saying that this excess fitness may be so gross that it would be unfair to hold the seller to the bargain. The protection thus accorded the seller still falls far short of that given to the buyer. He is entitled to complain of *any* deficiency in the fitness of the goods. By conventional modern English standards, *Sherwood* v *Walker* is probably wrong; certainly it is difficult to believe that the case would be followed if the contract were between two business parties. But the decision seems more acceptable if it is recognized as a consumer protection case; this would involve a recognition that an individual seller, selling to a buyer who buys in the course of business, requires greater protection than other sellers, just as the individual buyer buying from the seller who sells in the course of business has long been recognized to have greater rights than other buyers.

An alternative route by which an exception to the doctrine of *caveat vendor*, more acceptable to modern ideas than the doctrine of mistake, may be justified is as follows. In the more-or-less contemporaneous case of *Wood* v *Boynton*[386] a girl sold a stone the size of a canary's egg to a jeweller, who bought it in good faith professing himself unsure as to what it was. He paid $1 for it. It turned out to be a diamond. The contract was held not to be void for mistake. One possible way of distinguishing *Sherwood* v *Walker* is that the parties in *Wood* v *Boynton* were clearly contracting on the basis that the nature of the stone was uncertain. By contrast, in *Sherwood* v *Walker* the parties contracted on the basis that the cow was a cow for meat: the price might have been high or low for such goods, but that fundamental assumption set the limits of the risks exchanged by the parties. Accordingly, when matters proved to be otherwise, the seller might avoid the contract. This analysis, it will be realized, can also be applied to the doctrine of frustration: events beyond the control of the parties have affected the risk exchange intended by the parties.[387]

385 (1887) 33 NW 919.
386 25 NW 42 (1885).
387 Though from an economic point of view it has been argued that discharge should only be allowed where the promisee is the superior risk bearer. If the promisor is the superior risk bearer, non-performance should be treated as a breach of contract – see Posner and Rosenfield (1977) 6 Jo Leg Studies 83. On this analysis, cases such as *Krell* v *Henry* [1903] 2 KB 740 are doubtful. For an analysis of mistake in terms of efficiency of information gathering see Kronman (1978) 7 Jo Leg Studies 1.

Scots law

The Scots law of error has been much controverted and relatively little of the case law has been concerned with the subject-matter of sales of goods or with their quality.[388] The most recent analyses[389] have deployed a distinction between error in transaction (one related to a provision in the contract) and error in motive (where there will be no relief unless the error was induced by the other party's misrepresentation). Thus if A agrees to sell to B a painting declared in the contract to be a Picasso, and it is not, B could reduce the contract for error or sue for breach; while if A had merely represented that the painting was by Picasso, B could only claim reduction (unless A's misrepresentation was negligent or fraudulent, in which case B would have a delictual claim for damages). Either category of error will generally render the contract voidable. If an error of transaction is a unilateral error of expression – as where A, meaning to sell for £10,000, by a slip writes £1,000 – A may reduce the contract only if the other party knew or ought to have known of the error.

9. REFORM OF THE PRIVITY DOCTRINE

Privity issues crop up in all kinds of transaction, not merely those involving consumers, and for the reasons given below, it is considered appropriate to deal with this topic in this chapter. According to the privity doctrine in English law, where goods are sold by a manufacturer to a retailer, and then by the retailer to a customer, the customer cannot sue on the warranties implied in the contract between the manufacturer and the retailer, because a person cannot enforce a term of a contract to which he is not a party.[390] In fact, this is only one type of privity question. Four basic privity questions can be identified. These are as follows:

1 Can a person enforce a term of a contract to which he is not a party? (Questions of this sort can be labelled 'P$_1$'.)[391]
2 Can a person set up a defence based on the terms of a contract to which he is not a party in order to answer a claim brought by a person who is a party to the relevant contract ('P$_2$')?
3 Can a contracting party set up a defence based on the terms of his own contract in order to answer a claim brought by a person who is not a party to the relevant contract ('P$_3$')?
4 Can a contracting party enforce the terms of his own contract against a person who is not a party to the relevant contract ('P$_4$')?

---

388 There is, however, an extensive literature. See above, p. 45 *et seq*, for a summary overview; on error as to the quality of the thing contracted for, see Lawson (1936) 52 LQR 79; Gow (1952) 1 ICLQ 472, (1953) 65 JR 221, (1954) 66 JR 253; Smith (1955) 71 LQR 507; Stein, *Fault in the Formation of Contract* (1957), pp. 171–208.

389 See 15 *Laws of Scotland: Stair Memorial Encyclopaedia* paras 686–694; MacQueen and Thomson, *Contract Law in Scotland* (2000) paras 4.45–4.66.

390 See *Dunlop Pneumatic Tyre Co v Selfridge & Co Ltd* [1915] AC 847. Scots common law has always recognized third party rights in contract. For its doctrine of *jus quaesitum tertio*, see 15 *Laws of Scotland: Stair Memorial Encyclopaedia* (1996) paras 824–52.

391 This is the problem addressed by the 1999 Act – see below. The following two privity questions are addressed by the Act only in relation to the relaxation of P$_1$.

According to the doctrine of privity, each of these questions must be answered in the negative.[392] To answer P_1 and P_2 in the affirmative would be to allow a third party to take the benefit of a contract to which it was not a party; to answer P_3 and P_4 in the affirmative would involve burdening a person under a contract to which it was not a party.

A modest reform of the privity doctrine has now been effected by the Contracts (Rights of Third Parties) Act 1999 (which closely follows the draft appended to Law Com. No. 242). It modifies the rule in relation to P_1 and P_2 situations, but not in relation to P_4 situations. Its application to P_3 questions is not at all clear.[393]

Although this measure is not limited to consumer transactions, it is likely that in practice this is where (if anywhere) it is likely to be of application, since commercial contractors appear generally to be modifying their standard terms to ensure that the Act does not confer rights on a third party.

The key to the reform is the test of enforceability. By s. 1(1) of the 1999 Act, a third party is given the right to enforce a contract term if:

> the contract expressly provides that he may; or
> subject to s. 1(2) the term purports to confer a benefit on the third party.

According to s. 1(2), the second limb of the test (i.e., the test stated in s. 1(1)(b)) does not apply if on a proper construction of the contract it appears that the parties did not intend the contract to be enforceable by the third party. To take advantage of these provisions, the third party (as s. 1(3) stipulates):

> . . . must be expressly identified in the contract by name, as a member of a class or as answering a particular description but need not be in existence when the contract is entered into.[394]

Where the test enforceability is satisfied, the third party has the rights of a contracting party, but no greater rights.[395]

Lastly, s. 1(5) makes it clear that for the purpose of exercising his right, there shall be available to the third party any remedy that would have been available to him in an action for breach of contract if he had been a party to the contract, and also the benefit of any exclusion or limitation of liability.[396] Section 2 contains somewhat complicated provisions intended to preserve a third party's rights in certain circumstances if the contracting parties seek to vary or rescind a contract.

The Law Commission says that the second limb of the test would not normally cut across chains of sales contracts to give a purchaser of goods from a retailer a right to enforce a manufacturer's quality promises.[397] On the other hand, the Law Commission implies that the position might be different where B purchases goods from retailer A, making it clear that the goods are being purchased as a gift for C

---

392 The courts have cited *Dunlop v Selfridge* as a reason for answering each of the privity questions in the negative, though the question involved in that case was a P_1 question.
393 See *Butterworths Common Law Series: The Law of Contract*, 2003. Page 1065 *et seq.* See also p. 270 *et seq* below.
394 For discussion of the issues underlying the designation, existence and ascertainability of the third party, see Part VIII of the Law Commission's Report, *Privity of Contract: Contracts for the Benefit of Third Parties*, Law Com. No. 242, Cm. 3329, 1996.
395 See s. 1(4).
396 Section 1(6).
397 Op. cit., para. 7.18(iii).

(and with delivery to be direct to C).[398] Here, the Law Commission suggests that C might have a contractual claim against A for breach of the quality undertakings (although it qualifies this by saying that such a claim would be subject to rebuttal by A under the proviso).[399] What is to be made of this?[400] Nothing at all, is one possible view. What the Commission collectively thinks, or what individual Commissioners might think, matters little once legislation is in force. From that point on, the courts (with or without assistance from *Pepper* v *Hart*[401]) will gloss the statutory framework as they see fit. Another view is that, although the Act leaves the operation of s. 1(2) unclear, the Commission's fall-back position is that the parties can always cover themselves by express provision (and, perhaps, should be encouraged to do so). Thus, if the contractors do not intend the third party to have the right to enforce, they can simply say so and the presumption will be rebutted. Alternatively, if the contractors do intend the third party to have the right to enforce, they can say so and thereby invoke the first limb of the test of enforceability. Neither of these views, however, will satisfy those who want to know where they stand at the time of the Act's coming into force rather than after some later litigation – nor, of course, do they assuage the concern about the idea that parties are free to contract out of the reforms whenever it suits them.

---

398 Cf., p. 89, note 31: if delivery is not to be direct to C, there might be some difficulty in showing that the contract of sale was intended to confer a benefit on C.
399 See op. cit., para. 7.41 (illustrative example 14).
400 See also the discussion on p. 270 *et seq*.
401 [1993] 1 All ER 42 (noted by Miers (1993) 56 MLR 695).

14

EXCLUSION OF SELLER'S LIABILITY

EXEMPTION CLAUSES

Many contracts, especially 'standard-form contracts', contain exemption clauses the purpose of which is to negative the terms which would normally be implied in favour of a buyer. At first there was nothing legally objectionable in this course in contracts of sale of goods because s. 55 of the Act (now s. 55(1))[1] originally enabled the parties to negative or vary, by express agreement, any of the terms which were implied by the Act. Similarly, in hire-purchase agreements which did not fall within the ambit of the Hire-Purchase Acts, all implied conditions and warranties could be, and almost invariably were, excluded by the terms of the agreement. In cases governed by the Hire-Purchase Acts, however, the right to contract out of the implied terms was always severely restricted.

Although the courts did what they could to control the more extreme forms of abuse of this power of contracting out, the position became more and more unsatisfactory, as will be seen below.[2] Eventually it became clear that the task of controlling unreasonable exemption clauses was beyond the power of the courts and the position was radically altered by the Supply of Goods (Implied Terms) Act 1973. This Act greatly restricted the power of the seller to contract out of his liability for defective goods and also extended the restrictions formerly applicable to hire-purchase contracts. Then, in 1977, more general control of exclusion clauses was introduced by the Unfair Contract Terms Act (UCTA), which replaced the relevant provisions of the 1973 Act. On 1 July 1995, the EC's Directive on Unfair Terms in Consumer Contracts,[3] as implemented by the Unfair Terms in Consumer Contracts Regulations,[4] came into force. These added further controls. Because in some ways the implementing Regulations did not follow the Directive, they have now been replaced by Regulations which do so more exactly.[5] Since 2002 the Law Commissions have been working on combining these two sets of provisions into one set of rules on unfair terms – see joint consultation paper, 'Unfair Terms in Contracts', August 2002. In practice, UCTA and the Directive render the common

---

1 See above, p. 106.
2 See below, p. 232. For a history of the law relating to exemption clauses in standard form contracts see Adams, J.N., *Law Litigants and the Legal Profession*, Royal Historical Society, 1983, eds Ives and Manchester, p. 39; see also Adams, J.N., *Unconscionability and the Standard Form Contract* in 'Welfarism in Contract', eds Brownsword, R., Howells, G., and Williamsen, T., Dartmouth, 1994.
3 Council Directive 93/13/EEC.
4 SI 1994/3159.
5 SI 1999/2083. See p. 257.

law rules concerning exemption clauses of much less importance, but it will still be necessary to decide whether an exemption clause has been made part of the contract and at least in a general way what its effect is likely to be before the impact of UCTA and the new provisions need to be considered. Accordingly, a brief statement of the broadly similar common law position in England and Wales and Scotland follows and then UCTA is closely examined. Lastly, the Directive and the Regulations implementing it are dealt with.

If a seller relies on an exemption clause, he will first have to show that the clause was incorporated into the contract, that is that it was part of his offer which was accepted by the buyer. He can do this in one of two ways, namely by showing that the buyer has actually signed a contract incorporating the clause in question, or by showing that the clause was brought to the notice of the buyer.

In the first case, the fact that the buyer has not understood, or even read, the contract or the clause in question is immaterial.[6] Even in this case, however, there are some circumstances in which the seller may be disentitled from relying on the exemption clause. For example, if the seller has misrepresented the effect of the clause, whether fraudulently or innocently, he will not be able to rely on it;[7] similarly, if it is written on the reverse of the document in a foreign language, and the buyer's attention is not drawn to it.[8] So also, an express oral statement made by the seller may in some circumstances be treated as a term which overrides the terms of the written agreement.[9] Finally, there are some, though admittedly rare, circumstances in English law in which a party may plead that the contract was wholly void because the nature or effect or terms of the contract were radically different from what he had supposed.[10] In the absence of fraud, this plea is unlikely to arise in practice in cases of sale of goods because it must be rare indeed that a buyer (or seller) makes such a fundamental mistake as to justify holding the contract to be void.

Secondly, a party to a written contract can rely on an exemption clause, even where the other party has not signed it, if he has given reasonable notice of the existence of the clause before the contract is made, in such a way as to show that he intends it to be an integral part of the contract. This is a general principle of the law of contract which is not of such great importance in the law of sale of goods as it is in relation to certain other types of contract, and it would be outside the scope of this subject to discuss the cases in detail.[11]

---

6 *L'Estrange* v *Graucob* [1934] 2 KB 394.
7 *Curtis* v *Chemical Cleaning Co & Dyeing* [1951] 1 KB 805.
8 *Harvey* v *Ventilatoren-Fabrik Oelde GmbH* [1988] BTLR 138.
9 *Couchman* v *Hill* [1947] KB 554; *Harling* v *Eddy* [1951] 2 KB 739; *City & Westminster Properties* v *Mudd* [1959] Ch 129; *J Evans & Sons (Portsmouth)* v *Andrea Merzario* [1976] 1 WLR 1078; *Brikom Investments* v *Carr* [1979] QB 467.
10 This is the plea of *non est factum*, as to which see *Saunders* v *Anglia Building Society* [1971] AC 1104; Treitel, *Law of Contract*, 11th edn, p. 326 et *seq*; Cheshire, Fifoot & Furmston, *Law of Contract*, 14th edn, pp. 284–289; Atiyah, *Introduction to the Law of Contract*, 5th edn, 1995, pp. 184–5.
11 The leading cases are *Parker* v *SE Railway* (1877) 2 CPD 416; *Thompson* v *LMSR* [1930] 1 KB 41; *Chapelton* v *Barry UDC* [1940] 1 KB 532; *Thornton* v *Shoe Lane Parking* [1971] 2 QB 163; *British Crane Hire Corpn Ltd* v *Ipswich Plant Hire Ltd* [1975] QB 303; and *Interfoto Picture Library Ltd* v *Stiletto Visual Programmes Ltd* [1989] QB 433, followed in the Scottish case of *Montgomery Litho Ltd* v *Maxwell* 2000 SC 56. In Scotland, see *McCutcheon* v *David MacBrayne Ltd* 1964 SC (HL) 28, *Taylor* v *Glasgow Corporation* 1952 SC 440, *Hood* v *Anchor Line Ltd* 1918 SC (HL) 143 and *Grayston Plant Ltd* v *Plean Precast Ltd* 1976 SC 206.

A controversial type of exclusion of liability is the 'shrink wrap' licence commonly used in sales of computer software. As a condition for acquiring a copyright licence to enable the software to be loaded legally on to a computer, the purchaser is required to agree to the terms set out on the packaging (which may be reinforced by assent being required by the software itself as it is loaded on to the computer). In *Beta Companies (Europe) Ltd* v *Adobe Systems (Europe) Ltd*, the facts of which were given previously,[12] Lord Penrose accepted the efficacy of the shrink wrap licence, the unusual feature of the case being that it was in the interests of the acquirer of the software to argue for this, rather than the supplier. However, his view that no contract came into existence until acceptance of the licence terms is questionable. If he is right, there would seem to be no good reason for confining this to supplies of software, so that in the case of *any* goods supplied with conditions attached no contract would come into existence until the terms were accepted. Yet companies which habitually order goods by telephone would be surprised to learn that they had no contractual right to them if conditions (of which they had no knowledge) happened to be furnished with the goods. In order to avoid the difficulty that no contract would exist until the terms of the licence were accepted or rejected, it would be better to characterize the contract as a sale on approval, permitting the acquirer to rescind the transaction if the conditions are unacceptable.[13] It should not in principle affect this analysis whether the conditions which it is sought to impose are those of the supplier or of a third party.

Lord Penrose was also of the view that when the contract on the shrink wrap terms came into existence, it created a *jus quaesitum tertio* in favour of the software proprietor. But why? A licence is simply a permission in favour of the user to do that which would otherwise be unlawful.[14] The proprietor of the software did not need a *jus quaesitum tertio* since it had the copyright in the software.

It is also unfortunate that Lord Penrose did not address the question as to how his analysis that the licence terms constitute an offer which the defender could have accepted or rejected was consistent with the Software Directive as implemented by the Copyright (Computer Software) Regulations,[15] which amend the Copyright, Designs and Patents Act 1988. The Act gives the lawful user of a program the basic rights necessary to make use of the program.[16] Since the acquirer already has those rights, why should he or she be supposed to surrender those rights in return for no doubt lesser rights conferred by the shrink wrap licence? There are, however, good commercial reasons for saying that shrink wrap licences *ought* to be enforceable.[17] Perhaps the solution lies in technical means of protection. New software now often requires the user to register online. A condition of permitting this is that the user is required to accept the conditions imposed by the software house. Presumably, if the acquirer is not prepared to accept those conditions, he or she is entitled to reject the software. In this case, Lord Penrose's analysis would be more apposite, though modified by the suggestion made above that the transaction is a sale on approval.

---

12 1996 SLT 604. See p. 78.
13 See Sale of Goods Act 1979 s. 18 r. 4, and p. 78 above.
14 *Federal Commissioner of Taxation* v *United Aircraft Corporation* (1943) 68 CLR 525.
15 SI 1992/3233.
16 Copyright, Designs and Patents Act 1988 as amended, s. 50A(2).
17 See *ProCD* v *Zeidenberg* No. 96–1139 US Court of Appeals for the 7th Circuit, 86 F 3d 1447 (1996).

Difficulties can arise with regard to contracts made by business parties who use standard order forms, acknowledgments or similar documents, where the parties attempt to incorporate by reference their own standard terms – which of course invariably conflict.[18] This is the 'battle of the forms' situation, which is solved in accordance with general contractual principles,[19] though not always in a very satisfactory way. The difficulty with the usual legal solutions is that they seem to require the court to find either that there was no contract at all, or that there was a contract on one or other set of standard terms. Frequently, neither of these appears to be a fair or satisfactory result, and a better solution would be for the court to find a contract to exist (especially where performance has actually taken place), but not necessarily on either set of terms. However, this subject belongs to the general law of contract rather than to the law of sale, and it cannot be pursued here.[20]

An attempt to avoid the difficulties created by the 'battle of the forms' has been made following the adoption of the UN Convention on Contracts for International Sales of Goods by some 60 states,[21] which contains provisions which would deal with some of the battle of the forms problems in international sales of goods. Another approach is to encourage traders to use identical standard terms of trading. To this end, a standard set of trade terms, 'Intraterms', has been drawn up.[22] These are suitable for domestic non-consumer sales, as well as international sales. If widely adopted, they would obviate many of the difficulties mentioned in the previous paragraph.

CONSTRUCTION OF EXEMPTION CLAUSES

Where it is held that an exemption clause is incorporated into a contract, important and difficult questions of construction may arise.

The approach to such questions has varied over the years, but there is no doubt that for many years before the enactment of the Unfair Contract Terms Act 1977 the courts had tended to use strained methods of construction to avoid giving effect to what they regarded as unreasonably wide exemption clauses. The first case to reach the House of Lords after the passing of this Act, though it was in fact governed by the pre-Act law, was *Photo Production Ltd v Securicor Transport Ltd.*[23] In this case the House of Lords made it clear that they deprecated the use of such artificial methods of construction, now that legislative methods were available for the striking

---

18 Where these conflict with the provisions of a negotiated written contract, it is the terms of the written contract which prevail – *Indian Oil Corp v Vanol Inc* [1991] 2 Lloyd's Rep 634.

19 See *Butler Machine Tool Co v Ex-Cell-O Corpn* [1979] 1 WLR 401; *Santer Automation Ltd v H C Goodman (Mechanical Services) Ltd* [1986] 2 FTLR 239; *Hertford Foods Ltd and anor v TSB Commercial Finance Ltd*, 5 November 1999 (unreported); *Uniroyal Ltd v Miller & Co Ltd* 1985 SLT 101; and *Continental Tyre & Rubber Co Ltd v Trunk Trailer Co Ltd* 1987 SLT 58.

20 See Atiyah, *Introduction to the Law of Contract*, 5th edn, pp. 66–70 (1995); Adams and Brownsword, *Understanding Contract Law*, 4th edn, p. 57 et seq. (2004); MacQueen and Thomson, *Contract Law in Scotland* (2000), paras 2.40–2.43.

21 The Vienna Convention (1980).

22 Drafted by the Centre for Commercial Law Studies, Queen Mary College.

23 [1980] AC 827.

down of some unreasonable exemption clauses.[24] This is a welcome development, which should help free the law of much artificiality. It eliminates the fiction of 'interpreting' clauses in ways which are almost certainly contrary to their true intent, and keeps separate the two distinct questions of, on the one hand, interpretation or construction, and, on the other hand, the striking down of unfair clauses, properly interpreted.

Unfortunately, after that decision, the House of Lords appeared to endorse, in *Ailsa Craig Fishing Co Ltd* v *Malvern Shipping Co Ltd*,[25] a distinction which could perpetuate these artificial modes of construction in certain cases. In the *Ailsa Craig* case, the House distinguished between a limitation clause, and a complete exemption or exclusion clause. A limitation clause is a clause which limits the liability of a contracting party (for example, to damages not exceeding a specified figure) while an exclusion clause totally excludes any liability at all from arising. In the case of a limitation clause, it was stressed, the clause ought to be given its natural meaning without straining. No doubt, clear words are still necessary to protect a contracting party from the normal results of a breach of contract, but 'one must not strive to create ambiguities by strained construction . . . The relevant words must be given, if possible, their natural plain meaning.'[26] On the other hand, 'Clauses of limitation are not regarded by the courts with the same hostility as clauses of exclusion: this is because they must be related to other contractual terms, in particular to the risks to which the defending party may be exposed, the remuneration which he receives, and possibly also the opportunity of the other party to insure.'[27] The implication then was that complete exclusion clauses might remain subject to stricter, and perhaps still artificial, rules of construction. However, as noted above,[28] at least so far as the present Court of Appeal is concerned, the move is perhaps away from such artificiality.

The distinction between a limitation clause and an exclusion clause is not very satisfactory for several reasons. First, the distinction between a limitation clause and an exclusion clause is often just a matter of degree. If a clause limits a party's liability to a trivial sum which bears no relationship at all to the amount of damage actually suffered, it is surely absurd to treat this as something wholly different from an exclusion clause. Secondly, exclusion clauses and limitation clauses are often entwined together, as indeed they were in both the *Photo Production* case and the *Ailsa Craig* case. In both cases there were clauses which protected the defendants from all liability of a certain kind, and limited their liability for other kinds of loss or damage. This sort of mix is quite normal with certain kinds of exclusion/limitation clauses and once again it seems absurd to distinguish between the two effects. Thirdly, it must be said that if the distinction survives, it will simply complicate the law unnecessarily because counsel will be driven to argue in many cases first whether the clause is of the one

---

24 See also *Fastframe Ltd* v *Lohinski*, 3 March 1993 (unreported – discussed by Adams (1994) 57 MLR 960) in which the Court of Appeal refused to construe a 'no deduction or set-off' clause as applying only to legal, not equitable, set-off. It simply applied the Unfair Contract Terms Act 1977 to the clause. As to the application of UCTA to 'no set-off' clauses see *Stewart Gill Ltd* v *Horatio Myer Ltd* [1992] 2 All ER 257 discussed below.
25 [1983] 1 All ER 101, 1982 SC (HL) 14.
26 [1983] 1 All ER 101, 124, 1982 SC (HL) 14, 57 per Lord Wilberforce.
27 Ibid.
28 See n. 24.

kind or the other, and secondly that different rules of construction apply in the two cases. All this really seems quite unnecessary; all that is needed is that the courts should approach these questions of construction from the commonsense viewpoint that the more drastic the effects of the clause on the plaintiff's normal rights, the clearer its words must be if it is to affect those rights. In the last resort, the Unfair Contract Terms Act can be resorted to where appropriate.

In *George Mitchell (Chesterhall) Ltd* v *Finney Lock Seeds*,[29] which is discussed further below,[30] Lord Denning, in the Court of Appeal, pointed out the unsatisfactory nature of the distinction between limitation and exclusion clauses, and suggested indeed that there was earlier authority rejecting such a distinction. In the House of Lords, Lord Denning's judgment was in general endorsed by the Law Lords who rejected the strained and artificial construction placed on the clause in question by the majority of the Court of Appeal; but at the same time the House appears to have reaffirmed the importance of the distinction between limitation and complete exclusion clauses, without reference to Lord Denning's criticisms.[31] It seems certain that this distinction will return to haunt the House of Lords, and it is very difficult to understand why they allowed their own decision in the *Photo Production* case to be glossed in this way; the natural implications of that decision are that all such artificial distinctions should be rejected, and contractual clauses construed naturally in accordance with their ordinary meaning.[32]

However, for the present, the distinction may still exist, though what it is likely to mean in practice is not easy to say. Perhaps, it must be accepted that exclusion clauses are still to be construed more strictly against the party relying on them than limitation clauses. But the general principle that all such clauses which derogate from common law rights must be construed *contra proferentem*, that is against the party relying on them, seems to apply to limitation clauses as well as exclusion clauses.[33] In *Stewart Gill* v *Horatio Myer*,[34] which involved a contract for the supply and installation of a conveyor system, the Court of Appeal held that the effect of UCTA s. 13 was to extend the effect of ss. 3 and 7 (these provisions are discussed below) to catch a 'no set-off' clause. In this case no argument seems to have been presented about the scope of the clause, but in *Fastframe Ltd* v *Lohinski*[35] the argument that the clause in question was apt to exclude equitable, but not legal, set-off (or *vice versa*)[36] was dismissed out of hand. In *Stewart Gill* Lord Donaldson MR seems to have considered a 'no set-off' clause to be an exclusion clause, because it excludes the right, or the remedy, or the procedural rules of set-off. By implication, though it must

---

29 [1983] 1 All ER 108, affirmed [1983] 2 AC 803.

30 See below, p. 248.

31 See especially the speech of Lord Bridge, with which all the other Law Lords agreed, [1983] 2 AC at 814.

32 Since these remarks were first written in the seventh edition, the Australian High Court has rejected the *Ailsa Craig* decision, and has adopted the approach advocated here: *Darlington Futures Ltd* v *Delco Australia Pty Ltd* (1986) 161 CLR 500.

33 See Lord Fraser in the *Ailsa Craig* case, [1983] 1 All ER 101, 105; 1982 SC (HL) 14, 60–1, a passage cited with approval by Lord Bridge in the *George Mitchell* case. Note, however, *Fastframe Ltd* v *Lohinski*, n. 24 above.

34 [1992] 2 All ER 257.

35 See n. 24.

36 An argument based on the analogy of the rule that if there is more than one head of liability a clause is apt to exclude only one unless it mentions both – see *White* v *John Warrick & Co Ltd* [1953] 2 All ER 1021.

be admitted that the point was not directly addressed, so did the Court of Appeal in *Fastframe*. It is submitted that the correct view is that such clauses are properly speaking exclusion clauses, as much as are 'no rejection' and 'no refund' clauses.

Beyond this, it is uncertain what remains of some of the older case law. At least three general propositions may be deduced from the great mass of authorities on the subject though it may well be that these will now only be applied to exclusion clauses and not to limitation clauses, and perhaps not very enthusiastically even then.

In the first place, the courts will interpret exemption clauses strictly, and in particular they will attribute precise legal meaning to technical terms. For example, in *Wallis, Son & Wells v Pratt*,[37] the plaintiff bought from the defendant seeds described as 'common English sainfoin', which were, as it transpired, a different and inferior variety known as giant sainfoin. The contract contained a term excluding all warranties express or implied. The plaintiff had accepted the goods and was therefore precluded by the predecessor of s. 11(4) from rejecting them, and was compelled to treat the breach of condition as a breach of warranty. Despite this it was held by the House of Lords that the exemption clause did not protect the sellers. The term in question was a condition and not a warranty, and its nature was not altered by the fact that the plaintiff was compelled to fall back on his remedy in damages. So also in *Baldry v Marshall*,[38] the defendants' obligation to deliver a car suited to the plaintiff's requirements was held to be a condition and was therefore not excluded by a clause which referred only to guarantees and warranties.

One of the most striking of the older cases on the construction of exemption clauses is the decision of the House of Lords in *Beck & Co Ltd v Szymanowski & Co Ltd*,[39] where the defendants had sold to the plaintiffs 2,000 gross six-cord sewing cotton thread reels, the length on each reel stated to be 200 yards. The contract provided that: 'The goods delivered shall be deemed to be in all respects in accordance with the contract, and the buyer shall be bound to accept and pay for the same accordingly, unless the sellers shall within fourteen days after the arrival of the goods at their destination receive from the buyers notice of any matter or thing by reason whereof they may allege that the goods are not in accordance with the contract.' The reels only had 188 yards of cotton instead of 200 but this fact was not discovered by the buyers until 18 months later. The buyers claimed damages. It was held that the above clause provided no defence to the sellers, and the ingenious reason given by their lordships for their decision was well summarized by Lord Shaw:[40]

> The damages are claimed not in respect of the goods delivered but in respect of goods which were not delivered.

This seems to have been an example of just that kind of strained and artificial construction deprecated in recent cases. Today, such a clause would probably be held to be caught by ss. 3 and 6 of UCTA as extended by s. 13.[41]

---

37 [1911] AC 394.
38 [1925] 1 KB 260.
39 [1924] AC 43.
40 At p. 50.
41 See *Stewart Gill* v *Horatio Myer* and *Fastframe Ltd* v *Lohinski* (above) – there would probably have been little room for argument on the case law on s. 13 as it had developed even before those cases: see Adams and Brownsword, 'The Unfair Contract Terms Act: A Decade of Discretion' (1988) 104 LQR 94.

The same might be said of *Minister of Materials v Steel Bros & Co Ltd*,[42] where a contract for the sale of goods contained a term limiting the right to complain of defects of quality to a period of 60 days after the discharge of the goods at their destination. The goods were damaged as a result of defective packing. The Court of Appeal held that the ground of complaint was not the quality of the goods within the meaning of the exemption clause. Yet in the converse position it has been held that the 'quality' of the goods within the meaning of s. 14(2) includes the state of the packing, and that if this is unsatisfactory the goods are not of merchantable quality (now satisfactory quality).[43] The case also illustrates another problem arising from the limitation/exclusion distinction, because a time-limit clause of this kind (very common in certain contracts) is neither a complete exclusion clause nor is it a limitation clause. In *R W Green Ltd v Cade Bros Farm*,[44] the facts of which are given later,[45] Griffiths J, however, held that it would not be fair and reasonable to allow reliance on such a clause.[46] It is highly unlikely, therefore, that at the present day the Court would attempt to limit the effect of such a clause by an artificial construction of the sort given by the Court in this case. It would, no doubt, give the clause its normal construction and then apply UCTA.

In the second place, it is a general principle of construction of exemption clauses that, where a party would, apart from the particular provisions of the contract in question, be liable in the absence of negligence, an exemption clause in general terms does not protect him from liability for negligence.[47] Negligence must be specifically covered by the clause, or at least it must be a necessary inference that it is so covered. Since a seller is liable on the implied terms under the Sale of Goods Act irrespective of negligence, an exemption clause in general terms would not exclude the liability of the seller for negligence. Again, however, this principle is not of great importance in consumer sales since, in these days of manufactured pre-packaged products, the circumstances in which a retail seller will be guilty of negligence will be few, and the liability of manufacturers etc. will now generally be dealt with under the Consumer Protection Act 1987 the provisions of which cannot be excluded.[48] But commercial sellers of goods which are potentially hazardous or dangerous may sometimes be liable both in negligence and under the Sale of Goods Act, and in such cases this principle of construction could be important.[49] On the other hand, clear words must be applied even if the result is to protect a negligent seller from liability. If it is once found that the clause clearly limits the liability of the party in breach, there is no principle which can be applied to confine the clause to breaches occurring without negligence.[50]

---

42 [1952] 1 TLR 499.

43 *Niblett v Confectioners' Materials Co Ltd* [1921] 3 KB 387 – see above, p. 113.

44 [1978] 1 Lloyd's Rep 602.

45 See p. 249 *et seq.*

46 The case was decided on the now repealed provisions of the Supply of Goods (Implied Terms) Act 1973, as to which see p. 249 below.

47 *Rutter v Palmer* [1922] 2 KB 87; *Alderslade v Hendon Laundry* [1945] 1 All ER 245; *Smith v South Wales Switchgear* [1978] 1 All ER 18. But cf. clauses merely designed to adjust the incidence of insurance: *Scottish Special Housing Assoc'n v Wimpey Construction UK Ltd* [1986] 1 WLR 995, 1986 SLT 559.

48 See p. 284 below.

49 See, e.g., *Vacwell Engineering Co Ltd v BDH Chemicals Ltd* [1969] 3 All ER 1681 (though there was no exemption clause in this case).

50 See the *George Mitchell* case [1983] 2 AC 803, 814 per Lord Bridge. Note, however, that negligence may be a relevant factor under the Unfair Contract Terms Act – below, p. 248.

Lastly, mention must be made of two particular provisions in the Act bearing on the general question of construction. First, reference should be made to s. 55(2), formerly (with verbal alterations only) s. 14(4), which says:

> An express condition or warranty does not negative a condition or warranty implied by this Act unless inconsistent with it.[51]

Secondly, in addition to exclusion or variation of implied terms by express agreement, s. 55(1) says that 'the course of dealing between the parties' or 'such usage as binds both parties to the contract' may have the same effect. So far as usage is concerned, nothing need be added to the observations made above dealing with the implication of terms by usage,[52] for they are equally applicable here. With regard to the expression 'course of dealing between the parties', this has been judicially explained to mean that previous dealings between the parties may raise an implication that certain terms are or are not to be included in the contract, if these have or have not been implied on previous occasions.[53] 'If two parties have made a series of similar contracts each containing certain conditions, and then they make another without expressly referring to those conditions it may be that those conditions ought to be implied.'[54] But in order to justify the implications of terms – and more particularly, it would seem, the implication of terms contrary to those normally implied – by reference to a course of dealing, it must be shown that in fact there has been a consistent course of dealing in which the same terms have been regularly if not invariably incorporated in the past.[55] Thus, where over a period of years parties have regularly contracted on the basis of certain written terms for the supply of goods, the terms may be held to be incorporated in oral contracts for the supply of the same goods between the same parties.[56] In general, it seems much easier to incorporate an exemption clause from a course of dealing in commercial than in consumer transactions, especially in the case of the standard terms laid down by trade associations.[57]

FUNDAMENTAL BREACH

In previous editions of this work extensive treatment was given of this body of doctrine. For some 15 or 20 years in the 1950s and 1960s, the English courts attempted to achieve some measure of protection for consumers by dealing with harsh or oppressive exemption clauses. In retrospect it is now easy to see this judicial activity as a response to a particular social situation. With the great post-war consumer boom well

---

51　See, for a case where an express warranty of the capacity of a machine 'negatived' any implied term as to quality, *Border Harvesters Ltd* v *Edwards Engineering (Perth) Ltd* 1985 SLT 128.
52　See above, p. 215.
53　*Pocahontas Fuel Co Ltd* v *Ambatielos* (1922) 27 Com Cas 148, 152 per McCardie J.
54　*McCutcheon* v *David MacBrayne Ltd* [1964] 1 WLR 125, 128, 1964 SC (HL) 28, 35 per Lord Reid. See also *British Crane Hire Corpn* v *Ipswich Plant Hire* [1975] QB 303.
55　Ibid.
56　*Kendall* v *Lillico* [1969] 2 AC 31. Dicta of Lord Devlin in *McCutcheon* v *David MacBrayne Ltd* (above, n. 54), to the effect that actual knowledge of the terms was required before they could be incorporated into an oral contract, were disapproved in *Kendall* v *Lillico*. See also *Hertford Foods Ltd and another* v *TSB Commercial Finance Ltd*, 5 November 1999 (unreported).
57　Compare *British Crane Hire Corpn Ltd* v *Ipswich Plant Hire Ltd* [1975] QB 303 with *McCutcheon* v *David MacBrayne Ltd* [1964] 1 WLR 124, 1964 SC (HL) 28 and with *Grayston Plant Ltd* v *Plean Precast Ltd* 1976 SC 206.

under way, with the huge increase in ownership of consumer durables and above all vehicles, and with inflation rapidly making nonsense of the early Hire-Purchase Acts,[58] the courts began to see a steady stream of really hard cases. Most of these cases involved contracts of hire-purchase for second-hand cars or other vehicles. Invariably all liability for defects was excluded and frequently real hardship to the consumer was the probable result of strict adherence to the law. The courts' answer to this was the invention of the doctrines of fundamental breach[59] and fundamental terms.[60] Those interested in pursuing the rise and fall of this body of doctrine should consult the standard textbooks.[61] At least in the case of the doctrine of fundamental breach, one of its legacies was the original test of reasonableness inserted in s. 55 of the Sale of Goods Act by the Supply of Goods (Implied Terms) Act 1973. This provided that a term exempting from all or any of the provisions of ss. 13, 14 and 15 of the Act was not enforceable to the extent that it was shown that it would not be fair and reasonable to allow *reliance* on the term.[62] In the event, when these provisions came to be replaced by the Unfair Contract Terms Act 1977, it was the view of the Scottish Law Commission which prevailed,[63] and the test is now that of the reasonableness of *incorporating* the term into the contract.[64] The second, more enduring, legacy was the approach laid down by Denning LJ in *Karsales* v *Wallis*:[65]

> The thing to do is to look at the contract apart from the exemption clause to see what are the terms, express or implied, which impose obligations on the party.

This approach is implicit in the drafting of the Unfair Contract Terms Act. It thereby rejected Professor Coote's point that in strict logic an exception clause is simply one method of defining a positive obligation.[66] Although logical, this argument paid no attention to the history of the subject,[67] and was rightly rejected.[68] In fact, this aspect of the Unfair Contract Terms Act has not, in practice, caused difficulties.[69]

It is also to be borne in mind that to the armoury of devices controlling exemption (or exception) clauses offered to the courts by the Unfair Contract Terms Act and the Unfair Terms in Consumer Contracts Regulations,[70] is now added the Human

---

58 The first Hire-Purchase Act of 1938 only applied where the total purchase price did not exceed £50, and this was only increased to £300 in 1951, where the figure remained until 1964.
59 A body of doctrine which developed from the judgment of Denning LJ in *Karsales* v *Wallis* (see n. 65 below), though the term appeared in the judgment of Devlin J in *Alexander* v *Railway Executive* [1951] 2 KB 882. For the Scottish position, see n. 60 below.
60 Insofar as this was an independent doctrine (which was not entirely clear), its origins for present purposes may be traced to the judgment of Devlin J in *Smeaton Hanscomb* v *Sassoon & Getty* [1953] 2 All ER 1471, 1473. Note that neither doctrine took root in Scotland, however: see *Alexander Stephen (Forth) Ltd* v *J J Riley (UK) Ltd* 1976 SC 151 and Unfair Contract Terms Act 1977 s. 22.
61 Atiyah, *Introduction to the Law of Contract*, 5th edn; *Cheshire, Fifoot and Furmston's Law of Contract*, 14th edn, pp. 193–6; *Treitel on Contract*, 11th edn, pp. 225 et seq.
62 See also Misrepresentation Act 1967 s. 3.
63 See Unfair Contract Terms Act 1977 s. 11(1).
64 Unfair Contract Terms Act 1977 s. 11(1).
65 [1956] 1 WLR 936, 940.
66 Coote, *Exception Clauses*, Sweet & Maxwell, 1964. See also *G H Renton & Co Ltd* v *Palmyra Trading Corp. of Panama* [1957] AC 194.
67 As to which see Adams in *Welfarism in Contract Law* (Brownsword, Howells and Wilmhelmsson, eds) Dartmouth, 1994.
68 See Adams (1978) 41 MLR 613.
69 Other aspects have – see Adams and Brownsword, 'UCTA: a Decade of Discretion' (1988) 104 LQR 94.
70 SI 1999/2083.

Rights Act 1998. This Act incorporates into UK law for the first time the European Convention on Human Rights. Although the UK was a founder member of this Convention, prior to the Act it was never given direct effect in domestic law. Section 6(1) of the Act provides:

> It is unlawful for a public authority to act in a way which is incompatible with one or more of the Convention rights.

Although the reference to 'public authority' would seem at first sight to make this provision irrelevant for present purposes,[71] s. 6(3)(a) includes 'courts and tribunals' within the definition of 'public authorities' for the purposes of this section. It would appear, therefore, that a court will be obliged, in deciding disputes between private individuals, e.g., in deciding whether to exercise its discretion to grant equitable remedies such as injunctions or rescission, to consider whether Convention rights will he harmed or promoted by its decision.[72] It could bite where existing provisions do not, e.g., contracts which are oppressive in that they impose continuing obligations on buyers which are difficult to terminate.

UCTA AND THE EC DIRECTIVE ON UNFAIR TERMS IN CONSUMER CONTRACTS

As noted above, the EC Directive on Unfair Terms in Consumer Contracts[73] is in effect from 1 July 1995. It is now implemented by the Unfair Terms in Consumer Contracts Regulations.[74]

The effect of these Regulations is to create two overlapping legal regimes in this area: the Unfair Contract Terms Act 1977 (UCTA) and the Regulations. Unfortunately, the two regimes differ in some important respects. Thus, the test of 'reasonableness' in UCTA is not the same as the test of 'fairness' in the Regulations. Perhaps the results will usually be the same, but the tests are different. It is accordingly necessary to expound the two legal regimes separately, as contracts will have to pass through the double barrier of UCTA and the Regulations.[75] The Law Commissions are currently attempting to combine these two regimes.[76]

THE UNFAIR CONTRACT TERMS ACT 1977

The Act is divided into three Parts, the first applying to England and Wales, the second to Scotland, and the third to the United Kingdom. It is therefore necessary to have separate treatments of the positions under English and Scots law, although the broad thrust of the provisions is very similar.

---

71 This at least seems to be the view of the government – see the Lord Chancellor's comment 'The Convention had its origins in a desire to protect people from the misuse of power by the state, rather than from actions of private individuals' – HL Deb Vol. 582, col. 1232, 3 November 1997.

72 See Wade, 'The United Kingdom's Bill of Rights' in Hare and Forsyth, *Constitutional Reform in the United Kingdom: Practice and Principles* (Hart, 1998); MacQueen and Brodie, in Boyle *et al.*, *Human Rights in Scots Law* (2002).

73 93/13/EEC.

74 SI 1999/2083, replacing SI 1994/3159 – see p. 257.

75 The concept of a double barrier is already familiar from the context of EU competition law – see *Wilhelm* v *Bundeskartellamt* [1969] CMLR 100; *Boehringer Mannheim GmbH* v *Commission* [1973] CMLR 864.

76 See 'Unfair Terms in Contracts: a joint consultation paper', August 2002. This contains a useful comparison between them.

England and Wales

The first relevant provision applies to all contracts, not merely to contracts for the sale of goods. Section 3 states:

(1) This section applies as between contracting parties where one of them deals as consumer or on the other's written standard terms of business.

(2) As against that party, the other cannot by reference to any contract term—

    (a) when himself in breach of contract, exclude or restrict any liability of his in respect of the breach; or

    (b) claim to be entitled—

        (i) to render a contractual performance substantially different from that which was reasonably expected of him, or

        (ii) in respect of the whole or any part of his contractual obligation, to render no performance at all,

except in so far as (in any of the cases mentioned in the above sub-section) the contract term satisfies the requirement of reasonableness.

The effects of this clause are extended by s. 13 discussed below.[77] The reasonableness test for the purposes of s. 3 is that set out in s. 11(1):

. . . that the term shall have been a fair and reasonable one to be included having regard to the circumstances which were, or ought reasonably to have been, known to or in the contemplation of the parties when the contract was made.

This test is in theory different from that applied in relation specifically to the sale and supply of goods provisions discussed below.[78]

By s. 6(1) of this Act, it is provided that liability in respect of breach of s. 12 of the Sale of Goods Act cannot be excluded or restricted by any contract term. Section 12 is, of course, the section containing the implied conditions as to title. Section 6(1) also applies to the corresponding implied condition in hire-purchase contracts in s. 8 of the Supply of Goods (Implied Terms) Act 1973 (though the actual wording must now be sought in Sch. 4 to the Consumer Credit Act 1974). And s. 7 of the Unfair Contract Terms Act 1977, as subsequently amended, contains restrictions on contracting-out of the similar implied terms in all other contracts for the supply of goods, which are dealt with by the Supply of Goods and Services Act 1982.[79]

Section 6(2) and (3), as they now apply, are as follows:

(2) As against a person dealing as a consumer, liability for breach of the obligations arising from—

    (a) section 13, 14 or 15 of the 1979 Act (seller's implied undertakings as to conformity of goods with description or sample, or as to their quality or fitness for a particular purpose);

    (b) section 9, 10 or 11 of the 1973 Act (the corresponding thing in relation to hire-purchase);

cannot be excluded or restricted by reference to any contract term.

---

77 See p. 241 *et seq.*

78 See, however, *Danka Rentals Ltd* v *Xi Software* (1998) 7 Tr LR 74, where the judge suggested it made little practical difference – see p. 251.

79 Except that the conditions as to title are subject to the reasonableness test, rather than a prohibition on their exclusion or restriction. See below, p. 243 *et seq*, as to the reasonableness test.

(3) As against a person dealing otherwise than as a consumer, the liability specified in subsection (2) above can be excluded or restricted by reference to a contract term, but only
insofar as the term satisfies the requirement of reasonableness.[80]

Although s. 6(1) provides that there can now be no contracting out of s. 12 at all,
this is slightly misleading because s. 12 itself envisages a limited form of contracting-
out in that it now clearly recognizes the possibility of a sale of a limited interest in
goods. The Law Commission did not think that there was any reason why a seller
should not make it plain that he is only selling such title as he may have or, where he
acts only as agent, such title as some third party may have. But the Commission proposed that even in such a case the seller should be held liable if there should turn out
to be some charge or encumbrance on the goods known to the seller but not known
to the buyer or disclosed by the seller. Thus a seller who (for example) knows that the
goods he sells are held under some hire-purchase agreement should not be allowed to
conceal this fact and protect himself merely by purporting to sell only the hirer's interest in the goods. Section 6(1) of the 1977 Act gives effect to these recommendations.

The effect of s. 6(2) and (3) on contracting-out of ss. 13–15 is, of course, much
more dramatic and more radical. Under s. 6(2), no exclusion of the seller's duties
under ss. 13–15 is permissible at all 'as against a person dealing as a consumer', and
is only permissible subject to a test of reasonableness in other cases. In evaluating the
significance of these provisions, there are three important matters to be considered:
first the meaning of 'dealing as a consumer', secondly, the extent to which some limited forms of contracting-out may still be possible through the inherent operation of
ss. 13–15 themselves, and, thirdly, the requirement of reasonableness.

Consumer sales
As to the first point, s. 12 of the 1977 Act declares:

(1) A party to a contract 'deals as consumer' in relation to another party if—
    (a) he neither makes the contract in the course of a business nor holds himself out as
doing so; and
    (b) the other party does make the contract in the course of a business; and
    (c) in the case of a contract governed by the law of sale of goods or hire-purchase, or
by section 7 of this Act, the goods passing under or in pursuance of the contract are
of a type ordinarily supplied for private use or consumption.
(1A) But if the first party mentioned in subsection (1) is an individual paragraph (c) of that
subsection must be ignored.
(2) But the buyer is not in any circumstances to be regarded as dealing as consumer —
    (a) if he is an individual and the goods are second hand goods sold at public auction
at which individuals have the opportunity of attending the sale in person;
    (b) if he is not an individual and the goods are sold by auction or by competitive
tender.[81]
(3) Subject to this, it is for those claiming that a party does not deal as consumer to show
that he does not.

---

80 Section 7 also contains analogous provisions to s. 6(2) and (3) with respect to other contracts for the transfer of the possession or ownership of goods – see p. 251, *Danka Rentals Ltd* v *Xi Software* (1998) 7 Tr LR 74.
81 These provisions (subss. (1A) and (2)) were added and substituted, respectively, by the Sale and Supply of Goods to
Consumer Regulations 2002, SI 2002/3045.

The wording of this section (as amended) differs somewhat from that of the corresponding provisions of the 1973 Act, though there is little change in substance. In general, this section is clear enough, though there may be some points of difficulty. Broadly speaking, the position is that a sale is a consumer sale if the buyer is not buying in the course of business, and the seller is selling in the course of business, and the goods are of a type ordinarily supplied for private use or consumption. In addition, the following points must be noted.

First, a sale of second-hand goods by auction[82] which individuals have the opportunity of attending in person is not a consumer sale. Secondly, a sale by a seller not selling in the course of business is not a consumer sale. This means that in a transaction in which neither party acts in the course of a business (for example, a private sale of a second-hand car), neither party 'deals as consumer' within the section. Exclusion of liability under ss. 13–15 of the Sale of Goods Act would, therefore, be permissible subject to the requirement of reasonableness in such a case (in fact, only s. 13 would apply to such a case, anyhow).[83] Thirdly, a sale of goods of a type not ordinarily bought for private use or consumption is not a consumer sale unless the buyer is an individual.

The most difficult question concerns goods which are of a type ordinarily bought for private use or consumption, but which are sold to a person who does not buy for private use or consumption, or which are sold to a legal person[84] who buys or holds himself out as buying them 'in the course of business'. The term 'business' is defined in s. 14 of the 1977 Act to include a profession and also the activities of any government department, or local or public authority. The concept of a sale 'in the course of business' is familiar enough, but the concept of buying goods 'in the course of business' is more difficult. In *R & B Customs Brokers Co Ltd* v *United Dominions Trust*[85] the Court of Appeal held that the buyer only makes a contract 'in the course of a business' within the meaning of this section, either if the contract is one of a regular kind of contract made by the buyer, or if the purchase was an 'integral part of the business', that is (presumably) if the goods are bought for a distinctive business use. In that case, the plaintiffs purchased a motor car from the defendants under a conditional sale agreement. The car was the second or third which the plaintiffs had acquired on similar terms. The roof leaked, and the plaintiffs rejected the car.[86] The Court held that the plaintiffs 'dealt as consumer' for the purposes of s. 6(2) of UCTA. Where a transaction was only incidental to a business activity a degree of regularity was required before a transaction could be said to be an integral part of the business, and so entered into in the course of a business.[87] Clearly, however, a sale is not a consumer sale where the buyer buys for resale or

---

82 As to auctions, see *D & M Trailers (Halifax) Ltd* v *Stirling* [1978] RTR 468.
83 See p. 158.
84 I.e. a company.
85 [1988] 1 All ER 847, relying on *Davies* v *Sumner* [1984] 1 WLR 1301, 1305, a case under the Trade Descriptions Act dealing with an analogous point. See also *Peter Symmons & Co* v *Cook* (1981) 131 N LJ 758. See also discussion at p. 167 *et seq* as to what amounts to a sale in the course of a business for the purposes of s. 14(2). See also *Feldaroll Foundry plc* v *Hermes Leasing (London) Ltd* 12 May 2004 (CA) (as yet unreported).
86 See p. 172 above.
87 See p. 167.

where the goods are raw materials to be used by the buyer in his own manufacturing process.

A number of other points may be made about the meaning of 'dealing as consumer'. First, it seems that if there are several buyers, the position of each must be looked at individually.[88] Secondly, a company may buy as a consumer if it is a private company purchasing goods for the use of the members, even though, in one sense, any purchase by a company must be a business purpose.[89] Thirdly, it has also been held that if a consumer contracts to buy some article in such circumstances that he is dealing as a consumer, then if there is a novation under which a business party takes over the consumer's rights under the contract, the business succeeds to all the rights of the consumer.[90] The validity of any exemption clause must, therefore, be tested as though the business party were the original consumer in this situation.

It has been mentioned earlier that s. 2 of the 1977 Act totally bans the use of exemption clauses which exclude or limit business liability in negligence for personal injury or death. The meaning of 'business liability' for this purpose is obviously similar to the converse of a consumer sale, but the statutory language is not identical. Business liability is defined for this purpose by s. 1(3) of the 1977 Act as liability arising:

(a)   from things done or to be done by a person in the course of a business (whether his own business or another's); or
(b)   from the occupation of premises used for business purposes of the occupier.

Limited contracting-out still possible
Despite the apparently complete prohibition of clauses excluding or limiting the seller's liability under ss. 13–15 of the Act as against a person dealing as a consumer, the drafting of the Unfair Contract Terms Act 1977 does not in fact prevent the intention of the parties from having some control over liability under these sections. For instance, although the seller cannot escape liability under the implied condition that the goods must correspond with their description under s. 13 if the sale is a sale by description, yet the question whether the sale is indeed a sale by description is presumably still for the contract itself to determine. So, as we have seen,[91] it is still open to the court to hold that a sale is a contract for the sale of a specific unique chattel, and not a contract for sale by description. A seller may use descriptive words in selling specific goods, but if he makes it clear that it is for the buyer to examine the goods and satisfy himself of their proper description, he may escape liability on the ground that the sale is not by description at all. For instance, despite the decision in *Beale* v *Taylor*[92] about the '1961 Herald', it seems that if a seller of a second-hand car uses descriptive words, but qualifies them by saying that he does not guarantee their correctness, and makes it otherwise clear that the buyer must

---

88 *Rasbora Ltd* v *JCL Marine Ltd* [1977] 1 Lloyd's Rep 645.
89 *R & B Customs Brokers Co Ltd* v *United Dominions Trust* [1988] 1 All ER 847; *Rasbora Ltd* v *JCL Marine Ltd*, above, last note; *Stevenson* v *Rogers* [1999] QB 1028.
90 The *Rasbora* case, above, n. 88.
91 Above, p. 157.
92 [1967] 1 WLR 1193, above, pp. 150–1.

examine the car himself and take it 'as is', then the seller may escape liability even under s. 13.

A delicate line would, however, need to be trodden here to ensure that the courts do not drive a coach and four through the provisions of the Unfair Contract Terms Act. The key here, and elsewhere, to problems of this kind may lie in the concept of reasonable reliance as was suggested when we discussed *Harlingdon & Leinster Ltd v Christopher Hull Fine Art Ltd*.[93] If it is clear that the buyer has reasonably relied upon the words of description used by the seller, it would seem that the court ought not to allow the seller to escape liability by claiming that the sale is not really a sale by description; but if, on the other hand, a reasonable buyer would not have attached any weight to the descriptive words but would have relied entirely on his own examination of the goods, the sale may be held not to be by description and the seller may be permitted to escape liability. *A fortiori*, if the buyer actually sees that the goods do not conform with the seller's description it seems impossible that he could sue under s. 13. This still gives some weight to the Unfair Contract Terms Act; what it does, in effect, is to stress that the totality of the negotiations must be looked at, and that the seller cannot, just by procuring the buyer's signature to a document (for instance), eliminate from the picture the fact that descriptive words have been used and have been relied upon.

Similar problems may arise in relation to other implied terms. For example, under s. 14(2) the seller can point out defects to the buyer and no implied condition that the goods should be of satisfactory quality will exist as to those defects;[94] so also, if the buyer examines the goods, there is no implied condition that the goods should be of satisfactory quality as regards defects which his examination should have revealed. These provisions enable the parties to limit the responsibility of the seller despite the Unfair Contract Terms Act, with regard to defects which the buyer knew, or clearly ought to have known of.

It is to be expected that some sellers may attempt to take advantage of these provisions by incorporating written clauses into their conditions of sale, declaring (for example) that 'all defects have been drawn to the attention of the buyer and the buyer acknowledges this fact' or that 'the seller offers no opinion as to the suitability of the goods for any particular purpose and the buyer acknowledges that he does not rely on the seller's skill or judgment'.[95] Today it is likely that such clauses would be ineffective as attempts to exclude the liability of the seller by agreement under s. 6 of the 1977 Act. Under s. 14(2) and (3) of the Sale of Goods Act, it is the *facts* which matter and not the agreement.[96] The questions under these sections will be: Were the defects in fact drawn to the buyer's attention? Did the buyer in fact rely or reasonably rely on the seller's skill or judgment? It should also be noted that where a person deals as

---

93 See p. 150. Note also the case of *Smith* v *Eric S. Bush* [1989] 2 All ER 514 discussed below.

94 See Twigg-Flesner, Ch. 1 in Howells, Janssen & Schulge 'Information Rights and Obligations: a Challenge for Party Autonomy and Transactional Fairness', Ashgate, 2004.

95 *Lowe* v *Lombank Ltd* [1960] 1 WLR 196, which of course was decided long before UCTA, suggests that a clause reciting that the buyer has examined the goods would be effective only if it operated to raise an estoppel against the buyer.

96 See *Lutton* v *Saville Tractors (Belfast) Ltd* [1986] 12 NIJB 1, 19, where Carswell J in the High Court of Northern Ireland approved this passage, and held void a 'declaration' that the buyer did not rely on the seller as a 'transparent attempt to escape the operation of s. 6(2)(a) of the 1977 Act'.

consumer or (in Scotland) the contract of sale is a consumer contract,[97] s. 35(3) provides that the buyer cannot lose his right to have a reasonable opportunity to examine the goods under s. 25(2) by agreement, waiver or otherwise.

Another way in which, despite the Unfair Contract Terms Act, the seller may be able to escape a prima facie liability under s. 14(2) arises from the fact that the concept of satisfactory quality is so flexible. Thus, a buyer may actually order goods from a seller which are, or would in other circumstances be, of unsatisfactory quality.[98] If the seller supplies exactly what the buyer has ordered, the buyer may be unable to complain that the goods are of unsatisfactory quality. But once again, a delicate line needs to be trodden between two types of case: on the one hand, a buyer is clearly not to be deprived of his rights under s. 14(2) if, for example, he orders goods under their trade name, and the goods supplied, while complying with their trade name, happen to be defective specimens. On the other hand, if the buyer actually provides a detailed specification to the seller and says, in effect, 'Make me these goods to this specification', and the goods are so made in all respects in accordance with the specification, it would be remarkable if the buyer could complain that the resulting goods were still not of satisfactory quality. Yet the only way to avoid this result, if in fact the goods have defects rendering them unfit for normal use, is to hold that the goods, in the particular circumstances of the case, are of satisfactory quality despite the defects. Again, the key may lie in the question of reasonable reliance: if the buyer who orders goods to be made to a particular specification knows what he is doing, and relies entirely on his own ability to draw up the specification, the goods ought to be held to be satisfactory. If, however, it is clear that the buyer is still partially at least relying on the seller, it may be that the seller ought at least to advise the buyer that the goods may turn out to be of no use if made in accordance with the buyer's instructions.

Where a consumer buyer supplies material to be manufactured into finished goods, it is relevant to have regard to Article 2(3) of the Consumer Goods and Associated Guarantees Directive.[99] It provides:

> There shall be deemed not to be a lack of conformity for the purposes of this Article if, at the time the contract was concluded, the consumer was aware, or could not reasonably have been unaware, of the lack of conformity, or if the lack of conformity has its origin in materials supplied by the consumer.

Section 14(2C) already covered the first aspect of this Article so far as the warranty that the goods be of satisfactory quality is concerned, but if the non-conformity is in correspondence with description, fitness of purpose, or correspondence with sample, the Regulations[100] implementing the Directive have made no changes to these other provisions, and it would seem therefore that resort would have to be had to normal principles, which, it is submitted, would lead to a similar outcome to that set out in Article 2(3) of the Directive.[101] If the lack of conformity has its origin

---

97 As to the meaning of these terms see pp. 236 and 253.
98 See above, p. 169.
99 99/44/EC – see p. 299 *et seq.*
100 Sale and Supply of Goods to Consumers Regulations 2002, SI 2002/3045.
101 See pp. 149, 162 and 199. It should be noted, however, that Article 8(2) permits member states to have more stringent provisions to ensure a higher level of consumer protection.

in materials supplied by the consumer, it would appear that this would not be a contract for the sale of goods in any event,[102] and the duty of the manufacturer would be to exercise reasonable care and skill.[103]

Similar problems arise, or can arise, as already noted, with respect to the implied conditions in a sale by sample. As we have observed, the two most important conditions in a sale by sample are the implied condition of satisfactory quality and the implied condition that the bulk corresponds to the sample. But this does not mean that, even in a consumer sale, where prima facie the Unfair Contract Terms Act prohibits contracting-out, there is no way in which a seller can restrict his liability. Suppose, for instance, that a consumer orders a carpet after being shown a sample of carpeting, but he is clearly told by the sellers that they do not guarantee that the colours will be identical with those on the sample. If this is actually held to be a sale by sample, the sellers will be liable for the failure of the carpet to correspond with the sample, despite the specific warning given to the buyer. However, in such circumstances, this may well be regarded as an unreasonable result,[104] and it is open to the court to hold that the sale is not strictly speaking a sale by sample at all. In that event, although the carpet must still be of satisfactory quality under s. 14(2), the implied conditions applicable to a sale by sample will not attach.

Lastly, the implied condition in s. 14(3) about fitness for purpose raises similar issues. If the buyer *does* make known the purpose for which he wants the goods, and *does* rely (reasonably) on the seller's skill or judgment, the seller cannot escape liability by use of an exclusion clause; but it is possible for the seller to show that he does not guarantee that the goods will be suitable for the buyer's purposes. He may simply tell the buyer that he does not know if the goods will suit the buyer's needs, or that the buyer must make up his own mind as to this. Once again, the key concept is reasonable reliance, and in this case the Act recognizes this by actually introducing the concept in s. 14(3). If the seller can show that the buyer did not rely, or did not reasonably rely, upon his skill or judgment, then he is not liable at all, and the application of the Unfair Contract Terms Act does not arise. Clearly, it is once again the facts which matter. What the two Acts together rule out is the 'small print' exclusion clause; and it seems clear that it will not help the seller to replace a 'small print' exclusion clause by one declaring that the buyer has not relied on his skill or judgment, or that the seller gave no opinion on the suitability of the goods for the buyer's purposes.[105] This kind of purely formal agreement will not defeat the buyer's claims; but a real, and reasonable, agreement will show that the buyer has not relied upon the seller in such a way as to attract the implied condition in the first place.

Exemption clauses affected by the Unfair Contract Terms Act 1977
The question as to what precisely is an exemption clause the use of which is regulated by the Unfair Contract Terms Act is also one of no small difficulty. As we have seen,

102 See p. 21.
103 Supply of Goods and Services Act 1982 s. 13.
104 In practice slight differences of colour between the samples and the carpets provided are very common and probably unavoidable.
105 See *South Western General Property Co Ltd* v *Marton* (1982) 263 EG 1090; *Lutton* v *Saville Tractors (Belfast) Ltd*, above, n. 96.

the words of s. 6 of the Unfair Contract Terms Act say that the liability of a seller under ss. 13–15 cannot, as against a person dealing as consumer, 'be excluded or restricted by reference to any contract term'. Then s. 13(1) of the same Act goes on to say that the Act also prevents:

(a) making the liability or its enforcement subject to restrictive or onerous conditions;
(b) excluding or restricting any right or remedy in respect of the liability, or subjecting a person to any prejudice in consequence of his pursuing any such right or remedy;
(c) excluding or restricting rules of evidence or procedure.

Further, the section adds that it applies to 'terms and notices' which exclude or restrict liability. Section 13(2), however, makes it clear that this does not prevent the parties incorporating an arbitration clause in their contract.

Some things are reasonably clear. An outright attempt to say that implied terms do not apply or are excluded, or that some express condition is given in lieu of all statutory conditions, is simply ineffective if the other conditions of the Act are met. Similarly, a clause which says that breach gives no right of rejection would be ineffective as excluding 'a remedy in respect of the liability' under s. 13(1)(b) above. So also a clause which entitles the buyer to have the goods replaced but not to recover payment of the price would be void for the same reason. So also would a clause limiting the seller's liability for damage to a specified figure, or excluding liability for consequential losses.

But other points raise much more difficulty. What of a clause attempting to exclude or limit the seller's liability by claiming that a person acting on his behalf had no authority to say or do certain things? This question has arisen, and is more likely to arise, in connection with clauses attempting to limit or exclude liability for misrepresentation, which are not wholly void under s. 6 of the 1977 Act, but are subject to the test of reasonableness. But similar questions could arise under s. 6, for example where the seller's agent has offered an opinion as to the suitability for use of the goods being sold, and the seller later claims that the agent had no authority to give such an opinion. In the cases on misrepresentation it has so far been held that clauses (or even notices) about the authority of an agent must be treated in accordance with ordinary principles of contract law, and do not fall within the Act's control of exclusion or limitation clauses.[106] Their *effect* may be to limit the liability of the seller but their validity has not so far been tested by asking what their effect is, but by asking whether legitimate legal means have been used to achieve this effect.[107] On the other hand, a different result has been arrived at in a somewhat comparable situation, that is where a clause provides that one party is not to rely upon any representations made by the other party but is to make his own inquiries.[108] Here again, the issue arose in the context of a misrepresentation and an attempt to exclude liability for such a misrepresentation, but the issue is closely analogous to that which arises (for instance) under s. 14(3) of the Sale of Goods Act.[109]

---

106 *Overbrooke Estate Ltd* v *Glencombe Properties Ltd* [1974] 1 WLR 1335, approved by the CA in *Collins* v *Howell-Jones* (1980) 259 EG 331, criticized in (1981) 97 LQR 522.

107 Cf. *The Hollandia* [1983] 1 AC 565 where, in a different context, the HL applied an 'effects' test.

108 See cases cited in n. 105, above.

109 Thus a shop which displayed notices saying, 'Assistants are not authorized to give their opinion on the suitability of goods for particular purposes', might escape liability, while a shop displaying a notice saying, 'Customers must rely on their own judgment, not that of the assistant', would not. But cf. *Smith* v *Eric S. Bush* [1989] 2 All ER 514 which suggests that the first of these conclusions may now be challengeable.

Many other issues still lack authority. For instance, does s. 13(1)(a) of the 1977 Act prevent a seller from requiring a claim to be made against him within some specified period, or requiring notice of defects in the goods to be given within a certain time? If the time is so short that it is not practicable for the buyer to comply with it, then the restriction is within the Act, and will be void.[110] If the period is not as short as that it might be held that this is permissible simply because this would not be a restrictive or onerous condition, or alternatively it might be held to be within the Act but valid as reasonable.

Another problem which was canvassed by the Law Commissions in their Final Report, *Sale and Supply of Goods*,[111] concerns consumers who are asked to sign 'acceptance notes' when goods are delivered to them stating that they thereby accept the goods; the normal effect of an acceptance under s. 35 of the Act[112] is that the buyer is no longer able to reject them for defects but is confined to a claim for damages. But these 'acceptance notes' are not, and do not profess to be, contract 'terms': they are 'intimations' of acceptance within s. 35, and therefore may fall outside the statutory controls dealing with implied terms. This does not, however, mean that the 'acceptance note' must be taken at face value, since it would be open to a court to hold that such a note, if signed before any examination of the goods is possible, must be nothing more than a mere receipt for the goods.[113] In any event the Law Commissions proposed that the law should be amended on this point, and the Act now contains provisions to this effect which are dealt with further below.[114]

The requirement of reasonableness

The provisions relating to clauses excluding liability under the implied terms of the Sale of Goods Act in favour of a person dealing as consumer are, as we have seen, independent of any requirement of reasonableness. Insofar as the statutory terms are excluded or reduced in their effect, the exclusion clause is simply ineffective against a person dealing as consumer. But in other cases, exclusion clauses are now subject to the requirement of reasonableness by s. 2 (which deals with the exclusion of negligence liability), and s. 3 set out above. As noted at the outset,[115] the requirement of reasonableness is, at least theoretically, different for clauses relating to the implied terms in contracts for the sale or supply of goods, than it is for clauses relating to other contract terms.[116] Moreover, this requirement will operate in a number of different circumstances, of which the most important for present purposes are as follows.[117]

---

110 *R W Green Ltd* v *Cade Bros Farm* [1978] 1 Lloyd's Rep 602 – see below, pp. 249–50.
111 See paras 5.20–5.24 of the Report.
112 See below, p. 510 *et seq.*
113 See below, p. 510 *et seq*
114 See below, ibid.
115 See above, p. 235.
116 But see p. 235.
117 It should be stressed that the 1977 Act is a very intricate piece of legislation, and the following summary concentrates on essentials only. For details, reference to the Act itself is indispensable.

1   First, if the exclusion clause does not relate to the implied conditions under the
    Sale of Goods Act, but to some express term of the contract, as, for example, a
    requirement that goods be 'shipped in good condition'.[118] In this case, s. 3 pro-
    vides that the requirement of reasonableness applies whether or not the buyer is
    dealing as a consumer but, if he is not, then the requirement of reasonableness
    only applies if the buyer is dealing on the other party's 'written standard terms of
    business'.[119] The same position holds if the exclusion clause relates to some other
    liability under the Sale of Goods Act, for instance the quantity of the goods to be
    delivered.

2   Secondly, if the exclusion clause relates to the implied conditions in ss. 13–15 of
    the Act, the reasonableness requirement[120] will apply, but only where the buyer is
    not a consumer. It is immaterial whether the buyer is buying on the other's writ-
    ten standard terms of business.

3   Thirdly, the requirement of reasonableness[121] applies to any contractual term
    excluding business liability for negligence[122] (except for negligence leading to
    death or bodily injury, liability for which cannot be excluded at all).[123] In this
    case, it is immaterial whether the buyer is dealing as a consumer or on written
    standard terms or not. These factors may be relevant in the application of the test,
    but here we are only concerned with the preliminary question, whether it applies
    at all.

4   Fourthly, the requirement of reasonableness[124] applies to all cases where a clause
    relates to the effect of a misrepresentation, and here again, as in the third case, it
    is immaterial whether the buyer is a consumer or buying on written standard
    terms or not; indeed, the position is the same if the clause relates to the liability of
    the buyer rather than the seller.

In these four cases, therefore, the Unfair Contract Terms Act requires any exclusion clause to pass the appropriate test of reasonableness if it is to be upheld.
However, it will be seen that a number of preliminary questions may be relevant
before that test is applied to the exclusion clause. For instance, it may be necessary
to decide whether the exclusion clause is incorporated into the contract and what its
effect is as a matter of construction.[125] Secondly, it may be necessary to decide
whether the case does indeed fall within one of the above four classes of cases –
something which may not be nearly so clear as may be thought from this summary
of the Act. It would be beyond the scope of this book to examine these questions in
any detail, but a number of critical points must be mentioned.

---

118 See *Cehave NV v Bremer Handelsgesellschaft*, p. 92 above.
119 On the meaning of the equivalent phrase in s. 16 which is the corresponding, though somewhat differently worded,
     Scottish provision, see the Scots decision, *McCrone v Boots Farm Sales Ltd* 1981 SC 68, where Lord Dunpark said
     that the term is wide enough 'to include any contract, whether wholly written or partly oral, which includes a set
     of fixed terms or conditions which the proponer applies without material variation to contracts of the kind in
     question'.
120 I.e. that set out in s. 11(2).
121 I.e. that set out in s. 11(1).
122 Section 2(2).
123 Section 2(1).
124 I.e. that set out in s. 11(1).
125 See above, p. 225 *et seq.*

The first is that there may often be problems in deciding whether a clause is indeed an exclusion clause which is caught by the Act and so (in these four classes of cases) subjected to the relevant requirement of reasonableness. As we have seen, this problem is not wholly absent, even in the case of the consumer buyer who contends that an exclusion clause is ineffective because it restricts his rights under the implied conditions of the Sale of Goods Act; but the problem is likely to be much more acute in the cases presently under discussion. The difficulty can be illustrated by considering the ordinary commercial sale where the contract allows the seller a margin of tolerance, for instance as to the quality or quantity of the goods. If a seller contracts to deliver 5,000 tons of grain, but the contract proceeds to give the seller a tolerance by saying he may deliver 'five per cent more or less', is the seller's right to deliver five per cent less than the contract quantity an exclusion clause, or merely a clause defining his obligation? In a simple case of this kind, where tolerances are common (and where exact compliance would anyhow not always be practicable) it is surely unthinkable that the court would hold the clause to be an exclusion clause at all.

But other cases may be much more problematic. As noted above, there is now authority holding that a clause limiting the authority of an agent to bind his principal is not a clause excluding or limiting the liability of the principal within the meaning of the Act,[126] while a clause simply declaring that one party 'acknowledges' that no representations have been made to him, or that he has not relied on the other party, is within the statutory controls.[127] The leading authority on this question is now the decision of the House of Lords in *Smith* v *Eric S. Bush*[128] where a broad view was taken of the effect of the Act. Here it was held that a surveyor engaged by a mortgagee to value a house was liable for negligence even though the mortgagee had specifically declared that the valuation was only obtained on the basis that the surveyor accepted no responsibility. The argument that this was not a disclaimer subject to the 1977 Act, but a denial of responsibility which prevented a duty of care arising in the first place, was rejected by the House of Lords. So where there is or would prima facie be a legal liability, any clause denying that liability (no matter how phrased) would appear to be subject to the reasonableness requirements of the Act. But where there is not even a prima facie liability, because the contract is one which does not in itself impose such a liability, this argument presumably fails, and the Act will not apply.

These problems are likely to be most important in relation to s. 3 of the 1977 Act set out above,[129] which contains the general provision subjecting exclusion clauses to the reasonableness requirement, apart from clauses excluding the statutory implied terms under the Sale of Goods Act. It will be seen that two alternative cases are contemplated here. Under the first, a clause is caught by the section if it excludes or restricts a liability in the ordinary way (s. 3(2)(a)). Under the second, even where this is not the case – that is, even where the clause does not appear to be an exclusion clause in the ordinary sense – the section will bite if the effect of a clause is to permit

---

126 Above, n. 106.
127 Above, n. 105.
128 [1989] 2 All ER 514.
129 See p. 235.

a performance substantially different from that which could reasonably be expected, or no performance at all (s. 3(2)(b)). To some extent this last provision may be said to be a statutory recreation of the old doctrine of fundamental breach, though its results are very different from those of that doctrine.

The next question which arises with cases falling into these four groups, that is where the test of reasonableness is to be applied, is the ordinary question of construction. This question, too, might in theory be applied even in the consumer cases concerning the implied terms under the Sale of Goods Act, but it would have no practical importance in those cases. For whether the clause is held inapplicable to the circumstances which have occurred as a matter of construction or whether it is held ineffective under the statute, the result will be the same. But in the present group of cases, it is to be assumed that ordinary principles of construction will remain more important, for if the exclusion clause is found not to cover the events which have occurred, then there will be no need to apply the reasonableness test at all.

If, on the other hand, the construction question leads to the conclusion that the clause is intended to apply to the events which have occurred, the court must then go on to answer the reasonableness question. But it is unlikely that the old rules of construction will continue to be applied as though nothing has changed as a result of the 1977 Act. For it would be idle to pretend that the traditional rules of construction of exclusion clauses are ordinary rules of interpretation designed to ascertain the real intent of the parties. Frequently they were applied so as to defeat the manifest intent of the parties, but to give effect to the courts' views as to what was fair and reasonable. There are distinct signs in the decisions of the House of Lords in the *Securicor* and *Ailsa Craig* cases,[130] and also in the first House of Lords decision on the reasonableness condition,[131] that things are moving in this direction.[132] But as we have already seen,[133] some residue of the old law seems to have survived so far. At present, the position appears to be that total exclusion clauses, and also cases of fundamental breach, may still be subject to somewhat strict rules of construction, while limitation clauses (at least if there is no fundamental breach) are to be construed in their ordinary, natural meaning. This distinction has been criticized above,[134] and, as suggested,[135] it would not be surprising if strict methods of construing all exclusion clauses were abandoned on the ground that the problem could be better coped with by use of the Unfair Contract Terms Act.[136]

The reasonableness test is itself set out in s. 11 of the 1977 Act, and as we have noted differs at least in theory according to whether the appropriate provision is s. 11(1) or s. 11(2). In relation to the latter provision, there are guidelines set out in Sch. 2.[137]

---

130 Often referred to as 'the two *Securicor* cases' because in each Securicor had provided a patrolman to guard the property concerned – *Photo Production v Securicor Transport* [1980] AC 827, and *Ailsa Craig Fishing Co Ltd v Malvern Fishing Co Ltd* [1983] 1 All ER 101; 1982 SC (HL) 14.
131 *George Mitchell (Chesterhall) Ltd v Finney Lock Seeds Ltd* [1983] 2 AC 803.
132 See *Stewart Gill Ltd v Horatio Myer & Co Ltd* and *Fastframe Ltd v Lohinski*, p. 229 above.
133 Above, p. 228 *et seq.*
134 Ibid.
135 Ibid.
136 See above, p. 230.
137 Though, as noted below, in applying the test of reasonableness under s. 11(1), courts tend to take into account the guidelines of Sch. 2.

Section 11(1) was set out above.[138] The first point to note about this section is that it requires that the term should have been fair and reasonable *at the time when it was included in the contract.* This is somewhat different from the requirement of reasonableness which was originally contained in the Misrepresentation Act and in the Supply of Goods (Implied Terms) Act 1973, both of which have now been replaced by the new provisions.[139] Under the earlier Acts what had to be shown was that *reliance* on the exclusion clause was fair or reasonable. The difference is quite significant, because a very wide exclusion clause may easily be held to be unreasonable under the new Act, even though it would have been quite reasonable to have a narrower exclusion clause which would have actually covered what has in fact happened. Under the earlier Acts, reliance on the clause might well have been held fair and reasonable; under the new Act, it might be held unreasonable.[140] One effect of the Act could have been to compel those responsible for drafting standard conditions of contract to limit the width of exclusion clauses in the hope that narrower clauses were more likely to be upheld as reasonable. It is not permissible to maintain very broad unreasonable clauses and then claim that reliance on the clause in particular narrow circumstances is not unreasonable.

The next part of s. 11 which needs to be noted is s. 11(4), which declares that where an exclusion clause seeks to restrict the liability of a party to 'a specified sum of money', regard is to be had in particular to:

(a) the resources which he could expect to be available to him for the purpose of meeting the liability should it arise; and
(b) how far it was open to him to cover himself by insurance.

Section 11(5) goes on to say that the onus is on the party who claims an exclusion clause is reasonable to satisfy the court that it was.

The guidelines in Sch. 2 are more or less the same as those which were originally contained in the Supply of Goods (Implied Terms) Act, and they do not strictly speaking apply in all cases where the reasonableness test has to be applied but only to cases involving contracts for the sale (or supply) of goods.[141] The court must have regard to the following, where relevant:

(a) the strength of the bargaining positions of the parties relative to each other, taking into account (among other things) alternative means by which the customer's requirements could have been met;
(b) whether the customer received an inducement to agree to the term, or in accepting it had an opportunity of entering into a similar contract with other persons, but without having to accept a similar term;
(c) whether the customer knew or ought reasonably to have known of the existence and extent of the term (having regard, among other things, to any custom of the trade and any previous course of dealing between the parties);

---

138 See p. 235.

139 The present provisions reflect the recommendations of the Scottish Law Commission.

140 This emerges quite clearly from the judgment of Lord Denning in the *Howard Marine* case [1978] QB 574 where he held (under the original Misrepresentation Act) that reliance on the exclusion clause was reasonable, even though the clause as a whole was possibly unreasonably wide. The majority of the court, however, held that even reliance on the clause was unreasonable (though they gave no reasons).

141 But they have been taken into account – see *Danka Rentals Ltd* v *Xi Software* (1998) 7 Tr LR 74; and see *Farrans Construction Ltd* v *Ready Mixed Concrete (Scotland) Ltd* 2004 GWD 13-283 Outer House, Court of Session.

(d) where the term excludes or restricts any relevant liability if some condition is not complied with, whether it was reasonable at the time of the contract to expect that compliance with that condition would be practicable;

(e) whether the goods were manufactured, processed or adapted to the special order of the customer.

So far, only one sale of goods case[142] on the modern statutory control of exception and limitation clauses[143] has reached the House of Lords, and it is appropriate to begin with that case. It must be noted at the outset, however, that this case was governed by the provisions contained in the Sale of Goods Act 1979.[144] The significance of this is dealt with below. The case was *George Mitchell (Chesterhall) Ltd v Finney Lock Seeds Ltd*[145] where the plaintiffs were farmers who had ordered late cabbage seed from the defendants who were seed merchants. They were supplied with an inferior seed which was not indeed a late cabbage seed at all. The plaintiffs suffered considerable losses (over £60,000) which were not (it was stressed in the House of Lords) purely losses of profit; the losses included large sums of wasted expenditure in planting and later clearing the fields where there was a total crop failure. The contract contained a clause limiting the defendants' liability to the cost of replacing or refunding the price of the seeds sold – a relatively trivial sum. It was held that, applying the ordinary meaning of the words, the limitation clause did apply to the circumstances, but it was void under the Unfair Contract Terms Act as unreasonable.

In arriving at the second part of this decision, which is the material part for present purposes, the House of Lords balanced a number of considerations. In favour of the sellers was the fact that the parties knew and understood the terms clearly enough, and also that the damages claimed were out of all proportion to the price. But, in favour of the buyers, it was pointed out that (1) all seeds were sold on these terms by seed merchants – buyers had no opportunity to pay more and obtain protection from such risks, (2) the sellers could insure against this kind of liability without a material increase in the price of seeds, (3) the sellers had been negligent in supplying the wrong kind of seed, and (4) most important of all, it was shown that seed merchants did often negotiate settlements and offer some compensation where they were convinced that claims of this kind were genuine. This last factor was considered almost decisive by the House of Lords because it demonstrated that those in the trade did not themselves think it reasonable to rely on the limitation clauses in their full rigour. It suggested rather that the purpose of the clause was to enable the sellers to decide which claims to pay and which to reject, without control from the courts. In effect, the purpose of the clause thus seems to have been to enable the sellers to be judges in their own cause, rather than to exclude or limit their liability.

Two further points should be made about the *George Mitchell* case. The first is that, as noted above, because of the time when the facts arose, the case was governed by the Sale of Goods Act 1979 and not by the Unfair Contract Terms Act. Although the present Act is almost identical with the 1979 Act on many points, there are a

---

142 Though the House of Lords has considered the application of the Unfair Contract Terms Act in a consumer credit case: *Director General of Fair Trading v First National Bank plc* [2002] 1 All ER 97 – see p. 259.

143 There are early examples such as the Carriers Act 1830 and the Railway and Canal Traffic Act 1854.

144 Consolidating the identical provisions of the Supply of Goods (Implied Terms) Act 1973.

145 [1983] 2 AC 803.

number of points of difference; for instance, the 1979 Act provided that exclusion clauses were void 'to the extent that' they did not comply with the requirement of reasonableness; the present Act declares that in non-consumer sales, the implied conditions in ss. 13–15 can only be excluded by a term 'in so far as the term satisfies the requirement of reasonableness'. In the *George Mitchell* case, it was thought by the House of Lords (though no definite opinion was expressed) that the former of these provisions did not authorize a court to sever the offending part of an exclusion clause and uphold the remainder. In *Stewart Gill Ltd v Horatio Myer & Co Ltd*,[146] however, Lord Donaldson MR said that the issue is whether the term, the whole term, and nothing but the term, is a fair and reasonable one to have been included.

A second point of difference between the two Acts is that (as we have previously noted) in the 1979 Act the test of reasonableness was to be applied taking account of all the circumstances of the case. In *George Mitchell* the House of Lords held that this meant that the reasonableness of a clause was to be judged having regard to the circumstances prevailing at the time of the breach, rather than when the contract was made. In the 1977 Act the requirement of reasonableness, as we have seen, is that a term shall have been a fair and reasonable one to be included having regard to the circumstances which were, or ought reasonably to have been, known to or in the contemplation of the parties *when the contract was made*. In the *George Mitchell* case, therefore, the House of Lords took account of all the circumstances, including the fact that in the past the sellers had not relied on their limitation clause,[147] that the supply of the defective seed was due to negligence, and that the sellers could have insured against the losses. The fact of the crop failure itself was clearly a material circumstance under the 1973 Act; would it be material under UCTA? It seems unlikely that the change made by the 1977 Act would affect this, because the fact of crop failure is obviously readily foreseeable if the wrong, or inferior, seeds are supplied by a seed merchant, and if the reasonableness of the term limiting liability had been considered as at the time of the making of the contract, this foreseeable result would have been just as relevant as the actual result which had to be taken into account. But in other circumstances, this change made by the 1977 Act may be more significant, as already indicated. For instance, a minor breach, with small losses, might have been held to make it permissible to rely on an exclusion clause under the 1979 Act when it would no longer be held reasonable to have included the term in the contract within the 1977 Act. Even bearing in mind the differences between the two Acts with which the respective courts were concerned, it must be admitted that *George Mitchell* seems to represent a more interventionist approach to commercial contracts than the House of Lords seemed to signal in *Photo Production*.[148]

By comparison with the *George Mitchell* case, a different result was reached in *R W Green Ltd v Cade Bros Farm*[149] where the contract was for the sale of seed potatoes by

146 [1992] 2 All ER 257, 261.

147 Lord Bridge took it that this indicated that reliance on the clause would not be fair and reasonable. The clause in question was a standard in the seed trade, but on the sellers' own evidence was rarely, if ever, invoked – see [1983] 1 All ER 108, 117 per Lord Denning MR. For a critique of Lord Bridge's approach, see Adams and Brownsword (1988) 104 LQR 94.

148 See Adams and Brownsword (1988) 104 LQR 94. *Photo Production* did not directly involve UCTA but is recognized as authoritative so far as it dealt with the Act's application.

149 [1978] 1 Lloyd's Rep 602.

potato merchants. Here too the contract excluded liability for consequential damage and limited the responsibility of the sellers to returning the price. The potatoes proved to be infected with a virus which was not detectable in advance (by sellers or buyers) and the buyers suffered loss. Thus far, the facts were almost on all fours with those in *George Mitchell*, but one important difference was that the potatoes in question were uncertified, and hence somewhat cheaper. Certified potatoes were free from the virus infection. In the result Griffiths J upheld the limitation clause as reasonable though he struck down as unreasonable a clause requiring the buyers to give notice of a claim within three days of delivery. This was impractical because the fault could not be discovered until the potatoes began to grow, so the clause was clearly unreasonable. This case was not mentioned in the speeches in the House of Lords in *George Mitchell*, so it is uncertain whether it survives that case, but it would seem clearly distinguishable, both on the ground that the buyer had the choice to buy certified potatoes, and also on the ground that there was no negligence on the part of the sellers.

Amongst other decisions on the reasonableness requirement, brief mention may be made of a few. In *Stag Line Ltd v Tyne Repair Group Ltd ('The Zinnia')*[150] Staughton J suggested that the fact that terms are in very small print, or difficult to understand, is an argument against their reasonableness. In *Rasbora Ltd v JCL Marine*,[151] the subject-matter of the sale was a power boat sold for some £22,000. As a result of serious electrical faults, the boat caught fire and sank on its first outing. Lawson J held that in fact the sale was a consumer sale so that the exclusion clause was void insofar as it excluded the implied conditions under the Sale of Goods Act. But he went on to say that even if the sale had not been a consumer sale, he would have held the exclusion clause unreasonable inasmuch as it purported to exclude completely the implied condition of merchantability. In *R & B Customs Brokers Co Ltd v United Dominions Trust*,[152] where a car was bought by a company for the use of a director, on conditional sale terms, excluding all liability on the part of the sellers (who were mere financiers), it was held that the sale was a consumer sale and so the requirement of reasonableness did not arise. But the Court was inclined to think that if it had been a non-consumer sale the requirement of reasonableness would have been satisfied, because the sellers were mere financiers, who never saw the car, and the buyers were business parties, not devoid of commercial experience. It is, however, somewhat strange to see it suggested that mere financiers can reasonably exclude their liability in credit sales, because for a very long time the hire-purchase legislation has imposed liability on financiers just as though they were sellers.[153]

In the *Howard Marine* case,[154] which has been referred to previously and which involved the former s. 3 of the Misrepresentation Act, Lord Denning gave his reasons for regarding the exclusion clause as reasonable. The parties were of equal bargaining position, the representation was quite innocent and the plaintiffs (on the misrepresentation issue) could have discovered the truth themselves by further

---

150 [1984] 2 Lloyd's Rep 211, 222.
151 [1976] 2 Lloyd's Rep 645.
152 [1988] 1 All ER 847. See also discussion of this case at p. 237.
153 See p. 13 *et seq.*
154 [1978] QB 574.

inquiry. The majority of the court held the exclusion to be unreasonable without giving any reasons for their decision, other than to say that the matter was one of discretion for the trial judge, who was entitled to find the clause unreasonable. This last point may prove to be of some importance, because the House of Lords in the *George Mitchell* case has stressed that appeals on the question of reasonableness will not be broadly entertained. The decision on a reasonableness question is primarily for the trial judge and appeals will only be available where he has gone wrong in principle, or perhaps has failed to take account of the relevant considerations.[155]

The next case to be mentioned concerned not a contract of sale, but of hire. In *Phillips Products v Hyland and Hamstead Plant Hire*,[156] the plaintiffs hired a crane and driver for a short period from the defendants. The driver, through negligence, caused damage to the plaintiffs' own factory, but the conditions of hire excluded liability for the negligence of the driver. The condition was held to be unreasonable on the ground that the hire period was short, the plaintiffs had little time to arrange insurance, and were not regular hirers of such equipment.[157] However, a great deal of mechanical plant is regularly hired under similar conditions to these, so further litigation on this question may be expected.[158] *Danka Rentals Ltd v Xi Software*[159] is a case from outside the field of mechanical plant hire. In this case an exemption clause which purported to exclude all express and implied warranties in a lease of a photocopier which turned out to be a 'complete disaster', was held to be too wide and therefore unreasonable.[160]

Reference may be made again to the House of Lords' decision in *Smith v Eric S. Bush*[161] although this was not a sale of goods case. In this case it was held that it was not reasonable under the 1977 Act for surveyors who value houses on behalf of mortgagees to disclaim all liability for negligence towards the purchaser who in reality pays the surveyor's fees, though through the mortgagee. This decision was based on the general view that purchasers (at any rate in ordinary house-purchase transactions) have little or no bargaining power on these matters, especially because the arrangements are made by the mortgagee, and that it is impractical and expensive for purchasers to protect themselves by commissioning a second survey on their own behalf. Much of this reasoning is directed to the peculiar nature of the average

155 As to the implications of this, see Adams and Brownsword, 'The Unfair Contract Terms Act: A Decade of Discretion' (1988) 104 LQR 94.
156 (1985) 4 Tr LR 98.
157 The standard form clause in question, clause 8 of the Model Conditions of the Construction Plant Hire Association, has since been reworded to include a duty on the part of the owner to provide a competent operator. It is believed that this change was made having regard to the words of Slade LJ [1987] 2 All ER 620, 630. On these provisions generally, see Adams, *Commercial Hiring and Leasing*, Butterworths (1989), para. 6.103 *et seq.*
158 Indeed, in two cases following soon after *Phillips v Hyland*, *Paul v Ruddle Bros* (26 April 1985 – unreported) and in *Thompson v Lohan Plant Hire Ltd* [1987] 2 All ER 631, it was distinguished. In these latter cases, the relevant issues against which the reasonableness of the clause fell to be determined were between the owner and the hirer, rather than between either of them and the injured third party. In most such cases, the dispute is, in reality, between insurance companies.
159 (1998) 7 Tr LR 74. See also *AEG (UK) Ltd v Logic Resources Ltd*, 20 October 1995 (unreported).
160 Since the contract was on the lessor's standard terms the judge applied both ss. 3 and 7 to trigger the tests of reasonableness, and suggested that although the guidelines set out in Sch. 2 apply only in relation to the latter, it made little practical difference as there was nothing to prevent him from taking into consideration the guidelines in relation to s. 3.
161 [1989] 2 All ER 514.

house-purchase transaction and is unlikely to be especially relevant to the law of sale of goods. But there is one point about the decision which may be of wider importance. It emerged during the case that some building societies actually gave the house purchaser an option between obtaining a survey with liability and obtaining a survey without liability, and it might have been thought that this at least would have been reasonable in terms of the 1977 Act. But it also emerged that the additional cost of the survey with liability was so great that few buyers took advantage of it, and the judges were clearly doubtful whether the additional charge was truly justified. So it seems that, where options of this character are offered to a buyer, it may be necessary to show that the extra charge for the option which carries liability is itself a justifiable charge if the reasonableness requirement is to be satisfied. The availability of insurance cover is a relevant consideration in determining reasonableness,[162] as the *St Albans City and District Council* case discussed in the next paragraph illustrates.

The case of *St Albans City and District Council* v *International Computers Ltd*[163] involved a number of interesting questions. The defendants had installed a computerized database for the plaintiff's community charge register. An error in the software significantly overstated the population in the area, and as a result the plaintiffs lost £1,314,846.[164] The contract contained a clause limiting the defendant's loss to £100,000. Scott Baker J held that this term was subject to s. 3 of UCTA and that in addition either s. 6 or s. 7 applied.[165] Section 11(4) also applied because the defendants sought to restrict their liability to a specified sum. Under this latter provision, in considering the question of reasonableness, regard had to be paid to the defendants' resources to meet potential liability and how far it was open to them to obtain insurance cover. He went on to hold that the following factors had to be taken into account: that the parties were of unequal bargaining power; that the defendants had not justified the figure of £100,000 which was small in relation to the potential risk and the actual loss; that the defendants held an aggregate of £50 million insurance cover worldwide; and the practical consequences. On the last point, he went on to ask which of the two parties was the better loss bearer? The defendant was well able to insure, and had insured and no doubt passed the premium on to its customers. If the loss were placed on the plaintiffs, it would be borne by the local population in the form of increased taxes or reduced services. These

---

162 See s. 11(4)(b).

163 [1995] FSR 686, upheld by the Court of Appeal on the points material to the present discussion [1996] 4 All ER 481. See also *Horace Homan Group Ltd* v *Sherwood International Group Ltd*, TCC, 12 April 2000 (unreported) which also involved a computer software installation, and was made between two substantial concerns, but again, the Unfair Contract Terms Act 1977 was applied. It was held that the onus was on the defendants, under s. 11(5), to show that the term was reasonable and the defendant had failed to discharge the burden. Compare *SAM Business Systems Ltd* v *Hedley & Co (a firm)* [2002] EWHC 2733 (TCC) where the software installation contract provided machinery whereby the purchaser could get its money back, and the exclusion of liability for breach and misrepresentation was upheld as reasonable. In *Messer UK Ltd and anor* v *Britvic Soft Drinks Ltd and ors* [2002] EWCA Civ 548 it was pointed out that the provision of software is an exercise notoriously liable to give rise to problems, and that an ordinary supply of manufactured goods, CO_2 gas, is different. Accordingly, an exemption clause in such a supply contract was held to be unreasonable – see also *Bacardi-Martini Beverages Ltd* v *Thomas Hardy Packaging Ltd* [2002] EWCA Civ 549.

164 This amount was reduced by the Court of Appeal for reasons not germane to the present discussion.

165 From which it appears he considered the contract in question to involve a sale or supply of *goods* – see p. 77 *et seq* for a discussion as to whether a software contract involves a sale or supply of goods. On the approach taken by the judge the outcome would have been the same, however, even if no sale or supply of goods were involved – see ibid.

factors outweighed the fact that bodies such as the plaintiff and the defendant should be free to make their own bargains, that the plaintiffs contracted with their eyes open, and that these limitations were common in the computer industry which was an area of developing technology (in fact only two or three companies offered competing software packages, and each used similar terms). The burden was on the defendants to show the clause was fair and reasonable, and they had not discharged the burden.

Scots law

Part II of the Unfair Contract Terms Act 1977 provides the Scottish version of the controls just described. While the broad thrust of this Part is very similar to that for England and Wales, the language and structure are rather different. But in this section there will be reference back as appropriate to the previous section, since English authorities on the Act can be, and indeed are, cited freely in Scotland despite the differences in the statutory wordings.

Exemption clauses in contracts generally, i.e. not just in contracts for the supply of goods, are controlled by s. 17, which corresponds to s. 3 of the English Part of the Act.[166] But this section applies only to clauses in consumer contracts and standard form contracts. A consumer contract is one in which one party deals in the course of business and the other party does not deal in the course of business; and, in contracts involving the transfer of ownership or possession of goods, the goods are of a type ordinarily supplied for private use or consumption.[167] The Sale and Supply of Goods to Consumers Regulations[168] provide for the following exclusions from the definition of 'consumer contract':[169]

> (1B) The expression of 'consumer contract' does not include a contract in which—
> (a) the buyer is an individual and the goods are second hand goods sold by public auction at which individuals have the opportunity of attending in person; or
> (b) the buyer is not an individual and the goods are sold by auction or competitive tender.

As a result of this definition, s. 17 does not apply to contracts between private individuals. In any dispute over the nature of the contract, the onus lies on the party who is contending that the contract is *not* a consumer contract, to establish this is the case.[170]

A standard form contract is not defined in the Act. However, the protections of s. 17(1) are for the benefit of the customer, who is defined as a party to a contract on

---

166 See above, p. 235.
167 See further the English authorities on the meaning of 'consumer contract', discussed above, p. 236 *et seq.* There is Scottish authority that contracts of employment will almost always be consumer contracts for these purposes: *Chapman v Aberdeen Construction Group Ltd plc* 1993 SLT 1205 per Lord Caplan at 1209.
168 SI 2002/3045.
169 Regulation 14(4).
170 Section 25(1).

the other party's written standard terms of business.[171] Thus the contract must be in writing or refer to written standard terms.[172] The proponer of the standard terms must deal in the course of business. But unlike a consumer contract, the customer can also be dealing in the course of business, i.e. a standard form contract can be between two businesses. In a standard form contract, the majority of the terms are prearranged and not subject to negotiation, i.e. the terms offered are the same for all the party's transactions. Where, for example, the price of goods or services is altered for particular transactions, the contract will still be on standard terms if none of the other terms is altered. A proof may be necessary to establish that the contract is a standard form one.[173]

Provided the contract is a consumer contract or standard form contract, any clause which enables a party:

(a) who is in breach of a contractual obligation to exclude or restrict any liability of his to the consumer or customer[174] in respect of the breach; or

(b) in respect of a contractual obligation, to render no performance, or to render a performance substantially different from that which the consumer or customer reasonably expected from the contract,

has no effect if it was not fair and reasonable to incorporate the term into the contract.[175] The onus rests on the party wishing to rely on the clause to establish that it was fair and reasonable to incorporate the clause.[176]

Further rules apply specifically to contracts of sale of goods and hire-purchase contracts under ss. 20 and 21 of the Act, which correspond to ss. 6 and 7 in the English Part.[177] In *all* sales – including sales between private parties – and hire-purchase agreements, an exemption clause excluding the implied obligation of the seller or hirer to pass good title is void.[178] In consumer sales and hire-purchase, any clause excluding or restricting the implied obligation that the goods conform to description or sample, or to their reasonable quality or fitness for purpose, is void as against the consumer.[179] In any other case,[180] such a clause is unenforceable unless it is shown to have been fair and reasonable to incorporate the clause.[181] There are similar controls in respect of the contract of barter, contracts for the supply of works and materials and contracts of hire.[182]

---

171 Section 17(2).

172 *McCrone v Boots Farm Sales Ltd* 1981 SC 68 per Lord Dunpark at 74.

173 *Border Harvesters Ltd v Edwards Engineering (Perth) Ltd* 1985 SLT 128.

174 'Customer' is defined as 'a party to a standard form contract who deals on the basis of written standard terms of business of the other party to the contract who himself deals in the course of a business' (s. 17(2)).

175 Section 17(1).

176 Section 24(4). The defender must provide averments to assist the court in reaching a decision; see, for example, *Continental Tyre & Rubber Co Ltd v Trunk Trailer Co Ltd* 1987 SLT 58; *Landcatch Ltd v Marine Harvest Ltd* 1985 SLT 478.

177 See above, pp. 235 *et seq.*

178 Section 20(1).

179 Section 20(2).

180 E.g. sales between two businesses, whether or not on standard forms: i.e. these controls are not restricted to sales on standard form contracts. A private sale is included only insofar as conformity to description is concerned, as the other obligations arise only when the goods are sold in the course of business.

181 Section 20(2).

182 Section 21.

Section 16(1), which is the equivalent of s. 2 in the English Part of the Act, provides that where an exemption clause excludes or restricts liability for breach of duty arising in the course of any business or from the occupation of business premises, the term or provision is void if it purports to exclude or restrict liability in respect of death or personal injury.[183] Personal injury includes any disease and any impairment of a person's physical or mental condition.[184] When the clause excludes or restricts liability for breach of duty in respect of damage to property or economic loss, the clause has no effect unless the party relying on the clause can show it was fair and reasonable to incorporate the clause into the contract or non-contractual notice.[185] Breach of duty is breach of a contractual obligation to take reasonable care or exercise reasonable skill in performance of the contract, breach of the common law delictual duty to take reasonable care or exercise reasonable skill and breach of the duty of reasonable care imposed by s. 2(1) of the Occupiers' Liability (Scotland) Act 1960.[186] It does not matter whether the breach occurs as a result of an intentional act or negligence, while liability can be direct or vicarious.[187] The clause can be a contract term or a provision in a non-contractual notice, provided it would otherwise be effective.[188] Thus s. 16 provides an important control in respect of clauses exempting a business from delictual liability or liability for breach of contract which arises from a party's negligence.

What kinds of clauses are caught by the Act?[189] The sections quoted above often refer to the 'exclusion or restriction' of liability. The Act states that this includes:

(a) making the liability or its enforcement subject to any restrictive or onerous conditions;
(b) excluding or restricting any right or remedy (e.g. rejection or damages) in respect of liability, or subjecting a person to any prejudice in consequence of his pursuing any such right or remedy;
(c) excluding or restricting any rule of evidence or procedure;
(d) excluding or restricting any liability by reference to a notice having contractual effect;

but this does not include an agreement to submit any question to arbitration.[190] Section 17 also refers to clauses which allow a party to render no performance, or to render a performance substantially different from that which the consumer or customer reasonably expected from the contract. In *Macrae & Dick v Phillip*,[191] the defender purchased a Rolls-Royce from the pursuers and then attempted to re-sell it in the face of a pre-emption clause in favour of the sellers contained in the original contract of sale. When the sellers sought to enforce this clause, the defender argued that it enabled the pursuers to render a performance substantially different from that which he had reasonably expected, namely a right to prevent him selling to whomsoever

---

183 Section 16(1)(a).
184 Section 25.
185 Sections 16(1)(b) and 24(4). On the reasonableness test, see below, p. 256.
186 Section 25(1).
187 Section 25(2).
188 Section 16(1A).
189 See discussion above, pp. 241 *et seq.*
190 Section 25(3). Compare s. 13(1) of the English Part.
191 1982 SLT (Sh Ct) 5.

he wished. In the face of evidence that the defender had been well aware of the clause at the time of contracting, his argument was unsuccessful; but the case illustrates the potential reach of s. 17, going well beyond the conventional exemption clause.[192]

The reasonableness test is set out in s. 24. The reasonableness and fairness of the incorporation of the exemption clause is determined by having regard to the circumstances which were, or ought reasonably to have been, known to or in the contemplation of the parties at the time the contract was made.[193] Where, however, the exemption clause is in a non-contractual notice, whether or not it is fair and reasonable to rely on the notice is determined in accordance with the circumstances when liability arose.[194] When applying the test in the context of ss. 20 or 21, the court is expressly enjoined to consider 'in particular' the factors in Sch. 2 to the Act:[195] however, there is nothing to prevent them also being taken into account in any case when the reasonableness test is applied or, in supply of goods cases, taking other factors into account. When a limitation clause 'purports to restrict liability to a specified sum of money', the court has to have regard to (1) the resources of the party relying on the clause to meet the liability; and (2) how far it was open to that party to cover himself with insurance.[196] Once again, it is submitted that these factors – in particular the availability of insurance – can, and indeed should, be considered in any application of the reasonableness test and are therefore not restricted to limitation clauses. A clause is fair and reasonable if it has been approved by a competent authority which is not a party to the contract.[197]

In *Knight Machinery (Holdings) Ltd* v *Rennie*,[198] the court was called upon to adjudicate upon the fairness and reasonableness of a clause which provided that a buyer was deemed to have accepted defective goods unless he had given notice of the defect to the seller within seven days of receipt of the goods. Since teething problems were common with the machinery bought in this case, an Extra Division of the Court of Session held that it was not reasonable at the time of the contract to expect that it would be practicable for the buyer to give the requisite notice. The court rejected the seller's contention that the clause only demanded that the buyer should inform the seller that he was having problems with the machine. Before it could pass the reasonableness test, the least that could be expected of a term conceived wholly in the interests of its proponer, at the expense of the other party's rights, was that the term should be clear and unambiguous. On the other hand, in *Denholm Fishselling Ltd* v *Anderson*[199] a clause in a standard form contract used by fishsellers, placing an onus upon buyers to

---

192 See also *Elliot* v *Sunshine Coast International Ltd* 1989 GWD 28-1252, in which a holiday company's clause allowing it to alter the form of transport for customers without notice was found to allow it to render a performance substantially different from that which a customer reasonably expected as the result of oral discussions at the booking point, and that this was unreasonable.

193 Section 24(1). Compare the English s. 11(1), and see discussion above, pp. 246–7. In *Farrans Construction Ltd* v *Ready Mixed Concrete (Scotland) Ltd*, 2004 GWD 13–283, held that while those guidelines do not apply expressly to cases under s. 17, they have in practice been taken into account in considering what is fair and reasonable under that section (citing *Chitty on Contracts* §14–082).

194 Section 24(2A).

195 For these factors, see above, pp. 247 *et seq.*

196 Section 24(3).

197 Section 29(2).

198 1995 SLT 166.

199 1991 SLT (Sh Ct) 24.

satisfy themselves as to the quality of fish bought in a busy fish-market, was held to be reasonable, the court taking into account both market conditions and the fact that the buyers had alternative sources of supply: '[T]he fact that one party tenders to the other a set of non-negotiable contractual terms is not in itself evidence of inequality of bargaining power or that the terms themselves are unfair and unreasonable.'[200]

THE EC DIRECTIVE ON UNFAIR TERMS IN CONSUMER CONTRACTS

As explained at the beginning of this chapter, this Directive is additional to the Unfair Contract Terms Act 1977: contracts must pass through both barriers to be enforceable. It is implemented by the Unfair Terms in Consumer Contracts Regulations.[201] These revoke and replace earlier Regulations.[202] Regulations 3–9 re-enact regs 2–7 of the earlier Regulations, but with the modifications to reflect more closely the wording of the Directive. As was pointed out in the previous edition, where differences in wording between a Directive and UK legislation exist, it is the Directive as interpreted by the European Court of Justice which governs.[203]

Field of application

The Regulations apply to any term in a contract concluded between a seller or supplier and a consumer.[204] The Regulations do not apply in relation to contractual terms which reflect:

(a) mandatory statutory or regulatory provisions (including such provisions under the law of any member state or in Community legislation having effect in the United Kingdom without further enactment);

(b) the provisions or principles of international conventions to which the member states or the Community are party.[205]

The Regulations go on to provide that a contractual term which has not been individually negotiated shall be regarded as unfair if, contrary to the requirements of good faith, it causes a significant imbalance in the parties' rights and obligations arising under the contract, to the detriment of the consumer.[206] A term is always regarded as

---

200 At p. 25.
201 SI 1999/2083.
202 SI 1994/3159.
203 National courts are required to interpret national law in the light of the wording and purpose of Directives – see *Marleasing SA* v *La Comercial Internacional de Alimentación SA* Case C-106/89 [1990] ECR I-4135. Failure to implement a Directive can give rise to liability on the part of the member state to a person suffering damage thereby – *Francovich* v *Italy* Cases C-6 and C-9/90 ECR I-5357. Directives are binding only on member states to whom they are addressed. Consequently they cannot be invoked in personal disputes between private individuals – see, e.g., *Paolo Faccini Dori* v *Recreb Srl* Case C-91/92 [1995] 1 All ER (EC) 1.
204 Regulation 4(1).
205 Regulation 4(2).
206 Regulation 5(1). See *Director-General of Fair Trading* v *First National Bank* [2001] UKHL 52, [2002] 1 All ER 97; and see *Bairstow Eves London Central Ltd* v *Smith* [2004] EWHC 263 (QB) discussed below. In *Benincasa* v *Dentalkit Srl* Case C- 269/95 A-G Colomer expressed the view that consumer means a private final consumer, not one engaged in trade or professional activities (ibid. para. 36). Although this view was specifically expressed in relation to Articles 13 and 14 of the Brussels Convention, it would seem relevant to the likely meaning of 'consumer' in the present context. (See 93/13/EEC Art 2(b).) So that an individual who is not carrying on a business at the time, who enters for the first time into a commercial contract with a view to starting to trade, is not a consumer.

not having been individually negotiated where it has been drafted in advance and the consumer has therefore not been able to influence the substance of the term.[207] Even though a specific term, or certain aspects of it in a contract, has been individually negotiated, the Regulations still apply to the rest of the contract if an overall assessment of the contract indicates that it is a pre-formulated standard contract.[208] Although the wording of the Regulations is not altogether happy, it seems that what is intended is that if part of a *term* is individually negotiated, the test of fairness applies to the remainder of the term.

'Consumer' means a *natural* person who in contracts covered by the Regulations is acting for purposes which are outside his business.[209] There is no requirement equivalent to the original s. 12(1)(c) of UCTA that the goods passing under or in pursuance of the contract are of a type ordinarily supplied for private use or consumption.[210] 'Seller or supplier' means a natural or *legal* person who, in contracts covered by the Regulations, acting for purposes related to his business, sells goods.[211] The onus is on the seller or supplier to show that a term was individually negotiated.[212]

Because of the way in which the field of application of the Regulations is defined, the difficult question as to what an exemption clause is, which needed to be dealt with in relation to the Unfair Contract Terms Act, does not arise.

Unfair terms

The Regulations provide that the unfairness of a contractual term shall be assessed, taking into account the nature of the goods or services for which the contract was concluded and by referring, *at the time of conclusion of the contract*, to all the circumstances attending the conclusion of the contract and to all the other terms of the contract or of another contract on which it is dependent.[213] Although the words 'of another contract' follow the English text of the Directive, and suggest that reference can be made to only one other contract, this is clearly not what is intended, otherwise the result would be absurd. What is clearly intended is that reference may be made to '*any other* contract'. It should be noted that the relevant time under this Regulation is the time of the conclusion of the contract.[214] Although the Regulations, like UCTA, make it clear that it is the time the contract is concluded which is relevant for judg-

---

207 Regulation 5(2).
208 Regulation 3(4).
209 Regulation 3(1). Thus, the plaintiff in the *R & B Customs Brokers Co Ltd* case, discussed at p. 172 above, would seem not to be a consumer for the purposes of the Regulations, though it was held to 'deal as consumer' for the purposes of UCTA. See also *Stevenson v Rogers*, discussed at p. 167.
210 SI 2002/3045 inserts subsection 12(1A) which provides to the effect that if a party to a contract who 'deals as consumer, is an individual, paragraph (c) of s. 12(1) is to be ignored.
211 Regulation 3(1).
212 Regulation 5(4).
213 Regulations 6(1). See discussion of Unfair Contract Terms Act 1977 s. 11(1) at p. 247.
214 Compare the approach taken by Misrepresentation Act 1967 s. 3, where the question was whether it would be fair and reasonable to allow reliance on the term in the circumstances of the case. This was also the approach adopted in Sale of Goods Act 1893 s. 55, inserted by Supply of Goods (Implied Terms) Act 1973 s. 4 (now repealed) – see p. 247. However, in enacting the Unfair Contract Terms Act 1977 s. 11(1), which supersedes these provisions, the government preferred to follow the recommendations of the Scottish Law Commission, so that reasonableness is judged by circumstances in the contemplation of the parties when the contract was made (see Law Com. No. 69 (1975), para 177).

ing a term's unfairness, this is not so clear from the Directive itself which states that:

> A contractual term which has not been individually negotiated shall be regarded as unfair if, contrary to the requirement of good faith, it causes a significant imbalance to the parties' rights and obligations arising under the contract, to the detriment of the consumer.

On this wording, it is not clear that it would not be open for a court to adopt a *George Mitchell* type approach.[215] It is also unclear how the Regulations might apply to the 'acceptance note' problem,[216] but this is probably largely of academic interest in view of s. 35(3) introduced by the 1994 Act.[217]

The test of unfairness no longer lists matters to be taken into account in judging unfairness. The 1994 Regulations specified matters to be taken into account which overlapped considerably with the test of 'reasonableness' set out in Sch. 2 of the Unfair Contract Terms Act 1977; it is improbable, however, that courts will not have regard to such things as the strength of bargaining position of the parties.

An important qualification follows, in that insofar as it is plain, intelligible language, assessment of the unfair nature of the term must relate neither to the definition of the main subject-matter of the contract nor to the adequacy of the price and remuneration.[218]

In the important decision in *Director-General of Fair Trading* v *First National Bank*[219] the House of Lords had to consider the application of reg. 3(2), the predecessor of these exclusionary provisions,[220] to a term in a standard-form consumer credit agreement, requiring the borrower to pay interest after judgment at the contract rate. It concluded that the fairness of this provision fell to be adjudicated on under the Regulations. Regulation 3(2)(now reg. 6(2)) must be given a restrictive interpretation, otherwise, as Lord Steyn pointed out, these provisions 'will enable the main purpose of the scheme to be frustrated by endless formalistic arguments as to whether a provision is definitional or exclusionary.'[221] The House of Lords had then to consider whether the term in question satisfied the requirement of fairness. It concluded that it did. Lord Bingham observed:

> A term falling within the scope of the regulations is unfair if it causes a significant imbalance in the parties' rights and obligations under the contract to the detriment of the consumer in a manner or to an extent which is contrary to the requirement of good faith. The requirement of significant imbalance is met if a term is so weighted in favour of the supplier as to tilt the parties' rights and obligations under the contract significantly in his favour.[222]

He considered that substantive unfairness was complimented by the requirement of good faith, which was evidenced by fair and open dealing. Openness required that the terms should be expressed fully, clearly and legibly, containing no pitfalls or traps,

---

215 See p. 248.
216 See p. 243.
217 See p. 509.
218 Regulation 6(2).
219 [2001] UKHL 52.
220 SI 1994/3159.
221 Ibid. at para. 34.
222 Ibid. para. 17.

with prominence being given to terms which might operate disadvantageously to the consumer. Fair dealing required that the supplier should not, whether deliberately or unconsciously, take advantage of the consumer's necessity, indigence, lack of experience, unfamiliarity with the subject-matter of the contract, weak bargaining position, or any other factor listed in, or analogous to, those listed in Sch. 3 of the then Regulations.[223]

In *Bairstow Eves London Central Ltd* v *Smith*[224] an estate agent's commission was 3%, but this was discounted to 1.5% if payment was made within 10 days of completion. The court held that because the vendor would assume that all payments are made on completion, as is usual, the 1.5% rate was the normal, whereas the 3% rate only came into effect if the buyer defaulted. It was not a term therefore describing the price, and not covered by reg. 6(2).[225] This decision is probably specific to the type of transaction it covers.

Although the *First National* case did not concern a sale of goods transaction and although it concerned the predecessor of the present Regulations, it provides useful guidance as to the way in which the application of the present Regulation is to be approached. It should also be noted that the Office of Fair Trading takes the view that the requirement of good faith does not equate with the absence of bad faith in the narrow English sense,[226] which would appear to accord with Lord Bingham's views set out above.

A seller must ensure that any written term of a contract is in plain, intelligible language.[227] In the case of doubt about the meaning of a term, the interpretation most favourable to the consumer must prevail.[228] This rule does not apply to proceedings brought under reg. 12.[229]

An unfair contract term concluded with a consumer by a seller or supplier is not binding on the consumer,[230] but the contract continues to bind the consumer if it is capable of existing without the unfair term.[231]

An indicative and non-exhaustive list of terms which will be regarded as unfair is annexed to the Regulations:[232]

1. Terms which have the object or effect of—
    (a) excluding or limiting the legal liability of a seller or supplier in the event of the death of a consumer or personal injury to the latter resulting from an act or omission of that seller or supplier;
    (b) inappropriately excluding or limiting the legal rights of the consumer *vis-à-vis* the seller or supplier or another party in the event of total or partial non-performance or inadequate performance by the seller or supplier of any of the contractual obligations,

---

223 Ibid. para 17. See now SI 1999/2083 Sched.2.
224 [2004] EWHC 263 (QB).
225 The reasoning is somewhat reminiscent of the type of reasoning, that held the conditional bond used in the middle ages did not contravene the laws against usury – see Simpson *History of the Common Law of Contract*, Clarendon Press, 1975, p. 101 *et seq.* Similar devices are in use in the Islamic banking system at the present day.
226 See Office of Fair Trading Briefing Note *Unfair Contract Terms* available on the OFT's website or free of charge directly from the OFT.
227 Regulation 7(1).
228 Regulation 7(2), i.e. a statutory version of the common law *contra proferentum* rule.
229 Ibid.
230 Regulation 8(1).
231 Regulation 8(2).
232 Schedule 3.

including the option of offsetting a debt owed to the seller or supplier against any claim which the consumer may have against him;

(c) making an agreement binding on the consumer whereas provision of services by the seller or supplier is subject to a condition whose realisation depends on his own will alone;

(d) permitting the seller or supplier to retain sums paid by the consumer where the latter decides not to conclude or perform the contract, without providing for the consumer to receive compensation of an equivalent amount from the seller or supplier where the latter is the party cancelling the contract;

(e) requiring any consumer who fails to fulfil his obligation to pay a disproportionately high sum in compensation;

(f) authorising the seller or supplier to dissolve the contract on a discretionary basis where the same facility is not granted to the consumer, or permitting the seller or supplier to retain the sums paid for services not yet supplied by him where it is the seller or supplier himself who dissolves the contract;

(g) enabling the seller or supplier to terminate a contract of indeterminate duration without reasonable notice except where there are serious grounds for doing so;

(h) automatically extending a contract of fixed duration where the consumer does not indicate otherwise, when the deadline fixed for the consumer to express this desire not to extend the contract is unreasonably early;

(i) irrevocably binding the consumer to terms with which he had no real opportunity of becoming acquainted before the conclusion of the contract;

(j) enabling the seller or supplier to alter the terms of the contract unilaterally without valid reason which is specified in the contract;

(k) enabling the seller or supplier to alter unilaterally without valid reason any characteristics of the product or service to be provided;

(l) providing for the price of goods to be determined at the time of delivery or allowing a seller of goods or supplier of services to increase their price without in both cases giving the consumer the corresponding right to cancel the contract if the final price is too high in relation to the price agreed when the contract was concluded;

(m) giving the seller or supplier the right to determine whether the goods or services supplied are in conformity with the contract, or giving him the exclusive right to interpret any term of the contract;

(n) limiting the seller's or supplier's obligation to respect commitments undertaken by his agents or making his commitments subject to compliance with a particular formality;

(o) obliging the consumer to fulfil all his obligations where the seller or supplier does not perform his;

(p) giving the seller or supplier the possibility of transferring his rights and obligations under the contract, where this may serve to reduce the guarantees for the consumer, without the latter's agreement;

(q) excluding or hindering the consumer's right to take legal action or exercise any other legal remedy, particularly by requiring the consumer to take disputes exclusively to arbitration not covered by legal provisions, unduly restricting the evidence available to him or imposing on him a burden of proof which, according to the applicable law, should lie with another party to the contract.

2. Scope of paragraphs 1(g), (j) and (l)

(a) Paragraph 1(g) is without hindrance to terms by which a supplier of financial services reserves the right to terminate unilaterally a contract of indeterminate duration without notice where there is a valid reason, provided that the supplier is required to inform the other contracting party or parties thereof immediately.

(b) Paragraph 1(j) is without hindrance to terms under which a supplier of financial services reserves the right to alter the rate of interest payable by the consumer or due to the latter, or the amount of other charges for financial services without notice where there is a valid reason, provided that the supplier is required to inform the other contracting party or parties thereof at the earliest opportunity and that the latter are free to dissolve the contract immediately.

Paragraph 1(j) is also without hindrance to terms under which a seller or supplier reserves the right to alter unilaterally the conditions of a contract of indeterminate duration, provided that he is required to inform the consumer with reasonable notice and that the consumer is free to dissolve the contract.

(c) Paragraphs 1(g), (j) and (l) do not apply to:
— transactions in transferable securities, financial instruments and other products or services where the price is linked to fluctuations in a stock exchange quotation or index or a financial market rate that the seller or supplier does not control;
— contracts for the purchase or sale of foreign currency, traveller's cheques or international money orders denominated in foreign currency.

(d) Paragraph 1(l) is without hindrance to price indexation clauses, where lawful, provided that the method by which prices vary is explicitly described.

Prevention of continued use of unfair terms

The Regulations provide for the first time that statutory regulators and trading standards departments may apply for an injunction,[233] and Consumers' Associations[234] may also apply for an injunction, to prevent the continued use of an unfair contract term,[235] provided they have notified the Director General of their intention at least 14 days before the application is made.[236] Any of these bodies is under a duty to consider a complaint if it has told the Director General that it will do so.[237]

There is a new power for the Director General and the bodies mentioned in the previous paragraph to require traders to supply copies of their standard contracts, and give information about their use, in order to facilitate investigation of complaints and ensure compliance with undertakings or court orders.[238] Such bodies must also notify the Director General of undertakings given to them about the continued use of an unfair term and of the outcome of any court proceedings.[239] The Director General is given the power to arrange for the publication of this information in such form and manner as he considers appropriate, and to offer information and advice about the operation of these Regulations.[240] In addition, the Director General will supply enquirers about particular standard terms with details of any relevant undertakings and court orders.

233 Regulation 12(1).
234 Described in the Regulations as 'a qualifying body' – reg. 11(1) and Sch. I Part Two.
235 Regulation 12(1).
236 The Director General can consent to a shorter period – reg. 12(2)(b).
237 Regulation 11.
238 Regulation 13.
239 Regulation 14.
240 Regulation 15.

Moreover, in *Océano Grupo Editorial & Salvat Editores, SA*[241] the ECJ held that the Directive empowers a domestic court to raise the unfairness of a term, even where this issue has not been pleaded by the parties. It is not clear from that judgment to what extent domestic courts are obliged to do so, but that it even allows a court to declare of its own motion that a term is unfair may prove surprising to the parties involved. This decision has now given rise to further questions in *Cofidis SA v Fredout*,[242] where a consumer credit transaction was thought by the national court to be unfair but there was a national provision that such cases were time-barred if not brought within two years of the events to which they related. The ECJ held that the Unfair Terms Directive precluded national provisions prohibiting the national court from finding, of its own motion or following a plea raised by the consumer, that a term was unfair.

Choice of law clauses

The Regulations apply, notwithstanding any choice of the law of a non-member state, if the contract has a close connection with the territory of the member states.[243] This provision, which seeks to make the application of the Regulations mandatory, could clearly be of relevance to e-commerce transactions, where, as was pointed out in Chapter 5,[244] the deal will usually be set up in such a way that it is the seller's law which applies, and a choice of law clause will normally provide for this expressly. Provided, therefore, a court in the UK has jurisdiction over such a transaction,[245] it would appear that it must apply the Regulations. A literal interpretation of this provision, as of the Directive, is that a contract must have a close connection with the territory of all the member states of the European Union for it to affect a choice of law clause. This is clearly absurd: what must be intended is that the contract must have a close connection with the territory of *a* member state.

---

241 Cases C-240/98 to C-244/98 [2000] ECR I-4941.
242 Case C-473/00 [2002] ECR I-10875.
243 Regulation 7.
244 See pp. 56–7. Since this is a mandatory provision of domestic law, the reservations expressed earlier (p. 57) about the constitutional difficulties of construing EC Directives (and even Regulations) as mandatory, do not apply.
245 See p. 64 *et seq.*

15

PRODUCT LIABILITY AND CONSUMER
PROTECTION

In recent years the problem of consumer protection has received a good deal of publicity and (although this problem extends well beyond the law of sale of goods) many legislative changes justified the decision taken in the fourth edition to collect together a number of questions for discussion in this chapter. The most important of these questions relate to the quality and fitness of goods sold under consumer sales and therefore this seems a convenient place in which to consider them.

PRODUCT LIABILITY AT COMMON LAW

In a claim by a buyer based on breach of the statutory implied terms it is unnecessary, as a rule, to distinguish between a claim for damages arising from defects[1] *in the goods themselves*, and a claim for damages for damage *caused by the goods* – for example, personal injury caused by a dangerous electrical product or a defective car. In this chapter, however, we are concerned with possible complaints in respect of defective goods, arising outside the contract, which may be made *against third parties* (for example, manufacturers) or which may be brought *by third parties* (for example, non-buyer users of the goods). And in dealing with claims of this nature, it is necessary to distinguish between claims in respect of damage caused by the goods, and claims in respect of defects in the goods themselves. In this and the next sections we are concerned with claims in respect of damage caused by the goods.

We have seen that in general a seller who is sued under s. 14(2) or (3) is liable irrespective of all due care and skill; and we have also referred to many cases which illustrate that the seller's strict liability extends to consequential loss caused by the defective goods and is not limited to losses arising under the contract itself. Thus if the buyer suffers personal injury through use of defective goods, he can claim damages from the seller under the implied terms in the Sale of Goods Act, despite the fact that the seller has not been guilty of any negligence. In this respect the buyer is in a privileged position compared to most persons who suffer personal injury. Normally, claims for damages for personal injury must be made in tort or delict and generally speaking, of course, such claims require proof of negligence on the part of the defendant.

---

1 The word 'defect' here is used rather loosely to cover goods in respect of which there is, or may have been, a breach of ss. 13–15 of the Sale of Goods Act. As we shall see, there are several different definitions of 'defect' for the purposes of this chapter, and important differences exist between them. For a useful analysis of the meaning of 'defect' see Keeton (1973) 5 St Mary's LJ 30 – see p. 279.

Privity of contract: liability confined to the seller

But it will also be seen that the doctrine of privity of contract imposes serious limitations on this form of liability[2] – now generally called 'product liability'.[3] The buyer's remedy is only available against the actual seller. If the buyer wishes to sue the manufacturer he cannot prima facie invoke the strict liability involved in a breach of condition or warranty.[4] At common law his principal possible sources of remedies against a manufacturer lay in negligence, showing breach of a collateral contract, or through third party proceedings.[5] However, there is now a major statutory modification of the common law position in Part I of the Consumer Protection Act 1987. Because the 1987 Act provides remedies *in addition to*, rather than in substitution of, those previously available, it is still necessary to consider the position at common law.

Negligence or delict

In the famous case of *Donoghue* v *Stevenson*[6] it was held that the pursuer, who had consumed part of the contents of a bottle of ginger beer which allegedly contained the remains of a decomposing snail, and who as a result suffered physical illness, might sue the manufacturer of the ginger beer, notwithstanding that the bottle had been bought for her at a café by a friend. It is beyond the scope of a work of this nature to deal in detail with the complexities of the tort or delict of negligence; however, its principal problems from the plaintiff's point of view must be noted.

In the first place, the claimant must establish negligence on the part of the manufacturer. The fact that it can be shown that a defect in the product was the cause of the injury will suffice to throw the onus onto the manufacturer to show that he exercised proper care, but he may be able to discharge that onus. In *Daniels* v *R W White & Sons and Tabard*[7] the plaintiff's husband bought a bottle of lemonade manufactured by the first defendant from the second defendant's shop. The lemonade contained carbolic acid, and both were injured when they consumed some of it. The husband was able to recover against the shopkeeper for breach of the old merchantable quality warranty,[8] but the wife's remedy depended on proof of negligence on the part of the manufacturer, and it was held that the manufacturer had exercised reasonable care and accordingly was not liable in negligence.

The second limitation of the tort of negligence or delict is that in general it permits recovery only in respect of physical damage, not economic loss. The buyer of goods *may* have a claim in tort or delict for economic loss against the manufacturer for the defects *in the goods themselves* where there is some real proximity between the

---

2 As to the effect of the Contracts (Rights of Third Parties) Act 1999 on this doctrine, see p. 221 *et seq.*

3 This book follows the Consumer Protection Act 1987 in referring to 'product liability' in preference to 'products liability', the term usually used in America, and until now, also here.

4 It would appear that the Contracts (Rights of Third Parties) Act 1999 is not intended to alter this, though the right to sue on manufacturers' warranties is given by the Sale and Supply of Goods to Consumers Regulations 2002, SI 2002/3045 implementing the Directive on Certain Aspects of the Sale of Consumer Goods and Associated Guarantees – see p. 299 *et seq.*

5 And this was generally so even in a system which, like Scots law, recognizes the enforceability of benefits arising under contracts for third parties (*jus quaesitum tertio*) if the contracting parties so intended.

6 [1932] AC 562, 1932 SC (HL) 31.

7 [1938] 4 All ER 258.

8 Which, of course, as with the present satisfactory quality requirement, was a condition.

buyer and the manufacturer, but, for the reasons explained below, even this is now doubtful. If the manufacturer, for instance, gives advice or information to the owner, it is possible that the owner may be able to establish liability under the *Hedley Byrne*[9] principle. And this also explains why, even on the restrictive view of the law adopted by the Canadian Supreme Court, and approved by the House of Lords in *D & F Estates* v *Church Commissioners*,[10] the plaintiffs succeeded in part in *Rivtow Marine* v *Washington Iron Works*.[11] If it is once held that a manufacturer of a product owes a duty to warn owners of any design defects that come to his attention after it has been put into circulation, it may be possible to claim damages on the basis, as in the latter case, that the warning was unreasonably delayed and thereby increased the damage. In the unreported case of *Walton* v *British Leyland*[12] the rear wheel of a car manufactured by the defendants came off whilst the car was being driven, causing injury to the plaintiff. The cause of the accident was faulty design. The defendants had become aware of the problem because numerous incidents had been reported. They had failed, however, to mount a major recall campaign in case it damaged their sales. It was held that the defendants were liable in negligence for selling cars with a design fault, but it was also said obiter that the failure to recall itself amounted to negligence.

One case where a sufficient degree of proximity was established was *The Diamentis Pateras*[13] where the defendants were manufacturers of ships' furnaces which were installed in the plaintiffs' ship. Defects in the furnaces led to their cracking and replacement at high cost, and Lawrence J would have been prepared to hold that the defendants owed a duty of care in these circumstances, but negligence was not established. It is, however, not clear whether the duty arose out of the advice given by the defendants or perhaps out of the need to replace the boilers to avoid danger.

Beyond this point, it is not possible to go very far. For some years it seemed that the decision of the House of Lords in *Junior Books*,[14] which followed *Anns* v *Merton London Borough Council*,[15] might have heralded a willingness to see a great expansion in the law on this point. In that case the House upheld a claim for damages by the owner of a building against a subcontractor who had laid a floor so negligently that the work had to be redone. The owner had no direct contractual relationship with the subcontractor so the action had to be an action in delict (tort); furthermore, there was no suggestion that it was necessary to relay the floor in order to avoid danger to persons using the building. The claim thus seems to have been a claim to pure economic loss, and yet it was allowed, Lord Brandon dissenting. But there is little point in discussing the case at any length, because it has, in effect, now been

---

  9 [1964] AC 465.
 10 [1988] 2 All ER 992.
 11 [1974] SCR 1189.
 12 (1976) unreported.
 13 [1966] 1 Lloyd's Rep 179.
 14 [1983] 1 AC 520, 1982 SC (HL) 244. It is not clear from the Report why the pursuer chose to sue the subcontractor rather than the main contractor, but it appears that the reason for this course was that, before the defects in the floor became apparent, the owner had settled a large number of other claims against the main contractor in such terms as precluded all further action against him.
 15 [1978] AC 728.

repudiated by the House of Lords in the *D & F Estates* case, and in *Murphy* v *Brentwood Council*, where Lord Brandon's speech was largely endorsed. The case must now be interpreted as a case, on its own facts, where a high degree of proximity existed between the parties so as to justify the imposition of a duty of care. The owners, or their architects, had nominated the subcontractors, and thus the relationship between the parties, as the majority held, fell just short of a contractual relationship. It can be argued, therefore, that the case is really an application of the proximity principle established in *Hedley Byrne & Co* v *Heller & Partners Ltd*.[16] It is clear that a similar result will not be reached in future on such facts unless the relationship between the client and the subcontractor differs substantially from the ordinary commercial relationship between such parties.[17]

Certainly, there is now fairly general agreement that the mere fact that a manufacturer has made a defective product which may cause economic loss to a buyer does not, by itself, render the manufacturer liable unless there is a close degree of proximity between the parties. Even in *Junior Books* this does not seem to have been seriously doubted. But precisely what will be needed to establish the requisite degree of 'proximity' remains in some doubt. If contract and tort/delict liability are getting closer in this area, as seems to be the case, it may well be, indeed, that proximity will only be found when the facts are sufficient to establish a collateral contract, or at least come very close to doing so. At the very least, it seems certain that some direct contact between the buyer (or his agent) and the manufacturer will be necessary, and mere reliance on the manufacturer's reputation, or perhaps even on his promotional literature, will probably not by itself suffice.[18]

The reason for this refusal of the courts to impose direct manufacturer liability for defective products is that, as was suggested by Lord Fraser in the *Junior Books* case, there appears to be no way of judging what is the appropriate standard to which the goods have to be made except by invoking a contract. Goods may be of high quality or of low quality, but a manufacturer can hardly be guilty of negligence just because he makes low-quality goods. Thus Lord Fraser said:[19]

> A manufacturer's duty to take care not to make a product that is dangerous sets a standard which is, in principle, easy to ascertain. The duty is owed to all who are his 'neighbours'. It is imposed on him by the general law and is in addition to his contractual duties to other parties to the contract. But a duty not to produce a defective article sets a standard which is less easily ascertained, because it has to be judged largely by reference to the contract.

This is no doubt a good reason for not placing liability on a manufacturer for making a product to a low-quality standard which is intended to be sold as such. But it is far

16 [1964] AC 465.

17 It should be noted that the decision in *Junior Books* caused great concern to the construction industry and its legal advisers; accordingly, when the Law Commission deliberating on the relaxation of the privity rule, they received strong representations from that quarter. The construction industry appeared to have been quite happy with the law as it was prior to *Junior Books*, and is now again.

18 See *Muirhead* v *Industrial Tank Specialities Ltd* [1986] QB 507. As to the possibility of such promotional literature giving rise to a collateral contract, see below. In the case of consumer sales, public statements about the specific characteristics of the goods made by the seller or producer, can give rise to liability: s. 14(2D) of the Sale of Goods Act 1979 as amended by SI 2002/3045 – see p. 183.

19 [1983] 1 AC 520, 533.

from clear why this is an adequate reason for not imposing liability on a manufacturer for making a product which is not of satisfactory quality when the product was *originally* sold as being of satisfactory quality.[20] But, once again, the search for reasoned argument in this difficult area of the law does not seem to have been carried very far. Perhaps the best reason which can be suggested for the present law is that, leaving aside the possibility of a producer's liability on a consumer guarantee,[21] it is simply easier and less costly if buyers look to their sellers for redress for defective goods. If purchase and sale contracts in the marketplace are entered into with the appropriate degree of care and foresight by all parties, there should be less need for buyers to look to third parties for redress. This is doubtless a reasonable argument when commercial contracts are in question;[22] it is perhaps less convincing when consumers are under consideration. At all events, in many cases the Consumer Protection Act 1987 will provide consumers with a remedy against, *inter alia*, a manufacturer. This is dealt with below.

Collateral contracts

One common law expedient whereby a buyer may be able to hold a manufacturer strictly liable despite the apparent absence of privity is the collateral contract. For instance, in *Wells v Buckland Sand*[23] the plaintiff bought sand for growing chrysanthemums in reliance on an express assurance that the sand was suitable for this purpose. This assurance was not given by the seller but by the manufacturer. It was held that there was a collateral contract, and the buyer was entitled to damages when the sand proved unsuitable and the buyer suffered loss. This was a case in which a specific and personal assurance was given to the buyer by the manufacturer. What is not clear is whether such a claim could be based on statements made in a manufacturer's advertisement. Apart from the famous case of *Carlill v Carbolic Smoke Ball Co*,[24] there are hardly any illustrations of this possibility in English law. But in America it has been held that a person who buys a car in reliance on an advertisement that it has 'shatterproof' windscreens can sue the manufacturers for breach of warranty if the windscreen is not in fact shatterproof.[25]

But in the most recent English case on this subject, the Court of Appeal declined to hold that statements made by a manufacturer in his brochures could be construed as collateral warranties, on the ground that they were not 'intended' to create contractual liability.[26] This is open to criticism because manufacturers issue their promotional literature plainly intending to influence buyers, and it would seem perfectly reasonable to hold that simple statements of fact relied upon by buyers should be held to create collateral contracts. Of course, in the case of consumer sales public

---

20 In the USA, starting with *Greenman v Yuba Power Products Inc* 377 P 2d8 97 (Cal 1962), a doctrine of strict liability in tort applies where a person has been injured by a defective product. This line of cases is summarized in 402A Restatement 2d. In most jurisdictions this liability does not extend to economic losses, including damage to the product itself.

21 See p. 297 *et seq.*

22 As in the *Muirhead* case, and also in *Simaan v General Contracting Co v Pilkington Glass Ltd* [1988] 1 All ER 791.

23 [1965] QB 170. See also *Shanklin Pier Ltd v Detel Products Ltd* [1951] 2 KB 854.

24 [1893] 1 QB 256.

25 *Baxter v Ford* 12 P 2d 409 (1932); 15 P 2d 1118 (1932); 35 P 2d 1090 (1934). See also now the amendments to the Sale of Goods Act 1979 s. 14 effected by SI 2002/3045 with regard to public statements – see p. 183.

26 *Lambert v Lewis* [1980] 2 WLR 289, [1980] 1 All ER 978, reversed on different grounds, [1982] AC 225.

statements about the specific characteristics of the goods can give rise to liability under the Sale of Goods Act 1979 s. 14.[27] 'Puffs' and other vague advertising language are a different matter, but simple statements of fact ought to be held to create collateral contracts, when calculated to be relied on and in fact relied upon.[28]

This possible liability is wider in scope than the statutory liability under the Consumer Protection Act, because (as we shall see later) that Act only applies to *defective* goods – though the meaning of that expression causes problems. But the common law liability arising under a collateral contract can extend to cases where the goods are in no real sense defective, but are merely unsuitable for the buyer's purposes, or fail to live up to some claim made by the manufacturer. But even so, the collateral contract has serious limitations as a device for holding a manufacturer strictly liable. In particular, it only helps a buyer where he can find some *express* statement or assurance that can be construed as a warranty,[29] or a public statement on the specific characteristics of goods, within the meaning of the Sale of Goods Act 1979 s. 14, in the case of consumer sales.[30]

There is, as yet, no authority which goes so far as to hold that a manufacturer could be liable for breach of implied warranties on the basis of a collateral contract. The step from express to implied warranties would be a momentous one in practice, but in legal theory it seems a small extension.[31] A manufacturer markets his products through retailers; he advertises directly to the public, inviting them to buy his products. It does not seem unreasonable to hold that he is impliedly offering a warranty of reasonable fitness for ordinary use to a member of the public who buys the product. However, in view of the Consumer Protection Act 1987, which is largely based on this theory, and the changes effected by the Sale and Supply of Goods to Consumers Regulations,[32] it is perhaps unlikely that the courts will feel the need to develop the common law further in this area.[33]

Part 20 (formerly third-party) proceedings

The second common law expedient by which strict liability may be effectively imposed on the manufacturer is through third- and (if necessary) fourth-party proceedings. In the interests of making the law more 'user-friendly', under the Civil Procedure Rules 1998 these are now referred to as 'Part 20' proceedings in England and Wales! If the buyer sues the seller for breach of warranty, the seller may claim an indemnity from his own supplier, and that supplier (if not himself the manufacturer) may in turn claim an indemnity from the manufacturer. As between each pair of parties, the relationship will be contractual and liability for breach of warranty can be established. For instance, in *Dodd* v *Wilson*,[34] the plantiff farmer employed a veterinary surgeon to inoculate his cattle with some serum; it proved to be defective and many of the cattle died or became diseased. The plaintiff recovered damages from the

---

27 As amended by SI 2002/3045.
28 As in the cases cited at n. 23 above.
29 See Bradgate (1991) 20 Anglo-Am LR 327, 342.
30 As amended by SI 2002/3045.
31 This step is taken in the Uniform Commercial Code Art. 2-318, reflecting earlier case law developments.
32 SI 2002/3045.
33 Even though the Act is much more limited than a warranty of fitness would be, as we shall see below.
34 [1946] 2 All ER 691.

surgeon as on an implied warranty; the surgeon brought in his suppliers as third parties and the suppliers brought in the manufacturers as fourth parties. The surgeon obtained an indemnity from the third parties and they, in turn, obtained an indemnity from the fourth parties. In this way liability was imposed on the manufacturer for breach of implied warranty from the manufacturer through the intermediaries. Furthermore, the House of Lords has given the existence of such rights of indemnity as itself a good ground for imposing strict liability on a supplier in contracts for work and materials.[35] This is, however, a somewhat clumsy and costly expedient. Why should not the plaintiff have a direct remedy against the manufacturer for breach of warranty? Moreover, the expedient may not always work, for example if one of the intermediaries is insolvent, cannot be found, only carries on business overseas or has gone out of business.

In *Lambert* v *Lewis*,[36] retailers bought a defective coupling through a wholesaler whom they were subsequently unable to identify. In the Court of Appeal, where the retailers were held liable to pay damages to the ultimate buyer of the coupling, they were refused an indemnity from the manufacturers on the ground that, in the absence of a direct contract between the retailers and the manufacturer, any such claim would have to be made in tort, and tort law did not recognize such a claim as it was a claim for pure economic loss.[37] In the House of Lords the decision was reversed on a different ground,[38] but the House left open the possibility that such a claim for economic loss might be recognized by the law, where the economic loss consisted of a liability to pay damages in respect of some personal injury (or, presumably, property damage). However, such a development looks improbable in the foreseeable future in the light of *Murphy* v *Brentwood District Council*.[39]

Privity of contract: remedy confined to the buyer

The doctrine of privity of contract is also very material in the law of product liability in another major respect. Not only does the doctrine normally restrict liability to the seller; it also normally confines the remedy to the buyer. A sub-buyer, a donee, a member of the buyer's family, an employee of the buyer, a mere bystander – none of these can sue the seller (nor, *a fortiori*, the manufacturer) for breach of condition or warranty, but only for negligence.[40] Thus if any of these persons should be injured through the use of a defective product they can only sue the retailer or manufacturer if they can establish liability under the Consumer Protection Act 1987 or through negligence. Even in Scots law, which allows third parties to acquire rights under contracts to which they are not privy by means of its doctrine of *jus quaesitum tertio*, it

---

35 *Young & Marten Ltd* v *McManus Childs* [1969] 1 AC 454. Furthermore, the House of Lords made it quite clear that the same rule would apply in contracts of sale of goods.

36 [1980] 2 WLR 289.

37 This outcome would be unaffected by the Contracts (Rights of Third Parties) Act 1999 – see p. 221.

38 [1982] AC 225 – see p. 208.

39 [1991] 1 AC 398 – see above p. 266 *et seq*. And it must be noted that no reference to the dicta in *Lambert* v *Lewis* was made in the case of *D & F Estates* v *Church Commissioners* [1988] 2 All ER 992 which signalled a stop to the expansion of liability for economic loss in that *Junior Books* v *Veitchi Ltd* [1983] 1 AC 20, 1982 SC (HL) 244 was not followed.

40 As to the application of the Contracts (Rights of Third Parties) Act 1999 in this regard, see below and p. 221 *et seq*.

is rare for a contract of sale to show the necessary irrevocable intention of the parties to confer such an enforceable benefit.[41] Given the limitations of the 1987 Act, and the difficulty of establishing negligence on the part of the manufacturer,[42] such third parties are in a significantly worse situation than buyers and it seems unlikely that the Contracts (Rights of Third Parties) Act 1999 will do much to ameliorate this situation. In their Report,[43] the Law Commission contrasted two cases:[44]

1   On Mr and Mrs C's marriage, their wealthy relative B buys an expensive three-piece suite as a wedding gift from A Ltd, a well-known department store. She makes it clear at the time of purchase that it is a gift for friends, and that it is to be delivered to Mr and Mrs C's house and left with the housekeeper there as a gift. After two weeks serious faults in the suite become apparent. According to the Law Commission, Mr and Mrs C can sue A Ltd because A Ltd have promised to confer a benefit (a suite of satisfactory quality) on Mr and Mrs C who have been expressly identified by name.
2   The previous example, but A Ltd are unaware that the suite is a gift for anyone, and it is delivered to B's house. Mr and Mrs C cannot sue A Ltd because the contract between B and A Ltd does not purport to confer a benefit on Mr and Mrs C, who have not been expressly identified.[45]

Of course, there may be cases on the borders between these two examples, and it remains to be seen whether the courts will give the Act a broad or a narrow interpretation in such cases.[46]

In some situations the courts have struggled against the apparent logic of the doctrine of privity. For instance, in *Lockett* v *A M Charles Ltd*,[47] a husband and wife went into a hotel for a meal and the wife was made ill by being served infected food. Negligence on the part of the hotel was not made out so the claim had to be made in contract as on a breach of warranty. The hotel argued that the only contract was with the husband as it was a reasonable presumption that he would pay the bill.[48] This argument was rejected by Tucker J who held that, in the absence of evidence to the contrary, both husband and wife were in a contractual relationship with the hotel. He held that the normal inference where a person orders food in a hotel or restaurant is that he makes himself liable to pay for it, whatever the position may be as between

---

41   But see, e.g., *Cullen* v *McMenamin Ltd* 1928 SLT (Sh Ct) 2 and, possibly, *Scott Lithgow Ltd* v *GEC Electrical Projects Ltd* 1989 SC 412.
42   See p. 221 *et seq.*
43   *Privity of Contract: Contracts for the Benefit of Third Parties*, Law Com. No. 242 (1996), Cm. 3329.
44   Ibid., paras 7.41 and 7.42.
45   The Act, which follows the Law Commission's draft, provides as follows:

   1. (1) Subject to the provisions of this Act, a person who is not a party to a contract (a 'third party') may in his own right enforce a term of a contract if—
      (a)   the contract expressly provides that he may, or
      (b)   subject to subsection (2), the term purports to confer a benefit on him.
   (2) Subsection (1)(b) does not apply if on a proper construction of the contract it appears that the parties did not intend the term to be enforceable by the third party.
   (3) The third party must be expressly identified in the contract by name, as a member of a class or as answering to a particular description but need not be in existence when the contract is entered into.

46   See also observations at p. 223 as to the relevance of the Law Commission's views.
47   [1938] 4 All ER 170.
48   Times have perhaps changed in this regard.

the person ordering the food and his companions. But it would be difficult to apply this reasoning (say) where a person ordered a meal for a child.[49] Similarly, if somebody books a private room at a hotel to entertain a large party, it would be clear that only he was in a contractual relationship with the hotel.[50] Or again, where it is plain from the circumstances that the meal is to be paid for by a man and that a lady companion is only his guest, the lady will have no claim for breach of warranty.[51]

There is no doubt that the doctrine of privity can lead to some apparently anomalous results in these cases. A man buys a bottle of perfume (say) and gives it to his wife as a present. If the bottle explodes and injures her, she cannot sue the seller for breach of warranty (though she might have a remedy under the Consumer Protection Act or possibly in negligence). If, however, he has bought the bottle at his wife's request, and therefore as her agent, the position is different. One possible way of escaping these results has been opened up, though it is not yet possible to say how far it may be taken. In *Jackson* v *Horizon Holidays Ltd*[52] the Court of Appeal awarded damages for the inconvenience and disappointment of a ruined holiday, not merely for the inconvenience and disappointment of the plaintiff himself, but also for that of his family. Whether this would extend to personal injury cases is still uncertain, but it seems unlikely.[53]

Despite various signs of tentative movement in some directions, then, the broad position remained, until the coming into force of Part I of the Consumer Protection Act 1987,[54] that, unless the plaintiff could sue on a contract, he had to prove negligence to found his cause of action. But, at least in the case of personal injury and death, if such negligence can be proved, there can be no exclusion of business liability by contract or notice.[55]

In the United States, both by virtue of §402A Restatement 2d, and the various versions of Article 2-318 of the Uniform Commercial Code (which extend the benefit of the quality warranties to third parties), third parties physically injured by defective products generally have a remedy against the producer. Set against this, the Contracts (Rights of Third Parties) Act 1999 is a very modest measure.

Assignment and novation

Where goods are sold by the original purchaser to a third party, normally the sale will be treated as a sub-sale, and the third party will have no remedy against the original seller. It would appear, however, that the rights that the original purchaser had against the seller can pass to the third party by assignment, at least where such a sub-sale is contemplated by the original parties.[56] Any burden under the original contract, such as transferring to the purchaser the liability to pay service charges to the original

---

49 Though the 1999 Act might apply in this situation.
50 This situation would seem closer to the Law Commission's second example.
51 *Buckley* v *La Reserve* [1955] Cr Law Rev 451. But again, the 1999 Act might alter this outcome.
52 [1975] 1 WLR 1468, approved to a limited extent in *Woodar Investment Ltd* v *Wimpey UK Ltd* [1980] 1 All ER 571.
53 But see *Donnelly* v *Joyce* [1974] QB 454.
54 As to which, see p. 273 *et seq.*
55 See s. 2 of the Unfair Contract Terms Act 1977. For the meaning of the term 'business liability', see above, p. 167 *et seq.*
56 *Darlington Borough Council* v *Wiltshier Northern Ltd* [1995] 1 WLR 68. This case involved a building contract, but the same point would appear to be relevant in sales of goods.

seller, could only pass by novation or, in Scots law, delegation. It would appear that such assignments and novations are not uncommon when complex pieces of commercial equipment are sold. In English law, if no formal assignment has taken place complying with s. 136 of the Law of Property Act 1925, the assignment might nevertheless be effective in equity, but the assignee would have to sue in the name of the original purchaser. There is no equivalent to this in Scots law.

PRODUCT LIABILITY UNDER THE CONSUMER PROTECTION ACT 1987

In 1985 the Council of the EC promulgated a Directive on liability for defective products.[57] This introduced a regime of so-called 'strict' product liability. Part I of the Consumer Protection Act 1987 was passed to give effect to this Directive, and it applies equally in Scots law as in English law.[58] So far as the background to this Act is concerned, it will be enough to mention four points. First, one of the main sources of initiative behind the Directive was undoubtedly the view that the previous law created unacceptable anomalies in the way it distinguished between the remedies of a buyer and a non-buyer, the latter generally requiring proof of negligence. Second, another major concern was the view that it was anomalous that it was generally much easier to establish liability against a retailer than against the manufacturer, who was often the party primarily responsible for defective goods. Third, American law was thought to have demonstrated that it was possible to impose strict product liability in tort on manufacturers without undue strain.[59] And fourthly, the EC involvement arose because it was thought desirable that all manufacturers in member states should face similar legal liabilities so as to avoid distortions of competition which might arise if manufacturers had to bear different liabilities, according to varying laws in the member states.[60] Various countries had proposed reforms, but governments were hesitant to act, largely out of fear of imposing costs on their industries which industries in other member states did not have to incur.[61]

The new form of legal liability created by Part I of the Consumer Protection Act raises a very large number of difficult and intricate questions which could generate a huge volume of litigation.[62] In this work it will be necessary to offer a summary view

---

57 85/374/EEC, now amended by Directive 99/34/EC. The original Directive was preceded by the Strasbourg Convention of 1977. The Convention differs from the Directive in a number of respects: it includes primary agricultural products and game; it does not have the developments risks defences; and, it covers only personal injuries. Moreover, it does not have the mandatory character of the Directive.

58 For a useful study of the implementation of the Directive in the various member states of the European Union see Howells, *Comparative Product Liability*, Dartmouth, 1993.

59 See in particular s. 402A of the Restatement of Torts, 2d (1965). An enormous body of case law has grown up in America since then, but there is no evidence that this body of experience was seriously studied by the EC bureaucracy or anybody else responsible for the Directive.

60 Yet there is no uniform product liability law in the United States, where this is a matter left to the law of each individual state; and there are indeed many variations – the Uniform Commercial Code §2-318 has three alternatives, any of which may be chosen by a particular jurisdiction, and some states have introduced their own variations. It seems amazing that if the United States has been able to manage with such widely different laws of product liability it should be considered essential that EU nations, with their much more varied traditions, need a uniform law.

61 Germany had, however, introduced legislation dealing with pharmaceutical products.

62 But note the warning given at the beginning of this work about the effect of the Civil Procedure Rules 1998 on the number of *reported* cases.

of some of the essentials. The basic principle of the statutory product liability is that (1) any person who suffers damage, which is (2) caused by a defective product, is entitled to sue (3) the producer (and various other possible parties) without being required to prove fault.

Claimant or pursuer must show 'damage'

The first requirement to the application of the Act is that the claimant or pursuer must show that he has suffered 'damage'. By s. 5(1) 'damage' means 'death or personal injury or any loss of, or damage to any property (including land)'. There is no particular difficulty here with regard to personal injury. It is defined by s. 45(1) so as to include 'any disease and any other impairment of a person's physical or mental condition'. Presumably this is wide enough to cover the cases dealt with at common law under the term 'nervous shock'. So far as death is concerned, the new Act is tied in with the existing tort statutes relating to death, so that liability will only arise on behalf of financial dependants under the Fatal Accidents Act 1976, or, in the case of non-dependants, in the very limited cases (and to the very limited extent) provided for by the Law Reform (Miscellaneous Provisions) Act 1934, as amended. In Scotland, the tie-in is with the Damages (Scotland) Act 1976 and Part II of the Administration of Justice Act 1982. There are reform recommendations by the Scottish Law Commission.[63]

So far as property damage is concerned, there are more complications. First, the Act excludes claims for £275 or less.[64] Secondly, no claims for pure economic loss can be entertained under the Act. It is unclear to what extent consequential economic loss claims can be attached to claims for material loss or damage to property. If the consequential loss does not derive from the value of the damaged goods themselves, or is not parasitic on that damage,[65] it would seem not to be claimable under the Act. If the claim can be said to concern the quantification of the value of the physical damage itself, the consequential loss might be claimable, but that will not generally be the case with goods intended for private use as opposed to business use, and (as we shall see) there are severe limits on the extent of liability for goods intended for business use. It would appear that 'property' for these purposes includes intellectual property; consequently if, for example, a virus in a computer program[66] were to damage other software belonging to the claimant or pursuer presumably he could sue under the Act. In the case of software which is merely licensed (the usual situation) strictly speaking the licensee has no property in the software. It is to be hoped that a court would

---

63 *Report on Title to Sue for Non-Patrimonial Loss* (Scots Law Com. No. 187, 2002).

64 Section 5(4). If the claimant is awarded £250 damages, nothing will be recovered. But if he or she is awarded £280, the whole sum, including the first £275, is recoverable. The exclusion applies to the amount to be awarded; so if the claimant/pursuer claims £500, but half is deducted for contributory negligence, nothing will be awarded under the Act. Section 5(4) is a correct implementation of the English language text of the Directive, but in the French and German texts it is an excess, and this is the way in which it has been implemented in most member states including, significantly, the Republic of Ireland (Liability for Defective Products Act 1991 s. 3(1)). The effect in other member states is that if the claimant/pursuer recovers more than the excess, the excess will be deducted from the global damages recovered. If he recovers less, he gets nothing.

65 See *Spartan Steels & Alloys Ltd v Martin & Co (Contractors) Ltd* [1973] 1 QB 27; *Muirhead v Industrial Tank Specialities Ltd* [1986] QB 507.

66 As to whether computer software is a 'product' within the meaning of the Act, see p. 77 *et seq.*

construe 'property' non-technically to avoid this anomaly. Any data damaged, of which the plaintiff was author, would be his property in any event.

Next, it is made clear by s. 5(2) that damage to the defective product *itself* is not covered by the statutory liability. Nor does the statutory liability cover damage to a product 'which has been supplied with the product in question comprised in it'. So, arguably, if a defective tyre, which has been supplied with a car, bursts causing damage (a) to the tyre itself, and (b) to the car, then neither the damage to the tyre nor the car is covered, assuming that the tyre can be said to be 'comprised in' the car. If the tyre is comprised in the car, would the statutory liability extend to an accessory, such as an expensive stereo?[67] If the tyre is bought separately from the car, then the damage to the car will be covered. As we shall see later, it is not clear whether the Act differs from the common law on these intricate questions.[68] This result is illogical. In order to reach a more rational solution, a distinction might be drawn between those aspects of a product having no reality as articles of commerce apart from forming part of the complete unit such as a motor vehicle, and parts such as in the case of motor vehicle tyres, batteries, lamps, steering wheels, etc., which are customarily dealt with as accessories.[69] In practice, such items may be specified by the customer when the car is bought from the dealer, and it seems absurd that the result might be different where on the one hand the customer has requested the item to be fitted when the car is supplied, and on the other if he goes back a week later and purchases the item which causes the damage to the car. In other words, it is not stretching things too far to argue that such accessories or 'add-ons' are not really 'comprised in' the item supplied, but are bought *along with* it. It is often useful to look at German law in attempting to predict the way in which the European Court of Justice is likely to interpret a Directive. In a well-known German case, where a safety switch which functioned separately from the cleaning plant to which it was attached, failed and damaged the plant, it was held that the producer of the switch had brought a separate product into existence.[70] A domestic example might be the thermostats commonly supplied with central heating apparatus. By contrast, in a decision of the Austrian Supreme Court (German and Austrian law are similar on this point) it was held that a water-hose which caused damage to a car engine when it failed was not purchased as a separate product, and consequently neither the producer nor the importer of the car were liable.[71]

Section 5(3) largely confines the liability for property damage to property which is intended for private use, occupation or consumption. The section disallows an action for damage to property if the property is not:

(a) of a description of property ordinarily intended for private use, occupation or consumption; and

(b) intended by the person suffering the loss or damage mainly for his own use, occupation or consumption.

---

67 For a discussion of this, and various other points arising on these difficult provisions, see Bradgate and Savage (1987) 137 NLJ 929, 953, 1025 and 1049.

68 See p. 285 *et seq.*

69 This suggestion is based on the analogy of registered designs law – see *Ford Motor Company's Design Applications* [1994] RPC 545 (upheld by HL, [1995] RPC 167). The Directive merely excludes 'damage to the defective product itself' which begs the question as to what the product itself is.

70 The *'Floating Switch'* decision (*'Schwimmerschalter'* – *Entscheidung*, BGHZ 67, 359 (1976)).

71 3 February 1994 (8 OB 536(93)).

So the claimant or pursuer must show *both* that the property is ordinarily intended for private use, occupation or consumption, *and* that he did so intend it. The first requirement is similar to that contained in the Federal Warranties Act,[72] that the product concerned be a 'consumer product' which is defined as tangible personal property 'normally used for personal, family or household purposes', and presumably the cases on the interpretation of that provision might provide some guidance on the interpretation of s. 5(3)(a) and (b). The second requirement rules out the property of public authorities and business corporations,[73] and also, presumably, claims by professional firms who could hardly say that their property is intended for 'private' use, etc., even if it is property ordinarily used for private purposes. But the position may be different with a single self-employed professional, such as an author, who could reasonably claim that even goods used for the purposes of his profession (especially if these are kept in his home) are intended for 'private use'.

It must also be remembered that under s. 5(1) 'property' includes land and therefore a house, so damage to a house caused by a defective product will be recoverable under the Act if the house is occupied by the owner (presumably it is intended 'mainly' for his private occupation even if he has a wife and 10 children). On the other hand, if the house is merely rented, the damage will not be recoverable unless the tenant is legally answerable for it under the lease, in which case he will still be the person 'suffering the loss or damage'. Otherwise the landlord will be the person suffering the loss or damage, and he will not be able to recover it under the Act.

Damage must have been caused by a defective product

The next requirement is that the claimant or pursuer must show that his loss or damage was caused by a defective product. The term 'product' is defined by s. 1(2) of the Act[74] as 'any goods or electricity';[75] the definition also includes any product which is comprised in another product, for example as a raw material or as a component part. This formulation raises the interesting question as to whether computer software is a 'product' within the meaning of the Act. Software loaded on magnetic disks essentially consists of encoded electrical impulses. That embedded in CDs *when loaded* essentially works in the same way, and drawing a distinction between the two

---

72 The Magnuson-Moss Act of 4 January 1975, Pub L No 93-637, Title 1, §101, 88 Stat. 2183, 15 USCA §2301(1) Supp 1979.

73 Even a company car, it seems, would not be covered, because it is not intended by the person 'suffering the loss or damage' (the owner company) mainly for the owner's own use, occupation or consumption.

74 Following the original wording of Art 2. This Article is deleted by Directive 1999/34/EC and a new definition substituted:

> Article 2
> For the purposes of this Directive, 'product' means all movables even if incorporated into another movable product or into an immovable. 'Product' includes electricity.

> This Directive, which must be implemented by 4 December 2000, will require removal of the definition of 'agricultural product' from s. 1(2) of the Consumer Protection Act 1987, and of the exception from liability for 'agricultural producer' in s. 2(4).

75 For an American example of liability for electricity, see *Ransome* v *Wisconsin Electric Power Co* 275 NW 2d 641 (1979). For this and many other references and thoughts Professor Atiyah acknowledged his debt to Dr Simon Whittaker's article (1989) 105 LQR 125. See also discussion p. 77 *et seq*.

media (or software acquired online) would seem undesirable for the reasons given above.[76] Certainly, at the time damage is caused to the claimant's system, e.g. by a virus, the software *is* electrical impulses, and it would seem that the claimant should be able to recover under the Act.[77] Next, the word 'goods' is defined by s. 45(1) so as to include:

> . . . substances, growing crops and things comprised in land by virtue of being attached to it and any ship, aircraft or vehicle.

This is a little wider than the definition of 'goods' in the Sale of Goods Act in that it includes things attached to land, but probably not actual buildings[78] – though *damage* to buildings is covered. Presumably this means that there could be liability under the Act for damage done by defective parts of a new building, as if window glass or roof tiles fall off and injure a passer-by.

A number of questions which arise in the law of sale, and which have previously been considered, may also arise in connection with the new statutory liability. For instance, there is the question whether human blood (or plasma) supplied for transfusion is a 'product', which in turn must depend on whether it is 'goods' within the meaning of the Act.[79] Perhaps the inclusion of the word 'substances' in the statutory definition makes it more likely that blood and similar products would fall within the 1987 Act.[80] On the other hand, it may well be that the Act does not affect the general tendency to hold that professional liability is a matter of fault only, and should not be converted into strict liability merely because some product is incidentally supplied.[81] In America it has, for instance, been held that a supplier of contact lenses is strictly liable for injury caused by them if the lenses were defective, but not if the cause of the injury was improper fitting.[82]

The question has even been raised whether authors and publishers may be liable in respect of 'defective books', where the defects likewise lie in the intellectual content of the work rather than in its physical make-up.[83] This somewhat alarming possibility would add new terrors to authorship, though it would of course only matter anyhow where personal injury or property damage is caused by the misinformation.[84]

Although the definition of 'goods' includes growing crops, and also, no doubt, foodstuffs and so on, by s. 2(4) as originally drafted there was no liability under the Act for agricultural produce[85] and game, unless it had undergone 'an industrial

---

76 See p. 77 *et seq.*

77 'Off-the-shelf' software would probably be held to be a product in any event – see p. 77 *et seq.*

78 As Whittaker points out (above, n. 75) the Directive only applies to movables, and s. 1(1) of the Act makes it clear that the Directive must be taken into account in the construction of the Act. But 'product' includes movables incorporated into an immovable. This was so under the original definition of 'product' in Art. 2.

79 See *A* v *National Blood Authority* [2001] 3 All ER 289 discussed p. 279 below. This point, however, was passed over no doubt as a result of the defendant's concession in relation to Art. 6 of the Directive.

80 The Directive simply states that 'product' means all movables – Art. 2 as amended by Directive 1999/34/EC. See above, p. 276, for the position under the Sale of Goods Act.

81 See Whittaker, above, n. 75, at p. 22 *et seq.*

82 *Barbee* v *Rogers* 425 SW 2d 342 (1968).

83 Whittaker, above, n. 75.

84 But see above, p. 26.

85 Defined by s. 1(1) as 'any produce of the soil, of stockfarming or of fisheries'. The terminology seems somewhat restrictive, e.g. as to dairy farming. Are chickens and eggs the products of 'stockfarming'? Presumably the intention is that they should be.

process'. However, as a result of Directive 1999/34/EC, the exception regarding 'primary agricultural products and game' has been deleted.[86]

The next, and vital, requirement is that the claimant or pursuer must be able to show that the product was 'defective'. The meaning of a 'defect' is closely defined in s. 3 of the Act, though subject to an important defence in s. 4, which is considered later. Broadly s. 3(1) says that a product is defective if 'the safety of the product is not such as persons generally are entitled to expect'.[87] Section 3(2) then goes on to say that all the circumstances must be taken into account in deciding what persons generally are entitled to expect,[88] including the way the goods are marketed, their get-up, and any warnings and instructions. In addition, it is necessary to take account of what 'might reasonably be expected to be done with or in relation to the product'. Further, it is provided that the time of supply must be taken into account, and that it is impermissible to infer that a product was defective *merely* because later versions of the product are safer (a rather important qualification).[89] However, later versions may provide valuable evidence as to what might have been achieved at the time.

Plainly, the need to show that the product was defective is the heart of this statutory liability. Equally plainly, it raises similar questions in some respects to some of the requirements of s. 14(2) and (3) of the Sale of Goods Act; and (it may be suggested) the statutory definition of a defective product is about as helpful and vacuous as the former statutory definition of merchantable quality, as well, perhaps, as the new statutory definition of 'satisfactory quality'. No doubt there will be many obvious cases where the Act will be easily applied, because a product will be obviously 'defective' in some very simple way. But (to judge from American experience) there will be very many borderline cases where the statutory definition will not provide any easy solutions. To suggest that products should be as safe 'as persons generally are entitled to expect' does not help a great deal when the question at issue is, precisely what are persons generally entitled to expect? Nor does it help a great deal when the alleged defect is of an esoteric or complex nature as to which 'persons generally' probably have no expectations at all. Do 'persons generally' expect blood for transfusion (for instance) to be free from unknown and undiscoverable viruses as was the case at first with the AIDS virus? (Perhaps they now expect it to be free from the AIDS virus, but that is because that issue has received a great deal of publicity.) Again, when the person injured was not the buyer of the product, but (say) some innocent bystander, it is not clear why it should be relevant to ask what persons generally are entitled to expect of the goods in question. So far the case law on this has been somewhat 'black letter' and unreflective, and whilst this may accord with continental notions of strict liability, it seems to pay scant regard to economic theory, and it has potentially harmful consequences in that many pharmaceutical products have to be launched with known serious side-effects,

---

86 By the Consumer Protection Act 1987 (Product Liability) (Modification) Order 2000, SI 2000/2771. This change was in part precipitated by the BSE affair.

87 See Butterworths Common Law Series, *Law of Product Liability*, ed. Grabb and Howells. 2000.1.13 *et seq.*

88 In *Richardson* v *LRC Products* [2000] Lloyd's Rep Med 280, the claimant had become pregnant by an act of sexual intercourse during which the condom failed. She sued the defendant manufacturer. After considering expert testimony, the court found in favour of the defendant. No one had ever said that this method of contraception was 100 per cent effective. Fractures happened by chance. There was no evidence of a weakness in the system of testing used, and the condoms were manufactured to the standard required.

89 Directive Art. 6.2.

e.g., chemotherapy for terminal cancer patients. Are the manufacturers to be held liable for those known but unavoidable side-effects?

In *A v National Blood Authority*[90] the claimants had been infected with hepatitis C through contaminated blood transfusions, or blood products, administered in the course of surgery. At the time, the risk of infection was known to the medical profession, but it was impossible to detect with the screening tests then available. Burton J held that the avoidability of the harmful characteristic was not a relevant circumstance to take into account in determining whether a product was defective, but that persons generally were entitled to expect that the blood would be free from what was in effect an unavoidable risk.[91] In *Abouzaid v Mothercare (UK) Ltd*[92] where a twelve-year-old boy, helping his mother attach a product to a pushchair, was injured in the eye when one of the product's elasticated straps snapped back, the defendants were held liable though the danger had not previously been contemplated.

The American experience suggests that defects can generally be classified into three groups. There are first, manufacturing defects; second, design defects; and third, defects due to inadequate warnings or instructions.[93] The first are the easiest to deal with, because manufacturing defects generally mean that the product does not comply with the manufacturer's own specifications and design. It is difficult for a manufacturer to claim that the goods are not defective when they fail to comply with his own designs and specifications. (But it must be remembered, the Act only deals with 'safety', so defects of a purely cosmetic nature would presumably not be 'defects' within the Act.) In this respect there is unlikely to be much difficulty about the definition of 'defect'. The court will be performing an exercise which does not greatly differ from what it already does under s. 14(2) of the Sale of Goods Act, or even from what it does in an ordinary action for negligence. No court is likely to have much difficulty in concluding that the presence of a snail in an opaque bottle of ginger-beer renders the drink 'defective'. Although the liability under the 1987 Act is strict, and liability in negligence is of course fault-based, such manifestly faulty goods can usually be taken to be proof of negligence anyhow.

The second type of relevant defect is a design defect; where a product emerges from the supplier exactly as it is intended to be, but it nevertheless possesses unsafe attributes, claims may be made that it was defective because of those attributes. It is here that the statutory definition appears so inadequate, because again, though there may sometimes be gross design defects so glaring and simple to remedy that no court would have difficulty with them, there are bound to be many borderline situations where it is very difficult to say what 'persons generally are entitled to expect'.

Although it is not possible in this book to discuss the matter in any detail, it must be said that most modern American case law has abandoned, or anyhow supplemented, the 'reasonable public expectations' test. It is now widely held in America[94]

---

90 [2001] 3 All ER 289.

91 It should be noted that the defendants accepted that a producer's liability under Art. 6 of the Directive was irrespective of fault. Accordingly, there was no real discussion in the case of the sort that has taken place in many US decisions of the meaning of 'strict liability'.

92 [2000] EWCA Civ 348.

93 See Keeton (1973) 5 St Mary's LJ 30. On the distinction between warnings and instructions see Dillard and Hart (1955) 41 Virg LR 145, 172, and see above, p. 182 *et seq.*

94 See, e.g., *Barker v Lull Engineering Co* 573 P 2d 443 (1978) which is one of the leading cases on this point. See also *Richardson v LRC Products*, n. 88 above.

that design defects must be tested by a multi-factorial test not essentially dissimilar to that involved in the law of negligence.[95] It is necessary to ask how difficult or expensive it would have been to eliminate the defect, and what benefits would have been lost if that had been done. A simple example is provided by the release of new medicines and drugs. It is now well known that many drugs may have side-effects which cannot always be detected in advance, simply because some of these effects may only become apparent when the drug has been taken by a very large number of people (because the side-effect only affects one person in 100,000 for instance), or when it has been taken continuously for many years. If new drugs were held up until all such risks had been eliminated many people would be deprived of the benefit of the drugs (perhaps life-saving drugs) while this was being done (marketing approval takes some years to obtain, as it is). So it seems clear that some balance must be struck between avoiding unnecessary risks, and an over-cautious policy which only eliminates risk at huge cost. Before a product can be labelled defective in design, therefore, some sort of balance must be made, some attempt at a kind of cost-benefit analysis of the risks versus the gains. In some respects, this raises similar questions to the law of negligence, and so it may appear that the new strict liability is not in practice likely to prove very different from negligence liability, save – and this is important – that the burden of proof is in effect reversed.[96]

It must also be remembered that many goods are inherently unsafe, in that their use always involves some element of risk. A sharp kitchen knife can cut fingers as well as meat; a ladder is something that people fall off, despite all precautions. The mere fact that such goods are inherently risky does not make them defective under the new Act, any more than their production would be negligent at common law.

One point is, however, made reasonably explicit by s. 3(2)(b) which has already been referred to. Manufacturers must expect that goods will sometimes be misused, or that they will be involved in accidents. So, for instance, goods may be defective if they would be dangerous even if not used strictly as they should have been. A car (it has often been held in America) may be defective in design if it does not stand a crash as well as it should have done, because, for instance, the petrol tank is so situated that it is liable to explode in a rear-end collision. It is no defence for the manufacturer to claim that a car is designed to be driven and not to be crashed.

The 'state of the art' or 'development risks' defence
A special defence (popularly known as 'the state of the art' defence or sometimes the 'development risks' defence) is incorporated in s. 4(1)(e) which says that there is no liability if the defendant can show:

> that the state of scientific and technical knowledge at the relevant time was not such that a producer of products of the same description as the product in question might be expected to have discovered the defect if it had existed in his products while they were under his control . . .

---

95 That is, the so-called 'Learned Hand' negligence test – see *US* v *Carroll Towing Co Inc* 159 F 2d 169 (2nd Circ. 1947).
96 See below, p. 284.

This very controversial defence was included in the Directive at the insistence of the United Kingdom government, but its effects are almost as controversial as its political genesis. Indeed, there was considerable doubt whether the statutory defence correctly gave effect to the Directive, because the wording of the two differs somewhat.[97] If this were the case, the United Kingdom would be in breach of its obligations under the EC Treaty, and, of course, in cases of conflict with the provisions of domestic law it is the Directive, as interpreted by the Court of Justice, which at the end of the day must govern.[98] However, the Court of Justice ruled that the Commission had failed to establish that Art. 7(e) had been incorrectly transposed.[99] The Directive says that the defence arises if 'the state of scientific and technical knowledge . . . was not such as to allow the existence of the defect to be discovered'. This appears to mean that liability exists if somewhere there is scientific or technical knowledge which could have led to the discovery of the defect, even though it was not reasonably discoverable by the defendant.[100] But the UK legal advisers apparently took the view that 'scientific and technical knowledge' cannot be said to exist merely because somewhere in the world some obscure research worker has the relevant knowledge in his mind, or perhaps even has published it in some equally obscure journal. In other words, scientific and technical knowledge only exist in the relevant sense if it is reasonably discoverable knowledge.[101]

The effect of the defence, as interpreted in the Act, is plainly to reincorporate something very like a no-negligence defence into the statutory cause of action; and it is for this reason that the Act has been seen to be a somewhat illusory piece of reform which largely takes away with one hand what it has given with the other. Clearly, there will be many cases in which the statutory defence under this section will enable the defendant to escape liability by proving, in substance, that he was not negligent. However, this does not mean that the new statutory cause of action is in all respects identical to the law of negligence. First, the onus of proof of this defence is on the defendant, and this may be a very important point in respect of many types of allegedly defective products.[102] Second, the defendant may be liable, even though he has not been negligent, because the defect in question may anyhow

---

97 The wording of Art. 7(e) of the Directive is as follows:
  . . . that the state of scientific and technical knowledge at the time when he put the product into circulation was not such as to *enable the existence* [emphasis supplied] of the defect to be discovered.

98 National courts are required to interpret national law in the light of the wording and purpose of Directives – see *Marleasing SA* v *La Comercial Internacional de Alimentación SA*, Case C-106/89 [1990] ECR I-4135. Failure to implement a Directive can give rise to liability on the part of the member state to a person suffering damage thereby – *Francovich* v *Italy*, C-6 and C-9/90 [1991] ECR I-5357. Directives are binding only on the member states to which they are addressed. Consequently, they cannot be invoked in disputes between private individuals – see, e.g., *Paolo Faccini Dori* v *Recreb Srl* (Case C-91/92) [1995] All ER (EC) 1.

99 Case C-300/95 *EC Commission* v *United Kingdom* [1997] 3 CMLR 923.

100 Though any disclosure (or at least any enabling disclosure) would be sufficient to bar patentability or to invalidate a patent in European Patent Convention countries. Although the issues involved in patent law and product liability are different, on this point, given the close *practical* link between research and development and patenting, it might not be unreasonable to give the Directive its wider meaning. There are, after all, in existence today very efficient databases which enable the 'state of the art' to be established fairly rapidly, and which are utilized by those involved in R & D projects.

101 In the above case the court used the word 'accessible', which seems an appropriate criterion bearing in mind the comment made in the previous footnote. See *Vacwell Engineering Co Ltd* v *BDH Chemicals Ltd* [1971] 1 QB 111 where the relevant information was available in books in the defendant's own library.

102 Compare *Daniels* v *White & Sons Ltd and Tabard* [1938] 4 All ER 258 above, p. 265.

not have arisen from a lack of scientific and technical knowledge, but from the failure to put together obvious facts to appreciate and eliminate (or reduce) a risk. For instance, child-proof medicine bottles are hardly an invention based on 'scientific and technical knowledge', so conceivably (if the statute had been in force before their widespread use) a defendant supplying an ordinary medicine bottle might have been held strictly liable on the ground that the bottle was defective.[103]

A third possible difference, depending on the meaning attributed to 'scientific and technical knowledge', arises from the practical impossibilities of perfect quality control at places of production. Suppose one heart pacemaker in a thousand fails to work properly, and that this failure rate cannot be reduced, not because of a lack of scientific and technical knowledge in the ordinary sense, but because it is impractical (or far too costly) to raise the level of factory quality control to such a point as to eliminate the risk.[104] The actual product which fails is clearly defective under the Act, but could the defendant escape liability under 'the state of the art' defence? The answer is far from clear, though *Richardson* v *LRC Products* suggests that the defendant might escape liability on this ground.[105] Whether a product is defective in this sense under s. 3(1) might depend upon the existence of warnings or general knowledge of these things. If there were no evidence on these matters, a defence on the basis of s. 4(1)(e) would still seem to be available. Whether it would be available on the wording of Art. 6.1 of the Directive is less clear.[106]

In *US* v *Carroll Towing Co*[107] Learned Hand CJ suggested that negligence is a function of three variables: (1) the probability of harm; (2) the gravity of the resulting injury; and (3) the burden of adequate precautions. If we include opportunity costs in quantifying this last variable, we have a reasonable explanation as to why it might be negligent to market a headache cure which killed one person in ten thousand, but not a treatment for a terminal disease.

However, as observed above, the courts have approached the matter in a somewhat unreflective manner. In *A* v *National Blood Authority*[108] it was held that the defence in Art. 4.7(e) of the Directive did not apply where the existence of the generic defect was known or should have been known in the context of accessible information. Once the existence of the defect was known, there was the risk of that defect materialising in any particular product, and it was immaterial that the known risk was unavoidable in the particular product. It would be inconsistent with the purpose of the Directive if a producer, in the case of a known risk, continued to supply products simply because, and despite the fact that, he was unable to identify in which of his products that defect would occur or recur, or, more relevantly in a case where the producer was obliged to supply, he continued to supply without accepting the responsibility for any injuries resulting, by insurance or otherwise. The defence also

---

103 But if it is not 'scientific and technical knowledge' the defendant may be able to argue with more plausibility that persons generally would not have expected their medicine bottles to be safer than they had normally been in the past. (Or are persons generally 'entitled to expect' more than they do expect?)

104 See Newdick [1988] CLJ 455.

105 See n. 88 above.

106 Failure to take steps to warn the public after a dangerous defect in a product range becomes known to the manufacturer may be a basis for negligence liability – *Walton* v *British Leyland*, p. 266.

107 159 F 2d 169 (1947).

108 [2001] 3 All ER 289.

failed in *Abouzaid* v *Mothercare (UK) Ltd.*[109] If these cases were expressly based on risk spreading theory[110] they would be understandable, but they seem to be based neither on this nor on Learned Hand negligence, but rather on a somewhat 'black letter' approach to a Directive.[111]

Producers, and other parties liable

The third essential question under the Act is: who is liable? The answer broadly is that under s. 2 three parties are in principle made liable for damage done by a defective product: (1) the 'producer' of the product, (2) anyone who has 'held himself out to be the producer of the product', for instance by putting his trade mark on the product,[112] and (3) anyone who has imported the product into a member state from a place outside the member states. In addition, any supplier of the goods can also be liable if he fails, on request, to identify to the claimant one of the parties in the first three groups.

On the other hand, any party (including the producer) can escape liability if he can show that he did not supply the goods in the course of business or with a view to profit. 'Supply' is defined in an elaborate s. 46: it includes in particular selling, hiring or lending, furnishing by way of hire-purchase, supplying the goods under a contract for work and materials, or giving the goods away as a prize or gift. The coverage is fairly wide, but it is not exhaustive. Even a producer of a defective product would not be liable if he did not supply the product at all, but (say) the product was stolen from his factory, and ultimately sold to the claimant (or anyone else). It also means that a party who causes injury while using the goods will not be liable for product defects under the Act because he does not supply the goods to anyone. And this is true even if the user is also the producer – so if (say) the maker of fork-lift trucks uses them in its own factory, and a defect causes injury to a workman, there will be no statutory liability.

There may be more than one 'producer' of a defective product within the Act. Because of the definition of 'product', the term covers the finished product as well as component parts and raw materials. So if a product is defective because of a defective component, the producers of both the finished product and the component will be liable, assuming each has 'supplied' the relevant product, as will usually be the case.[113] The liability of the producer of the finished product in this particular respect may well be genuinely strict, and may easily extend beyond common law liability for negligence.

---

109 [2000] EWCA Civ 348 – see p. 279 above.
110 See *Goldberg* v *Kollsman Instruments Co* 191 NE 2d 81 (1963), p. 284 below.
111 In the sense that although the Directive is interpreted in accordance with its purposes, these are determined entirely within the legislation.
112 Section 2(1)(b). Where a mark is applied by a licensee, it would appear, therefore, that it is the *licensor* who is liable under this provision, because by licensing the application of his mark he has 'held himself out to be the producer of the product'. The licensee will be liable as 'the producer' if such he is. But if he is buying in goods and applying the mark, he presumably will not be liable as producer. In such a case the original producer is liable, together with the trade mark licensor.
113 Though there may be good economic grounds for not holding a component manufacturer liable – see *Goldberg* v *Kollsman Instruments* 191 NE 2d 81 (1963) at p. 284 below.

Relation of the statutory liability to other forms of liability

The cause of action under the 1987 Act is in addition to, and does not in any way supersede, any other cause of action.[114] Further, the Act prohibits any party from contracting-out of (or limiting) his liability under the Act.[115] It is therefore possible in theory for a person who acquires goods from a producer of those goods to have a statutory cause of action under the Act, which overlaps with his contractual causes of action under the Sale of Goods Act, or otherwise. And occasionally, this may help a buyer because (for instance) the definition of a defective product is wider than the implied terms under the Sale of Goods Act, or because the prohibition on limiting or excluding liability is wider than that imposed under the Unfair Contract Terms Act. But this will not often be a matter of much practical importance, because consumers rarely buy goods direct from the manufacturers,[116] and businesses who do so will find that there is virtually no liability for business damage under the Act.

So the main practical importance of the Act will lie in the fact that a buyer will sometimes be enabled to sue parties other than the seller without having to prove fault, and that a non-buyer will likewise be enabled to sue the producer (though not a mere seller) without proving fault.

It still remains to be seen how far this legislation will prove to have been worthwhile. Although many European lawyers have been for some years casting envious eyes at American developments, it is far from clear that they have really achieved a great deal to benefit consumers. The truth is that in the great majority of cases, the Act will produce the same outcome as the law of negligence.[117] Defects in products are usually the result of negligence.[118] Indeed, as suggested above,[119] 'negligence' in the Learned Hand sense may provide useful guidance in applying the Act and the Directive. Only in special and unusual circumstances is it likely that a manufacturer would be held strictly liable where he has not been negligent, though it may be that the reversal of the burden of proof under the 'state of the art defence' may have some practical importance.

A good illustration of the difference between 'strict' liability and negligence is provided by the American case of *Goldberg* v *Kollsman Instruments*[120] in which passengers were killed when an airliner crashed due to a defective altimeter. The manufacturer of the aircraft had not been negligent, but was held liable, whereas the manufacturer of the altimeter was held not liable. The reason for this seems to have been that the aircraft manufacturer was felt to be the better loss distributor: a sensible result which, for the reasons given above, could not be reached under the 1987 Act.

---

114 Section 2(6).
115 Section 7.
116 An exception would be goods that are commonly built to order such as bicycles.
117 As in the case of negligence, the claimant must prove that the defect was the cause of the damage, and in cases of physical injury whose effects only become apparent after a considerable lapse of time, that may be a considerable problem. Even where the product can be established as the cause of the damage, there ought to be a defence if it can be established that it is a natural side-effect of the product, as in the case of a drug: the 'Learned Hand' test suggested in the text (see above, pp. 282–3) gives an explanation as to why it is not negligent to supply cancer chemotherapy with serious side-effects, but it would be to market a cure for a minor ailment with similar side-effects.
118 See, e.g., *Walton* v *British Leyland*, p. 266.
119 See p. 282.
120 191 NE 2d 81 (1963).

It must be said that the move to strict product liability against manufacturers in America has led to a huge amount of litigation as it has been necessary to work out what is meant by a 'defective product'; the original view that this would be a much simpler matter than deciding issues of negligence has been completely falsified by events. It has also been necessary to reconsider many doctrines of tort and delict law (for instance, the application of the rules of contributory negligence and remoteness of damage) to see if they need adaptation to a strict liability regime as opposed to a negligence liability regime.[121] It seems hardly going too far to say that the American experience suggests that the main beneficiaries of these changes are lawyers and insurers.

NON-CONTRACTUAL CLAIMS IN RESPECT OF DEFECTS IN THE GOODS

A person who buys goods which prove defective may wish to claim damages in respect of the defects themselves, for instance because the goods may have to be repaired, or because they are simply worth less than the buyer had expected, or because they are less efficient in use. Such cases are outside the Consumer Protection Act which excludes liability for loss or damage to the product itself, or any part of any product which has been supplied with the product in question comprised in it.[122] If the buyer sues the seller, such a claim raises no particular problem and is governed by the same principles as apply to actions for damages in respect of defective goods.[123] But if the buyer wishes to sue the manufacturer or anyone else responsible for the state of the goods, then apart from the possibility of recovering through the device of the collateral contract, or through intermediate suppliers,[124] the action must be brought in tort. And a tort action of this nature is still the subject of very considerable legal difficulty, because it appears to be (at least in many cases) a claim for pure economic loss. Recent developments, moreover, suggest that this form of liability will rarely be available in tort or delict to supplement contractual liability.[125]

Since the case of *Murphy* v *Brentwood*, which was mentioned above, overruled *Anns* v *Merton London Borough Council*, the possibility of suing in negligence for economic losses has virtually ceased to exist.[126] It will be best to consider the interplay of the various areas of law having a bearing on this issue through a series of examples arising from the following hypothetical situation. Suppose A buys a second-hand car from B, the car having originally been made by C, and suppose also that B had fitted a *new* tyre[127] made by T which was dangerous because of some negligence in manufacture on the part of T. While A is using the car, the tyre bursts.

---

121 Though liability under the 1987 Act does specifically attract the operation of the Law Reform (Contributory Negligence) Act 1945, some case law may well be needed before the application of that Act is sorted out in its relation to s. 3(2)(b) of the 1987 Act, dealing with misuse, etc.
122 See p. 275.
123 See p. 534 *et seq.*
124 See above, p. 268.
125 As to tort and delict liability see p. 265.
126 See pp. 267–8.
127 If the tyre was bought with the car there will be no recovery for damage to the car – see Case 5 below.

Case 1. If no injury or damage is caused by the tyre burst, except to the tyre itself, A cannot sue T in respect of the damaged tyre under the Consumer Protection Act because s. 5(2) excludes damage to the product itself.[128] Since *Murphy* v *Brentwood* it is likely that, as damage to the product itself, this will be treated as pure economic loss, which is not generally recoverable in tort. And even though the original defect in the tyre may have caused the burst, which may itself be a much more serious piece of damage than the original defect (so the tyre indeed becomes worthless) this does not alter the situation.

Case 2. If the result of the tyre burst is that A is injured, or that any property belonging to A (other than the tyre itself) is damaged, then A still cannot recover for the damage caused to the tyre itself by its bursting,[129] but he can recover damages for that other injury or damage from T in an ordinary action in tort under the principle of *Donoghue* v *Stevenson*.[130] This possibility extends also to a claim for damage to the car itself, because this is A's property and was not itself made by T and was bought separately. It appears to be immaterial in this case how closely connected the two chattels are, even where they are plainly sold as one item, so long only as the two items were made by separate manufacturers. So a buyer of plastic pails who fills them with waterproofing compound for resale can sue the maker of the pails if they were so negligently made that they leak, causing the compound to be lost, and a buyer of a bottle of wine can sue the maker of the cork (assuming he is a different party from the wine-maker) if it is so defective that it causes the wine to go bad.[131]

The effect of the Consumer Protection Act in these cases appears somewhat erratic, because s. 5(2) of that Act only denies liability for damage to the defective product itself, or to 'any product which has been supplied with the product in question comprised in it'. An amelioration of the apparent anomaly that the results are different if the tyre is bought separately than if it is bought with the car was suggested above.[132] The problem caused by the words 'with the product in question comprised in it' could not in any case apply to the examples of the defective pails and wine-corks. In neither case would the defective product be 'comprised' in the damaged goods.[133] So there could occasionally be liability under the Act, in which case, of course, it would be necessary to show that the product in question was defective, rather than that there had been negligence at common law.

Case 3. If the defect in the tyre does not cause it to burst, but (say) to deflate suddenly, without other damage to the tyre itself, and if this deflation should itself cause

---

128 See Directive 85/374/EEC, Art. 9(b).

129 See *D & F Estates* v *Church Commissioners* [1988] 2 All ER 992, at 1012 per Lord Oliver, where he accepts that there may be liability in such a case where buildings are concerned, but rejects the idea of liability in the case of chattels. Lord Bridge appears to draw no distinction between buildings and chattels (see p. 1006 at letter j) but it seems that he also would reject liability for the tyre damage on these facts.

130 [1932] AC 562, 1932 SC (HL) 31.

131 See *Aswan Engineering Establishment Co Ltd* v *Lupdine Ltd* [1987] 1 WLR 1, 21 per Lloyd LJ (but here the loss caused by the failure of the pails was not foreseeable).

132 See p. 275 *et seq.*

133 This assumes, however, that normal literal English methods of statutory interpretation are applied to s. 5(2), an assumption which may be incorrect. See Whittaker, above, n. 75 where it is suggested that because the Directive must be taken into account in the construction of the Act, and because the European Court will be the ultimate authority on the construction of the Directive, it may be necessary to use different methods of interpretation. If so, the precise wording of s. 5(2) may eventually turn out not to be of so much importance as the general purport.

an accident in which some injury or other damage occurs, then it seems that any additional damage to the tyre caused by the accident, and not by the original deflation, may be recoverable in tort. The reason for this is that the additional damage to the tyre here is parasitic on the other injury or damage, and it still seems to be a recognized principle that such parasitic damage will be recoverable in tort, even if it is economic loss alone.[134] The only rational justification for this appears to be that where actionable damage has already occurred, it will not open the door to a multitude of additional possible claimants to allow the victim of economic loss to latch on his claim for economic loss to his other claims for injury or damage.

Again it seems that the result under the Consumer Protection Act could be different because of s. 5(2) because it is the product itself that is damaged, so the claim could only be brought at common law if negligence can be proved.

Case 4. If A discovers that the tyre is defective and dangerous before any accident occurs, and replaces the tyre, it now seems that there can be no claim against T for the cost of the tyre. The law on this point has undergone some vicissitudes in the last few years. At one time, it seemed established by *Anns* v *Merton London Borough Council*[135] that the cost of this replacement would have been recoverable in tort. This decision has now been overruled by *Murphy* v *Brentwood District Council*,[136] and although this case involved a building, the dicta in it extend to chattels. It suggests that whilst the manufacturer of, for example, a central heating boiler may be liable for damage to property caused by it, that liability would not extend to the repair costs of the chattel itself, since this would, in effect, introduce product liability and transmissible warranties of quality into the law of tort by judicial legislation. The result under the Consumer Protection Act is the same.

Case 5. Suppose now that the defective tyre was originally made and fitted by the manufacturer of the car, and the defect in the tyre causes a burst which leads to an accident in which the car is damaged. The problem here is whether the car and tyre should be considered as one item, so as to fall within the principle in Case 1, that a defect in some good which causes damage to itself is not recoverable; or whether it falls within the principle in Case 2, that the damage to the car should be considered independently, so that that would be recoverable as ordinary physical damage under the rule in *Donoghue* v *Stevenson*. In *Murphy* v *Brentwood District Council* it was observed that it was unrealistic to regard a chattel which had been manufactured by the same person as a complex structure. In consequence, this suggests that the House of Lords would view the situation as falling within Case 1. In the case of complex structures the result might be different. In the *D & F Estates* case Lord Bridge reserved his opinion on the question whether, in the case of complex structures and chattels made up of distinct parts, physical damage done by one part to another could qualify as ordinary physical damage under the rule in *Donoghue* v *Stevenson*. Lord Oliver, while agreeing that this might be possible in the case of buildings, appeared more firm against accepting this in the case of complex chattels. It is difficult to offer comment

---

134 *Spartan Steels* v *Martin & Co* [1973] QB 27; *Muirhead* v *Industrial Tank Specialities Ltd* [1986] QB 507.
135 [1978] AC 728.
136 [1991] AC 398, [1990] 2 All ER 908.

or prediction in this area of the law, where everything now seems dictated by prag-
matic considerations, and arbitrary lines abound in preference to reasoned arguments.
But it really would seem an outrage to common sense if an ordinary consumer whose
negligently made car battery causes a fire destroying his car along with the battery
cannot sue the manufacturers of the battery just because they also happen to be the
manufacturers of the car.[137] But this means, of course, that some principle will be
needed to identify a 'complex' chattel. The law is perhaps still some way from sorting
this problem out. The Consumer Protection Act would possibly provide a remedy in
this situation if the 'separate market' argument set out above is accepted.[138]

Case 6. If the defect in the tyre is not one which renders it dangerous, but (say)
simply unlikely to wear as well as such a tyre ought to, then the buyer's prospects of
succeeding against the manufacturer are now slim indeed. Even here the law does in
principle recognize some situations in which recovery is possible, but the circumstances would have to be very exceptional.

There is no liability under the Consumer Protection Act in this case.

Case 7. If the tyre had been damaged in an accident (or otherwise – for instance,
by negligent fitting) caused by the negligence of a third party before A bought the car
it seems that A will have no cause of action in tort against the third party,[139] and it
makes no difference that the damage was not manifest at the time of the purchase.
Only a person who has a proprietary or possessory interest in goods *at the time they
are damaged* can sue a third party in tort for causing that damage.[140] This rule has
arisen in commercial situations where it does not usually cause a great deal of trouble, because the buyer of goods liable to have suffered damage (that is, principally
goods being transported by land or sea) normally receives a transfer of the contract
of carriage,[141] which enables him to sue for the damage in contract. In other contexts
the present rule may be less justifiable, but it does not appear in fact to cause much
practical difficulty. Once again the principal justification for it appears to be the view
that the buyer of the goods should look to his contract to protect him against defects
and damage done before he acquires the goods, though hard cases are conceivable in
which a court might try to distinguish the *Aliakmon*, e.g. on the basis that the plaintiff was a consumer. The situation would also be different where personal injury was
caused: here the plaintiff could recover on usual *Donoghue* v *Stevenson* principles.

STATUTORY DUTIES

A great deal of consumer protection is today provided for by particular statutes.
Some of these, like the Food Safety Act 1990, are concerned, to some extent, with the
quality and fitness of particular types of goods, such as those supplied for public consumption. Some, like the Weights and Measures Act 1985, are designed to see that

---

137 The suggestion made at p. 275 *et seq* may be another way out of this problem, because car batteries are acces-
     sories dealt in separately.
138 Ibid.
139 *The Aliakmon* [1986] AC 785.
140 Ibid.
141 See p. 427.

the consumer is not supplied with short measure. In addition, there is the very comprehensive Trade Descriptions Act 1968, which is mainly designed to prohibit false or misleading statements or advertisements by retail sellers. In addition, there is Part II of the Consumer Protection Act 1987 (replacing earlier legislation) which deals with the sale and supply of safe goods, and which gives the Secretary of State the power to make regulations to ensure the safety of goods, to restrict the availability of goods or to ensure that they are supplied with proper information.[142]

These statutes all rely on the criminal law for their enforcement, together with enforcement officers and inspectors, etc., appointed by local authorities, usually in departments now known as Trading Standards or Consumer Protection Offices. It is generally assumed by Parliament and public alike that, when the consumer feels aggrieved, his reaction is to complain to a public authority rather than to take legal proceedings. Hence few of these modern statutes provide any form of civil remedy to the aggrieved consumer, though there is one notable exception. Under s. 41(1) of the Consumer Protection Act 1987, a breach of any safety regulations made by the Secretary of State under that Act is civilly actionable as a breach of statutory duty. But a breach of the 'general safety requirement' created by s. 10 of that Act (a broad offence of supplying or offering, etc., unsafe goods for sale) is not civilly actionable. Earlier regulations made under previous Acts are continued in force until replaced. At present such regulations cover a wide variety of goods including, in particular, toys, carry-cots, nightdresses, children's clothes, electrical appliances, certain cooking utensils, upholstered furniture and oil heaters.

A person who buys goods not complying with the regulations would, therefore, have an action for breach of statutory duty against the seller. Although it is not necessary to prove negligence in such an action, the defendant may be able to escape liability if he can prove that he took all due diligence to avoid the commission of an offence, and he is also provided with a statutory defence whereby he may be able to prove that the contravention was due to the act or default of another.[143] Apart from these defences, however, the cause of action is a form of strict liability. Contracting out is also prohibited. Moreover, the action for breach of statutory duty which the Act provides would also be available at the suit of a plaintiff who is not himself the buyer. For example, if a child or other member of the buyer's family were injured by goods sold in contravention of regulations under the Act, an action would lie.

This provision of the Consumer Protection Act (when first enacted) was something of a statutory innovation which appears to have been prompted by the appeal made by Lord du Parcq in *Cutler* v *Wandsworth Stadium* Ltd[144] that Parliament should make its intention clear where it intends penal legislation to confer civil rights. There is no similar provision in other consumer protection legislation such as the Food Safety Act 1990, and it has been held that breach of these Acts gives no civil remedy.[145]

---

142 The current regulations are the General Product Safety Regulations 1994, SI 1994/1328.
143 Sections 39 and 40 of the Consumer Protection Act 1987. See, as to s. 39, *Taylor* v *Lawrence Fraser (Bristol) Ltd* [1978] Crim LR 43.
144 [1949] AC 398, 410.
145 *Square* v *Model Farm Dairies (Bournemouth) Ltd* [1939] 2 KB 365. Cf. *Read* v *Croydon Corpn* [1938] 3 All ER 631 (breach of statutory duty to supply wholesome water does not give cause of action); *Lonrho Ltd* v *Shell Petroleum Co Ltd* [1982] AC 173; *RCA* v *Pollard* [1983] FSR 9.

Although it is understandable perhaps that no individual remedy should be provided for breach of standards of purity (for instance in water supplies) where the dangers to the public consist of long-term risks rather than immediate and actual injury, it is less easy to understand why no remedy exists for genuine injuries. The traditional argument that such statutory provisions are intended for the benefit of the public as a whole seems pure sophistry. A statute laying down requirements as to the purity of food or drink supplied to the public would seem obviously to be for the benefit of every consumer likely to consume the food and drink. To say that the Act is intended for the benefit of the public as a whole seems merely to beg the question, for what is meant by such an assertion is not that the Act is literally not meant for the benefit of individuals, but that the Act is not meant to benefit individuals by providing an action for breach of statutory duty. But since the whole question in such cases is whether the Act does confer such a civil remedy, this reasoning is plainly circular.

Parliament's own policy on these questions also seems hard to understand. While the Consumer Protection Act expressly allows for an action for breach of statutory duty (as mentioned above) some modern legislation expressly disallows the possibility of civil remedies. For instance, the Trade Descriptions Act 1968, s. 35, expressly provides that failure to comply with that Act does not render any contract void or unenforceable. And s. 17 of the Merchandise Marks Act 1887, which gave a civil remedy for breach of that Act, was repealed and not reproduced by the Trade Descriptions Act. It is not easy to understand why Parliament does not make greater use of the action for breach of statutory duty as a consumer remedy. It sometimes has the great advantage from the public point of view that statutory regulations become to some degree self-enforcing. If the aggrieved party can himself take proceedings, no public expenditure is required to enforce the statute. Moreover, it seems strange that a seller can, in a civil court, hold a buyer to a contract on terms imposed by him in contravention of clear statutory provisions.[146] However, in the last few years there has been one major development which goes some way to offering an alternative to the action for breach of statutory duty. This is the introduction of the power to make compensation orders, which is dealt with in the next section.

Future developments in this area are likely, in the main, to be driven from Brussels. The EU's Directive on General Product Safety[147] aimed to standardize safety requirements, in order to remove obstacles to free movement in a single market. It introduces a general obligation on producers and importers, and, in certain circumstances, others in the supply chain.[148] The general principle of the Directive is that producers may place only safe products on the market, and must provide consumers with information on the risks associated with the product, and monitor the safety of products after sale. 'Product' is defined as intended for consumers or likely to be used by consumers whether for consideration or not, and whether new, used or reconditioned. The supply must take place in the course of a

---

146 It is to be noted, however, that the Director General of Fair Trading in discussions of the duty to trade fairly in his Report 'Trading Malpractices' (1990) retreats from the proposal to have one measure providing both standards and redress.

147 92/59, OJ 1992 L228/24, 11 August.

148 The text was adopted by the Council of Ministers on 29 June 1992. Its operative date was 29 June 1994. The UK Regulations to implement the Directive came into force on 3 October 1994 – SI 1994/2328.

business. The Directive applies only to consumer goods. There are other European measures covering various aspects of product safety, but it is beyond the scope of this work to consider these.[149]

CONSUMER REMEDIES

The above discussion of statutory regulations relating to contracts of sale leads directly on to another point. The law of sale of goods appears on the face of it to confer satisfactory civil remedies to a buyer who has bought goods which prove defective or otherwise unsatisfactory. But in practice there is a good deal of evidence that the expense and trouble of civil litigation are so great that the average consumer gets no real protection from them in minor cases. In 1969, the Consumer Council conducted a sample survey of a number of county court cases involving 'small' claims, these being defined as mainly in the £20 to £100 area.[150] Out of a total of 1,104 cases investigated, not a single one was an action brought by a consumer. While business firms and tradesmen frequently launched claims for £10 or even £5, consumers were invariably advised by solicitors not to sue unless a claim was for at least £30, which would today be perhaps £200. The only cases in which consumer claims were regularly put forward appeared to be those in which consumers were sued for the price of goods and then set up breach of warranty as a defence. The Consumer Council also addressed a questionnaire to a large number of solicitors about consumer claims. The almost unanimous response was that consumer claims were unsatisfactory for plaintiff (claimant) and solicitor alike. Some solicitors took the attitude that it was pointless even to write letters of complaint because of the cost; all advised against legal proceedings by the consumer. The Consumer Council concluded that it was doubtful whether the county courts were a suitable forum for consumer claims.

The Civil Procedure Rules 1998 establish a 'small claims track'[151] for claims of under £5,000.[152] If the parties consent, adjudication can be on paper rather than at a public hearing (which the parties need not attend in any event).[153] Tailored directions are given for the most common small claims, such as spoiled holidays and wedding videos, motor accidents and building disputes. It remains to be seen what impact these reforms will have on the problems alluded to above. Certainly, their predecessor, the old small claims procedure, which was also informal and in effect an arbitration, had little effect.[154]

It is not easy to know what the ultimate solution of these problems is likely to be. It seems clear that the trend towards use of the criminal law as the main method of

---

149 See Miller, *Product Liability and Safety Encyclopaedia*, Butterworths Looseleaf Part V.
150 See *Focus*, the Consumer Council journal, July 1969, p. 2.
151 CPR Pt 27.
152 For personal injuries, the limit is £1,000, where the value of the whole claim is less than £5,000.
153 Provided they give the court and the other party notice. This will guarantee that the court will take into account any written evidence the non-attending party has submitted.
154 For other developments of a similar nature see Cranston, *Consumers and the Law*, London, 1978, pp. 88–95; C.J. Whelan, *Small Claims Courts: A Comparative Study*, Clarendon, 1990. For the Scottish small claims procedure, which has an upper limit of £1,500, see 6 *Laws of Scotland: Stair Memorial Encyclopaedia*, para. 169, 2002 Cumulative Supplement and Updating Service; and for more detail, W.C.H. Ervine, *Small Claims Handbook*, 2nd edn, 2003.

consumer protection is likely to increase. But some method must be found of enabling the consumer to enforce the legal rights given to him by the Sale of Goods Act without paying out more in legal costs than the claim is worth. At present it must be admitted that in many circumstances the most effective remedy of the aggrieved consumer is to write a letter of complaint to a daily newspaper rather than to resort to litigation in the courts. This is no credit to the legal system. The EU produced a Green Paper on the access of consumers to justice and the settlement of consumer disputes.[155] Its main themes include comparability of injunctions throughout the Union, legal aid, simplified settlement of transfrontier disputes, self-regulation, a dialogue between consumers and professionals, and transfrontier co-operation.

Compensation orders

As mentioned above, there has been a major development in recent years in the field of consumer remedies with the introduction of compensation orders in criminal cases. At one time, the use of such orders was generally confined to cases of serious crime and damage to property, but under the Powers of Criminal Courts Act 1973 (as subsequently amended) a court which convicts a person of any offence may (instead of,[156] or in addition to, dealing with him in any other way) order him to pay compensation for any personal injury, loss or damage resulting from that offence. The power has been extended to cover an award for funeral expenses or bereavement in cases where death ensues.[157] It has been held that compensation can be awarded not only for pecuniary losses but also for distress and anxiety, where this can be said to be 'personal injury . . . resulting from the offence' and there is a manifestly direct causal connection between the offence and the distress.[158] If damages are subsequently awarded, credit must be given for the amount awarded under the compensation order.[159] In a magistrates' court, the total compensation awarded against one person must not exceed £5,000,[160] but in Crown Courts there is no limit on the amount.

These orders are most widely used in cases of assault and personal injury, on the one hand, and in cases of theft or property damage on the other. But there is no reason why they should not be used in many other cases and they are, in fact, now also commonly made where a breach of the Trade Descriptions Act is proved. There is also no reason why other consumer complaints (for example, in cases under the Food Safety Act) should not be remedied by a compensation order. Given the width of the powers available and the amounts which may be awarded, even in magistrates' courts, many consumer complaints could be adequately compensated by such orders without the necessity for civil proceedings to be taken. However, the making of a compensation order is discretionary, and appellate courts have insisted over and

---

155 COM (93) 576.
156 This change was made by s. 67 of the Criminal Justice Act 1982.
157 This change was introduced by s. 104 of the Criminal Justice Act 1988. A similar scheme was introduced in Scotland under the Criminal Justice (Scotland) Act 1980 and is now governed by the Criminal Procedure (Scotland) Act 1995 ss. 249–253. See 6 *Laws of Scotland: Stair Memorial Encyclopaedia*, para 171, 2002 Cumulative Supplement and *Shaw* v *Donnelly* 2002 SCCR 804 (compensation order made for sum stated by prosecutor quashed as no proof held on true cost of repair).
158 *Bond* v *Chief Constable of Kent* [1983] 1 All ER 456.
159 Powers of Criminal Courts Act 1973 s. 38.
160 Criminal Justice Act 1991.

over again that orders are not to be made where the issues are complex or seriously controverted.[161] Nevertheless, there are many simple consumer complaints which can be remedied by these means if magistrates are so minded, so it is worth devoting some attention to the possibility, especially as private individuals may instigate proceedings in the magistrates' court.

The essential requirement is that there must be personal injury, loss or damage before an order can be made. So where a buyer dishonestly bought some goods, which he took before payment, but the goods were recovered by the seller, and no loss ensued from the theft, it was held that no compensation order should have been made.[162]

On the other hand, it has been held that a compensation order can be made even where there is no civil liability so long as the statutory requirements are met.[163] But the results are so anomalous that it seems unlikely that courts will encourage the making of orders where there is obviously no civil liability. But it is, anyhow, clear that the courts will not take technical and pedantic points of law – however good they might be in a civil case – to defeat the possibility of a compensation order being made. For example, in *R v Thomson Holidays Ltd*,[164] the defendants were convicted of an offence under the Trade Descriptions Act in respect of a misleading holiday brochure. It was held that a compensation order could be made in favour of a disappointed holidaymaker who complained that he did not obtain the amenities which he had been led to expect by the brochure. The defendants argued that the holidaymaker's real complaint was that the defendants had not provided him with the holiday which he was entitled to under his contract and not that he had been misled by the brochure. In other words, they were arguing that the complaint was really of breach of contract rather than misrepresentation. But the court rejected this argument, holding that the Act was not intended to import into the criminal law complex causation questions from the civil law.

The amendments to s. 35 of the Powers of Criminal Courts Act made by the Criminal Justice Act 1982 enable the court to make a compensation order where an offence is merely taken into consideration as well as where a conviction is actually recorded. In addition, there is the rather obscure s. 35(1A) inserted by the 1982 Act which appears to have been intended to amend the ruling in *R v Vivian*[165] to the effect that an order can only be made where the amount of the loss or damage is either proved or admitted and not where it remains uncertain. The effect of this provision is to enable the court to make an order which is well within the limits of the damage or loss, even though the full amount remains uncertain.[166] The Criminal Justice Act also provides that where an offender cannot pay both fine and compensation the court is to give priority to the compensation order.

So far as the buyer of goods is concerned, it is likely that the Trade Descriptions Act 1968 will be the main source of compensation orders. It would not be appropriate in

---

161 See, generally, *R v Miller* [1976] Crim LR 694; *R v Roger Scott* (1986) 83 Cr App Rep 227; *R v Broughton* (1986) 8 Cr App Rep (S) 379; *R v Holden* [1985] Crim LR 397; *R v Swan and Webster* (1984) 6 Cr App Rep (S) 22.
162 *R v Boardman* (1987) 9 Cr App Rep (S) 74.
163 *R v Chappel* [1984] Crim LR 574.
164 [1974] QB 592.
165 (1978) 68 Cr App Rep 53.
166 See *R v Horsham Justices, ex parte Richards* [1985] 1 WLR 986.

this book to explore this Act at any length,[167] but some illustrations of cases in which orders have been made may be useful. The main provision relevant to the law of sale of goods is s. 1 of the Act, which makes it an offence for a person in the course of a trade or business to apply a false trade description to any goods, or supply any goods to which a false trade description is applied.[168] Sections 2, 3 and 4 of the Act contain elaborations of some complexity on this basic provision, but it is unnecessary here to go into the details. It is clear that a written or verbal application of a trade description will suffice. Moreover, mere words of commendation, which might be held to be simple 'puffs' in civil law, may fall within these statutory provisions. For example, in *Hawkins* v *Smith*,[169] a car sold by the defendants, who were second-hand car dealers, was described as 'in showroom condition throughout'. In fact, the car had many mechanical defects and the defendants were convicted. Similarly, in *Chidwick* v *Beer*,[170] a car sold for £320 and, described as being 'in excellent condition through-out', was found to need immediate repairs costing £36 and, shortly afterwards, was found to have some 17 other defects, some of which rendered it unsafe to use. It was held that nobody could say that the car was in excellent condition throughout, and magistrates were directed to convict. It was also said quite specifically in this case that it was immaterial that the buyer may not have been misled by the description, and in other cases it has been said to be immaterial whether the buyer has got a bad bar-gain.[171] It has also been stressed that the question in these cases is not whether on the 'true construction' of some descriptive words they may be held to be true, but whether the description is capable of misleading the average buyer.[172] In all these cases, it would seem that compensation orders could have been made.

A mileometer (or odometer) reading on a motor vehicle is a trade description within the Act, and a person who sells a vehicle in the course of his trade or business is supplying the vehicle with the description attached. He may, therefore, be guilty of an offence and be ordered to pay compensation if the reading turns out to have been false.

If the defendant has himself *applied* the false trade description, that is has himself been responsible (either personally or through his employees) for turning back the mileage indicator, or in some other way has warranted the genuineness of the mileage, he will be guilty of an offence under s. 1(1)(a) of the Act even, apparently, if there was no dishonesty or intent to deceive.[173] If there is *mens rea*, the offence is complete when the indicator is turned back, or the warranty is given, and no other application of the description needs to be proved, such as by sale or offer to sell. Further, in this event, there is no way in which the defendant can escape liability by use of a disclaimer.[174]

---

167 For further reading see Richard J. Bragg, *Trade Descriptions*, Clarendon, 1991.
168 'Supply of goods' includes the return of goods to the owner after repairs have been carried out on them, so that a false statement, say, as to new parts fitted, can be a false trade description – *Formula One Autocentres Ltd* v *Birmingham City Council* [1999] RTR 195.
169 [1978] Crim LR 578.
170 [1978] RTR 415; see also *Furniss* v *Scholes* [1974] RTR 133.
171 *Furniss* v *Scholes* – see last note.
172 *Routledge* v *Ansa Motors Ltd* [1980] RTR 1.
173 *Norman (Alec) Garages* v *Phillips* [1985] RTR 164.
174 *Newman* v *Hackney London BC* [1982] RTR 296; *R* v *Southwood* [1987] RTR 273.

But if, on the other hand, the defendant has not himself been responsible for turning back the indicator, but this was (for instance) done by a previous owner, the defendant can only be charged with supplying or offering to supply goods to which a false trade description has been applied under s. 1(1)(b) of the Act. In that event he may be able to escape liability by showing that he disclaimed any responsibility for the accuracy of the mileage indicator. Strictly speaking, this defence 'which is a court-created defence distinct from the statutory defence of "due diligence" under s. 24(1) of the Trade Descriptions Act'[175] amounts to a defence that no false description was in fact *applied* to the goods. Clearly the simplest and most effective way of achieving this is to cover up the mileage indicator so that the buyer cannot see it. But a seller may be able to escape liability under this provision of the Act even if he does not cover up the indicator, so long as he makes it quite clear by notice or disclaimer that he in no way accepts responsibility for the accuracy of the indicator.

But it has several times been held that a seller who seeks to rely on a notice warning buyers that mileage readings may be inaccurate must show that the notice was 'bold, precise and compelling'.[176] This is, perhaps, especially important where a car or other vehicle is sold by auction. For even in such a case, disclaimer notices may be held insufficient to nullify the effect of a mileage reading, and so compensation could be awarded; yet (as we have seen) under the Unfair Contract Terms Act, a sale by auction, even to a consumer, is not treated as a consumer sale. Consequently, as a matter of civil law, where goods are sold by auction, the seller may be permitted to rely on printed exclusion clauses provided they satisfy the test of reasonableness in the 1977 Act. It now seems clear that there could nevertheless be a conviction under the Trade Descriptions Act in such circumstances.[177] And, consequently, a buyer could get a compensation order, despite the absence of civil liability.

Apart from the possibility of escaping liability by use of a disclaimer, a seller may here (as elsewhere under the Trade Descriptions Act) rely on the general defence under s. 24(1)(b) of that Act that he took all reasonable precautions and exercised all due diligence to avoid committing an offence.[178] This defence has sometimes been confused with the court-created defence by which disclaimers may be held to show that no false description has been applied at all, but strictly it is a separate defence altogether.[179] For the purposes of s. 24, supervised shop managers and employees transacting business under their instructions are neither the ego, nor the alter ego, of their employers.[180] Accordingly, the section provides a defence to employers who can show that they took all reasonable precautions and exercised due diligence.

Another case of some interest under the 1968 Act is *Fletcher* v *Budgen*,[181] where a person sold a second-hand car to a dealer, who told him the car would have to be

---

175 See *Cook* v *Howells Garages (Newport) Ltd* [1980] RTR 434, 439; *Wandsworth London BC* v *Bentley* [1980] RTR 429, 433.
176 *Zawadski* v *Sleigh* [1978] RTR 113; *Stainthorpe* v *Bailey* [1980] RTR 7. There are a great many cases on these provisions regarding false odometer readings.
177 *Zawadski* v *Sleigh*, above, last note.
178 As to the standard of due diligence required under the Act, see *Simmons* v *Ravenhill* [1984] RTR 412. See also *Hurley* v *Martinez & Co* (1990) 154 JP 821; *Denard* v *Smith & Dixons* [1991] Crim LR 63.
179 See cases cited above, nn. 174 and 175.
180 See *Beckett* v *Kingston Bros (Butchers) Ltd* [1970] 1 QB 606; *Tesco Supermarkets Ltd* v *Nattrass* [1972] AC 153.
181 [1974] 1 WLR 1056.

scrapped and paid £2 for it. In fact, this was untrue as the defendant was able to repair and resell the car. It was held that even a buyer (if acting in the course of a trade or business) can be guilty of applying a trade description under the Act. However, it is not everything said by a contracting party which falls within the Act. Broadly, a trade description must refer to some present or past fact, and the Act does not cover mere breaches of promise.[182]

Quite how far the courts will be willing to go in making compensation orders for offences under statutes of this kind remains to be seen. For instance, it is not clear if an order could be made upon a conviction under s. 20 of the Consumer Protection Act 1987 of giving a misleading indication as to the price at which goods are offered for sale.[183] If, for example, goods in a supermarket are wrongly priced and a customer is charged the correct, or higher, price it is likely that an offence has been committed under s. 20 of the Consumer Protection Act. But it is not clear whether the customer could be said to have suffered any 'loss'. On the other hand, the Act does not apply only to misdescriptions in the ordinary sense. It seems quite likely that the possibility of obtaining a compensation order in a criminal case will be one of the growth areas of the law in the future. Certainly, even as matters stand now, a consumer who wishes to complain of defective goods – at least where the complaint relates to some misdescription – may be well advised to approach his local Consumer Protection or Trading Standards Office, at any rate in the first instance.

---

182 *British Airways Board v Taylor* [1976] 1 WLR 1395. See, e.g., *British Gas Corpn v Lubbock* [1974] 1 WLR 37.
183 It should be noted that s. 20(1) of that Act restricts liability for such things as misleading price indications to the owner of the business – see *Warwick CC v Johnson* [1993] 1 All ER 299. The Code of Practice on Price Indications approved under s. 25 of the Consumer Protection Act is set out in SI 1988/2078.

16

MANUFACTURERS' GUARANTEES

INTRODUCTION: A WORD ABOUT THE WORD 'GUARANTEE'

The word 'guarantee' is used in law in four very different senses:

1. It is the promise to answer for the debt or default of another. Under the Statute of Frauds[1] such contracts must be evidenced in writing, signed by the party to be charged. Guarantees in this sense are commonly met with in consumer credit transactions, for example, where a parent might be required to guarantee his or her child's hire-purchase debt to a finance company. We are not concerned with guarantees in this sense in this chapter.
2. Product guarantees, of which the most common is the manufacturer's product guarantee, commonly found printed as a standard form purporting to take effect as a contract between the buyer of the goods in question and the manufacturer. These are dealt with in the following section.
3. 'Extended warranties' or 'guarantees' routinely offered with more expensive consumer electrical goods and the like. In return for a lump sum[2] or regular payments to a company which may be (but is not necessarily) independent of either the retailer or the manufacturer,[3] the costs of repair should the goods break down will be covered. These are dealt with in the section following 'manufacturers' guarantees'.
4. 'Satisfaction guarantees': these are typically in a form such as 'Money back in 30 days if not completely satisfied'. These are in fact sale-on-approval transactions, which are dealt with elsewhere in this book.[4]

MANUFACTURERS' GUARANTEES

A useful working definition of the manufacturer's guarantee is as follows:

> ... a voluntary undertaking given by a manufacturer[5] (the 'guarantor') without charge to provide a remedy, should the product covered by the guarantee become defective as a result of poor workmanship or the use of faulty materials in the manufacturing process during a specified period of time after purchase.[6]

---

1 29 Car. 2 c. 3 (1677) s. 4.
2 Which may be covered by the moneys lent under the credit agreement covering the price of the goods.
3 Which may be an insurance company – from the consumer's point of view, as explained below, there are certain advantages in it being an insurance company.
4 See p. 329 *et seq.*
5 Which term includes producers.
6 This definition is taken from Twigg-Flesner *Consumer Product Guarantees*, Ashgate, 2003, p. 1.

Similar guarantees are offered by some retailers, and these too are within the scope of this chapter, though, to avoid complicating matters, we will in general be focusing on manufacturers' guarantees. Since there will be a contractual nexus between the buyer and the retailer, retailers' guarantees will operate either as part of the sales transaction, or as collateral contracts, the consideration for which in English law can be found in the buyer entering into the sales contract.[7] The contractual aspect of manufacturers' guarantees in English law was more problematic.

As was pointed out in previous editions of this work, there is scarcely any English or Scottish authority on the effect of manufacturers' guarantees. Were the buyer of goods aware of the guarantee, then it would be possible to analyse it as a collateral contract, the consideration for which was the purchase of the goods from the dealer.[8] It would, however, be difficult to apply this analysis where the buyer only became aware of the guarantee when he or she got home and opened the box. In fact, this will commonly be the case, as most consumer (and many non-consumer) goods are delivered from the retailer's stockroom in sealed boxes, after the buyer has selected a model from the samples on display. Thus, the first time that the consumer will see the guarantee is when he or she opens the box at home. Formerly, it was possible to argue that by completing and posting the guarantee, which invariably excluded common law rights, the consideration was the surrender of these rights in return for the manufacturer's undertakings given under the guarantee. This line of argument might still have some validity in non-consumer cases, but because (as we have seen) the consumer buyer is no longer able to surrender his or her common law rights,[9] this analysis is no longer useful in consumer cases. Another possibility is that the English courts may now be prepared to hold such guarantees binding as unilateral contracts.[10] This would certainly provide a sensible solution in non-consumer cases,[11] where otherwise the absence of consideration would mean that the buyer has no legal rights under the guarantee.[12] This problem does not arise under Scots law, as it has no consideration requirement;[13] manufacturers' guarantees are characteristically seen as unilateral promises rather than contracts.

A further problem with manufacturers' guarantees is whether or not they are limited to the original buyer, or whether they run to persons who subsequently become owners of the goods within the period of the guarantee. This problem was discussed in the European Commission's Green Paper of 1993,[14] and has been discussed by the

---

7 On the analogy of the series of hire-purchase cases starting with *Webster* v *Higgings* [1948] 2 All ER 127 where dealers said 'If you buy the [*car*] we will guarantee that it is in good condition'. In reliance on this statement, the defendant entered into a hire-purchase transaction with a third party. The car turned out to be in poor condition, and the dealers were held liable on their 'guarantee'. See also V*A Industries (UK) Ltd* v *Bostock & Bramley & others* [2003] EWCA Civ 1069.

8 See *Shanklin Pier Ltd* v *Detel Products Ltd* [1951] 2 KB 854.

9 See p. 235.

10 See *Blackpool and Fylde Aero Club Ltd* v *Blackpool Borough Council* [1990] 3 All ER 25 – see Adams and Brownsword (1991) 54 MLR 301.

11 The situation in consumer cases is now covered by legislation, as explained below.

12 It would also seem to be in accordance with the slightly curious wording of the Sale and Supply of Goods to Consumers Regulations in consumer cases – see Reg. 2.

13 See Cusine 1980 JR 185. On the Scots law of unilateral promise, see MacQueen & Thomson *Contract Law in Scotland* (2000) paras 2.54–2.63.

14 Green Paper on Guarantees for Consumer Goods and After-sales Service COM (93) 509 final.

Office of Fair Trading.[15] In both cases the view was taken that these guarantees should run with ownership of the goods in question. As yet, no action has been taken on this, however, and the current situation is that manufacturers can limit the guarantee to the first buyer.[16]

A related question is who should be liable to the consumer under the guarantee. Clearly, the manufacturer giving the guarantee is liable on it, subject to the legal questions discussed above in relation to non-consumer sales. It has been suggested, however, that the retailer should additionally be liable, since the manufacturer's guarantee is often specifically mentioned by the retailer as a selling point for the goods in question. The Department of Trade and Industry took this view in their consultation paper.[17] However, nothing has been done about this, though, as noted above, many reputable retailers do offer their own guarantees, which may extend for a longer time than the manufacturer's. Obviously, there is a cost in this, and probably the answer is best left to consumer choice. If goods are bought at a low price from the warehouse type establishments sometimes referred to as 'box shifters', no doubt the price will be lower than from a reputable department store, but by buying from the latter type of establishment, the consumer does often acquire additional security in the form of the store's guarantee. This is particularly useful where, as is often the case, it is more convenient to return defective goods to the store than to the manufacturer.

The situation under manufacturers' guarantees so far as the consumer buyer is concerned is now significantly altered by the Sale and Supply of Goods to Consumers Regulations.[18] These bring into force the Sale of Consumer Goods and Associated Guarantees Directive.[19] The Directive both gives additional remedies to consumers,[20] and harmonises the law on manufacturers' guarantees. The former are dealt with in Part VII, Chapter 26A. Here we are concerned with the latter.

Overview of the Sale of Consumer Goods and Associated Guarantees Directive and the Sale and Supply of Goods to Consumers Regulations[21]

The Directive's field of application is limited to sales of 'consumer goods' to 'consumers'.[22] The Directive applies, moreover, only where goods are sold by a 'seller' within the meaning of the Directive. For these purposes, 'consumer goods' are 'any tangible movable item, with the exception of goods sold by way of execution or otherwise by authority of law, water and gas where they are not put up for sale in a limited volume or set quantity[23] and electricity'.[24] 'Consumer' means 'any natural

---

15 Most recently in OFT 2001c Unfair Contract Terms Guidance.
16 Sale and Supply of Goods to Consumers Regulations 2002, SI 2002/3045, reg. 15 does not appear to preclude this.
17 Consumer Guarantees Consultation Paper para. 14.
18 SI 2002/3045.
19 Directive 99/44/EC on Certain Aspects of the Sale of Consumer Goods and Associated Guarantees OJ 1999 L 177/12.
20 They add an entirely new Part 5A to the Sale of Goods Act, providing buyers with additional rights in consumer cases.
21 SI 2002/3045.
22 Article 1.
23 Article 1(2)(b). Sales of cylinders of camping gas *would* therefore fall within the Directive, as would sales of bottled mineral water.
24 Ibid.

person who, in the contracts covered by the Directive, is acting for purposes which are not related to his trade, business or profession'.[25] 'Seller' means 'any natural or legal person who, under a contract, sells consumer goods in the course of his trade, business or profession'.[26] There is no requirement in the Directive that a manufacturer's guarantee be given, but, if it is, the provisions of the Directive are applicable. A 'guarantee' for these purposes is 'any undertaking by a seller or producer[27] to the consumer, given without extra charge,[28] to reimburse the price paid or to replace, repair or handle consumer goods in any way if they do not meet the specifications set out in the guarantee statement or in the relevant advertising'.[29]

The Regulations do not exactly reproduce the provisions of the Directive, but rather paraphrase them. Thus the important definition of 'consumer guarantee' is as follows:

> ... any undertaking to a consumer by a person acting in the course of his business, given without extra charge, to reimburse the price paid or to replace, repair or handle consumer goods in any way if they do not meet the specifications set out in the guarantee statement or in the relevant advertising.[30]

Whilst the above wording seems to be in accordance with Art. 1 of the Directive,[31] though differently worded, there is at least one instance, noted below, where the Regulations do not seem correctly to implement the Directive.

The Regulations make a number of amendments to the Sale of Goods Act 1979 and parallel legislation. It has been thought appropriate to note these changes where the relevant provisions of these Acts are discussed in the text.

The provisions dealing with consumer guarantees are contained in reg. 15. Regulation 15(1) lays to rest the doubts (mentioned above) that existed at common law about the effectiveness of manufacturers' guarantees as legal documents.[32] Consumer guarantees now take effect at the time the goods are delivered as a contractual obligation owed by the guarantor under the conditions set out in the guarantee statement and the associated advertising. Because a guarantee is treated as a unilateral promise, rather than as a contract, in Scots law,[33] reg. 15(1) does not state that the guarantee forms a contract between the manufacturer and the buyer. Perhaps so far as the law in England and Wales is concerned, the use of the

---

25 Article 1(2)(a).
26 Article 1(2)(c). The definition of 'seller' in s. 61(1) of the Sale of Goods Act 1979 is unamended by the Regulations implementing the Directive, presumably because the drafters thought that the present definition is in accordance with the Directive.
27 Article 1(2)(d). Section 61(1) of the Sale of Goods Act 1979 is amended accordingly: '"producer" means the manufacturer of goods, the importer of goods into the European Economic Area or any person purporting to be a producer by placing his name, trade mark or other distinctive sign on the goods' – SI 2002/3045, reg. 6 – see p. 283.
28 Accordingly, the Regulations do not have any application to the extended warranties or guarantees discussed in the next section.
29 Article 1(2)(e).
30 Regulation 2.
31 The equivalent is to be found in Art. 1(2)(e) which defines 'guarantee' as:
    '... any undertaking by a seller or producer to the consumer, given without extra charge, to reimburse the price paid or to replace, repair or handle consumer goods in any way if they do not meet the specification set out in the guarantee statement or in the relevant advertising.'
32 See p. 298 above.
33 See Hogg (2001) 9 ERPL 337; Ervine 2003 SLT (News) 67, 70.

term 'contractual obligation' is also intended to signal that these documents are unilateral contracts, a possibility suggested above for analysing guarantees in non-consumer cases.[34]

As was pointed out above, manufacturers are under no legal obligation to provide guarantees, but, if they do, they are legally binding and must comply with the terms of the Regulations. In particular the guarantee must set out in plain intelligible[35] language the contents of the guarantee and the essential particulars necessary for making claims under the guarantee, notably the duration and territorial scope of the guarantee as well as the name and address of the guarantor.[36] If the consumer requests, the guarantee must be made available in writing or other durable medium available and accessible to him within a reasonable time.[37] Enforcement is by injunction, or in Scotland specific implement, applied for by the enforcement authority, i.e. the Director General of Fair Trading.[38] Where the guarantor is outwith the UK, this will give rise to the problems alluded to above.[39]

EXTENDED WARRANTIES OR GUARANTEES[40]

As noted above, these are usually offered with more expensive types of domestic electrical appliance such as fridges, washing machines and dishwashers. These are known in the trade as 'white goods'. Such warranties or guarantees are also offered with a range of 'brown goods' such as television sets and television recorders.[41] These contracts cover three types of risk: (1) the risk of product breakdown;[42] (2) the financial risk if an expensive part needs replacing; and (3) the risk that a suitable repairer may be difficult to find (the warrantor should offer a network of repairers who can carry out the repair quickly and efficiently). These contracts add to the remedies provided to the consumer under the Sale of Goods Act and the Sale and Supply of Goods to Consumer Regulations, but how much they add is problematic, because obviously at the outset the reliability of goods is unknowable, and many manufacturers' guarantees will cover most breakdowns that are likely to occur, and the retailers are liable for defects existing at the time of sale under the Sale of Goods Act. As noted previously, reputable retailers often themselves offer guarantees equivalent to manufacturers' warranties for a period that may even be longer than the manufacturer's guarantee. Where goods are heavily used by different persons, as will be the case with goods present in furnished lettings, they may well prove to need more

---

34 See p. 298.
35 Ibid., reg. 15(2). Where goods are offered within the UK this language must be English – reg. 15(5).
36 Ibid.
37 Ibid., reg. 15(3).
38 Ibid., reg. 2.
39 At p. 63.
40 For a useful discussion of this sparsely covered topic see Twigg-Flesner *Consumer Product Guarantees*, Ashgate, 2002, Ch 2.5, and [2002] 4 Web JCLI by the same author.
41 Leaving aside the situation under extended warranties, an important practical difference between the two categories of goods is that in the case of white goods, the manufacturer will usually have its own repair network, and the consumer will deal with that directly. In the case of brown goods, traditionally the dealer maintained its own repair facilities. Today, not all retailers maintain these facilities, and, where they do not, the manufacturer will provide a list of approved repairers.
42 This could be due to inherent lack of reliability, accidental damage, or simply wear and tear.

repair and maintenance than those in homes under single-family occupation. In this case these extended warranty contracts can offer a good way of making outgoings predictable, which will usually be what the owners in such cases want. It may also be that those on a tight budget will find that the predictability that these contracts offer is of value. In practice, however, it would appear that these contracts are offered by retailers whose margins on their sale can be very high, as a way of inflating their profits.[43] In fact, the claims made seem to be lower than for insurance generally.[44] In short, for most consumers they offer poor value.

A further cause of concern is that whereas the real nature of these contracts is that of insurance, many are not made with insurance companies. Where, as has happened, the warranty providers become insolvent and unable to provide the contracted services, the consumer has been left without recourse, and the premiums paid are unrecoverable. By contrast, if an insurance company were involved and became insolvent, the Financial Services Compensation Scheme, operated by the Financial Services Authority, would cover the case.[45]

In consequence of these concerns, in July 2002 the Competition Commission was asked to investigate and report on the existence or possible existence of a monopoly situation in relation to the supply of extended warranties for domestic electrical goods in the UK. Its report appeared in 2003.[46] Four overlapping characteristics of market behaviour suggested that, given the point of sale advantage that the offer of such contracts possesses, practices that might otherwise be unexceptionable could act to restrict or distort competition:

(a) Almost all extended warranties are purchased at point of sale; few consumers seek information on extended warranties prior to their purchase;[47] and consumers have little opportunity to consider alternatives to the extended warranty on offer at point of sale.

(b) Extended warranties on offer at point of sale are nearly always all from one provider, usually the retailer (or a third party which is the sole supplier to the retailer).

(c) There is generally no information available at point of sale on prices, or terms and conditions, of extended warranties available from alternative providers (such as manufacturers, insurers, credit card companies or others).

(d) There is generally no information available on domestic electrical goods' reliability, likely repair costs, or the probability of theft or accidental damage.

Based on their consultation on remedies and further consideration, the Competition Commission developed two packages of possible remedies.

---

43 Competition Commission Report 'Extended warranties on domestic electrical goods: a report on the supply of extended warranties on domestic electrical goods within the UK – Volumes 1, 2 and 3' accessible at website http://www.competition-commission.org.uk [accessed 30 December 2003]. See section headed 'EW [*i.e. Extended warranties*] pricing and profitability'.

44 Office of Fair Trading, 'Extended Warranties on Domestic Electrical Goods' 2002b, para. 4.31.

45 Ibid., para. 4.59.

46 See Competition Commission Report n. 43 above.

47 Or indeed intend to purchase an extended warranty before they go out to buy electrical goods. It is the element of surprise that tends to reinforce the retailer's point of sale advantage.

Package 1:

This was founded in three core aspects of their assessment: the need for consumers to know extended warranty prices at the time that they choose the domestic electrical goods; the need for consumers to have time to compare extended warranties and to have the opportunity to switch; and the need for consumers to have better information when deciding whether to buy an extended warranty. This package therefore comprises:

(a) the requirement to display the price of an applicable extended warranty along-side domestic electrical goods in store and in press advertisements and other publicity;
(b) cancellation and termination rights, including the right to cancel an extended warranty with a full refund within 45 days from purchase if no claim has been made (and the provision of a written postal reminder of the right to cancel), and the right to terminate an extended warranty and obtain a pro-rata monetary refund at any time;
(c) the provision of a written quotation in a standard format stating that the extended warranty remained available for 30 days on the same terms (which a customer purchasing an extended warranty must sign to confirm issue and acceptance), and the requirement that offers of a discount on domestic electrical goods prices contingent on the purchase of an extended warranty should be available to the consumer for the period of the quotation; and
(d) the requirement to make available to consumers a standard information leaflet set-ting out information on statutory rights, on the availability of extended warranties from other organizations, on the possible relevance of household insurance for some consumers, on cancellation rights and on the nature of the warranty.

Package 2 was founded on the belief that the point of sale advantage is so strong that it can only be addressed by delaying the purchase of extended warranties which provide cover for more than one year. Thus consumers would retain the convenience of being able to purchase an extended warranty (for one year only) at the same time as the domestic electrical goods, and would then have that one-year period to consider whether they wanted longer-term cover, and to shop around. Other providers would have the opportunity to market their extended warranties in this period. It comprises:

(a) a requirement that prevented point of sale providers selling an extended war-ranty providing cover for more than one year on the day of sale of the relevant domestic electrical goods or for 30 days thereafter (but there would be no restriction on the point of sale provider selling a one-year extended warranty at point of sale, so that consumers that wanted extended cover for, for example, accidental damage, can obtain it immediately);
(b) a requirement to display an applicable extended warranty price (the one-year extended warranty) alongside the display of the price of the domestic electrical goods;
(c) the same rights to cancel a one-year extended warranty or to terminate an extended warranty which may have been purchased after the 30-day prohibition as in package 1; and
(d) the same requirement for a standard information leaflet as in package 1.

The Competition Commission considered the likely effectiveness of the two pack-ages in remedying the adverse effects, and the restrictions and costs they would impose on providers and consumers, in order to assess the reasonableness both of each individual remedy and of the packages. Both packages would reduce the point of sale advantage which is at the heart of the Commission's adverse public interest finding. However, the majority felt that the impact of package 1 would be adequate to remedy the adverse effects and that package 2 would be excessively restrictive. It would appear that the government intend to accept this advice, and that package 1 will be adopted.[48]

48 Regulations giving effect to the Competition Commission's recommendations are expected in summer 2004 follow-ing consultations with interested parties.

Part III

THE DUTIES OF THE BUYER

17

THE DUTY TO PAY THE PRICE

PAYMENT OF THE PRICE

It is the duty of the buyer to pay the price of the goods he has bought or agreed to buy, and, in the absence of a contrary agreement, he is not entitled to claim possession of the goods unless he is ready and willing to pay the price in accordance with the contract. Whether it is necessary that the buyer should actually have tendered the price before he can insist on delivery has been discussed earlier.[1]

If no time is fixed for payment, the price is due immediately on the conclusion of the contract, provided that the seller is ready and willing to deliver the goods. Unless otherwise agreed, the seller is not bound to accept payment in anything but cash, and if he does accept payment by bill of exchange he is entitled (in the absence of agreement to the contrary) to retain the goods until the bill is met. But if the seller accepts payment by a bill not maturing immediately, he must be taken to have agreed to allow the buyer credit and cannot claim to retain the goods.

Where the seller accepts payment by cheque, bill of exchange or other negotiable instrument, this is normally treated as conditional payment only[2] and, if it is not honoured, the seller may sue either on the instrument as a contract in itself (in which case he will benefit from procedural advantages[3]) or he may sue on the contract of sale for the price of the goods.[4] It is theoretically possible for a cheque or other instrument to be accepted as absolute payment, so that the seller has no further claim if the instrument is not honoured, but an intention to accept in absolute payment must be strictly shown.[5] Similarly, agreement to furnish a letter of credit in payment for goods sold would not normally be treated as depriving the seller of his right to sue for the price if, in exceptional circumstances, the goods are delivered to the buyer but payment is not made under the credit.[6]

---

1 See above, p. 125.
2 In Scotland, see *Leggatt Bros* v *Gray* 1908 SC 67.
3 In particular, the buyer cannot set up defences based on breaches of contract by the seller in respect of defects in the goods or the like; in an action on a cheque, or other bill of exchange, the buyer must first pay, and then counter-claim for damages – see, e.g., *Jade International Steel Stahl und Eisen GmbH & Co KG* v *Robert Nicholas (Steels) Ltd* [1978] QB 917.
4 By s. 38(1)(b) of the Sale of Goods Act 1979 the seller is deemed to be an 'unpaid seller' when a bill of exchange or other negotiable instrument has been received as a conditional payment, and the condition on which it was received has not been fulfilled by reason of the dishonour of the instrument, or otherwise.
5 *Maillard* v *Argyle* (1843) 6 M & G 40.
6 *W J Alan & Co Ltd* v *El Nasr Export & Import Co* [1972] 2 QB 179; *Saffron* v *Société Minière Cafrika* (1958) 100 CLR 231; *E D & F Man Ltd* v *Nigerian Sweets & Confectionery Co Ltd* [1977] 2 Lloyd's Rep 50; see below, p. 445.

However, it has been held by the Court of Appeal that there is no general rule that all forms of payment deriving from a third party must be treated as conditional payments only.[7] Each method of payment must be considered in light of all the circumstances, and it was held in the same case that payment by credit card (issued by a third party[8]) is in many circumstances an absolute payment, so that the failure of the credit card company to pay the retailer does not mean that the retailer has any residuary claim against the customer. Further, the situation is not altered merely because the customer has not yet paid the credit card company in respect of the transaction in question. The card holder's liability is to pay the credit card company, and his liability is not affected by the relationship between the credit card company and the retailer.

There are several reasons why this method of payment differs in its legal results from payment by cheque. First, in the case of cheques there is no contractual relation between the seller who accepts the cheque, and the bank on whom the cheque is drawn, so if the cheque is not met the seller has no redress against the bank.[9] In the case of a credit card transaction, however, there is a prior contract in existence between the seller and the credit card company under which the company accepts liability for relevant credit card transactions, subject, no doubt, to compliance with the specified conditions. Furthermore, it is the seller who chooses to do business with the credit card company,[10] while it is the buyer who selects the bank with whom he banks, and whose cheques he uses. Secondly, the ordinary credit card transaction leaves the seller with no record of the buyer's address, so it is a reasonable implication that the seller does not expect under any circumstances to look to the buyer for the price.[11] Thirdly, it is the clear understanding of all parties that the customer can never be expected to pay twice for such a transaction, so if he has paid the credit card company, nobody expects the customer to be liable to pay the seller merely because the credit card company fails to pay the seller. Indeed, in the case in question this point was conceded by counsel, who merely argued that if the buyer had not yet paid the credit card company the seller ought to be able to intercept the money, as it were, and obtain payment direct from the buyer. But the court found this an unacceptable implication.

---

7 *Re Charge Card Services Ltd* [1988] 3 All ER 702. The analysis in this case would also, it would seem, apply where payment is by Provident 'cheque' and the like. These are treated for VAT purposes as sales at the full value of the voucher, notwithstanding that they will be discounted by the finance house – see *Kingfisher plc v Customs and Excise Commissioners*, 7 December 1999 (unreported). Arguably, therefore, if the finance house became insolvent, the seller would have no claim against the buyer for the price.

8 Some retailers issue their own credit cards, which can only be used in their own stores. If the issuing company and the seller are legally the same company, the position is obviously different. Presumably, in the event of the seller's insolvency, the credit terms contained in the credit card contract would control recovery of the purchase price from the buyer.

9 There is an important distinction between the common law rules concerning cheques and that of many civil law systems where cheques can operate as assignments of a part of the drawer's bank account so that the payee can acquire rights against the bank. In principle, there is a possibility that an equitable assignment might be found to accompany the delivery of a cheque if it could be established that that was the intention of the parties – see Farnsworth (1962) 36 Tulane LR 245.

10 This is the reason for the suggestion in n. 7 with regard to Provident cheques and the like.

11 By contrast, when a cheque is taken which is not covered by a cheque guarantee card, the usual practice is to require the drawer buyer to write his or her address on the back of the cheque.

Payment made by cheque backed by a bank guarantee card appears to be different from payment by credit card.[12] It is true that here also the bank accepts a direct obligation to meet the payment, assuming it falls within the terms of the bank's undertaking to honour such transactions,[13] but this obligation is clearly by way of guarantee of the buyer's obligation which remains primary.[14] But the point is anyhow of very little practical importance because the buyer can be sued on the cheque itself even if he cannot for some reason be sued on the underlying transaction.

Where payment is made by cheque and the cheque is later met, the payment relates back to the time when it was handed over.[15] Consequently, if the cheque reaches the seller on the date agreed, he cannot complain that there has been delay in payment, provided that it is met in due course. If the seller agrees that the price shall only be due on request, he is bound to afford a reasonable time to the buyer for payment after making his request,[16] and if he writes to the buyer asking him for his cheque the mere posting may be a sufficient payment, even if the cheque is stolen en route and cashed by the thief.[17]

Section 10 of the Act says:

(1) Unless a different intention appears from the terms of the contract, stipulations as to time of payment are not of the essence of a contract of sale. . . .

(3) In a contract of sale 'month' means prima facie calendar month.

It has been said that this section is 'seriously at odds' with ss. 27 and 28[18] but it is submitted that this is not in fact the case. Although it is obviously the duty of the buyer to pay the price agreed at the appointed time, the effect of s. 10 is to create a presumption that this duty is not a condition. In other words, a buyer who fails to pay the price on the day fixed is guilty of a breach of contract for which the seller may be able to recover damages if he has in fact suffered any, but he is not entitled to treat the contract as repudiated and resell the goods elsewhere.[19] Although this rule has been criticized on the ground that it extends compulsory credit to the buyer,[20] the seller can of course decline to deliver the goods until the buyer pays, and

---

12 See *Re Charge Card Services Ltd* [1987] Ch 150, 166 per Millett J, a point on which the Court of Appeal expressed no opinion.

13 In *First Sport Ltd* v *Barclays Bank plc* [1993] 3 All ER 789 it was held that where a cheque and cheque card were presented to a retailer by a thief, who forged the account holder's signature, the bank was liable to the retailer on its undertaking to honour the cheque. The statement on the card that it could only be used by an authorized signatory did not make the offer conditional on the cheque being signed by the authorized signatory.

14 See *Belshaw* v *Bush* (1851) 11 CB 191; *Edwards* v *Hancher* (1875) 1 CPD 111.

15 *Marreco* v *Richardson* [1908] 2 KB 584. But as between a trustee in bankruptcy and the payee the payment is only deemed to be made when the cheque is met: *In re Hone A Bankrupt, Ex Parte the Trustee* v *Kensington BC* [1951] Ch 85; cf. *Bolt & Nut Co (Tipton) Ltd* v *Rowlands, Nichols & Co Ltd* [1964] 2 QB 10.

16 *Brighty* v *Norman* (1862) 3 B & S 305.

17 *Norman* v *Ricketts* (1886) 3 TLR 182; *sed qu*: it does seem strange if the mere request of the seller that the buyer should mail him a cheque puts the seller at risk of the cheque being stolen. Does a request for a cheque invite the buyer to post an uncrossed cheque? Cf. also *Comber* v *Leyland* [1898] AC 524.

18 Stoljar (1955) 71 LQR 527, 539. Sections 27 and 28 of the Act are set out above, pp. 124 and 125.

19 *Payzu Ltd* v *Saunders* [1919] 2 KB 581. An important exception to this is that where the price is to be paid by means of a letter of credit opened by the seller, the failure to open the credit on the due date justifies immediate repudiation – see Chapter 24. And see also, for a similar case, *Warde (Michael I)* v *Feedex International* [1985] 2 Lloyd's Rep 289.

20 Stoljar (1955) 71 LQR 527, at 540.

there seems no reason why the seller should be entitled to repudiate the contract merely because the buyer is late in paying the price, perhaps by only a day or two. Indeed, even repeated failure by the buyer to pay on time (for example, in an instalment contract) may not justify repudiation by the seller, at least where there is no serious fear that the buyer will not pay at all.[21] It can make little difference to the seller in the usual way whether he is paid one day earlier or later, and if it does make a difference he should stipulate for a right of immediate termination, or of resale on default in payment by the buyer. Moreover, damages may be obtained for the late payment where additional costs have been imposed on the seller[22] and, anyhow, interest may be awarded to the seller by a court where he has been kept out of his money.[23]

In any event, the compulsory credit which the seller has to extend to the buyer is severely limited, for s. 48(3) provides that:

> Where the goods are of a perishable nature, or where the unpaid seller gives notice to the buyer of his intention to re-sell, and the buyer does not within a reasonable time pay or tender the price, the unpaid seller may re-sell the goods and recover from the original buyer damages for any loss occasioned by his breach of contract.

The indirect result of this subsection is to create an exception to s. 10(1) in the case of perishable goods, for in such a case the seller may resell the goods without notice to the buyer as soon as there is default in payment. As regards non-perishable goods, the period of compulsory credit can be brought to an end by the seller giving notice to the buyer of his intention to resell.

Although failure to pay the price at the appointed time is not *per se* a breach of condition or a material breach, it was at one time thought that if the delay was of inordinate length it might be possible to infer an intention to abandon the contract, so that the seller could thus be justified in reselling even without notice.[24] But it now seems established that this is not a permissible result unless there is some ground on which the court can find that the buyer has repudiated the contract, and that the seller has accepted that repudiation.[25]

It is desirable to stress again a point that has also been made before, that the mere fact that the buyer is under an obligation to pay the price of the goods does not necessarily mean that he can be *sued for the price* if he fails to pay. The seller's remedy against the buyer for non-payment of the price is often limited to an action for damages, as we shall see in Chapter 26.

---

21 *Decro-Wall International SA* v *Practitioners in Marketing Ltd* [1971] 1 WLR 361.
22 See *Wadsworth* v *Lydall* [1981] 1 WLR 598, approved by the HL in *President of India* v *La Pintada Compania Navigacion SA* [1985] AC 104, subject to the limitation that the damages must fall within the second rule in *Hadley* v *Baxendale* (1854) 9 Ex 341 by reason of special facts known to the defendant. In Scots law, see the authorities discussed in MacQueen, 1996 JR 295.
23 Under s. 3 of the Law Reform (Miscellaneous Provisions) Act 1934 in English law and at common law in Scotland (following 'wrongful withholding'). There is also a right to statutory interest under the Late Payment of Commercial Debts (Interest) Act 1998 (in both England and Wales, and Scotland), which applies when both the purchaser and the supplier are acting in the course of a business – s. 2(1).
24 See *Pearl Mill Co Ltd* v *Ivy Tannery Co Ltd* [1919] 1 KB 78 and the use made of this case in *The Splendid Sun* [1981] QB 694.
25 See *Allied Marine Transport Ltd* v *Vale do Rio Doce Navegacao SA (The Leonidas D)* [1985] 2 All ER 796, 806–7.

18

THE DUTY TO TAKE DELIVERY

Under ss. 27 and 28 of the Act (which have been set out earlier[1]) it is the duty of the buyer to accept and pay for the goods in exchange for the delivery of the goods by the seller. We have seen that the general rule is that it is for the buyer to take delivery of the goods from the seller's place of business and not for the seller to send the goods to the buyer. We have also seen that the time of delivery of the goods by the seller, or the time at which he is to have the goods ready for collection, is prima facie of the essence, but that the time for payment is prima facie not of the essence. The question now has to be answered whether the buyer's duty to take delivery at a particular time is of the essence.

The general rule seems to be that this is no more of the essence than the time of payment[2] and, consequently, the buyer's failure to take delivery of the goods at the time agreed does not by itself justify the seller in forthwith disposing of them to someone else. But, in accordance with ordinary principles of contract law, if the buyer accompanies his failure to take delivery with words or conduct which justify the seller in thinking that the buyer is repudiating the whole contract, the seller may accept the repudiation, and he is then free to resell the goods and to sue the buyer for damages for non-acceptance.

Moreover, if the contract is for the sale of goods of a perishable nature,[3] the buyer's duty to take delivery at the right time is of the essence, and default by the buyer justifies the seller in reselling immediately.[4] In this respect the position is also the same in regard to payment for, as we have seen, s. 48(3) enables the seller to resell perishable goods without notice to the buyer if the price is not paid when due.

It also seems that in a 'spot contract', that is a contract for almost immediate delivery and payment, there will be a breach of condition if the buyer fails to take delivery at the time agreed.[5] It may well be that in such a case there will be a contrary intention which makes the time of payment also of the essence.

It is important that the rules as to the times of payment and taking delivery should be the same, because otherwise difficulties would arise if the seller refused to allow the buyer to take delivery on the ground of non-payment. If the seller could transform a breach of the term as to payment into a breach of condition as to taking

---

1 See above, pp. 123 and 125.
2 *Woolfe v Horn* (1877) 2 QBD 355; *Saint v Pilley* (1875) LR 10 Ex 137; *Kidston v Monceau Iron Works Co Ltd* (1902) 7 Com Cas 82.
3 This rule probably also applies to a sale of livestock: *Harrington v Browne* (1917) 23 CLR 297.
4 *Sharp v Christmas* (1892) 8 TLR 687.
5 *Thames Sack & Bag Co Ltd v Knowles* (1918) 88 LJKB 585.

delivery by the simple expedient of exercising his lien, this would in effect turn every agreement for time of payment into a condition. If the time of payment is not of the essence, therefore, it would seem illogical (at any rate in ordinary circumstances) to hold that the time for taking delivery is of the essence. But there is nothing to prevent an express agreement that the time for taking delivery shall not be of the essence, but that the time for payment shall be.

It must be borne in mind that even where the time of delivery is not of the essence, s. 20 casts on the buyer, where there is delay in taking delivery, the risk of accidental destruction of, or damage to, the goods which might not have occurred but for the delay.

Where a contract provides for delivery 'as required', the buyer may be under a duty to give notice of his requirements to the seller as a preliminary to actually taking delivery.[6] Where a buyer contracts to take delivery of goods as speedily as possible although no time limit is actually imposed, he is under an obligation to remove the goods within a reasonable time.[7] And in such circumstances the measure of damages for breach may, in an appropriate case, be the benefit to the buyer rather than the loss to the seller.[8]

If the contract provides for the delivery of the goods in instalments and the buyer wrongfully refuses to accept one or more of them, the question whether the seller may treat the whole contract as repudiated is dealt with by s. 31(2). As will be seen later,[9] this merely provides that the answer to this question depends on the terms of the contract and all the circumstances of the case. In practice, the issue usually involves breach by the seller rather than the buyer, and it has been held that the question to be considered is the gravity of the breach in relation to the whole contract and the probability of its recurrence.[10]

Where the contract does not provide for delivery by instalments, there is nothing in the Act corresponding to s. 30(1) entitling the seller to repudiate the contract if the buyer refuses to accept some part of the goods only. Whether such refusal amounts to repudiation, therefore, depends on general principles of contract law, that is on whether the breach goes to the root of the contract. Where a buyer refused to take 728 sheep out of a total contract quantity of over 6,000, and he was entitled to refuse 448 sheep, it was held that the seller could not repudiate the whole contract.[11]

It should be noted that in some contracts, especially f.o.b. contracts, the buyer's duty to take delivery often involves many incidental obligations, for example the duty to nominate a ship for the transport of the goods, etc. Breach of these duties usually discharges the seller as a necessary consequence.[12]

---

6 *Jones* v *Gibbons* (1853) 8 Ex 920 – see above, p. 133.
7 *Penarth Dock Engineering Co Ltd* v *Pounds* [1963] 1 Lloyd's Rep 359.
8 Ibid.
9 See below, p. 501.
10 *Maple Flock Co Ltd* v *Universal Furniture Products (Wembley) Ltd* [1934] 1 KB 148 – see below, p. 502.
11 *Francis* v *Lyon* (1907) 4 CLR 1023.
12 Because it will be a breach of condition – see, e.g., *Bunge Corp* v *Tradax Export SA* [1981] 1 WLR 711. As to f.o.b. contracts, see below, p. 420.

Part IV

====

THE EFFECTS OF THE CONTRACT

19

THE TRANSFER OF PROPERTY

THE MEANING OF 'PROPERTY'

Part III of the Act is divided into two sections, headed 'Transfer of Property as Between Seller and Buyer' and 'Transfer of Title'. It must be said at once that there is something rather curious about this terminology. The term 'property', defined by s. 61 as 'the general property in goods', is commonly used by lawyers to signify title or ownership, and in everyday usage this terminology is also applied to the sale of goods. Yet the Act talks of a transfer of property as between seller and buyer, and contrasts this with the transfer of title.[1] It is trite learning, however, that the distinguishing feature of property rights is that they bind not merely the immediate parties to the transaction, but also all third parties. How, then, can there be such a legal phenomenon as a transfer of property *as between seller and buyer*?[2] Either there is a mere transfer of rights and duties from seller to buyer, or there is a transfer of property which affects the whole world. Nor is it possible to adopt the solution of saying that 'property' is here used in its medieval sense of right to possession[3] when at least it would make sense to talk of a transfer as between seller and buyer. The Act itself precludes the adoption of this view because it lays down the clear rule that the buyer's right to possession depends either on payment of the price or on the granting of credit, not on the passing of the property. In other words, the mere fact that the property in the goods has passed to the buyer does not confer on him a title good against the whole world, nor does it confer on him the right to possession as against the seller. What then is this peculiar legal conception which the Act calls 'the property in the goods'? The answer can only be given by considering what precisely are the consequences which flow from the passing of property. What rights does the passing of the property give to the buyer?

In the first place, then, what is the position of the buyer if he wishes to obtain possession from the seller? The answer, which has already been intimated, is that he can only do so if he pays the price or if the seller sees fit to grant him credit.[4] Nor can the buyer avoid this consequence under English law by framing his action in tort and

---

1 For an interesting discussion of dual terms, see Ho (1997) 56 CLJ 571.
2 See Lawson (1949) 65 LQR 362, especially at 359–60. Cf., for a different view, Battersby and Preston (1972) 35 MLR 268. See also critique in Ho, n. 1 above. For Scottish perspectives, see Smith, *Property Problems in Sale* (1978); Reid, *The Law of Property in Scotland* (1996), paras 624 *et seq*.
3 This is a loose translation of the complex medieval concept of 'seisin'.
4 Section 28 makes delivery conditional on payment of the price – see p. 125. Indeed, a buyer who takes the goods without the consent of the seller, when he has no right to possession, may well be guilty of theft. See *R v Boardman* (1987) 9 Cr App R (S) 74, where the only question was as to the suitability of a compensation order.

suing for conversion, basing his claim on the fact that the goods are now his goods. The reason for this is that the action for conversion will only lie at the hands of someone with an immediate right to possession and this the buyer does not have until he tenders the price.[5] Again, if the buyer resells the goods before obtaining possession, the sub-buyer can only obtain possession on the same terms as the original buyer, that is to say by payment of the price, unless the original seller has assented to the second sale.[6] The same applies if the buyer pledges the goods instead of selling them. In all these cases the buyer's property avails him nothing, because the position would be precisely the same even if no property had passed.

The same is true if the buyer goes bankrupt before delivery of the goods and payment of the price. The seller cannot be compelled to deliver up the goods to the trustee in bankruptcy, and be relegated to his right to prove in the bankruptcy for the price, even though the property in the goods has passed to the buyer. Indeed, quite the contrary, the law goes out of its way to protect the seller from the bankruptcy of the buyer by conferring on him the right of stoppage in transit should the buyer go bankrupt after the seller has dispatched the goods to him, but before the buyer has received them.[7]

Suppose, next, that the buyer has actually obtained the possession of the goods. Once again the practical effect of the passing of the property is somewhat limited because s. 25(1) of the Act enables the buyer in possession to pass a good title to a third party, binding on the first seller, whether or not the property had already passed to the original buyer. Moreover, it is arguable that s. 25(1) has the strange result that the buyer, even if in possession, and even if he has the property, cannot pass a good title to a *mala fide* transferee.[8] However, it is true that if the goods are delivered to the buyer with a stipulation that the seller reserves title and property is only to pass on payment, the seller may be able to recover the goods in the event of the buyer's bankruptcy.[9] Moreover, the practice of incorporating these 'reservation of title clauses' is widespread. This then is a case where the passing (or non-passing) of the property may have important practical effects, and indeed, many modern cases dealing with the passing of property hinge on these reservation of title clauses. But as we shall see later, these clauses cause a great deal of trouble, and some of them are void unless registered under the Companies Act 1985, because they amount in substance to the grant by the buyer of a charge by way of security, falling under s. 395 of that Act.[10]

What then is the position if the seller, being still in possession of the goods, resells them to a third party, whether rightfully or wrongfully? Again the answer is that the transfer of property has little effect, for s. 24 enables the seller who is in possession to pass a good title to a *bona fide* transferee, even though the transfer may be wrongful as against the first buyer. And since the Privy Council's decision in *Pacific Motor*

---

5 Ibid.
6 Section 47 – see below, p. 373. But if the buyer has passed documents of title to the third party the seller's rights are defeated – see below, p. 404.
7 For the right of stoppage in transit, see below, p. 459 *et seq.*
8 But as to this, see below, p. 407 *et seq.*
9 *Aluminium Industrie BV v Romalpa Aluminium Ltd* [1976] 1 WLR 676. See further as to these reservation of title clauses, below, p. 470.
10 See, e.g., *Re Bond Worth* [1980] Ch 228, below, p. 478. Amendments to these provisions of the Companies Act 1985 are effected by the Companies Act 1989, which is not yet in force, however – see p. 477, n. 122.

Auctions Pty Ltd v *Motor Credits (Hire Finance) Ltd*,[11] it is immaterial in what capacity the seller retains possession. Of course if the goods are actually delivered to the buyer and then returned to the seller to hold as bailee he will not be able to pass a good title to a third party, but once again the same result would follow if property passed on delivery instead of by mere agreement.

The next case to be considered is that in which goods are sold and the property passes to the buyer but, for some reason, the seller remains in possession. If the seller becomes insolvent, can the buyer claim the goods by virtue of his property? As against the seller himself, or a liquidator or receiver, the answer at common law and in Scots law is prima facie, yes, but in England sometimes the Bills of Sale Acts or the Companies Act operate to invalidate the sale or the buyer's rights in these circumstances.[12] So this is again a case where the passing of property may have important practical consequences. And here too there are a number of modern cases demonstrating the important practical effects which attach to the passing of property in this situation, and the difficulties which arise when the property has not passed, or cannot pass because the goods remain in bulk, and no physical separation of the buyer's goods from the remainder has yet been effected.[13] So also, the buyer's chances of obtaining equitable or specific relief seem to be greater if property has passed to him, especially if the seller claims no proprietary or possessory rights of any kind over the goods. A buyer's right to goods of which he is undisputed owner will be specifically enforced against a seller who proposes to convert them and pay damages in lieu.[14]

Next, reference must be made to three[15] other important results which generally follow from the passing of property. The first of these is that the risk in the goods prima facie passes with the property. The second consequence is that generally speaking the seller is not entitled to sue for the price of the goods unless the property has passed. If the buyer repudiates the contract before this happens the seller's remedy is prima facie an action for damages for non-acceptance. Yet even here one cannot say that these consequences follow naturally or logically from the passing of the property. Roman law had much the same rules as English law so far as risk is concerned, yet it refused to recognize that property passed merely by virtue of a contract of sale. Nor is there any necessary or logical connection between the right to sue for the price and the passing of property. Indeed, it will be suggested later[16] that a number of unfortunate consequences follow from the present rules on this subject.

The next consequence is that the passing of property may in some circumstances determine who is the proper plaintiff to sue a third party who has damaged or destroyed the goods, for example when they are en route to the buyer. But property

---

11 [1965] AC 867 – see below, p. 395.
12 For the Bills of Sale Acts which do not apply in Scots law, see above, p. 20. If the seller is a company rather than a private individual, the buyer's property may have to be registered under s. 395 of the Companies Act 1985 (as amended by the Companies Act 1989) as a charge on goods within the meaning of s. 396(1)(b) (as amended) – these amendments are not yet in force.
13 As to bulk sales and changes effected by the Sale of Goods (Amendment) Act 1995, see p. 346 *et seq.*
14 *Redler Grain Silos Ltd* v *BICC Ltd* [1982] 1 Lloyd's Rep 435 – see below, p. 561.
15 Formerly, a fourth consequence was that, when the property in specific goods had passed to the buyer, he could no longer reject them for breach of condition. The law on this point was altered by the Misrepresentation Act 1967, s. 4 – see below, p. 507.
16 See below, p. 484 *et seq.*

alone will rarely be decisive. Usually, it is combined, either with a right to possession,[17] or with a contractual right against the third party, such as a carrier. Prima facie, the person who is entitled to sue in respect of goods damaged at sea is usually the person who holds the bill of lading,[18] and that person has a contractual right both against the shipowner and also the property. So it is rarely necessary to ask whether it is the one or the other which gives him the right to sue. But a contractual right without property will not usually enable the plaintiff to sue because he will not have suffered any damage.[19] And it has been decided by the House of Lords that a right of property (or a possessory right) is necessary to establish a cause of action in tort against someone who has been responsible for damaging or destroying goods.[20] In particular, in circumstances where the buyer does not have the benefit of the Carriage of Goods by Sea Act 1992,[21] where goods are lost or damaged while en route from a seller to a buyer, the buyer will now have no right to sue the carrier in tort unless the property had passed to him before the damage or loss occurred, or he has a possessory title to the goods.[22] In most cases of carriage by sea this will not matter, because the buyer will have contractual rights against the carrier, either because he made the contract of carriage (or it was made on his behalf),[23] or because the Carriage of Goods by Sea Act 1992 applies. But there are some unusual circumstances in which these contractual rights are absent, and in that case it will now be a matter of considerable practical importance whether property has passed to the buyer, and, if so, when.[24]

To sum up, it may be said that the most important practical consequences which flow from the mere passing of the property are as follows:[25]

1   If the property in the goods has passed to the buyer he will generally have a good title to them if the seller becomes insolvent while the goods remain in the seller's possession.

2   If the goods are delivered subject to a reservation of title (or property) by the seller, the seller *may*[26] have a good title to the goods should the buyer become insolvent.

---

17   *Lord* v *Price* (1874) LR 9 Ex 54. Cf. *Lee Cooper* v *C H Jeakins & Sons Ltd* [1967] 2 QB 1.

18   The Carriage of Goods by Sea Act 1992 also confers rights on holders of certain other types of shipping document – see pp. 427–8.

19   *The Albazero* [1977] AC 774. But there can be exceptional cases – see *Obestein Inc* v *National Mineral Devp't Corp Ltd* [1987] 1 Lloyd's Rep 465; *Linden Gardens Trust* v *Linesta Sludge Disposals Ltd* [1994] 1 AC 85. In both of these cases *The Albazero* was distinguished and the old case of *Dunlop* v *Lambert* (1839) 6 Cl & F 600 applied. *Dunlop* v *Lambert* was a Scots case, reported also at (1839) 1 Macl & Rob 663.

20   *Leigh & Sillivan Ltd* v *Aliakmon Shipping Co Ltd (The Aliakmon)* [1986] AC 785; *Transcontainer Express Ltd* v *Custodian Security Ltd* [1988] 1 Lloyd's Rep 128. The actual outcome of *Leigh & Sillivan* would now be different because of the Carriage of Goods by Sea Act 1992, but the principle stated in the text is unaffected. In Scotland, see, e.g. *Nacap Ltd* v *Moffatt Plant Ltd* 1987 SLT 221.

21   Or the situation is not covered by one of the conventions governing international carriage by rail (COTIF Convention: CIM Rules Art. 54), road (CMR Convention Art. 13) and air (Amended Warsaw Convention Arts 13, 14 and 24).

22   *Margerine Union GmbH* v *Cambay Prince Steamship Co Ltd (The Wear Breeze)* [1969] 1 QB 1; *Transcontainer Express Ltd* v *Custodian Security Ltd* [1988] 1 Lloyd's Rep 128, 138.

23   It is not unusual that the circumstances may indicate that the seller made the contract of carriage as agent for the buyer – see, e.g., *Texas Instruments Ltd* v *Nason (Europe) Ltd* [1991] 1 Lloyd's Rep 146.

24   It must be noted, however, that in the international carriage of goods by rail, road and air, the relevant conventions (see n. 21 above) state who is entitled to claim against the carrier, and the rights under these conventions do not depend on ownership of the goods – see, e.g., *Texas Investments Ltd* v *Nason (Europe) Ltd* [1991] 1 Lloyd's Rep 146.

25   Another result is that in time of war, the ownership of a cargo for prize purposes depends upon the property, but this is obviously of limited application.

26   See text at n. 9.

3   The right to sue a third party for damage to, or loss of, the goods may depend on who has the property.

4   The risk passes prima facie when the property passes.

5   Generally speaking, the seller can only sue for the price if the property has passed.

It will be observed that only the first three of these consequences affect third parties and that, although the passing of the property may have important results as *between buyer and seller*, its effect on third parties in ordinary circumstances is minimal.[27] Still, a buyer or seller, relying on his property, against an insolvent seller or buyer, may well have a title good against a liquidator or trustee in bankruptcy claiming through the seller or buyer. Of course, parties claiming through a contracting party are not treated by the law as third parties in this sense, although in another, more realistic sense, trustees in bankruptcy and liquidators should perhaps be treated as third parties.[28] Indeed, one of the chief problems of the existing law is that matters relating to the passing of property are treated as though they only concern the parties to the contract, and can be adjusted entirely according to the intention of the contracting parties. Yet, as we have now seen, by far the most important results of the passing of property relate to the rights of trustees in bankruptcy and liquidators who in a realistic commercial sense represent third party creditors of buyer or seller. So it is a serious question whether contracting parties should be permitted to adjust the passing (or non-passing) of the property in a contract of sale to protect themselves against the risk of the other party's insolvency, without any regard to the interests of third party creditors. At present the rights of third parties are occasionally protected by the provisions of the Companies Act requiring the registration of charges, but the right to property under a contract of sale is not usually regarded by the law as a charge in the relevant sense.[29]

In earlier editions of this work it was suggested that the Sale of Goods Act adopted the policy of allowing property to be transferred by contract alone, and then contained many elaborate provisions designed to reverse the practical effects of this policy. It was also suggested that the law would have been simpler if the Sale of Goods Act had adopted the rule of Roman (and Scots common) law that the property in the goods passes on and not before delivery. Had this been done, all the special rights of the unpaid seller might have been unnecessary, as also would ss. 24 and 25. But it is today perhaps less clear that this is so than it seemed at the time when this book was first written. The truth is that the problems concerned cannot be eliminated by changing the rules about the transfer of property. Questions will still arise (for instance) as to who is the proper plaintiff to sue a third person when goods are damaged en route; questions will still arise about risk, and the right to sue for the price. Above all, questions will still arise about the claims of a buyer against an insolvent seller (and those claiming through him) as well as about the claims of

---

27 Lawson (1949) 65 LQR 352 at 359 went so far as to say: 'If we look at the other effects [than passing of risk] of the transfer of property as between seller and buyer in the common law systems, we shall see that they are for the most part, if not entirely, illusory.' As we have seen, this was an exaggeration, and anyhow there have been marked signs of an increase in the importance attached to the passing of property in recent years.

28 Under §544 of the US Federal Bankruptcy Code, trustees in bankruptcy are in the position of lien creditors.

29 See below, p. 476 *et seq.*

a seller against an insolvent buyer (and likewise those claiming through him). These claims must be disposed of by the law somehow. One way of doing it is the traditional common law way of trying to use a concept like 'property' to decide most of the problems, while recognizing that many exceptions must be made. This has the disadvantage, as indicated above, that the exceptions sometimes seem to eat up the rule.

Alternatively, the law might have abandoned the 'conceptual' approach altogether and adopted the 'specific issue' approach, that is, have dealt with each specific question, such as the buyer's ability to pass title to a third party, the passing of risk, liability for the price, etc., without reference to the passing of property. This is the approach of Article 2 of the Uniform Commercial Code which is now in force throughout nearly all of the United States.[30] But the alternative approach, while it has many attractions, fails to provide answers to new problems unforeseen by the law, or indeed to problems newly created by subsequent laws. For the 'specific issue' approach avoids general solutions by use of organizing concepts like property, and therefore may offer no solution at all (except perhaps by way of arguments by analogy) to new problems. The traditional common law approach has at least the virtue that in principle there is always a way of meeting new problems, namely by looking to see who has the property in the goods at the relevant moment, and treating that person as owner, with consequences which are assumed to meet the new problems.

A good illustration of this ability of the traditional approach to meet new problems is to be found in some cases concerning conflicts over fuel oil on board chartered vessels. In *The Span Terza*[31] the House of Lords held that a dispute between a charterer and a mortgagee of the ship in question could be resolved by simply asking whether the fuel oil (which had been bought and paid for by the charterers) had been sold to the shipowners so that property had passed to them. It was held that it had not, so that the charterers still owned the oil and had a prior right to that of the mortgagees, who could only claim through the owners. Editor Adams considers that in most cases the 'specific issue' approach leads to clearer answers. After all, under the Uniform Commercial Code the issue would probably have been resolved simply by asking if the mortgagee had a perfected security interest covering the fuel oil under Art. 9. The need to resort to such devices as reservation of title clauses[32] does not arise, for the same reason. It is the deficiencies of our law of sale of goods that makes it useful to have a workhorse concept such as the 'property in goods.'

THE PASSING OF PROPERTY: I. SPECIFIC GOODS

The exact moment at which the property passes depends upon whether the goods are specific or unascertained, and this cleavage is so fundamental that the subject will be dealt with under two separate headings.

---

30 It is enacted in all states except Louisiana, which adopted the Code Napoleon in the early nineteenth century.
31 [1984] 1 Lloyd's Rep 119.
32 See Ch. 19.

Section 17 of the Act is as follows:

(1) Where there is a contract for the sale of specific or ascertained goods the property in them is transferred to the buyer at such time as the parties to the contract intend it to be transferred.

(2) For the purpose of ascertaining the intention of the parties regard shall be had to the terms of the contract, the conduct of the parties, and the circumstances of the case.

Although this section only applies to specific or ascertained goods, it is well settled that, as a matter of general contract law, the principle expressed in subsection (2) also holds true for unascertained goods.[33]

Section 18 (which applies to both specific and unascertained goods) goes on to state:

Unless a different intention appears, the following are rules for ascertaining the intention of the parties as to the time at which the property in the goods is to pass to the buyer.

And the section then sets out five Rules for ascertaining the intention of the parties.

In practice, these Rules are of the greatest importance, for the parties often do not have any clear intention, still less express any, as to the passing of the property.[34] Moreover, it appears that even if the parties do express such an intention it will have no effect if the property has already passed in accordance with the rules laid down in s. 18. In *Dennant v Skinner and Collom*,[35] the plaintiff sold a car to X by auction. X, who was a swindler, gave a false name and address and asked to be allowed to take the car away in return for his cheque. The plaintiff allowed X to do this on obtaining his signature to a document which stated that the title to the vehicle would not pass until the cheque was met. X sold the car, which was ultimately resold to the defendant. Hallett J held that the intention of the parties as expressed in this document was too late to prevent the property from passing since it had already done so on the fall of the hammer,[36] in accordance with Rule 1 of s. 18.

Rule 1

This Rule is as follows:

Where there is an unconditional contract for the sale of specific goods, in a deliverable state, the property in the goods passes to the buyer when the contract is made, and it is immaterial whether the time of payment or the time of delivery, or both, be postponed.

This Rule gives rise to a number of difficult questions.

---

33 *Ginzberg v Barrow Haematite Steel Co* [1966] 1 Lloyd's Rep 343. But this is subject to the qualification laid down in s. 16 – see below, pp. 332 and 339 *et seq.*

34 *Smyth & Co Ltd v Bailey Son & Co Ltd* [1940] 3 All ER 60, 67 per Lord Wright.

35 [1948] 2 KB 164.

36 It is odd that the defendant did not rely on s. 25(1) which would appear to have been decisive of this part of the case. It may be that this case turned on the fact that the sale was by auction. It might, however, have been argued on behalf of the seller that the intention of the transaction was that the seller released his lien on the vehicle in consideration of the revesting of property in him – see *Hain SS Co Ltd v Tate & Lyle Ltd* [1936] 2 All ER 597 (as to the unpaid seller's lien, see p. 452). In a sale in a shop it seems that no contract is made (and hence no property passes) until the mode of payment is agreed: see *Ingram v Little* [1961] 1 QB 31, 49; and in a supermarket, no property passes until the price is actually paid: *Lacis v Cashmarts* [1969] 2 QB 400, 407; *Davies v Leighton* [1978] Crim LR 575. These remarks may need qualification where the sellers advertise their willingness to accept payment by credit card as in Internet sales – see *Re Charge Card Services Ltd* [1988] 3 All ER 702, but so far as risk of loss is concerned, the effect of the amendment of s. 32 is that in the case of consumer sales, risk of loss after goods are delivered to a carrier, is the seller's – see p. 359.

'Unconditional contract'

In the first place, what is an unconditional contract within the meaning of this Rule? This may mean either (a) a contract not subject to a condition precedent or subsequent (*Scoticé*, suspensive or resolutive conditions), or (b) a contract not containing any conditions in the sense of essential stipulations, the breach of which gives the buyer the right to treat the contract as repudiated. At first sight it seems too clear for argument that the former of these interpretations is the correct one. Throughout the Act, the term 'conditional contract' is used in this sense. Thus s. 1(2) says: 'A contract of sale may be absolute or conditional', which clearly means subject to a condition precedent, for otherwise there would be no point in the contrast. Again, Rules 2, 3 and 4 of s. 18 all deal with contracts subject to conditions precedent, so that the natural inference is that Rule 1, by contrast, deals with contracts not subject to such conditions. Furthermore, and this is surely conclusive, it is difficult to see how there can be any such thing as an unconditional contract if 'condition' here means 'essential stipulation'. Every contract must contain at least some essential stipulations and most contracts contain a great many. In every contract of sale there must be some fundamental conditions or obligations, namely that of the seller to deliver the goods to the buyer, and that of the buyer to accept the goods and pay the price. If the presence of these obligations makes all contracts of sale conditional within Rule 1 it is deprived of all effect.

Yet despite these arguments the question has not been free from difficulty, though it is thought that these difficulties have now been set at rest in England at least. The trouble arose largely from s. 11(4) of the Act which, in its original form (then s. 11(1)(c) of the 1893 Act), deprived the buyer of the right to reject goods for breach of condition 'where the contract is for specific goods, the property in which has passed to the buyer'. If the term 'unconditional contract' in Rule 1 was given its natural meaning, the result appeared to be that in the vast majority of sales of specific goods there was no real right to reject for breach of condition at all. The property passed when the contract was made and at that very same time the right to reject was lost under s. 11(1)(c). This was such a startling result that the judges, consciously or unconsciously, strove to avoid it by giving a forced interpretation to the words 'unconditional contract' in Rule 1. Thus in *Varley* v *Whipp*,[37] to which reference has already been made, it was held that the sale of a reaping machine was not an unconditional sale despite the fact that it was clearly not subject to any conditions precedent, but no reasons were given for this part of the decision. Similarly in *Ollett* v *Jordan*,[38] a case dealing with the meaning of 'unconditionally appropriated' within Rule 5, it was held that the property in fish did not pass to the buyer owing to the fact that there was a breach of the implied condition that the fish was fit for human consumption, although there was no condition precedent. Finally, in *Leaf* v *International Galleries*,[39] and again in *Long* v *Lloyd*,[40] there were dicta which supported the conclusion reached in *Varley* v *Whipp*.[41] Fortunately these difficulties now

---

37 [1900] 1 QB 513.
38 [1918] 2 KB 41.
39 [1950] 2 KB 86.
40 [1958] 1 WLR 753.
41 [1900] 1 QB 513.

seem to be a matter of past history. The Misrepresentation Act 1967 s. 4 repealed the words formerly appearing in s. 11(1)(c), 'where the contract is for specific goods the property in which has passed to the buyer'. As a result, there is now no need for judges to give an unnatural construction to the words 'unconditional contract' in s. 18 Rule 1 in order to avoid depriving a buyer of his right to reject goods.

The issue has not been discussed by the Scottish courts, but it has been suggested that (a) the contract need only be unconditional in the sense of having no conditions relevant to the passing of property rather than having no conditions at all; and (b) the conditions in question must be suspensive (rendering the contract an agreement to sell) rather than resolutive; if they are the latter, the contract may nonetheless be regarded as 'unconditional' for the purposes of Rule 1.[42]

The most important kind of condition which may need to be satisfied before property passes is a condition as to payment. Express terms may make the passing of property conditional on payment even after delivery.[43] Similarly, such a term may be readily implied in circumstances where payment is normally required before delivery, for example in a supermarket.[44] Other types of conditional contract are dealt with later.[45]

Specific goods

The next question which arises under Rule 1 is as to the meaning of the term 'specific goods'. It has already been observed that this term does not necessarily mean the same thing wherever it appears in the Act, despite the single definition by s. 61 of specific goods as goods 'identified and agreed upon at the time a contract of sale is made'. At any rate, so far as the passing of property is concerned, it seems settled that future goods can never be specific, although they may possibly be sufficiently specific to come within the doctrine of frustration.

The meaning of 'identified' still remains to be examined. In most cases this gives rise to no difficulty – it is usually obvious enough when the goods are identified by the contract. But sometimes difficulty arises because general descriptive words are used which are not entirely easy to apply. In *Kursell* v *Timber Operators & Contractors Ltd*,[46] the plaintiff sold to the defendants all the trees in a Latvian forest which conformed to certain measurements on a particular date, the buyers to have 15 years in which to cut and remove the timber. Almost immediately afterwards the Latvian Assembly passed a law confiscating the forest. The Court of Appeal held that the property in the trees had not passed to the defendants as the goods were not sufficiently identified, since not all the trees were to pass but only those conforming to the stipulated measurements.[47] An Australian decision provides an interesting

---

42 Reid, *The Law of Property in Scotland* (1996), para. 631.
43 *Aluminium Industrie BV* v *Romalpa Aluminium Ltd* [1976] 1 WLR 676 – see below, p. 470 *et seq.* Although generally speaking a cheque operates only as a conditional discharge for the obligation to pay the price (see p. 307), this will not usually prevent the property passing under Rule 1 – see *Anderson* v *Havana Horse and others*, 18 August 1999 (unreported).
44 See *Davies* v *Leighton* [1978] Crim LR 575.
45 See below, p. 327 *et seq.*
46 [1927] 1 KB 298. Cf. *Lord Eldon* v *Hedley Bros* [1935] 2 KB 1 – sale of haystacks held to be of specific goods though buyer not bound to take mouldy or unmerchantable hay.
47 Note that the Sale of Goods (Amendment) Act 1995 would not affect the situation in a case like this, because even if the buyer had paid for a quantity of goods, it is questionable whether the bulk was sufficiently identified to constitute an identified bulk.

contrast to this case. In *Joseph Reid Pty Ltd v Schultz*,[48] a sale of all the millable or marketable hardwood timber on a certain site was held to be a sale of specific goods. In *Commissioners of Customs & Excise v Everwine Ltd*[49] as liquor was delivered to a bonded warehouse it was allocated a 'rotation number'. The totality of alcohol held by the Everwine Ltd was sold by a series of contracts to a specific buyer. It was held that property had passed applying *Wait & James v Midland Bank Ltd*.[50] However, where release notes did not cover all of the claimant's stock under the specified rotation numbers, the goods were unascertained and property could not pass.[51]

Deliverable state

The third question arising out of s. 18 Rule 1 is the meaning of the term, 'deliverable state'. Under s. 61(5):

> Goods are in a 'deliverable state' within the meaning of this Act when they are in such a state that the buyer would under the contract be bound to take delivery of them.

It is to be noted that s. 61(5) does not purport to give a comprehensive definition of 'deliverable state'. In particular, it does not say that, if the buyer would not be bound to take delivery of the goods, then the goods are *not* in a deliverable state. The buyer is not bound to take delivery of defective goods, but it does not follow that all defective goods are not in a deliverable state within the meaning of this provision. If this were so, property would never pass in defective goods,[52] but it seems to be generally accepted that defects do not prevent property passing.[53] (If the buyer rejects the goods, property revests in the seller.) Section 61(5) was probably intended to cover the case where the goods could not be said to be in a deliverable state physically, yet the buyer had agreed to take delivery as they stood. This means that the words 'deliverable state' cannot be construed by reference to the definition of delivery in s. 61 as 'a voluntary transfer of possession'. The possession of goods can probably always be transferred in law if the parties intend to transfer it, no matter what the physical condition of the goods may be. If this was what 'deliverable state' meant, therefore, goods would probably always be in a deliverable state.

The authorities on this point are not of great assistance, because there has been a tendency to interpret the words literally by reference to the physical moveability of the goods. In *Underwood Ltd v Burgh Castle Brick & Cement Syndicate*[54] the plaintiffs sold a condensing engine to the defendants f.o.b. The engine weighed over 30 tons and was cemented to the floor. The engine had to be dismantled after being detached from the floor, a task which of course fell on the sellers under the f.o.b. contract, and which was expected to take about two weeks and to cost about £100 (in 1922). It was held that the engine was not in a deliverable state and that the property

---

48 (1949) SR (NSW) 231.

49 [2003] EWCA Civ 593.

50 (1926) 24 Ll Rep 313 – see p. 343 below.

51 See also *Re Stapylton Fletcher Ltd* [1994] 1 WLR 1181, which was distinguished – see p. 346 below.

52 In the first edition Professor Atiyah argued that this was indeed so. But this argument was largely a response to the difficulties created by s. 11 of the 1893 Act which have now been removed by s. 4 of the Misrepresentation Act 1967. See below, p. 507.

53 Reid, *The Law of Property in Scotland* (1996), para 631, also accepts this view.

54 [1922] 1 KB 343.

had not passed when the contract was made.[55] But the judges also thought that there was anyhow a sufficient contrary intention to be inferred from the fact that clearly some element of risk was involved in the work of dismantling the engine and dispatching it to the buyer, so it seemed that the property was not intended to pass on the sale.

Philip Head & Son Ltd v *Showfronts Ltd*[56] was a case under s. 18 Rule 5(1) which also contains the phrase 'in a deliverable state'. Here the plaintiffs sold carpeting to the defendants, which they were required to lay. The carpet was delivered to the defendants' premises, but was stolen before it could be laid. It was held that the carpet was not in a deliverable state, apparently because it was a heavy bundle and difficult to move. But importance was attached to the fact that the carpet had to be laid by the sellers. This seems a better ground for holding that the property had not passed, because the mere weight of the goods cannot mean they are not in a deliverable state – after all, goods of enormous weight are in fact commonly delivered under contracts of sale.

Factors indicating a contrary intention

As we have seen, express agreement that property is not to pass, for instance, until payment, is effective in law. In consumer cases, such 'conditional sale' agreements have long been known. But they can also be found in commercial contexts.[57] Where there is no express provision, it is a matter of inference whether the prima facie operation of Rule 1 is displaced.[58]

There is no doubt that the rule that property passes when the contract is made does not fit easily into the pattern of consumer sales.[59] It is therefore not surprising to see the suggestion being made that in modern times very little is needed to rebut the inference that property passes on the making of the contract.[60] It seems that in an ordinary sale in a shop, property does not pass at least until the parties have agreed on the mode of payment;[61] and on a sale in a supermarket, property does not pass until the price is paid.[62] At a petrol filling station, property in the petrol passes when it is put into the vehicle's petrol tank,[63] but that is not a case of a sale of specific goods so much as of unascertained goods, so it is dealt with later.

---

55 Compare *Broadcrest CD Ltd* v *Ruddick & ors* 5 May 2000 (unreported) where the machines in question were not fixed, but only needed to be disconnected into their constituent parts, held to be in a deliverable state and that property had passed on payment of the price. Similarly *Anderson* v *Havana Horse (UK) Ltd or ors* 31 July 1999 (unreported) Mercedes with crack in its windscreen and some scratches on its wheels (both of which were to be fixed before delivery to the buyer) in a deliverable state.

56 [1970] 1 Lloyd's Rep 140.

57 See the *Romalpa* case, above, p. 12, and below, p. 470 *et seq*.

58 The onus is on the seller to displace the statutory presumption – *Higgins* v *Farmer*, 8 December 1999 (unreported).

59 See below, p. 358.

60 *R V Ward Ltd* v *Bignall* [1967] 1 QB 534, 545 per Diplock LJ.

61 *Ingram* v *Little* [1961] 1 QB 31, 49. But this case did not concern a sale in a shop, and it is not easy to see why the contract should not be held to be made as soon as the sale is agreed, on the assumption that the basic position is that the buyer must pay cash unless the seller agrees to accept some alternative.

62 *Lacis* v *Cashmarts* [1969] 2 QB 400, 407; *Davies* v *Leighton* [1978] Crim LR 575; cf. *Watts* v *Seymour* [1967] 2 QB 647.

63 *Edwards* v *Ddin* [1976] 1 WLR 943; *Re Charge Card Services Ltd* [1988] 3 All ER 702, 706 – see below, p. 341.

Despite the fact that Rule 1 states that it is immaterial for purposes of passing of property whether the time of payment or the time of delivery, or both, be postponed, it is not possible to ignore such postponement completely. For, if payment or delivery or both be postponed, this may be some indication of a contrary intention which excludes the operation of Rule 1 altogether. In an Irish case,[64] where the plaintiff had agreed to trade in his old car with the defendants in part-exchange for a new one, and was allowed to retain and use the old one pending delivery of the new one,[65] it was held that property and risk had both passed to the defendants. The decision seems a curious one, and it is thought that on such facts a court would be fully justified in finding a contrary intention which would negative an intention to pass property before delivery.[66] It certainly seems quite wrong that the risk should be held to be on the buyer while the seller still has the use of the car.

Another factor which may point to a contrary intention is any specific agreement on the transfer of risk. As will be seen, the risk in the goods prima facie passes with the property. If the risk has passed, therefore, this may be some indication that the property has also passed.[67] Conversely, where the risk is still on the seller this may be evidence that the property has not passed.[68] But it is possible to draw precisely the opposite inference from the passing of risk. In *Re Anchor Line Ltd*,[69] the Court of Appeal inferred that the property in goods had not passed because there was a specific clause in the contract placing the risk upon the buyer, and (the Court reasoned) if the property had passed such a clause would not have been necessary. One can only say, therefore, that the proper inference to be drawn from an agreement placing the risk on the buyer must depend on all the circumstances of the case.[70]

An obligation to insure placed upon one party by the contract is also an indication that he bears the risk,[71] and it has been said that this is an indication that he also has the property. But once again, the proper inference to be drawn must depend upon all the circumstances of the case, for it could well be that the intention is simply that one party insures the other's risk.

In trying to determine what is the correct inference to draw from a contractual provision about the transfer of risk, or an obligation to insure, the following appear to be relevant factors to bear in mind. First, it seems that, where the seller advises the

---

64 *Clarke* v *Michael Reilly & Sons* (1962) 96 ILTR 96.
65 As to whether a part-exchange is a sale at all, see above, p. 10.
66 The decision seems to have been influenced by an admission by the defendants that they would have regarded it as a breach of contract had the plaintiff sold his car to a third party. This may well have been correct but it does not follow that property had passed. There are good policy reasons for holding that the 'seller' in such a case bears the risk, because he should have the burden of looking after the goods, and is the more likely carrier of insurance cover – see *Martin* v *Melland's* 283 NW 2d 76 (1979), a case on Art. 2 of the Uniform Commercial Code. Although the UCC is explicit on this policy consideration, the court in that case could within the terms of the Code have reached the same conclusion as the Irish court.
67 *The Parchim* [1918] AC 157, 168. But this decision can no longer be treated as supporting any general inference that the passing of risk (especially in shipped goods) means that property has also passed: *Mitsui & Co Ltd* v *Flota Mercante Grancolombiana SA* [1989] 1 All ER 951.
68 *Carlos Federspiel & Co SA* v *Charles Twigg & Co Ltd* [1957] 1 Lloyd's Rep 240, 255; *President of India* v *Metcalfe Shipping Co* [1970] 1 QB 289.
69 [1937] Ch 1.
70 For a review of some earlier conflicting cases and dicta on the inference to be drawn from such a stipulation, see the Australian case of *McPherson, Thorn, Kettle & Co* v *Dench Bros* [1921] VLR 437.
71 *Allison* v *Bristol Marine Ins Co Ltd* (1876) 1 App Cas 209, 229 per Blackburn J.

buyer to insure, this is some indication that risk and property have passed to the buyer.[72] Such advice does not suggest that the seller retains any property in the goods, as might be argued if he actually stipulated for insurance. Secondly, there may be cases in which a seller may retain some interest in the goods even where the property has passed, for example he may still have a lien or some sort of charge on the goods. In such circumstances the seller may very well wish to require the buyer to insure the goods in order to protect his own interest, and this would be no indication that risk had not passed, although the property remained in the seller.[73] Conversely, where the contract requires the buyer to insure the goods, but the seller would have, on the face of it, no interest in the goods if the property and risk had passed from him, the correct inference may well be that property and risk have not passed.

Another kind of case in which the presumption contained in Rule 1 would normally be rebutted is a contract for the sale of goods and land together. For example, where a person contracts to sell a house, together with some furnishings, the presumption that property passes on the making of the contract would be rebutted. The normal inference in such a case would be that the property is only to pass on conveyance.[74] Indeed, where (contrary to the normal English practice) the vendor is not fully paid on conveyance and the price is to be paid by instalments, the property may not even pass on delivery of possession.[75]

Where goods are to be supplied and installed or fitted by the seller in a building or construction so that the goods will become fixtures in the technical sense, the property does not normally pass until the work of installation has been completed.[76] But cases of this nature are more likely to involve unascertained goods, so this point is dealt with more fully later.[77]

Rules 2 and 3

In contrast to Rule 1 which deals with the unconditional sale of specific goods, Rules 2, 3 and 4 deal with the conditional sale of specific goods. But unlike Rule 1 which deals with all unconditional contracts, Rules 2 to 4 deal only with certain types of conditional contract, so there is in fact no general or residuary rule dealing with conditional contracts not falling within Rules 2, 3 or 4. (Section 19 also deals with certain conditional contracts, but as these mostly concern unascertained goods, this section is dealt with under the next heading.) So a conditional contract which does not fall within Rules 2, 3 or 4 (or s. 19) must be dealt with under the very general terms of s. 17 which simply require the court to ascertain the presumed intention of the parties by taking account of all the circumstances of the case. Rules 2 and 3 are as follows:

---

72 See, e.g., *Donaghy's Rope and Twine Co Ltd v Wright, Stephenson & Co* (1906) 25 NZLR 641.
73 This is certainly the case, for example, in hire-purchase contracts. In the case of vehicles, and other expensive goods, such contracts always require the hirer to insure.
74 *Commissioner of Stamps v Queensland Meat Export Co Ltd* [1917] AC 624. The same result could be arrived at by holding that the sale is conditional on conveyance and so not within Rule 1 at all.
75 *Warren v Forbes* [1959] VR 14.
76 *Clark v Bulmer* (1843) 11 M & W 243; *Aristoc Industries Pty Ltd v R A Wenham (Builders) Pty Ltd* [1965] NSWR 581.
77 See below, p. 335.

Rule 2. Where there is a contract for the sale of specific goods and the seller is bound to do something to the goods, for the purpose of putting them into a deliverable state, the property does not pass until the thing is done, and the buyer has notice that it has been done.

Rule 3. Where there is a contract for the sale of specific goods in a deliverable state, but the seller is bound to weigh, measure, test, or do some other act or thing with reference to the goods for the purpose of ascertaining the price, the property does not pass until the act or thing is done, and the buyer has notice that it has been done.

It is not clear why Rule 2 is confined to cases where the seller is bound to do something to put the goods 'into a deliverable state'. Thus it seems that the Rule would not apply where the seller has agreed to repair the goods, for example to overhaul a second-hand car which the buyer has agreed to purchase 'as is'. On the other hand, such a sale may still be a conditional sale, but one to which none of the Rules in s. 18 would apply. In such a case, the court may simply fall back on s. 17 and hold that property is not to pass until the repairs have been done as this is the presumed intention of the parties.[78] In a Scottish case about the sale of growing potatoes, the seller undertook to lift and put the goods in pits at maturity, and to cart them to the railway station. It was held that the goods were in a deliverable state when put into the pits, the obligation of carting relating only to actual delivery.[79]

Rule 3 requires little comment. It clearly deals with cases where the passing of the property is conditional upon the performance of some act with reference to the goods. The presumption embodied in this rule is probably somewhat weaker than those in Rules 1 and 2 because it is easy to imagine circumstances in which the parties intend the property to pass at once, especially if the price has been paid. So, for instance, where a seller sold haystacks for delivery at the buyer's convenience and the price was paid at once, though liable to adjustment when the hay was weighed on delivery, it was held that the property passed at once.[80] Similarly, it is probable that the property would be held to have passed if the goods have been delivered, although the seller has still to do something to ascertain the price, for example to look up the list price in a catalogue. If the seller is not *bound* to do some act to the goods to ascertain the price, Rule 3 is inapplicable.[81]

At all events, Rule 3 only applies to acts to be done by the seller. In *Nanka Bruce v Commonwealth Trust Ltd*,[82] A sold cocoa to B at an agreed price per 60 lb, it being arranged that B would resell the goods and that the cocoa would then be weighed by the purchasers in order to ascertain the total amount due from B to A. It was held that the weighing did not make the contract conditional and that the property passed to B before the price was ascertained.

---

78 *Anderson* v *Ryan* [1967] IR 34, 37.
79 *Cockburn's Tr* v *Bowe* 1910 2 SLT 17. See also *Brown Bros* v *Carron Co* (1898) 6 SLT 231 and *Paton's Trs* v *Finlayson* 1923 SC 872.
80 *Lord Eldon* v *Hedley Bros* [1935] 2 KB 1. See also *Kennedy's Tr* v *Hamilton* (1897) 25 R 252. It is very common for export contracts for the sale of goods in bulk to provide for final adjustment of the price on weighing (or measuring) the goods on discharge from the vessel. It seems clear that this would not prevent property passing at the usual time, namely on transfer of the bill of lading – see below, p. 426. (These contracts would normally be for the sale of unascertained goods and so not within Rule 3, anyhow.)
81 *Woodburn* v *Motherwell* 1917 SC 533.
82 [1926] AC 77.

Rule 4

Rule 4 deals with two different types of transaction altogether, although they are very similar to a conditional sale and may become a sale in due course; they are:

> When goods are delivered to the buyer on approval or on sale or return or other similar terms . . .

There is little authority on the meaning of the terms 'sale on approval' or 'sale or return', and it has been suggested that they are very different transactions in commercial function, and perhaps also in intent.[83] One possible difference is that a sale on approval may legally amount to a contract of sale with a condition subsequent which permits the buyer to rescind the transaction if he finds the goods unsuitable,[84] while a 'sale or return' transaction may not even be a contract of sale at all, but rather an offer to sell, accompanied by delivery, which must actually be accepted before it becomes a contract of sale (i.e. up to that point it is a mere bailment). The Act does not differentiate between them, however, and as the Rule also applies to transactions on 'other similar terms', it may be that no difference was intended. It has at least been held that there is no difference between a transaction where the goods are delivered to a prospective buyer who may keep or return the goods, on the one hand, and cases where the goods are delivered to a dealer who is expected either to resell or return the goods, on the other hand. Both these transactions fall within Rule 4.[85] In Scotland, a sale or return has been taken to be a sale, albeit subject to a suspensive condition.[86]

Rule 4, having set out the transactions to which it applies, then goes on to say that in these transactions the property passes to the buyer:

> (a) When he signifies his approval or acceptance to the seller or does any other act adopting the transaction.

It has been held that any action by the buyer inconsistent with his free power to return the goods is an act adopting the transaction within the meaning of the Rule. Thus where a person obtains goods on sale or return or similar terms and then resells or pledges them, this is an act adopting the transaction, and the third party is therefore protected against the seller. Nor is it material that the first buyer is guilty of a criminal offence.[87] An express stipulation that the property is not to pass until the goods are paid for is effective to protect the seller, because this is evidence of a contrary intention which overrides Rule 4.[88]

---

83 See generally, Adams, Ch. I, in *Essays for Clive Schmitthoff*, ed. J.N. Adams, Professional Books, 1983. Note also *Brown v Marr Barclay & Co* (1880) 7 R 427.
84 But cf. *Cranston v Mallow* 1912 SC 112, in which it was held that when a horse was sold under a warranty and with a week's trial, the contract was not a sale on approval, because the buyer's right to return the goods was not unqualified but dependent on non-fulfilment of the warranty.
85 *Poole v Smith's Car Sales (Balham) Ltd* [1962] 2 All ER 482. See also *Michelin Tyre Co Ltd v Macfarlane (Glasgow) Ltd* 1917 2 SLT 205, HL, distinguishing between sale and return and agency.
86 *Ross v Plano Manufacturing Co* 1903 11 SLT 7, 9. Cf. *Bell Rannie & Co v White's Trustee* (1885) 22 SLR 597.
87 *Kirkham v Attenborough* [1897] 1 QB 201; *London Jewellers Ltd v Attenborough* [1934] 2 KB 206; *Genn v Winkel* (1911) 28 TLR 483.
88 *Weiner v Gill* [1906] 2 KB 574; *R v Eaton* (1966) 50 Cr App Rep 189. Cf. in Scotland, *Bryce v Ehrmann* (1904) 7 F 5.

Rule 4 tells us what acts of the buyer cause property to pass, but it does not indicate what he must do if he decides to return the goods. Under Rule 4(b), property passes if the buyer retains the goods beyond a certain time without giving 'notice of rejection'. Clearly, this cannot be 'notice of rejection' in the same sense as this term is used in relation to defective goods, simply because in the case of sale or return contracts what suffices for this purpose will be controlled by the terms of the original contract, which will frequently spell out what is to be done; whereas when goods are rejected as defective, the contract will rarely say what is to be done. In *Atari Corporation* v *Electronics Boutique Stores*,[89] the Court of Appeal held that in the absence of a specific provision controlling the matter, in a sale or return contract any intimation to the 'seller' that the 'buyer' does not wish to exercise his option to purchase suffices. In modern commercial conditions, where goods are bought centrally and distributed around a chain of retailers, it will often be impractical to return the goods at the time of the notice, or even to specify what goods are being returned. In *Atari* the Court of Appeal recognized this commercial reality. It is sufficient if after giving notice, the 'buyer' collects in the goods within a reasonable time so that the 'seller' can resume possession of them.[90] This case also supports the view, set out above, that sale or return contracts are contracts of bailment up to the time property passes. This is a matter of some importance, because if the passing of property and time of payment are separate, the goods will remain at the seller's risk notwithstanding payment by the buyer. So if the 'buyer' must pay for the goods by 30 November, but has until 31 January to reject them,[91] the goods will remain at the 'seller's' risk until 31 January. Since these are in reality financing transactions, time of payment merely indicates the point of time up to which the 'seller' is prepared to finance the 'buyer's' inventory. It is submitted that Rule 4 still controls the passing of property,[92] and therefore risk, in the absence of contract provisions dealing with this.

In modern times, the extensive use of 'reservation of title' clauses (under which goods are delivered but the seller reserves title until he is paid[93]) sometimes leads to a transaction which is rather similar to a sale on approval or a sale or return, although these are more likely to be transactions relating to unascertained goods to which, strictly, Rule 4 has no application. Where goods are delivered to a buyer under a reservation of title clause, and he is authorized by the seller to use the goods even before payment, such use may – if it deprives the goods of their identity – amount to an act which necessarily transfers the property to the buyer, despite the terms of the reservation of title clause. So, for instance, resin delivered to a buyer who used it in a matter of days in the manufacture of chipboard, was held to have ceased to exist as a separate commodity, despite a reservation of title clause,[94] and a similar result was reached when leather was sold which was intended to be used in the making of handbags.[95] It was held that as soon as the buyer started to work

---

89 [1998] 1 All ER 1010.
90 Ibid. pp. 1023–24.
91 As in *Atari*.
92 See Adams (1998) 61 MLR 432.
93 See below, p. 470 *et seq.*
94 *Borden (UK) Ltd* v *Scottish Timber Products Ltd* [1981] Ch 25.
95 *Re Peachdart Ltd* [1983] 3 All ER 204. But cf. *Hendy Lennox Ltd* v *Grahame Puttick Ltd* [1984] 2 All ER 152.

the leather, the property passed to him, despite the reservation of title clause. These decisions can be explained by saying that the reservation of title clause must be read subject to the paramount intent of the parties that the buyer is to be entitled to use the goods in the process of his business, and that this intent is inconsistent with any real intention that property is to remain in the seller after the process has begun. None of these cases actually refers to s. 18 Rule 4, presumably because they related to unascertained goods. It was suggested in previous editions that the result in these cases is in line with Rule 4 in that they appear to be examples of acts 'adopting the transaction' under this Rule if the contracts are characterized as transactions 'on sale or return or other similar terms'. This is true in a sense, but perhaps is slightly mis-leading, because a fundamental difference between retention of title and sale or return transactions is that usually the buyer in the former type of transaction is committed to buy, whereas the whole point of the latter arrangement is that he is not. The legal basis of retention of title clauses under the Act is s. 19 (as already explained), and the rule expressed in s. 17 that property passes when the parties intend it to.

A slightly different problem arises where the buyer under a sale or return trans-action sells the goods to a third party despite a clause providing that property is not to pass until payment. Although such a clause overrides s. 18 Rule 4 because it shows a contrary intention as to the time when property is to pass, there are many other ways in which the third party buyer may be protected. For example, the seller may be caught by the doctrine of estoppel,[96] or by the provisions of s. 2 of the Factors Act 1889.[97] In *Weiner v Harris*,[98] the plaintiff sent jewellery to F, a retailer, under a standing contract, whereby the property was to remain in the plaintiff until the goods were sold or paid for. F pledged the jewels in question with the defendant. Cozens-Hardy MR posed the following question: 'Was the transaction the ordinary well-known transaction of goods taken on sale or return, or was it a transaction under which F was constituted agent for sale, with author-ity to sell, and bound to account to his principal for the proceeds of such sale?' In the former case, s. 18 Rule 4 would be overridden by a contrary intention and the seller would be protected. In the latter case, F would be a mercantile agent enabled by s. 2 of the Factors Act to pass a good title to a buyer or pledgee. The Court of Appeal had no doubt that in this case F was a mercantile agent, and the defendants were protected.

It has been held that a person who has obtained goods on sale or return cannot pass a good title to a third party under s. 25(1) of the Act, if there is a contrary inten-tion which excludes the operation of Rule 4.[99] The reason for this is not very clear, but it seems to depend on the view that such a person is not, within the meaning of s. 25(1), a person who has 'bought or agreed to buy goods'. He has an option to pur-chase, but that is all; until he exercises his option by accepting the goods or adopting the transaction, there is no sale. But there is one difficulty about this analysis, and that is that the buyer can 'adopt' the transaction without communicating his

---

96 On estoppel, see below, p. 372.
97 On the Factors Act, see below, p. 385.
98 [1910] 1 KB 285.
99 *Edwards v Vaughan* (1910) 26 TLR 545.

intention to the seller. If this were really a mere option, it would seem that the buyer would have to communicate his acceptance to the seller. It may be, therefore, that the right view is that there must actually be a contract of sale of goods and *then* an act adopting the transaction before the property passes.[100] In Scotland it has been held that goods on sale or return do not pass to the buyer's trustee in sequestration.[101]

The second alternative given by Rule 4 is:

> (b) If he does not signify his approval or acceptance to the seller but retains the goods without giving notice of rejection, then, if a time has been fixed for the return of the goods, on the expiration of that time, and, if no time has been fixed, on the expiration of a reasonable time.

Thus if a time has been fixed for the return of the goods, the buyer is deemed to have exercised his option to buy them if he retains them after this time. Here again, therefore, the transaction may be completed without a communication of acceptance. It is clear that an unsolicited delivery of goods with an offer to sell them does not have this effect,[102] and it is therefore arguable that delivery on sale or return must be more than a mere option or offer to sell. The buyer may, of course, waive the time limit and accept the goods at once by so informing the seller, or by doing some act which adopts the transaction.

If the goods are not returned within a reasonable time because of the defaults of employees of the buyer, the property will be held to have passed to him even though he may have given instructions for the return of the goods.[103] But the sub-rule does not apply if the goods are detained by someone for whose acts the buyer is not responsible. Thus where goods were delivered to X on sale or return within one week, and two days later they were seized by execution creditors of X, who retained them until after the week was over, it was held that the property had not passed under Rule 4(b).[104]

THE PASSING OF PROPERTY: II. UNASCERTAINED GOODS

The meaning of the term 'unascertained goods' has already been discussed and it has been seen to cover three possibilities: first, goods to be manufactured or grown by the seller; secondly, purely generic goods; and, thirdly, an unidentified portion of a specified bulk or whole.[105] Although the Act does not distinguish between these three types of unascertained goods, the rules as to the passing of property and risk may well differ in the three cases. In particular, it will be seen that the passing of risk in an unidentified portion of a specified whole may sometimes take place at a different time

---

100 Rule 4 does not start by saying 'Where there is a contract for the sale of specific goods' etc., so it appears to apply to a delivery of the goods even where there is no contract then in being – see generally Adams, above, n. 83.
101 *Macdonald* v *Westren* (1888) 15 R 988.
102 Indeed, the goods may become the property of the buyer without payment under the Unsolicited Goods and Services Act 1971.
103 *Poole* v *Smith's Car Sales (Balham) Ltd* [1962] 2 All ER 482.
104 *In re Ferrier* [1944] Ch. 295.
105 See p. 85.

from the usual. And, secondly, it will be seen that what amounts to an 'unconditional appropriation' – which is what is usually required to transfer the property – in one type of sale may not be so in another.

The fundamental rules are laid down by ss. 16 and 17. Section 16 provides that:

> Subject to section 20A below, where there is a contract for the sale of unascertained goods no property in the goods is transferred to the buyer unless and until the goods are ascertained.

Then s. 17 (which has been set out above[106]) provides that on a sale of specific or ascertained goods, the property passes when the parties intend it to pass, and that intention is to be gathered from the terms of the contract, the conduct of the parties and the circumstances of the case. Section 18 Rule 5 then says that, subject to a contrary intention:

> (1) Where there is a contract for the sale of unascertained or future goods by description, and goods of that description and in a deliverable state are unconditionally appropriated to the contract, either by the seller with the assent of the buyer, or by the buyer with the assent of the seller, the property in the goods thereupon passes to the buyer; and the assent may be express or implied, and may be given either before or after the appropriation is made.

Relationship of ss. 16, 17 and 18

It is clear that s. 16 must be the starting point in considering the passing of property in a sale of unascertained goods. The section lays down the fundamental rule that subject to s. 20A the property cannot pass until the goods are ascertained, and this appears to be a mandatory provision which takes precedence over the intention of the parties.[107] Indeed, s. 17, which deals with the intention of the parties, only operates in a sale of 'specific or ascertained goods'. There was thus no provision covering the passing of property in goods which are still unascertained for the good reason that the Act clearly did not contemplate this as a legal possibility at all. No matter what the parties may have intended, property could not pass until the goods are ascertained.

> Whatever the intentions of the parties, where there is a contract for the sale of unascertained goods, no property can pass until the goods are ascertained: see s. 16 of the Sale of Goods Act 1893.[108] Once ascertainment has taken place, the passing of property depends on the intention of the parties and the circumstances of the case: see s. 17.[109]

This rule still applies to contracts made before 19 September 1995 when the Sale of Goods (Amendment) Act 1995 came into force. After that date the position is regulated by the new s. 18 Rule subsections 5(3) and (4), but it is submitted that the last

---

106 See above, p. 321.
107 Before amendment by the Sale of Goods (Amendment) Act 1995, which added s. 20A, this led to certain problems – see p. 343 *et seq*.
108 Now of course the 1979 Act: there is no change on this point.
109 *Karlshamns Oljefabriker* v *Eastport Navigation Corp* [1982] 1 All ER 208, 212 per Mustill J. See also *Hayman & Son* v *McLintock* 1907 SC 936.

sentence of this dictum is still relevant. We now turn to an examination of the wording of s. 18 Rule 5.

Deliverable state

The meaning of this term, which also appears in Rule 1, has already been discussed in connection with that Rule.

Unconditional appropriation

Under the terms of Rule 5, an 'unconditional appropriation' is the usual method by which the property will pass. Put very briefly, the requirement of unconditional appropriation means that some ascertained and identified goods must be irrevocably attached or earmarked for the particular contract in question.[110] Subject to the question of assent, which is dealt with below, the property in the goods will then pass to the buyer. So the first and most vital question is, how do unascertained goods become unconditionally appropriated to the contract? One of the commonest and simplest ways in which this happens is by delivery. If the seller actually delivers to the buyer goods answering the contract description, this is an appropriation which, assuming it to be unconditional, and subject to the question of assent, will thereupon pass the property to the buyer, at least if the goods are delivered to the correct destination.[111]

Rule 5(2) gives another illustration of an unconditional appropriation:

> Where, in pursuance of the contract, the seller delivers the goods to the buyer or to a carrier or other bailee . . . (whether named by the buyer or not) for the purpose of transmission to the buyer, and does not reserve the right of disposal, he is to be taken to have unconditionally appropriated the goods to the contract.[112]

This sub-rule, like the whole of s. 18, had to be read subject to the unamended s. 16 because it was clear that if the seller delivered the goods to a carrier still mixed with other goods, no property could pass, because the goods were still unascertained, despite what would otherwise amount to an unconditional appropriation. So, for instance, in *Healy* v *Howlett & Sons*,[113] the defendant ordered 20 boxes of mackerel from the plaintiff, a fish exporter carrying on business in Ireland. The plaintiff dispatched 190 boxes and instructed the railway officials to earmark 20 of the boxes for the defendant and the remaining boxes for two other consignees. The train was delayed before the defendant's boxes were earmarked, and by the time this was done

---

110 For example, in the case of bottled drinks sold on licensed premises, property in both the bottle and its contents pass when the bartender removes the cup and hands the bottle to the customer. Property in the bottle also passes where the contents are poured into a glass and the bottle disposed of by the bartender – *R* v *Environment Agency, ex parte Valpak* [2002] Env LR 36.

111 If the goods are not delivered to the correct destination, they remain at the seller's risk – see *CTN Cash and Carry Ltd* v *Gallagher Ltd* [1994] 4 All ER 714.

112 See also s. 32 (1), but note that this latter provision does not apply in the case of consumer sales – s. 32(4).

113 [1917] 1 KB 337. Conversely, if the seller delivers goods to the buyer with the intention that the goods will lose their identity by being mixed with other goods, it is almost impossible to hold that property has *not* passed: *Borden (UK) Ltd* v *Scottish Timber Products Ltd* [1981] Ch 25; *South Australian Insurance Co* v *Randell* (1869) LR 3 PC 101. But see below, p. 470, as to the *Romalpa* case.

the fish had deteriorated. It was held that the property in the fish had not passed to the defendant before the boxes were earmarked and that they were, therefore, still at the seller's risk when they deteriorated. Because it was not possible to say which of the boxes belonged to the buyer until the earmarking had been done, no identified or ascertained goods had yet been appropriated to the contracts of each individual buyer.[114]

Apart from the particular instance given in Rule 5(2), the meaning of the term 'unconditional appropriation' has been considered on many occasions by the courts. The possibility of the appropriation being conditional is discussed further below. Here we shall concentrate on the concept of appropriation itself. Despite the fact that the word 'appropriated' has been said to be 'a term of legal art [which] has a certain definite meaning',[115] it is extremely difficult to define it with precision. One thing at least was clear, that where an unidentified part of a bulk was sold there could be no appropriation until there was a severance of the part sold from the rest and thus no passing of property. *Healy* v *Howlett & Sons*[116] is one authority for this. Another is *Laurie & Morewood* v *John Dudin & Son*.[117] Here the defendants were warehousemen who were in possession of some maize belonging to A. A sold part of it to B and B resold it to the plaintiffs, who obtained a delivery order and lodged it with the defendants. A, not having been paid by B, stopped delivery, and the plaintiffs then brought an action of detinue against the defendants. The Court of Appeal disposed of the case on the short ground that without severance no property could have passed to the plaintiffs because the goods were not identified. The outcome of similar cases occurring today will be unaffected by the 1995 Act.

The question of appropriation has arisen in a number of different situations. One common type of case concerns builders or contractors who leave a contract uncompleted (often because they have become insolvent) and disputes then arise as to the ownership of materials brought onto the site by the builder. Of course if the site itself belongs to the builder and he has merely contracted to sell or convey the completed building, it is almost impossible that the property in such materials could pass to the client before the building is completed and the land conveyed to the buyer. But if the site is already owned by the client, or the builder is working on renovation or repairs to an existing building, the owner of the site may claim that the property in the materials has passed to him, while the builder's creditors may dispute this, and claim that the property remains in the builder.

As we have already seen, where goods are to be supplied and installed or fixed by the seller in a building or construction, so that the goods will become fixtures in the technical sense, becoming attached to the land or a building on the land, the general rule or presumption is that property does not pass until the work of installation has been completed, or anyhow, until the materials are 'affixed to or in a reasonable sense

---

114 As to the passing of property in such fact situations under the Sale of Goods (Amendment) Act 1995, see p. 346. Of course, what ultimately was at issue in *Healy* v *Howlett* was the passing of risk, and, for the reasons explained above, the questions of the passing of risk and passing of property need to be considered separately. It is certainly possible that had the goods been specific in *Healy* v *Howlett*, they might have travelled at the seller's risk even though property in them had passed to the buyer.

115 *Re Blyth Shipbuilding Co Ltd* [1926] Ch 494, 518 per Sargant LJ.

116 [1917] 1 KB 337.

117 [1926] 1 KB 223. See also *Wardar's (Import and Export) Co Ltd* v *W Norwood & Sons Ltd* [1968] 2 QB 663.

made part of the corpus'.[118] This is often explained by saying that the contract is for work and materials in such a case, rather than a sale of goods. Hence, if the contract is clearly intended to be for the sale of goods to be afterwards installed,[119] even by the seller, the Sale of Goods Act will apply, and property may pass on the making of the contract under Rule 1 if the goods are specific goods. It seems best, however, to explain these differences as resting on the intention of the parties and the nature of the transaction rather than on its technical classification. Whether it is a contract for the sale of goods or for work and materials is itself immaterial.[120]

So also, an ordinary supply of goods to a building site for ultimate incorporation in a building or construction will usually be a simple sale of goods, and property will normally pass on delivery, if not sooner, though subject to any express contractual conditions which are indeed quite normal in such cases. For instance, in *Santer-Automation Ltd v H C Goodman (Mechanical Services) Ltd*[121] the plaintiffs were subcontractors who had brought materials onto a site for incorporation into a building being constructed by the defendants, the main contractors, for the Property Services Agency, a public body. The main contractors became insolvent, and the Agency determined the contract with them, and proposed to use the materials and equipment brought onto the site by the plaintiffs. The plaintiffs claimed that the property in these materials was still vested in them under their conditions of work, but it was held that these conditions had never been accepted, and that the Agency's conditions governed because the plaintiffs must have known of these conditions when they contracted with the main contractors. The Agency's conditions provided that the property in materials and equipment brought onto the site vested in them, so here the question of appropriation under Rule 5 simply did not arise.[122] The passing of property was governed by express contractual provision, not by the Act.

Where a seller, who is not himself in any way involved in the construction works, delivers goods to a site in pursuance of a contract with a contractor, the passing of property will depend on the contract between them. Prima facie the delivery would be an appropriation of the goods under Rule 5, but the position is today often complicated by reservation of title clauses which enable the seller to claim title until he is paid.[123] Again, therefore, the question of appropriation would not strictly arise, although it may well be that the courts would decline to uphold a reservation of title where the goods have actually been incorporated into the building works.[124]

The question of appropriation has also arisen in a number of shipbuilding cases. In such cases, as in the case of all goods to be manufactured by the seller, the general

---

118 *Seath v Moore* (1886) 1 App Cas 350, 381 per Lord Watson. Of course the installation may not involve a transfer of property at all, as where a tenant installs furniture and fittings which do not become fixtures, and so remain his property. See, e.g., *Young v Dalgety PLC* (1987) 281 EG 427.

119 *Pritchett and Gold and Electrical Power Storage Co v Currie* [1916] 2 Ch 515.

120 See *Young & Marten Ltd v McManus Childs* [1969] 1 AC 454.

121 [1986] 2 FTLR 239.

122 Cf. *Dawber Williamson Roofing Ltd v Humberside CC* (1979) 14 Build LR 70, where the subcontractor succeeded, but standard building terms have been altered since this case.

123 See *Hanson (W) (Harrow) Ltd v Rapid Civil Engineering & Usborne Developments Ltd* (1987) 38 Build LR 106.

124 Possibly such incorporation might amount to a wrongful conversion on the part of the building owner, and, because this is not a contract of sale, he cannot rely on s. 24 of the Act. See the *Dawber Williamson* case, cited above, n. 122.

presumption is that no property is to pass until the article is completed.[125] This is still the case even if the price is to be paid by instalments during the construction of the ship.[126] But it was said 'there is no doubt that a contract might be so framed as to give the purchaser power to claim the property in those parts which, when they are put together, make the complete ship'.[127] And since then it has become customary for shipbuilding contracts to do something like this where the price is payable by instalments as the work proceeds. Thus in *Re Blyth Shipbuilding Co*[128] A agreed to build a ship for B, the price to be paid by instalments as the work proceeded. The contract provided that on the payment of the first instalment 'the vessel and all materials and things appropriated for her should thenceforth . . . become and remain the absolute property of the purchaser'.[129] A went bankrupt before the ship was complete. A certain amount of worked and unworked material was lying about the yard at the relevant time, some of which had been fashioned and was ready to be incorporated into the ship. It was held by the Court of Appeal that the property in the incomplete ship had passed to the buyers, but the worked and unworked material gave rise to more difficulty. In the result it was held that neither had been sufficiently appropriated to pass the property, mainly because they had not yet been fixed to the body of the ship. Although complete and final fixing to the body of the ship was perhaps not necessary, it was held that the goods must be substantially in position so that to remove them would have involved undoing work already done.

Another kind of case arises where a seller manufactures goods for subsequent delivery to the buyer, and the goods are completed or virtually completed, and ready for delivery, and the seller then becomes bankrupt or insolvent. If the buyer has paid the price, or part of the price in advance, he may wish to claim that the property in the goods has passed to him, while the seller's creditors, or liquidator, may argue that the property was still in the seller. In *Carlos Federspiel & Co SA v Charles Twigg & Co Ltd*[130] sellers manufactured bicycles to the buyers' order. The bicycles were made and packed in containers with the buyers' name and address on them, but before the goods could be shipped, the sellers became insolvent. It was held that the property had not passed to the buyers. After a comprehensive review of the authorities, old and new, Pearson J summed up the law relating to appropriation in the following passage, the whole of which merits citation:

> First, Rule 5 of s. 18 of the Act is one of the Rules for ascertaining the intention of the parties as to the time at which the property in the goods is to pass to the buyer unless a different intention appears. Therefore the element of common intention has always to be borne in mind. A mere setting apart or selection by the seller of the goods which he expects to use in performance of the contract is not enough. If that is all, he can change his mind and use those goods in performance of some other contract and use some other goods in performance of

---

125 *Reid v Macbeth* [1904] AC 223.
126 *Laing & Sons v Barclay, Curle & Co* [1908] AC 35.
127 Ibid., at p. 43 per Lord Halsbury.
128 [1926] Ch 494. Strictly speaking this case did not involve the meaning of a statutory 'appropriation' within Rule 5, but since the contract itself used the same term, the decision would seem an authority on the application of Rule 5.
129 A clause of this kind does not deprive the buyer of any right of rejection he may have when the vessel is completed: *McDougall v Aeromarine of Emsworth Ltd* [1958] 1 WLR 1126.
130 [1957] 1 Lloyd's Rep 240, 255–6.

this contract. To constitute an appropriation of the goods to the contract the parties must have had, or be reasonably supposed to have had an intention to attach the contract irrevocably to those goods, so that those goods and no others are the subject of the sale and become the property of the buyer.

Secondly, it is by agreement of the parties that the appropriation, involving a change of ownership, is made, although in some cases the buyer's assent to an appropriation is conferred in advance by the contract itself or otherwise.

Thirdly, an appropriation by the seller with the assent of the buyer may be said always to involve an actual or constructive delivery.[131] If the seller retains possession, he does so as bailee for the buyer. There is a passage in Chalmers' *Sale of Goods Act*, 12th edn at p. 75 where it is said—

> In the second place, if the decisions be carefully examined, it will be found that in every case where the property has been held to pass, there has been an actual or constructive delivery of the goods to the buyer.

I think that is right, subject only to this possible qualification, that there may be after such constructive delivery an actual delivery still to be made by the seller under the contract. Of course, that is quite possible, because delivery is the transfer of possession, whereas appropriation transfers ownership. So there may be first an appropriation, constructive delivery, whereby the seller becomes bailee for the buyer, and then a subsequent actual delivery involving actual possession, and when I say that I have in mind in particular the cases cited, namely *Aldridge* v *Johnson*[132] and *Langton* v *Higgins*.[133]

Fourthly, one has to remember s. 20 of the Sale of Goods Act, whereby the ownership and the risk are normally associated. Therefore, as it appears that there is reason for thinking, on the construction of the relevant documents, that the goods were, at all material times, still at the seller's risk, that is prima facie an indication that the property had not passed to the buyer.

Fifthly, usually, but not necessarily, the appropriating act is the last act to be performed by the seller. For instance, if delivery is to be taken at the seller's premises and the seller has appropriated the goods when he has made the goods ready and identified them and placed them in position to be taken by the buyer and has so informed the buyer, and if the buyer agrees to come and take them, that is the assent to the appropriation. But if there is a further act, an important and decisive act, to be done by the seller, then there is prima facie evidence that probably the property does not pass until the final act is done.

Probably the decisive fact in this case was that the sellers were responsible for arranging shipment of the goods. By contrast, in *Hendy Lennox Ltd* v *Grahame Puttick Ltd*[134] the sellers assembled generators which had been ordered by buyers, and it was held that the property in the generators passed when they were ready for delivery, and buyers received from the sellers the invoices, together with delivery notes, containing the serial numbers of the generators sold. At this stage the sellers had done everything they needed to do under the contract; the serial numbers enabled

---

131 The concept of a 'constructive delivery', though sometimes relied upon in older cases, involves use of a fiction and does not seem particularly helpful. But the concept may be important in some cases concerning the transfer of title by a non-owner – see below, p. 396 *et seq*, and in solving the apparent conflict between the Act's risk provisions and the seller's duty to deliver goods of the right quality, see p. 147.

132 (1857) 7 E & B 885.

133 (1859) 4 H & N 402.

134 [1984] 2 All ER 152.

the particular generators sold to be identified, and nothing remained except for the buyers to pay the invoices and take delivery.

A New Zealand case has gone so far as to hold that where sellers made rope for the buyers' order and stored it in a warehouse from which deliveries were made as requested, there was an unconditional appropriation.[135] This case is also authority for saying that, even if the goods are stored with other similar goods, they are sufficiently earmarked if the sellers can identify the particular goods set aside for the buyers. It is immaterial that nobody else could tell which goods were meant for which buyer.[136] However, it is doubtful whether this would be an acceptable rule where the only 'appropriation' is in the seller's mind, and there is no independent objective evidence of the 'appropriation', for example in the seller's books or records.

Where goods are in the possession of a third party, such as a warehousekeeper, and the third party sets the goods aside for delivery to the buyer, the goods are unconditionally appropriated at the latest when a delivery order is accepted.[137]

It may well be that what is necessary to constitute an unconditional appropriation will vary according to the type of goods in question and the general circumstances of the case. In particular, where goods are being manufactured by the seller, the courts will not too readily infer that the materials have been appropriated since this might hamper the freedom of the seller to manufacture the goods as he thinks best. This consideration does not apply in the case of goods to be grown by the seller, and here it might well be held that the property in the goods, if sufficiently designated, passes as soon as they come into existence. So, also, where an unidentified part of a specified bulk is sold, the only thing necessary for appropriation is the separation of the part sold from the rest, with the assent of the parties.[138] Thus in *Aldridge* v *Johnson*,[139] the plaintiff agreed to buy 100 quarters of barley out of a particular parcel of 200 quarters which he had inspected. It was held that, as soon as the seller filled some sacks sent by the buyer with the barley, the property passed, even though the sacks were still in the seller's possession.

Conditional appropriation

As to the qualification that the appropriation must be 'unconditional' if it is to pass the property, the general and most important rule is that the appropriation is not unconditional if the seller only means to let the buyer have the goods on payment.[140] Prima facie any express or implied contractual stipulation[141] showing that the seller

---

135 *Donaghy's Rope and Twine Co Ltd* v *Wright, Stephenson & Co* (1906) 25 NZLR 641.
136 See also *Re Stapylton Fletcher* [1994] 1 WLR 1181 discussed at p. 346 below.
137 *Wardar's (Import & Export) Co Ltd* v *W Norwood & Sons Ltd* [1968] 2 QB 663. Cf. *Hayman & Son* v *McLintock* 1907 SC 936.
138 This point concerning appropriation is still valid, but before that occurs the effect of the Sale of Goods (Amendment) Act 1995 in such cases must now be noted – see p. 346 *et seq.*
139 (1857) 7 E & B 885.
140 *Stein, Forbes & Co Ltd* v *Country Tailoring Co Ltd* (1916) 86 LJKB 448; see also *Cheetham & Co Ltd* v *Thornham Spinning Co Ltd* [1964] 2 Lloyd's Rep 17, which could perhaps have been decided on this ground. See too *Mitsui & Co Ltd* v *Flota Mercante Grancolumbiana SA* [1989] 1 All ER 951, discussed below, p. 420.
141 Moreover, a condition can be imposed on appropriation, even if not in the contract – see Bradgate [1988] JBL 477, and see p. 470, n. 93 below.

intends to reserve some rights over the goods themselves (and not just contractual rights) until he has been fully paid makes the appropriation conditional, and prevents the property from passing until that happens.

Some important types of conditional contracts of sale are considered in s. 19, which actually applies to the sale of both specific and unascertained goods, but as, in practice, its application to unascertained goods is far more common, it has been reserved for consideration here. Section 19(1) is as follows:

> Where there is a contract for the sale of specific goods or where goods are subsequently appropriated to the contract, the seller may, by the terms of the contract or appropriation, reserve the right of disposal of the goods until certain conditions are fulfilled; and in such a case, notwithstanding the delivery of the goods to the buyer, or to a carrier or other bailee . . . for the purpose of transmission to the buyer, the property in the goods does not pass to the buyer until the conditions imposed by the seller are fulfilled.

The courts have been very ready to find that the seller has reserved the right of disposal and that the buyer does not acquire property in the goods before actual delivery. In *Re Shipton Anderson & Co Ltd and Harrison Bros & Co Ltd*[142] the owner of a specific parcel of wheat in a warehouse sold it on the terms 'payment cash within seven days against transfer order'. The goods were requisitioned by the government under emergency powers before delivery to the buyer. It was held by the Court of Appeal that the express term quoted above was in effect a right of disposal reserved by the seller, as he was not bound to hand over a delivery order until payment. Consequently, the property had not yet passed and the contract was frustrated by the seizure of the goods.

Section 19(1) is only a generalization of the specific case dealt with by s. 19(2), which is concerned with goods sent by sea. Under this subsection, a shipper who receives from the carrier bills of lading whereby the goods are deliverable to him or to his order is taken to reserve the right of disposal, because he can hold onto the bill of lading until he is paid or otherwise satisfied. Nobody can obtain the delivery of the goods without the bills of lading (at any rate without giving the shipping company an indemnity against the possible consequences), and the seller's possession of these, where the goods are deliverable to him, therefore enables him to treat the goods as continued security for payment. As this is by far the most important illustration of the reservation of the right of disposal, more detailed consideration of this question will be postponed until Chapter 22, where export sales are dealt with.[143]

Yet another type of conditional contract is dealt with by s. 19(3):

> Where the seller of goods draws on the buyer for the price, and transmits the bill of exchange and bill of lading to the buyer together to secure acceptance or payment of the bill of exchange, the buyer is bound to return the bill of lading if he does not honour the bill of exchange, and if he wrongfully retains the bill of lading the property in the goods does not pass to him.

In other words, the transfer of the property by the bill of lading in such a case is conditional upon the bill of exchange being honoured, and if, for example, the buyer

142 [1915] 3 KB 676.
143 See below, p. 419.

should become bankrupt with the bill of lading still in his possession, not having accepted the bill of exchange, the seller will be able to claim the goods. Similarly, if the buyer retains the bill of lading without paying for it, he is in breach of his duties to the seller, for example if he takes delivery of the goods or sends the bill of lading on to a sub-buyer. In such circumstances, the buyer may be sued either for the tort of conversion or for the price of the goods, and his liability will be precisely the same in either case.[144]

It should be noted, however, that even if the property does not pass to the buyer because of the operation of this section, the seller is at risk in one important respect. Although he may be protected against the risk of the buyer becoming insolvent before he has paid for the goods, the seller is at risk that the buyer may resell the goods to a third party. As will be seen more fully in Chapter 21, the buyer may in this situation be able to pass a good title to a third party under various provisions of the Act, even though property has not yet passed to him, because the seller has reserved a right of disposal. If the buyer actually obtains the possession of the goods or of the bill of lading, and transfers them to a sub-buyer who takes in good faith and for value, the sub-buyer gets a good title under s. 25(1), s. 47(2), and s. 10 of the Factors Act 1889.[145]

Reference was previously made to Rule 3 under which, in a sale of specific goods, the passing of the property is postponed if the seller is bound to weigh, measure, test or do some other act for the purpose of ascertaining the price. Although this Rule is confined to sales of specific goods, it seems that the position is the same in a sale of unascertained goods. In *National Coal Board* v *Gamble*,[146] the appellants supplied coal as part of a bulk sale to a purchaser by loading it onto the buyer's lorry at a colliery. The coal was loaded by means of a hopper and subsequently driven to a weighbridge, where the weight of the coal was ascertained and the statutory weight-ticket supplied. It was held that the property did not pass until the coal had been weighed and the ticket given to and accepted by the buyer. The court had no doubt that if too much had been loaded onto the lorry the seller could have insisted on the excess being unloaded. It seems (although this was not stated in the judgments) that the correct analysis of the facts was that, although the coal was appropriated to the contract by being loaded onto the lorry, the appropriation was not unconditional until it was weighed and the weight-ticket accepted by the buyer. On the other hand, in *Edwards* v *Ddin*[147] (a prosecution under the Theft Act 1968) a different result was arrived at. Here it was said that when a person buys petrol at a filling station, the property passes as soon as it is put in the tank of the buyer's vehicle. There is no reservation of rights by the seller, and the appropriation is unconditional. If the buyer does not pay, he may be guilty of an offence and can, of course, be sued for the price, but the property will have passed. It is perhaps unclear if the seller can detain the buyer's vehicle or attempt to drain the petrol out of the tank in exercise of his lien. (For further discussion of the seller's lien, see Chapter 25.)

---

144 *Ernest Scragg & Sons Ltd* v *Perseverance Banking & Trust Co Ltd* [1973] 2 Lloyd's Rep 101.
145 *Cahn* v *Pockett's Bristol Channel Co Ltd* [1899] 1 QB 643 – see p. 404.
146 [1959] 1 QB 11.
147 [1976] 1 WLR 943. And see also *Re Charge Card Services Ltd* [1988] 3 All ER 702, 706 where it was accepted by the CA that the contract is made in such a case when the tank is filled.

Assent

The assent which Rule 5 requires for the appropriation may be express or implied. Where, therefore, the defendant sold some rice to the plaintiff from a specified parcel at a particular place, and sent the plaintiff a note of appropriation, his assent was implied from his failure to reply for a whole month.[148] Consequently, although Rules 2 and 3 only require notice to be given to the buyer of the fulfilment of conditions in a sale of specific goods while Rule 5 requires the buyer's assent, there may often be little difference in practice.

Rule 5(1) says that the assent may be given before or after the appropriation is made, and in some cases the assent may be inferred from the facts which take place when the contract is made, or when or before the appropriation takes place. So it has been held that the dispatch and receipt of invoices and delivery orders which clearly identified the goods being sold were enough to transfer property even though there was no further act or indication of assent to the appropriation by the buyer.[149]

As we have seen, Rule 5(2) states that where the goods are delivered to a carrier for shipment to the buyer the goods are taken to be unconditionally appropriated to the contract. Although this sub-rule does not actually say that the buyer's assent must be taken to have been given in these circumstances, it is nevertheless clear that the customary course of business rests on the assumption that shipment is an unconditional appropriation with the assent of the buyer.[150] The buyer's assent is to be inferred from the nature of the transaction itself. It does not follow that property is always transferred on shipment; whether it is transferred then or later depends on the nature and terms of the contract. These questions are discussed in Chapter 22. Here it is merely desired to stress that the apparent absence of a prior assent to the appropriation does not prevent property passing on shipment.

Unfortunately, this appears to be one of those areas in which a rule suitable for commercial contracts is not necessarily suitable for consumer contracts. When a consumer orders goods by post, it is not necessarily appropriate for the law to treat the dispatch of the goods to him by the seller as passing the property, because the result is that the goods will be at the buyer's risk in the course of post. In *Badische Anilin und Soda Fabrik v Basle Chemical Works*,[151] the question was whether by posting the goods in Switzerland a Swiss seller had made, used, exercised or vended the invention within the ambit of a UK patent. The House of Lords held that it had not, the implication being that it was the buyer, who had ordered the goods, who was the infringer.[152]

---

148 *Pignataro v Gilroy & Son* [1919] 1 KB 459. But this is of course subject to the need for the goods to be ascertained.
149 *Hendy Lennox Ltd v Grahame Puttick Ltd* [1984] 2 All ER 152.
150 The most explicit authority on this point appears to be in dicta of the Australian High Court – see *James v Commonwealth* (1939) 62 CLR 339, 377; *Saffron v Société Minière Cafrika* (1958) 100 CLR 231, 242.
151 [1898] AC 200; cf. *The Albazero* [1974] 2 All ER 906, 927 where Brandon J discusses this case. It was not discussed in the higher courts. The suggestion made in *Badische* that the Post Office is the buyer's agent, which echoes views expressed in *Household Fire Insurance v Grant* (1879) 4 Ex D 216, cannot be sustained today – see Corbin on *Contracts* §78.
152 This result seems consistent with the view that the seller is not in breach of the warranty of merchantable quality where an importer orders goods which cannot legally be sold in the importer's territory (see *Sumner Permain & Co v Webb* [1922] 1 KB 551), and the related point on the fitness for purpose warranty which arose in *Teheran Europe Co Ltd v S T Belton (Tractors) Ltd* [1968] 2 QB 545 – see p. 200 above. It is also consistent with the rules which have developed in answering the question as to which party, the buyer or the seller, has the duty, in the absence of express agreement, to get an export licence – see p. 435 below.

Although it appears to have been held that the posting of ordered goods effected delivery to the buyer, and would thereby, presumably, have passed the property to him, this case is perhaps not decisive because this point was not disputed and the real issue in the case related to the patent law issues set out above. Moreover, there are other cases which suggest that the point may still be open in some contexts, although it cannot be said that any of them are directly in point.[153]

Transfer of property without unconditional appropriation

As we have seen, under s. 18 Rule 5(1) the usual way in which property in unascertained goods is transferred to the buyer is by the goods becoming unconditionally appropriated to the contract; but it is not the only possible way. In *Karlshamns Oljefabriker* v *Eastport Navigation Corp*[154] the plaintiffs bought 6,000 tons of copra c.i.f. Karlshamns. The sellers shipped 16,000 tons of copra on one ship, part of which was intended for the plaintiffs and part for other buyers. A small quantity, surplus to all the contractual requirements of the various buyers, was bought by F from the sellers and resold by them to the plaintiffs. The plaintiffs thus obtained bills of lading first for the 6,000 tons, and second for the small extra quantity sold to F. But all the copra was shipped in undivided bulk, and it was held that no property could have passed on shipment, nor on the transfer of the bills of lading. The ship called first at Rotterdam and then at Hamburg, discharging all the copra meant for other buyers, so that at this stage the only copra left was that destined for the plaintiffs. It was held by Mustill J that at this stage the property passed to the plaintiffs because the goods had become ascertained by a process of 'exhaustion'. Mustill J went on to hold that it is not always necessary that the goods should be appropriated to the contract under Rule 5, although this is the commonest method by which the goods are ascertained. The essential requirements of the law, he held, are (1) that the goods should be, or have become, ascertained, and (2) that the parties should intend that the property be transferred. There is no independent third requirement that the goods should be unconditionally appropriated to the contract.[155] Appropriation is only one way of ascertaining the goods. Mustill J also held that there was no reason why property should not pass even though it was not possible to say which part of the copra was to be taken to be the 6,000 tons sold by the sellers direct, and which the extra quantity sold through F.[156] The result of this case is confirmed by s. 1 of the Sale of Goods (Amendment) Act 1995, discussed below, which adds subsections (3) and (4) to s. 18 Rule 5.

Sale of unidentified part of an identified bulk

We have seen above that, no matter what the intention of the parties may be, the effect of s. 16 in its original form was that the property in goods could not pass until they

---

153 See *Noblett v Hopkinson* [1905] 2 KB 214; *Pletts v Campbell* [1895] 2 QB 229; *Pletts v Beatty* [1896] 1 QB 519; and cf. *Preston v Albuery* [1964] 2 QB 796, 805 per Ashworth J.
154 [1982] 1 All ER 208, following *Wait and James v Midland Bank* (1926) 31 Com Cas 172.
155 This was also accepted by Oliver J in *In re London Wine Co (Shippers) Ltd* (1986) PCC 121.
156 In other words, the plaintiffs were entitled to the whole, albeit under separate contracts.

had been ascertained; and we have also seen that this meant that where an unidentified and unascertained part of some bulk or whole was sold, then even though the
bulk itself might be identified and ascertained, no property could pass until the part
sold had been in some way physically severed or segregated from the remainder of the
bulk, or at least earmarked so that the parts appropriated could readily be identified.
The effect of s. 16 in this respect caused some concern in certain contexts, and the Law
Commissions published a Report on the subject.[157] It is now necessary to say something further by way of explanation of these concerns, and the reforms effected by the
Sale of Goods (Amendment) Act 1995 consequential on them.[158]

The legal problems which arise from the sale of an unidentified part of a definite
bulk or whole involve two sets of relationships, although only one of them is of direct
concern to the subject-matter of this book. These two relationships are, first, that
between seller and buyer; and, secondly, that between the buyer and the carrier where
the goods are in process of being transported (by sea or air, for instance) from seller
to buyer. The relationship which concerns us is that of the seller and buyer.

It often happens that the transaction between seller and buyer is completed in all
essentials, even to the extent of the buyer actually paying for the goods, while the goods
are still in the possession of the seller himself, or of a carrier. If at that stage the goods
were ascertained and identified, the property in them would pass to the buyer and two
consequences would follow from this. First, the buyer would be protected from the risk
of the seller's insolvency, because if the property has passed to the buyer he can simply
lay claim to the goods themselves if the seller becomes bankrupt. And secondly, the
goods would prima facie be at the buyer's risk, so that any subsequent deterioration or
damage to the goods would no longer be the responsibility of the seller. But where the
goods were an unidentified part of a bulk so that property could not pass as a result of
s. 16 in its original form these consequences would not follow, and the results often
seemed largely fortuitous. We have already seen one example of these fortuitous results,
namely *Healy* v *Howlett & Sons*[159] where the property in the fish being sold to the
defendant would in the ordinary way have passed to him, and with it the risk of delay
and deterioration, when the goods were dispatched to the buyer. But because in that
particular case the goods were dispatched with similar goods to other buyers, and were
not physically earmarked for the defendant himself, the property could not pass, and
neither did the risk. That result was somewhat unsatisfactory, because the outcome
depended on the happenstance of when the railway officials allocated the defendant his
boxes. This particular problem is, however, unusual because in most cases of this
nature (particularly where the goods are dispatched by sea) there is no doubt that the
risk will pass on shipment, even if the property does not or cannot pass; and there is,
indeed, one leading authority which suggests that even in other circumstances the risk
in an unidentified part of a specified bulk may pass before the property.[160]

A more disturbing consequence of s. 16 was that a buyer might find that although
he *thought* he had obtained the property in the goods and had paid for them, he had

---

157 'Sale of Goods Forming Part of a Bulk', Law Commission No. 215 (1993).
158 See comments on the Law Commissions' Report and on the Act by Bradgate and White [1994] LMCLQ 315;
     Ulph [1996] LMCLQ 93; Burns [1996] MLR 260; and Gullifer [1999] LMCLQ 93.
159 [1917] 1 KB 337 – but see comments at p. 334.
160 See p. 423.

no property and remained vulnerable to the risk of the seller's insolvency because of the purely accidental or fortuitous fact that the goods were not ascertained. This problem was perhaps most acute where part of a large cargo of goods was sold while they were at sea, as happened in the *Karlshamns Oljefabriker* case, which was discussed above. This is today a more frequent occurrence than it used to be, because ships are larger, cargoes bigger, and buyers therefore are more often buying proportionately smaller quantities. Buyers often receive bills of lading from sellers (who have, of course, received the bills from the shipping company concerned) and bills of lading are universally regarded by commercial parties as firm documents of title. So buyers (and also banks) quite happily pay good money in exchange for bills of lading in the confident belief that the bills give an unqualified right to the possession of the goods; yet in these cases where the bills of lading only cover part of a bulk cargo it was clear that no unqualified title was passed because of s. 16 of the Act.

That these difficulties could also arise in other contexts is shown by the facts of *In re London Wine Co (Shippers) Ltd*,[161] a case decided in 1975 though not fully reported until 1986. In this case a company sold wine to customers, while retaining possession of the wine. The customers paid for the wine, as well as for subsequent storage charges, and the seller gave the buyers 'certificates of title', but there was no actual earmarking or physical segregation of the wine sold to the different customers. The wine company became insolvent, and the receiver (representing mortgagees or chargees) claimed that all the wine still belonged to the company, a claim which was ultimately upheld by Oliver J in a lengthy and complex judgment.[162]

The situation was further complicated in this case because separate claims were made on behalf of several different groups of buyers. One group claimed that in some cases the buyer had bought the whole stock of a particular description of wine owned by the company, so that the property might have passed by 'exhaustion' as in the *Karlshamns Oljefabriker* case, discussed above. But this claim failed because the wine had not been sold *as part of a particular consignment or bulk*, but had merely been described as 'lying in bond'. So although the sellers may quite genuinely have intended in their own minds to tie in the sales with a particular stock of wine of that description, they were under no legal obligation to do so. That particular stock of wine belonged to them, not the buyers; the sellers could have disposed of it elsewhere and bought further stocks to satisfy the buyers without any breach of contract.

A second group of buyers who had together bought the whole stock of a particular description of wine argued that between them they could have been treated as co-buyers, so that property could have passed to them jointly. But this claim failed for the same reason as in the case of the first group of buyers. A third group of buyers had actually received acknowledgments (attornments) either from the company itself, or from independent warehousemen who held the stock, but their claims also failed

---

161 (1986) PCC 121.
162 Oliver J's judgment was approved by the Privy Council in *Re Goldthorp Exchange Ltd* [1994] 2 All ER 806, in which, however, the facts were not precisely the same – the case involved claims to unallocated stocks of bullion, and the PC was of the view that the parties could not have intended to create an interest in its general stock of bullion which would have inhibited the (now insolvent) bullion company's dealings in it. See also *Mac-Jordan Construction Ltd* v *Brookmount Erostin Ltd* [1992] BCLC 350.

because of the basic fact that no ascertainment had taken place under s. 16. However, it must be noted that in *Re Stapylton Fletcher*,[163] in which cases of wine were *separately* stored for a group of customers, it was held that for the purposes of s. 16 property had passed to the customers, the customers taking as tenants in common.[164] Judge Paul Baker QC, citing Staughton J's review of the authorities in *Indian Oil Corp Ltd* v *Greenstone Shipping Co SA (Panama)*,[165] concluded that it was possible to use the tenancy in common as a tool for remedying unforeseen mixing, and that if the creation of a tenancy in common could be brought about by construction of law, it could equally be brought about by agreement express or to be inferred from the circumstances. He concluded that from the evidence it could readily be inferred that the parties intended the property in the goods to pass when they were set aside for storage. It was the separation of the goods from the company's trading assets, whether done physically, or by giving instructions to a bonded warehouse keeper, which caused the goods to be ascertained for the purposes of s. 16.[166]

As a result of these difficulties (as well also as difficulties arising from the relations between buyer and carrier which are not strictly within the subject-matter of this book) the Law Commissions suggested that there should be a new rule on sale of goods out of a bulk which would enable property in an undivided share to pass before ascertainment of goods relating to specific sales contracts.[167] We must now deal with this.

The Sale of Goods (Amendment) Act 1995[168]

This Act, which came into force on 19 September 1995 (but had no retrospective effect on any contract concluded before that date),[169] implements the recommendations of the English and Scottish Law Commissions in the Report discussed above. The Act does two things: (1) it puts into statutory form the doctrine of 'ascertainment by exhaustion';[170] and (2) it enables property in an undivided share forming part of an identified bulk to pass before ascertainment of the goods relating to the specific sales contract or contracts. We will deal with these in turn, but first we must consider what is meant by 'bulk' for these purposes.

The definition of 'bulk' for the purposes of these subsections
Section 2 of the 1995 Act provides that in s. 61(1) of the 1979 Act, after the definition of 'action' there shall be inserted the following definition:

> 'bulk' means a mass of goods of the same kind which—
> (a) is contained in a defined space or area; and
> (b) is such that any goods in the bulk are interchangeable with any other goods therein of the same number or quantity; . . .[171]

---

163 [1994] 1 WLR 1181.
164 See also *Indian Oil* v *Greenstone Shipping* [1988] QB 345, below, p. 350.
165 [1988] QB 345.
166 Compare *Everwine Ltd & ors* v HM *Commissioners of Customs & Excise* [2003] EWCA Civ 593 – p. 324 above.
167 As is the case under the Uniform Commercial Code, s. 2-105(4). See Law Commission No. 215 (1993) para 2.21.
168 1995 c. 28.
169 So that the old rules set out above still apply to such contracts – 1995 Act s. 3(2).
170 See pp. 343 above.
171 For illustrations, see n. 175 below.

Ascertainment by exhaustion

As recommended by the Law Commissions, the effect of the doctrine of ascertainment by exhaustion[172] is now confirmed by s. 1 of the Sale of Goods (Amendment) Act 1995. This inserts the following words:

(2) In section 18 of the 1979 Act, at the end of rule 5 there shall be added the following—

    (3) Where there is a contract for the sale of a specified quantity of unascertained goods in a deliverable state forming part of a bulk which is identified either in the contract or by subsequent agreement between the parties and the bulk is reduced to (or to less than) that quantity, then, if the buyer under that contract is the only buyer to whom goods are then due out of the bulk—

        (a) the remaining goods shall be taken as appropriated to that contract at the time when the bulk is so reduced; and

        (b) the property in those goods then passes to that buyer.

    (4) Paragraph (3) above applies also (with the necessary modifications) where a bulk is reduced to (or less than) the aggregate of the quantities due to a single buyer under separate contracts relating to that bulk and he is the only buyer to whom goods are then due out of that bulk.

It should be noted that this section applies not only where there is only one contract with one buyer, but also where there is more than one contract with one buyer, as was the case in *The Elafi* mentioned above.[173] It also applies where there is more than one buyer initially, but, because of deliveries to the other buyers, there is left only one buyer entitled to the residue of the bulk.

The situation where there is more than one buyer entitled to the identified bulk is dealt with by the next subsection of s. 1 of the 1995 Act.

Undivided shares in goods forming part of a bulk

Section 16 of the Sale of Goods Act 1979 is amended by insertion of the words 'Subject to section 20A below . . .'. After s. 20 of the 1979 Act the following section is inserted:

20A (1) This section applies to a contract for the sale of a specified quantity of unascertained goods if the following conditions are met—

        (a) the goods or some of them form part of a bulk which is identified either in the contract or by subsequent agreement between the parties; and

        (b) the buyer has paid the price for some or all of the goods which are the subject of the contract and which form part of the bulk.

    (2) Where this section applies then (unless the parties agree otherwise), as soon as the conditions specified in paragraphs (a) and (b) of subsection (1) above are met or at such later time as the parties may agree—

        (a) property in an undivided share in the bulk is transferred to the buyer, and

        (b) the buyer becomes owner in common of the bulk.

    (3) Subject to subsection (4) below, for the purposes of this section the undivided share of a buyer in a bulk at any time shall be such share as the quantity of

---

172 See p. 343 above.
173 See p. 343 above.

goods paid for and due to the buyer out of the bulk bears to the quantity of goods in the bulk at that time.

(4)   Where the aggregate of the undivided shares of buyers in a bulk determined under subsection (3) above would at any time exceed the whole of the bulk at that time, the undivided share in the bulk of each buyer shall be reduced proportionately so that the aggregate of the undivided shares is equal to the whole bulk.

(5)   Where a buyer has paid the price for only some of the goods due to him out of a bulk, any delivery to the buyer out of the bulk shall, for the purposes of this section, be ascribed in the first place to the goods in respect of which payment has been made.

(6)   For the purposes of this section payment of part of the price for any goods shall be treated as payment for a corresponding part of the goods.

Thus for the section to apply three conditions must be satisfied: (1) there must be a sale of a specified quantity;[174] (2) the bulk must be identified;[175] (3) the buyer must have paid for some or all of the goods.[176] The new section is not limited to goods in a deliverable state.[177] It is also concerned with *quantity*, not shares expressed as fractions or percentages. The effect of s. 20A(3) is that the buyer's undivided share is such a share as the goods paid for and due to him bear to the quantity of goods in the bulk *at that time*. Where deliveries have been made to the buyer of some of the goods forming part of the bulk, and the buyer has paid for only some of the goods, the deliveries are to be ascribed in the first place to the goods paid for.[178]

Section 20A(1)(b), (3) and (5) make reference to the case where a buyer has paid for some only of the goods due from the bulk under the contract. Part-payments would not normally be treated as relating to any particular portion of the goods due under the contract, it was necessary therefore for s. 20A(6) to provide that part-payments are to be treated as payments *for* part.

The aggregate shares of two or more buyers can never exceed the whole of the bulk.[179] In such cases the undivided share of each buyer is reduced proportionately so that the aggregate of the undivided shares is equal to the whole of the bulk.[180]

---

174 As opposed to a sale of a fraction such as a third of a bulk – see Law Com. No. 215, para. 6.3.
175 1995 Act s. 2(a) amending 1979 Act s. 61(1) as indicated above. The Law Commissions give the following illustrations of an identified bulk: (a) a cargo of wheat in a named ship; (b) a mass of barley in an identified silo; (c) the oil in an identified storage tank; (d) cases of wine (all of the same kind) in an identified cellar; (e) ingots of gold (all of the same kind) in an identified vault; (f) bags of fertilizer (all of the same kind) in an identified storehouse; (g) a heap of coal in the open at an identified location. See ibid. para. 4.3. Thus the seller's general stock is not intended to be an identified bulk – ibid.
176 Section 20A(1)(b) added by 1995 Act s. 1(3) and ibid., para. 6.4. The reason for this exclusion is that the buyer who has not paid suffers no loss, because payment and delivery are concurrent conditions – s. 28. Unfortunately, this appears to have the consequence that a seller's liquidator can decide whether or not to deliver according to whether the market price of the goods is above or below the contract price.
177 Ibid. para. 5.6 – goods forming part of an undivided share would never be in a deliverable state within the meaning of s. 61(5), 1979 Act.
178 Section 20A(5), added by 1995 Act s. 1(3). The definition of 'delivery' in s. 61(1) is amended by adding the words 'except that in relation to sections 20A and 20B above it includes such appropriation of goods to the contract as results in property in the goods being transferred to the buyer'. As to 'unconditional appropriation', see p. 334.
179 Section 20A(4).
180 Ibid.

Unless otherwise agreed, property in an undivided share passes as soon as the buyer has paid for all, or some, of the contract goods, and the buyer thus becomes an owner in common of the bulk.[181] This does not seem to answer the question about the allocation of risk between buyer and seller. Section 20B(3)(c) provides that nothing in the section shall affect the rights of any buyer under his contract, and the Report indicates that the co-ownership of the bulk is without prejudice to the buyers' contractual rights.[182] They are still entitled to goods which conform to the contract in quantity and quality. Presumably, then, risk passes when property passes under s. 18 Rule 5, though delay on the part of the buyer in taking delivery could affect this.[183]

Deemed consent by co-owner to dealings in bulk goods

The effect of creating undivided shares in an identified bulk would be similar to the situation which existed in relation to undivided shares in land in England before 1926: it would require all the part-owners to be joined in order to transfer any part of the bulk, and in turn the tracing of title to each part share.[184] Section 20B deals with this by deeming consent by the other co-owners to a sale by one co-owner:

(1) A person who has become an owner in common of a bulk by virtue of section 20A above shall be deemed to have consented to—
   (a) any delivery of goods out of the bulk to any other owner in common of the bulk, being goods which are due to him under his contract;
   (b) any dealing with or removal, delivery or disposal of goods in the bulk by any other person who is an owner in common of the bulk in so far as the goods fall within that co-owner's undivided share in the bulk at the time of the dealing, removal, delivery or disposal.
(2) No cause of action shall accrue to anyone against a person by reason of that person having acted in accordance with paragraph (a) or (b) of subsection (1) above in reliance on any consent deemed to have been given under that subsection.
(3) Nothing in this section or section 20A above shall—
   (a) impose an obligation on a buyer of goods out of a bulk to compensate any other buyer of goods out of that bulk for any shortfall in the goods received by that other buyer;
   (b) affect any contractual arrangement between buyers of goods out of a bulk for adjustments between themselves; or
   (c) affect the rights of any buyer under his contract.

Subsection (1)(b) above makes it clear that each co-owner can deal with goods within his or her share without needing the consent of the other co-owners. As noted above, the definition of 'delivery' is amended in relation to this subsection.

The purpose of s. 20B(2) is to protect liquidators and other such persons who step into the buyer's shoes on his or her insolvency.[185] They are protected against any action by other co-owning buyers who may receive short delivery because the bulk is

---

181 Section 20A(2), added by 1995 Act s. 1(3).
182 Paragraph 4.34.
183 Under s. 20(2) – see *Sterns Ltd* v *Vickers Ltd*, discussed at p. 354 below.
184 See Co. Litt. L.3.C.4.S.292; *Williams on Real Property*, 23rd edn (1920) p. 150.
185 Paragraph 6.7.

insufficient to meet all claims, as a result of any dealing with the goods of the sort specified in s. 20B(1)(a) or (b).

Section 20B(3) makes it clear that the rules do not: (a) impose any obligation on a buyer who takes delivery of goods out of a bulk to compensate others who receive short delivery as a result; (b) affect any contractual arrangements between the buyers for adjustments between themselves; or (c) alter or diminish contractual rights of the buyer against the seller. If a seller, having sold 50 tonnes out of an identified bulk of 100 tonnes, were subsequently to sell 60 tonnes to a second buyer who bought in good faith without notice, the second buyer would acquire a good title by virtue of s. 24 of the Act,[186] but the first buyer would still have a remedy against the seller for non-delivery of 10 tonnes. Similarly, any sub-buyer of the first buyer who had been sold 50 tonnes would have a remedy for the shortfall of 10 tonnes against the first buyer.

The effect of these provisions

Thus, if a buyer who has agreed to buy 50 tonnes out of a bulk of 100 tonnes, has paid 50 per cent of the price, and taken delivery of 10 tonnes, he would be taken to have paid for a further 15 tonnes. The buyer's entitlement *as a proportion* will necessarily fluctuate as the size of the bulk fluctuates. If the bulk is reduced to such a point that it is the same or less than the buyer's entitlement, the buyer will be entitled to the whole under s. 18 Rule 5(3), introduced by the 1995 Act s. 1(2).

It was perfectly possible for two or more persons to own goods in common under suitably drafted contracts under the law as it was before the 1995 Act came into force (to own 'undivided shares' as the law puts it).[187] Indeed, it has been held that if a seller appropriates goods to the contract, so that property passes to the buyer, and the seller *thereafter* wrongfully (even accidentally) mixes goods of his own with the goods sold (as where an oil cargo, for instance, is sold and then other oil is placed in the same tanks) the buyer and the seller would thereupon become co-owners of the resulting whole.[188] And presumably it must be possible for one person to sell an undivided share in specific goods to another so that the buyer thereupon becomes a co-owner with the seller. It is, indeed, quite common for several persons to be co-owners of certain types of property, for example racehorses, and there seems no reason why one owner cannot sell a share in a horse so that the buyer becomes a co-owner.[189] Similarly the parties could become co-owners where a buyer or buyers are sold a specified share in an identified bulk expressed as a fraction of the whole,[190] provided it was clear from the terms of the contract or the surrounding circumstances that that was the intention of the parties. Any lingering doubts about these matters should be put to rest by the amendments to s. 61 of the 1979 Act effected by the 1995

---

186 See p. 395 *et seq.*

187 See *Re Stapylton Fletcher*, p. 346 above.

188 *Indian Oil Corp Ltd* v *Greenstone Shipping Co SA* [1988] QB 345.

189 In *Re Sugar Properties (Derisley Wood) Ltd* [1988] BCLC 146 it was held that a charge of such a share did not require registration under s. 395 of the Companies Act 1985.

190 Section 2(2) recognizes a sale between one part owner and another, but there was nevertheless some doubt whether the sale of an undivided share was a sale of goods. The Law Commissions' Report No. 215 recommended that the point be clarified – para. 5.3.

Act.[191] 'Goods' now includes an undivided share in goods. 'Specific goods' includes an undivided share, specified as a fraction of the goods identified or agreed upon, so that the sale of a quarter share in a racehorse is a sale of specific goods. But such a transaction is quite different from a sale where the intention is that goods forming part of an unascertained bulk will ultimately be divided and part transferred to the buyer, while parts either remain with the seller or are to be transferred to a different buyer or buyers. This is the situation in which ss. 16 and 17 of the Act prevented the property from passing and which is addressed by the provisions of the 1995 Act discussed above.

The position in equity prior to the 1995 Act

While common law insisted on identification of the particular thing sold, English equity was apparently less stringent.[192] In *Tailby v Official Receiver*[193] Lord Watson stated the single requirement of equity 'which must be fulfilled in order to make the assignee's right attach to a future chose in action, which is that on its coming into existence it shall answer the description in the assignment, or, in other words, that it shall be capable of being identified as the thing, or as one of the very things assigned'. It seems to have been thought that physical identification or ascertainment might not be required in equity so long as the thing sold belonged to an identified bulk or whole. If the contract was one which a court of equity would enforce by a decree of specific performance, it was thought that an equitable interest in the property might be held to pass as soon as the property came into existence and could be made identifiable, presumably by physical separation.

It was never entirely clear before the passing of the Sale of Goods Act whether (and, if so, to what extent) this equitable doctrine applied to an ordinary sale of unascertained goods. It certainly applied to the assignment of a future chose in action and to a covenant to convey or mortgage real estate. In these cases the equitable doctrine meant that once the property came into the hands of the seller, or the chose in action became currently due, the assignee or buyer was entitled to the property or chose in preference to judgment creditors or a trustee in bankruptcy of the seller or assignor. But an ordinary contract of sale of goods has never been specifically enforceable in equity, though there are dicta in *Holroyd v Marshall*[194] suggesting that a contract for the sale of specific goods or of an unspecified part of a specified bulk may be so enforceable.

For some years after the passing of the 1893 Act it was an open question whether this equitable rule was applicable to contracts of sale of goods, but the question seems to have been settled. In *Re Wait*[195] Wait bought 1,000 tons of wheat which was expected to be loaded on a named vessel, the *Challenger*, on 20 November 1925. The following day he contracted to sell 500 tons of this to X. The wheat was shipped in one undivided load, and one bill of lading for the whole load was issued. X paid Wait on 5 February, and Wait went bankrupt on 24 February. The ship arrived on 28

---

191 See the Law Commissions' Report para. 5.3 *et seq.*
192 *Holroyd v Marshall* (1862) 10 HLC 191.
193 (1888) 13 App Cas 523, 533.
194 See n. 192.
195 [1927] 1 Ch 606. On the equitable doctrine prior to *Re Wait*, see Pennington (1975) 27 IC Law Q 277.

February. Wait's trustee claimed the whole 1,000 tons as assets in the bankruptcy, while X claimed either that he had an equitable assignment or charge on the 500 tons, or that he was entitled to specific performance of the contract under s. 52. A majority of the Court of Appeal decided against X on both grounds.[196] There had clearly been insufficient appropriation at law to pass the property and Lord Hanworth MR was of the opinion that even if the equitable doctrine of *Tailby* v *Official Receiver* survived the Sale of Goods Act, the goods were not sufficiently identified even in equity. But Atkin LJ went much further than Lord Hanworth. He denied that equity would ever have applied its doctrines to an ordinary sale of future goods. He went on to say that even if equity would ever have applied its doctrine to such a case, it could not do so now having regard to the Sale of Goods Act. He said:[197]

> The Code was passed at a time when the principles of equity and equitable remedies were recognized and given effect to in all our courts, and the particular equitable remedy of specific performance is specially referred to in s. 52. The total sum of legal relations (meaning by the word 'legal' existing in equity as well as in common law) arising out of the contract for the sale of goods may well be regarded as defined by the Code. It would have been futile in a Code intended for commercial men to have created an elaborate structure of rules dealing with rights at law, if at the same time it was intended to leave, subsisting with the legal rights equitable rights inconsistent with, more extensive, and coming into existence earlier than the rights so carefully set out in the various sections of the Code.
>
> The rules for transfer of property as between seller and buyer, performance of the contract, rights of the unpaid seller against the goods, unpaid seller's lien, remedies of the seller, remedies of the buyer, appear to be complete and exclusive statements of the legal relations both in law and equity.

These are powerful arguments and they have the support of subsequent authority.[198] Accordingly, the only issue in cases of this kind is whether or not the property in the goods has passed in accordance with the rules set out in s. 18 (as amended) and s. 20A inserted by the 1995 Act.[199]

---

196 As to the second ground, see below, p. 560.
197 [1927] 1 Ch 606, 635–6.
198 In *London Wine Co (Shippers) Ltd* (1986) PCC 121 Oliver J largely agreed with Atkin LJ on this point. Atkin LJ's views were also substantially supported though only on a 'provisional view' by the House of Lords in *Leigh & Sillivan Ltd* v *Aliakmon Shipping Corp Ltd (The Aliakmon)* [1986] AC 785. This passage was applied by the Privy Council in *Re Goldthorp Exchange Ltd* [1994] 2 All ER 806, and approved in *Re Stapylton Fletcher* [1994] 1 WLR 1181. Accordingly, this point would appear to be settled beyond doubt.
199 Section 1(3).

20

RISK AND FRUSTRATION

RISK AND FRUSTRATION DISTINGUISHED

When a person is bound to bear the accidental loss of, or damage to, goods, they are said to be at his risk. Sometimes, also, a contract for the sale of goods, like any other contract, may be totally frustrated by some extraordinary and (usually) unforeseeable event. Because frustration is sometimes also relevant where goods are destroyed or even severely damaged, the two sets of legal principles are interconnected in various ways. Indeed, the doctrine of frustration is sometimes said to be merely an aspect of the general rules as to risk, but this is not entirely accurate. If an executory contract is frustrated, neither party is under any liability to the other. On the other hand, if the goods are at the seller's risk and they perish or deteriorate, although the buyer is not liable to the seller for the price, it by no means follows that the seller is not liable to the buyer for non-delivery if the buyer can prove that he has suffered loss therefrom. The rules as to risk have nothing to say in such a case, and if the seller is to be exempted from liability, it must be by the doctrine of frustration. Conversely, if the goods are at the buyer's risk, he is clearly liable for the price even though the goods have perished or deteriorated. But it does not follow that he may not also be liable for damages for non-acceptance if the seller can prove that he has suffered any.[1] Only frustration can discharge the buyer from the liability for non-acceptance.

Nonetheless, the doctrines of risk and frustration are undoubtedly related, and it is convenient to consider them in the same chapter. The next three sections will be devoted to an examination of the transfer of risk, frustration, and effects of frustration. As the following pages will demonstrate, the whole subject of risk and frustration is bedevilled by the distinction between specific and unascertained goods, and by the failure of the Sale of Goods Act to draw any distinction between different types of unascertained goods. Indeed, it is difficult at times to avoid the conclusion that the draftsmen of both the Sale of Goods Act and the Law Reform (Frustrated Contracts) Act 1943 forgot that there were sales of unascertained goods other than purely generic goods.

TRANSFER OF RISK IN NON-CONSUMER CASES[2]

The general rule laid down by s. 20(1) is that prima facie the risk passes with the property:

---

1 For example, for storage charges: see the Sale of Goods Act s. 37.
2 As to the passing of risk in consumer cases see s. 20(4) added by the Sale and Supply of Goods to Consumers Regulations 2002, SI 2002/3045 reg. 4 – p. 359 below.

Unless otherwise agreed, the goods remain at the seller's risk until the property in them is transferred to the buyer, but when the property in them is transferred to the buyer, the goods are at the buyer's risk whether delivery has been made or not.

If there is an express agreement that one party is to bear the risk even though he has no property (as, for example, there always is in contracts of sale subject to reservation of title clauses), effect must no doubt be given to the agreement, but in the absence of such an express contract, it has been said that 'the rule *res perit domino* is generally an unbending rule of law arising from the very nature of property'.[3] While this is no doubt largely true in a static situation where property remains with one person throughout, it is not necessarily true of the dynamic situation where property is being transferred from one party to another. In this situation, there is nothing peculiar about separating the transfer of risk from the transfer of property and this commonly happens where goods are shipped under a c.i.f. or an f.o.b. contract.[4] Apart from these cases, two other exceptional cases seem to be established by the authorities, in one of which the risk passes before the property and, in the other, the risk passes after the property. The best example of the former exception is *Sterns Ltd* v *Vickers Ltd*.[5] The defendants in this case sold to the plaintiffs 120,000 gallons of spirit, which was part of a total quantity of 200,000 gallons in a storage tank belonging to a third party. The plaintiffs obtained a delivery order which the third party accepted, but the plaintiffs decided to leave the spirit in the tank for the time being for their own convenience. The spirit deteriorated in quality between the time of sale and the time when the plaintiffs eventually took delivery of the 120,000 gallons. Despite the fact that the property clearly had not passed because the goods sold had not been ascertained in the technical sense, and therefore there had been no appropriation, the Court of Appeal held that the risk had passed to the buyers.

Although the decision in *Sterns Ltd* v *Vickers Ltd* appears to have been approved by the House of Lords[6] and must therefore be accepted as correct on its particular facts, the case raises many problems which are closely related to the difficulties arising with regard to the passing of property. As we saw in the last chapter,[7] a sale of an unidentified part of a bulk, as in this case, could not, before the changes effected by the Sale of Goods (Amendment) Act 1995,[8] pass property in the goods because of s. 16. The 1995 Act permits property in an *undivided share* to pass to the buyer, but otherwise, as we have seen, the passing of property, and therefore risk, seems still to be governed by s. 18 Rule 5. But although property in the goods could not, and still cannot pass, the facts of *Sterns Ltd* v *Vickers Ltd* illustrate a situation where, for all practical purposes, the goods 'belong' to the buyers and so it seems desirable that they should be treated as being at the buyers' risk, as the court there held. But of course the problems which prevented the law from treating the property as passing can also affect the question of risk. Suppose, for example, that the spirit had been

---

3 See the Scots case, *Hansen* v *Craig & Rose* (1895) 21 D 432, 438 per Lord President Inglis, cited by Lord Normand in *Comptoir d'Achat et de Vente SA* v *Luis de Ridder Limitada (The Julia)* [1949] AC 293, 319.
4 See Chapter 22.
5 [1923] 1 KB 78.
6 In *The Julia*, above, n. 3.
7 Above, p. 343 *et seq.*
8 See p. 346 *et seq.*

stored in two separate tanks each containing 100,000 gallons and that the contents of one tank only had deteriorated, would the buyer have been compelled to take all the deteriorated spirit, or would he have been able to claim all the spirit from the other tank? Or should the good and bad spirit be divided between the parties in proportion to their respective interests? This latter solution appeared to be the logical conclusion from *Sterns Ltd v Vickers Ltd*, since it gives effect to the holding that the risk is on the buyer and, at the same time, it offers a fair solution to the problem. The 1995 Act, for the reasons explained above, does not seem to add anything to this problem.[9]

At all events, the exceptional nature of this case was emphasized by the House of Lords in *Comptoir d'Achat et de Vente SA v Luis de Ridder Limitada (The Julia)*,[10] where Lord Porter said:

> It is difficult to see how a parcel is at the buyer's risk when he has neither property nor possession except in such cases as *Inglis v Stock*[11] and *Sterns Ltd v Vickers Ltd*[12] where the purchaser had an interest in an undivided part of a bulk parcel on board a ship, or elsewhere, obtained by attornment of the bailee to him.[13]

And Lord Normand observed:

> In those cases in which it has been held that the risk without the property has passed to the buyer it has been because the buyer rather than the seller was seen to have an immediate and practical interest in the goods,[14] as for instance when he has an immediate right under the storekeeper's delivery warrant to the delivery of a portion of an undivided bulk in store, or an immediate right under several contracts with different persons to the whole of a bulk not yet appropriated to the several contracts.[15]

It can be seen, therefore, that the acceptance of the delivery warrant in *Sterns Ltd v Vickers Ltd* was regarded as the crucial factor in the case, since it was this which gave the buyer an immediate right to possession.[16] This may serve to distinguish *Healy v Howlett & Sons*,[17] which is otherwise very similar on its facts to *Sterns Ltd v Vickers Ltd*. Here, it will be recalled, it was held that the risk in 20 boxes of fish, which were dispatched to the buyer as part of a total of 190 boxes, none of which had been earmarked for him, was still on the seller. The court pointed out the difficulties which would have arisen if some only of the boxes had deteriorated or perished. As we have seen,[18] the Law Commissions' proposals on

---

9 See p. 349.
10 [1949] AC 293.
11 (1885) 10 App Cas 263, an f.o.b. case in which risk was held to have passed on shipment before the goods were specifically appropriated to the contract.
12 [1923] 1 KB 78.
13 [1949] AC 293 at p. 312.
14 But this is not really so as regards c.i.f. contracts, for the seller retains the general property, and the buyer has not even an immediate right to possession. See the remarks of Lord Wright in *Smyth & Co Ltd v Bailey & Co Ltd* [1940] 3 All ER 60, 67, quoted below, pp. 426–7.
15 [1949] AC 293 at p. 319.
16 Where the goods are still in the possession of the seller himself, though not yet ascertained, it seems that the risk may pass on the making of the contract, or at least when delivery falls due: see the New Zealand case, *Donaghy's Rope & Twine Co Ltd v Wright, Stephenson & Co* (1906) 25 NZLR 641, 651–2.
17 [1917] 1 KB 337.
18 See pp. 334–5.

the sale of goods forming part of a bulk and the 1995 Act[19] did not deal with this problem directly. The Report indicated that the buyer should be entitled to delivery of goods which conform to the contract in quantity and quality, and that nothing in the new provisions should affect the buyer's rights under the contract.[20] The Commissions are not intending to affect the result in situations similar to those in the cases discussed above in which it was held that the risk of loss or damage to goods forming part of a bulk *could* pass to a buyer prior to delivery.

It should, moreover, be remembered that it is only in the sale of an unidentified part of a specific whole that it can ever be held that the risk passes before the property in a sale of unascertained goods. It clearly cannot do so in the case of goods not owned or possessed by the seller, except in the sense that the buyer may conceivably have contracted to pay the price whether or not the goods are delivered.

It is not easy to imagine circumstances in which the risk remains with the seller after the property has passed in the absence of express agreement to this effect, but if the decision in *Head* v *Tattersall*[21] has survived the Act, it may provide an illustration of such a case. The plaintiff in this case bought a horse from the defendant, warranted to have been hunted with the Bicester hounds, and the plaintiff was given a week in which to return the horse if it did not answer the description. The horse was accidentally injured before the week was up, and the plaintiff claimed to return it, having discovered that it had not been hunted with the Bicester hounds. It was held that the plaintiff was entitled to return the horse and recover the price. The risk was thus held to be on the seller although the property had probably passed to the buyer, subject to the possibility of being divested.[22] There is no reason to think that the case would not be decided in the same way today, but in most such cases, of course, the property does not pass until the expiry of the time fixed in accordance with s. 18 Rule 4(b). However, the decision may well illustrate a broader principle of some importance, namely that the risk always remains on the seller when the buyer has a right of rejection. Thus if the seller ships or delivers defective goods (or if there is a shortfall in quantity[23]) so that the buyer is entitled to reject, it seems that the risk remains on the seller unless and until the buyer accepts the goods. Although this rule is not actually spelt out in the Act,[24] it seems to follow from the rules as to acceptance.[25] As will be seen later, there is nothing in these rules to prevent rejection merely because the goods have been accidentally lost or damaged, and by exercising his right to reject the buyer can thus effectively throw the risk on the seller.

A fairly common instance of an express agreement, under which the property passes before the risk, occurs where the seller agrees to dispatch specific goods at his

---

19 Law Commission No. 215 – see above, p. 344.
20 Ibid., para. 4.34.
21 (1870) LR 7 Ex 7.
22 This, at least, appears to have been the view of Cleasby B. Neither Kelly CB nor Bramwell B expressed any view on the matter. Given that the underlying nature of the transaction in that case appears to have been a sale subject to a right of rescission, it is suggested that Cleasby B's view was correct – see Adams, *Essays for Clive Schmitthoff*, Professional Books, 1983, 1, 3.
23 See *Vitol SA* v *Esso Australia Ltd (The Wise)* [1989] 1 Lloyd's Rep 96, below, p. 506.
24 Compare Art. 2-510 of the UCC.
25 See below, p. 506 *et seq*. The Law Commissions regarded the position as doubtful, but decided against recommending any changes – see Final Report, *Sale and Supply of Goods*, para 5.40.

own risk to the buyer. In this event, the seller is only liable for deterioration or destruction not necessarily incident to the course of transit, for s. 33 provides:

> Where the seller of goods agrees to deliver them at his own risk at a place other than that where they are when sold, the buyer must, nevertheless (unless otherwise agreed), take any risk of deterioration in the goods necessarily incident to the course of transit. •

It seems that the words 'any risk . . . necessarily incident to the course of transit' must be confined to risks which would have arisen with any goods answering the contract description.[26] Thus, a risk of deterioration which is only incidental to the course of transit because of the defective condition of the goods at the commencement of the transit is not covered by this provision. Reference has already been made to *Mash & Murrell v Joseph I Emmanuel Ltd*,[27] where it was held that the implied condition that the goods are of merchantable quality involves a continuing obligation as to the condition of the goods for a reasonable time after shipment in a c.i.f. contract, and to the apparent affirmation of this principle by the House of Lords.[28]

These cases prompt the question whether there is any need for a separate 'doctrine' of risk, at least so far as deterioration of the goods is concerned. It seems to accord more with the techniques of the English and Scottish law of sale to approach such questions by asking whether the seller has continuously warranted the condition of the goods. If so, then clearly the seller remains liable for the deterioration in their condition. If not, then indeed the risk is the buyer's, but it is perhaps misleading to think of the risk of deterioration in almost tangible terms as something which 'passes' from seller to buyer. There is no distinction in principle between the risk of deterioration, which is treated by s. 20 as passing with the property, and the ordinary risk which every buyer takes in respect of matters not covered by conditions and warranties imposed on the seller.

It may, indeed, be that a similar analysis could be made of the risk of accidental destruction of the goods. The question which is most likely to arise in such circumstances is whether the buyer remains liable to pay the price or whether the seller's inability to deliver the goods discharges the buyer. Prima facie, one would have thought that the latter should be the case because payment and delivery are, under s. 28 of the Act, concurrent conditions. But this is not the law, because if the goods are accidentally destroyed after the property has passed, the presumption is that the risk has also passed, and the buyer must therefore pay the price even though the seller cannot deliver the goods. It is, however, far from obvious why the risk of accidental destruction should be on the buyer prior to delivery, except in the case of goods which are shipped for dispatch to the buyer, where special considerations arise. Indeed, in retail sales the technical legal position is so grotesque that it is difficult to believe that a seller would ever take advantage of it. If, for example, in a non-consumer

---

26 See (1965) 28 MLR 180, 189 and [1962] J Bus L 352. As suggested above, it is arguable that the risk in non-conforming goods always remains with the seller – see *Head v Tattersall* (1871) LR 7 Ex 7, p. 356 above. The proposition may gain support from *Kinnear v Brodie* (1901) 3 F 540; Gow, *Mercantile Law*, pp. 149, 184, 185. See also Scottish Law Commission Memorandum No. 25, *Corporeal Moveables: Passing of Risk and of Ownership* (1976); T.B. Smith, *Property Problems in Sale* (1978), Ch. II.

27 [1961] 1 All ER 485, above, p. 188 *et seq.*

28 *Lambert v Lewis* [1982] AC 225, 276.

case[29] a person buys an article in a shop for later delivery and the shop is burned down with its stock overnight, the buyer would probably be astonished to learn that he might still be liable for the price.[30] In fact, the goods would almost certainly be insured and, if the buyer were required to pay the price, it is possible that the seller would be a constructive trustee of the proceeds of the insurance policy for the buyer.[31]

The question of who should bear the risk of accidental destruction, therefore, boils down in modern conditions to who should be required to insure them. It is surely very doubtful whether the present rule which lays the obligation to insure (or more strictly, the risk of not insuring) on the party who has the property, is in most circumstances the right solution. Certainly in retail sales and similar transactions, a powerful case could be made for saying that the most appropriate person to insure would nearly always be the party with physical possession, if only because in practice this is what would normally happen.[32] To take a simple example, in a hire-purchase agreement the person who ought to insure the goods is clearly the person in possession and, of course, all hire-purchase agreements of vehicles impose an obligation to insure on the hirer.

Even in bulk sales, it seems doubtful whether the present rule is the most appropriate one. Here again it seems probable that the right person to insure normally is the person in physical possession, although it may be that special provision would be necessary in relation to insurance while the goods are in the hands of a carrier for transmission to the buyer. And it may well be that commercial practice would, in many other circumstances, rebut the prima facie presumption that the person in possession should insure.

At all events, the concept of 'risk' is concerned only with accidental destruction or deterioration and does not cover damage to the goods caused by the fault of either party. Section 20, therefore, has the following further provisions:

(2) But where delivery has been delayed through the fault of either buyer or seller the goods are at the risk of the party at fault as regards any loss which might not have occurred but for such fault.

(3) Nothing in this section affects the duties or liabilities of either seller or buyer as a bailee . . . of the goods of the other party.

Subsection (2) was applied in *Demby Hamilton & Co Ltd* v *Barden*.[33] Here the seller contracted to sell 30 tons of apple juice to be delivered to the buyer in weekly loads. The seller crushed the apples and put the juice in casks pending delivery. The buyer was late in taking delivery and some of the juice went bad. Applying subs. (2), the learned judge held that the buyer was liable. But it is important to note that the

---

29 For the situation in consumer sales see p. 359 *et seq.* below.
30 Perhaps a court would hold today that property in such a case does not pass on the making of the contract: see the dictum of Diplock LJ in *R V Ward* v *Bignall* [1967] 1 QB 534, 545.
31 See s. 47 of the Law of Property Act 1925, and *Maurice* v *Goldsborough Mort & Co Ltd* [1939] AC 452, and cases there cited.
32 The Uniform Commercial Code adopts this approach fairly consistently – see generally Art. 2 Part 5, and especially Art. 2-509 Comment 3. As to the situation in the case of consumer sales, see p. 359 *et seq.* below. See also Scottish Law Commission Memorandum No. 25 (1976), cited above n. 26.
33 [1949] 1 All ER 435. See also *Pommer* v *Mowat* (1906) 14 SLT 373.

party in fault is not liable for all risks, but only for those which 'might not have occurred but for such fault'.[34]

Subsection (3) means that the mere fact that one party is in fault does not discharge the other from his obligations to take due care as a bailee. In particular, the fact that the buyer is late in taking delivery does not mean that the seller is not still bound to take all reasonable care of the goods.[35] If he also is in fault, questions might arise as to the possibility of apportioning the damage between the parties, either by the application of the Law Reform (Contributory Negligence) Act 1945,[36] or possibly, in some cases, on the basis of causation at common law.[37] In *Knight* v *Wilson*,[38] the seller of a boat, the property and risk in which had passed to the buyer, negligently caused damage to it while sailing it without permission, and was held liable to the buyer under the custodian's duty of care.

TRANSFER OF RISK IN CONSUMER CASES

In cases where the buyer deals as consumer, the above rules set out in s. 20(1)–(3) no longer apply. Instead, the following rule is subsituted.[39]

> (4) In a case where the buyer deals as consumer or, in Scotland, where there is a consumer contract in which the buyer is a consumer, subsections (1) to (3) above must be ignored and the goods remain at the seller's risk until they are delivered to the consumer.

This rule seems eminently sensible, as it is likely both to accord with the fact that the buyer's household insurance policy will cover the goods only when they are in his possession, and with the need for a clear rule as to when risk has passed.[40]

In the case of consumer sales there is a further modification to the risk provisions. Section 32(1)–(3) deal with cases where goods are to be delivered to a carrier who is to transport them to the buyer. These provisions are dealt with in Chapter 22. However, these provisions too are disapplied in the case of consumer sales.[41]

---

34 It is, however, to be noted that there appears to be no justification in terms of insurance for this rule. Generally, the party in possession of the goods will have them insured, and it makes no difference that, the delivery to a particular buyer is delayed. It appears to be a weakness of the Uniform Commercial Code that, having adopted a general principle of placing the risk of loss on the party in possession, it then permits breach to affect the risk of loss – see Art. 2-510.

35 In the Tasmanian case of *Sharp* v *Batt* (1930) 25 Tas LR 33, 56, it was said that the buyer remained liable in the absence of gross negligence by seller, but today it is unlikely that a court would require the negligence to be gross.

36 See *Forsikringsaktieselskapet Vesta* v *Butcher* [1988] 2 All ER 43, in which the Court of Appeal clarified the circumstances in which the 1945 Act may be applicable to an action in contract. (The decision was affirmed on a different point: [1989] 1 All ER 402.) The Act has no application where the defendant is in breach of a strict contractual duty as under the Sale of Goods Act 1979 – *Barclays Bank* v *Fairclough Buildings Ltd* [1988] 2 All ER 43 – see Law Commission Report No. 219 (1993).

37 See, for an example of such apportionment at common law, *Tennant Radiant Heat* v *Warrington Devp't Corpn* [1988] EG LR 41 (CA).

38 1949 SLT (Sh Ct) 26.

39 Substituted by the Sale and Supply of Goods to Consumers Regulations 2002, SI 2002/3045 reg. 4(2).

40 As noted at p. 320 above, under the American Uniform Commercial Code the general rule where the seller is a merchant is that risk passes on the buyer's receipt of the goods (Art. 2-509(3)). The policy underlying this provision is set out in Comment 3 to this subsection, namely that a merchant who is to make physical delivery of the goods can be expected to insure his interest in them. By contrast, it is extremely unlikely that a buyer will carry insurance over goods not yet in his possession. Where the seller is not a merchant, risk passes on tender of delivery under this subsection.

41 Sale and Supply of Goods to Consumers Regulations 2002, SI 2002/3045 reg. 4(3).

(4) In a case where the buyer deals as consumer or, in Scotland, where there is a consumer contract in which the buyer is a consumer, subsections (1) to (3) above must be ignored, but if in pursuance of a contract of sale the seller is authorised or required to send the goods to the buyer, delivery of the goods to the carrier is not delivery of the goods to the buyer.

This too seems a sensible modification, as the rules contained in s. 32 were developed in the context of commercial sales, and do not correspond to the reasonable expectations of most consumer buyers. In point of fact, it seems likely that many responsible retailers already operated on a principle akin to that set out in the new s. 32(4).

FRUSTRATION

It has already been suggested that the doctrine of frustration covers a wider field than the rules as to risk. The drafting of s. 7 supports this view:

> Where there is an agreement to sell specific goods, and subsequently the goods, without any fault on the part of the seller or buyer, perish before the risk passes to the buyer, the agreement is thereby avoided.

The doctrine of risk simply lays down that prima facie if the goods perish before the property passes, the seller must bear the loss and cannot claim the price. Were the doctrine of frustration merely an aspect of the rules as to risk, this section would be an absurdity for it would, in effect, be saying that where the risk is on the seller he must bear the risk of the goods perishing. But s. 7 does more than this, for it provides that in the circumstances there mentioned the contract is avoided. This means that both parties are discharged from their obligations; in other words, not only is the buyer not liable for the price, but the seller is not liable for non-delivery.

Application of s. 7

The scope of s. 7 is comparatively narrow. It only applies to a contract for the sale of specific goods in which neither the property nor the risk[42] has passed but, as we have seen, the general presumption is that a contract for the sale of specific goods passes both the property and the risk at once. Section 7 therefore only applies where s. 18 Rule 1 does not apply for some reason, or where, if it does apply, in the case of non-consumer sales, s. 20 does not apply. Section 7 will prima facie apply wherever there is a case of a conditional sale of specific goods under s. 18 Rules 2 and 3.

The meaning of the word 'perish' in s. 7 is presumably the same as in s. 6 and the discussion there may be referred to.[43] Destruction of part only of specific goods also raises similar questions in the two sections. If a person agrees to sell specific goods, part only of which perish before the risk passes to the buyer, does s. 7 operate to frustrate the contract and discharge the seller? *Barrow Lane & Ballard Ltd v Phillip*

---

42 Note that s. 7 only applies 'where there is an *agreement* to sell specific goods', not 'where there is a sale', etc., which shows that it has no application where property passes. See, e.g., *Horn v Minister of Food* [1948] 2 All ER 1036.
43 See above, p. 109 *et seq*.

Phillips & Co Ltd[44] suggests that if the contract is unseverable it is frustrated by the perishing of part of the goods, whereas if it is severable it is frustrated only as to the part which has perished. But this conclusion seems suspect in the light of *H R & S Sainsbury* v *Street*.[45] This case, although not itself falling under s. 7, suggests that where part only of the goods perish, the seller may well be obliged to offer the remaining goods to the buyer. The buyer, however, may not be obliged to take them.

It is thought that the perishing of the goods cannot frustrate a contract otherwise than under s. 7. If the property and the risk have both passed, it surely cannot be said that the subsequent destruction of the goods can frustrate the contract. Frustration cannot apply to a fully executed contract.[46] Nor is it easy to see how the result can be different if the property has passed but the risk has not. If the property has passed, it can hardly be said that the object of the contract can be defeated by supervening events. There remains the possibility that the risk may have passed before the property, and the goods may have perished after the one and before the other. Here, again, it is submitted there cannot be frustration, for this would discharge the buyer's obligation to pay the price, or enable him to recover it if already paid, and this would mean that the risk was on the seller and not the buyer.[47]

Whatever the true basis of the doctrine of frustration, it would appear that s. 7 is only a prima facie rule of construction and nothing more, so that it does not necessarily apply merely because the facts fall within its purview. Once again there are at least three possible constructions similar to those which were discussed in connection with *Couturier* v *Hastie*[48] and *Howell* v *Coupland*[49] (and again, in commercial cases[50] yet further constructions may be possible where part only of the goods perish):

1   There may be an implied condition that if the goods perish the contract will be discharged and neither party will be liable, that is the contract may be frustrated.
2   The seller may contract that the goods will not perish, in which case the seller will not only have to bear the loss of the goods, that is will be unable to claim the price, but he may also be liable for damages for non-delivery.
3   The buyer may contract that he will take the consequences of the goods perishing, in which case he will have to pay the price whatever happens to the goods, and he may also be liable for damages.

Frustration of contract of sale at common law

Perishing of specific goods is the only instance of frustration provided for by the Act, but there is no doubt that at common law a contract for the sale of specific goods may be frustrated by any event which destroys the whole basis of the contract and

---

44 [1929] 1 KB 574.
45 [1972] 1 WLR 834 – see above, p. 109.
46 See *Re Shipton Anderson & Co Ltd and Harrison Bros & Co Ltd* [1915] 3 KB 676, where the CA clearly thought that there could be no frustration if property and risk had both passed.
47 *Horn* v *Minister of Food*, above, n. 42. Certainly in c.i.f. contracts where risk usually passes before property, the perishing of the goods after passing of risk does not frustrate the contract, even though there is then no property to pass.
48 (1856) 5 HLC 673 – see above, p. 103.
49 (1876) 1 QBD 258 – see above, p. 108.
50 In consumer sales goods remain at the seller's risk until delivery – s. 20(4), see p. 359 above – so that for practical purposes the possibilities set out below would not be realistic.

radically alters the obligations of the parties, provided that the event occurs before the property and risk have passed to the buyer.[51]

The question remains whether a contract for the sale of unascertained goods can be frustrated by perishing of the goods or otherwise. The answer depends upon the type of unascertained goods in question. In the first place, it is probable that an agreement to sell purely generic goods cannot be frustrated by the destruction of the goods, because a whole species of goods cannot perish – as the Latin maxim has it, *genus numquam perit*. A particular stock of the goods in question may perish, of course, but it is no concern of the buyer that the seller had a particular stock in mind which is accidentally destroyed after the making of the contract.

> Suppose A has contracted to sell to B unascertained goods by description, for example 'a' Bentley Mark VI (not 'this' Bentley Mark VI) and suppose, further, that the seller expects to acquire the goods from a particular source, which may, indeed, be the only source available, the bare fact, without more, that when the time for delivery comes, that source has dried up and that the seller cannot draw on it, does not absolve the seller. He is still, in the absence of some contractual term excusing him, liable for non-delivery.[52]

It does not follow from this that a contract for the sale of unascertained goods of the other two types discussed above[53] cannot be frustrated by the perishing of the goods. For example, if a person agrees to sell a crop to be grown on a particular field, the contract may be frustrated by the failure of the crop;[54] or, if a person agrees to construct machinery in a building owned by another, and the whole building with the machinery is accidentally destroyed before it is completed, the contract may be frustrated.[55]

There also seems to be no reason why, in an appropriate case, a contract for the sale of any type of unascertained goods may not be frustrated by some event other than the perishing of the goods. It may, of course, be more difficult to persuade the court that the event which has occurred has destroyed the basis of the contract where the goods are unascertained and, indeed, in *Blackburn Bobbin Co Ltd v Allen & Son*,[56] McCardie J went so far as to say:

> In the absence of any question as to trading with the enemy, and in the absence also of any administrative intervention by the British Government authorities, a bare and unqualified contract for the sale of unascertained goods will not (unless most special facts compel an opposite implication) be dissolved by the operation of [the doctrine of frustration].

But although this case was affirmed in the Court of Appeal,[57] none of the Lords Justices was as cautious as McCardie J. On the contrary, they all treated the case as though the doctrine of frustration might have applied, but that it did not do so

---

51 For example, *Re Shipton Anderson & Co Ltd and Harrison & Bros & Co Ltd* [1915] 3 KB 676. On the Scots common law of frustration, see McBryde, *Law of Contract in Scotland*, 2nd edn (2001) Ch. 21.
52 *Monkland v Jack Barclay Ltd* [1951] 2 KB 252, 258 per Asquith LJ.
53 Above, pp. 83–4 *et seq.*
54 *Howell v Coupland* (1876) 1 QBD 258.
55 *Appleby v Myers* (1867) LR 2 CP 651.
56 [1918] 1 KB 540, 550.
57 [1918] 2 KB 467.

because the alleged frustrating event only affected the way in which the seller was going to perform the contract. Such being the case, as Pickford LJ observed:

> Why should a purchaser of goods, not specific goods, be deemed to concern himself with the way in which the seller is going to fulfil his contract by providing the goods he has agreed to sell?[58]

A striking instance of the application (in effect) of this principle is to be found in the Suez Canal cases,[59] where the House of Lords held that the closure of the canal did not frustrate c.i.f. contracts for the sale of Sudanese groundnuts to European buyers, despite the fact that the only alternative route was via the Cape of Good Hope, several thousand miles longer. The decisive point may have been that these were contracts for the sale of goods c.i.f. in which the buyers were only concerned with the shipment of the goods at the port of shipment, and their ultimate arrival at their destination. Precisely how the sellers got the goods to the buyers was their own business. Conversely, the unloading of the goods from the vessel at the port of destination in a c.i.f. contract is prima facie the sole responsibility of the buyer. If the goods cannot be so unloaded because the buyer has not obtained any necessary import licence, he will bear the loss.[60] The inability to unload the vessel is not a frustrating circumstance because the buyer could (for instance) have diverted the ship to take delivery elsewhere. This is, anyhow, no concern of the seller. Similarly, the contract is not frustrated merely because the buyer is unable to export the goods for resale as he had intended.[61]

But in *Re Badische Co Ltd*[62] Russell J held that a contract to supply unascertained goods which both parties knew could only be obtained from Germany was frustrated by the outbreak of war. He said:[63]

> Speaking for myself, I can see no reason why, given the necessary circumstances to exist, the doctrine should not apply equally to the case of unascertained goods. It is, of course, obvious from the nature of the contract that the necessary circumstances can only very rarely arise in the case of unascertained goods. That they may arise appears to me to be undoubted.

More recently it has been affirmed that there is no legal principle excluding the doctrine of frustration in the case of a c.i.f. contract, though also confirming that the doctrine would only apply rarely in practice.[64] In this case, a seller carrying on business in Malta agreed to sell potatoes c.i.f. London, shipment between 14 and 24 April. In fact, only one vessel called at Malta during this period and the seller was unable to obtain space on it. It was held that the seller took the risk of being unable to get shipping space and was liable.

---

58 Ibid., at p. 469. Cf. *Re Thornett & Fehr & Yuills Ltd* [1921] 1 KB 219.
59 *Tsakiroglou & Co v Noblee & Thorl GmbH* [1962] AC 93, overruling *Carapanayoti & Co Ltd v E T Green Ltd* [1959] 1 QB 131.
60 *Congimex v Tradax* [1983] 1 Lloyd's Rep 250.
61 *McMaster & Co Ltd v McEuen & Co Ltd* 1921 SC (HL) 24. But where an English company orders goods from a foreign company, both parties being aware that an export licence is necessary, the failure to obtain the licence may frustrate the contract – see *A V Pound & Co Ltd v M W Hardy & Co Inc* [1956] AC 588. (Cf. *Peter Cassidy Seed Co v Osuustukkuk-Auppa IL* [1954] 2 Lloyd's Rep 586.). See below, p. 435 *et seq.*
62 [1921] 2 Ch 331.
63 Ibid., at p. 382.
64 *Lewis Emmanuel & Son Ltd v Sammut* [1959] 2 Lloyd's Rep 629.

Force majeure clauses

Although it is thus difficult to invoke the doctrine of frustration when restrictions are imposed by governments on the export or import of goods sold under c.i.f. and similar contracts, business contracts often include *force majeure* clauses (as they are known) to protect the parties against liabilities arising from such governmental activity, or other similar events. These clauses are usually very strictly interpreted by the courts against those relying on them so that liability is often imposed on the ground that, despite embargoes, prohibitions and the like, the party relying on the clause might still have been able to perform, for example by buying goods afloat, by shipping earlier (or later) or by making more strenuous efforts to obtain a licence. What is particularly striking about the legal approach to these problems is that the liability in question is nearly always a liability for pure expectation, or loss of bargain, damages. There is surely a case for a less strict form of liability, where the plaintiff claims damages of this nature, even apart altogether from the presence of *force majeure* clauses. To interpret such clauses very narrowly where these are the only damages claimed suggests that the courts are imposing their own view of commercial morality (or economics) in the teeth of commercial expectations.

A whole series of cases, which came before the courts in the second half of the 1970s and early 1980s out of one major commercial embargo, illustrates very well the extreme stringency with which such clauses are usually interpreted. These cases arose out of a disastrous failure of the soya bean crop in the United States in 1973 which led to an embargo being placed on the export of soya beans for a short period late in 1973. Many contracts for the sale of this crop, to the value of millions of pounds, were affected, and sellers relied on *force majeure* clauses in the standard contract used in that trade.[65] But in a whole series of decisions the Court of Appeal, and in one or two cases the House of Lords, approached the clause so strictly that the result was almost always to render the seller liable, despite the *force majeure* clause. Sometimes, the courts held that the burden of proof was on the sellers to show that they could not have found adequate supplies already afloat; sometimes it was held that sellers had failed to give notice, as required by the clause, at the right time; sometimes it was held that the sellers could have shipped before the embargo was imposed, or after it was lifted. The story was reviewed by the Court of Appeal in *André et Cie v Tradax*[66] in which the judges acknowledged that the courts had perhaps been too legalistic in their approach, or at least that they had tended to look at the problems from a strictly legal, rather than a more realistic commercial, viewpoint. In particular, the courts had sometimes failed to appreciate the aggregate effects of the embargo as a whole, looking too closely at individual contracts to see whether (for instance) a particular seller might in theory have been able to buy the soya beans for his contract without regard to the fact that hundreds of other sellers were all at the same time desperately looking for any soya beans available for export. It is still unclear whether this case foreshadowed a greater willingness on the part of the courts to allow *force majeure* clauses to be

---

65 The GAFTA form.
66 [1983] 1 Lloyd's Rep 254.

invoked.[67] Of course, as a matter of strict law, all depends on the proper construction and application of each clause in its own context, and it is beyond the scope of this work to attempt to look at typical clauses.

EFFECTS OF FRUSTRATION[68]

In English law, the consequences of frustration of a contract for the sale of goods depend upon whether the Law Reform (Frustrated Contracts) Act 1943[69] applies or not.

Cases to which the Frustrated Contracts Act does not apply

Section 2(5)(c) of the Frustrated Contracts Act excludes from its operation:

> Any contract to which section 7 of the Sale of Goods Act, 1979 . . . applies, or [to] any other contract for the sale, or for the sale and delivery, of specific goods, where the contract is frustrated by reason of the fact that the goods have perished.

With regard to contracts to which s. 7 of the Sale of Goods Act applies this is clear enough, but the interpretation of the second part of this clause is a matter of some difficulty. As we have seen, it is probable that no contract for the sale of specific goods is frustrated 'by reason of the fact that the goods have perished' otherwise than in accordance with s. 7. Yet if this is so there is no room at all for the application of the second half of s. 2(5)(c) of the Frustrated Contracts Act. Moreover, even if, contrary to the above contention, a contract may be frustrated in such circumstances, it is still not easy to understand the object of this clause. Three cases may be considered.

First, where there is a contract for the sale of specific goods in which the property and the risk have both passed to the buyer. Even if such a contract could be frustrated by the perishing of the goods, which seems highly improbable, the Frustrated Contracts Act does not apply. It may be that this was intended to avoid any possible doubt that in such an event the buyer is still liable to pay the whole price and cannot ask the court for any relief under the Act of 1943.

Secondly, where there is a contract for the sale of specific goods in which the property has not yet passed, but in which the risk has passed to the buyer. Once again it seems inconceivable that such a contract could be frustrated at all, because this would render meaningless the statement that the risk is on the buyer, but if such a contract can be frustrated the Act does not apply. The intention here may have been to avoid all difficulty in c.i.f. contracts should the goods perish after the risk has passed but before the bill of lading is transferred. In this event, the buyer is still bound to pay the whole price and cannot invoke the Act of 1943.

Thirdly, where the property has passed but the goods are still at the seller's risk. If such a contract is frustrated by the perishing of the goods, which again seems

---

67 For a possible straw in the wind, see *Pagnan SpA v Tradax Ocean Transportation SA* [1987] 3 All ER 565. On the other hand, cases arising from the great soya embargo of 1973 show the courts finding against the sellers on almost every occasion; see, e.g., *Cook Industries Inc v Tradax Export SA* [1985] 2 Lloyd's Rep 454.

68 See Glanville Williams, *Law Reform (Frustrated Contracts) Act 1943*, pp. 81–90.

69 Hereafter referred to as the Frustrated Contracts Act.

unlikely, the Frustrated Contracts Act does not apply. Presumably this is to avoid any doubt that the seller must bear the whole loss and cannot transfer any of it to the buyer.

In considering the cases to which the Frustrated Contracts Act does not apply, therefore, it may be permissible to concentrate on cases under s. 7 of the Sale of Goods Act, that is to say where there is a sale[70] of specific goods in which neither property nor risk has passed to the buyer and the contract is frustrated by the perishing of the goods. To such a case, the ordinary common law rules of frustration apply. The most important of these are as follows.

In the first place, both parties are discharged from all obligations not yet accrued before the destruction of the goods. In other words, the seller is not liable for non-delivery of the goods and the buyer is not liable for non-payment of the price.

Secondly, if the price, or any part of it, has been paid, it can be recovered if there is a total failure of consideration. This was the law even before the decision in the *Fibrosa* case[71] because the rule in *Chandler* v *Webster*,[72] which was overruled in that case, was never applied to contracts for the sale of goods.[73] In the *Fibrosa* case buyers paid £1,000 in advance for some machinery to be manufactured by the sellers. The contract was frustrated before the machinery was completed and before any part of it was delivered, although the sellers claimed that they had already incurred considerable expense in performance of the contract. The buyers were held entitled to recover their prepayment as on a total failure of consideration, and the sellers were not allowed to set off any of their expenses against the prepayment.

Today the *Fibrosa* case would be subject to the operation of the 1943 Act, but comparable cases may still arise where the common law rules continue to operate, so that if there is a total failure of consideration and the buyer can recover the price, the seller is not entitled to set off anything for expenses which he may have incurred before the frustrating event. For example, suppose that A agrees to buy some goods from B and pays the price, or part of it, in advance, but B is to do something to the goods to put them into a deliverable state. Suppose, further, that the goods are accidentally destroyed after B has done some of the work. This is a case to which s. 18 Rule 2 applies and, therefore, prima facie the property and the risk do not pass until the work is completed and the buyer has notice thereof. The case, therefore, falls within the clear wording of s. 7 of the Sale of Goods Act, and the Frustrated Contracts Act does not apply. The common law rule therefore enables the buyer to recover the whole amount which he has paid in advance, and the seller is not entitled to retain any of it on account of the expenses incurred. It is difficult to see why this should be so, for as a matter of justice there seems no material distinction between such a case and the *Fibrosa* case[74] to which the Frustrated Contracts Act clearly would apply. Moreover, the arbitrary results of s. 2(5)(c) of the Frustrated Contracts Act are all the more apparent when it is remembered that s. 7 of the Sale of Goods

---

70 It must also be remembered that s. 7 only applies to contracts of sale of goods, so it does not apply to any contract for services, nor to a contract for the supply of goods which is not strictly a sale.

71 [1943] AC 32.

72 [1904] 1 KB 493.

73 *Logan* v *Le Mesurier* (1847) 6 Moo PC 116.

74 [1943] AC 32.

Act only deals with frustration through perishing of the goods. If the contract is frustrated by some other event, for example the outbreak of war or the like, s. 7 has no application and the Frustrated Contracts Act can be invoked. It is submitted that this is quite unjustifiable, and it is hard to see why s. 2(5)(c) of the Act of 1943 was thought necessary at all, especially as the workings of the Act are left to the discretion of the court.

The fourth rule at common law is that payments made under a contract which is subsequently frustrated cannot be recovered if there is only a partial failure of consideration. Suppose, for example, A agrees to buy a specific parcel of 100 tonnes of wheat now in a warehouse, the price to be paid in advance, but the goods to remain the property of the seller, B, until delivery, and delivery to be by instalments of 10 tonnes each. One instalment is delivered, and the rest of the wheat is then accidentally destroyed by fire. Prima facie the risk remains with the seller until the property has passed, so that this is a case within s. 7 of the Sale of Goods Act. The question whether the goods have perished within the meaning of that section probably depends upon the construction of the contract. Prima facie it would appear that the destruction of the undelivered part of the goods avoids the whole contract. To this case the Frustrated Contracts Act does not apply and the position at common law remains. These common law rules, however, are by no means easy to apply to a case of this kind. At first sight, it might be thought that nothing can be recovered because there is only a partial failure of consideration, but in fact it is submitted that the buyer can recover the amount of the price which is to be attributed to the goods which have perished. The reason for this is that the risk in respect of those goods was on the seller when they perished. The same applies if the buyer has not paid the price in advance, so that the buyer should only be liable for a proportionate part of the price.

In these cases, therefore, the Frustrated Contracts Act is not needed and does not apply, because the common law can achieve a satisfactory result through the rules as to risk. Yet, illogically, if the contract is frustrated by some event other than the perishing of the goods, the Frustrated Contracts Act does apply.

Finally, the usual common law rule, known as the 'entire contracts rule', is that if a contract is frustrated it is not possible to compel one party to pay for a benefit received where the contract was to perform one indivisible service, and nothing has been paid in advance. So if one party has partly (but not 'substantially')[75] performed his contract and finds that he cannot complete it as a result of frustration, he is not entitled at common law to any part of the agreed price, even though some benefit has been received by the other party,[76] and perhaps even if that benefit survives the frustrating event.

But although this is the general rule at common law, it can hardly be applied without qualification to contracts of sale of goods. Even if the party who has received the benefit before the frustrating event cannot be made to pay for that benefit under the contract, he may be liable in a restitutionary action, based upon his acceptance of the benefit and his refusal to disgorge it. So, for example, if part of the goods under

---

75 As to substantial performance see Adams and Brownsword (1990) 53 MLR 536 at 538.
76 *Cutter* v *Powell* (1795) 6 TR 320; *Appleby* v *Myers* (1867) LR 2 CP 651.

a contract of sale have been delivered and then a frustrating event prevents the seller from delivering the remainder, the buyer may be liable in a restitutionary claim for the goods delivered, which is based at least in part on the benefit received, and his refusal to return the goods. Hitherto, it has been established law that this restitutionary claim is only available where a new promise is capable of being implied in fact.[77] If, therefore, the buyer still has the goods in his possession when the contract is frustrated, no doubt such a new promise can be implied, but if he has already disposed of them it may be that he cannot be made liable to pay a proportionate part of the price for them.[78] This seems a harsh and unreasonable result which is due to the fact that restitutionary remedies were originally based on the idea of an 'implied' contract or promise, and it is ripe for reconsideration in light of modern ideas about the basis of the law of restitution. Once again, the position is different under the Frustrated Contracts Act, though it is hard to see why sales of specific goods should be distinguished from sales of unascertained goods, nor is it easy to see why the result should differ according to the nature of the frustrating event. Yet such is the effect of s. 2(5)(c) of the Frustrated Contracts Act 1943.

Cases to which the Frustrated Contracts Act does apply

The Frustrated Contracts Act applies *inter alia* to all contracts for the sale of unascertained goods, and to contracts for the sale of specific goods which are frustrated by some event other than the perishing of the goods. The Act effects three main changes in the law.

First, it enables a person to recover any payments made under a contract which has since been frustrated even though there has only been a partial failure of consideration. This is the effect of s. 1(2) of the Frustrated Contracts Act:

> All sums paid or payable to any party in pursuance of the contract before the time when the parties were so discharged . . . shall, in the case of sums so paid, be recoverable from him as money received by him for the use of the party by whom the sums were paid, and, in the case of sums so payable, cease to be so payable.

So, for example, if a person agrees to buy 1,000 tons of wheat, payment in advance and delivery by instalments, and the contract is frustrated after only one instalment is delivered, this subsection applies. The seller is therefore bound to repay the price paid in advance even though there is no total failure of consideration.

The same result could be reached by applying s. 2(4) of the Act of 1943:

> Where it appears to the court that a part of any contract to which this Act applies can properly be severed from the remainder of the contract, being a part wholly performed before the time of discharge, or so performed except for the payment in respect of that part of the contract of sums which are or can be ascertained under the contract, the court shall treat that part of the contract as if it were a separate contract and had not been frustrated and shall

---

77 *Sumpter* v *Hedges* [1898] 1 QB 673.
78 Section 30(1) (above, p. 139) probably has no application to such a case, because it postulates circumstances in which the delivery of only part of the goods is a breach of contract, and in which the buyer may reject that part at once. The case put here is one in which the delivery of part of the goods is not a breach of contract, and the buyer cannot therefore reject them when delivered.

treat the foregoing section of this Act as only applicable to the remainder of that contract.

By severing the executed from the frustrated part of the contract, the court can in effect turn a partial failure of consideration in respect of the whole contract into a total failure of consideration in respect of the frustrated part, and in this way enable the payer to recover his payment.

The second main change made by the Act is to enable the seller to retain part or all of a sum which would otherwise be recoverable as on a total (or now, a partial) failure of consideration, if he has incurred expenses in or for the purpose of the performance of the contract. Thus s. 1(2) continues:

> Provided that, if the party to whom the sums were so paid or payable incurred expenses before the time of discharge in, or for the purpose of, the performance of the contract, the court may, if it considers it just to do so having regard to all the circumstances of the case, allow him to retain or, as the case may be, recover the whole or any part of the sums so paid or payable, not being an amount in excess of the expenses so incurred.

Apart from imposing upper limits, the Act leaves the question of the amount of the set-off to the discretion of the court, and one possible consequence of this is that the seller will not be allowed to retain a sum equivalent to the whole of the expenses which he has incurred. The object of the Act was to avoid the injustices which followed at common law of throwing the whole loss on to one party or the other, and it is not likely that the Act merely contemplated shifting this loss from one party to the other. Probably, therefore, the court would, in a suitable case, divide the loss between the two parties and permit the seller to recover accordingly.

The third main change in the law effected by the Act is the creation of a special exception to the 'entire contracts' rule, commonly known as the rule in *Cutter* v *Powell*.[79] This case laid down that, where there is a contract to perform a complete action and nothing is payable in advance, no part of the agreed amount can be recovered if the contract is not completely (or anyhow 'substantially') performed as a result of frustration or any other cause. The position is now regulated by s. 1(3) of the Frustrated Contracts Act:

> Where any party to the contract has, by reason of anything done by any other party thereto in, or for the purpose of, the performance of the contract, obtained a valuable benefit (other than a payment of money to which the last foregoing subsection applies) before the time of discharge, there shall be recoverable from him by the said other party such sum (if any), not exceeding the value of the said benefit to the party obtaining it, as the Court considers just, having regard to all the circumstances of the case . . .

Thus where part only of the goods has been delivered and the contract is then frustrated, we have seen that at common law the seller may be unable to recover anything if the circumstances are such that it is not possible to imply a new promise to pay. Where the Frustrated Contracts Act applies, however, s. 1(3) thus enables the court to compel the buyer to pay for the part which he has received, although it would not have been possible to imply the existence of a promise to pay at common law.

---

79 (1795) 6 TR 320 – but see n. 76 above as to the modification of the strict application of this rule in modern contexts.

Many intricate questions, mostly turning on the application of s. 1(3) of the Act, were discussed by Robert Goff J (now Lord Goff) in *BP Exploration Co (Libya) Ltd* v *Hunt*.[80] In his view, this subsection is properly to be regarded as the statutory creation of a restitutionary right for benefits rendered. In the application of s. 1(3), the learned judge held that the key question was the identification and measurement of the benefit rendered before the frustrating event. The value of the benefit is the upper limit of the amount which may be awarded but, subject to that, the amount to be awarded is that sum which the court finds to be just having regard to the circumstances mentioned in the Act. He also held that where goods are delivered and retained until the frustrating event, they must be valued for the purposes of the Act as at the date of the frustrating event. But if the goods have been disposed of by the defendant prior to the frustrating event, then they must be valued at the date of disposal and no allowance can be made for any benefits which the defendant may have had from the proceeds of sale; thus if many years elapse before the frustrating event, the defendant cannot be made to pay for the valuable benefits he may have received as a result of having in his hands the proceeds of sale during that time. Robert Goff J also expressed the view that no sum should be awarded for any benefit conferred if, as a result of the frustrating event, the benefit is in effect completely nullified. For example, if goods are delivered to a buyer which have some value, but a subsequent embargo is placed on all dealings with the goods (before the buyer has the chance to dispose of any of them) then, if this is indeed a frustrating event, the buyer will have been deprived by the frustration of the contract of the whole value of the goods. In this event, no compensation can be awarded to the seller under the Act. If this is right, the decision in *Appleby* v *Myers*[81] would be no different under the Act, but the judge's views on this were *obiter* and the point remains open.[82]

Despite the fact that the Frustrated Contracts Act was passed to mitigate the harshness of the common law rules, it still leaves a substantial area for their operation. The Act only alters the common law where something has been paid in advance or where one party has received a valuable benefit under the contract before the frustrating event (and, if Goff J is right, where that benefit survives the frustrating event). But in contracts for the sale of goods to be manufactured by the seller there is rarely any benefit obtained before the contract is fully executed, so the Frustrated Contracts Act does nothing unless there has been some prepayment. Suppose, for example, that A orders machinery from B, nothing to be paid until delivery. After B has incurred considerable expense in the construction of the machinery, the contract is frustrated by the outbreak of war or the like. Although this is not a case within s. 7 of the Sale of Goods Act and the Frustrated Contracts Act could apply, it provides no remedy to the seller. Yet surely his position is no less meritorious because he has not insisted on being paid in advance. The same result follows where there is a payment in advance, but the seller has incurred expense in excess of this amount.[83] If, for example, in the *Fibrosa* case[84]

---

80 [1979] 1 WLR 783; affirmed briefly by the CA [1981] 1 WLR 236, and (on one point only) by the HL [1982] 1 WLR 253.

81 (1867) LR 2 CP 651, above, p. 362.

82 See Treitel, *Law of Contract*, 11th edn, p. 915, where a different view is offered.

83 Unless the seller has incurred expenses at least twice as great as the prepayment the problem may not arise because, as has been suggested, the court would probably divide the loss and not permit the seller to throw the whole of it onto the buyer.

84 [1943] AC 32.

the sellers had spent well over £1,000 on the machinery before the frustrating event they would not, even under the Frustrated Contracts Act, have been able to recover anything from the buyers over and above the amount of the advance payment. Here again, therefore, the seller's rights depend on the purely fortuitous question of how much has been paid in advance.[85]

It seems, therefore, that although the Frustrated Contracts Act is a useful measure of reform, it still leaves much to be desired. In particular, it is submitted that s. 2(5)(c) could safely be repealed, and provision should be made for the case where the seller has incurred expenditure before the frustrating event, but where nothing has been paid in advance, and where the buyer has had no valuable benefit.

It is, however, possible that the whole question is a somewhat academic one. The strangest aspect of the law relating to the Frustrated Contracts Act is that there is still only one reported case in which it has been applied. The reason for this is not entirely clear, but it is possible that businessmen are less attracted than lawyers by the justice of dividing a loss between the contracting parties.

In Scots law the consequences of frustration fall to be dealt with under the common law of unjustified enrichment. In *Cantiere San Rocco SA* v *Clyde Shipbuilding & Engineering Co*,[86] Austrian purchasers of marine engines to be supplied by a Scottish company had paid the first instalment of the price before the contract was frustrated when the outbreak of the First World War made the purchasers enemy aliens. No engines were ever delivered. After the conclusion of the war, the purchasers claimed restitution under the *condictio causa data causa non secuta*, and eventually succeeded in the House of Lords. The availability of enrichment remedies of this kind has so far provided a satisfactory solution to the problems of post-frustration adjustment, although whether it can deal well with all cases remains unclear.

85 But if the sum is payable before the frustrating event, the mere fact that it has not been paid will not deprive the payee of his right to sue, subject to appropriate deductions, of course.
86 1923 SC (HL) 105. See criticism by Evans-Jones (1993) 109 LQR 663.

21

TRANSFER OF TITLE BY A NON-OWNER

NEMO DAT QUOD NON HABET[1]

The second half of Part III of the Act is entitled 'Transfer of Title' and deals with those cases in which a seller with no right to the goods may nonetheless pass a good title to a third party. In most of these cases the question which arises is which of two innocent people is to suffer for the fraud of a third. A thief steals goods and sells them to someone who buys in good faith and for value; a person hands goods to an agent to obtain offers and the agent sells them without authority and disposes of the proceeds; a swindler buys goods, induces the seller to let him have them on credit and promptly resells or pledges them for whatever he can get; a person sells goods, but retains possession of them and fraudulently resells them to a third party. In all these cases the law has to choose between rigorously upholding the rights of the owner to his property, on the one hand, and protecting the interests of the purchaser who buys in good faith and for value on the other hand. As Lord Denning once put it:

> In the development of our law, two principles have striven for mastery. The first is for the protection of property: no one can give a better title than he himself possesses. The second is for the protection of commercial transactions: the person who takes in good faith and for value without notice should get a better title. The first principle has held sway for a long time, but it has been modified by the common law itself and by statute so as to meet the needs of our times.[2]

The first of these principles is of course still the general rule, and is affirmed by the Act in s. 21(1):

> Subject to this Act, where goods are sold by a person who is not their owner, and who does not sell them under the authority or with the consent of the owner, the buyer acquires no better title to the goods than the seller had, unless the owner of the goods is by his conduct precluded from denying the seller's authority to sell.

This rule is frequently dignified by the use of Latin in the tag *nemo dat quod non habet*, or more shortly *nemo dat*. Some difficulty has arisen with the words 'where goods are sold' in this section, and it has been held that this does not encompass a mere agreement to sell.[3] But this is a somewhat confusing decision: the first part of s. 21(1) – the negative part stating that a non-owner cannot pass title – is merely a

---

1 For a broad, comparative, and somewhat academic, survey of this area of law, see Davies (1987) 7 Leg St 1. For a Scottish perspective, see Reid, *The Law of Property in Scotland* (1996), para. 669 *et seq*.
2 *Bishopsgate Motor Finance Corpn v Transport Brakes Ltd* [1949] 1 KB 332, 336–7.
3 *Shaw v Commissioner of Met Police* [1987] 1 WLR 1332.

re-enactment of the common law principle so it would seem that that part of the sub-section, or the common law in lieu, is applicable whether there is a sale or a mere agreement to sell. The second part of the subsection (beginning with the word 'unless') has the positive effect of enabling a non-owner to pass a good title, although this also appears to be merely a restatement of the common law doctrine of estoppel. The only substantive question, therefore, is whether a person who has merely agreed to buy the goods can rely upon the doctrine of estoppel. This point is discussed below.[4]

The consent of the owner

Where the goods are sold with the express authority of the owner, the ordinary rules of principal and agent apply and no special difficulty arises. But s. 21(1) also refers to the 'consent' of the owner, and reference should also be made to s. 47(1):

> Subject to this Act, the unpaid seller's right of lien . . . or stoppage in transit is not affected by any sale, or other disposition of the goods which the buyer may have made, unless the seller has assented to it.

If, therefore, the buyer, not being in possession, resells the goods and the seller assents to such sale, the sub-buyer obtains a good title free from the first seller's lien or right of stoppage in transit. The effect of such assent on the part of the seller is very similar to that of estoppel, but the difference seems to be that whereas estoppel can only operate if the assent is communicated to the sub-buyer, the seller may assent to the resale within the meaning of s. 47 even though he only communicates his assent to the buyer. But the mere fact that the seller has been informed of a resale and has not objected to it does not amount to an assent within s. 47.

In *Mordaunt Bros* v *British Oil & Cake Mills Ltd*,[5] the defendants sold oil to X, who resold part of it to the plaintiffs and gave them delivery orders in respect of that part. The plaintiffs paid X for the oil and sent the delivery orders to the defendants, who accepted them without comment. The defendants delivered instalments of the oil direct to the plaintiffs as and when they were paid by X, but, on X's falling into arrears with the payments, they refused to deliver any more. Pickford J held that the defendants had not assented to the resale within s. 47. 'In my opinion', he said,[6] 'the assent which affects the unpaid seller's right of lien must be such an assent as in the circumstances shews that the seller intends to renounce his rights against the goods. It is not enough to shew that the fact of a sub-contract has been brought to his notice and that he has assented to it merely in the sense of acknowledging receipt of the information.'[7]

On the other hand, in *D F Mount Ltd* v *Jay & Jay Co Ltd*[8] Salmon J came to a different conclusion on the following facts. The defendants were owners of 500 cartons

---

4 See below, p. 375.
5 [1910] 2 KB 502.
6 At p. 507.
7 The case might well have been different if the goods had been specific goods, because in that case the acceptance might have been an attornment which would have passed property, but no property can pass in unascertained goods. Cf. *Laurie & Morewood* v *John Dudin & Sons* [1926] 1 KB 223.
8 [1960] 1 QB 159.

of tinned peaches lying at the wharf of D. The defendants were approached by M at a time when the market was falling, and M told them that he had a customer for 250 cartons. He made it clear that he, M, would pay the defendants out of the price he obtained from the sub-purchaser. The defendants agreed to sell the cartons to M and gave him a delivery order. M sent the order to D, who received it without acknowledgment. Later M sold the cartons to the plaintiffs, who paid M. The defendants, never having received the price from M, subsequently claimed to be still entitled to the cartons. Salmon J held that the defendants had assented to the sale within the meaning of s. 47:

> In the present case the defendants were anxious to get rid of the goods on a falling market. They knew that M could only pay for them out of the money he obtained from his customers, and that he could only obtain the money from his customers against delivery orders in favour of those customers. In my view the true inference is that the defendants assented to M reselling the goods, in the sense that they intended to renounce their rights against the goods and to take the risk of M's honesty.[9]

The maxim *nemo dat* has a wider application than s. 21 of the Sale of Goods Act, because the latter only applies to a sale of goods by a non-owner, while the maxim also covers those cases where an owner sells goods, but is unable to sell them free from some encumbrance or charge existing in favour of a third party. In fact, this is an unusual situation because the law generally sets its face against the recognition of encumbrances which run with chattels into the hands of third parties[10] and, of course, equitable rights are always subject to those of a purchaser for value in good faith without notice. But there is one not uncommon situation where the law does recognize such encumbrances as binding on third parties. Where a person pledges goods, or the documents of title to goods, and subsequently the pledgee returns the goods or the documents to the pledgor for a limited purpose, for example to obtain clearance of the goods from the warehouseman, any unauthorized disposition by the pledgor will not prejudice the rights of the pledgee.[11] In other words, the seller, although owner of the goods, cannot sell them free from the pledgee's right. It may be that, technically, this result depends upon the pledgee's retention of possession, but since the courts are prepared to hold that the return of the custody of the goods or documents of title does not transfer possession back to the pledgor, this is not much consolation to the innocent third party. It might well be thought that the extension of the rule *nemo dat* to these cases is unjustifiable, for it seems extraordinary that an owner who is in actual possession of his goods with the consent of the pledgee cannot transfer a good title free from the pledge to an innocent third party. The hardship on the third party who buys goods from the admitted owner in actual possession is so obvious as to need no stressing. At all events, there are two limitations on the rule *nemo dat* in this connection.

---

9 At p. 167.
10 *McGruther* v *Pitcher* [1904] 2 Ch 306; *Dunlop Pneumatic Tyre Co Ltd* v *Selfridge & Co Ltd* [1915] AC 847. But see *Lord Strathcona* v *Dominion Coal Co Ltd* [1926] AC 108.
11 *North Western Bank* v *Poynter* [1895] AC 56, (1894) 22 R (HL) 1, revsg (1894) 21 R 513; *Reeves* v *Capper* (1838) 5 Bing NC 136; *Official Assignee of Madras* v *Mercantile Bank of India Ltd* [1935] AC 53; *Mercantile Bank of India Ltd* v *Central Bank of India Ltd* [1938] AC 287. For Scots law perspectives on this whole area, see Rodger, 1971 JR 193, and Gretton, 1990 JR 23.

In the first place, if the pledgee returns the goods to the pledgor with an unrestricted authority to sell them, an innocent buyer from the pledgor obtains a good title free from the pledge, even though the pledgor fraudulently absconds with the purchase money.[12] And in the second place, if the pledgor is a mercantile agent, the return of the goods to him by the pledgee will enable the third party to plead that the pledgor was in possession of them with the consent of the owner and consequently that he is protected by s. 2(1) of the Factors Act 1889.[13]

The exceptions to *nemo dat*

As the opening words of s. 21 indicate, there are a number of exceptions to the general rule *nemo dat* which are of considerable importance, though they do not, of course, swamp the main rule itself, at any rate so far as the sale of goods is concerned. It is perhaps worth pointing out that the exceptions are all cumulative from the point of view of the party seeking protection against the original owner. He need only bring his case under one of the exceptions to obtain protection against the former owner. Failure to bring his case under this or that exception does not prevent him succeeding under a different exception. We proceed now to examine the exceptions.

ESTOPPEL

The first exception is provided by the doctrine of estoppel, which is embodied, in this connection, in the concluding words of s. 21(1) itself, which may be repeated here:

> . . . unless the owner of the goods is by his conduct precluded from denying the seller's authority to sell.

This provision merely throws us back on the common law doctrine of estoppel, for it gives no indication when the owner is by his conduct precluded from denying the seller's authority to sell.[14] It seems that there are two distinct cases where the owner is so precluded. The first is where he has by his words or conduct represented to the buyer that the seller is the true owner, or has the owner's authority to sell, and the second is where the owner, by his negligent failure to act, allows the seller to appear as the owner or as having the owner's authority to sell. These are generally called estoppel by representation and estoppel by negligence respectively. The terminology of the subject is, however, somewhat confusing. On the one hand, estoppel by representation is sometimes subdivided into estoppel by words and estoppel by conduct, while the wording of the Act suggests that estoppel by words is merely a species of estoppel by

---

12 *Babcock v Lawson* (1880) 5 QBD 284.
13 *Lloyds Bank v Bank of America* [1938] 2 KB 147. On the Factors Act, see below, p. 385 *et seq.*
14 There had been suggestions (to which *Shaw v Commissioner of Met Police* [1987] 1 WLR 1332 appeared to give some countenance) that s. 21 actually operates independently of the doctrine of estoppel, and so perhaps the 'duty' requirement of common law estoppel does not then apply. But this idea was rejected by the New South Wales Court of Appeal in *Thomas Australia Wholesale Vehicle Trading Co Pty Ltd v Marac Finance Australia Ltd* [1985] 3 NSWR 452, and (at p. 470) McHugh JA specifically endorsed the sentence set out above in the text, then appearing in the 4th edn of this work at p. 180. Note further the Scots law comments in Reid, *The Law of Property in Scotland* (1996), para. 680, emphasizing that the Scottish doctrine of personal bar is not precisely analogous to estoppel and that care is therefore needed in handling the English authorities on this topic. There are no Scottish cases in point, however.

conduct. But there is also much controversy about the propriety of the term 'estoppel by negligence'. Strictly speaking, it seems there is no such thing as estoppel by negligence.[15] All these estoppels rest in the last resort on a *representation* of some kind.[16]

A person may make a representation by words or by conduct, but how does a person make a representation by negligence? The answer appears to be that this is really a representation through an omission.[17] A person who negligently omits to inform another of certain facts may be said to be representing that the facts calling for report do not exist. Again, a person who omits to correct a misrepresentation made by a third party may in certain circumstances be treated as responsible for that representation. Thus if A stands by while B makes a representation to C which A knows to be incorrect, and which he has a duty to correct, A may be said, loosely, to be guilty of misrepresentation by negligence. In truth, what has happened is that A, by his negligence, has allowed B to mislead C by a misrepresentation. Thus, the correct approach is that this kind of estoppel rests in every case on a representation. The representation may be (1) by words, or (2) by conduct, or (3) by a negligent omission.

Although the point is not free from doubt, it seems that in the first two cases it is unnecessary to show fraud or an intent to deceive or negligence as a foundation for the estoppel.[18] The only requirements are those common to all estoppels, namely that the representation must be one of fact, that it must be unambiguous and that it must be acted upon. But although neither fraud nor negligence needs to be shown the representation must at least be *voluntary*, as that term is used in the law. A person who is induced by violence or duress to sign a piece of paper containing a representation in circumstances where the violence or duress would justify a plea of *non est factum* if the document was a contractual document cannot be held to have made a representation, even where some third party has relied upon it.[19]

In the third type of case referred to above, however, it seems that negligence, in the sense of a breach of a duty of care (or, of course, fraud) must be proved. So where a person is charged with having omitted to correct a misleading statement by a third party, and that is the basis of the alleged estoppel, it must be shown that the defendant had some duty to correct the misstatement.

Estoppel by words

A good example of estoppel by words is the decision of the Court of Appeal in *Henderson & Co v Williams*.[20] In this case G & Co were induced by the fraud of one F to sell him goods lying in certain warehouses of which the defendants were

---

15 See *Saunders v Anglia Building Society* [1971] AC 1004, 1038 per Lord Pearson, and also Atiyah, *Essays on Contract*, pp. 316–19 (1986).

16 This suggestion was approved by Popplewell J in *Lenn Mayhew-Lewis v Westminster Scaffolding plc*, 5 March 1999 (unreported).

17 Ibid.

18 A good example of the confusion in this branch of the law is provided by *Seton, Laing & Co v Lafone* (1887) 19 QBD 68 where the whole discussion was in terms of estoppel by negligence, and yet the only representation was that of the defendant himself. This was a simple example of estoppel by representation, and negligence ought not to have been relevant.

19 *Debs v Sibec Developments Ltd* [1990] RTR 91.

20 [1895] 1 QB 521.

warehousemen. The circumstances were such that the contract between G & Co and F was void for mistake. On the instructions of G & Co, the defendants transferred the goods in their books to the order of F. F sold the goods to the plaintiffs who, being suspicious of the bona fides of the seller, made inquiries of the defendants. The latter supplied the plaintiffs with a written statement that they held the goods to the order of F, and when this did not satisfy them, they endorsed it with a further statement that they now held the goods to the plaintiffs' order. G & Co, not having been paid by F, instructed the defendants not to deliver the goods to the plaintiffs but to themselves, and they gave them an indemnity against so doing. It was held that both G & Co and the defendants were estopped from denying the plaintiffs' right to the goods, the former because they had represented that F was the owner by ordering the defendants to transfer the goods into his name in their books, and the latter because they had attorned to the plaintiffs, that is represented to them, that they held the goods to their order.[21]

A more modern case of estoppel by words is *Shaw v Commissioner of Metropolitan Police*[22] where the plaintiffs agreed to buy a car from one L who had obtained it from the true owner, together with a certificate signed by him saying that he had sold the car to L. In fact this was untrue, as the owner had not sold the car to L – he had merely authorized L to sell it on his behalf. L was a swindler who did not pay for the car, and when suspicions were aroused he disappeared, leaving the title to the car in doubt. The plaintiffs had the effrontery to claim that they had acquired title under s. 21 of the Act even though they had not paid the price to L or anyone else. The Court of Appeal denied the plaintiffs' claim, though on the rather unsatisfactory ground (as noted above) that s. 21 did not apply where the buyer had merely *agreed to buy* the goods, but only where he had bought them. This is unconvincing, because if (as has been submitted) s. 21 is merely a statement of the common law principle of estoppel, it ought to protect anyone who has acted to his prejudice on the representation in question. It would therefore have been better to have held that the plaintiffs' claim failed because they had not acted to their prejudice since they had not paid the price.[23]

Estoppel by conduct

An early leading case on estoppel by conduct is *Farquharson Bros v J King & Co Ltd*.[24] The plaintiffs here were timber merchants who owned timber housed with a dock company. The plaintiffs' clerk had authority to send delivery orders to the

---

21 The position of the warehouseman in this sort of case is unenviable, because if he had delivered the goods to the plaintiffs he would have been liable to G & Co for disobeying their instructions: *Rogers v Lambert* [1891] 1 QB 318. His proper course is to take interpleader proceedings, under which he disclaims title himself, and leaves the court to sort out the claims of the other contending parties.

22 [1987] 1 WLR 1332.

23 A difficulty was caused by the fact that they had given a banker's draft for the price, but this was never cashed, and the bank refunded the money, subject to an undertaking to indemnify them if the draft was later cashed in circumstances in which the bank was liable. It is probable that this was thought sufficient action in reliance to raise an estoppel, which may explain why the court was anxious to avoid placing its decision on estoppel. But the result could perhaps have been avoided by application of the principle in *Société Italo-Belge v Palm Oil & Vegetable Oils* [1982] 1 All ER 19 (trifling acts of reliance do not justify estoppel when it would be inequitable).

24 [1902] AC 325.

dock company, and the latter were instructed to act on the clerk's delivery orders, but the clerk had no authority to sell the timber himself. The clerk fraudulently transferred some of the timber to himself under an assumed name and gave the dock company instructions accordingly. He then sold the timber to the defendants under his assumed name and instructed the dock company to deliver the goods to their order. The plaintiffs, having discovered the clerk's fraud, brought an action for conversion. The House of Lords held that the defence of estoppel failed because the defendants had not acted on any representation made by the plaintiffs concerning the authority of the clerk. Even the dock company would not have needed, or been able to plead, estoppel. As Lord Halsbury pointed out, they would not have been liable simply because they had done nothing more than obey their principal's instructions. Despite the vigorous speeches of Lord Halsbury[25] and Lord Macnaghten in this case, and the expressions of astonishment that the defence should ever have been set up, let alone accepted (as it was by the Court of Appeal), it is by no means easy to lay down what sort of conduct is sufficient to invoke the doctrine of estoppel.

One thing, at any rate, is clear, that merely allowing another person to have possession of goods which he does not own is not *by itself* enough to bring into operation the doctrine of estoppel. There are so many different circumstances in which an owner of goods may allow another to have possession of them that it cannot be claimed that such conduct amounts to an unambiguous representation that the party in possession is the owner or has the owner's authority to sell. Although the Privy Council accepted a proposition of almost this width in *Commonwealth Trust Ltd* v *Akotey*,[26] this case was virtually overruled by the Privy Council itself in *Mercantile Bank of India Ltd* v *Central Bank of India Ltd*.[27] In this latter case, X pledged railway receipts, which in this case were documents of title,[28] with the Central Bank in return for an advance. In accordance with the usual practice the Bank then returned them to X to enable him to obtain clearance of the goods, but X fraudulently pledged them with the Mercantile Bank in return for an advance from them. It was held that there was no estoppel because the possession of the railway receipts 'no more conveyed a representation that the merchants (X) were entitled to dispose of the property than the actual possession of the goods themselves would have done'.[29] If estoppel by conduct is to be invoked there must be some act which positively misleads the third party beyond merely allowing a non-owner to have possession of the goods.[30]

In *Central Newbury Car Auctions Ltd* v *Unity Finance Ltd*,[31] a swindler called on the plaintiffs and offered to buy a Morris car on hire-purchase terms, leaving with the

---

25 Lord Halsbury's speech was a little too vigorous, for he thought the clerk was guilty of larceny: see the note by Pollock in [1902] AC at p. 329.

26 [1926] AC 72.

27 [1938] AC 287. Lord Denning in *Central Newbury Car Auctions* v *Unity Finance Ltd* [1957] 1 QB 371 was willing to support it, but his opinion is inconsistent with a mass of other authority.

28 In English commercial practice railway receipts are not usually documents of title, but if they were the result on such facts would probably be different in England because of the Factors Act which did not apply in India. See below, p. 385 *et seq.*

29 At p. 303 per Lord Wright.

30 *Jerome* v *Bentley* [1952] 2 All ER 114.

31 [1957] 1 QB 371, followed in *J Sargent (Garages) Ltd* v *Motor Auctions Ltd* [1977] RTR 121.

plaintiffs in part-exchange a Hillman car which, as it transpired, was also let on hire-purchase. The swindler signed hire-purchase forms whereby the Morris was to be sold to a finance company and then hired to him, and he was thereupon given the registration book and permitted to drive the Morris away. The finance company refused the hire-purchase proposal and the car was later discovered in the possession of the defendants, who had bought it in good faith from an unknown person, who was presumed to be the swindler. The Court of Appeal (Denning LJ dissenting) held that there was no estoppel and that the plaintiffs were entitled to recover the car. The registration book (now, registration document) of a car is not a document of title,[32] and in fact it contains a warning that the person in whose name the car is registered may or may not be the owner. Hence it was not possible to say that the plaintiffs had in any way represented the swindler to be the owner, or to have the owner's authority to sell. The case for invoking estoppel was based entirely on the fact that the owner had entrusted possession of the goods to another party, and this (as we have seen) is normally insufficient to raise an estoppel. Nevertheless, the result in this kind of case is a serious anomaly, having regard to the fact that a buyer from a person in possession under a hire-purchase agreement is now protected by Part III of the Hire-Purchase Act 1964.[33]

On the other hand, in *Eastern Distributors Ltd* v *Goldring*[34] where, in pursuance of a plan to deceive a finance company, one M signed and delivered forms to C which enabled C to represent that he had M's authority to sell a car belonging to him, it was held by the Court of Appeal that M was estopped from setting up his title against the plaintiffs who had bought the car from C. It was also held that the estoppel in fact operated to pass a good title to the plaintiffs not only against M himself, but also against a buyer in good faith from M. It is, however, not entirely clear why the case was not disposed of on the simpler ground that C had M's apparent authority to sell, although in fact he exceeded that authority.[35]

So also, if the owner of goods entrusts the possession of them to a dealer with authority to sell, or to obtain offers or something of that kind, the owner would normally be estopped if the dealer sold without authority or in excess of his authority. But this form of estoppel is now of little practical importance because it has been largely overtaken by the statutory protection conferred on innocent purchasers by the Factors Act 1889.[36]

There is an important distinction between a representation (or conduct equivalent to a representation) that the seller has authority to sell the goods as agent, on the one hand, and a representation that the seller is himself the owner, on the other hand. Where the true owner represents the seller to be the owner, or enables the seller to represent himself as owner, and knows that the seller will or may sell as an owner, it is immaterial that the seller sells outside the ordinary course of business unless this demonstrates lack of good faith on the buyer's part. In *Lloyds and Scottish Finance*

---

32 *Joblin* v *Watkin & Roseveare (Motors) Ltd* (1948) 64 TLR 464.
33 See below, p. 410 *et seq.* See also *Shogun Finance Ltd* v *Hudson* [2003] UKHL 62 discussed at p. 43 *et seq.* above.
34 [1957] 2 QB 600.
35 See per Devlin LJ at p. 606.
36 See below, p. 385.

Ltd v *Williamson*,[37] the plaintiff entrusted his car to a dealer and authorized him to sell at or above a certain price. The dealer sold the car above this price but the price was not paid in cash but set off against a debt owed by the dealer to a friend of the buyer. For this reason, the sale was outside the ordinary course of business but it was held that this was immaterial. Since the owner knew that the seller might very well sell as a principal and not as an agent and had authorized him to do so, it made no difference how he sold the goods.

But if the case is one of ostensible agency the position is different. For it is reasonably implicit that an agent is only authorized to sell in the ordinary course of business and if he does not do so there will be no estoppel. Ostensible agency may arise in one of two ways: it may arise where the owner authorizes an agent to sell as agent only, or it may arise where the buyer knows that the agent is not himself the owner and acts on the assumption that he is an agent only. This latter possibility is illustrated by *Motor Credits (Hire Finance) Ltd* v *Pacific Motor Auctions Pty Ltd*.[38] In this case M Ltd, who were dealers in vehicles, sold a number of vehicles to the plaintiffs under a 'display agreement' whereby M Ltd remained in possession of the cars for display in their showrooms. They were paid 90 per cent of the price and were authorized to sell the vehicles as agents for the plaintiffs. M Ltd got into financial difficulties and the plaintiffs revoked their authority to sell the vehicles, but M Ltd nevertheless sold a number of them to the defendants who were bona fide purchasers for value. The sale was outside the ordinary course of business, partly because it took place after business hours and partly because the defendants agreed to sell the cars back to M Ltd in certain events (in fact it is clear that the defendants really wanted the vehicles as security for pre-existing debts owed to them). The defendants knew all about the display plan agreement and could not therefore have supposed that M Ltd were owners, though they did suppose M Ltd to have authority to sell. On these facts the Australian High Court held that the defendants were not protected; as this was a case of ostensible agency and not ostensible ownership the defendants would only have been protected if the sale had been in the ordinary course of business. This decision was reversed on appeal to the Privy Council,[39] without consideration of this point, on the ground that the defendants were protected by s. 24 of the Act. This aspect of the case is considered later.[40]

Estoppel by negligence

As we have already seen, estoppel by negligence may be established where the owner of goods has, by his negligence, allowed a third party to represent himself as owner or as having the owner's authority to sell. But the application of the principle of estoppel by negligence is severely restricted by the fact that, as in the law of tort, there can be no negligence unless there is a duty to take care. It is for this reason that:

---

37 [1965] 1 WLR 404.
38 (1963) 109 CLR 87.
39 [1965] AC 867.
40 See below, p. 395.

If I lose a valuable dog and find it afterwards in the possession of a gentleman who bought it from somebody whom he believed to be the owner, it is no answer to me to say that he would never have been cheated into buying the dog if I had chained it up or put a collar on it, or kept it under proper control. If a person leaves a watch or a ring on a seat in the park or on a table at a cafe and it ultimately gets into the hands of a bona fide purchaser, it is no answer to the true owner to say that it was his carelessness and nothing else that enabled the finder to pass it off as his own.[41]

Since there is no duty of care on an owner of property to see that it does not get lost or stolen, it is comparatively rare to find a clear case of estoppel by negligence in this connection. The dictum of Ashurst J in *Lickbarrow v Mason*,[42] which is frequently quoted in this connection by despairing counsel, that 'wherever one of two innocent persons must suffer by the acts of a third, he who has enabled such third person to occasion the loss must sustain it', has been more qualified than any other case in the books and has been dissented from more often than it has been followed.[43]

The necessity for establishing a duty of care often precludes the operation of the doctrine of estoppel in those cases where an owner is induced to part with goods to a buyer under a contract void for 'mistake'. In those cases, the owner can claim the goods even from a bona fide purchaser from the fraudulent buyer, and it is no defence to say that it was the owner's negligence, however gross, which enabled the buyer to obtain the goods unless a duty to take care can be established.[44] Similarly, just as entrusting goods to another has been held not to amount to a representation that he is the owner or has authority to sell, so also if that party represents himself to be the owner or to have authority to sell, the owner will not normally be defeated by the plea of estoppel by negligence. Once again the reason given is that there is no duty of care on the owner of goods to protect the possible interests of third parties.[45] On the other hand, estoppel by negligence was applied in *Coventry Shepherd & Co v Great Eastern Rly Co*,[46] where the defendants negligently issued two delivery orders relating to the same load of goods. The person to whom they were issued was thereby able to represent to the plaintiffs (to whom he pledged the goods) that the goods were in fact available after they had already been disposed of.

A more modern case where a duty to take care was established, although on the facts it was held not to be broken, is *Mercantile Credit Co Ltd v Hamblin*[47] in which the facts were these. The defendant wished to borrow some money on the security of her car. She consulted a dealer who was apparently solvent and respectable and he gave her some hire-purchase forms to sign in blank. She signed the forms thinking

---

41 *Farquharson Bros v C King & Co Ltd*, per Lord Macnaghten [1902] AC 335–6.

42 (1787) 2 TR 63.

43 See, e.g., *Farquharson Bros v C King & Co* [1902] AC at 342 per Lord Lindley, 'Such a doctrine is far too wide'; *London Joint Stock Bank v MacMillan* [1918] AC 777, 836 per Lord Parmoor; *Jones v Waring & Gillow Ltd* [1926] AC 670, 693 per Lord Sumner; *Wilson & Meeson v Pickering* [1946] 1 KB 422, 425 per Lord Greene. The truth is that the dictum is really a statement of *principle*, rather than a *rule*.

44 See, e.g., *Cundy v Lindsay* (1878) 3 App Cas 459; *Ingram v Little* [1961] 1 QB 31; *Lewis v Averay* [1972] 1 QB 198. The House of Lords reviewed these cases in *Shogun Finance Ltd v Hudson* [2003] UKHL 62 – see p. 43 *et seq.*

45 See the *Mercantile Bank of India* case [1938] AC 287, above, pp. 374–5.

46 (1883) 11 QBD 776.

47 [1965] 2 QB 242, followed in *Beverley Acceptances Ltd v Oakley* [1982] RTR 417.

they were some sort of mortgage transaction, but retained possession of her car throughout. The dealer told her that he would find out what sum he could arrange for her to raise and would let her know. He also gave her a blank cheque which she was to fill in for the agreed figure on the scheme being completed. In fact, the dealer completed the hire-purchase forms so as to constitute an offer by himself to sell the car to the plaintiffs, a finance company, and an offer by the defendant to take the car on hire-purchase terms from the plaintiffs. Without further reference to the defendant, he sent the forms to the plaintiffs who purported to accept both offers. The defendant repudiated the alleged agreement and it was held by the Court of Appeal that she was not bound by it because she had not in fact authorized the dealer to make any offer to the plaintiffs and was not estopped from denying that she had done so. Although the court held that the defendant did owe a duty of care sufficient to raise an estoppel, they held that she had not in fact failed to take care. In the particular circumstances of the case, it was not unreasonable for her to have trusted the dealer.

The importance of the case lies in the fact that the court treated the existence and the nature of the duty to take care in such circumstances as the same as those which arise in the ordinary law of negligence. Thus, Pearson LJ found a 'sufficient relationship or proximity' between the defendant and the plaintiffs from the fact that the defendant intended that the documents which she signed should constitute an offer to contract subject to certain conditions being fulfilled, and that she had entrusted the documents to the dealer and was thereby arming him with 'the means to make a contract ostensibly on her behalf'.[48]

On the other hand, a majority of the House of Lords arrived at a different conclusion in the important decision in *Moorgate Mercantile Co Ltd* v *Twitchings*.[49] This case arose out of the activities of a body called HPI (Hire-Purchase Information).[50] It was a private body which kept a register of vehicles which were the subject of hire-purchase agreements, or which had been notified to have been stolen. Any finance company which let a vehicle on such an agreement could register the agreement with HPI, and any dealer who was offered a vehicle for purchase could easily find out from HPI whether the vehicle was registered with them. At the time when this case arose there was no express obligation on the plaintiff (the claimant) as a member of HPI to register agreements,[51] although in practice this was the whole purpose of membership, and the great majority did so.

---

48 [1965] 2 QB 242, 275.
49 [1977] AC 890; followed in *Cadogan Finance Ltd* v *Keith Lavery* (1982) Com LR 248 (omission to notify registration authorities of finance interest in aircraft).
50 In the early 1990s HPI was sold. It is now owned by Equifax, a credit referencing organization. In 1997 it was merged with the independent Mileage Verification Association and it provides information both to the motor industry and to consumers. Information about outstanding hire-purchase agreements is now provided by applying to Equifax or Experium. See p. 412.
51 In the 7th and earlier editions of this book it was stated that HPI had altered its rules since the *Moorgate Mercantile* case so as to impose an obligation to register agreements on its members. This was an unfortunate error which was based on some remarks in the speeches in the House of Lords, where the judges were clearly labouring under the same mistake. What seems to have happened was that, at the time of the *Moorgate Mercantile* case, some members were under an obligation to register agreements, but not all, and in particular not the plaintiff in that case. Following the decision, the obligation to register was totally removed from the HPI rules so that members were no longer bound to register agreements. Professor Atiyah acknowledged in previous editions that he was obliged to HPI for correspondence on this subject.

Dealers, in practice, relied on the information given by HPI as there was rarely any other means of discovering whether a vehicle was subject to a hire-purchase agreement. In the case in question, the plaintiffs had omitted to register a particular agreement and this was held to be careless on their part. The hirer under this agreement sold the vehicle to the defendants, who inquired from HPI if the agreement was registered and were told that it was not. The plaintiffs then sued the defendants for conversion and the defendants argued that the plaintiffs were estopped from asserting their title.

The defendants' plea was put in two alternative ways. First, they argued that there was estoppel by actual representation. This argument depended on the assumption that HPI gave the information as agents for the plaintiffs, but it failed in any event because the information which HPI gave the defendants was in fact (as the majority of the House of Lords held) true. HPI said the agreement was not registered; they did not say that there was no such agreement in existence.

The defendants' second argument was more difficult. They argued that the plaintiffs were guilty of an omission (to register) and that this gave rise to an estoppel. It was accepted on all hands that the question to which this led was whether the plaintiffs were under a duty to the defendants to register the agreement, or, more strictly, a duty to take reasonable care to register. By a majority, it was held there was no such duty. Membership of HPI specifically did not impose a duty on the defendants to register agreements and the majority did not see where else such a duty could come from. In earlier editions of this book it was suggested that the dissenting speeches of Lords Wilberforce and Salmon carried more conviction. As Lord Wilberforce pointed out, in practice everyone in the motor trade relied heavily on the registration of hire-purchase agreements with HPI, and it would not seem unreasonable to hold that a duty to register arose out of these facts. But today, it seems that the majority decision in a sense anticipated the current trend to restrict the growth of liability in negligence, and to reassert the view that tort duties are only to be imposed with great caution on parties who have expressly restricted their contractual obligations.[52]

Effect of estoppel

It should finally be added that if estoppel does operate it will do so whether the transaction is a sale, pledge or other disposition, but that it will not bind anyone who does not claim under the person estopped. A person claiming under title paramount cannot be bound by an estoppel to which he was not privy.

It is not entirely clear whether the effect of estoppel is actually to pass a title good against the party estopped. On one view, estoppel is merely a rule of evidence which precludes a person from adducing certain evidence before a court – he is not permitted to deny statements which he has previously made where the doctrine operates. On this view, the 'real' legal position remains unaffected by estoppel. The former owner remains owner, but simply cannot claim the goods as against anyone entitled to the

---

52 So *a fortiori* it has been held there can be no duty on the part of a member of the public to warn the police that a car has been stolen (which information would also normally be passed on to and registered by HPI or now its successors – see p. 412): *Debs v Silbec Developments Ltd* [1990] RTR 91.

benefit of the estoppel.[53] But in *Eastern Distributors Ltd* v *Goldring*[54] the Court of Appeal said that the effect of estoppel anyhow in some cases relating to the sale of goods is to pass a real title, and not merely a 'metaphorical title by estoppel', though precisely when this is the case remains obscure. Since then it has been asserted that estoppel anyhow cannot help transfer a title in cases where s. 16 prevents property passing because the goods are unascertained.[55]

Somewhat akin to the doctrine of estoppel in this connection are cases in which a person who sells goods without title subsequently acquires the title, for example by paying off the true owner. In such circumstances, it has been suggested[56] that the seller's subsequent acquisition of title 'goes to feed' the defective title of the buyer and any person deriving title through the buyer. This concept has not, however, been fully worked out and may give rise to some interesting questions, for example: can a title be acquired and 'fed' in goods which have already been consumed?[57]

Relationship between estoppel and other principles

It will be apparent that the doctrine of estoppel is closely connected with other legal principles. The ostensible authority of an agent to transfer the title of goods in excess of his actual authority is based on principles similar to, if not identical with, those in the doctrine of estoppel. It must be admitted that legal theory in these areas is in a state of some confusion and it is not always easy to understand the basis for a decision. Estoppel, in particular, sometimes appears to be invoked to justify decisions which can be explained more simply. For instance, in *Snook* v *London West Riding Investments Ltd*[58] the plaintiff was held estopped from denying the title of the defendant's predecessors to a car, although he had intended to transfer the property to them.

The use of estoppel in such cases seems merely confusing. The whole purpose of the doctrine is to prevent the plaintiff from denying his real intentions when he has misled other parties as to those intentions. Where in fact his real intention was to transfer title it is surely unnecessary to invoke estoppel.

SALE BY AGENT

This exception may be quickly disposed of.[59] Section 21(1) says, *inter alia*, that if the goods are not sold with the authority or consent of the owner, the buyer acquires no title. But this section is subject to the provisions of the Act, and s. 62 preserves the rules of common law regarding principal and agent. It follows that, according to the ordinary principles of common law, a sale within the usual or 'ostensible' authority

---

53 See, e.g., *Simm* v *Anglo-American Telegraph Co* (1879) 5 QBD 188, 206 per Brett LJ. The idea that estoppel is a mere rule of evidence is challenged in Atiyah, *Essays on Contract*, pp. 306–12 (1986).
54 [1957] 2 QB 600, 611.
55 *In re London Wine Co (Shippers) Ltd* (1986) PCC 121.
56 *Butterworth* v *Kingsway Motors Ltd* [1954] 1 WLR 1286; *Anderson* v *Ryan* [1967] IR 34.
57 See p. 116.
58 [1967] 2 QB 786.
59 For analysis from a Scots law perspective, see Reid, *The Law of Property in Scotland* (1996), para. 670.

of an agent, even though outside his actual authority, will bind the owner. It is not of course every agent who has a 'usual' authority. Unless the agent belongs to a certain class of agents who usually have a certain authority, it cannot be said that the agent has any 'usual' authority wider than his actual authority.[60]

It is not within the scope of this work to analyse in detail the circumstances in which an agent can pass a title to a third party where he acts beyond his actual authority. It seems, however, that in addition to cases in which the agent acts within his 'usual' or 'ostensible' authority, there is an independent principle which, at least in some circumstances, enables an agent to pass a title beyond his actual authority. If, for example, an agent is authorized to sell at a certain price and sells below this price to a bona fide purchaser, it seems that the purchaser gets a good title, irrespective of whether the agent has any usual or ostensible authority or, indeed, whether he is known to be an agent at all. In such circumstances, the courts draw a distinction not unlike that drawn in vicarious liability in the law of tort.[61] If the agent has acted within the course of his employment as an agent, he binds the principal even though he exceeds his actual authority; if, on the other hand, he acts right outside the course of his employment, he does not bind his principal.[62] Another view, however, is that this line of authorities is an anomaly and should not be extended.[63] On this view the third party will only be protected if the agent had apparent or usual authority beyond his actual authority. Of course, if the buyer is aware that the agent is exceeding his authority, no property will pass.[64]

A person who is not the owner of goods but sells with the consent or authority of the owner may, of course, sell expressly as agent, in which case the only contract of sale is that created between the owner and the buyer; whether the agent is entitled to sue, or liable to be sued on, such a contract depends on ordinary principles of agency. But it can also happen that the party actually arranging the sale sells as principal and not as agent, even though he is not the owner. For example, where goods are sold by S to B1 under a contract with a 'retention of title clause' which provides that property is to remain in S until payment in full, but permits B1 to resell the goods in the ordinary course of business, then a resale by B1 to B2 may create a contract of sale between these two parties. B1 may thus be reselling with the consent of the owner S, but he sells as a principal, not as an agent. S will not be a party to the sale contract between B1 and B2.[65]

SECTION 2 OF THE FACTORS ACT 1889

The next exception to the rule *nemo dat* is provided by s. 2 of the Factors Act 1889, which was extended to Scotland by the Factors (Scotland) Act 1890.[66] Section 21(2) of the Sale of Goods Act runs:

---

60 *Jerome* v *Bentley* [1952] 2 All ER 114.
61 Treitel, *Law of Contract*, 11th edn, p. 717.
62 See, e.g., *Brocklesby* v *Temperance Building Society* [1895] AC 173; *Fry* v *Smellie* [1912] 3 KB 282; cf. *France* v *Clark* (1884) 26 Ch D 257. Despite some rather loose dicta in *Mercantile Credit Co Ltd* v *Hamblin* [1965] 2 QB 242, it is thought that negligence is not an essential feature of this type of liability. The question was left open in *Moorgate Mercantile Ltd* v *Twitching* [1977] AC 890.
63 See *Chitty on Contract*, 28th edn, §32–077.
64 *Cressman & anor* v *Coys of Kensignton* [2004] EWCA Civ 47.
65 See *Aluminium Industrie BV* v *Romalpa Aluminium Ltd* [1976] 1 WLR 676; *Re Bond Worth Ltd* [1980] Ch 228.
66 For analysis from a Scots law perspective, see Reid, *The Law of Property in Scotland* (1996), para. 671.

Nothing in this Act affects—

(a) The provisions of the Factors Acts, or any enactment[67] enabling the apparent owner of goods to dispose of them as if he were their true owner.

At common law, the doctrine of estoppel (or usual or ostensible authority) would normally have protected a third party who bought goods from a dealer in the ordinary course of business, where the goods had been entrusted to the dealer by the true owner.[68] But the common law did not protect a person who lent money on the security of the goods, that is in legal terms a pledgee; the courts took the view that a 'factor' was acting outside the normal course of business if he pledged goods rather than resold them.[69] This was a somewhat unreal approach when applied to the commercial agents of import merchants who regularly pledged imported goods (or documents of title) to banks or other financial institutions in order to provide finance pending the arrival and resale of the goods.[70] Accordingly, Parliament took a hand and passed a series of Factors Acts, beginning in 1823 and culminating in the present Act of 1889. The Acts were partly declaratory of the common law and partly an extension of it;[71] but the present Act specifically declares that it is not to be construed in derogation of the common law,[72] and it now appears that there may be circumstances in which the common law is wider than the Act. Thus (as seen above) a sale by an agent outside the ordinary course of business is protected at common law if the true owner has authorized the agent to sell as an owner, and not merely as an agent.[73]

By a somewhat strange twist, the provisions of the Factors Act are now usually applied to situations quite different from those for which they were enacted. The typical Factors Act case envisaged by Parliament was that of the commercial agent who pledged or resold goods (or documents of title to goods) consigned by foreign merchants to English ports; the typical case to which the Act is applied today concerns a motor vehicle entrusted to a motor dealer for sale or to obtain offers.

Section 2(1) of the Factors Act is as follows:

Where a mercantile agent is, with the consent of the owner, in possession of goods or of the documents of title to goods, any sale, pledge, or other disposition of the goods, made by him when acting in the ordinary course of business of a mercantile agent, shall, subject to the provisions of this Act, be as valid as if he were expressly authorized by the owner of the goods to make the same; provided that the person taking under the disposition acts in good faith, and has not at the time of the disposition notice that the person making the disposition has not authority to make the same.

The meaning of this subsection requires the most careful consideration.

---

67 The words 'any enactment' were thought to refer to the reputed ownership clause of the Bankruptcy Act 1914 (under which goods in the possession of a bankrupt in such circumstances that he was the reputed owner could pass to the trustee in bankruptcy); this clause disappeared with the Insolvency Act 1985.
68 The leading case was *Pickering* v *Busk* (1812) 15 East 38, but there is no doubt that the principle itself was older than this.
69 *Paterson* v *Task* (1743) 2 Str 1178 was the first of a long line of decisions to this effect.
70 See Holdsworth, *History of English Law*, vol. XIII, pp. 380–1.
71 See *Cole* v *North Western Bank* (1875) LR 10 CP 354, 362.
72 Section 13 of the Factors Act 1889.
73 *Lloyds and Scottish Finance Ltd* v *Williamson* [1965] 1 WLR 404.

Mercantile agent

A mercantile agent is defined by the statutes as 'a mercantile agent having in the customary course of his business as such agent authority either to sell goods or to consign goods for the purpose of sale, or to buy goods, or to raise money on the security of goods'.[74] Whether a person is a mercantile agent or has merely obtained goods on sale or return is sometimes a difficult question. In the ordinary way it makes no difference to the result, because a sale or other disposition by the party entrusted with the goods will be valid in either event. If the party entrusted with the goods is a mercantile agent, a sale by him will be validated by the Factors Act, while, if he is held to have the goods on sale or return, a sale by him will normally be treated, under s. 18 Rule 4, as an act 'adopting the transaction' which passes property to him and through him to the sub-buyer. But in some cases it does make a difference whether the party with the goods is a mercantile agent or has the goods on sale or return, because it is possible to contract out of s. 18 Rule 4, while it is not possible to contract out of the provisions of s. 2 of the Factors Act 1889.[75]

A person may be a mercantile agent although he is only acting for a single principal,[76] but he must be more than a mere servant or employee. A person who induces another to let him have goods on a representation that he knows a third party who will buy them is not, without more, a mercantile agent.[77] But a person may be a mercantile agent without carrying on the business of being a mercantile agent.[78] And as every business must have a beginning, a person may be held to be a mercantile agent in respect of the transaction in question even though he has never acted as one before.[79] If the person who obtains the goods is not a mercantile agent at the time he obtains them, the fact that he becomes such later while the goods are still in his possession will not bring the case within the Factors Act[80] unless, presumably, the owner later consents to his possession as mercantile agent.

In possession of goods or of the documents of title to goods

The Act requires that the mercantile agent should be in possession of the goods or of the documents of title to the goods. It has been held that he must actually be in possession at the time of the sale, pledge or other disposition if the buyer is to be protected under the Factors Act. In *Beverley Acceptances Ltd* v *Oakley*,[81] one O pledged two Rolls-Royce cars to the defendant G for a large loan. The cars were parked in G's locked compound but O borrowed the keys of the compound telling G that it was a matter to do with insurance, but in reality to show the cars to the plaintiffs, who were contemplating advancing money on their security. The cars were duly returned to G. Some days later, the plaintiffs did advance money to G, and G

---

74 Section 1(1) of the Factors Act, also reproduced in s. 26 of the 1979 Sale of Goods Act.
75 See *Weiner* v *Harris* [1910] 1 KB 285, discussed on p. 331, above.
76 *Lowther* v *Harris* [1927] 1 KB 393.
77 *Jerome* v *Bentley* [1952] 2 All ER 114.
78 *Weiner* v *Harris*, above.
79 *Mortgage Loan & Finance Co of Australia* v *Richards* (1932) SR (NSW) 50, 58.
80 *Heap* v *Motorists' Advisory Agency Ltd* [1923] 1 KB 577.
81 [1982] RTR 417.

executed a bill of sale in their favour which was duly registered. It was held that, even if G was to be taken to be the 'owner' of the cars[82] and even if O was a mercantile agent, and even if O had been allowed temporary possession when he was lent the keys of the compound, still the buyer was not protected. The sale to the buyer had taken place at a time when any temporary possession obtained by O had long disappeared, and the section only applies where the mercantile agent 'is in possession', not where he once has been in possession.

The consent of the owner

The next requirement of the subsection is that the mercantile agent must be in possession of the goods with the consent of the owner. The meaning of these last words, which also appear in s. 25(1),[83] gave rise at one time to considerable difficulty where a person was induced to part with goods as a result of fraud and, in particular, where he parted with the goods in circumstances amounting to larceny by a trick under the old law of theft. It was at one time thought that in such a case the goods could not be said to be in the possession of the agent with the consent of the owner,[84] but it is probably safe to say that this view would not be accepted since the decision in *Pearson* v *Rose & Young*.[85] In this case, the plaintiff delivered his car to X, a mercantile agent, in order to obtain offers, but with no authority to sell it. The agent obtained possession of the registration book by a trick in such circumstances that the owner had clearly not consented to parting with the possession of it, and then promptly sold the car, as he had intended to do from the first. The Court of Appeal held that the question whether the agent had committed larceny by a trick was quite immaterial and that in each case the only question was whether the goods were in his possession with the consent of the owner. In this case, the mercantile agent had possession of the car with the consent of the owner, but not of the registration book. The court further held that a sale without a registration book would not have been a sale in the ordinary course of business and that the defendants were therefore not protected by the Factors Act.[86]

The dicta in *Pearson* v *Rose & Young*[87] were applied by Sellers J in *Du Jardin* v *Beadman*,[88] a case under s. 25(1) of the Sale of Goods Act, where the learned judge held that although the goods were obtained by larceny by a trick, they were nonetheless in the possession of the buyer with the consent of the seller. Since the coming into force of the Theft Act 1968, the offence of larceny by a trick has disappeared from English law, but there can be no doubt that these cases represent the modern law on the subject.

---

82 Or at least if O and G were together to be treated as owner under *Lloyds Bank* v *Bank of America* [1938] 2 KB 147, below, p. 389.
83 See below, p. 395.
84 See dicta in *Oppenheimer* v *Frazer* [1907] 2 KB 50.
85 [1951] 1 KB 275. See also *Folkes* v *King* [1923] 1 KB 282.
86 See also *Stadium Finance Ltd* v *Robbins* [1962] 2 QB 664. See also *Dreveston* v *Regal Garage Ltd*, 9 October 1997 (unreported). It appears that 'goods' for the purposes of the Factors Act in relation to motor vehicles means the vehicle plus its registration documents – see (1951) 67 LQR 3.
87 [1951] 1 KB 275.
88 [1952] 2 QB 712.

It has been suggested that a purchaser cannot rely on the owner's consent to the mercantile agent's possession if that consent was given under an illegal contract.[89] But this would produce the strange result that the owner of the goods could rely on his own illegal agreement with the agent to defeat the claims of an innocent third party. Moreover, the suggestion bears some resemblance to cases prior to *Pearson* v *Rose & Young* which (as we saw above) gave an artificial meaning to the word 'consent' in s. 2 of the Factors Act. It is submitted that this suggestion is wrong.

Not only the requirement of consent, but also the word 'owner' has given rise to difficulty in this section. First, the 'owner of the goods here referred to is the owner with whose consent the agent is in possession of them'.[90] Clearly, the section does not adversely affect the title of any person except the person who has entrusted the goods or documents of title to the mercantile agent. It does not thus affect the title of a person whose goods have been stolen, and later come into the possession of a mercantile agent from the thief.

Another difficulty arose in *Lloyds Bank* v *Bank of America*,[91] where the plaintiffs lent money to X, a mercantile agent, on the security of documents which were pledged with them. The documents were then returned to X under a 'trust receipt'[92] to enable him to sell the goods as trustee for the plaintiffs, but X fraudulently pledged them with the defendants for an advance. The defendants pleaded that they were protected by s. 2 of the Factors Act 1889, but the plaintiffs argued that as X, the mercantile agent, was himself the owner of the goods, it could not be said that he was in possession with the consent of the owner within the meaning of the Act. The Court of Appeal rejected these arguments, however. In the words of Lord Greene MR:

> Where the right of ownership has become divided among two or more persons in such a way that the acts which the section is contemplating could never be authorized save by both or all of them, these persons together constitute the owner.[93]

In this case the plaintiffs were the legal pledgees and, in equity, beneficiaries of the proceeds of sale, while X was the legal and beneficial owner, subject to the prior claim of the plaintiffs. Consequently, these two persons together constituted the owner within the Act, and the goods were nonetheless in the possession of X with the consent of the owner, because he was himself one of those two persons.

Goods entrusted to the mercantile agent as such

The purchaser from the mercantile agent will not be protected if the goods were entrusted to him for some purpose quite unconnected with his business as a mercantile agent. As Lord Denning once said:

---

89 *Belvoir Finance Co Ltd* v *Harold G Cole & Co Ltd* [1969] 1 WLR 1877.
90 *National Employers Mutual General Insurance Association Ltd* v *Jones* [1990] 1 AC 24, 60 per Lord Goff.
91 [1938] 2 KB 147.
92 A 'trust receipt' (now apparently usually called a 'letter of trust') is a document obtained by a bank or other finance institution which has advanced money against documents in respect (usually) of imported goods, when the documents are released to the buyer before the advance is paid off. See *Sale Continuation Ltd* v *Austin Taylor & Co* [1967] 2 All ER 1092, 1098 per Paull J.
93 [1938] 2 KB 147, 162.

The owner must consent to the agent having them for a purpose which is in some way or other connected with his business as a mercantile agent. It may not actually be for sale. It may be for display, or to get offers, or merely to put in his showroom; but there must be a consent to something of that kind before the owner can be deprived of his goods.[94]

So if the owner does not even know that the bailee to whom he entrusts the goods carries on business as a mercantile agent, his consent to the bailee's possession cannot suffice under the Act.[95]

Subsections (2), (3) and (4) of s. 2 of the Factors Act are also concerned with the meaning of the consent referred to in s. 2(1). Section 2(2) lays down that, if the agent obtains the goods with the consent of the owner, the subsequent withdrawal of the consent will not affect the rights of a purchaser who had no notice of the withdrawal. Section 2(3) provides that, if the agent is in possession of the goods with the consent of the owner and obtains possession of the documents of title by virtue of his possession of the goods, he shall be deemed to have such possession also with the consent of the owner. Finally s. 2(4) enacts that 'For the purposes of this Act the consent of the owner shall be presumed in the absence of evidence to the contrary.'

Sale in ordinary course of business

The purchaser claiming the protection of s. 2 must next prove that the mercantile agent acted in the ordinary course of business. This cannot be read literally because, obviously, in one sense a sale without the authority of the owner can rarely, if ever, be in the ordinary course of business, and it is only in this event that the Factors Act is needed at all. Consequently this should probably be taken as meaning 'appearing to act in the ordinary course of business'.[96] Alternatively, it may mean that the mercantile agent must act in the ordinary course of business except for the fact that he does not have the owner's authority.

It is immaterial that the third party dealt with the mercantile agent as a principal and did not know him to be an agent; and it is also immaterial that the agent entered into a transaction not normally sanctioned by the custom of the trade unless, perhaps, the custom is so notorious that the third party would normally be taken to have knowledge of it as, for example, if an auctioneer were to pledge goods entrusted to him for sale. In other words, the phrase 'acting in the ordinary course of business of a mercantile agent' means 'acting in such a way as a mercantile agent in the ordinary course of business as a mercantile agent would act, that is to say, within business hours, at a proper place of business, and in other respects in the ordinary way in which a mercantile agent would act, so that there is nothing to lead the pledgee to suppose that anything is done wrong, or to give notice that the disposition is one which the mercantile agent had not authority for'.[97] So also, if a

94　*Pearson* v *Rose & Young* [1951] 1 KB 275, 288. There is a long line of authority supporting this viewpoint, dating back to *Cole* v *North Western Bank* (1875) LR 10 CP 354. It has also been held that the decision in the *Pacific Motor Auctions* case [1965] AC 867 (see p. 395) has not affected the law on this point: *Astley Industrial Trust* v *Miller* [1968] 2 All ER 36.
95　*Henderson* v *Prosser* [1982] CLY 21.
96　See (1951) 67 LQR 6. Cf. *Oppenheimer* v *Attenborough* [1908] 1 KB 221.
97　*Oppenheimer* v *Attenborough* [1908] 1 KB 221, 230–1 per Buckley LJ.

mercantile agent sells goods on the terms that the price is not to be paid directly to him but to one of his creditors, this may well be outside the ordinary course of business.[98] But a sale is not necessarily outside the ordinary course of business because the price is not paid in cash.[99] Whether the mercantile agent has acted in the ordinary way in which a mercantile agent would act in any particular case is a question of fact.[100]

It seems that the requirement that the agent must act in the ordinary course of business is distinct from the requirement that the buyer must take in good faith and without notice.[101] A buyer may be in good faith even though the sale is outside the ordinary course of business. To this extent the dictum above, from Buckley LJ's judgment in *Oppenheimer* v *Attenborough*, must be modified. For if the agent is only held to act outside the ordinary course of business in circumstances in which the buyer would have notice of his lack of authority, it would seem that the buyer would necessarily fail on the second requirement in any event.[102]

These decisions give rise to the question whether the requirement that the agent must act in the ordinary course of business serves any useful purpose. It would seem that the owner is already adequately protected by the requirement that the buyer must act in good faith and without notice, and this additional requirement could well be dropped in any future reform of the law.[103]

Sale, pledge or other disposition

What sort of transaction amounts to a 'disposition' has been dealt with by the courts in relation to s. 24 of the Sale of Goods Act, so the point is discussed in connection with that section.[104]

Good faith and notice

The next requirement of s. 2 is that the buyer must prove that he took in good faith and without notice that the sale was made without the owner's authority, and the burden of proof is apparently on him in this respect,[105] although under s. 23 lack of good faith must be proved by the original owner.[106]

---

98 *Lloyds & Scottish Finance Ltd* v *Williamson* [1965] 1 WLR 404, 408.
99 *Tingey & Co* v *John Chambers* [1967] NZLR 785.
100 *Biggs* v *Evans* [1894] 1 QB 88.
101 *Lloyds & Scottish Finance Ltd* v *Williamson* – see above, n. 98; *Pacific Motor Auctions Ltd* v *Motor Credits (Hire Finance) Ltd* [1965] AC 867.
102 In both the cases cited in the last note sales were made outside the ordinary course of business, but the buyers were in good faith and were both held to be protected though for different reasons.
103 The UCC retains the requirement that the sale must be in the ordinary course of business on the ground that purchasers (in the USA) were frequently held to be in good faith in cases where this result outraged common sense. See the Commentary to Art. 2-403(2). But this is of course the result of jury trial and is no longer relevant here where commercial cases are hardly ever tried by jury today.
104 See below, p. 406.
105 *Heap* v *Motorists Advisory Agency Ltd* [1923] 1 KB 577; although the reasons given are not convincing, the result seems sensible. It is not difficult for the buyer to prove his good faith, but it is very hard for the owner to disprove it. Hence the Law Reform Committee recommended the endorsement of this case: Cmnd. 2958, para. 25.
106 *Whitehorn Bros* v *Davison* [1911] 1 KB 463. The Law Reform Committee recommended reversal of this decision – see previous note.

Pledges

Although a pledge is included within the protection of this section, s. 4 of the same Act excludes a pledge made for an antecedent debt. Thus if a mercantile agent pledges goods in his possession with the consent of the owner, the pledgee will have to prove that the pledge was made in return for a loan given at the same time, and not before the pledge was made.

SPECIAL POWERS OF SALE

Section 21(2) says that:

> Nothing in this Act affects—
> (b) The validity of any contract of sale under any special common law or statutory power of sale, or under the order of a court of competent jurisdiction.

This provision covers a large number of miscellaneous cases where a non-owner may pass a good title to goods, some of which are considered below.[107]

Common law powers

The most important of these is the power of sale of a pledgee, but if the pledge is made under a 'regulated agreement', that is, it is taken by a provider of credit from a consumer, the power must be exercised under the Consumer Credit Act 1974 (see below).

Statutory powers

There are a large number of these; the most important include the power of a sheriff to sell goods seized under a writ of execution;[108] the power of an innkeeper to sell goods upon which he has a lien under s. 1 of the Innkeepers Act 1878; the powers conferred by the Torts (Interference with Goods) Act 1977; and the powers relating to pawns under the Consumer Credit Act 1974. Under s. 120 of this Act, a pawn for under £75 can be forfeited at the end of the redemption period, but a pawn for a sum exceeding £75 can only be realized in accordance with the procedures laid down in s. 121.[109]

The only one of these provisions calling for any further comment is the Torts (Interference with Goods) Act 1977. This Act repealed the Disposal of Uncollected Goods Act 1952, which had not worked very satisfactorily. Section 12 of the new Act confers power on a bailee to sell goods after due notice given in various circumstances

---

107 For Scots law, see Reid, *The Law of Property in Scotland* (1996), para. 667.
108 Companies Act 1985 ss. 621, 622 (as amended by Insolvency Act 1985 s. 235 and Sch. 10 Pt II); Insolvency Act 1986 s. 346; Supreme Court Act 1981 s. 138B (inserted by Statute Law Repeals Act 1989 s. 1(2) and Sch. 2). The buyer acquires a good title even if the goods did not belong to the person against whom execution issues, and even if he knew of the rights of the true owner: *Curtis* v *Maloney* [1951] 1 KB 736; *Dyal Singh* v *Kenyan Insurance Ltd* [1954] 1 All ER 847.
109 The figure of £75 was substituted for £25 by the Consumer Credit (Further Increase in Monetary Limits) Order 1998.

specified in the Act. If the bailee is unable to trace the bailor, he may still be able to sell the goods subject to the conditions laid down in the Act. A sale under this Act gives a good title to the purchaser as against the bailor, but not against the true owner if the bailor had no authority to bail them.

Sale by order of the court

The court has a wide jurisdiction under the Civil Procedure Rules 1998 to order the sale of goods which 'for any just and sufficient reason it may be desirable to have sold at once', for example because they are of a perishable nature, or because the market is falling. The court has power to insist on a sale despite the objections of the owner, where such a course seems necessary or desirable.[110]

SALE IN MARKET OVERT[111]

The fifth exception to the *nemo dat* rule in England and Wales was the case of a sale in market overt (another concept unknown in Scots law). Section 22 of the Act provided:

(1) Where goods are sold in market overt, according to the usage of the market, the buyer acquires a good title to the goods, provided he buys them in good faith and without notice of any defect or want of title on the part of the seller.

This exception could be explained, but scarcely justified, on historical grounds only, and it may be regretted that it was included in the 1893 codification. Reform of the rule was proposed as long ago as 1966, but not acted upon.[112]

In January 1994, the government produced a Consultation Paper[113] which recommended the abolition of the rule, replacing it with a rule which would confer a good title on bona fide purchasers through retail outlets or auctions. The Sale of Goods (Amendment) Act 1994, however, abolishes the rule with effect from 3 January 1995. Accordingly, a good faith purchaser will no longer get a good title even in the limited circumstances provided by the market overt rule. This abolition would appear to be untimely, as currently the European Commission is considering a Directive intended to harmonize the laws of member states, and the majority of member states have a general rule in favour of innocent purchasers, so that it is likely this will form the basis of harmonization. Goods covered by the European Commission's Regulations on 'cultural goods'[114] and goods registered in the International Art Loss Register will no doubt be outside the operation of any rule which may be promulgated by the Commission favouring good faith purchasers. No title will pass in such goods.

SALE UNDER A VOIDABLE TITLE

Section 23 confirms the common law rule that a person cannot avoid a voidable contract to the prejudice of third-party rights acquired in good faith and for value:

---

110 *Larner* v *Fawcett* [1950] 2 All ER 727.
111 See (1956) 9 *Current Legal Problems* 113.
112 Report of the Law Reform Committee, Twelfth Report (1966) Cmnd. 2958.
113 'Transfer of Title: ss. 21–26 of the Sale of Goods Act 1979'.
114 Regulation 3911/92, OJ 1992 L395/1, 31.12.92 (as amended). See also Council Directive 93/7/EEC on the return of cultural goods unlawfully removed from the territories of member states. See – http://europa.eu.int/scadplus/leg/en/lvb/l11017a.htm (accessed 17.08.04).

When the seller of goods has a voidable title to them, but his title has not been avoided at the time of the sale, the buyer acquires a good title to the goods, provided he buys them in good faith and without notice of the seller's defect of title.

The great practical importance of this rule is that, if a person buys goods by fraud[115] and disposes of them before the other party avoids the contract, a buyer in good faith[116] from the fraudulent party acquires a good title. Where, however, the fraud is such as to nullify the offer or acceptance (or where there is a fundamental mistake) so that no real contract comes into existence, the buyer acquires no title at all and cannot therefore pass anything on to the innocent third party.[117] Consequently, this section does not protect such a buyer and unless he can invoke one of the other exceptions to the *nemo dat* rule, such as estoppel or s. 2 of the Factors Act 1889, he will have no defence to an action of conversion by the owner.

In general, the defrauded party can only rescind the contract by communicating with the other party to the contract and notifying him of the rescission. But in *Car & Universal Finance Ltd* v *Caldwell*[118] the Court of Appeal held that the seller can rescind the contract by evincing an intention to do so and taking all steps open to him (such as informing the police) where he is unable to communicate with the fraudulent party, at least where this is because the fraudulent party is deliberately keeping out of the way. The court left open the question whether the law would be the same where the innocent party's inability to communicate with the other is not due to the fact that the latter is deliberately keeping out of the way. At first it seemed that this decision had fundamentally affected the protection afforded to the innocent third party by the Act because it had previously been assumed that a contract could not be rescinded without communication. Where the contract is fraudulently induced, it was generally thought that in practice there was little that the innocent party could do to defeat a bona fide purchaser. This view of the law was, moreover, adopted in Scotland in *McLeod* v *Kerr*,[119] which was decided in the same year as *Caldwell's* case. The facts in this case were substantially identical with those in *Caldwell's* case and the Court of Session held that 'by no stretch of imagination' could the seller's conduct amount to rescission of the contract. However, as will be seen later, it is now clear that the decision in *Caldwell's* case will be of limited application in practice because in circumstances to which it applies the third party will often get a good title under s. 25(1) of the Act.[120]

Although s. 23 only refers to the possibility of a sale, the common law rule is the same and presumably still applies to pledges, so a person with a voidable title to goods who pledges them before the other party avoids the title can pass a good title to the pledgee.[121] But a trustee in bankruptcy takes no better title than the bankrupt

---

115 Or other invalidating case such as duress, which also renders a contract voidable – see *North Ocean Shipping Co Ltd* v *Hyundai Construction* [1979] QB 705; *Pao On* v *Lau Yiu* [1980] AC 614; *Atlas Express Ltd* v *Kafco (Importers and Distributors) Ltd* [1989] 1 All ER 641. Cf. *Universe Tankships of Monrovia Ltd* v *ITWF* [1983] 1 AC 366; *Dimskal Shipping Co SA* v *International Transport Workers Federation* [1992] 2 AC 152.

116 The onus of proving lack of good faith is on the original owner: *Whitehorn Bros* v *Davison* [1911] 1 KB 463. But cf. *Thomas* v *Helas*, 27 November 1986, only noted in (1986) 3 CL 295a.

117 As, for example, in *Cundy* v *Lindsay* (1878) 3 App Cas 459 and similar cases.

118 [1965] 1 QB 525. It was apparently followed in *Thomas* v *Helas*, above, n. 116.

119 1965 SC 253. See further, Reid, *The Law of Property in Scotland* (1996), paras 606–10.

120 See below, p. 399.

121 See, e.g., *Phillips* v *Brooks* [1919] 2 KB 243.

had, and if the bankrupt had a voidable title the seller can still avoid that title and retake the goods even after they have vested in the trustee.[122]

SELLER IN POSSESSION

The last two exceptions to the *nemo dat* rule are contained in ss. 8 and 9 of the Factors Act 1889 (extended to Scotland by the Factors (Scotland) Act 1890[123]), which are reproduced with the omission, in each case, of a few words in s. 24 and s. 25(1) of the Sale of Goods Act, though the sections of the earlier Act were not repealed. Because the sections of the Factors Act are wider than those of the Sale of Goods Act, the discussion here will be in terms of the former. Section 8 of the Factors Act is as follows:

> Where a person, having sold goods, continues, or is, in possession of the goods or of the documents of title to the goods, the delivery or transfer by that person, or by a mercantile agent acting for him, of the goods or documents of title under any sale, pledge or other disposition thereof [or under any agreement for sale, pledge or other disposition thereof], to any person receiving the same in good faith and without notice of the previous sale, shall have the same effect as if the person making the delivery or transfer were expressly authorized by the owner of the goods to make the same.

The words placed in square brackets in the text are the words omitted in s. 24 of the Sale of Goods Act.[124]

'A person, having sold goods, continues, or is, in possession'

There was for some years a continuous stream of authority holding that it was not enough that the seller was simply in possession of the goods when he resold them, but that the third party claiming under this section must go further and show that the seller was in possession as seller, and not in some other capacity, for example as bailee.[125]

However, the authority of these decisions was severely shaken by the decision of the Privy Council in *Pacific Motor Auctions Pty Ltd* v *Motor Credits (Hire Finance) Ltd*,[126] the facts of which have already been given.[127] The Privy Council held that the defendants obtained a good title under a section of the New South Wales Sale of Goods Act identical with s. 24 of the 1979 Act. In delivering the opinion of the Board, Lord Pearce rejected the earlier English decisions as wrongly decided. The Privy Council held that the words 'continues . . . in possession' in the section were intended to refer to the continuity of physical possession, regardless of any

---

122 *In re Eastgate* [1905] 1 KB 465.
123 For a Scottish perspective, see Reid, *The Law of Property in Scotland* (1996), paras 681 and 682.
124 The omitted words in ss. 24 and 25 are one of the oddities of the Sale of Goods Act. If Parliament thought that ss. 8 and 9 of the Factors Act were too wide, why did it not repeal them; and if it did not think they were too wide, why did it leave out these words?
125 *Staffs Motor Guarantee Ltd* v *British Wagon Co Ltd* [1934] 2 KB 305; *Eastern Distributors* v *Goldring* [1957] 2 QB 600; *Dore* v *Dore*, *The Times*, 18 March 1953; *Halfway Garage (Nottingham)* v *Lepley*, *Guardian*, 8 February 1964.
126 [1965] AC 867.
127 See above, p. 380.

private transaction between the seller and the first buyer which might alter the legal title under which the possession was held. Accordingly, unless there is an actual transfer of physical possession, the seller is to be treated as continuing in possession and as able to pass a good title under the section.[128] The Privy Council approved the New Zealand case of *Mitchell* v *Jones*,[129] where the seller sold and delivered a horse to the buyer, but later borrowed it back and wrongfully sold it again. In such a case the second buyer is not protected; the seller is 'in possession' in a literal sense, but the fact that he was a seller originally is no longer relevant. He is a bailee, not a seller.[130]

This decision was later followed by the Court of Appeal[131] and was much to be welcomed. It rid the law of an unnecessary complication for it replaced the previous imprecise criteria for determining whether a seller was in possession 'as seller' by the simpler criterion of whether he remained in physical possession throughout. It is also thought that the result is more equitable than that reached in the earlier cases since, if a buyer chooses to leave the seller in possession, the risk of the seller proving dishonest should rest on him rather than on a bona fide purchaser.

In the application of this provision it must be borne in mind that there is nothing in the section to alter the usual commercial meaning of the word possession. Consequently, it has been held that goods which were at the seller's disposal though physically in the custody of warehousemen were in the possession of the seller within s. 8 of the Factors Act.[132]

The delivery or transfer . . . of the goods or documents of title

On the face of it the section appears to require that the goods should be *delivered* (or anyhow transferred) to the second buyer if he is to obtain a title binding on the first buyer. So if the seller sells goods to B1, *but retains possession of them*, and then sells them again (whether rightfully or wrongfully is immaterial) to B2, but still retains possession of them, it seems that B2 obtains no title under the section, and B1 has the better claim. In *Nicholson* v *Harper*[133] a merchant owned some wine stored with warehousemen, the defendants; he sold 250 dozen old port to the plaintiffs who left the wine in the possession of the defendants, and apparently gave them no notice of their purchase, nor obtained any delivery orders or other acknowledgment of their claim. Later the original seller pledged all his wine to the warehousemen, and he subsequently became insolvent. North J held that the property in the wine had passed to the plaintiffs under the first sale, and that the warehousemen obtained no title under s. 25 (now s. 24) of the Sale of Goods Act. Although the merchant was

---

128 Prima facie a dealer in possession under such an agreement would be able to pass a title under s. 2 of the Factors Act. (See, e.g., the CA decision in *St Margaret's Trust Ltd* v *Castle*, 28 July 1964 (1964) 10 CL §175a.) But the transaction in this case was not 'in the ordinary course of business' and the buyers were therefore compelled to rely on s. 24.
129 (1905) 24 NZLR 932.
130 The words 'or is in possession' give rise to some difficulty, but were explained as covering the case where the seller did not originally have possession of the goods but only acquired it later.
131 *Worcester Works Finance Ltd* v *Cooden Engineering Co Ltd* [1972] 1 QB 210.
132 *City Fur Co Ltd* v *Fureenbond* [1937] 1 All ER 239.
133 [1895] 2 Ch 415.

a seller who had retained possession under that section, there had been no delivery or transfer of possession to the warehousemen after the sale.

However, *Nicholson v Harper* was rejected as bad law by the Australian High Court in *Gamer's Motor Centre (Newcastle) Pty Ltd* v *Natwest Wholesale Australia Pty Ltd*,[134] a case concerning the parallel provisions of s. 9 of the Factors Act and s. 25(1) of the Sale of Goods Act. In this case the defendants agreed to sell eight cars to car dealers under an agreement whereby the sellers retained title until payment. The cars were delivered to the dealers who immediately resold them under a financing plan to the plaintiffs, while retaining possession of them for stock display. It was held (by a bare majority of the High Court) that the plaintiffs obtained a title to the cars, good against the defendants, because they had bought the cars from a buyer who had obtained the possession of the goods with the consent of the seller. Like s. 8, s. 9 of the Factors Act appears only to protect a buyer when there has been a delivery or transfer of the goods to him, but the High Court held that it was already well established at the time that the original Sale of Goods Act was passed that this did not necessarily require a physical transfer of possession. The law recognized the concept of a 'constructive delivery' where the physical possession remained unaltered, but the right to possession was transferred. So if S sells goods to B1, and retains possession of them, and then sells them again to B2, although he may still retain the physical possession of the goods unaltered, there may then be a constructive delivery to B2, at least if B2 has an immediate right to possession. The section would then be satisfied, and B2 would have a better claim than B1.[135]

Constructive doctrines are today often regarded as fictions, somewhat out of fashion,[136] and the High Court's decision in the *Gamer* case may appear, at first sight, inconsistent with the general approach of the Privy Council in the *Pacific Motor Auctions* case, where the continuity of physical possession was stressed as the basis of s. 8 of the Factors Act, and where the Privy Council reversed another decision of the High Court on these statutory provisions. But the two cases are not entirely comparable, if only because the *Gamer* decision protects the bona fide purchaser for value, while the High Court's decision in the *Pacific Motor Auctions* case did not. Furthermore, the policy of the Act suggests that the *Gamer* decision is preferable to *Nicholson v Harper* because (in a s. 8 case) the second buyer who pays the price of the goods is acting in reliance on his belief that the original seller retains title, having regard to his continued possession of the goods.[137] Moreover, the other exceptions to the *nemo dat* principle, such as estoppel, ss. 22 and 23 of the Act and s. 2 of the Factors Act, all appear to operate to protect the buyer as from the moment of the sale

---

134 (1987) 163 CLR 236. But *Nicholson v Harper* was followed in New Zealand: *New Zealand Securities & Finance Ltd v Wright Cars Ltd* [1976] 1 NZLR 77.

135 See *Forsythe International (UK) Ltd v Silver Shipping Co Ltd* [1994] 1 WLR 1334.

136 Though there is modern case law applying the concept of constructive delivery in a different context: *Four Point Garage Ltd v Carter* [1985] 3 All ER 12. See also pp. 147 and 353.

137 In the NSW Court of Appeal McHugh JA suggested that it was 'curious that the legislature, having penalized the owner for allowing the buyer to have possession, intended the sub-buyer to obtain a good title even though he leaves the same goods in the possession of the same person': *Gamer's Motor Centre (Newcastle) Pty Ltd v Natwest Wholesale Australia Pty Ltd* [1985] 2 NSWLR 475, 490. But the answer to this is that the seller has induced the injurious reliance of the second buyer by allowing the first to have possession, while the second buyer has induced no reliance at all.

to him, provided at least that he has paid the price, or acted to his prejudice so as to constitute himself a bona fide purchaser for value. None of these provisions appears to require an actual delivery to the person claiming to be protected.[138] What is more, the second buyer is protected although he has only agreed to buy the goods and the property has not yet passed to him,[139] so it would seem strange to insist on an actual physical delivery to him. In *Michael Gerson (Leasing) Ltd* v *Wilkinson*[140] counsel for the claimant accepted that delivery in s. 24 includes constructive delivery and that it is not confined to physical delivery. Clarke LJ accepted that both concessions were correctly made. They accorded with the decision of the High Court of Australia in *Gamer's Motor Centre (Newcastle) Proprietary Ltd* v *Natwest Wholesale Australia Proprietary Ltd*[141] which he had followed at first instance in *Forsythe International (UK) Ltd* v *Silver Shipping Co Ltd*.[142]

Sale, pledge or other disposition

In most cases, the party claiming the protection of this section will rely on a sale or pledge, but the section also refers to other 'disposition'. In *Worcester Works Finance Ltd* v *Cooden Engineering Co Ltd*,[143] the Court of Appeal held that this was a very wide word, but that it did not cover a mere transfer of possession; there must be some transfer of an interest in the goods to constitute a disposition. In this case one G bought a car from the defendants, paying the price with a cheque which was not met. He then sold the car to another finance company – the plaintiffs – but retained the possession of the car as he had induced the plaintiffs to accept a hire-purchase proposal for the benefit of an accomplice. Subsequently the defendants, with the consent of G, retook the car from him. It was held that the defendants were protected as against the plaintiffs. So far as the plaintiffs were concerned, G was a seller who remained in possession. Moreover, the retaking of the car by the defendants was a 'disposition' by G to them inasmuch as it amounted to a rescission of the contract between them and, therefore, it revested the property in the defendants.

This case is also authority for the proposition that a party relying on s. 8 of the Factors Act need not prove that the seller remained in possession with the consent of the buyer. The difference in wording between ss. 2 and 8 in this respect clearly shows that s. 8 was intended to apply even where the seller wrongfully retains possession after the sale.

Good faith and notice

The second buyer is only protected if he acts in good faith and without notice of the previous sale. Notice presumably has its usual commercial meaning here, so that it applies only to actual and not to constructive notice; 'there is no general duty on a

---

138 But as to estoppel, see *Shaw* v *Commissioner of Met Police* [1987] 1 WLR 1332, above, p. 377.
139 This is the effect of s. 8, differing in this respect from s. 24 of the 1979 Act.
140 [2000] 2 All ER (Comm) 890.
141 (1987) 163 CLR 236.
142 [1994] 1 WLR 1334.
143 [1972] 1 QB 210. See Preston (1972) 88 LQR 239.

buyer of goods in an ordinary commercial transaction to make inquiries as to the right of the seller to dispose of the goods'.[144] There is no independent requirement in this section that the transaction should be made 'in the ordinary course of business', though of course a transaction outside the ordinary course of business may sometimes be sufficient to put the buyer on inquiry.

Application of s. 8

As is to be expected, s. 8 only applies when the property in the goods has passed to the buyer under the contract of sale, because if the property has not so passed, obviously the seller sells by virtue of his property in the goods and no statutory exception to the *nemo dat* rule is needed. Hence s. 8 only applies where the seller has 'sold' (not 'agreed to sell') the goods.

BUYER IN POSSESSION

Section 9 of the Factors Act and s. 25(1) of the Sale of Goods Act contain provisions parallel to those of s. 8 and s. 24. Section 9 is as follows:

> Where a person, having bought or agreed to buy goods, obtains with the consent of the seller possession of the goods or the documents of title to the goods, the delivery or transfer, by that person or by a mercantile agent acting for him, of the goods or the documents of title under any sale, pledge or other disposition thereof [or under any agreement for sale, pledge or other disposition thereof], to any person receiving the same in good faith and without notice of any lien or other right of the original seller in respect of the goods, shall have the same effect as if the person making the delivery or transfer were a mercantile agent in possession of the goods or documents of title with the consent of the owner.

The words placed in square brackets in the text are omitted in s. 25(1) of the Sale of Goods Act, so the ensuing discussion is in terms of s. 9 because it is the wider provision. Section 26 of the Sale of Goods Act defines the term 'mercantile agent', but the definition merely repeats that incorporated in s. 1(1) of the Factors Act 1889. This has already been discussed in connection with s. 2 of the Factors Act.[145]

A person 'having bought or agreed to buy goods'

It has already been seen that s. 8 only applies where the property has passed to the first buyer before the second sale, because otherwise the special provision is not necessary. But s. 9 applies where the first buyer has 'bought or agreed to buy goods', that is to say, it applies whether or not the property has passed to the first buyer. This is a strange provision for it is not easy to see why there should be any special enactment to protect a person who has bought goods from a buyer in possession when the property has already passed to this buyer. Prima facie the buyer can sell the goods in these circumstances and pass a good title by virtue of his own property. It is to be hoped that

---

144 *Feuer Leather Corp* v *Frank Johnstone* (1981) Com LR 251, 253.
145 See above, p. 385 *et seq.*

a court would dismiss as mere surplusage the words 'bought or' in s. 9 even though the section imposes certain restrictions on the buyer's ability to pass a good title to a third party;[146] in fact (as appears below) it is not easy to envisage circumstances in which these restrictions would become applicable. But possibly they do not matter anyhow because it is arguable that a buyer can always pass property even at common law if it has already passed to him, and therefore s. 9 could be ignored in such a case.

Where a buyer has resold goods supplied under a reservation of title clause,[147] a sub-purchaser can acquire a good title under this provision (as well as s. 2(1) of the Factors Act). But if the goods are in turn supplied by the buyer to the sub-purchaser under the reservation of title clause, it would seem that the words in s. 9 which do not appear in s. 25 of the Sale of Goods Act (in square brackets where the section is set out above) do not serve to defeat the original seller's retention of title clause. Unless and until the sub-purchaser has paid for the goods, or satisfied such other conditions as may have been stipulated by the buyer for the passing of property to the sub-purchaser, the original seller is entitled to repossess.[148]

The fact that s. 9 only applies where a person has bought or agreed to buy goods means that there must be a contract of sale within the meaning of the Act.[149] If a supplier contracts to sell goods to a building contractor who is engaged on building works and the goods are delivered direct to the building site, and the contractor subsequently becomes insolvent without having paid his supplier, title to the goods may be disputed between the original supplier and the owner of the site for whom the work is being done. If the goods have been delivered to the site under a contract of sale, title can pass under s. 9 of the Factors Act. The supplier is a seller, the contractor has undoubtedly bought or agreed to buy the goods, and delivery to the site is a delivery to the contractor who is thus in possession of the goods. So his contract with the building owner may be a sale or other disposition which transfers title.[150] But if the first relevant contract is not a contract of sale but (for instance) a contract for services s. 9 will not apply at all, and the original owner may be able to reclaim the goods. So where a contractor had agreed to do certain building works, and a subcontractor had agreed to supply and fix the roof slates, the delivery of the slates to the site by the subcontractor did not pass title to the building owner under s. 9.[151] The first relevant contract here was that between the contractor and the subcontractor which was not a contract of sale at all, so s. 9 simply did not apply. In practice the position is today often complicated by special conditions of sale as well as special conditions in building contracts which may provide that the title to goods delivered to a site passes forthwith to the building owner.[152]

---

146 See the dicta of Brennan J in the *Garner* case (1987) 163 CLR 236, 251.
147 See p. 470 *et seq.*
148 *Re Highway Foods International Ltd* [1995] BCC 271. A similar conclusion was reached in *Hanson (W) (Harrow) Ltd v Rapid Civil Engineering & Usborne Developments Ltd* (1987) 38 Build LR 106, which argued on the basis of s. 2(1) of the Factors Act and the narrower s. 25(1) of the Sale of Goods Act. As to circumstances in which the seller can trace his security interest into the proceeds of sale, see p. 473 *et seq.*
149 See the Scots decision in *Archivent Sales & Developments Ltd v Strathclyde Regional Council* (1984) 27 Build LR 98, 1985 SLT 154. See also *Thomas Graham & Sons Ltd v Glenrothes Development Corp* 1967 SC 284.
150 Ibid.
151 *Dawber Williamson Roofing Ltd v Humberside CC* (1979) 14 Build LR 70.
152 See, e.g., *Hanson (W) (Harrow) v Rapid Civil Engineering & Usborne Developments Ltd* (1987) 38 Build LR 106.

Other problems which arise from the need to show that there was a contract of sale in the strict sense, before s. 9 can apply, relate to hire-purchase and similar agreements. Because a contract of sale is defined by s. 2(1) of the Act as a contract under which the seller transfers or agrees to transfer the property in goods to the buyer in return for a money consideration, a mere option to purchase cannot be a contract of sale until the option is exercised. It is for this reason, as we have seen, that the ordinary hire-purchase agreement is drafted in the form of a bailment with an option to purchase. A person in possession of goods under such an agreement is not a person who has 'bought or agreed to buy goods' within the meaning of s. 9 of the Factors Act.[153] On the other hand, 'A contract of sale may be absolute or conditional',[154] and a person in possession of goods under a contract in which the transfer of the property is conditional, whether on payment[155] or on the occurrence of some other event,[156] was until 1965 treated as a person who had agreed to buy goods within s. 9. Between 1889 and 1965, then, the law distinguished fundamentally between cases where a person obtained possession of goods under a hire-purchase agreement, to which s. 25(1) of the Sale of Goods Act and s. 9 of the Factors Act did not apply (*Helby* v *Matthews*)[157] and cases where a person obtained possession under a conditional sale agreement, to which those sections did apply (*Lee* v *Butler*).[158]

However, the law on this point was profoundly modified by the Hire-Purchase Act 1964. In accordance with the general assimilation of conditional sale agreements to hire-purchase agreements since that Act, it is now provided that, for the purposes of s. 9 of the Factors Act (and s. 25(1) of the Sale of Goods Act), 'the buyer under a conditional sale agreement is to be taken not to be a person who has bought or agreed to buy goods'.[159] A conditional sale agreement for the purposes of this provision is an agreement for the sale of goods which is a consumer credit agreement, and under which:

> ... the purchase price or part of it is payable by instalments, and the property in the goods is to remain in the seller (notwithstanding that the buyer is to be in possession of the goods) until such conditions as to the payment of the instalments or otherwise as may be specified in the agreement are fulfilled.[160]

An agreement in which the price is not payable by instalments is not, therefore, a conditional sale agreement for this purpose and remains within the protection of s. 9 of the Factors Act even though it is conditional upon some other event.[161]

It is important to observe that the provisions of the law relating to conditional sales mentioned above are confined to agreements which are consumer credit agreements within the protection of the Consumer Credit Act 1974. In other words, a buyer in possession under a conditional sale agreement can still pass a good title under s. 9 of

---

153 *Helby* v *Matthews* [1895] AC 471; *Belsize Motor Supply Co Ltd* v *Cox* [1914] 1 KB 244.
154 Section 2(3).
155 *Lee* v *Butler* [1893] 2 QB 318.
156 *Marten* v *Whale* [1917] 2 KB 480.
157 [1895] AC 471.
158 [1893] 2 QB 318.
159 Section 25(2)(a) of the 1979 Act.
160 Section 8 of the Consumer Credit Act 1974.
161 So, for instance, *Marten* v *Whale* (above, n. 156) would still be decided in the same way today.

the Factors Act if the total credit provided exceeds £15,000 or if the buyer is a corporation.

It is apparent, then, that these Acts have to a large extent done away with the distinction between conditional sale agreements and hire-purchase agreements which
formerly existed as a result of the celebrated cases of *Lee* v *Butler*[162] and *Helby* v
Matthews.[163] In view of the fact that the tendency over the last century has been to
widen the circumstances in which a non-owner can transfer a good title, this particular move may seem a retrograde step. The justification for it appears to be that, in
practice, conditional sale agreements of this kind have not been commonly used as a
method of consumer finance, and that it was desirable to assimilate the law relating
to conditional sale and hire-purchase, partly in order to prevent evasion of the Acts
and partly in the interests of simplicity. Moreover, the practical effect of this statutory
modification of *Lee* v *Butler* is much qualified by the special provisions relating to
motor vehicles. As will be seen later, Part III of the Hire-Purchase Act 1964 protects
a bona fide purchaser of a motor vehicle from a person in possession under a
hire-purchase or a conditional sale agreement.[164]

A person who obtains goods on 'sale or return' has also been said to be outside the
provisions of s. 9 because he also is not a person who has agreed to buy goods,
although in a certain sense he has made a conditional contract of sale.[165] We have
already seen that in many cases it makes no difference whether a person who has
taken goods on sale or return comes within s. 9 or not, because if he sells or pledges
the goods he does an act adopting the transaction within s. 18 Rule 4(b) and the
property passes to him, with the result that the sub-buyer or pledgee is protected. We
have also seen that it is possible to contract out of s. 18,[166] but it is not possible to
contract out of s. 9 of the Factors Act, so that in this event it is of vital importance
to decide whether the case comes within s. 9 or not.

A person who is entrusted with goods as a mere agent to sell them is not within the
section,[167] for the obvious reason that he has not bought or agreed to buy them
within the meaning of the section. But if he is a mercantile agent, as defined in the
Factors Act, then he can pass a good title under s. 2 of that Act; and it may also be
possible for a buyer from him to claim that he has acquired title at common law
simply on the ground that the agent sold the goods within his actual, usual or ostensible authority.

The consent of the seller

The protection afforded to a third party by s. 9 is only available if the goods were in
the possession of the buyer with the consent of the seller. This is similar to the
requirement which appears in s. 2, and, *mutatis mutandis*, the law is the same.
Consequently, it is not material that the buyer obtained the goods by a criminal

---

162 See below, p. 409–10.
163 *Edwards* v *Vaughan* (1910) 26 TLR 545. See the doubts expressed about this case at p. 331, above.
164 See p. 410 *et seq.*
165 *Edwards* v *Vaughan* (1910) 26 TLR 545. See the doubts expressed about this case at p. 331.
166 *Weiner* v *Harris* [1910] 2 KB 285 – see above, p. 331.
167 *Shaw* v *Commissioner of Met Police* [1987] 1 WLR 1332.

offence, the only question being whether the seller in fact consented to the buyer having possession.[168] Nor is it material that the seller has revoked his consent to the buyer having possession. As we have seen, s. 2(2) of the Factors Act specifically states that the subsequent withdrawal of his consent by the seller does not prevent the operation of the Act. This means that the decision in *Car & Universal Finance Co v Caldwell*[169] is of little practical importance. In that case, as we have seen, it was held that a contract of sale induced by fraud could be rescinded without communicating with the fraudulent party. But it is now clear that the only result of this is to force the third party to rely on s. 9 of the Factors Act instead of s. 23 of the Sale of Goods Act.[170]

Possession of the goods

It is clear that the section only applies where the first buyer has actually obtained possession of the goods[171] or documents of title to the goods, and it is not enough that he has merely bought or agreed to buy them. So long as the seller retains possession he cannot be affected by a resale by the first buyer unless he has assented to it in terms of s. 47(1) which we have already examined,[172] or unless he is affected by an estoppel. On the other hand, if the seller, at the request of the first buyer, himself delivers the goods direct to a sub-buyer, this is enough to bring the second buyer within the protection of the section. There is a constructive delivery to the first buyer, and a constructive delivery by him to the second buyer, and that is sufficient for the section to operate.[173]

It is, however, uncertain if the section will apply whatever the nature of the buyer's possession. For instance, would the section apply if a person agrees to sell a car, but insists on a cash price, and then allows the buyer to take the car to a garage for an emergency repair?[174] Despite some doubts expressed in Australia,[175] it is thought that the section would apply. In *Marten v Whale*,[176] it was applied even though the goods were temporarily loaned to the buyer, and the analogy of the *Pacific Motor Auction*[177] case appears virtually conclusive.

In *Forsythe International (UK) v Silver Shipping Co and Petroglobe International (The Saetta)*[178] the plaintiff had supplied bunkers to the charterer of a vessel under a retention of title clause. The charterer did not pay for the bunkers. The owner subsequently withdrew the vessel from service for non-payment of hire, and used the

---

168 *Du Jardin v Beadman* [1952] 2 QB 712; *National Employers' Insurance Ltd v Jones* [1990] AC 24 – see p. 388, above.
169 [1965] 1 QB 525 – see p. 394, above.
170 But there is one important respect in which s. 9 may be narrower than s. 23 – below, p. 408.
171 Rutherford and Todd (1979) 38 CLJ 346 argue, on the basis of the legislative history of the Acts, that s. 25(1) and s. 9 of the Factors Act were not intended to apply to a buyer in possession of goods (as opposed to documents of title). But the argument is of historical interest only because the wording of the sections and the uniform current of case law extending for almost a century preclude this narrow interpretation today.
172 See p. 373, above.
173 *Four Point Garage Ltd v Carter* [1985] 3 All ER 12.
174 See *Langmead v Thyer Rubber Co Ltd* (1947) SR (SA) 29, 34.
175 Ibid.
176 [1917] 2 KB 480.
177 [1965] AC 867 – see above, p. 395.
178 [1993] 2 Lloyd's Rep 268.

bunkers. The plaintiff sued in conversion, and it was held that there would be conversion unless there was a delivery to the owner justified by s. 25(1) of the Sale of
Goods Act. It was held that 'possession' had the same meaning in the Factors Act
1889 and in s. 25(1), and was not limited to physical possession. However, the owner
succeeded, because it was held that the transfer of the bunkers was not achieved by a
voluntary act on the part of the charterer, but by termination by the owner.[179]

Documents of title

Where the buyer has obtained the documents of title to the goods with the consent of
the seller, the position is a little more complicated as a result of the seller's right of lien
and of stoppage in transit, if he is still unpaid. Section 47 of the Sale of Goods Act
reproduces in almost identical terms s. 10 of the Factors Act 1889, although the latter
is not repealed. Section 47(2) is as follows:

> Where a document of title to goods has been lawfully transferred to any person as buyer or
> owner of the goods, and that person transfers the document to a person who takes it in good
> faith and for valuable consideration, then—
> (a) if the last-mentioned transfer was by way of sale the unpaid seller's right of lien . . . or
>   stoppage in transit is defeated, and
> (b) if the last-mentioned transfer was made by way of pledge or other disposition for value,
>   the unpaid seller's right of lien . . . or stoppage in transit can only be exercised subject
>   to the rights of the transferee.

It is sometimes suggested[180] that this section is more favourable to the third
party than s. 9 of the Factors Act because it says nothing about the requirement
that he must not have notice of the rights of the original seller, but it may be
doubted whether this really adds anything to the requirement of good faith.

It must be added that s. 19(3) of the Sale of Goods Act[181] is subject to these sections. In *Cahn v Pockett's Bristol Channel Steam Packet Co Ltd*,[182] the sellers
shipped copper on the defendants' ship and sent bills of lading, together with a
draft, to the buyers. The buyers, being insolvent, did not accept the draft, but they
transferred the bills of lading to the plaintiffs in pursuance of a contract previously
made. The sellers, learning of the buyers' bankruptcy, stopped the goods in transit.
The Court of Appeal held that, although the buyers had acted wrongfully in transferring the bills of lading when they did not accept the draft, this breach of s. 19(3)
did not deprive the plaintiffs of the protection afforded by s. 47 of the Sale of Goods
Act.[183]

Although s. 47 only talks of a transfer of a document of title, it has been held that
it applies also where the documents are issued by the seller to the buyer and transferred by the latter to a third party taking in good faith and for value.[184] On the other

---

179 See p. 405.
180 For example, Schmitthoff, *Sale of Goods*, 2nd edn, p. 168.
181 See above, p. 340.
182 [1899] 1 QB 643.
183 And s. 25(1) and ss. 9 and 10 of the Factors Act, an extraordinary duplication of statutory provisions.
184 *Ant Jurgens & Margarinefabrieken v Louis Dreyfus & Co Ltd* [1914] 3 KB 40.

hand, s. 47(2) apparently applies only where it is the same document which is transferred (or issued) to the buyer, and by the buyer to the third party.[185] In contrast, s. 9 applies even where there are two separate documents.[186]

Delivery or transfer of the goods[187]

The first buyer, having acquired possession of the goods (or of the documents of title) must make a delivery or transfer of them (or of the documents) before the section can apply. In *Forsythe International (UK) v Silver Shipping Co and Petrograde International (The Saetta)*[188] it was held that 'delivery or transfer' required some voluntary act, though actual physical delivery was not required, so that where the owner of a vessel terminated for non-payment of hire, there was no 'delivery or transfer' within the meaning of s. 25(1) of the Sale of Goods Act. The same would equally apply in relation to s. 8 of the Factors Act 1889.

As we saw in considering the parallel provisions of s. 8 of the Factors Act, there is some uncertainty as to the possibility of recognizing a 'constructive delivery' for the purposes of this section.[189] It has at least been held that if the seller, at the request of the first buyer, delivers the goods direct to the second buyer, this is a sufficient constructive delivery to the first buyer, and by him to the second buyer.[190] But it is less clear whether, if the goods are delivered to, and remain in the possession of, the first buyer, a contract for the sale of the goods to the second buyer can itself be treated as enough to amount to a constructive delivery. The cases in this connection were discussed earlier, when considering s. 8.[191]

There are a number of cases in which it has been assumed, without argument, that a sub-buyer can obtain title under s. 9 even in part of an undivided bulk.[192] But it has been pointed out that this may be inconsistent with s. 16 of the Act which (as seen above)[193] does not permit a transfer of property in an undivided bulk of goods except in the circumstances set out in s. 20A inserted by the 1995 Act.[194] The argument rests on the assumption that a sub-buyer of an undivided part of a bulk cannot sue the seller in conversion because he has no property, and if he cannot sue in conversion, he cannot acquire a title under s. 9. No doubt there may be cases where difficulties arise, but so long as the dispute lies solely between a seller and a sub-buyer (which is the usual case dealt with by s. 9) there seems nothing in policy against (and everything in favour of) recognizing a distinction between 'property' in the s. 16 sense, and a right of possession necessary to maintain an action of conversion. If the

---

185 *D F Mount Ltd* v *Jay & Jay Co Ltd* [1960] 1 QB 159, 168.
186 Ibid.
187 See also discussion of the equivalent provision in s. 24 at p. 396.
188 [1993] 2 Lloyd's Rep 268 – see p. 403 above.
189 See above, p. 394 *et seq.*
190 *Four Point Garage Ltd* v *Carter* [1985] 3 All ER 12.
191 See above, p. 397.
192 *D F Mount Ltd* v *Jay & Jay Co Ltd* [1960] 1 QB 159; *Ant Jurgens Margarinefabrieken* v *Louis Dreyfus & Co Ltd* [1914] 3 KB 40; *Capital & Counties Bank* v *Warriner* (1896) 1 Com Cas 314.
193 Above, p. 343.
194 See Nicol (1970) 42 MLR 129; Law Commission No. 215, para. 2.8. The sub-buyer may, of course, prevail if the original seller, not having been paid, attempts to exercise the *possessory* rights of an unpaid seller – ibid.

sub-buyer has an immediate right to possession in the sense that he may demand separation of his share of the goods from the remainder of the bulk, it would be pure pedantry to deny him the right to claim a title under s. 9, merely because as between himself and the intermediate seller there has not been a separation of the part sold from the rest sufficient to pass property. But it must be admitted that more difficulty may arise where insolvency is in issue, or where there is also a dispute between the sub-buyer and intermediate seller.

Sale, pledge or other disposition

One difference between the wording of s. 9 and s. 25(1) of the Sale of Goods Act is the presence which we noted at the outset of the words 'or under any agreement for sale, pledge or other disposition' in s. 9. If the buyer were to sell the goods on under a retention of title clause,[195] the sub-buyer could not acquire title under s. 25(1) until title had passed to him.[196] But s. 9 of the Factors Act applies where the goods are obtained under any '*agreement* [emphasis supplied] for sale, pledge or other disposition'. It had been suggested that a sub-purchaser might be able to rely on this provision when in possession under a reservation of title clause.[197] In *Re Highway Foods International Ltd*[198] it was held that in such a situation the original seller could claim title to the goods, however.[199] The effect of s. 9 is that in favour of a bona fide purchaser an agreement for sale has the same effect as if the person making the transfer were a mercantile agent in possession with the consent of the owner.[200] But s. 2(1) of the Factors Act, which deals with the powers of a mercantile agent in possession, only provides that any *sale* etc. by a mercantile agent in possession with the consent of the owner shall be as valid as if the mercantile agent were authorized by the owner.

What amounts to a sale, pledge or other disposition has been considered in connection with s. 24 of the Act.[201] In the present context it may also be relevant to draw attention to some cases dealing with a delivery of goods by a seller to a building site, where the buyer, a contractor, has contracted to install or incorporate them into a building. The contract between the contractor and the building owner may in this situation not be a strict contract of sale, because of the contractor's obligations to install or affix the materials; but it seems that this is at least another 'disposition' within the meaning of the section.[202] This situation must be distinguished from that in which the *first* contract relied upon is not a sale of goods, because in that case the section does not apply at all.[203]

---

195 As to which see p. 470.
196 *Hanson (W) (Harrow) Ltd v Rapid Civil Engineering Ltd* (1987) 38 Build LR 106.
197 *Benjamin on Sale*, 4th edn, §5-128.
198 [1995] BCC 271.
199 The judge declined to follow the suggestion in *Benjamin on Sale*, 4th edn, §5-128, that the sub-purchaser in such a case might be able to rely on the words of s. 9. See now *Benjamin on Sale*, 6th edn, §5–156. See also p. 472.
200 See p. 385 *et seq.*
201 Above, p. 398.
202 *Archivent Sales & Developments Ltd v Strathclyde Regional Council* (1984) 27 Build LR 98, 1985 SLT 154.
203 *Dawber Williamson Roofing Ltd v Humberside CC* (1979) 14 Build LR 70.

Good faith and notice

The third party must take the goods 'in good faith and without notice of any lien or other right of the original seller in respect of the goods'. Clearly, if the seller retains the property in the goods after delivery and the buyer has no right to dispose of the goods pending payment of the price or fulfilment of some other condition, any sub-buyer who takes the goods with notice of the circumstances will not be protected by the section. Notice, as usual in commercial law, means actual and not constructive notice.[204]

So far the effect of the section is clear enough. It is much less easy to understand the effect of the section with regard to two other questions, namely the effect of a sub-sale on the seller's lien, and the possible application of the section where the property in the goods has passed to the buyer. Where the buyer is in possession of the goods with the consent of the seller, it is difficult to see how the seller can have any lien or other right in respect of the goods. Under s. 43(1), the unpaid seller loses his lien:

(b) when the buyer or his agent lawfully obtains possession of the goods.

If the buyer has obtained possession with the consent of the seller, it seems to follow of necessity that he has lawfully obtained possession and it is submitted that this is still the case if the buyer has obtained possession by a criminal offence. This question was discussed in the New Zealand Court of Appeal in *Jeffcott v Andrews Motors Ltd*[205] where, however, the court bypassed the issue. It was there held unnecessary to decide whether the seller's lien could survive where the buyer obtained possession of the goods by criminal fraud, on the ground that in any event the third party was protected by the terms of s. 9. If the lien survives in such circumstances the survival must be purely academic and, it seems, quite meaningless as it gives the seller no right to obtain the possession of the goods from the third party. It is therefore submitted that in whatever capacity the buyer obtains control of the goods, provided it is with the consent of the owner, s. 9 applies and the buyer can pass a good title to an innocent third party free from the seller's claims.

However, if the buyer merely obtains possession of the documents of title to the goods and not of the goods themselves, it may be that in some circumstances the seller could still have a lien on the goods themselves, and effect could then be given to the section by holding that a purchaser with notice of the lien would take subject to the lien, whether or not the property had passed to the original buyer. This is an unlikely eventuality, however, for possession of the documents of title normally carries with it possession of the goods themselves – this is certainly the case with bills of lading – and it could only be in the most extraordinary circumstances that the seller could transfer the documents to the buyer while retaining a lien on the goods themselves.

Apart from the possibility of the seller retaining his lien, the section also requires that the third party should take without notice of any 'other right of the original

---

204 Above, pp. 398–9.
205 [1960] NZLR 721.

seller in respect of the goods'. But where the buyer has already bought the goods so that the property has passed to him, it is again not easy to see of what 'other right of the original seller' the third party can have notice. The mere fact that the price has not been paid to the knowledge of the third party surely cannot bring this clause into operation, because it is a common business occurrence for a seller to be paid for goods before he himself has paid for them, and knowledge of these circumstances can scarcely be held to put the buyers upon inquiry.[206] In any event, this would not seem to be a right 'in respect of the goods' but a personal right in respect of the contract of sale. Moreover, if the property has passed to the buyer it is hard to see how there can be any question of bad faith on the part of the sub-buyer. Even if he is aware that the buyer has not paid the seller and cannot do so because he has become insolvent, it is clear that the original seller cannot impugn the sub-buyer's title on the ground of bad faith, otherwise a person could never safely buy goods which he knew had not been paid for. It is, therefore, submitted that the requirement that the third party must receive the goods 'in good faith and without notice of any lien or other right of the original seller in respect of the goods' can generally only be applicable where the property has not passed to the buyer, and even then it is difficult to see how any question of lien can arise.[207]

Effect of s. 9

There is one curious but important difference in the wording of ss. 8 and 9. The former says that a sale by a seller in possession shall, subject to the conditions laid down, 'have the same effect as if the person making the delivery or transfer were expressly authorized by the owner of the goods to make the same'. On the other hand, s. 9 says that a sale by a buyer in possession shall, subject to the conditions already discussed, have the same effect 'as if the person making the delivery or transfer were a mercantile agent in possession of the goods or documents of title with the consent of the owner'. What exactly is the significance of these last words? If read literally they would appear to create a serious difficulty because, it may be recalled, an unauthorized sale by a mercantile agent in possession of goods with the consent of the owner is only made effective to pass a title by s. 2(1) of the Factors Act 1889 if the mercantile agent is *acting in the ordinary course of business*. If a person is not a mercantile agent, how can he be said to act in the ordinary course of business of a mercantile agent? As Pearson LJ said in *Newtons of Wembley Ltd v Williams*,[208] 'It seems on the face of it to be an impossible position.' Nevertheless, the Court of Appeal thought that the buyer must somehow be treated as a notional mercantile agent, and the court has to ask whether the sale would have been in the ordinary course of business had he been a mercantile agent. In this case, the court decided that the sale would have been in the ordinary course, so it may be that the court's

---

206 See *Forsythe International (UK) v Silver Shipping Co and Petroglobe International (The Saetta)* [1993] 2 Lloyd's Rep 268, the facts of which are given at p. 405 above.

207 On the whole of this difficult question, see a review of the second edition of this book by the late Professor J. C. Smith in the *Journal of the SPTL*, Vol. VII, p. 226, to which, in previous editions, Professor Atiyah acknowledged his indebtedness.

208 [1965] 1 QB 560, 578.

view on the main issue could be regarded as *obiter*. But this cannot be said of the earlier and unreported case of *Lambert v G & C Finance Corporation Ltd.*[209] In this case, the plaintiff sold his car to X, who offered him a cheque for the price. The plaintiff reluctantly accepted the cheque but insisted on keeping the log book until the cheque was met. In fact, the cheque was worthless and X sold the car to a dealer, who disposed of it to the defendants. The learned judge held that the retention of the log book showed an intention that the property was not to pass until the cheque was met and that the defendants did not obtain a title under s. 9 of the Factors Act. Since X had sold the car without the log book, the learned judge had no difficulty in holding that the sale was not in the ordinary course of business, or rather would not have been in the ordinary course of X's business had he been a mercantile agent.[210]

In the *Lambert* and the *Newtons of Wembley* cases, it may well be that substantial justice was done. But if the dicta in the latter case are followed this may not always be possible. For example, a sale by a mercantile agent outside business premises would not generally be in the ordinary course of business.[211] But if a private individual who is not a mercantile agent were, for example, to sell a second-hand car, the sale would almost certainly take place outside business premises, and a strict application of the *Newtons of Wembley* case would take the case outside s. 9. In the circumstances, it is unfortunate that the court was not referred to dicta in Australia[212] and New Zealand,[213] which take a contrary view. On this view, the effect of a sale by a buyer in possession is the same 'as if' the buyer were a mercantile agent and the sale was in the ordinary course of his business. 'The section operates to validate a sale as if the buyer in possession were a mercantile agent; it does not require that he should act as though he were a mercantile agent.'[214] There is no doubt that this was thought to be the law in *Lee v Butler*[215] and was assumed to be the law ever since that case until the *Newtons of Wembley* case. In 1966 the Law Reform Committee recommended that the law be amended to restore the position to what it was formerly thought to be,[216] but nothing has been done to implement this recommendation.

On the other hand, in a case in Northern Ireland[217] the dicta in the *Newtons of Wembley* case were followed by Lord Lowry CJ, who insisted that it would be absurd if a buyer from an ordinary seller was in a better position than a buyer from a mercantile agent, because this would make s. 9 of the Factors Act a greater invasion of title than s. 2.

> The key to the meaning of s. 9's 'shorthand' [said Lord Lowry] must be that innocent purchasers can be protected not only (as they were originally meant to be) when dealing with mercantile agents acting in the ordinary course of a mercantile agent's business, but also

---

209 See (1963) Sol Jo 666.
210 This issue causes some difficulties with the Scottish cases of *Thomas Graham & Sons Ltd v Glenrothes Development Corp* 1967 SC 284 and *Archivent Sales & Development Ltd v Strathclyde Regional Council* 1985 SLT 154; on which see Reid, *The Law of Property in Scotland* (1996), para. 682(5).
211 *Oppenheimer v Attenborough & Sons* [1908] 1 KB 221, above, pp. 390–1.
212 *Langmead v Thyer Rubber Co Ltd* (1947) SR (SA) 29, 39. And see now also the dicta of the High Court in the *Gamer* case, (1987) 163 CLR 236, 243 and 252–3, though the point was ultimately left open.
213 *Jeffcott v Andrew Motors Ltd* [1960] NZLR 721, 729 per Gresson P.
214 Ibid.
215 [1893] 2 QB 318.
216 Twelfth Report, Cmnd. 2958, para. 23 (1966).
217 *Martin v Duffy* [1985] 11 NIJB 80.

with ordinary persons acting in the way in which a mercantile agent would be expected to act in the ordinary course of business.[218]

Although Lord Lowry may be correct in suggesting that this was the original intention behind s. 9, the contrary view was acted on for so long (beginning, indeed, with *Lee* v *Butler* in 1893) that it seems very late in the day to return now to that view. Moreover, as a matter of policy, one may disagree with his suggestion that it would be absurd to protect the bona fide purchaser where the intermediate buyer has not acted as though he were a mercantile agent. A seller who actually delivers the goods to a buyer before being paid chooses to trust to that buyer's credit, and there seems every reason why he should take the risk if that buyer wrongfully resells the goods to an innocent purchaser in good faith.

Effect of s. 9 where seller is not the owner

One difficult point remains to be mentioned. What is the effect of s. 9 where the seller was not himself the owner of the goods and had no authority to sell from the owner? For instance, if a thief steals a car and sells it to a car dealer who resells it, does s. 9 apply to the resale? A literal reading of the section might suggest that it would protect the second buyer in this situation, on the ground that the first buyer is a person who has bought or agreed to buy the goods, and that the sale by him to the second buyer is then to have the same effect as if it had been made by a mercantile agent in possession of the goods with the consent of the owner. But this literal reading of the section was rejected by the House of Lords in *National Employers Mutual General Insurance Association Ltd* v *Jones*.[219] The words 'with the consent of the owner' at the end of the section were here interpreted to mean, 'with the consent of the owner who has entrusted him with, or consented to his having the possession of, the goods or of the documents of title to the goods'.[220] The whole point of these provisions is that they are designed to protect someone who buys from a person who has been entrusted with the goods or documents of title. No rational policy could defend protecting a second buyer after a theft, but not a first buyer.[221]

PART III OF THE HIRE-PURCHASE ACT 1964

Part III of the Hire-Purchase Act 1964 (as re-enacted by the Consumer Credit Act 1974) provides, in essence, that a bona fide purchaser for value of a motor vehicle from a person in possession under a hire-purchase agreement or a conditional sale agreement[222] obtains a good title. The simplicity of result contrasts starkly with the

---

218 At p. 84.
219 [1990] 1 AC 24, upholding the view contended for in earlier editions of this work. See the 7th edn, pp. 302–3 for some Commonwealth cases no longer of importance in England.
220 For a useful note on this case see Battersby (1991) 54 MLR 752.
221 If the views of Battersby and Preston (1972) 35 MLR 268 are correct, the effect of a theft is to create a second title within which the Factors Act would apply in the normal way to defeat the rights of the 'owner' under that title, but not of course the rights of the true owner.
222 It must therefore be the debtor named in the agreement. So title could not be gained under s. 27 from a rogue masquerading as a real person who was named as the debtor in a hire-purchase agreement – *Shogun Finance Ltd* v *Hudson* [2003] UKHL 62.

complexity of the statutory language, which occupies four full pages in the Queen's printer's copy of the Act. Section 27(1) and (2) of the 1964 Act are as follows:

(1) This section applies where a motor vehicle has been bailed or (in Scotland) hired under a hire-purchase agreement, or has been agreed to be sold under a conditional sale agreement, and before the property in the vehicle has become vested in the debtor, he disposes of the vehicle to another person.

(2) Where the disposition referred to in subsection (1) is to a private purchaser, and he is a purchaser of the motor vehicle in good faith without notice of the hire-purchase agreement or conditional sale agreement (the 'relevant agreement'), that disposition shall have effect as if the creditor's title to the vehicle had been vested in the debtor immediately before that disposition.

Thus, the power of a person in possession under a conditional sale agreement to pass a title which was taken away by the sections already discussed was, so far as concerns motor vehicles, in effect restored by this section. There is, however, one important limitation on this power to pass title and that is that a 'trade or finance purchaser' is not protected. The 'private purchaser' referred to in s. 27(2) is any purchaser other than a trade or finance purchaser, and this term is defined by s. 29(2) to mean a person who carries on a business which consists wholly or partly:

(a) of purchasing motor vehicles for the purpose of offering or exposing them for sale, or
(b) of providing finance by purchasing motor vehicles for the purpose of bailing or (in Scotland) hiring them under hire-purchase agreements or agreeing to sell them under conditional sale agreements.

It will be seen that these provisions do not deprive all business concerns of protection under Part III. A large company which buys an expensive lorry may obtain title under Part III. It is only the car dealer and the finance company who are outside the protection of these sections. It has been held that what matters under these provisions is the status of the buyer and not the capacity in which he buys. Thus a person who deals in motor vehicles is a trade purchaser and outside the protection of the sections, even though he buys a vehicle for his own private use.[223]

If a trade or finance purchaser, having acquired a vehicle from a hirer in possession under a hire-purchase agreement, proceeds to dispose of it to a third party, the third party will be protected by s. 27(3). The section also deals with the possibility that a vehicle which has been disposed of by a hirer to a finance company is then relet under a new hire-purchase agreement to a new hirer. In this event, the new agreement is itself a disposition by virtue of the definition in s. 29(1) and the new hirer is protected. Moreover, his protection is not displaced by the fact that, before he exercises his option to purchase, the true facts may have come to light. Section 27(4) provides, in effect, that in such circumstances the time for determining whether the new hirer is in good faith or not is when he enters into the hire-purchase agreement and not when he exercises his option to purchase. It may be noted that the trade or finance purchaser will not itself be better off as a result of the subsequent disposition because it will remain liable in conversion to the original owner

---

223 *Stevenson v Beverley Bentinck Ltd* [1976] 2 All ER 606.

under s. 27(6). In Scotland, the trade or finance purchaser is liable to the deprived owner insofar as the former is enriched by the transaction. Arguments that he might also be liable under the doctrine of *specificatio* have been authoritatively rejected.[224]

A trade or finance purchaser, though unprotected by *these* sections,[225] can apply to either Equifax or Experian for information.[226] But, as we have seen,[227] there was no redress where the owner of a vehicle let under a hire-purchase agreement had failed to notify the predecessor of the first of these bodies, Hire Purchase Information, of the agreement. The position would appear to be the same in relation to Equifax or Experian. Accordingly, a purchaser will buy in good faith if he or she has been told there is no agreement registered with either of them.

The first requirement of these provisions, then, is that the vehicle must have been let under a hire-purchase agreement or been agreed to be sold under a conditional sale agreement. The Act does not, therefore, apply where the vehicle has been let under a simple hiring agreement. Nor does the Act have any bearing on the situation which arose in *Central Newbury Car Auctions Ltd* v *Unity Finance Ltd*,[228] where a dealer allowed a swindler to have possession of a vehicle on his signing hire-purchase proposal forms which were later rejected by the finance company. It seems anomalous that the dealer is not at risk in this sort of case for he clearly takes a much greater chance than a dealer who actually enters into a hire-purchase agreement himself. If the finance company accepts the hirer's proposals in this sort of case, then presumably his power to pass title becomes effective as from the moment when the contract is completed, that is, in most cases, when the acceptance is posted to him.

It is important to note that the Act does not require the hirer to be in possession *under* the hire-purchase agreement.[229] It merely requires that the vehicle 'has been bailed under a hire-purchase agreement' and that the hirer should have disposed of it before the property has passed to him.[230] And the definition of 'debtor' in s. 29(4) makes it clear that even if the agreement has already been determined, the former hirer is still the debtor for the purposes of s. 27. So also is a hirer who is in possession under a time order made under s. 130(4) of the Consumer Credit Act.[231]

The next requirement of these provisions is that there must have been a 'disposition' by the hirer or buyer. This is defined by s. 29(1), from which it appears that a disposition includes a sale, a contract of sale and a letting under a hire-purchase agreement. These provisions are narrower than those of the Factors Act and the Sale of Goods Act in that the definition of 'disposition' is exhaustive, whereas under the other Acts any disposition is protected. This is, however, largely an academic point for ordinary vehicles are unlikely to be pledged, and the only other type of disposition

---

224 *North West Securities Ltd* v *Barrhead Coachworks Ltd* 1976 SC 68, overruling *FC Finance Ltd* v *Langtry Investment Co Ltd* 1973 SLT (Sh Ct) 11.
225 Though in appropriate cases other exceptions to the *nemo dat* rules may apply.
226 See p. 382.
227 See above, p. 382.
228 [1957] 1 QB 371 – see above, p. 382.
229 Though, as noted above, he or she must be the person named in the agreement – see nn. 43–4 above.
230 *Carlyle Finance Ltd* v *Pallas Industrial Finance and anor* [1999] RTR 281.
231 A 'time order' is an order made by a court which gives the hirer or debtor extra time to pay the instalments.

which is likely to be encountered, namely the creation of a lien, would almost inevitably be in favour of a trade or finance purchaser who would not be protected anyhow.[232]

Finally, the purchaser must buy in good faith and without notice of the hire-purchase or conditional sale agreement. For this purpose, it is immaterial that the buyer may know that the vehicle was the subject of a hire-purchase agreement if he believes that the finance company has been paid off.[233]

Section 28 of the 1964 Act contains a number of elaborate presumptions to meet the not uncommon situation where a person in possession of a vehicle which was once the subject of an unfulfilled hire-purchase agreement does not know precisely what has happened to the vehicle before he acquired it.[234] The net effect of these presumptions appears to be as follows. The onus of proof that the defendant (or an earlier purchaser) was himself a purchaser in good faith and without notice lies on the defendant. But once this has been proved, there appear to be only two ways in which the finance company will be able to establish its title against the defendant. One will be to show that the first private purchaser to acquire the vehicle was not a purchaser in good faith. If this can be established, then no subsequent purchaser can acquire a title under s. 27 even if he is himself in good faith. Secondly, the finance company may be able to establish that the vehicle was not in fact disposed of by the hirer at all, but was, for example, stolen from him, or was disposed of by someone who had obtained temporary control of the car with the hirer's consent.

WRITS OF EXECUTION

Section 26 of the 1893 Act dealt with writs of execution; it was concerned with the ability of a debtor to pass title to goods after a writ of execution has been issued with respect to those goods. It was thus dealing with matters in some respects similar to those involved in the exceptions to the *nemo dat* maxim. But the section was not included in the 1979 consolidated version of the Sale of Goods Act, and it was subsequently repealed and replaced by s. 138 of the Supreme Court Act 1981. This seems to mark the recognition that the section is more appropriately dealt with in works on the enforcement of judgments, and it will therefore no longer be dealt with here.

PROPOSALS FOR REFORM

There can be no doubt, after the above discussion, that the law relating to the transfer of title to goods is in a complex and confused state. It has been complained that 'statutory protection for the bona fide purchaser has developed in a piecemeal and haphazard fashion; and some of the relevant provisions have been so drafted and

---

232 Similarly, the unusual transaction held to be a disposition in *Worcester Works Finance Ltd* v *Cooden Engineering Co Ltd* [1972] 1 QB 210 (see above, p. 398) is unlikely to occur except in favour of a trade or finance purchaser.

233 *Barker* v *Bell* [1971] 1 WLR 983.

234 The presumptions do not operate where it is known what transactions have actually taken place: *Soneco Ltd* v *Barcross Finance Ltd* [1978] RTR 444.

interpreted as to make their application depend not on principles of equity or justice but on fine technicalities which have little rhyme and less reason'.[235] In his judgment in *Ingram* v *Little*[236] Devlin LJ, as he then was, suggested that it might be possible to apportion the loss which occurs when an innocent owner and an equally innocent bona fide purchaser are left to dispute over the title to goods after some dishonest middle party has quit the scene. The result of this suggestion was that the whole topic was referred to the Law Reform Committee.[237] The Committee in fact rejected Lord Devlin's suggestion as impractical, largely because of the complications which would ensue where the goods pass through several hands. For example, a thief steals a car belonging to O and sells it to A, who sells to B, who resells to C, and so on. In such circumstances, there would be great difficulty in any system of law which allowed apportionment of the loss: should apportionment be only as between O and A? Or between all the parties? And how should the loss be apportioned?

The Committee did, however, go on to make a number of other recommendations for reform of the law. They rejected the notion of fundamental alteration in the law such as would prima facie protect any bona fide purchaser for value, but went on to propose the following detailed changes.

1 The Committee recommended[238] the abolition of the distinction between contracts void for mistake and contracts voidable for fraud. Hence, in cases like *Cundy* v *Lindsay*[239] and *Ingram* v *Little*,[240] it would become immaterial whether the contract is void or voidable. In either event, the third party should be protected.[241]

2 The Committee recommended[242] reversal of the decision in *Caldwell's*[243] case: rescission of a voidable contract should require communication.

3 The third recommendation[244] is that the dicta in the *Newtons of Wembley*[245] case should be reversed and s. 9 of the Factors Act amended to make it clear that it enables the buyer in possession to pass a good title without requiring him to act as a mercantile agent.

4 The Committee rejected the suggestion that any bailee should be able to pass a good title.[246]

5 The Committee strongly criticized the market overt rule as 'capricious', and recommended that the rule should be replaced by a wider protective provision applicable to a sale at any retail premises. As we have seen, however, this is not the path which Parliament saw fit to follow, as the effect of the Sale of Goods (Amendment) Act 1994 is that bona fide purchasers do not acquire a good title.

---

235 See the *Report of the Crowther Committee on Consumer Credit*, Cmnd. 4596, para. 4.2.8 (1971).
236 [1961] 1 QB 31. See discussion of this case in *Shogun Finance* v *Hudson*, pp. 43–4 above.
237 Twelfth Report, Cmnd. 2958 (1966).
238 Paragraph 15.
239 (1878) 3 App Cas 459.
240 [1961] 1 QB 31.
241 This result is achieved by Art. 2-403 of the UCC.
242 Paragraph 16.
243 [1965] 1 QB 525.
244 Paragraph 23.
245 [1965] 1 QB 560.
246 Paragraph 29.

Within the context of the existing law, the first three of these recommendations appear to be sensible and would have been unlikely to rouse much opposition, although some scepticism may be felt about whether the first recommendation would actually have achieved very much in practice. The fourth recommendation was more controversial, but the fifth appears to have been the real stumbling block to the implementation of the Report. This recommendation raised fears that it would facilitate the disposal of stolen goods by underworld channels. Generally, the Report was a disappointing document largely because of its complete failure to search for any empirical evidence as to the way in which the law operated.[247] The continuing lack of this evidence makes it very difficult to justify positive proposals for change of a fundamental character. The most important question to which insufficient attention has usually been paid is the likelihood of the original owner of lost or stolen goods being protected by insurance.[248] Where this is the normal situation, there seems good reason for giving greater protection under the law to bona fide purchasers than is done at present. A less drastic approach would, as a minimum, amalgamate some of the existing statutory provisions by reducing them to a common principle. Thus ss. 2, 8 and 9 of the Factors Act could well be replaced by a principle (along the lines of Art. 2-403 of the UCC) enabling any dealer to pass a title to goods which have been entrusted to his possession. At all events, as noted above, future developments in this area may well be at the behest of Brussels.

In 1976 the Scottish Law Commission produced some tentative proposals for consideration.[249] It suggested that the law should provide protection for *bona fide* onerous acquirers of another's property, provided that the acquirer had taken possession in good faith and provided that the goods were not infected by a real vice resulting from involuntary dispossession of the owner (e.g. theft). The purchaser should have the onus of proving his own good faith, or facts from which it could be inferred, while the owner should be obliged to prove real vice. The basic principle would be to protect the good faith purchaser where the owner's voluntary parting with possession had facilitated wrongful disposal. But these proposals did not even reach the status of a Law Commission Report, and there has been no legislation in Scotland.

A different, and in some ways far more radical, approach was advocated by the Crowther Committee on Consumer Credit.[250] This Committee proposed that legislation, along the lines of Art. 9 of the American UCC, should be enacted to cover all situations in which a security interest is reserved over goods, as a form of mortgage or charge, irrespective of its legal nature. Thus, this legislation would replace (*inter alia*) the Bills of Sale Act 1882, s. 25 of the Sale of Goods Act and s. 9 of the Factors Act, and would also cover the post-Crowther development of the *Romalpa* reservation of title clauses. The basic idea behind such legislation is that the law should not differentiate between different types of transaction which have the same fundamental commercial purpose, merely because a different legal form has been adopted. To a considerable extent, this policy has already been adopted in the Consumer Credit

---

247 See Professor Atiyah's criticisms of the Report in (1966) 29 MLR 541.
248 See Battersby, n. 220 above.
249 Memorandum No. 27, *Corporeal Moveables* (1976).
250 See the Report of the Crowther Committee, Cmnd. 4596, paras 5.5.1–5.7.83 (1971); and see also R. M. Goode (1984) 100 LQR 234.

Act, which was the first product of the Crowther Committee recommendations. But the second major legislative development envisaged by the Committee – a new Lending and Security Act – remains to be enacted, and there is little sign at present of any action being taken on the most recent proposals.[251] The legislation which the Committee, and the later DTI Green Paper,[252] envisaged would cover all agreements by which one person attempts to obtain an interest over goods by way of security, irrespective of the form of the agreement. This would thus cover hire-purchase agreements, sales under which title is reserved by the seller as a security, bills of sale (which are not designed as outright sales) and other arrangements of a similar character.

Such a law would, to some degree, regulate the rights of borrower and lender *inter se*, by providing, for instance, when and how the security rights of the lender could be exercised, and what kind of limits might be imposed on the freedom of the parties to make their own contract; but more importantly, it would regulate the rights of the holder of the security as against third parties, in particular as against creditors of the borrower. It would also provide for some kind of registration system for certain sorts of security. Legislation along these lines would not replace all the provisions of the Sale of Goods Act dealing with the transfer of title – for instance, s. 24 of the Act (sales by seller in possession) and s. 23 (sale under voidable title) would not necessarily be encompassed within such legislation, nor would s. 2 of the Factors Act. But many other provisions dealt with above would fall within the scope of such a new law. The recent huge growth of reservation of title clauses in commercial sales is rendering reform a matter of some urgency.[253] Again, it is possible that further developments in this area will be initiated from Brussels.[254]

---

251 See the DTI's Green Paper 'A Review of Security Interests in Property' by Professor A. L. Diamond, 1989 – see also below, p. 470. For Scotland see above, p. 17 n. 57.
252 See n. 251 above.
253 See p. 470 *et seq* below for further discussion of this topic.
254 See ETAN Working Paper 'Strategic Dimensions of Intellectual Property Rights in the Context of Science and Technology Policy', 1999, para. 6.3.

Part V

EXPORT SALES

22

EXPORT SALES

The sale of goods which are to be shipped to their destination gives rise to a host of difficult questions, adequate discussion of which would require a whole volume.[1] This is not a task which it is proposed to undertake here, but because the Sale of Goods Act contains provisions relevant to these transactions something must be said of the principal types of export contract, of the problems raised by export and import licences, and of the method of payment by bankers' commercial credits. In the first place, four types of contract will be considered, the central two kinds being contracts whose essential terms have become standardized by commercial practice, although there is considerable variation in matters of detail. These four are ex-works contracts, f.o.b. contracts, c.i.f. contracts and ex-ship contracts.[2] Many export and import transactions are made subject to INCOTERMS.[3] Where the parties have adopted these, the duties of the parties under a contract on these terms are clearly spelled out. The rules of the common law set out below apply in the absence of such specific agreement.

Care must be taken not to assume that a contract which is said to be an ex-works contract, or a c.i.f. or f.o.b. contract, necessarily carries all the incidents which may be associated with these contracts in the absence of a contrary intention. Terms of this kind are often used by businessmen in agreements which contain other terms inconsistent with any such possibility. As was said by Roskill LJ in *The Albazero*:[4]

> It is a trite observation that what is sometimes called a true f.o.b. or a true c.i.f. contract is a comparative commercial rarity. Contracts vary infinitely according to the wishes of the parties to them. Though a contract may include the letters f.o.b. or c.i.f. amongst its terms, it may well be that other terms of the contract clearly show that the use of those letters is intended to do no more than show where the incidence of liability for freight or insurance will lie as between buyer and seller, but is not to denote the mode of performance of the seller's obligations to the buyer or the buyer's obligations to the seller. In other cases, though the letters c.i.f. are used, other terms of the contract may show that the property is intended to pass on shipment and not upon tender of and payment against the documents so tendered, or though the letters f.o.b. are used, other terms may show that the property was not

---

1 See de Battista, *Sale of Goods Carried by Sea*, 1998; *Schmitthoff's Export Trade*, 10th edn; *British Shipping Laws*, Vol. 5.
2 Of importance in the present day also are the terms especially suited to container transport, but it is beyond the scope of this work to consider these. Reference should be made to the works listed in n. 1 above.
3 The current version is *INCOTERMS 2000*.
4 [1977] AC 774, 809.

intended to pass on shipment but upon tender and payment, the seller by the form in which he took the bill of lading intending to reserve his right of disposal until he was paid against the shipping documents.

It should be noted that in American practice the term f.o.b. is used as a shipment *and* as a destination term.[5] It is also used in relation to carriage by 'vessel, car or other vehicle'.[6]

EX-WORKS OR EX-STORE CONTRACTS

Ex-works or ex-store contracts present few difficulties in this connection. In fact, these can hardly be considered as export sales at all, since it is the buyer's duty to take delivery at the works or store in question, and what he does with them after that is entirely his own affair. The property and risk will, in the absence of any contrary indication, pass when the goods are delivered in most contracts of this kind, since they are almost invariably sales of unascertained goods and it is unlikely that there will be any appropriation (except perhaps where provision is made for inspection at an early date) prior to delivery.

F.O.B. CONTRACTS

In an f.o.b. contract, the seller's duty is to place the goods free on board a ship to be named by the buyer during the contractual shipment period. Prima facie at least it seems that 'The expression f.o.b. determines how the goods shall be delivered, how much of the expense shall be borne by the sellers and when the risk of loss or damage shall pass to the buyers. It does not necessarily decide when the property is to pass.'[7] The seller's obligations extend to all charges incurred before shipment, including loading charges, but not freight or insurance.

In the absence of a contrary intention, the buyer has the right and the responsibility of selecting both the port and the date of, and generally making the arrangements for, the shipment of the goods.[8] He must nominate a ship on which the goods may be loaded by the seller and give adequate notice to the seller of that nomination. The ship must be an 'effective' ship, that is capable, both physically and otherwise, of receiving the cargo.[9] If the buyer nominates a ship which cannot receive the cargo or which cannot load in time, he may, if he still has sufficient time, substitute another vessel in place of the one first nominated.[10] Where the contract provides for a range of ports from which the goods are to be shipped, it is the buyer's right and duty to select one

---

5 UCC Art. 2-319(a) and (b).

6 Ibid., subs. (c).

7 *Mitsui & Co Ltd* v *Flota Mercante Grancolumbiana SA* [1989] 1 All ER 951, 956 per Staughton LJ.

8 *Ian Stach Ltd* v *Baker Bosley Ltd* [1958] 2 QB 130.

9 But compare *Eurico SpA* v *Philipp Bros* [1987] 2 FTLR 213 (where buyer buys goods afloat, it is not his responsibility if the vessel cannot enter the port of discharge).

10 *Agricultores Federados Argentinos* v *Ampro SA* [1965] 2 Lloyd's Rep 157. It would appear, however, that there is no common law right to withdraw an effective nomination – *Coastal (Bermuda) Petroleum* v *VTT Vulcan Petroleum* [1993] 1 Lloyd's Rep 329.

out of the permitted number of ports and to give the seller sufficient notice of his selection.[11] On receiving the necessary notices from the buyer, the seller must be ready to ship the goods within a reasonable time (which must also be within the contractual time for shipment), but he does not necessarily have to have the goods available for immediate shipment.[12] Compliance with the obligation to ship at the port nominated is a condition of the contract.[13] On the other hand, if the nomination is subject to acceptance by the terminal operator, the duty of the seller to obtain this acceptance is an innominate term,[14] but failure to fulfil it timeously will be a ground for repudiation by the buyer.[15]

The type of transaction described above is sometimes known as the 'classic' f.o.b. contract.[16] A second type of f.o.b. is a variant on this: the seller arranges for the ship to come on berth, but the legal incidents are the same. In these two types of f.o.b. transaction, the buyer is not a party to the contract of carriage. A third type is where the seller puts the goods on board, takes a mate's receipt and gives this to the buyer or his agent who then takes a bill of lading. In this latter type, the buyer is a party to the contract of carriage *ab initio*.[17] The significance of the buyer being, or not being, a party to the contract of carriage is explained below.[18]

The time of delivery in an f.o.b. contract binds the buyer as much as the seller. As was said by Donaldson J in *Bunge & Co Ltd v Tradax England Ltd*,[19] 'Under an f.o.b. contract, the obligation to deliver and the obligation to accept delivery are mutual and both are confined to the shipment period.'[20] The ship nominated by the buyer must arrive in time to load the goods, having regard to holidays and normal working hours.

In the 'classic' f.o.b. contract, the contract for the carriage of the goods is made between the seller and the shipowners. In modern times, however, as noted above, there are variants. In particular, it is nowadays very common for the seller to be required to make some or all of the arrangements for shipping and insuring the goods, particularly where the seller is an exporter,[21] or where small parcels rather than whole cargoes are being shipped.[22] Where the seller is making the shipping arrangements he normally obtains a mate's receipt, which he transmits to the buyer who exchanges this for the bill of lading. Hence there may be no privity of contract between sellers and shipowners; this may cause difficulty where goods are damaged

---

11 *David T Boyd & Co Ltd v Luis Louca* [1973] 1 Lloyd's Rep 209. Compare *Miserocchi & Co SpA v Agricultores Federados Argentinos SCL* [1984] 1 Lloyd's Rep 202 – the buyer to nominate but the choice of ship to be made by the seller.

12 *Tradax Export SpA v Italgrani Di Francesco Ambrosio* [1986] 1 Lloyd's Rep 112.

13 *Petrograde Inc v Stinnes Handel GmbH*, *The Times*, 27 July 1994.

14 As to which see p. 91 *et seq*.

15 *Phibro Energy AG v Nissho Iwai Corp and Bomar Oil Inc* [1991] 1 Lloyd's Rep 38.

16 *Pyrene & Co v Scindia Navigation Co* [1954] 2 QB 402, 424 per Devlin J.

17 Ibid., approved in *The El Amria and El Mina* [1982] 2 Lloyd's Rep 28, 32.

18 See p. 422.

19 [1975] 2 Lloyd's Rep 235.

20 Ibid., at p. 239.

21 An f.o.b. sale, though contemplating the export of the goods, is not necessarily an export contract itself, but may be made between parties carrying on business in the same country. For example, a company which has contracted to sell goods to a foreign buyer may itself buy goods in order to fulfil that contract, f.o.b. an English port. In that case the first sellers will not be exporters.

22 *D H Bain v Field & Co Ltd* (1920) 3 Ll LR 26, 29.

in the course of loading by the shipowners before property and risk have passed to the buyers.[23]

Seller's duties as to contract of carriage

Because it is the seller who makes the contract for the carriage of the goods with the shipowner in the 'classic' f.o.b. contract, he must comply with s. 32(2) of the Act. This provides:

> Unless otherwise authorized by the buyer, the seller must make such contract with the carrier on behalf of the buyer as may be reasonable having regard to the nature of the goods and the other circumstances of the case and if the seller omits to do so, and the goods are lost or damaged in course of transit, the buyer may decline to treat the delivery to the carrier as a delivery to himself, or may hold the seller responsible in damages.

In other words, if this subsection applies the buyer can either reject the goods or accept them and claim damages. It may be observed that this differs from the provisions of s. 20(2), which is in certain respects parallel to this provision. Under the present subsection, it appears that the buyer's remedies for the damage to or loss of the goods operate whether or not the loss or damage was the consequence of the seller's failure to make a reasonable contract with the carrier, whereas under s. 20 if either party is at fault in taking delivery of the goods, the goods are at the risk of the party in fault, but only in respect of damage which might not have occurred but for such fault.

What is a 'reasonable' contract for the seller to make must be judged in the light of the circumstances existing when the contract of carriage is made and not at the date of the contract of sale.[24] Thus a contract to carry the goods by an unusual route may be reasonable if the more usual route is unavailable when the contract of carriage is made.[25]

A simple illustration of the workings of s. 32(2) is provided by *Thomas Young & Sons Ltd* v *Hobson & Partners*,[26] where goods were damaged in transit owing to their being insecurely fixed. Had the sellers made a reasonable contract with the carriers, that is had they sent the goods at the company's risk as was the usual practice for goods of that kind instead of at the owner's risk, the loss would not have occurred. The Court of Appeal held that the buyers were entitled to reject the goods. On the other hand, in a later decision (on a c.i.f. contract) it was held that the seller was under no obligation to make a contract for the carriage of oil of an unusual kind providing that the oil was to be heated *en route*; in fact such heating was not necessary for the kind and length of voyage contemplated, although in the event the oil suffered damage which would have been averted if it had been heated.[27]

---

23 See *Pyrene* v *Scindia Navigation* [1954] 2 QB 402, where Devlin J solved this problem in an ingenious way. The Contract (Rights of Third Parties) Act 1999 does not affect this situation because contracts for the carriage of goods by sea under a bill of lading etc. are excluded from the Act's application – s. 6(5) and (6).
24 *Tsakiroglou & Co Ltd* v *Noblee Thorl GmbH* [1962] AC 93.
25 Ibid. See also the Australian case, *Plaimar Ltd* v *Waters Trading Co Ltd* (1945) 72 CLR 304.
26 (1949) 65 TLR 365. The contract here was f.o.r. (free on rail) but the legal results are the same as with an f.o.b. contract.
27 *The Rio Sun* [1985] 1 Lloyd's Rep 350.

Where the seller is responsible for shipping the goods, it may be an important question whether he does so on his own account as a principal or merely as agent of the buyer. In particular, if the seller ships as principal, the presumption against property passing on shipment is strong, whereas if he ships as agent, it is more likely that property will be held to pass on shipment.[28] But apart from this crucial distinction, many other ancillary questions may turn on whether the seller acts as principal or agent in shipping the goods. For example, if the seller is unable to secure shipping space despite all reasonable efforts, he would normally be liable for non-delivery if it was his duty as seller to arrange shipping,[29] whereas he would not be so liable if he were required to arrange shipping as the buyer's agent. And other issues may also turn on whether the seller ships as principal or as agent, for example who is to bear any increase in shipping or insurance charges after the contract of sale is made, or whether the seller is entitled to charge commission on the contract of carriage.

Whether the seller acts as principal or agent in shipping the goods usually depends on whether the parties intend that the seller should retain the bill of lading as security for payment. If this is the intention of the parties, the presumption is that the seller is acting as principal. This in turn may be determined by the bill of lading itself. If it is made out in the seller's name (that is, if goods are deliverable to, or to the order of, the seller) then the seller is reserving a right of disposal which would suggest that he is acting as principal.

Of course, in the last resort everything depends on the terms of the particular contract and it must not be assumed that every f.o.b. contract is identical in the obligations imposed on the parties. It would, however, be very unusual for the property to pass before shipment in an f.o.b. contract,[30] or for the risk not to pass on shipment.

Passing of risk and property

In this sort of f.o.b. contract the almost universal rule is that risk passes on shipment – as soon as the goods are over the ship's rail, and, if it should be material, the risk in each part of the cargo will pass as it crosses the ship's rail.[31] This is not because of any peculiarity of f.o.b. contracts but because in this type of contract the seller's duty is to deliver the goods f.o.b. Once they are on board, the seller has delivered them to the buyer and it is natural that they should thereafter be at the buyer's risk.[32] However, so far as the exact point at which risk passes, two views are possible: one is that risk literally passes as the goods cross the ship's rail, the other is that the risk passes when the goods are safely loaded on board the vessel.[33]

As regards the passing of property, the position is that prima facie property may also pass, like risk, on shipment. The loading of the goods may be an 'unconditional

---

28 For a modern illustration, see *President of India* v *Metcalfe Shipping Co* [1970] 1 QB 289, and see below, p. 424.
29 See, e.g., *Lewis Emmanuel & Son Ltd* v *Sammut* [1959] 2 Lloyd's Rep 629.
30 See *Carlos Federspiel & Co SA* v *Chas Twigg & Co Ltd* [1957] 1 Lloyd's Rep 240, where the authorities are comprehensively reviewed by Pearson J. See above, pp. 337–8.
31 *Colonial Insurance Co of New Zealand* v *Adelaide Marine Insurance Co* (1886) 12 App Cas 128.
32 *Frebold* v *Circle Products Ltd* [1970] 1 Lloyd's Rep 499.
33 See *Schmitthoff's Export Trade*, 10th edn §2–013. Both INCOTERMS and the UCC Art. 2-319(1) define the seller's duty as being to load the goods '*on board*'.

appropriation' which passes the property under s. 18 Rule 5. If the goods are loaded together with other goods of the same description so that an unconditional appropriation of the actual goods sold then takes place, but the goods subject to the contract are still unascertained, property cannot pass on shipment,[34] but the risk will still do so.[35]

In modern times, any general presumption that property passes with risk on shipment in an f.o.b. contract has probably largely disappeared. Although this may still sometimes be the case if the contract contains no contrary provision, the practice of treating the shipping documents as security for the payment of the price is now so well established in international sales that contractual terms requiring payment against (i.e. in exchange for) the shipping documents is probably the norm in f.o.b. contracts these days, just as much as in c.i.f. contracts where this practice may have first originated. Where payment is only to be made against documents, the seller will normally have himself named as the consignee in the bill of lading (that is, the goods will be deliverable under the bill of lading to, or to the order of, the seller), so that s. 19(1) and (2) become relevant. Section 19(1) has already been set out above.[36] Section 19(2) provides:

> Where goods are shipped, and by the bill of lading the goods are deliverable to the order of the seller or his agent, the seller is prima facie to be taken to reserve the right of disposal.

This reservation of the right of disposal makes the appropriation conditional under s. 19(1) so that property does not pass until the condition is satisfied. It is clear that today there is nothing contrary to the nature of the f.o.b. contract in the seller doing this, and indeed, as already said, it is nowadays very common. The result is that the shipment is treated under s. 19 as only amounting to a conditional appropriation, the condition being that the seller must be paid before property passes.

But the terms of the bill of lading are only evidence of the intention of the parties. The fact that the bill of lading is taken in the seller's name is not conclusive proof that the seller is shipping the goods as principal, or is reserving the right of disposal. There are cases where the seller does not want or need to keep the documents as security for the price, as where (for instance) seller and buyer are associated companies, or where the seller has agreed to grant the buyer credit. In such a case the seller may in fact transfer the bill of lading to the buyer as soon as he receives it, which would probably indicate that he was acting as agent all along.[37] And although the taking of the bill of lading in his own name by the seller prima facie indicates that the property does not pass on shipment, it does not follow that if the bill of lading is taken in the buyer's name it must be held that the property does pass on shipment. The retention of the bill of lading by the seller may be inconsistent with an intention to pass the property until it is handed over.[38]

---

34 Though the buyer may acquire an undivided share in the bulk under the Sale of Goods (Amendment) Act 1995 – see p. 346 *et seq*.

35 *Inglis v Stock* (1885) 10 App Cas 263.

36 See above, p. 340.

37 *The Albazero* [1977] AC 774, and see p. 423 above.

38 Compare the classic f.o.b. described at p. 420 *et seq*. See *The Kronprinsessan Margareta* [1921] 1 AC 486; cf. *The Parchim* [1918] AC 157, but this case can no longer support any general inference of passing of property merely by reason that risk has passed on shipment; see *Mitsui & Co Ltd v Flota Mercante Grancolumbiana SA* [1989] 1 All ER 951, 957.

It must be stressed that even where property does not pass on shipment, the seller normally retains the property only as security for payment or, in modern times, as a means of obtaining bridging finance to cover the period of shipment.[39] Hence, once the goods are shipped, the buyer has an interest in the goods so that the seller must transfer goods to the buyer from that shipment; if he transfers them to anyone else so that he cannot supply the buyer from that shipment, he breaks his contract with the buyer, although today the seller will normally be able to pass a good title to the third party. But in the ordinary way, in the absence of privity of contract,[40] the buyer cannot sue a third party (such as the carrier) in tort for damage to the goods where he had no property, or possessory interest, at the time the damage occurred.[41] On the other hand, the seller may sue and recover damages for the full value of the loss to the amount permitted by the Carriage of Goods by Sea Act 1971,[42] even though the seller himself had only a limited interest in the goods;[43] any surplus will be held on trust for the buyer.[44]

The above analysis of the way the sections of the Sale of Goods Act fit in with modern commercial practice has been reaffirmed by the Court of Appeal, and applied even to a case in which the buyer had paid 80 per cent of the price by letter of credit before the goods were shipped.[45] In such a case, although property does not pass under s. 19 until the conditions imposed by the seller have been fulfilled, the buyer may nonetheless acquire an undivided share in the part of an identified bulk paid for under the Sale of Goods (Amendment) Act 1995.[46]

Seller's duties as to insurance

It has already been seen that under s. 32(1), delivery to the carrier is prima facie deemed to be delivery to the buyer himself, but despite this it has been held that s. 32(3) applies to f.o.b. contracts. This subsection states that:

Unless otherwise agreed, where goods are sent by the seller to the buyer by a route involving sea transit, under circumstances in which it is usual to insure, the seller must give such notice to the buyer as may enable him to insure them during their sea transit, and if the seller fails to do so, the goods are at his risk during such sea transit.

---

39 *Ross T Smyth & Co Ltd* v *Bailey Son & Co* [1940] 3 All ER 60, 68.
40 But once the bill of lading is transferred to the buyer, the buyer becomes a party to the contract of carriage under the Carriage of Goods by Sea Act 1992 – see p. 428.
41 *Leigh & Sillivan Ltd* v *Aliakmon Shipping Co Ltd (The Aliakmon)* [1986] AC 785, and see p. 343 above.
42 Giving effect to the Hague/Visby Rules. The Act applies to all shipments where the contract expressly, or by implication, provides for the issuance of a bill of lading or similar document of title. Its effect is to limit the carrier's liability for loss or damage to a certain amount. Where there is no privity of contract, but the buyer is able to sue by virtue of ownership or a possessory title, it is believed that the limits would nevertheless apply under the rules developed in relation to the law of bailments – see *Southcote's Case* (1601) 46 Co Rep 86a; *Gibbon* v *Payton* (1769) 4 Burr 2298. The baroque complexity of this area of law is due to the over-rigid adherence of the courts to the doctrine of privity of contract. As to the effect of the Sale of Goods (Amendment) Act 1995 (ascertainment by exhaustion), see p. 346 *et seq*.
43 *Obestain Inc* v *National Mineral Development Corp Ltd* [1987] 1 Lloyd's Rep 465; *Linden Garden Trust* v *Linesta Sludge Disposals Ltd* [1994] 1 AC 85, though this is subject to the qualification laid down in *The Albazero* [1977] AC 774. So the effect of *The Aliakmon* (above, n. 41) may only be to force the buyer to sue in the shipper's name.
44 See *The Winkfield* [1902] P 42.
45 See under s. 19 – p. 340. *Mitsui & Co Ltd* v *Flota Mercante Grancolumbiana SA* [1989] 1 All ER 951.
46 See p. 346 *et seq*.

The construction of this subsection was the subject of some widely differing views in the Court of Appeal in *Wimble Sons & Co Ltd* v *Rosenberg & Sons*,[47] where the plaintiffs sold goods to the defendants f.o.b. Antwerp. The buyers sent instructions for shipping the goods, leaving it to the sellers to select the ship. The sellers shipped the goods, but did not insure and the cargo was lost at sea. Vaughan Williams and Buckley LJJ agreed that s. 32(3) applied to f.o.b. contracts, differing from Hamilton LJ who thought it had no application at all to such contracts because the seller does not send the goods to the buyer but only puts them on the ship for dispatch to the buyer. The majority thought, however, that dispatch was something different from delivery and that the seller does dispatch or send the goods to the buyer although he only delivers them to the ship, and such delivery is deemed to be delivery to the buyer by s. 32(1). This was not the end of the disagreements because Buckley LJ thought that the sellers were not liable in this case since the buyers already had sufficient information to enable them to insure if they wished. They knew what the freight was, they knew the port of loading and they knew the port of discharge. The only information lacking was the name of the ship, which would not have prevented insurance. On the other hand, Vaughan Williams LJ thought that such a construction would destroy the efficacy of the section since it is always possible for the buyer to insure the goods by a general cover policy. However, Buckley LJ answered this fairly by pointing out that in this case the buyer had enough information to enable him to make a particular insurance, but he agreed that the mere fact that the buyer can take out a general cover policy would not prevent the operation of s. 32(3).

The net result of this case is that, though the subsection in theory applies to f.o.b. contracts, in practice it will rarely be of much importance because in most cases the buyer will already have enough information to insure the goods specifically.

Seller's duties as to documents

Where a seller under an f.o.b. contract must tender documents, his duties are the same as a c.i.f. seller discussed in the following section. Thus the tender must be made with all reasonable dispatch.[48]

C.I.F. CONTRACTS

The main features of a c.i.f. contract were summarized by Lord Wright in *Smyth & Co Ltd* v *Bailey Son & Co Ltd*:[49]

> The contract in question here is of a type familiar in commerce, and is described as a c.i.f. contract. The initials indicate that the price is to include cost, insurance and freight. It is a type of contract which is more widely and more frequently in use than any other contract used for purposes of sea-borne commerce. An enormous number of transactions, in value amounting to untold sums, are carried out every year under c.i.f. contracts. The essential characteristics of this contract have often been described. The seller has to ship or acquire

---

47 [1913] 3 KB 743, followed in *Northern Steel Co Ltd* v *Batt* (1917) 33 TLR 516.
48 *Concordia Trading BV* v *Richco International Ltd* [1991] 1 Lloyd's Rep 475.
49 [1940] 3 All ER 60, 67–8.

after that shipment the contract goods, as to which, if unascertained, he is generally required to give a notice of appropriation. On or after shipment, he has to obtain proper bills of lading and proper policies of insurance. He fulfils his contract by transferring the bills of lading and the policies to the buyer. As a general rule, he does so only against payment of the price, less the freight which the buyer has to pay. In the invoice which accompanies the tender of the documents on the 'prompt' – that is, the date fixed for payment – the freight is deducted, for this reason. In this course of business, the general property remains in the seller until he transfers the bill of lading . . .

By mercantile law, the bills of lading are the symbols of the goods. The general property in the goods must be in the seller if he is to be able to pledge them. The whole system of commercial credits depends upon the seller's ability to give a charge on the goods and the policies of insurance.[50]

Seller's duties in c.i.f. contract

The seller's duties in a c.i.f. contract, as summarized in the above passage, relate to the following matters. First, he must ship the goods or buy goods already shipped. It would not be very common nowadays for a c.i.f. seller to buy goods afloat and in the great majority of cases the seller either already has the goods or himself buys them for shipment.[51] Stipulations as to the time and place of shipment as specified in the contract must be strictly complied with and are almost always treated as conditions.[52] Delay of even one day in shipping the goods will justify rejection by the buyer. Indeed, the buyer is equally justified in rejecting the goods if they are shipped too soon.[53] The seller must also insure the goods at his own expense.

Secondly, the seller must make a contract for the carriage of the goods to, and for their delivery at, the c.i.f. destination. Thirdly, the seller must, with all reasonable dispatch,[54] tender to the buyer proper shipping documents. These comprise (1) the seller's invoice for the price, (2) the bill of lading and (3) an insurance policy covering the goods against marine risks. The most essential feature of the bill of lading is the requirement that it should evidence a contract for the carriage of the goods to the agreed port of discharge.[55] The bill of lading and the insurance policy are, in a commercial sense, the buyer's guarantee that he will receive the goods in due course or, if they are lost or damaged, that he will have recourse either against the shipowners or

---

50 In one respect Lord Wright's speech differs from the judgment of Kennedy LJ in *Biddell* v *E Clemens Horst* [1911] 1 KB 934, 956 (the *locus classicus*), because Kennedy LJ thought that the property passed on shipment, conditionally or unconditionally, but according to the modern view, expressed by Lord Wright, property does not pass until the bill of lading is transferred.

51 This has been recognized by decisions holding that a *force majeure* clause can often be invoked where actual shipment is prohibited, even though in theory the seller might still be able to buy goods afloat – see *Tradax Export SA* v *André et Cie SA* [1976] 1 Lloyd's Rep 416, approved in *Bremer* v *Vanden Avenne* [1978] 2 Lloyd's Rep 109, 114 per Lord Wilberforce. But a seller may still be expected to buy afloat where he is a trader rather than a shipper, and the contemplation of the parties was that he would buy from other suppliers, before or after shipment: *Bunge SA* v *Deutsche Conti* [1979] 2 Lloyd's Rep 435; *André et Cie* v *Tradax Export* [1983] 1 Lloyd's Rep 254.

52 *Bunge Corp* v *Tradax* [1981] 1 WLR 711, above, p. 94.

53 *Bowes* v *Shand* (1877) 2 App Cas 455.

54 Where the contract requires the buyer to pay against documents within so many days of the bill of lading, the seller is under a correlative duty to deliver the shipping documents within this period: *Toepfer* v *Lenersan-Poortman NV* [1980] 1 Lloyd's Rep 143.

55 *SIAT Di Dal Ferro* v *Tradax Overseas* [1980] 1 Lloyd's Rep 53.

against the insurers. Recourse against the shipowners is now secured by the transfer to the buyer of the contract of carriage under the Carriage of Goods by Sea Act 1992.[56] Generally the buyer must pay the price in exchange for these shipping documents. But in practice, as we shall see more fully in Chapter 24, payment will often be made through a bank by means of a letter of credit, and the documents are in this case sent to a bank and not to the buyer direct.

Non-conforming documents

The shipping documents are therefore very important commercial and legal documents, because buyers pay the price in exchange for the documents, long before they receive the goods. Similarly, where the price is payable by letter of credit, banks will pay in exchange for the documents, thereby treating the documents as security for the money they advance. It is thus of critical importance that the documents be accurate, and that they comply with the terms of the contract. In practice, documents very often do not so comply, and this is an extremely common source of commercial and legal difficulty. If buyers and banks always rejected non-complying documents, international trade would probably grind to a halt, but many of the instances of non-compliance are trivial or technical and do not lead to rejection. If at a later date the buyer decides that he wants to reject after all there will often be arguments about waiver and estoppel, which we discussed earlier.[57] Where it is banks who in the first instance discover discrepancies in the documents, they often inform their buyers and act on their instructions. Sometimes, where the discrepancies appear particularly doubtful or technical, the bank may accept the documents in return for an indemnity, that is an undertaking to repay any moneys advanced and make good any loss if the buyer (or another bank on whose behalf the bank accepts the documents)[58] should then reject the documents.

Dating of the bill of lading

A point of critical importance in commercial practice, and also in law, is that the bill of lading must be correctly dated. The date on the bill of lading recording when the goods have been shipped is the buyer's guarantee that shipment has occurred during the contractual shipment period. It is a separate breach of contract for the seller to tender to the buyer incorrectly dated bills of lading, so that (in theory, and indeed for some purposes in practice also) the seller commits two breaches by shipping the goods late and then procuring misdated bills of lading. Regrettably, bills of lading are

---

56 This Act implements the recommendations of the Law Commission No. 196. By s. 2 the rights of suit under the contract of carriage contained in or evidenced by the bill of lading are to be transferred to or vested in the lawful holder of a bill of lading, by virtue of his having become the lawful holder of the bill so that the holder can sue on the contract as if he had been a party to it. The Act repealed the Bills of Lading Act 1855. That Act required property in the goods to pass 'upon or by reason of . . . consignment or indorsement [of the goods or bill of lading]'. This gave rise to difficulty where the property passed either before or after these events – see, e.g., *The Aliakmon* [1986] AC 785, p. 343 above. The 1992 Act also confers rights of suit to a person to whom goods are to be delivered under a sea waybill – such documents are not transferred and do not have to be presented in order to obtain delivery of the goods.

57 Above, p. 134.

58 See Chapter 24.

often misdated (with the connivance of shipping companies or shipping agents) in order to conceal the fact that the goods were shipped outside the contract period,[59] and this practice often gives rise to legal difficulties, especially where the buyer does not discover the incorrect dating until much later.

The present law is very strict in its requirements about the date of shipment, and the dating of the bills of lading, and this sometimes seems to encourage an over-technical approach to commercial matters. Buyers are sometimes enabled by these rules to reject documents or goods on the grounds of late shipment by a bare day or two, even where no loss has been caused thereby, but (for instance) the market has fallen significantly since the contract was made. On the other hand, it is not always a mere technicality that the law gives the buyer the right to insist on correctly dated bills of lading. The value of bills of lading may well depend upon the date of shipment shown, because, for example, this may indicate the probable date of arrival, and in a rapidly moving market this may be a matter of importance.[60] Moreover, in the hands of an innocent third party, a backdated bill is valid and the bank must pay against its presentation on a confirmed documentary credit.[61]

Contract of carriage

Section 32(2), which has been set out above,[62] also applies to c.i.f. contracts. This section requires the seller to make a 'reasonable' contract with the shipowner. It has already been seen that what is reasonable must be judged at the time the contract of carriage is made and not when the contract of sale is made.[63] So far as c.i.f. contracts are concerned, one of the most important requirements of a 'reasonable' shipping contract is that it should give the buyer a right of action against the shipping company for loss or damage to the goods throughout the whole period of the voyage.[64] This means that if the goods have to be transhipped, the first shipowner (who contracts with the seller and will be liable to the buyer when the documents are transferred to him) must accept liability for the defaults of subsequent shipowners who will not be in privity with the sellers nor, therefore, with the buyers. But this may no longer be true in practice because most bills of lading today exonerate the shipowner from liability after transhipment, and if these are the only available bills of lading the seller is entitled to ship on those terms.[65]

It follows from the nature of a c.i.f. contract that s. 32(3) does not apply because there is always an express agreement as to the insurance of the goods. This is still the

---

59 See the judgment of Kerr LJ in *Procter & Gamble Philippine Manufacturing Corp v Kurt A Becher GmbH* [1988] 2 Lloyd's Rep 21, where it is said that bills of lading dated on the last date of the month are often viewed with suspicion by lawyers because of the probability that they have been ante-dated so as to make it appear that goods have been shipped during a contractual shipping period.

60 The price may be calculated by reference to the bill of lading, and if the price falls between the date of the bill of lading and the true date of shipment, the buyer will pay more than he legally should – see *Rudolph A Oetker v IFA International Frachtagentur AG (the 'Almak')* [1985] 1 Lloyd's Rep 557.

61 *United City Merchants (Investments) Ltd v Royal Bank of Canada* [1983] 1 AC 168.

62 Above, p. 422.

63 Above, p. 422.

64 *Hansson v Hamel & Horley Ltd* [1922] 2 AC 36.

65 *Plaimar Ltd v Waters Trading Co Ltd* (1945) 72 CLR 304.

case even if special circumstances occur as a result of which the ordinary insurance cover is not effective and it would be advisable to take out a special cover.[66]

Passing of property and risk

Although s. 32(1) states, as we have seen, that delivery to a carrier is prima facie deemed to be delivery to the buyer, this has no application to c.i.f. contracts in which delivery of the goods to the buyer occurs when, but not before, the documents are handed over. The peculiar feature of c.i.f. contracts has always been the importance attached to the shipping documents, delivery of which transfers the property in, and the possession of, the goods to the transferee. The seller's duty to deliver the goods in these cases means only that he must deliver the documents, for even if the goods are lost at sea the seller can still insist on payment of the price in return for the documents.[67] Indeed, the position is the same if the goods are damaged after loading and are discharged before the ship sails, and even before the bill of lading is issued.[68] But 'that does not mean that a c.i.f. contract is a sale of documents and not of goods. It contemplates the transfer of actual and conforming[69] goods in the normal course. If the goods are lost, the insurance policy and bill of lading contract – that is, the rights under them – are taken to be, in a business sense, the equivalent of the goods'.[70] Moreover, a seller does not fulfil his duty by delivering a bill of lading which is regular on its face if, in fact, no goods have been shipped. Thus where a seller in good faith bought goods afloat and was given a bill of lading, apparently in order, and proceeded to sell the goods c.i.f. to another buyer, he was held in breach of contract when it was discovered that there were no goods.[71]

Not only does a transfer of a bill of lading transfer the property and the possession in the goods, but a pledge of the documents also operates as a pledge of the goods although this is not generally true of documents of title. This transferability is of crucial importance both in law and in practice. Indeed, negotiability (in this sense) is of the very essence of a bill of lading. A non-negotiable document is not strictly speaking a bill of lading at all.[72] But a bill of lading is not a negotiable instrument in the sense that a bill of exchange is, so a transferee of a bill of lading does not get a better title than the transferor.[73]

In c.i.f. contracts the risk once again passes on shipment, and if the goods are lost at sea the buyer is still bound to pay the price, although he will as a rule have the benefit of the insurance policy. The law is the same even if the seller knows that the goods have been lost when he tenders the shipping documents.[74] So also, the inability of the buyer to have the goods discharged at the port of destination (because, for instance, he cannot obtain an import licence) is of no concern to the seller, and

---

66 *Law & Bonar v American Tobacco Co Ltd* [1916] 2 KB 605.
67 *Manbré Saccharine Co Ltd v Corn Products Ltd* [1919] 1 KB 198.
68 *Golodetz (M) & Co Inc v Czarnikow-Rionda Co Inc* [1980] 1 All ER 501.
69 See *Trasimax Holdings SA v Addax BV ('The Red Sea')* [1999] 1 Lloyd's Rep 28.
70 *Smyth & Co Ltd v Bailey Son & Co Ltd* [1940] 3 All ER 60, 70 per Lord Wright.
71 *Hindley & Co Ltd v East India Produce Co Ltd* [1973] 2 Lloyd's Rep 515.
72 *Kum v Wah Tat Bank* [1971] 1 Lloyd's Rep 439.
73 *Nippon Yusen Kaisha v Ramjiban Serowgee* [1938] AC 429, 449 per Lord Wright.
74 *Manbré Saccharine Co Ltd v Corn Products Ltd* [1919] 1 KB 198.

cannot be a frustrating event.[75] The delivery of the goods on board the vessel, followed by the delivery of correct documents, is a complete performance by the seller of his duties under a c.i.f. contract; what happens after that is of no concern to him, subject to some special cases (for instance, where goods are shipped in an undivided bulk[76]).

At one time c.i.f. contracts differed fundamentally from f.o.b. contracts with regard to the time at which property passes, although today the tendency may well be for f.o.b. contracts to be treated in the same way as c.i.f. contracts.[77] At any rate, in c.i.f. contracts, it is quite clear that the general rule, which is not easily displaced,[78] is that the property only passes when the documents are transferred and paid for.[79] Where the bill of lading is taken in the seller's name, this accords with s. 18 and s. 19(1) and (2) which have already been discussed. Where, contrary to the usual practice, the bill is taken in the buyer's name, the prima facie rule is that delivery to the carrier is deemed to be an unconditional appropriation,[80] but this presumption is rebutted by the very nature of the c.i.f. contract. Under s. 19(3), which has been set out above,[81] it is expressly provided that if the seller sends a bill of exchange to the buyer with the shipping documents, the property does not pass unless the buyer accepts the bill of exchange. Even if the seller draws a bill of exchange on the buyer and discounts it with a bank before it has been accepted by the buyer, the property will still not pass. Although the seller may obtain payment in this way he remains under a secondary liability as drawer of the bill of exchange and so property remains in him as security for this contingency.[82] Indeed, even when the seller has received the full price in advance there may be special circumstances which give him some interest in retaining the property and it may be held that the transfer of the documents remains necessary to pass property.[83]

There have been a few unusual cases in which property has been held to pass in a c.i.f. contract at some other time than the transfer of documents. For instance, where the relationship between the parties was such that the seller was not concerned over the immediate payment of the price, then the property was held to pass on shipment or at latest on transfer of the bill of lading, even though no price was then paid. In *The Albazero*,[84] the sellers and buyers were both companies which were members of one corporate group, and the sale was not a genuine arm's length transaction. It was held that property passed on the posting of the bill of lading. Conversely, where a seller sold goods 'c.i.f.' but it was intended that he should store the goods in his warehouse and make deliveries as required, payment being made only after the goods left the ware-

---

75 *Congimex* v *Tradax* [1983] 2 Lloyd's Rep 250.
76 See below.
77 Above, p. 424.
78 See, e.g., *Cheetham & Co Ltd* v *Thornham Spinning Co Ltd* [1964] 2 Lloyd's Rep 17 (property held to have been retained by sellers even after the goods had been deposited in the buyers' warehouse, sellers not having been paid, and having retained bill of lading). A similar case is *Ginzberg* v *Barrow Haematite Steel Co Ltd* [1966] 1 Lloyd's Rep 343; and so also in *The Aliakmon* [1986] AC 785, the variation of the original c. & f. contract led to the same result – the buyers took possession but only as agents of the sellers, pending payment.
79 *Mitsui & Co Ltd* v *Flota Mercante Grancolumbiana SA* [1989] 1 All ER 951.
80 Section 18, Rule 5(2) – see above, p. 334.
81 Above, p. 340.
82 *The Prinz Adalbert* [1917] AC 586; *HM Procurator-General* v *M C Spencer* [1945] AC 124.
83 *The Gabbiano* [1940] P 166.
84 [1977] AC 774.

house, it was held that property had not passed prior to delivery of bills of lading.[85] This was plainly an unusual case in that the goods were imported by the seller but were not intended for immediate delivery, so it was hardly an ordinary c.i.f. contract.

Another case where property did not pass under a c.i.f. contract on transfer of the bill of lading is the case of the sale of an undivided share of goods carried in bulk. If a seller sold 5,000 tons of a cargo of wheat which totals 10,000 tons, the mere transfer of bills of lading for 5,000 tons could not pass the property because of s. 16 of the Sale of Goods Act which requires the goods to be ascertained before property can pass.[86] In such a case, however, the buyer can now acquire an individual share in the bulk,[87] and the property in the whole subject-matter of the contract will probably pass when the goods are discharged from the ship and appropriated to the particular contract in some way. Such a contract differs in various respects from an ordinary c.i.f. contract and indeed comes to resemble an ex-ship contract in that the seller must deliver the goods at the port of destination. If he procures the ship carrying the cargo to be directed elsewhere and the goods are unloaded there, he is therefore guilty of a breach of contract.[88] In an ordinary c.i.f. contract, however, any action of the seller to divert the ship and cargo after the goods are loaded and the documents delivered would not be a breach of the contract of sale; it might possibly involve a breach of the contract of carriage by the carrier, and the seller could conceivably be liable in tort, but he would have performed the contract of sale and so could not be liable for breach of that contract.[89]

In modern times a new problem has occasionally surfaced as a result of which property may pass at some other time than the transfer of the documents. This problem is that bills of lading are sometimes very late in being issued, and cargoes nowadays sometimes arrive before the bills of lading are ready for transfer to the buyer. When this happens, the seller may instruct the carrier to deliver the goods to the buyer without the production of bills of lading (agreeing to indemnify the carrier in case any holder of the bills of lading turns up with a right to demand the goods); of course the terms on which the seller is willing to do this will depend on his arrangements with the buyer – he may agree to give the instructions to the carrier only in return for payment if the contract was originally for cash against documents. If the goods are delivered to the buyer in this way, property will then pass to him,[90] in the absence of some express stipulation by the seller whereby he retains property despite the delivery.

As we saw in the quotation from Lord Wright's speech in *Smyth & Co Ltd v Bailey Son & Co Ltd*, in the sale of unascertained goods c.i.f. the seller is often under a duty to give notice of appropriation to the buyer, but this 'is not intended to pass and does not pass the property'.[91] The reason for this is that the notice is not an

---

85 *General Reinsurance Corpn v Forsakringsaktiebolaget Fennia Patria* [1982] QB 1022.
86 See above, p. 333, as to the effect of s. 16. The Sale of Goods (Amendment) Act 1995, which makes this provision subject to s. 20 A, is discussed at p. 346 *et seq.*
87 Under the Sale of Goods (Amendment) Act 1995 – see p. 346 *et seq.*
88 *Peter Cremer v Brinkers Grondstoffen BV* [1980] 2 Lloyd's Rep 605.
89 *Industria Azucarera Nacional v Expresa Exportadora De Azucar* (1982) Com LR 171.
90 *Enichmen Anic SpA v Ampelos Shipping Co Ltd* [1988] 2 Lloyd's Rep 599. The sale to the sub-buyers in this case was a c.i.f., but this is immaterial to the point about the passing of property, which was to occur on unloading. This had the effect that on unloading, the bills of lading ceased to be effective as transferable documents of title, and the sub-buyers, having no contract with the carriers, could not sue them for a shortfall in the quantity delivered.
91 *Smyth & Co Ltd v Bailey Son & Co Ltd* [1940] 3 All ER 60, 65 per Lord Wright – above, p. 426.

'unconditional' appropriation within the meaning of s. 18, Rule 5. It is conditional on the buyer taking up the documents and paying for the goods. The effect of such a notice of appropriation may be to convert the sale into one for specific or ascertained goods, so that it would thereafter be a breach of contract for the seller to deliver any other goods.[92] Otherwise, if the goods still form part of a bulk, the effect is that it will commit the seller to delivering goods from that bulk.

Variants on c.i.f. contracts

One very common variant of the c.i.f. contract is the c. & f. contract, in which the buyer arranges his own insurance, but in other respects the shipping arrangements are made by the seller, and, once again, property usually passes when the documents are transferred in exchange for payment of the price.

Buyer's duties

The duties of the buyer under a c.i.f. contract are to accept the shipping documents when tendered and to pay the contract price in exchange for the documents. Frequently, as we shall see more fully in Chapter 24, the price is payable by means of a letter of credit, in which case the documents are sent to a bank in the first instance, and the bank then passes the documents to the buyer, in exchange for payment or for some other method of satisfaction. Sometimes several banks are involved, and the documents are transferred from one to another, ultimately ending up with the buyer.

Sometimes the buyer is under a contractual duty to nominate a discharge port because the c.i.f. contract may not have originally specified a single port as the c.i.f. port, but may have envisaged a range of ports (e.g. any port in Italy), leaving the buyer to select the particular port at a later date. In this situation the buyer must obviously make his nomination in sufficient time for the vessel to sail to the port specified without interruption or delay.[93]

EX-SHIP CONTRACTS

In ex-ship contracts 'the seller has to cause delivery to be made to the buyer from a ship which has arrived at the port of delivery and has reached a place therein, which is usual for the delivery of goods of the kind in question'.[94] In other words, the seller really is under an obligation to deliver the goods to the buyer at the port of discharge in ex-ship contracts, and the buyer has no concern with the shipment itself. Section 32, therefore, has no application at all to this type of case. It also follows that if the seller fails to deliver the goods, the buyer is not liable for the price or, if he has paid it, he can recover it as on a total failure of consideration. Thus in *Comptoir d'Achat et de Vente SA* v *Luis de Ridder Limitada (The Julia)*,[95] the plaintiffs bought a

---

92 *The Vladimir Ilich* [1975] 1 Lloyd's Rep 322, 328.
93 *The Rio Sun* [1985] 1 Lloyd's Rep 350.
94 *Yangtsze Insurance Association* v *Lukmanjee* [1918] AC 585, 589 per Lord Sumner.
95 [1949] AC 293.

quantity of rye 'c.i.f. Antwerp', but the sellers retained the bill of lading and the insurance policy under the contract, and they also guaranteed the condition of the goods on arrival. It was held by the House of Lords that these terms were inconsistent with a true c.i.f. contract and that in fact the contract was for the sale and delivery of the goods ex-ship. Consequently, the seller's failure to deliver the goods through the outbreak of war enabled the buyers to recover the price as on a total failure of consideration.

Generally speaking, in contracts of this kind the property and risk will only pass on delivery.

23

EXPORT AND IMPORT LICENCES

In the modern world, where trade prohibitions and restrictions abound, the obtaining of an export or import licence, or both, is often a necessary prerequisite to the performance of a contract of sale. It is, therefore, a matter of considerable importance to decide which of the parties is to obtain the licence, and what happens if he fails to do so. As noted in the previous chapter, many export and import transactions are made subject to INCOTERMS. Where the parties have adopted these, the duties of the parties in this respect are clearly spelled out.[1] These duties are not always in conformity with the rules of English law set out below, which apply in the absence of such specific agreement.

WHOSE DUTY?

The courts have refused to lay down any general principles on this question and have insisted that each case must be decided according to its own special circumstances.[2] Nevertheless, some indications may be gleaned from the cases to show the sort of considerations which the courts will treat as relevant. It goes without saying, of course, that if the parties have expressed a clear intention as to who is to apply for a licence or what is to happen if it is not obtained then the courts will give effect to that intention. The difficulties arise when the parties have not expressed any such clear intention.

In ex-works or ex-store contracts, it is hardly possible to doubt that in the absence of a contrary intention it is the buyer's duty to obtain all necessary permits and licences. Indeed, one can go further and say that in such contracts the seller is not generally concerned with what the buyer does with the goods after he has taken delivery. Hence, in such cases the question of export and import licences will usually be irrelevant to the contract of sale.

At the other end of the scale, ex-ship contracts also do not give rise to much difficulty. In the absence of any contrary intention, it is plainly the seller's duty to obtain any necessary export licence, but probably the buyer's duty to obtain an import licence if required.

It is f.o.b. and c.i.f. contracts and their many variants which tend to give rise to the difficulties in this connection.[3] So far as f.o.b. contracts are concerned, it was for long thought that, as a result of the decision of the Court of Appeal in *H O Brandt & Co* v

---

1 The current version is *INCOTERMS 2000*.
2 *A V Pound & Co Ltd* v *M W Hardy & Co Inc* [1956] AC 588.
3 See *Schmitthoff's Export Trade*, 10th edn, p. 30 *et seq*.

H N Morris,[4] the obligation to obtain an export licence was generally on the buyer. It is obvious that this would in many circumstances be a highly inconvenient conclusion. Fortunately, it appears from the decision of the House of Lords in *A V Pound & Co Ltd v M W Hardy & Co Inc*[5] that *Brandt*'s case is not to be taken as laying down any general rule, and although the House refused to lay down any general rule itself, it is possible, without undue rashness, to say that prima facie in an f.o.b. contract the duty of obtaining the export licence is on the seller. *A fortiori* this is the case in a c.i.f. contract.

The points to which attention must be given in considering whether this is so in any particular case are, *inter alia*, the following. Is the seller exporting the goods from one country to the buyer in another, or are both parties carrying on business in the same country? The latter may, of course, be the position where the buyer is buying for export to a customer abroad, and hence himself buys the goods on f.o.b. or even c.i.f. terms. In this event, as in *Brandt*'s case, it is much easier to reach the conclusion that the duty to obtain an export licence is on the buyer, because the seller is not himself selling the goods for export. It is the buyer who wants to export the goods and, naturally, therefore it is for him to obtain the licence. The case is quite different in the normal position where the seller is exporting the goods to the buyer, for if the buyer's business is based in some country hundreds or thousands of miles away it would be unreasonable and impracticable to expect him to obtain the export licence.

Another point to consider is whether there are any particular circumstances rendering it easier for one party or the other to obtain the licence. If, for example, the buyer and seller are based in different countries, and only a member of a certain trade association may be granted an export licence,[6] or if the licences are granted according to a quota system based on the seller's previous shipments,[7] it becomes virtually impossible to hold that the buyer must obtain the licence.

A third relevant factor is whether the need for a licence existed when the contract was made (and, if so, whether the parties knew about it) or whether the need for a licence was only imposed after the contract was made by new legislation or controls.

The duty of obtaining an import licence must plainly be on the importer, that is the buyer, in most circumstances, if only because the relevant statutory provisions will generally impose the duty on him, and, in the absence of a contrary intention, 'the contract must be treated as made upon the assumption that the statutory law applicable . . . should be observed by the parties to the contract'.[8] This is *a fortiori* the case in an f.o.b. sale for the seller may not even know the destination of the goods. Indeed, in many international contracts the ultimate destination of the goods is of no concern to the seller, who performs his contract by shipping the goods and delivering the requisite documents. Thus failure by the buyer to obtain any required import licences is solely a matter for the buyer, and it is probably even incorrect to regard the buyer as under a contractual duty to obtain such a licence.[9]

---

4 [1917] 2 KB 784.
5 [1956] AC 588.
6 For example, *Peter Cassidy Seed Co Ltd* v *Osuustukkuk-Auppa IL* [1957] 1 All ER 484.
7 *Partabmull Rameshwar* v *K C Sethia Ltd* [1950] 1 All ER 51, affirmed (but no speeches reported) [1951] 2 All ER 352n.
8 *Mitchell Cotts & Co (Middle East) Ltd* v *Hairco Ltd* [1943] 2 All ER 552, 554–5 per Scott LJ.
9 *Congimex* v *Tradax* [1983] 1 Lloyd's Rep 250.

WHETHER DUTY ABSOLUTE OR TO USE BEST ENDEAVOURS

When it has been decided whether the duty to obtain the necessary licence is on the buyer or the seller, the next question which may arise is whether the duty is absolute, that is, is the party in question to be taken to have warranted that he will obtain the licence, or only that he will use his best endeavours to do so? If the latter is the true position, a failure to obtain the licence despite such best endeavours will generally mean that the contract is frustrated. Alternatively, the party unable to obtain the licence may be excused by an express *force majeure* clause, in which case the contract simply fails, since the detailed provisions of a *force majeure* clause usually leave no room for the application of the common law.[10]

Where a licence is required throughout the period of shipment, the party whose duty it is to obtain the licence must not delay too long in making his application or he may be held to have failed to use due diligence to obtain one.[11] On the other hand, the position is rather different where the need for a licence is only introduced during the shipment period. Here, the party who should obtain the licence cannot be blamed for not having acted before the requirement was introduced, and even though he might have shipped the goods then, he may still be excused by his later failure to obtain a licence.[12]

In *Re Anglo-Russian Merchant Traders Ltd*[13] the Court of Appeal held that generally speaking there is no absolute duty to obtain a licence, and that where a seller applies for and is refused an export licence, he is not generally liable in damages for non-delivery. In *Peter Cassidy Seed Co Ltd* v *Osuustukkuk-Auppa IL*[14] Devlin J agreed with this as a general principle.

> The person whose duty it is to apply for a licence may either warrant that he will get it, that is an absolute warranty, or he may warrant that he will use all due diligence in getting it. When nothing is said in the contract it is usually – probably almost invariably – the latter class of warranty which is implied, but each case must be decided according to its own circumstances, and the question of implication must be settled in the ordinary way in which implied terms are settled.[15]

But ultimately the learned judge held that in the particular circumstances of the case the sellers had warranted that they would obtain a licence. In this case, the contract stated: 'Delivery: prompt as soon as export licence granted' and the sellers had assured the buyers that this was a pure formality.

On the other hand, in *Mitchell Cotts & Co (Middle East) Ltd* v *Hairco Ltd*[16] Scott LJ inclined to the view that the buyers' duty to obtain a licence (in that case, an import licence) is generally absolute, and in *Partabmull Rameshwar* v *K C Sethia Ltd*[17] the House of Lords held, on somewhat unusual facts, that the sellers had bound themselves to obtain an export licence.

---

10 *Pagnan SpA* v *Tradax Ocean Transportation SA* [1987] 3 All ER 565.
11 *Agro Export State Enterprise* v *Compagnie Européenne de Céréales* [1974] 1 Lloyd's Rep 499.
12 *Ross T Smyth & Co Ltd* v *W N Lindsay Ltd* [1953] 1 WLR 1280, though in this case the seller was not discharged. Cf. *André* v *Tradax* [1983] 1 Lloyd's Rep 254.
13 [1917] 2 KB 679.
14 [1957] 1 All ER 484.
15 At p. 486.
16 [1943] 2 All ER 552. See also *Congimex* v *Tradax* [1983] 1 Lloyd's Rep 250.
17 [1950] 1 All ER 51, affirmed [1951] 2 All ER 352n.

Even an obligation by a party to use his best endeavours to obtain a licence is somewhat strictly applied by the courts. In *Brauer & Co (Great Britain) Ltd* v *James Clark (Brush Materials) Ltd*,[18] for instance, sellers had agreed to sell goods for shipment f.o.b. a Brazilian port, 'subject to any Brazilian export licence'. The sellers had applied for a licence, which was refused on the ground that the price was too low. On its appearing that the sellers might have obtained a licence if they had been prepared to pay the extra (some 20 per cent above the contract price) to their own suppliers, it was held that they had not used their best endeavours to obtain a licence. So too, a seller who contracts to ship from one of a number of ports is not excused if export from one only is prohibited, even though he may already have made all necessary arrangements to ship from that port.[19] Where the seller is under a duty to apply for a licence, the buyer may nevertheless be bound to supply the seller with any information (for example, as to the ultimate destination of the goods) which may be required by the licensing authority.[20] Where a seller, who is under a duty to use his best endeavours, fails even to apply for a licence, he has the heavy burden of proving that any application was foredoomed to failure.[21] A party whose licence is revoked is in the same position as one whose application is refused.[22]

On the other hand, total suspension of a licensing system and the banning of all imports (or exports) is a different matter from the mere refusal of a licence, and even though a party may prima facie have warranted to obtain a licence, he may be more readily excused by a *force majeure* clause in this situation.[23]

There is, perhaps, something slightly misleading in talking of an implied warranty by a party to obtain, or to use his best endeavours to obtain, a licence. If there is no mention of the matter in the contract, then the true position is simply this. The seller is bound to deliver the goods to the buyer and the buyer is bound to take delivery from the seller. If either party will not or cannot perform his obligations he is prima facie in default, unless he can show that the contract has been frustrated. Often he can show that the contract has been frustrated by proving that a necessary licence has been refused despite his best endeavours to obtain one.[24] But where the obligation to deliver (or to take delivery) is construed as an absolute obligation, then the failure to obtain the licence does not excuse non-performance. Strictly speaking, therefore, it does not seem accurate to talk of a person warranting that 'he will get a licence', or that 'he will use his best endeavours to get a licence'.

---

18 [1952] 2 All ER 497.
19 *Pagnan SpA* v *Tradax Ocean Transportation SA* [1987] 3 All ER 565.
20 *Warinco AG* v *Fritz Mauthier* [1978] 1 Lloyd's Rep 151; see too *Malik Co* v *Central European Trading Agency Ltd* [1974] 2 Lloyd's Rep 279.
21 *Phoebus D Kyprianou* v *Cyprus Textiles Ltd* [1958] 2 Lloyd's Rep 60.
22 *Société d'Avances Commerciales (London)* v *A Besse & Co (London)* [1952] 1 TLR 644.
23 *Czarnikow Ltd* v *Rolimpex* [1978] 2 All ER 1043.
24 It is now well established that a party who has failed to obtain a licence must himself prove due diligence: *Brauer & Co (Great Britain) Ltd* v *James Clark (Brush Materials) Ltd* [1952] 2 All ER 497; *Vidler & Co (London) Ltd* v *R Silcock & Sons Ltd* [1960] 1 Lloyd's Rep 509; *Tradax Export SA* v *André et Cie* [1976] 1 Lloyd's Rep 416; *Bremer* v *Vanden Avenne* [1978] 2 Lloyd's Rep 109.

24

BANKERS' COMMERCIAL CREDITS

PAYMENT OF PRICE BY BANKERS' COMMERCIAL CREDIT[1]

Where a person carrying on business in one country buys goods from a seller in another country, it is common practice for the price to be paid by means of a banker's commercial credit. The normal procedure is more or less as follows, although there may frequently be variations of detail.

The buyer instructs his own bank (the issuing bank) to open a credit in favour of the seller with a bank in the seller's country (the 'intermediary' or 'correspondent' or 'confirming' banker). Almost invariably, the buyer instructs the issuing bank that the seller is only to be allowed to draw on the credit on presentation to the paying bank of documents showing that the goods have been shipped and are on their way to the buyer. The shipping documents will comprise (at least) the seller's invoice for the goods, the bill of lading and, frequently (always in c.i.f. contracts), an insurance policy or certificate. The intermediary banker will then notify the seller that instructions have been received to open a credit in his favour and will inform him of the precise terms on which he will be allowed to avail himself of the credit. As soon as the goods are shipped and the seller has received the necessary documents himself from the carriers or their agents and the insurers, he will present these documents together with his invoice to the intermediary banker. The bank will check the documents with the terms of the credit to ensure that the goods shipped are (so far as can be seen from the documents) the contract goods and that everything appears to be in order and, if satisfied that this is the case, will permit the seller to draw against the credit. This may be done by accepting a bill of exchange, or discounting a bill drawn on the buyer, or by making funds available in cash.

The intermediary bank will then transmit the documents to the issuing bank, which will likewise have to check the documents against the terms of the credit, and which will pay the intermediary bank if satisfied that all is in order. The issuing bank will then inform the buyer that the documents have been received, and will be transferred to him against payment. The buyer will also satisfy himself that the documents are in order and will, in due course, pay the issuing bank an amount corresponding to the price paid to the seller, together with the bank's own charges. Of course the issuing bank may be providing credit to the buyer – that is a matter for the contract between them – in which case it will transmit the documents to him before receiving

---

1 See generally Gutteridge and Megrah, *The Law of Bankers' Commercial Credits*, 8th edn, 2001.

payment. Armed with the documents, the buyer will then be in a position to resell the goods and transfer the documents to a sub-buyer or, alternatively, to take delivery as soon as the goods arrive. The holder of the documents is prima facie the person to whom the carrier will deliver the goods.

Virtually all bankers' credits are today granted on the terms that they are to be governed by the Uniform Customs and Practice for Documentary Credits (and Supplement for Electronic Presentation) prepared by the International Chamber of Commerce.[2] The banks of nearly all the countries in the world use this document (hereafter referred to as the Uniform Customs) which is, therefore, to all intents and purposes a part of the law of bankers' commercial credits.[3] But this document is not a statute, and should not be interpreted as such; for instance, reasonable implications can be read into the Uniform Customs.[4]

There are many variations in the forms of commercial credits, the principal distinctions being between revocable and irrevocable credits, and confirmed and unconfirmed credits. Under the Uniform Customs, an irrevocable credit constitutes a definite undertaking by the issuing bank that the credit will be made available if the seller complies with the stipulated conditions. A revocable credit does not constitute a definite undertaking by the issuing bank and may be cancelled or modified without notice until payment is made or documents accepted under the credit. The distinction between a confirmed and an unconfirmed credit turns upon whether or not the intermediary bank accepts a direct obligation to the seller to honour the credit. In the former event, the intermediary bank 'confirms' the credit, that is undertakes (sometimes for an extra commission payable directly by the seller) to pay, whether or not it is put in funds by the issuing bank; in the latter event, the credit is unconfirmed, the intermediary bank merely informs the seller that the credit has been opened in his favour, and the seller will have no right of recourse against the bank in the event of its refusing to pay.

In the past, doubts have even existed as to whether the seller could sue the bank if it refused to honour a confirmed credit, anyhow prior to shipment, on the ground that there is no contract between seller and bank, owing to the absence of any consideration supplied by the seller. There is no difficulty when the goods have once been shipped, because this is action by the seller in reliance on the bank's undertaking, and that should suffice as a valid consideration by any modern test. But it is theoretically arguable that, if the bank repudiates the credit before shipment, the seller may be unable to enforce the letter of credit by direct action against the bank. In practice, banks never take this technical point and judicial pronouncements now seem to have put their liability beyond doubt.[5]

---

2 The current version was released in 2002.

3 Of course there must be something to justify incorporation of the Uniform Customs in the contract, and this is usually done expressly, but a bare marginal note has been held sufficient to achieve this result: *Forestal Mimosa Ltd* v *Oriental Credit Ltd* [1986] 1 WLR 631.

4 *Co-operative Centrale Raiffeisen-Boerenleenbank BA* v *Sumitomo Bank Ltd* [1987] 1 FTLR 233 (varied on appeal [1988] 2 FTLR 27).

5 See especially *Hamzeh Malas & Sons* v *British Imex Industries Ltd* [1958] 2 QB 127, 129 per Jenkins LJ; *Urquhart Lindsay & Co* v *Eastern Bank Ltd* [1922] 1 KB 318; *United City Merchants (Investments) Ltd* v *Royal Bank of Canada* [1983] 1 AC 168, 183 per Lord Diplock. Where applicable under choice of law rules (see p. 69 *et seq.*) the Contracts (Rights of Third Parties) Act 1999 would also seem to give the seller a remedy. Where Scottish law is applicable, the seller will have a remedy under the *jus quaesitum tertio*.

The vital element in this commercial machinery is that the seller must not be allowed to draw against the credit unless it is quite clear, so far as can be seen from an examination of the documents, that he has fulfilled his obligations under the contract. Hence it is of the first importance that the buyer should inform the issuing bank precisely what documents are required.[6] It is equally important that the documents presented by the seller to the intermediary bank should correspond exactly with the terms of the credit (which should, of course, represent the agreed terms of sale[7]) for otherwise the bank will refuse payment, or if it pays, it does so at its peril, because the buyer (or the issuing bank) may refuse to take up the documents.

In practice minor discrepancies between the shipping documents and the letter of credit are a very common source of trouble. The bank to whom the documents have been presented will often seek instructions from the buyer (or from an issuing bank) rather than immediately reject non-conforming documents, and very often the letter of credit will be amended, or the discrepancies will be waived. Although the bank is entitled thus to seek instructions it must act with reasonable dispatch, and must ultimately either accept or reject the documents.[8]

As we have seen, the main documents are the bill of lading, the invoice and any necessary insurance documents. The bill of lading must cover shipment from and to the agreed ports. It was for long a requirement that the bill of lading should be a 'shipped' bill of lading,[9] that is it had to acknowledge that the goods had actually been shipped and not merely received for shipment,[10] but new types of commercial documentation (such as combined road and shipping documents) have now led to an abandonment of this requirement by Art. 27 of the 1994 Uniform Customs. But some letters of credit still require 'shipped' bills of lading.[11]

The invoice must describe the goods exactly as stated in the credit.[12] It was formerly held that even the *de minimis* rule was excluded in this situation,[13] but Art. 34 of the Uniform Customs permits a tolerance of 5 per cent more or less than the contract quantity unless the credit stipulates to the contrary.[14] In other matters than

---

6 See Arts 5, 14 and 22 of the Uniform Customs.
7 But in practice it is not uncommon for additional contract terms to be spelled out in the letter of credit which were not in the original contract. The buyer who inserts such terms does so at his peril, because the seller is under no duty to co-operate with him in filling in terms left uncertain in the original contract (*Siporex Trade SA v Banque Indosuez* [1986] 2 Lloyd's Rep 146) and any new terms may lead to rejection of the letter of credit as inconsistent with the contract of sale. If the letter of credit is accepted, this may amount to a variation of the original sale contract (*W J Alan & Co Ltd v El Nasr Export & Import Co* [1972] 2 QB 189) or it may amount to a waiver or forbearance giving rise to an estoppel (*Ficom SA v Sociedad Cadex* [1980] 2 Lloyd's Rep 118, 131).
8 *Co-operative Centrale Raiffeisen-Boerenleenbank BA v Sumitomo Bank Ltd* [1987] 1 FTLR 233, varied [1988] 2 FTLR 27.
9 *Diamond Alkali Export Corpn Ltd v Bourgeois* [1921] 3 KB 443.
10 For the difference between a 'shipped' and a 'received for shipment' bill of lading, see *Wespac Banking Corpn v South Carolina National Bank* [1986] 1 Lloyd's Rep 311.
11 See *Wespac Banking Corpn v South Carolina National Bank*, above, n. 10.
12 It was formerly held that even the bill of lading had to do this – see *Rayner & Co Ltd v Hambro's Bank Ltd* [1943] KB 37. But under Art. 41(c) of the Uniform Customs, it is sufficient if the bill of lading describes the goods in general terms. The invoice is in effect a representation by the seller to the buyer of the very goods he has shipped, so it is natural that this is the document where the goods must be described in precise conformity with the contract.
13 *Moralice (London) Ltd v E D & F Man* [1954] 1 Lloyd's Rep 526.
14 This does not apply where the credit specifies quantity in terms of packing units or containers or individual items. Nor does it entitle the seller to draw more than the amount of the credit. It simply means that the bank will pay even if the seller ships up to 5 per cent more or less than the contract quantity. (The tolerance is extended to 10 per cent if the contract quantity is qualified by words such as 'about' or 'circa'.) It remains the responsibility of the seller to draw the invoice for the correct amount shipped, of course.

quantity the position still is that the *de minimis* rule does not apply.[15] Generally, also, the credit requires 'clean' bills of lading, which means that the bill must 'not contain any reservation as to the apparent good order or condition of the goods or the packing'.[16]

Where the documents are to include insurance policies, a certificate will not suffice unless, as is customary, the credit expressly says so. Additional documents are often required by the contract, such as certificates of quality, or the like, to be provided by independent third parties after inspection of the goods.

Provided that the documents presented by the seller are in order, he is entitled to avail himself of the credit notwithstanding that the buyer may have some complaint about the quality of the goods.[17] The value of this method of payment would be considerably reduced if a claim by the buyer had the effect of preventing the seller from drawing on the credit. One of the principal purposes of a letter of credit is to assure the seller that he will be paid, leaving for later settlement and, if necessary, litigation any complaints by the buyer. A letter of credit thus throws the onus of litigation on to the buyer who must pay first and sue afterwards. As Lord Diplock put it in *United City Merchants (Investments) Ltd* v *Royal Bank of Canada*:

> The whole commercial purpose for which the system of confirmed irrevocable documentary credits has been developed in international trade is to give the seller an assured right to be paid before he parts with control of the goods and that does not permit of any dispute with the buyer as to the performance of the contract of sale being used as a ground for non-payment or reduction or deferment of payment.[18]

This general policy gives rise to the fundamental principle expressed in Art. 4 of the Uniform Customs that banks 'deal in documents and not in goods'. Thus the bank is expected to confine its attention to the documents and to examine them for regularity on their face. In the *United City Merchants* case (from which the above quotation comes), the shipping documents presented by the sellers misrepresented the date on which the goods had been shipped (though this was not in fact known to the sellers) and the bank became aware of this fact; but there was nothing on the face of the documents themselves to indicate that there was any irregularity. It was held that the bank must pay. The House of Lords, however, reserved the question whether the result would be the same if the documents were actually forged.

It is also well established that if the seller is guilty of actual fraud – if he knowingly presents documents which are false in some material respect, for instance – the bank

---

15 *Soproma SpA* v *Marine & Animal By-Products Corpn* [1966] 1 Lloyd's Rep 367, 390.

16 *British Imex Industries Ltd* v *Midland Bank* [1958] 1 QB 542, per Salmon LJ. See now Art. 34 of the Uniform Customs. In practice bills of lading usually only acknowledge that the goods are in apparent (not actual) good order and condition. That is enough for a clean bill. See also *Golodetz (M) & Co Inc* v *Czarnikow-Rionda Co Inc* [1980] 1 All ER 501.

17 *Hamzeh Malas & Sons* v *British Imex Industries Ltd* [1958] 2 QB 127. In many cases the buyer will not even see the goods until the seller has obtained payment, so this question can hardly arise; but sometimes the buyer may have grounds for suspecting non-compliance even before he receives the goods, e.g. because of a previous shipment.

18 [1983] AC 168, 183. See also *Nova Jersey (Knit) Ltd* v *Kammgarn Spinneiri* [1977] 1 WLR 713; *Power Curber International* v *National Bank of Kuwait* [1981] 1 WLR 1233.

is entitled to, indeed is under a duty to, refuse payment, even if the fraud is not apparent from the documents themselves: this also was accepted as settled law in the *United City Merchants* case. But the fraud must be clearly proved and a bank which has actually paid under the letter of credit against conforming documents cannot be refused reimbursement unless it is also shown that the bank had clear knowledge of the fraud.[19]

Where fraud can be established, the buyer may be able to obtain an injunction to restrain his own bank from paying under the letter of credit, or to restrain the seller from drawing under it.[20] Courts are, however, very reluctant to grant injunctions – even interim injunctions – to restrain banks from honouring their letters of credit, and a strong case must be made for an injunction against the bank itself. There are also difficulties in getting an injunction against a bank with whom the buyer has no direct dealings, even though the documents, and the duty to make payment, will eventually be passed down the line to him.[21] Moreover, an injunction is unlikely to be granted to restrain an issuing bank from paying a confirming bank, where the confirming bank has already paid the seller in good faith and looks to the issuing bank for an indemnity under the issuing bank's own obligations, unless it is apparent that the confirming bank has paid on non-conforming documents, or that it had clear knowledge of fraud by the seller.

From the legal point of view, a commercial credit as described above involves a pledge of the documents by the seller to the paying bank which is, in due course, transferred to the issuing bank. In the normal course of events, the pledge is discharged when the buyer takes up the documents and pays off the bank. If, however, something should go wrong in the performance of the contract, for example if the buyer should become insolvent, the bank is in a position to enforce and realize its security, if necessary through its possession of the documents. One result of this commercial machinery has been to reduce the importance of the seller's right of stoppage in transit, because if the buyer becomes insolvent there is no fear that he will obtain the goods since he has not got the necessary documents, and will not be able to get them except on paying the bank.

Although, in an ordinary contract of sale of goods, delivery and payment are concurrent conditions, in contracts in which the price is to be paid by means of a commercial credit 'the seller is entitled, before he ships the goods, to be assured that, on shipment, he will get paid'.[22] So where the contract specifies the time during which the letter of credit must be opened, there is a strong presumption that that time limit is a condition, and failure to comply justifies immediate repudiation by the

---

19 *United Trading Corpn SA v Allied Arab Bank* [1985] 2 Lloyd's Rep 554.
20 *Szeijn v J Henry Schroder Banking Corp* 31 NYS 2d 631, 634 (1941) ('fraud unravels all'); *Edward Owen Engineering Ltd v Barclays Bank International Ltd* [1978] 1 QB 178; *Hamzeh Malas & Sons v British Imex Industries Ltd*, above. A bare allegation of fraud will not suffice, even for interim relief: *Discount Records Ltd v Barclays Bank* [1975] 1 WLR 315. Nor does previous fraud necessarily suffice for interim relief, unless there is a strong probability of further fraud: *Tukan Timber Ltd v Barclays Bank* [1987] 1 FTLR 154. But the buyer does not have to disprove all possible explanations other than fraud, and an injunction will be granted if the only realistic inference is fraud: *United Trading Corpn SA v Allied Arab Bank* [1985] 2 Lloyd's Rep 554. The case law in this area was helpfully reviewed by Phillips J in *Deutsche Ruckversicherung AG v Wallbrook* [1994] 4 All ER 181.
21 *United Trading Corpn SA v Allied Arab Bank*, above, n. 19.
22 *Pavia & Co SpA v Thurmann-Nielsen* [1952] 2 QB 84, 88 per Denning LJ.

seller.[23] Where no time is specified in the contract the credit must (in the absence of some contrary indication[24]) be opened by the buyer a reasonable time before the beginning of the shipment period,[25] even if the seller has some weeks or even months in which to ship, and does not in fact ship until the end of the period. This is still the case, even where the contract is on f.o.b. terms in which the buyer is entitled to fix the date of shipment.[26] The seller cannot, of course, draw against the credit until the goods are shipped because the presentation of the shipping documents is a condition precedent to his right to use the credit, so that strictly speaking there is no violation of the rule that payment and delivery are concurrent conditions, at any rate if delivery is taken to encompass delivery of the documents. The point is that payment by means of a banker's credit is intended to operate, and does operate, not merely as a method of payment, but as a means of *guaranteeing* payment. Hence the seller is entitled to know before he ships the goods that the credit has been opened and that, as soon as he presents the documents, he will be paid.

It will be seen that payment of the price by banker's credit is very favourable to the seller in at least three respects. First, once the credit is issued, he is reasonably assured of payment, and almost certainly if the credit is irrevocable (which under the 1994 Revision, all credits are, unless stated to be revocable);[27] secondly, the buyer cannot delay payment by disputing the goods' conformity to the contract; and thirdly, the cost of financing the shipment period falls on the buyer. The result is that payment by this method becomes less common in a buyer's market.

Where the contract provides for payment by means of a banker's credit, and for payment against delivery of documents to a bank, the buyer fulfils his obligations by providing the credit on the agreed terms. If the seller delivers non-conforming documents to the bank, the bank and the buyer are fully entitled to reject the documents, and the contract will then be at an end, subject to the buyer's claim for damages. There is no remaining obligation on the buyer to accept the goods when they arrive, even if they conform to the contract.[28] So also, the seller is not entitled to disregard the credit and send the documents direct to the buyer and claim payment from him.[29] Accordingly, the buyer may reject documents tendered directly to him instead of to the bank. But this does not mean that the seller can never sue the buyer for the price even if the price was agreed to be payable by banker's credit. For example if, by some commercial mishap, the goods are actually delivered to and accepted by the buyer without payment by the bank, the seller retains his ordinary right to sue for the price,[30] unless perhaps in exceptional circumstances it may be held that he had

---

23 *Nichimen Corpn v Gatoil Overseas Inc* [1987] 2 Lloyd's Rep 46; *Warde (Michael I) v Feedex International* [1985] 2 Lloyd's Rep 289.

24 For an example of such a case, see *Tradax (Ireland) v Irish Grain Board* [1984] 1 IR 1 (contract made on 23 March, for shipment in April, May and June, term for letter of credit 'maturing on 1 May' – held not required to be opened before the shipment period).

25 *Sinason-Teicher Inter-American Grain Corpn v Oilcakes & Oilseeds Trading Co Ltd* [1954] 1 WLR 1394.

26 *Ian Stach Ltd v Baker Bosly Ltd* [1958] 2 QB 130.

27 Article 6. If the credit is revocable, it may be cancelled even though shipment of the goods has taken place – see *Cape Asbestos Co v Lloyds Bank* [1921] WN 274.

28 *Shanser Jute Mills Ltd v Sethia London Ltd* [1987] 1 Lloyd's Rep 388.

29 *Soproma SpA v Marine & Animal By-Products Corpn* [1966] 1 Lloyd's Rep 367, 385–6.

30 *W J Alan & Co Ltd v El Nasr Export & Import Co* [1972] 2 QB 179; *Saffron v Société Minière Cafrika* (1958–59) 100 CLR 231.

accepted the letter of credit as absolute payment.[31] So, also, if the goods are sold f.o.b. and the seller does not reserve the right of disposal, property may pass (as we have seen) on shipment. Therefore, if the bank wrongfully refuses payment in such a case, the seller may still sue the buyer for the price.[32] The same is true if the bank fails to pay because of insolvency.[33]

A contractual term requiring a letter of credit is, of course, no protection to the seller unless it is in fact issued, and though the seller can refrain from shipping the goods if the letter is not duly issued, his guarantee of assured payment will simply fail without the letter of credit. To protect the seller against the risk that the letter of credit may not be issued, the contract may require the buyer to provide a performance bond as soon as it is agreed. Such a bond is itself very like a letter of credit; it is an undertaking, usually given by a bank or other unimpeachable guarantor, to pay a specified sum to the addressee on various terms.[34] Sometimes the terms are (in effect) simply that the recipient of the letter writes to the bank asserting that there has been default by the other party and demanding payment under the bond. The bank must then pay, even though there was no default.[35] As with a letter of credit, any argument about whether the amount of the bond was payable is deferred until after the bond has been paid. Performance bonds are more often encountered in building and engineering contracts, but they may also be demanded in an ordinary export sale to cover the period before a letter of credit is issued.[36]

31 See Ellinger (1961) 24 MLR 530.
32 *Newman Industries Ltd* v *Indo-British Industries Ltd* [1956] 2 Lloyd's Rep 219, 236, reversed on the facts [1957] 1 Lloyd's Rep 211.
33 *E D & F Man Ltd* v *Nigerian Sweets and Confectionery Co Ltd* [1977] 2 Lloyd's Rep 50.
34 See Bennett, *Performance Bonds and the Principles of Autonomy* [1994] JBL 574.
35 *Edward Owen Engineering Ltd* v *Barclays Bank International Ltd* [1978] 1 QB 178.
36 See, e.g., *Siporex Trade SA* v *Banque Indosuez* [1986] 2 Lloyd's Rep 146.

Part VI

THE REMEDIES OF THE SELLER

25

REAL REMEDIES

SELLER'S RIGHTS AND POWERS AGAINST THE GOODS

Where the buyer defaults in his principal obligation, that is in payment of the price, the seller has, of course, his personal action on the contract itself, but if the seller were always compelled to fall back on this remedy, his position would be in many respects unsatisfactory. The law has, therefore, developed certain 'real' rights or remedies whereby the seller can still look to the goods as a kind of security for payment of the price. In considering these real remedies, four different fact situations must be distinguished.

First, there may be a sale of specific goods in which the property has passed to the buyer and the goods have been delivered to him. Here the seller has relinquished all right to look to the goods for his price and he is relegated to his personal right of action against the buyer. If the seller attempts to enforce his right to the price by seizing the goods from the buyer's possession, the seller's conduct will be a breach of s. 12 of the Act[1] and will doubtless constitute the tort of conversion in English law as well. It is possible for the parties to provide by express agreement that the property in the goods is to remain in the seller even after they have been delivered, in which case the seller may have the right to seize or reclaim the goods in certain events – for instance, if the buyer becomes insolvent before the price is paid. But such a right to reclaim the goods after delivery cannot be implied since it would be very rare for the property to be retained by the seller after delivery unless there is an express provision to this effect. But the use of such express provisions – reservation of title clauses – is widespread and giving rise to difficult questions. It will therefore be necessary to consider their effect,[2] even though they cannot arise by implication of law in the same way that the other real rights arise.

Secondly, there may be a sale of specific goods in which the property has passed to the buyer, but the goods have not yet been delivered. In this case, whether the goods are still in the possession of the seller or have been dispatched to the buyer (but not yet reached him), the law confers on the seller, subject to certain conditions, (a) the power to resell the goods and pass a good title to a third party as well as some incidental powers, and (b) the right to do so *vis-à-vis* the first buyer. It must be emphasized that these are two very different things, because the seller often has the power to pass a good title to a bona fide transferee without having the right to do so; in other words the resale may constitute a breach of contract as against the first buyer

---

1 *Healing (Sales) Pty Ltd* v *Inglis Electrix Pty Ltd* (1968) 121 CLR 584.
2 See below, p. 470.

although it validly transfers the property. Indeed, as we have already seen, a seller always has the power to transfer a good title to an innocent third party so long as he is in possession of the goods because of s. 24 of the Sale of Goods Act and s. 8 of the Factors Act 1889, but the right to do so is more severely restricted, as will become apparent in due course.

Thirdly, there may be an agreement to sell specific or unascertained goods in which no property has yet passed, but in which the seller is under a personal obligation to deliver certain particular goods and no others. This is always the case where there is an agreement to sell specific goods, and it may also occur in a sale of unascertained goods when there has been sufficient appropriation to place the seller under an obligation to deliver those particular goods, although there has not been sufficient appropriation to pass the property. This may happen, for example, in a c.i.f. contract when the seller gives notice of appropriation, or in a contract for the manufacture of an article where the personal obligation to deliver the goods may come into being before the property passes.[3] In these cases, the law does not need to confer a power of resale on the seller because he still has the property in the goods and can, simply by virtue of this property, transfer a good title to another buyer. But it does not follow that the seller does not need statutory protection from the consequences of exercising this power. For example, if the buyer defaults in payment of the price on the date agreed, the seller, being still the owner of the goods, has power to resell them (and the incidental powers of retaining them, or recovering them from a carrier), but the exercise of these powers might be a breach of contract. The law, therefore, protects the seller from the consequences of availing himself of these powers, subject to certain conditions.

Fourthly, there may be an agreement to sell unascertained goods in which no property has yet passed and in which there is no obligation to deliver any particular goods. Here no special provisions are needed at all, because the seller clearly has full power to exercise any control over the goods, and such exercise cannot be a breach of contract. For example, if a seller agrees to sell 1,000 tonnes of a certain type of wheat and procures wheat of that description intending to deliver it in performance of the contract, no property passes before appropriation, nor is the seller bound to deliver that particular 1,000 tonnes. If, therefore, the seller resells this 1,000 tonnes to a third party, he can pass a good title to this party, and his action will not be a breach of contract with the first buyer.

It must be said that the Act fails to draw clearly all the above distinctions, with the natural consequence that confusion results. One does not have to agree with all the conclusions of Hohfeld[4] to acknowledge that there is a world of difference between a power and a right of resale, yet even this clear distinction is obscured by the ambiguity of such phrases as 'the seller has the right to do such and such', or 'the seller may do such and such'.[5] An examination of s. 39, which confers the three real rights of the unpaid seller, illustrates some of these problems:

---

3 *Laidler* v *Burlinson* (1837) 2 M & W 602, 610–11 per Parke B; *Wait* v *Baker* (1848) 2 Ex 19, 8–9.
4 See *Fundamental Legal Conceptions as Applied in Judicial Reasoning*, ed. Cook, Yale University Press, 1923, Ch. 1.
5 Cf. ss. 39, 41 and 48.

(1) Subject to this and any other Act, notwithstanding that the property in the goods may have passed to the buyer, the unpaid seller of goods, as such, has by implication of law—
  (a) a lien on the goods or right to retain them for the price while he is in possession of them;
  (b) in case of the insolvency of the buyer, a right of stopping the goods in transit after he has parted with the possession of them;
  (c) a right of resale as limited by this Act.
(2) Where the property in goods has not passed to the buyer, the unpaid seller has (in addition to his other remedies) a right of withholding delivery similar to and co-extensive with his rights of lien and stoppage in transit where the property has passed to the buyer.

The first subsection is not likely to give much difficulty, although it is not so clearly drafted as it might have been. It is clear that its object is to confer on the seller not merely the power to deal with the goods, but also the right so to do as against the buyer. This section is for the benefit of the seller and not of the third party, so that a power without a corresponding right would have been useless in this respect. But the second subsection is not so innocuous and could give rise to trouble. The draftsman seems to have thought it necessary to put in the right of withholding delivery, but not the power of resale, because the seller who is still owner does not need a power of resale. But this appears to be a confusion of the right and the power. If s. 39(2) only means to lay down certain powers, then it is totally unnecessary because the owner of the goods has the power of withholding delivery no less than the power of passing a good title to a third person. On the other hand, if s. 39(2) is meant to confer a right to exercise the power, as one would have thought, it follows that the right to resell the goods should have been included as well. The omission of this right might have the remarkable result that an unpaid seller could, as against the buyer, resell the goods in accordance with the Act where the property had passed to the buyer, but could not do so where the property had not passed. But whatever the literal construction of these provisions may be, the courts have shown no inclination to be too literal-minded. On the contrary, it has been affirmed that the seller's rights of resale cannot be greater where the property has passed to the buyer than where it has not.[6]

The second apparent flaw in s. 39(2) is that it states that the owner-seller's right of withholding delivery is similar to and coextensive with the rights of lien and stoppage in transit where the property has passed. This fails to differentiate those cases where the seller is under a personal duty to deliver a particular lot of goods and those cases where there is no such duty. In the latter event, the seller's right of withholding delivery is by no means coextensive with his right of lien. It is a far wider right, because it arises without default on the part of the buyer. Obviously, where the seller's duty has not yet become attached to any particular goods, there can be no question of a breach of contract by him simply because he chooses to withhold delivery of some goods which he had intended to use in performance of the contract. It is inconceivable that this section should, by a side wind as it were, alter these fundamentals in the law of sale. In proceeding to examine the three real rights of the unpaid seller, then, it must be borne in mind that we are only

---

6 *R V Ward Ltd v Bignall* [1967] 1 QB 534, 545.

concerned with the second and third fact situations put above. In other words, we are concerned with those cases where, but for these special rights, the seller would have a power but no right to deal with the goods by withholding delivery or reselling, and those cases where the seller would have neither the power nor the right to do so.

Who is an unpaid seller?

These three real rights may only be exercised by an unpaid seller, and the first question is, who exactly is an unpaid seller within the meaning of the Act? The meaning of 'unpaid' is explained by s. 38(1) as follows:

> (1) The seller of goods is an unpaid seller within the meaning of this Act—
>   (a) when the whole of the price has not been paid or tendered;
>   (b) when a bill of exchange or other negotiable instrument has been received as conditional payment, and the condition on which it was received has not been fulfilled by reason of the dishonour of the instrument or otherwise.

The seller is therefore 'unpaid' within the meaning of the Act even though he has sold on credit, and he remains unpaid until the whole price has been paid or tendered.[7]

The meaning of a 'seller', for present purposes, is explained by s. 38(2) as follows:

> In this Part of this Act 'seller' includes any person who is in the position of a seller, as, for instance, an agent of the seller to whom the bill of lading has been indorsed, or a consignor or agent who has himself paid (or is directly responsible for) the price.

If, for example, the seller sells the goods through an agent and the agent has himself paid the price to the seller, or made himself liable to pay it, then the agent is entitled to exercise any of the rights of the unpaid seller.[8] A buyer who has rejected goods is not, however, in the position of a seller within the meaning of this section and cannot claim any of the unpaid seller's rights in order to secure repayment of the price.[9] It follows that a buyer who is minded to reject goods on the ground that they do not conform to the contract should, if he has paid the price, be careful to do so only if he is satisfied of the solvency of the seller. The rejection of the goods revests the property in the seller, so if he should prove insolvent the buyer will have worsened his position by the rejection.

We can now pass to examine in detail the three real rights conferred by the Act on the unpaid seller.

UNPAID SELLER'S LIEN

The seller's lien in ordinary contracts of sale of goods now depends entirely on the Sale of Goods Act, which is quite inconsistent with any suggestion that there may be any equitable lien differing from that provided for in the Act.[10]

---

7 See, e.g., *McDowall & Neilson's Trustee* v *Snowball Co* (1904) 7 F 35.
8 *Ireland* v *Livingston* (1872) LR 5 HL 395, 408; *Cassaboglou* v *Gibb* (1883) 11 QBD 797, 804.
9 *J L Lyons & Co Ltd* v *May & Baker Ltd* [1923] 1 KB 685.
10 *Transport & General Credit Corpn Ltd* v *Morgan* [1939] 2 All ER 17, 25 per Simonds J.

The seller's lien is a right to retain the goods until the whole of the price has been paid or tendered. It does not 'strictly speaking give to the seller any property in the goods subject to it'.[11] At common law, a lien does not confer a power of sale, but the unpaid seller has a statutory power and right of sale subject to certain conditions which will be examined in due course. In practice the lien is often exercised merely as a preliminary to a resale of the goods. The seller's right of lien is a qualification upon the duty to deliver the goods laid down by s. 27 and it only arises if three conditions are satisfied.

In the first place, the seller must be an unpaid seller as defined by s. 38. This section has already been set out and it is only necessary to emphasize here that the whole of the price must be paid or tendered before the buyer can claim to have discharged the lien. This raises important questions in connection with instalment contracts and it has been held that, generally speaking, the seller is entitled to exercise his lien over any part of the goods if any part of the price is outstanding. In other words, he is not confined to claiming a lien over those goods to which the unpaid part of the price may be attributed.[12] Reference should also be made here to s. 42, which is as follows:

> Where an unpaid seller has made part delivery of the goods he may exercise his lien . . . on the remainder, unless such part delivery has been made under such circumstances as to show an agreement to waive the lien . . .

Where, however, there is not one contract, but a number of separate contracts for goods to be separately paid for and delivered, it naturally follows that the seller cannot claim a lien over any part of the goods which have been paid for, merely because some others have not been paid for.[13] This would be a general lien, which may be conferred by express contractual terms, but the lien which the Act confers is only a special or particular lien. It does not follow, of course, from the mere fact that the goods are to be delivered and paid for in instalments that there is not still one contract only. On the contrary, the general rule is that a contract for the sale of goods by instalments is still one contract, and the lien may therefore be exercised over any part of the goods.[14]

In the second place, the seller is not entitled to a lien if the goods have been sold on credit. If a seller agrees to allow the buyer credit, this does not necessarily mean that he is prepared to deliver the goods before the price has been paid. It may only mean that the seller is not insisting on immediate payment to which he is prima facie entitled if he is ready and willing to deliver. Oddly enough, the Act appears to assume that an agreement as to credit necessarily means an agreement that the buyer shall be entitled to the goods before payment, because s. 41(1)(a) says:

> (1) Subject to this Act, the unpaid seller of goods who is in possession of them is entitled to retain possession of them until payment or tender of the price in the following cases, namely—
> (a) where the goods have been sold without any stipulation as to credit . . .

---

11 *Lord's Trustee* v *Great Eastern Rly* [1908] 2 KB 54, 63–4 per Fletcher-Moulton LJ, reversed [1909] AC 109 on grounds not affecting this dictum.
12 *Ex parte Chalmers* (1873) 8 Ch App 289; *Longbottom & Co Ltd* v *Bass Walker & Co Ltd* [1922] WN 245.
13 *Merchant Banking Co Ltd* v *Phoenix Bessemer Steel Co Ltd* (1877) 5 Ch D 205, 220.
14 *Ex parte Chalmers* (1873) 8 Ch App 289.

Read literally, this would mean that if a person buys goods and asks the seller for time to pay, which the seller grants, the buyer is forthwith, without more, entitled to demand delivery. Yet in granting credit, the seller may have meant no more than that he would not insist on immediate payment and, in this event, the court would no doubt give effect to the intention.

Although the seller, therefore, has generally no right of lien if he sells the goods on credit, there are two exceptions to this rule, for s. 41(1) proceeds to add two further cases where the lien may be claimed:

(b) where the goods have been sold on credit, but the term of credit has expired;
(c) where the buyer becomes insolvent.

The first of these exceptions clearly enables the seller to claim a lien on the goods where the buyer has not taken advantage of the sale on credit to take possession of the goods. But it also seems to confer a right of lien even where the seller acts wrongfully in refusing to allow the buyer delivery despite the agreement as to credit, although it may be that the buyer could recover damages for non-delivery in this event.

The second exception requires rather closer examination. This clause enables the seller to refuse delivery even where he has agreed to sell the goods on credit (and *a fortiori*, if he has not) if the buyer becomes insolvent. On the meaning of insolvency, reference should be made to s. 61(4):

A person is deemed to be insolvent within the meaning of this Act if he has either ceased to pay his debts in the ordinary course of business, or he cannot pay his debts as they become due, whether he has committed an act of bankruptcy[15] or not . . .

It is important to note that the mere fact that the buyer has become insolvent, or even that he has announced his insolvency, does not necessarily amount to a repudiation of the contract.[16] It is, therefore, open to the trustee in bankruptcy or to a sub-buyer to tender the amount due to the seller and claim delivery of the goods. But although the mere fact of insolvency is not therefore a repudiation of the contract, any clear indication by the buyer that he will not proceed with the contract may amount to a repudiation. 'If a person who has entered into a contract of this kind gives to the vendor before he has parted with the goods that which amounts in effect to this notice, "I have parted with all my property, and am unable to pay the price agreed upon", it is equivalent to a repudiation of the contract.'[17] This may be too rigidly stated. In modern cases the question whether a party is to be treated as having repudiated the contract has been said to depend upon whether the guilty party has made it quite plain that he will not[18] or cannot[19] perform his obligations.[20]

---

15 Acts of bankruptcy were abolished by the Insolvency Act 1985, and there is now only one ground for making a bankruptcy order.
16 *In re Phoenix Bessemer Steel Co Ltd* (1876) 4 Ch D 108; *Ex parte Chalmers* (1873) 8 Ch App 289.
17 *Ex parte Stapleton* (1879) 10 Ch D 586, 590 per Jessel MR.
18 See, e.g., *Woodar Investment Devpt Ltd* v *Wimpey Construction UK Ltd* [1980] 1 WLR 277.
19 *The Hazelmoor* [1980] 2 Lloyd's Rep 351.
20 And the usual burden of proof in civil cases requires the seller to establish the fact of the repudiation on the balance of probabilities – see *Alfred C Toepfer Int* v *Itex Italgrani Export* [1993] 1 Lloyd's Rep 361, which involved a seller's repudiation, but the point equally applies in relation to a buyer's repudiation.

In such a case, the seller can treat the contract as at an end and do as he pleases with the goods and, if he resells at a loss, he can claim in the bankruptcy for the remainder. For present purposes, the important point is that, even if the seller has sold the goods on credit, he can refuse to deliver them if the buyer becomes insolvent, except on payment of the whole price. He cannot be compelled to deliver up the goods and be relegated to his right to claim in the bankruptcy for the price.

The third essential requirement of the unpaid seller's right to a lien is that the seller must be in possession of the goods. The lien is the right of an 'unpaid seller of goods who is in possession of them . . . to retain possession of them'. It is not a right which enables the seller to regain a possession which has been given up.[21] Possession is always a difficult subject, perhaps largely because it has not always been appreciated that possession means different things in different branches of the law.[22] Indeed, it does not always seem to have the same meaning in the same branch of the law. In *Great Eastern Rly* v *Lord's Trustee*,[23] Lord Macnaghten expressly recognized that the seller's lien differs from other liens in certain respects. It seems highly probable, for example, that the degree of control necessary to retain a seller's lien differs from that necessary to retain an innkeeper's or repairer's lien. An innkeeper does not lose his lien although he permits the owner the most complete control over the goods, provided only that they are not taken out of the inn. A repairer may even retain his lien although he permits the owner to take the goods away for a limited purpose every day, provided they are returned at night.[24] It was, indeed, formerly thought that a seller likewise did not lose his lien if he merely delivered the goods to the buyer as his agent or bailee, but this is probably not so today, even if it ever was.[25] There is, however, no reason to doubt that some element of control over the goods by the buyer is not inconsistent with the seller's retention of his lien.

At common law, a seller was only entitled to his lien if he was still in possession in his capacity as seller, and he lost his right of lien if he only retained possession as agent or bailee of the buyer. But the law was altered by the 1893 Act; s. 41(2) of the present Act enacts that:

> The seller may exercise his lien . . . notwithstanding that he is in possession of the goods as agent, or bailee . . . for the buyer.

But if the seller agrees to hold the goods as agent or bailee, it may be held that he has waived his lien, the possibility of which is not excluded by this subsection.[26]

The seller's lien is twice said by the Act to be a lien for the price,[27] so presumably the seller is not entitled *as seller* to claim a lien for storage charges or the like. The decision of the House of Lords in *Somes* v *British Empire Shipping Co*[28] is usually

---

21 Scottish courts have held that where the seller retakes possession from the buyer, the former does not necessarily also regain the right of lien: *London Scottish Transport* v *Tyres (Scotland) Ltd* 1957 SLT (Sh Ct) 48; *Hostess Mobile Catering* v *Archibald Scott Ltd* 1981 SC 185.
22 This seems to have been recognized by the House of Lords: see *R* v *Warner* [1969] 2 AC 256.
23 [1909] AC 109, 115.
24 *Albermarle Supply Co* v *Hind & Co* [1923] 1 KB 307.
25 See *Tempest* v *Fitzgerald* (1820) 3 B & Ald 680. But this was a case of a buyer exercising some rights of dominion by permission of and under the supervision of the seller (exercising horse on seller's land).
26 See below, p. 458.
27 Section 39(1)(a) and s. 41(1).
28 (1860) 8 HLC 338.

cited as laying down that the seller has no lien for storage charges in any circumstances, but in fact the case only decided that the seller cannot claim a lien in respect
of storage charges which arise as a result of the seller's exercise of his lien for the
price. Indeed, the case also decides that the seller is not entitled to recover from the
buyer the cost or expenses incurred by the seller in maintaining his possession for his
sole benefit. But the case is not to be taken to decide that such costs or expenses can
never be recovered from the buyer where he does derive some benefit from them, and,
in particular, where they are incurred before the buyer demands possession, and
therefore before the seller is strictly exercising his lien.[29] However, it is not wholly
clear whether the seller has any lien on the goods for such additional costs or
expenses. If the goods are actually improved, or at least if they are saved from
damage by the expenditure incurred, it seems that in principle a lien could arise for
these expenses even though the lien conferred by the Act is confined to a lien for the
price. But the general principle is that a bailee cannot claim a lien (except by express
contract) unless he has in some way improved the goods, so that mere storage charges
would not, in any event, give rise to a lien.[30]

Loss of lien

The seller loses his lien in one of four ways. First, if the price is paid or tendered, the
seller ceases to be an unpaid seller and therefore loses his lien. But (apart from any
question of waiver to be considered shortly) he is entitled to retain possession until
payment or tender. If this is so it might seem that payment or tender is, strictly
speaking, a condition precedent to the buyer's right to claim delivery, but as we have
seen s. 28 expressly says that payment and delivery are concurrent conditions. It is
usually inferred from this that actual tender of the price is not necessary provided the
buyer is ready and willing to pay the price and there is judicial authority to the effect
that this at any rate is the limit of the seller's duty to deliver.[31] But if the buyer sues
for non-delivery without making tender it would usually be arguable that the seller
has waived the need for such a tender by making it quite plain that he is not going to
deliver the goods in any event.[32]

The remaining three ways in which the seller loses his lien are set out in s. 43 which
runs:

(1) The unpaid seller of goods loses his lien . . . in respect of them—
    (a) when he delivers the goods to a carrier or other bailee . . . for the purpose of trans-
        mission to the buyer without reserving the right of disposal of the goods;
    (b) when the buyer or his agent lawfully obtains possession of the goods;
    (c) by waiver of the lien . . .

We have already seen that for some purposes delivery to a carrier is deemed to be
delivery to the buyer,[33] but this section clearly differentiates between these two different possibilities and, as will be seen shortly, the seller's right of stoppage in transit

---

29 See *China Pacific SA v Food Corpn of India* [1981] AC 939, 962–3 per Lord Diplock.
30 See, e.g., *Re Southern Livestock Producers Ltd* [1963] 3 All ER 801.
31 *Levey & Co Ltd v Goldberg* [1922] 1 KB 688.
32 See *Peter Turnbull & Co Ltd v Mundas Trading Co Ltd* (1954) 90 CLR 235.
33 See above, p. 131.

depends on this very distinction. Although the seller loses his lien on delivery to the carrier, he may still have the right of stoppage in transit, but it is all the same important to decide when the goods pass into the possession of the carrier, because the extent of the right of lien differs from that of stoppage in transit. In particular, the seller can only stop the goods if the buyer is insolvent, whereas his right of lien only depends on the absence of a stipulation as to credit. It follows that the seller may well have a right of lien in circumstances in which he will have no right of stoppage once the goods have been delivered to the carrier.

The meaning of a right of disposal has already been discussed in considering s. 19[34] and, if it means the same thing here as it does in that section, it follows that a seller who takes a bill of lading in his own name will have a right of lien until he transfers the bill. It has, however, been argued that right of disposal means something different here, namely a right of disposal of the *possession*.[35] The point is a difficult one. On the one hand, it would be strange to find a different meaning attributed to the same phrase in a similar context in two parts of the same Act. On the other hand, by s. 39(1)(a) the seller only has a lien while he is in possession of the goods and delivery to a carrier normally means that the seller no longer has possession. Moreover, by s. 39(2) the seller's right to a lien is the same whether or not property has passed; but if the seller is held to 'reserve the right of disposal' within the meaning of s. 43 by taking a bill of lading in his own name, he will not lose his lien on shipment, but only when property passes. The answer to these difficulties probably lies in the principle that possession of a bill of lading (at least where it is in the name of the party in possession) confers possession of the goods. As a practical matter, it seems clear that shipping the goods will not normally deprive the seller of his lien if the goods are deliverable to him (or his order) under the bill of lading. In the absence of any contrary agreement, the seller may decline to transfer the bill of lading except against payment of the price.[36] This difficult point of interpretation has arisen largely because, since the Act of 1893 was passed, the practice of treating the shipping documents as conferring possession and property has become so much more widespread that it now seems inconsistent with commercial practice to treat shipment of the goods as a delivery to the buyer.

Since possession is essential to the maintenance of a lien, it naturally follows that when the buyer or his agent lawfully obtains possession of the goods the lien is lost. It is submitted that 'lawfully' here means 'with the consent of the seller', so that even if the goods are obtained in circumstances amounting to a criminal offence, provided that it is with the consent of the seller, the lien will be lost. It is only by such an interpretation that the section can be brought into harmony with s. 25(1) of the Sale of Goods Act and s. 9 of the Factors Act which, as we have seen, enable a buyer in possession with the consent of the seller to pass a good title to a third party. Although it may be a little odd to say that a possession obtained in circumstances amounting to

---

34 See above, pp. 424 and 340.

35 Schmitthoff, *The Sale of Goods*, 2nd edn, pp. 158–9.

36 If, by the bill of lading, the goods are deliverable to the buyer or his order, it would doubtless be more difficult for the seller to contend that he retained possession sufficient to maintain a lien, but the practice of demanding payment in exchange for the documents in international sales is so well established that, in the absence of a clear contrary intention, it would probably still be held that the seller could do this.

an offence may be 'lawfully' obtained, this interpretation seems more consonant with the rest of the Act and would probably be adopted.[37] But if the buyer obtains possession of the goods without the consent of the seller, the lien is not lost and, even if the property has passed to the buyer, it appears that he cannot pass a good title free from the lien to a third party.

It has already been suggested that the seller's lien cannot avail him as against third parties taking in good faith even if he delivers the goods to the buyer merely as his agent or bailee.[38] But it may be that in such a case the seller will retain his lien as against the buyer, a point which is only likely to assume practical importance in somewhat unusual circumstances.[39]

The fourth way in which the seller may lose his lien is by waiver. In a certain sense, delivery of the goods to the buyer on credit is but an instance of waiver of the lien, but the seller may waive his lien without giving up possession at all. If, for example, the seller should ask the buyer's permission to retain possession by way of temporary loan, he may be held to have waived his lien. Although s. 41(2) says that the seller may exercise his lien notwithstanding that he is in possession as the buyer's bailee or agent, the subsection does not say that the seller may exercise his lien notwithstanding that he has impliedly waived his lien. And, if the seller, having originally refused to sell on credit, were later to agree to the buyer taking possession before payment, this would presumably amount to a waiver of the lien and the seller would not be able to change his mind again and insist on the lien after all.[40] Moreover, if the seller wrongly deals with the goods in a manner inconsistent with the buyer's rights, he is held to have waived his lien and cannot therefore plead lack of payment or tender if sued by the buyer in conversion.[41]

Section 43(1)(c), dealing with waiver, is probably to be read subject to s. 41(1)(b) and (c), which confer a lien where the goods are sold on credit but the term of credit has expired, or where the buyer has become insolvent, since both these clauses contemplate a situation in which there is a waiver followed by later events causing the lien to revive. If, therefore, the seller originally refuses credit but later waives his lien, it is probable that the subsequent insolvency of the buyer will cause the lien to revive if the seller is still in possession of the goods. This, at any rate, was the position at common law.[42]

The seller's right of lien is not affected by any sub-sale or other disposition of the goods by the buyer unless he has assented thereto. The meaning of this has already been considered.[43] It must also be remembered that if the seller allows the buyer to

---

37 See, e.g., *Du Jardin v Beadman* [1952] 2 QB 712 (above, p. 388) which is inconsistent with any suggestion that the lien would bind a bona fide purchaser to whom the buyer disposes of the goods after having obtained possession by a criminal trick or fraud. This is also confirmed by the New Zealand decision in *Jeffcott v Andrews Motors Ltd* [1960] NZLR 721, holding that the bona fide purchaser is protected without deciding whether the lien survives or not. Although it may be argued that this does not preclude the possibility of the lien surviving as between seller and buyer in such circumstances, it is difficult to see how the seller could enforce the lien or what significance the survival of the lien could have. But it is, perhaps, arguable that if the lien does survive, a disposition by the buyer to a third party who takes with notice of the circumstances will not override the seller's lien.

38 See above, p. 407.

39 See n. 37.

40 Cf. *Bank of Africa v Salisbury Gold Mining Co Ltd* [1892] AC 281, 284 per Lord Watson.

41 *Jones v Tarleton* (1842) 9 M & W 675; *Mulliner v Florence* (1878) 3 QBD 484.

42 *Townley v Crump* (1835) 4 M & W 58.

43 See above, p. 373.

have possession of the documents of title, or of the goods themselves, a transfer of these to an innocent third party will defeat the right of lien.

A seller who has once lost his lien does not regain it merely because he obtains possession of the goods once more.[44] But a seller who exercises his right of stoppage in transit is in effect restored to his former position and regains his lien.

The exercise of the seller's right of lien does not of itself rescind the contract of sale. This naturally follows from the fact that failure by the buyer to pay the price at the agreed time is not a breach of condition which justifies the seller in repudiating the contract. This question will be more fully examined later.[45]

UNPAID SELLER'S RIGHT OF STOPPAGE IN TRANSIT

The seller's right of stoppage in transit is set out in s. 44:

> Subject to this Act, when the buyer of goods becomes insolvent, the unpaid seller who has parted with the possession of the goods has the right of stopping them in transit, that is to say, he may resume possession of the goods as long as they are in course of transit, and may retain them until payment or tender of the price.

It makes no difference whether or not the property has passed to the buyer.[46] Where the property has not passed the seller has, in virtue of his ownership, the power to stop the goods, and the Act makes the exercise of this power rightful as against the buyer; where the property has passed, the Act confers both the power and the right to stop.

The House of Lords introduced the doctrine of stoppage in transit into Scots common law in 1790, displacing the previous doctrine that a buyer who took delivery of goods within three days of stopping payment was presumed to have taken fraudulently, so that the seller could recover them against the buyer's trustee in sequestration.[47]

It has been said that 'the courts look with great favour on the right of stoppage in transit on account of its intrinsic justice',[48] and this is certainly borne out by judicial pronouncements.[49] It seems to accord with commercial morality that the seller should be treated as, in a sense, a secured creditor, looking to the goods as his security, until they have finally passed into the possession of the buyer. In modern times, the development of the system of payment against documents and, in particular, of payment by bankers' commercial credits has greatly reduced the importance of the right of stoppage.[50] Where the price is to be paid in this way, the seller has little to fear from the threat of the buyer's insolvency because the seller will retain the control of the goods through the documents of title until he is paid. The law relating to stoppage in

---

44 *Valpy v Gibson* (1847) 4 CB 837; *Pennington v Motor Reliance Works Ltd* [1923] 1 KB 127; *London Scottish Transport v Tyres (Scotland) Ltd* 1957 SLT (Sh Ct) 48; *Hostess Mobile Catering v Archibald Scott Ltd* 1981 SC 185.
45 See below, p. 465 *et seq*.
46 Section 39(2).
47 *Jaffrey v Allan, Stewart & Co* (1790) 3 Paton 191.
48 Chalmers, *The Sale of Goods*, 13th edn, p. 124. This passage was excised from later editions.
49 See, e.g., *Booth SS Co Ltd v Cargo Fleet Iron Co Ltd* [1916] 2 KB 570, 580.
50 See Ch. 24.

transit is therefore only important where the sale is on credit and there are virtually no modern cases on the subject, though the possibility of the right being needed must sometimes arise in the case of sales to buyers in other European Union countries, where sales on open account are quite usual.

When right of stoppage arises

Before the seller can exercise his right of stoppage in transit, three conditions must be satisfied. First, the seller must be an unpaid seller within the meaning of the Act. Secondly, the buyer must be insolvent, and, thirdly, the goods must be in course of transit. The first two of these have already been considered and it remains now to examine the meaning of the expression 'course of transit'. The decisions at common law on this subject were very numerous and in 1877 Jessel MR said: 'As to several of them there is great difficulty in reconciling them with principle; as to others, there is great difficulty in reconciling them with one another; and as to the whole, the law on this subject is in a very unsatisfactory state.'[51] Section 45 of the Act makes a determined and, on the whole, successful attempt to reduce this chaos to a number of definite rules.

The goods are in transit when they have passed out of the possession of the seller into the possession of a carrier,[52] but have not yet reached the possession of the buyer. Little difficulty is generally encountered with the question, 'When does the transit commence?', but one ambiguity must be cleared up. If the carrier is the seller's own agent no question of the right of stoppage arises at all, for the goods, while in the possession of such agent, are still sufficiently in the possession of the seller to enable him to exercise his lien and he need not invoke the less extensive right of stoppage. The right of stoppage only arises when the carrier is an independent contractor who holds possession of the goods on his own behalf, as carrier.[53]

It is now necessary to examine the question, 'When does the transit end?' In the first place, it must be clearly understood that, although s. 32(1) says that delivery to a carrier is prima facie deemed to be delivery to the buyer, this is only a constructive and not an actual delivery, and it is only an actual delivery which ends the right of stoppage.[54] If this were not so, of course, s. 32(1) would be inconsistent with the whole concept of stoppage in transit, because this right postulates delivery to a carrier, but not delivery to the buyer. This much is clear from s. 45(1):

> Goods are deemed to be in course of transit from the time when they are delivered to a carrier, or other bailee . . . for the purpose of transmission to the buyer, until the buyer, or his agent in that behalf, takes delivery of them from the carrier or other bailee . . .

---

51 *Merchant Banking Co Ltd* v *Phoenix Bessemer Steel Co Ltd* (1877) 5 Ch D 205, 220.
52 It has been held in New Zealand that the Post Office is not a carrier for this purpose and there is no right of stoppage over goods consigned by post: *Postmaster-General* v *W H Jones & Co (London) Ltd* [1957] NZLR 829. The effect of the Interception of Communications Act 1985 s. 1 is that an attempt by the seller to intercept the goods once they have come into the hands of the Post Office would be a criminal offence.
53 In *Badische Anilin un Soda Fabrik* v *Basle Chemical Works Bindschender* [1898] AC 200 discussed at p. 342 above it was held that the Post Office was the buyer's agent, but, having regard to the rule stated in the previous footnote, even if this view were correct, it is in the present context of academic interest only. The rule for private postal carriers is presumably the same as that for other carriers, namely that the right of stoppage will only be needed when the carrier is the buyer's agent.
54 *Ex parte Rosevear China Clay Co Ltd* (1879) 11 Ch D 560, 569.

Although, therefore, delivery to a carrier is not in itself delivery to the buyer for this purpose, there is no reason why the buyer should not be able to show that, in the particular circumstances of the case, the carrier was his agent and that, therefore, the transit was at an end, just as the seller can show that the carrier was his agent and that the transit had never started. This possibility is expressly recognized by s. 45(1) which refers to the buyer or 'his agent', and by s. 45(5) which says:

> When goods are delivered to a ship chartered by the buyer it is a question depending on the circumstances of the particular case, whether they are in the possession of the master as a carrier, or as agent to the buyer.

If the ship is owned by the buyer, clearly delivery of the goods to the master is a delivery to the buyer's agent which terminates the transit. Likewise, if the ship is demised to the buyer so as to vest complete control over the vessel in the buyer, the master is treated as being employed by the buyer, and then delivery to the ship is delivery to the buyer. But if the ship is merely chartered for a voyage or a fixed period, as is the usual case, the master remains the employee of the shipowner and does not become the agent of the buyer, so that delivery to the ship does not end the right of stoppage. If the seller is owner of the ship no question of the right of stoppage arises at all, of course, because the goods are still in the possession of the seller while on the ship.

The mere fact that the contract is for the sale of goods f.o.b. does not exclude the right of stoppage. Although the seller's duty in a contract f.o.b. may be complete when he has placed the goods on board, this does not mean that he is not still interested in them and that he cannot subsequently stop them if the buyer becomes insolvent.[55]

Similarly, the transit is not at an end merely because it is the buyer who gives the instructions for the dispatch of the goods for part or all of the voyage. 'Wherever it is part of the bargain between the vendor and the vendee that the transit shall last up to a certain time, the transit continues until that time has arrived.'[56] But if the buyer requests delivery to a certain place or person, the transit does not continue merely because the buyer intends ultimately to give, and does in fact give, fresh directions for the dispatch of the goods elsewhere. The law on this point was summed up by Brett LJ (as he then was) in *Bethell & Co Ltd* v *Clark & Co Ltd*:[57]

> Where the transit is a transit which has been caused either by the terms of the contract or by the directions of the purchaser to the vendor, the right of stoppage *in transitu* exists. But, if the goods are not in the hands of the carrier by reason either of the terms of the contract or of the directions of the purchaser to the vendor, but are *in transitu* afterwards in consequence of fresh directions given by the purchaser for a new transit, then such transit is no part of the original transit and the right to stop is gone. So also, if the purchaser gives orders that the goods shall be sent to a particular place, there to be kept till he gives fresh orders as to their destination to a new carrier, the original transit is at an end when they have reached that place.

It follows that, in the ordinary way, if the goods pass through successive stages of transit from one carrier to another in pursuance of the contract or of later directions

---

55 Ibid.
56 *Kendall* v *Marshall, Stevens & Co Ltd* (1883) 11 QBD 356, 369 per Bowen LJ.
57 (1888) 20 QBD 615, 617. Cf. *Lyons* v *Hoffnung* (1890) 15 App Cas 396.

given by the buyer to the seller, the transit continues and the seller retains his right to stop the goods until they reach their ultimate destination.[58] But if the buyer intercepts the goods at some stage in the course of the transit the right to stop is lost. Thus s. 45(2) says:

> If the buyer or his agent in that behalf obtains delivery of the goods before their arrival at the appointed destination, the transit is at an end.

Where, therefore, the seller of goods contracted to deliver them free of charge at the buyer's premises in London, but the carriers delivered the goods at dock warehouses in accordance with instructions from the buyer, it was held that there was no right to stop.[59]

The transit is normally brought to an end by actual delivery of the goods to the buyer, but the transit is also determined if the carrier in effect attorns to the buyer, or acknowledges to him on arrival at the destination that it holds the goods for the buyer, or if it wrongfully refuses to deliver to the buyer. Thus s. 45(3) and (6) say:

> (3) If, after the arrival of the goods at the appointed destination, the carrier or other bailee . . . acknowledges to the buyer, or his agent, that he holds the goods on his behalf and continues in possession of them as bailee . . . for the buyer, or his agent, the transit is at an end, and it is immaterial that a further destination for the goods may have been indicated by the buyer.
>
> (6) Where the carrier or other bailee . . . wrongfully refuses to deliver the goods to the buyer, or his agent in that behalf, the transit is deemed to be at an end.

Thus, where goods were sent by rail to a particular station, where the consignee signed a receipt, but did not take away the goods, the transit was held to have ended, making a subsequent stop notice too late.[60] If, however, the buyer rejects the goods the transit is not at an end, for s. 45(4) says:

> (4) If the goods are rejected by the buyer, and the carrier or other bailee . . . continues in possession of them, the transit is not deemed to be at an end, even if the seller has refused to receive them back.

It is not clear on the face of the Act whether subs. (4) is to be read subject to subs. (3) or vice versa. If the carrier informs the buyer that the goods have arrived and that it holds them on the buyer's behalf and, subsequently, the buyer inspects the goods and rejects them, does the transit continue or not? As the Act is doubtful, resort may be had to the decisions at common law, and these seem to show that in such a case the transit is not ended because the carrier's attornment (or acknowledgment) to the buyer only transfers the possession to the buyer on the assumption that the buyer assents thereto. Where he rejects the goods, the attornment[61] (or acknowledgment) has no effect and the right to stop continues.

As with the seller's lien, the right of stoppage may generally be exercised over part only of the goods where some other part has been delivered. Under s. 45(7):

---

58 *Reddall* v *Union Castle Mail SS Co* (1915) 84 LJKB 360.
59 *Plischke & Sohne GmbH* v *Allison Bros Ltd* [1936] 2 All ER 1009. Cf. *Valpy* v *Gibson* (1847) 4 CB 837; *Reddall* v *Union Castle Mail SS Co*, above, n. 58.
60 *Muir* v *Rankin* (1905) 13 SLT 60.
61 *Bolton* v *Lancs & Yorks Rly* (1866) LR 1 CP 431; cf. *Taylor* v *Great Eastern Rly* (1901) 17 TLR 394.

Where part delivery of the goods has been made to the buyer, or his agent in that behalf, the remainder of the goods may be stopped in transit, unless such part delivery has been made under such circumstances as to show an agreement to give up possession of the whole of the goods.[62]

It has been held in a Scots case that if the carrier ignores the stop notice and delivers to the buyer, the stoppage is defeated and the buyer's trustee in sequestration can claim the goods; however, the carrier is liable in damages to the seller.[63]

Transfer of the bill of lading

Somewhat surprisingly, the Act does not make it clear whether the transfer of the bill of lading to the buyer is by itself sufficient to terminate the seller's right of stoppage. The UCC (Art. 2-705(2)(d)) expressly provides that negotiation of any negotiable document of title to the buyer (which of course covers transfer of a bill of lading) terminates the right of stoppage. But it seems implicit in the Sale of Goods Act that mere transfer of the bill of lading to the buyer does not prevent the seller from stopping the goods in transit. Both s. 39(1) (which says that the seller's real rights exist even though property may have passed), and s. 47(2) (which postulates a transfer of the bill of lading to the buyer and further dealings with the bill by the buyer), seem to assume that the right may continue even after the bill is transferred to the buyer. Yet it is surprising that there are no modern cases on the subject, and it may be that in practice businessmen simply do not believe that they have the right to reclaim the goods from the carrier once they have transferred the bill of lading to a buyer even though he has bought on credit, and becomes insolvent before paying the price. Despite modern commercial practice, it must still sometimes happen that buyers buy on credit but become insolvent while the goods are at sea, and in this situation the right to stop could still be of practical importance.

But although the mere transfer of the bill of lading to the buyer may not defeat the right to stop the goods, the right may be lost by sub-dealings with the goods (or documents) by the buyer. Considerable difficulties have arisen here and it is essential to keep two points clearly distinct. The first question which arises is whether the sub-buyer or pledgee is entitled to possession of the goods free from the seller's right of stoppage, and the second question is whether, assuming the sub-buyer or pledgee to be so entitled, the seller can exercise his right of stoppage over the money paid by the sub-buyer in the event of a sale, or over the goods subject to the pledgee's rights in the event of a pledge. To take the latter possibility first, there can be no doubt that the seller can still exercise his right of stoppage, notwithstanding that the goods have been pledged, but, of course, he can only do so subject to the rights of the pledgee. In other words, the seller can claim the return of the goods from the carrier if he is prepared to pay off the pledgee. What is more, even if the pledgee obtains the goods in virtue of his pledge and sells them, the seller is entitled to claim that the balance of the price shall be paid directly to him and not to the insolvent buyer. This was decided by the House of Lords in *Kemp* v *Falk*[64] and the decision has been incorporated in s. 47(2)(b) of the Act, which says that, where the documents of title to goods which the seller

---

62 For an example see *Mechan* v *North-Eastern Railway* 1911 SC 1348.
63 Ibid.
64 (1882) 7 App Cas 573.

would otherwise be entitled to stop have been pledged, 'the unpaid seller's right of lien or stoppage in transit can only be exercised subject to the rights of the transferee'. It is true that this section is mainly concerned to give priority to the rights of the pledgee over those of the seller (hence the word 'only') but it seems necessarily to recognize that the right of stoppage may be exercised in these circumstances.

The problem is more difficult in the case of a sub-sale by the buyer. In *Ex parte Golding Davies & Co Ltd*,[65] A sold goods to B and B resold them to C before they were dispatched by A. The bill of lading was taken in C's name, but before it was transferred to C, B became insolvent. C not yet having paid the price, A claimed that he was entitled to intercept the money before it reached B, that is, in effect, A claimed the right of stoppage over the money. It was held by the Court of Appeal that A was entitled to do this.

In *Kemp v Falk*,[66] Lord Selborne clearly thought that *Ex parte Golding Davies & Co Ltd*[67] was wrongly decided, but the other members of the House in that case expressed no opinion on the point. *Ex parte Golding Davies & Co Ltd* is also not easy to reconcile with *Berndtson v Strang*.[68] In this case, the Chancery Court of Appeal held that where goods are damaged in transit, the unpaid seller has no right to the proceeds of an insurance policy covering the goods. His right of stoppage 'is a right to stop the goods in whatever state they are. If they arrive injured and damaged in bulk or quality the right to stop *in transitu* is so far impaired.'[69] Presumably, it follows that if the goods are entirely lost in transit the right to stop is similarly lost, yet there seems no difference in principle between such a case and a resale of the goods.[70] But even if *Ex parte Golding Davies & Co Ltd*[71] was rightly decided at common law, the question must still be answered whether it survives the Sale of Goods Act, and the answer to this, it is conceived, must be 'no'. Section 47(2)(a) says quite clearly that if the bill of lading is transferred by way of resale to a third party taking in good faith and for value, the unpaid seller's right of stoppage 'is defeated'. No mention is made of the possibility of transferring the right from the goods to the money. It should also be borne in mind that even if the above submissions are wrong, and *Ex parte Golding Davies & Co Ltd* does represent the modern law, yet there can be no shadow of a claim of stoppage when the purchase price from the sub-purchaser has actually been paid over to the insolvent buyer. This would be a blatant attempt to obtain full payment of a debt from an insolvent debtor and could not be permitted.

Position as between vendor and carrier

If a carrier, to whom a notice of stoppage has been sent, wrongly delivers the goods to the buyer, he is liable for conversion to the vendor, so it is of the utmost importance

---

65 (1880) 13 Ch D 628.
66 (1882) 7 App Cas 573, 577–8.
67 (1880) 13 Ch D 628.
68 (1868) 3 Ch App 588.
69 Per Lord Cairns at p. 591. But in most c.i.f. and many f.o.b. contracts, the policy would be taken out by the seller and he would therefore be able to claim the proceeds himself.
70 Presumably the result would be different if the damage or loss occurred after the seller had given notice of exercise of the right of stoppage.
71 (1880) 13 Ch D 628.

that the relationship between the carrier and the seller should be clearly defined. But the Act does no more than lay down the methods which the seller may adopt of exercising his right of stoppage, and imposes the burden of redelivery on the seller. Section 46 says:

(1) The unpaid seller may exercise his right of stoppage in transit either by taking actual possession of the goods, or by giving notice of his claim to the carrier or other bailee . . . in whose possession the goods are.
(2) The notice may be given either to the person in actual possession of the goods or to his principal.
(3) If given to the principal, the notice is ineffective unless given at such time and under such circumstances that the principal, by the exercise of reasonable diligence, may communicate it to his servant or agent in time to prevent a delivery to the buyer.
(4) When notice of stoppage in transit is given by the seller to the carrier, or other bailee . . . in possession of the goods, he must redeliver the goods to, or according to the directions of, the seller; and the expenses of such redelivery must be borne by the seller.

The carrier has a lien on the goods for the freight due, and this takes priority over the seller's right of stoppage. Hence the carrier can refuse to redeliver the goods to the seller unless the latter is first prepared to discharge the amount of the freight. But any general lien which the carrier may have by contract is postponed to the seller's right of stoppage unless the seller was a party to the contract which conferred this general lien.[72] A general lien, that is a right to retain the goods for other freights due upon other transactions, can only arise by express contract or from general usage, and such a lien, apart from contract, cannot affect the rights of the consignor.[73]

In some respects, the carrier's lien as against the unpaid seller is of a peculiar nature, because it confers on him the positive right of action to recover the amount of the freight. Moreover, an unpaid seller who stops the goods in transit is under a duty to give the carrier instructions as to the disposal or return of the goods and, if he fails to do so, the carrier is not responsible for the consequences.[74]

As is the case with the seller's lien, the exercise of the right of stoppage in transit does not of itself rescind the contract of sale. The exercise of the right to stop enables the seller to resume possession of the goods and to retain them until payment or tender of the price.[75] It follows that if the buyer's trustee in bankruptcy chooses to tender the whole price, the seller is bound to accept it and redispatch the goods to him, unless indeed there are grounds for inferring a repudiation of the contract by the buyer.

UNPAID SELLER'S RIGHT OF RESALE

It has already been pointed out that the seller's *power* of resale must be carefully distinguished from his *right* of resale. The seller has the power to resell the goods (a) if he still has the property in the goods, or (b) if, even though the property has passed, he is in possession of the goods within s. 24 of the Sale of Goods Act or s. 8 of the Factors Act, or

---

72 See *US Steel Products Co Ltd* v *Great Western Rly* [1916] 1 AC 189.
73 Ibid.
74 *Booth SS Co Ltd* v *Cargo Fleet Iron Co Ltd* [1916] 2 KB 570.
75 Section 44.

(c) if, even though the property has passed, the seller has exercised his right of lien or stoppage in transit. The first case does not call for comment, and the second has already been fully discussed, but the third needs to be briefly considered. Section 48(2) says:

> Where an unpaid seller who has exercised his right of lien . . . or stoppage in transit re-sells the goods, the buyer acquires a good title to them as against the original buyer.

This presumably means that, even though the property has passed to the first buyer, if the seller exercises his right of lien or stoppage, he has the power to resell the goods passing a good title to a third party although he could not have done so under s. 24 of the Sale of Goods Act and s. 8 of the Factors Act. In other words, this subsection envisages the possibility of a resale by a seller not in possession of the goods, and is to that extent wider than these two sections.

It is now necessary to examine the seller's right of resale. The seller is entitled as against the buyer to resell the goods in any of the following circumstances:

1   If the seller's obligation to deliver has not yet crystallized into an obligation to deliver any specific goods. Here it is clear that the seller incurs no liability if he resells the goods for the simple reason that it cannot be said which are 'the goods' which he must deliver.

2   If the buyer repudiates the contract, it is again clear on principle that the seller can accept the repudiation and may resell the goods if he chooses.[76] It is, of course, immaterial whether or not the property has passed to the first buyer. Refusal to accept the goods by the buyer is prima facie a repudiation of the contract, and if the seller accepts that repudiation, the contract is thereby rescinded, any title which has passed to the buyer will revest in the seller, and the seller may resell the goods and sue for damages for non-acceptance. If, however, the seller refuses to accept the repudiation, then prima facie he is not entitled to resell the goods. This is because either the property will have passed to the buyer or the seller will still be bound to transfer it to the buyer. In this situation, the seller can only resell if authorized to do so by s. 48(3) or (4), which are discussed below.[77] As we have seen the mere fact that the buyer is late in paying the price is not necessarily a repudiation of the contract, but may only amount to a breach of warranty for which the seller may recover damages, so late payment of itself does not justify a resale by the seller unless s. 48(3) or (4) is satisfied, except in cases where time of payment is of the essence.

3   In the third place, the seller has a right of resale if he has expressly reserved this right in the original contract, on default by the buyer. In this event, s. 48(4) comes into play:

> Where the seller expressly reserves the right of re-sale in case the buyer should make default, and on the buyer making default re-sells the goods, the original contract of sale is rescinded, but without prejudice to any claim the seller may have for damages.

As we have seen, s. 48(1) states that:

> Subject to this section, a contract of sale is not rescinded by the mere exercise by an unpaid seller of his right of lien . . . or stoppage in transit.

---

76 See, e.g., *Compagnie de Renflouement v W Seymour Plant Sales* [1981] 2 Lloyd's Rep 466, 482.
77 *R V Ward Ltd v Bignall* [1967] 1 QB 534 – see below, p. 467.

4   Lastly, the unpaid seller is given a right of resale if the buyer fails to pay the price, and the goods are perishable or, in other cases, if he gives notice to the buyer that he intends to resell, and the buyer still does not pay the price due. Section 48(3) states that:

> Where the goods are of a perishable nature, or where the unpaid seller gives notice to the buyer of his intention to re-sell, and the buyer does not within a reasonable time pay or tender the price, the unpaid seller may re-sell the goods and recover from the original buyer damages for any loss occasioned by his breach of contract.

The first of these four possibilities has already been discussed and the second does not need enlarging upon here. The question what exactly amounts to a repudiation of the contract is never an easy one, but it is a question which belongs more properly to the general law of contract. It is enough here to say that the party claiming that the contract has been repudiated must show that the other party has made it quite plain that he will not[78] or cannot[79] perform his obligations. The third and fourth cases, however, require further consideration.

Resale under s. 48(3) or (4)

It will be noted that s. 48(4) explicitly provides that, where the seller resells in the exercise of an express power of resale in the contract, then 'the original contract of sale is rescinded'. Section 48(3) contains no such provision to cover the case where the goods are perishable or where the seller resells after notice. In *Gallagher* v *Shilcock*,[80] it was held by Finnemore J that this meant that a sale under s. 48(3) did not rescind the original contract of sale. Accordingly, if the property in the goods had already passed to the buyer, then the seller was reselling the buyer's goods and was acting as a quasi-pledgee rather than as an owner. Hence, the buyer remained liable for the price (subject to credit for the resale price) and would indeed have been entitled to claim any profit made if the resale were at a higher price.

This decision was unsatisfactory in many ways and it was overruled by the Court of Appeal in *R V Ward Ltd* v *Bignall*.[81] In this case, the plaintiffs sold two used cars to the defendant, who almost at once repudiated the purchase and refused to pay or take delivery of the goods. The sellers at first wrote to the buyer insisting that the property in both cars had passed to him and that he was therefore liable for the price. But the sellers also gave notice that if the buyer did not pay the price within five days they would resell the cars. The buyer did not pay and the sellers only succeeded in reselling one car. They therefore sued for the price of the other plus their loss on the resale of first car. The court held that the sellers were not entitled to the price of the remaining car as the resale of the first had rescinded the original contract. Hence the buyer was only liable for damages for non-acceptance, assessed in the usual way as the difference between the contract price and the market price of the remaining car.

---

78   *Woodar Investments Ltd* v *Wimpey Construction UK Ltd* [1977] 1 WLR 277.
79   *The Hazelmoor* [1980] 2 Lloyd's Rep 351.
80   [1949] 2 KB 765.
81   [1967] 1 QB 534.

The court explained away the difference in the wording of s. 48(3) and (4) on somewhat ingenious grounds. Failure by the buyer to pay the price is not *per se* a breach which justifies repudiation, but, once the seller has given notice to the buyer to pay, time is made of the essence of the contract. Hence failure to pay now amounts to repudiation and the seller accepts this by reselling the goods. The resale therefore necessarily amounts to a rescission of the contract, property revests in the seller and the buyer is no longer liable for the price. If, however, the contract contains an express provision for resale, then such a resale (apart from s. 48(4)) would not necessarily amount to rescission. For in this event the resale would be an exercise of a contractual right and not an acceptance of repudiation by the buyer. Therefore, s. 48(4) expressly provides that resale is a rescission of the contract. Thus the reason for the contrast is not that s. 48(3) is intended to have a different result – in both cases the resale rescinds the original contract – but the express provision to this effect is not necessary in s. 48(3), while it was thought necessary in s. 48(4).

In order to avoid confusion, it must now be pointed out that the statutory use of the term 'rescission' in s. 48 is out of line with the modern usage adopted by the House of Lords in *Johnson* v *Agnew*.[82] In this case a sharp line was drawn for English law between *rescission* of a contract *ab initio* on grounds of contractual invalidity such as fraud or duress, and *termination* of the contract for breach. Only the former is strictly 'rescission' which has retrospective effect.[83] Termination for breach is not retrospective in operation, and leaves standing, not only claims for damages for the breach itself, but also claims which have already accrued due at the time the contract is terminated. Now clearly, a failure to pay the price, and a subsequent resale of the goods by the seller under s. 48(3) or (4), involve termination and not rescission in this terminology. The seller still has a claim for damages for breach of contract, and accrued claims may survive the termination. At the same time it must be pointed out that even termination must have some retrospective effects in a contract of sale of goods, a point which the House of Lords appear to have overlooked in *Johnson* v *Agnew*, and perhaps even more seriously in *Hyundai Heavy Industries Co Ltd* v *Papadopoulos*.[84] The termination of a contract of sale of goods almost always involves the restoration of the property in the goods from the buyer to the seller if the property has already passed, and to that extent a termination is just as retrospective as a rescission; similarly, if the property has not yet passed when the contract is terminated, the seller's duty to pass the property disappears, even though the duty existed before the contract was terminated.[85]

Who is entitled to profit on resale?

The decision in *R V Ward Ltd* v *Bignall*[86] means that when the unpaid seller resells the goods, either under s. 48(3) or (4), he sells on his own account, and not in the sort of quasi-pledgee capacity envisaged by Finnemore J in *Gallagher* v *Shilcock*.[87] This

---

82 [1980] AC 367.
83 Scots law continues to use the term 'rescission' to describe termination for breach.
84 [1980] 1 WLR 1129 – see below, p. 558.
85 For Scots law on this point, see MacQueen [1997] *Acta Juridica* 176, 192–8.
86 [1967] 1 QB 534.
87 [1949] 2 KB 765.

means that if the seller actually succeeds in reselling the goods at a higher price he will retain any profit thereby made. In the ordinary case, that seems a perfectly sensible result; indeed, the contrary result suggested in *Gallagher* v *Shilcock* is absurd. It would be outrageous if a buyer who has defaulted in his obligations was entitled to collect from the seller the additional profit earned by the seller's efforts in reselling the goods.

However, this result may be less absurd and outrageous in one particular type of case. Where the seller sells and delivers goods to the buyer under a 'reservation of title' clause, giving the buyer the right to deal with the goods in the ordinary course of business, but reserving the right to reclaim the goods if the buyer fails to pay or to meet other conditions, the contract clearly envisages the possibility that the seller may sometimes reclaim and then resell the goods. Even in this situation, if the seller first terminates the contract before reclaiming and reselling the goods, it seems clear that the buyer cannot claim any surplus profit made on the resale.[88]

But in *Clough Mill Ltd* v *Martin*[89] the Court of Appeal assumed that such a resale of the goods could take place without a rescission (or termination) of the contract, and that the seller would then have to account to the buyer for any surplus made by him on the resale. Unfortunately no reference was made in this case to s. 48(4) of the Act which prima facie at any rate suggests that this is incorrect, because the subsection appears to insist that in this situation the contract is rescinded. Possibly the analysis in *Clough Mill Ltd* v *Martin* could be supported by arguing that there is in this case an implied term which negatives s. 48(4) and enables the resale to take place without rescission of the original contract. Moreover, there might be good sense in this in the case where the seller reclaims and resells under a reservation of title clause, because the right of the seller to reclaim and resell the goods is very much in the nature of a mortgage or charge. So it is not unreasonable in this case that the first buyer should be entitled to claim the profit on the resale. It is no different, in substance, from the position which arises where the buyer of a house defaults, and the house is sold by the mortgagee: here also the buyer is entitled to any surplus gain made on the resale, even though he may have defaulted in payment of the very first instalment on the mortgage. Paradoxically, though, *Clough Mill Ltd* v *Martin* is the leading authority for saying that a reservation of title clause does not operate like a mortgage or charge, but is to be treated as a straightforward sale on special terms. There seems, in truth, to be an irreconcilable conflict at the root of this case, which is discussed further under the next heading.

Claim by seller in respect of payments due before rescission

Recently another difficult problem has also surfaced in connection with the effects of a resale. If the seller resells the goods can he still sue the buyer for any part of the price which was payable before the contract of sale was rescinded? If the seller resells at a loss, this question is not of great importance, because the seller is entitled to damages for the buyer's breach, and the damages should fully compensate him for his loss anyhow. But if the seller resells at a profit, or if he resells at a loss which is less than

---

88 See *Clough Mill Ltd* v *Martin* [1984] 3 All ER 982.
89 See n. 88.

the sum which should have been paid by the buyer before rescission, the question does assume practical importance. Indeed, the question recently arose in a difficult case[90] which requires further consideration, but is more conveniently dealt with at a later point.[91]

RESERVATION OF TITLE CLAUSES

Reservation of title clauses and real remedies

It has been noted in a number of places that there has in recent years been a growing practice of incorporating in contracts of sale 'reservation of title' clauses (sometimes called *Romalpa* clauses, after the first case upholding their utility[92]). Some of these clauses are of considerable complexity, and there are many different versions in use, but the essence of a reservation of title clause is to reserve the property in the goods to the seller until the price is paid in full, notwithstanding that the goods are delivered to the buyer. The purpose of such a clause is, of course, to confer upon the seller some degree of security against the insolvency of the buyer. Prima facie at least, if the buyer becomes insolvent before the price is fully paid, the seller will be able to reclaim possession of the goods. From a functional or commercial viewpoint, therefore, reservation of title clauses operate like a more extended version of the real rights of lien and stoppage in transit. The lien operates while the seller is still in possession, the right of stoppage after he has dispatched the goods but before they have arrived, and a reservation of title clause operates after the goods have actually been delivered to the buyer. But a reservation of title clause must be expressly imposed;[93] there is no implied real right to reclaim goods from the buyer once they have been delivered merely because the price has not been paid. In theory, such a right might exist even without express reservation if there are any grounds for arguing in some particular case that property has not passed on or before delivery; but it would be rare indeed that property does not pass at the latest on delivery, in the absence of some express provision to this effect. So it can be assumed for all practical purposes that a reservation of title clause must be expressly imposed if the seller is to retain any title after delivery.

This area of law has been examined in a number of jurisdictions recently, and proposals for reform along the lines of Art. 9 of the Uniform Commercial Code have been made.[94]

---

90 *Damon Cia Naviera* v *Hapag-Lloyd* [1985] 1 All ER 475.

91 See below, p. 556.

92 See *Aluminium Industrie* v *Romalpa Aluminium Ltd* [1976] 1 WLR 676. The power to reserve title derives from ss. 17 and 19 of the Sale of Goods Act – see pp. 320–1 and p. 339 *et seq*. above.

93 In contracts for the sale of specific goods the reservation of title clause generally *must* be contained in the contract of sale, because otherwise property in the goods will usually pass as provided by s. 18 r. 1. In the case of unascertained goods, however, s. 19(1) gives the power to impose a reservation in the terms of the appropriation of the goods to the contract – see Bradgate [1988] JBL 477.

94 See A. L. Diamond, *A Review of Security Interests in Property* (DTI 1989) HMSO; DTI Consultation Paper 'Security over Moveable Property in Scotland', November 1994. For a succinct overview of the Scottish authorities, see Reid, *The Law of Property in Scotland* (1996), para. 638. See also Law Reform Commission (Ireland) Report on Debt Collection (2), *Retention of Title*; Australian Law Reform Commission, *Personal Property Securities*, Discussion Paper 52 (August 1992); New Zealand Law Com. Report 8 (1989). For a useful summary of the current situation in New Zealand, see also Ahdar [1993] LMCLQ 382.

Resale of goods by buyer

In principle, there is nothing new about the possibility of the seller trying to reserve title after delivery, by way of security. Indeed, the hire-purchase contract is a familiar device to achieve the same effect, though the use of such contracts has largely been confined to consumer transactions. But modern reservation of title clauses are being widely used in commercial sales rather than consumer sales;[95] they also differ from hire-purchase contracts in that they usually relate to goods not designed for consumer use, and therefore not suitable for contracts of *hire*. For example, cases have involved aluminium foil sold to be manufactured into other goods, resin sold for the manufacture of chipboards, leather sold to be made into handbags, and so on. Furthermore, these modern clauses often permit or authorize the buyer to use the goods in the process of manufacture, and also to resell the goods in the course of business. Such clauses therefore differ from hire-purchase contracts under which the hirer is not entitled to resell the goods, and, if he does, cannot pass a title to them, except in the case of motor vehicles to which Part III of the Hire-Purchase Act 1964 applies.

A reservation of title clause will not usually restrict the buyer's right to resell the goods in the course of his business, because that is not the purpose behind the clause. So such clauses quite often expressly authorize the buyer to resell, though there may be restrictions on his right to resell on credit. And even in the absence of an express authority to resell, such an authority will often be readily implied from the very nature of the transaction as a whole.[96] In *Four Point Garage Ltd* v *Carter*[97] the sellers were motor dealers who supplied cars to a company under a reservation of title clause. This company was believed by the suppliers to be in the business of letting cars on hire, rather than reselling them, but it was nonetheless held that between two commercial concerns like this, a power of resale would readily be implied, and therefore a buyer in good faith from the company obtained a good title binding on the suppliers even though they had never been paid for the vehicle in question.

Even where the reservation of title clause does impose restrictions on the resale of the goods, they will not be of any avail against a purchaser without notice. As we have already seen, a buyer in possession of the goods has the power to pass a good title to a purchaser for value without notice under s. 25 of the Sale of Goods Act and s. 9 of the Factors Act,[98] and it has been stressed that a sub-buyer is not to be treated as having notice of restrictions on the power of sale contained in a *Romalpa* clause merely because he failed to make inquiry about the buyer's right to resell.[99] In commercial contexts, a buyer is not generally under any duty to inquire into the seller's right to sell the goods. Doubtless there may occasionally be special circumstances putting the buyer on inquiry, or he may have actual notice of a *Romalpa* type clause restricting the seller's power of resale, but in that event the buyer has only himself to blame if he buys without ensuring that the seller complies with the requirements of the *Romalpa* clause.

---

95 But they are also found in some consumer contracts, for example sales of domestic fuel oil.
96 See *Aluminium Industrie BV* v *Romalpa Ltd* [1976] 1 WLR 676.
97 [1985] 3 All ER 12.
98 See above, p. 399 *et seq.*
99 *Feuer Leather Corpn* v *Frank Johnstone* (1981) Com LR 251. See also *Forsythe International* v *Silver Shipping* [1994] 1 All ER 851, 867.

The situation where the buyer *resells* is covered by s. 25(1) of the Sale of Goods Act, and s. 2(1) of the Factors Act, but what is the situation where the buyer merely *agrees* to resell? This would be the situation where the buyer sold on to a sub-buyer who took possession under a reservation of title clause. Section 25(1) does not cover that situation, but s. 9 of the Factors Act applies, as we have seen,[100] where the goods are obtained under any '*agreement* [emphasis supplied] for sale, pledge or other disposition'. But the effect of that provision is that the delivery or transfer in favour of a bona fide purchaser has the same effect as if the person making the delivery or transfer were a mercantile agent in possession with the consent of the owner,[101] and s. 2(1) of the Factors Act, which deals with the powers of a mercantile agent in possession, only provides that any *sale* etc. by a mercantile agent in possession with the consent of the owner shall be as valid as if the mercantile agent were authorized by the owner. In *Re Highway Foods International Ltd*[102] it was held that in such a situation the original seller could claim title to the goods.[103] The sub-buyer would only acquire title on payment of the price to the buyer.

Claims to the goods themselves

In the most straightforward case, the reservation of title clause applies to specific goods which remain identifiable as the goods sold after they have been delivered to the buyer. This sort of clause is effective to reserve title to the seller under ss. 17(1) and 19(1) of the Act. The passing of property in the goods is conditional on the payment of the price, and there is nothing contrary to the law in the parties making a contract to that effect. Nor, as we shall see more fully below, does this case raise any problems as to the need for registration of the clause as a mortgage or charge (though this in reality is what is being created[104]). In law, the clause is not regarded as a mortgage or charge which might require registration, but simply as an ordinary contractual provision deferring the passing of the property until certain conditions have been complied with. The seller is doing no more than ss. 17(1) and 19(1) permit. A company can create a charge only on its own property, and if it never acquires property in the goods the subject of an agreement for sale, it cannot charge them. In short, the courts have chosen to look at form rather than substance.[105] Usually, these conditions are that the price must have been fully paid, but it is now common to enlarge the conditions by requiring that all outstanding indebtedness of the buyer to the seller should be discharged before the property can pass – the so-called 'all moneys' clause. Thus – assuming always that the goods sold retain their identity and are still in the possession of the buyer – the seller is able to reserve title in all the goods sold by him to the buyer until all the prices due are fully paid. So where a seller makes regular deliveries to the buyer under contracts containing such

---

100 See p. 406.
101 See ibid.
102 *The Times*, 1 November 1994.
103 The judge declined to follow the suggestion in *Benjamin on Sale*, 4th edn, §5–128 (now changed) that the sub-purchaser in such a case might be able to rely on the words of s. 9. See also p. 406.
104 See Ahdar [1993] LMCLQ 382, 382–3.
105 *Clough Mill Ltd* v *Martin* [1984] 3 All ER 982, 983 per Oliver LJ; and see *Armour* v *Thyssen Edelstahlwerke* [1991] 2 AC 339, 1990 SLT 891; *Accurist Watches Ltd* v *King* [1992] FSR 80.

a clause, the property in the very first delivery may be retained long after the buyer has paid the full price of that delivery, so long only as some part of the price of subsequent deliveries is not yet paid.[106] In *Armour* v *Thyssen Edelstahlwerke*,[107] the House of Lords whilst upholding an 'all moneys' clause did not answer, as the facts of the case did not give rise to the problem, what the situation would have been if the seller had used the clause as a basis for repossessing paid-for goods, as well as unpaid-for goods.[108] Arguably, in this situation the seller would be required to refund the price of the paid-for goods, on the ground of a total failure of consideration, so that the clause would be self-defeating. On the other hand, if the clause operated as a charge the seller would in principle be able to satisfy its debt without an obligation to refund the price of the paid-for goods.[109] In short, this would suggest that such clauses should be treated as charges.

Claims to the proceeds of resale

Thus far, matters are reasonably simple. Complications start when a seller attempts to draft the relevant clause so as to give him some security even after the goods have been resold. As already mentioned, reservation of title clauses are not designed to prevent the buyer reselling the goods in the ordinary course of his business: to do that would freeze the buyer's business and frustrate the whole point of buying the goods. But a reservation of title clause may attempt to transfer the seller's preferential rights from the goods themselves to the proceeds of sale received by the buyer. For example, the clause may provide that all moneys received by the buyer through disposal of the goods in question are to belong in equity to the seller and to be paid into a separate bank account which is to be held on trust for the seller.[110] In the *Romalpa* case itself, the plaintiffs had sold large quantities of aluminium foil to the defendants on the terms that property was to remain in the plaintiffs until full payment was made. The defendants got into financial difficulties and a receiver was appointed. He found some £50,000 worth of foil still in the possession of the defendants, and he received from sub-buyers a further £35,000 odd, representing the price of goods made out of the foil and sold to sub-buyers. There was no problem as to the £50,000. This represented the foil which still belonged to the plaintiffs, and it could not be disputed that it was their foil. But even the £35,000 was held to be claimable by the plaintiffs on the ground that the defendants had been mere bailees of the foil, which they had sold with the implied authority of the owners,[111] and for which they had therefore to account in equity. At first instance, Mocatta J held that no registrable charge arose and this question was not further discussed on appeal.

---

106 It is arguable in England and Wales that the effect of such clauses here is to give rise to a floating charge which requires registration under Companies Act 1985 s. 395.
107 [1991] 2 AC 339, 1990 SLT 891.
108 The previous point was not argued in *Armour* v *Thyssen*.
109 See Goodhart (1986) 47 MLR 96, 97–8. For a contrary view, see McCormack, *Reservation of Title* (1990), pp. 107–9; Mance [1992] LMCLQ 35.
110 In Scotland, clauses of this kind were generally held not to constitute effective trusts: see *Clark Taylor & Co Ltd v Quality Site Development (Edinburgh) Ltd* 1981 SC 111, *Emerald Stainless Steel Ltd v South Side Distribution Ltd* 1983 SLT 162, and *Deutz Engines Ltd v Terex Ltd* 1984 SLT 273.
111 See above, p. 385.

The result was in many respects extremely artificial, because the decision of the Court of Appeal involved the conclusion that all the money received by the defendants from resale of the goods had to be held on trust for the plaintiffs, including even the profit made by the defendants from making and reselling these goods. Had the plaintiffs strictly enforced their right to have this money paid into a separate bank account, therefore, none of it would have been available for use by the defendants (except to pay the plaintiffs). It is very unlikely that the parties actually contemplated that the money would be used in this way: clearly the plaintiffs did not want to interfere with the daily business activities of the defendants, they merely wanted to be able to step in when the defendants' financial position became precarious and then seize hold of whatever could be found. Furthermore, the equitable ownership of the proceeds of sale which the plaintiffs claimed and which the Court of Appeal upheld was also artificial. Obviously, if these proceeds had actually exceeded the sums due to the plaintiffs, nobody intended that the plaintiffs could keep the excess. This fact alone demonstrates that what was really involved here was a mortgage or charge, since the plaintiffs were only entitled to the proceeds of sale insofar as they were necessary to pay off what was due to them. But that conclusion would have involved recognition that the arrangement was registrable as the grant of a mortgage or charge under the Companies Act, the requirements of which are further discussed below; and yet this was not the outcome of the case, partly because the question was not even argued in the Court of Appeal.

The *Romalpa* case itself is therefore a somewhat unsatisfactory authority, and it is not surprising that some subsequent cases should have restricted the authority of that case. These restrictions have so far taken two forms. First, it has been stressed that in the *Romalpa* case it was conceded that the defendants were *bailees* of the aluminium foil, so that there was some justification for the argument that the resale of the goods by the buyer involved a sale of the *plaintiff's* goods, and could therefore give rise to a duty to account for the price, the proceeds belonging in equity to the sellers. But the usual relationship created by a contract of sale, even subject to a reservation of title clause, does not involve a bailment. The mere fact that the seller may in some circumstances be entitled to reclaim the goods does not make the transaction a bailment. The relationship between the parties is simply that of buyer and seller, and if the buyer is authorized to resell the goods, the normal implication is that he has no duty to account for the proceeds or to treat them in any particular way.[112]

Even if the relationship between the parties can be said to be, or to involve, a bailment, it does not follow that there is a fiduciary duty on the buyer which gives the seller the right to claim the proceeds of sale in equity. Not all bailees have such fiduciary obligations; whether such an obligation is to be imposed depends upon the implications to be made in the contract,[113] but prima facie at least, it seems that there will be no duty to account for the proceeds unless the contract imposes some obligations on the buyer

---

112 *E Pfeiffer Weinkellerei-Weinemkauf GmbH v Arbuthnot Factors Ltd* [1987] BCLC 522, esp. at 530; *Compaq Computers Ltd v Abercorn Group* [1993] BCLC 602. In *A M Bisley v Gore Engineering & Retail Sales* (1989) 2 NZ BLC 103, 595, Holland J decided that the contractual arrangements between the parties did not create a fiduciary relationship, but merely a debtor–creditor relationship.

113 *Hendy Lennox (Industrial Engines) Ltd v Grahame Puttick Ltd* [1984] 2 All ER 152; *Tatung (UK) Ltd v Galex Telesure Ltd* (1989) 5 BCLC 325; *Re Weldtech Equipment Ltd* [1991] BCLC 393.

to deal with them in a particular way,[114] or expressly confers equitable rights to the proceeds of sale on the original seller, as in the *Romalpa* case itself.

In this connection a claim by the seller runs into certain practical difficulties of proof, unless there are express clauses covering the proceeds of resale. If the seller argues that the buyer was under some implied duty to account for the proceeds in a particular way, he will be faced with the difficulty that it is unlikely that the parties intended the *whole* of the proceeds of sale to be dealt with in this way. Probably the parties expected the buyer to keep for himself the difference between the sale and the resale prices; but if the seller concedes that the buyer only had to account for a *part* of the proceeds of the resale, this militates against any suggestion of a fiduciary relationship in the first place. It more clearly points to a simple debtor–creditor relationship.

Another restriction on the effect of the *Romalpa* case has also become apparent where claims are made against the proceeds of sale. A bailment involves that there may be some circumstances in which the bailee is obliged to redeliver the very same goods to the bailor. So if it appears from the nature of the goods that there will never be any such redelivery, the transaction simply cannot be a bailment (no matter what the parties may have called it); it must be a sale, and any attempt by the seller to claim title over the proceeds of resale – even if otherwise valid between the parties – will be a charge or mortgage requiring registration. This point is dealt with again later.

Transferred claims to other goods

Reservation of title clauses frequently give the seller not only the right to treat the very goods sold as still belonging to him but also the right to claim any other goods as his property, where those other goods have been made with the goods sold.[115] So where yarn was sold to buyers for the purposes of being made into material, the seller's conditions of contract reserved the title in the yarn until the sellers were paid, but also declared that any material made out of the yarn should belong to the sellers until they were paid.[116] The problem here is that the seller will obtain the benefit of the value the buyer has added to the goods. In consequence, such a clause is arguably a charge registrable under the Companies Act (as to which see below). Difficulties can also arise where (as can easily happen) two or more sellers sell materials under similar (or perhaps different) reservation of title clauses, and the goods of all these sellers are ultimately incorporated in some new goods made by the buyers.[117] So far this particular sort of problem has not come before the courts,

---

114 *Re Andrabell Ltd* [1984] 3 All ER 407.
115 It would seem that in the absence of clear provision, retention of title clauses will be construed narrowly. So where live animals were supplied to an abattoir, the terms 'livestock' and 'goods' applied only to the live animals, not to their carcasses – *Chaigley Farms Ltd* v *Crawford Kaye & Grayshire Ltd (t/a Leylands)* [1996] BCC 957.
116 See *Clough Mill Ltd* v *Martin* [1984] 3 All ER 982.
117 The situation may be different where goods of two or more sellers are only co-mingled, and the co-mingled goods form a separate and identifiable bulk. In *Indian Oil Corp Ltd* v *Greenstone Shipping* [1988] QB 345 it was held that where oil was mixed with a quantity belonging to another party already in a ship's hold, the resulting mixture was held in common, and the innocent party was entitled to receive out the same quantity of goods which went in. In *Re Stapylton Fletcher* [1994] 1 WLR 1181 it was held that property in a number of cases of wine, separately stored for a group of customers, had passed as the goods were ascertained for the purposes of s.16, the customers owning as tenants in common. It would appear to follow from this that each seller of goods under a reservation of title clause would, in a similar situation, have an undivided share in the whole of the resulting product – see p. 343 *et seq.*

but several other difficulties have come to light from these extended reservation of title clauses.

In *Borden (UK) Ltd* v *Scottish Timber Products Ltd*,[118] plaintiffs sold resin to the defendants which the defendants (as the plaintiffs knew) used in the manufacture of chipboard. A simple reservation of title clause provided that the property in the resin was to remain in the sellers until they were fully paid. It was held by the Court of Appeal that the sellers could have no claims to the chipboard in which the resin was incorporated. The resin itself had ceased to exist as an independent commodity. Consequently, there was no property of the sellers which they could claim; no question arose of a charge under the Companies Act. The plaintiffs' claim failed at an earlier point, since there was no property on which they could even claim a charge.

The reservation of title clause in this case did not contain an extended provision declaring that any goods made with, or incorporating, the resin were also to be the property of the sellers, even in equity. It seems, however, that even such a clause is unlikely to save the seller where a significant change in the identity of the goods is contemplated by the parties. In *Re Peachdart Ltd*[119] sellers sold leather to a company who used it for the manufacture of handbags. The contract contained a reservation of title clause providing that (a) all unworked leather remained the property of the sellers until full payment, (b) the ownership of goods made out of the leather was to vest in the sellers, and (c) the sellers were to have the right to trace the proceeds of sale of the handbags. It was held that, despite the language of the parties, the intention must have been that the sellers should lose their exclusive ownership in each piece of the leather as soon as work on it was commenced by the buyers. The sellers' rights would therefore become, at that point, rights in the nature of a mortgage or charge, and this was therefore registrable, and, being unregistered, it was void.

It follows from the above that use of a reservation of title clause in a repair contract, which purports to give the repairer ownership of the article into which any parts he has supplied have been incorporated, is unlikely to achieve its object. In *Specialist Plant Services Ltd* v *Braithwaite Ltd*[120] it was held that a clause of this sort created a charge, which was void for non-registration. Where the goods become fixtures on installation, the seller's title is destroyed, because the principle *quicquid plantatur solo, solo cedit* applies.[121]

Charges registrable under the Companies Act

The prime purpose of a reservation of title clause, as we have now seen, is to protect the seller against the insolvency of the buyer. For practical or commercial purposes, it is equivalent to a mortgage or charge upon the goods. However, there are policy arguments against permitting a seller to have the benefit of such a mortgage or charge because its main effect is simply to give the seller priority over other creditors of the

---

118 [1981] Ch 25. See also the Irish case of *Fried Krupp Huttenwerke AG* v *Quitman Products* [1982] ILRM 551.
119 [1983] 3 All ER 204. See also *Modelboard Ltd* v *Outer Box Ltd* [1993] BCLC 623; *Ian Chisholm Textiles* v *Griffiths* [1994] BCLC 96; *Chaigley Farms Ltd* v *Crawford, Kaye & Grayshire Ltd* [1996] BCLC 96; but cf. the *Hendy Lennox* case, above, n. 113.
120 [1987] BCCL 1.
121 See *Air-Cool Installations* v *British Telecommunications* [1995] CLY 821.

buyer in the event of the buyer's insolvency, and the law does not generally permit one creditor to obtain preferential treatment in this way unless the prior charge or mortgage is publicized by some form of registration.

In order to prevent a creditor from obtaining priority in this way, therefore, there are a number of statutory provisions requiring the registration of transactions under which a person grants a mortgage or charge over property while retaining the possession of that property. Under the Bills of Sale Acts a person who sells goods and remains in possession, or grants a mortgage or charge over goods by way of security, may have to register the bill of sale under which the transaction is effected or evidenced. In practice, these provisions are today important because they are applied to companies by ss. 395 and 396 of the Companies Act 1985,[122] which requires particulars of a charge to be delivered to the Registrar of Companies.[123] This includes charges over goods.[124] So a frequent problem arising from *Romalpa* clauses is to know whether they should have been registered under these provisions.[125] If particulars of a charge have not been delivered to Companies House within 21 days of their creation,[126] it is void as against creditors or the liquidator of the company.[127] So even though the reservation of title clause may be effective as between the seller and the buyer, the clause will fail in its main purpose – that is to protect the seller against the risk of the buyer's insolvency – where it should have been registered but was not. Particulars of few of these clauses are actually likely to have been sent to Companies House, so once it is held that the seller's rights are registrable, the result is usually that the seller will fail to get the priority that he seeks as against a liquidator or other creditors of the buyers.

A reservation of title clause is clearly an attempt to evade the registration requirements of the Companies Act, because its commercial purpose is to grant the seller preferential treatment in the insolvency of the buyer. And any rational system of registration of charges clearly ought to cover reservation of title clauses, as is done for instance by Art. 9 of the Uniform Commercial Code, but so far this result has not been achieved here. The courts have themselves deprecated any suggestion that these clauses should be narrowly construed or be treated with reserve because they escape the registration requirements.[128] It has so far been insisted that the parties are

---

122 For registration of charges by Scottish companies, see Companies Act 1985 Part XII chapter II. Both English and Scottish provisions may be amended by the Companies Act 1989 s. 93 – the new provisions are not yet in force, and at the time of writing it looks improbable that they will be brought into force.

123 Under the definition provided by the Companies Act 1989 'charge' means any form of security interest (fixed or floating) over property other than an interest arising by operation of law – Companies Act 1985 s. 395(2) (as amended – but see n. 122 above).

124 Companies Act 1985 s. 396(1). Note that in Scotland fixed securities over corporeal moveables other than ships or aircraft do not require to be registered – Companies Act 1985 s. 410.

125 The amendments effected by the 1989 Act, if brought into force, do not appear to affect the principles established under the former Acts.

126 It is sufficient that particulars of such charges have been delivered to the Registrar – Companies Act 1985 s. 395(1). The practice of Companies House is not to register them.

127 Companies Act 1985 s. 395(1). The equivalent provision in the amendments to be effected by the 1989 Act is to be found in s. 399 – but see n. 126 above. The extent to which a charge particulars of which have not been delivered to Companies House is void against a *receiver* is problematic. Parris, *Retention of Title on the Sale of Goods*, Granada (1982), Ch. 6 argues that such charges are void only against liquidators and creditors. However, a receiver represents the appointing creditor, notwithstanding he is agent of the company in receivership. Moreover, this point has never been taken in any of the cases.

128 See *Clough Mill Ltd* v *Martin*, above, n. 116. But see *Chaigley Farms* at n. 119 above.

entirely free to make whatever contracts they wish on whatever terms they choose, and that there is nothing illegitimate about the result if they succeed in evading the requirements of registration. So also, there is now widespread international support for the simple recognition of reservation of title clauses without need for registration, and indeed the Council of Europe drafted a convention to give effect to such clauses,[129] but it fell into abeyance. Under the Directive on late payments in commercial transactions[130] between enterprises in the private sector, and between such enterprises and the public sector, member states are required to take appropriate steps to ensure that national legislation contains provisions according to which the seller can retain title to the goods sold until the buyer has made payment and be able to recover them until payment is made.[131]

But all this seems most unsatisfactory. Total freedom of contract is inappropriate where the whole purpose of the contract is to affect the rights of third parties who have no say in the contract.[132] And the proposal of the Council of Europe was a strange and unhappy result of the fact that – especially in times of recession – governments are under pressure from their exporters to take measures to help them secure priority over the creditors of importers, despite the fact that each country ought to be just as much concerned with the interests of its own national creditors as with the interests of its exporters. If the proposals noted above[133] were ever acted upon, it is almost certain that many forms of reservation of title clauses would become registrable.

However, for the present, the law does not generally require reservation of title clauses to be registered. The technical reason given for this, as we have seen, is that the effect of such a clause is simply to prevent the property from passing to the buyer in the first place. He is not in the position of a person who is owner of the goods, and thereafter grants a mortgage or charge over them.[134] The analysis of the situation made by the courts is thus highly formal – the terms of the contract are given full effect, whatever their underlying purpose may be. In this respect the decisions on these clauses are precisely in line with the law relating to hire-purchase contracts. There also the underlying commercial purpose of the transaction is ignored, and effect is given to the legal form in which the transaction has been cast.

But there are limits to this general approach. In *Re Bond Worth*,[135] sellers sold synthetic fibre to buyers who (as the sellers knew) bought it to spin into yarn together with other fibres, and make carpeting out of the resultant yarn. A retention of title clause provided that the sellers were to retain 'equitable and beneficial ownership' of the yarn, and in the proceeds of sale of goods made with the yarn. Slade J held that this was in substance an outright sale with a mortgage or charge back by

---

129 See Latham (1983) J Bus Law 81.
130 Directive 2000/35/EC, OJ 2000 L200/35, Art. 4 is implemented by SI 2002/1674, but these Regulations do not mention retention of title because it is already recognized by law. See for comment Milo (2003) 11 ERPL 379.
131 Under the Sale of Goods Act an unpaid seller merely has a lien on the goods – see p. 452 *et seq.*
132 See Bradgate [1987] Conv 434.
133 At n. 94.
134 See Goff LJ in *Clough Mill Ltd v Martin* [1984] 3 All ER 982, 986–9.
135 [1980] Ch 228.

the buyer.[136] This 'equitable and beneficial ownership' was plainly not intended to be full ownership, but only a security right, because the plain intention of the parties was that (a) the buyers could pay off the sellers at any time the balance of the price due, and thereupon the charge would come to an end, and (b) if the proceeds of resale exceeded the sums due to the sellers they would not have been entitled to the excess. As a result, the transaction was registrable under the Companies Act, and, in default of registration, it was void against the liquidator of the buyers.

There seem to be strong grounds for thinking that any reservation of title clause which gives rights over the proceeds of a sale or sales by the buyer must be vulnerable to this sort of reasoning.[137] Almost always, it would seem, such a clause must carry the two implications (a) and (b) regarded as critical by Slade J.

So also in *Clough Mill Ltd* v *Martin*[138] there was a reservation of title clause which covered the yarn sold to the buyers, and also any goods into which the yarn was incorporated. When the buyers went into receivership, the receiver argued that the goods incorporating the yarn sold under the clause were subject to a charge which was void for non-registration under the Companies Act. The Court of Appeal upheld this argument. There was no reason, they held, why the property in these new goods should not be transferred to the sellers if their contract was intended to achieve this result, and the bare fact that the goods had not existed before did not by itself show that this was a transfer by way of charge. But the court went on to say that if these goods were seized and resold by the sellers under the clause it could not have been the intention of the parties that the sellers would be entitled to retain the whole proceeds of sale. Because these goods had never been the sellers' property, and because there might even be additional claimants to the goods under other reservation of title clauses, it must be assumed that the sellers could only keep the sums due to themselves under their own sales, and would have to refund any surplus to the buyers. This meant that the transfer of property in these goods to the sellers must have been intended to operate by way of charge, and not absolutely.

In practice, however, it might have been thought that it would almost always be the case that the parties intend any surplus from the resale of the seized goods over and above the price still due to the seller to belong to the buyer. But while the Court of Appeal in the *Clough Mill* case agreed that this was so with regard to the goods made out of or incorporating the goods sold, they insisted that it was not the case with regard to these goods themselves. They held that a seizure and resale of the actual goods sold might give the buyer the right to claim the surplus proceeds without this showing that the goods were charged. If the seizure and resale of the goods were made under the terms of the contract, it was suggested, the contract could still

---

136 In reaching this conclusion, Slade J distinguished the Court of Appeal decision in *Re Connolly Bros (No. 2)* [1912] 2 Ch 25. That case, however, was followed by the House of Lords in *Abbey National Building Society* v *Cann* [1990] 1 All ER 1085 which overruled the competing line of authority including *Church of England BS* v *Piskor* [1954] 1 Ch 553. It has been argued that the effect of this is to overturn the 'sale with a mortgage back or charge' analysis – Hicks [1992] JBL 398; Gregory (1990) 106 LQR 550. On this argument, the buyer would merely acquire an equity of redemption, which would not be registrable under either s. 395 of the Companies Act 1985 or its possible successor, s. 398(1) of the Companies Act 1989. However, as Hicks admits, the courts appear to have a policy of striking down clauses which claim rights to new products, or the proceeds of sale.

137 See *Compaq Computers* v *Abercorn Group* [1993] BCLC 602; *Modelboard Ltd* v *Outer Box Ltd* [1993] BCLC 623.

138 See above, n. 116.

subsist, and so the resale would be subject to the buyer's rights. However, as we saw earlier,[139] this discussion was conducted without reference to s. 48 of the Act and the decision in *R V Ward Ltd v Bignall*[140] which appear to be inconsistent with this analysis. That section makes it clear that if the seller resells the goods, whether under the contract or not, the resale effects a rescission of the original contract. Hence – as decided in *R V Ward Ltd v Bignall* – the buyer cannot claim any surplus on the resale. The only way to avoid this conclusion appears to be to hold that s. 48 of the Act is in such cases excluded by a contrary intention, but the only ground for arguing that there is a contrary intention appears to be that the transaction is really not intended to be an outright sale but is intended to operate by way of mortgage or charge. Consequently, if the court in *Clough Mill Ltd* was correct in thinking that the buyer might under the contract in that case be entitled to reclaim the surplus on any resale of the goods by the seller, it would seem they must have been wrong to hold that the actual goods sold were not the subject of a charge.

Many of these more recent decisions represent some move away from the ill-considered *Romalpa case*, though *Armour v Thyssen* appears to reaffirm the central point of the *Romalpa* case on the effectiveness of a simple retention of title clause in relation to the goods supplied.[141] To summarize: a reservation of title clause is effective so far as the original goods are concerned so long as they retain their identity and remain in the possession of the buyer. Moreover, attempts to extend the seller's preferential rights (a) to other goods made with or incorporating the goods sold, or (b) to the proceeds of sale of the goods by the buyer, are at present highly vulnerable to attack in England as unregistered charges. But (on the present authorities) it appears to be possible to avoid the requirement of registration by a carefully worded clause which stresses that the 'buyer' is not really a buyer but a bailee, which insists that the bailee is only entitled to use the goods to manufacture other goods as a trustee, and on behalf of the seller, and which provides that the proceeds of sale of such goods (or the original goods) are to be held on trust in a separate bank account. Furthermore, it must be made clear that the intention of the parties is that the buyer is not to have any residuary right (in the nature of an equity of redemption) to the balance of the proceeds of sale after payment of the price of the goods (and other goods, supplied by the seller, if the clause so provides). So if the seller reclaims and resells the goods it must be made clear that there will be no liability to account to the buyer for any surplus over and above the price of the goods sold to the buyer under the contract. It is unlikely that many buyers would willingly agree to such a Draconian clause if they fully understood its implications; and a clause drafted in this form must raise major doubts as to whether the parties seriously intend it to operate according to its terms, or whether it is in truth a complete sham.

---

139 See above, p. 467 *et seq.*
140 [1967] 1 QB 534.
141 See also *Clough Mill Ltd v Martin* (n. 116 above).

26

PERSONAL REMEDIES

ACTION FOR THE PRICE

In addition to the real rights, the seller has, of course, his personal action upon the sale for breach of contract by the buyer. This action may take one of two forms. It may be an action for the price of the goods sold or it may be an action for damages for non-acceptance. The distinction between an action for the price and an action for damages is of considerable importance. In purely monetary terms there will usually be a substantial difference between the price of the goods and damages for non-acceptance. Moreover, if the property has passed to the buyer and the seller is entitled to sue for the price, he is under no obligation to mitigate his damage[1] by attempting to resell the goods or otherwise.[2] The goods now belong to the buyer and not the seller, and it is the buyer's responsibility to take delivery of the goods or otherwise dispose of them.

The general rule laid down in s. 49(1) and s. 50(1) is that an action for damages is the appropriate remedy where the property has not passed and an action for the price is available when the property has passed. This simple principle is unfortunately complicated by the fact that the property in the goods may pass to the buyer before they have been delivered to and accepted by him. Section 49(1) says:

> Where, under a contract of sale, the property in the goods has passed to the buyer, and the buyer wrongfully neglects or refuses to pay for the goods according to the terms of the contract, the seller may maintain an action against him for the price of the goods.

Section 50(1) says:

> Where the buyer wrongfully neglects or refuses to accept and pay for the goods, the seller may maintain an action against him for damages for non-acceptance.

It is, of course, obvious that the property in the goods may have passed to the buyer, *and* he may have neglected or refused to accept and pay for them because, as we have seen, property in the goods often passes before delivery. In such an event, it seems to follow that the seller has the option of suing for the price under s. 49(1) or for damages under s. 50(1). In other words, the seller has:

---

1 As to the normal duty to mitigate, see below, p. 487.
2 In this sense an action for the price of goods in which property has passed is an illustration of the principle laid down by the HL in *White & Carter (Councils) Ltd* v *McGregor* [1962] AC 413, 1962 SC (HL) 1 – see per Lord Keith at pp. 437 and 19–20 respectively.

1   an action for the price where the property has passed and the buyer has accepted the goods;
2   an action for damages where the property has not passed and the buyer refuses to accept the goods;
3   an action for the price, or for damages where the property has passed and the buyer refuses to accept the goods.

The fact that the property has not passed, owing to some wrongful act of the defendant, does not enable the seller to claim the price, unless the buyer is estopped by his conduct from disputing the fact that the property has passed. So, for instance, if the buyer fails to name an effective ship in a sale f.o.b., the seller's remedy is an action for damages, not for the price.[3] And if the buyer in a c.i.f. contract refuses to take up the shipping documents when tendered, the seller's remedy is once again an action for damages, not for the price.[4]

Price payable on a 'day certain'

There is one exceptional case in which the seller may sue for the price although the property has not passed, for under s. 49(2):

> Where, under a contract of sale, the price is payable on a day certain irrespective of delivery, and the buyer wrongfully neglects or refuses to pay such price, the seller may maintain an action for the price, although the property in the goods has not passed, and the goods have not been appropriated to the contract.

The important point to note about this subsection is that it concerns a case where the price is payable irrespective of delivery. If the price is due on some specified date after delivery, no great difficulty arises. Clearly, the seller can sue for the price as soon as the date arrives. But s. 49(2) also applies to cases where the price is due before delivery, and one can see why this is necessary. If the price is payable before delivery, and the buyer fails to pay, the seller cannot sue for damages for non-acceptance because the date for acceptance has not yet arrived. Indeed, the buyer may very well intend to accept the goods: but he has in the meantime defaulted in his obligation to pay. So the seller clearly needs to be able to sue for the price (or an instalment) due on some date before delivery.

The main difficulty in interpreting the subsection is the meaning of 'a day certain'. Does it mean a named, fixed date, or is it possible to invoke the maxim *certum est quod certum reddi potest*, so that the section could be applied to a contract which contains machinery for ascertaining the date when the price is to be paid without actually fixing any date? In *Workman Clark & Co Ltd* v *Lloyd Brazileno*,[5] it was held that the seller, who was constructing a ship for the buyer, was entitled to sue for the instalments as they became due, although the date on which they became due was ascertained by reference to the stage which had been reached in the construction of the vessel. The Court of Appeal decided both that s. 49(2) applies to instalments payable

---

3 *Colley* v *Overseas Exporters Ltd* [1921] 3 KB 302.
4 *Stein, Forbes & Co Ltd* v *County Tailoring Co Ltd* (1916) 86 LJKB 448.
5 [1908] 1 KB 968.

on a day certain, and that these instalments were payable on a day certain.[6] It does not follow that the price can be sued for whenever the date for payment can be ascertained because in many cases an action for damages would be the more appropriate remedy. But in this case there would have been no ground for an action for damages and the seller would have been left without any remedy if he could not sue for the price.

But although a seller may need to be able to sue for the price before delivery if the contract provides for advance payment, this is liable to leave open one serious problem: what happens if the goods are never delivered at all? Of course, if this is due to breach by the seller, the buyer will have his own remedy. But suppose the goods are not delivered because the seller treats the non-payment as a sufficient repudiation to justify him in terminating the whole contract, either as a matter of common law or under some specific clause in the contract?

In *Hyundai Heavy Industries Co Ltd* v *Papadopoulos*,[7] which was also a shipbuilding case in which the price was payable by instalments, it was held by the House of Lords that the buyer could be sued for an instalment which fell due on 15 July despite the fact that the seller exercised a contractual right of cancellation on 6 September, with the result that the buyer would have had[8] to pay the instalment even though he would not have received the goods. This holding has somewhat alarming implications which do not appear to have been wholly thought through by the House of Lords; for it would seem to follow from the decision that even if the entire price had been payable in advance, the seller could have both exercised his right of cancellation, so sparing him the necessity of delivering the ship at all, and still have sued for the price. The House seems to have been led to its decision by its desire to stick to the newly established distinction between a rescission of a contract *ab initio*, and a mere termination as a result of breach.

This distinction, which originated with the House's own decision in *Johnson* v *Agnew*,[9] was a great simplification of the law, but the decision concerned land law, and the relationship of a right to specific performance and a claim for damages for breach of a contract to sell land. In transferring this decision to the law of sale of goods, the House seems to have overlooked the fact that there are special features to a contract of sale of goods, which mean (for instance) that even a termination of such a contract has retrospective effect in certain respects.[10] They appear also to have overlooked the categorical pronouncement by Lord Wilberforce in *Johnson* v *Agnew* (with whom all the other Law Lords concurred) that:

> If the vendor treats the purchaser as having repudiated the contract and accepts the repudiation, he cannot thereafter seek specific performance. This follows from the fact that, the purchaser having repudiated the contract, and his repudiation having been accepted, both parties are discharged from further performance.[11]

---

6 On the meaning of 'day certain' see: *Shell Mex Ltd* v *Elton Cop Dyeing Co Ltd* (1928) 63 Comm Cas 29; *Henderson & Keay Ltd* v *AM Carmichael Ltd* 1956 SLT (Notes) 58; *Stein Forbes & Co* v *County Tailoring Co* (1916) 86 LJKB 448

7 [1980] 1 WLR 1129. See for Scottish perspectives on this case, *Lloyds Bank plc* v *Bamberger* 1993 SC 570 and MacQueen [1997] *Acta Juridica* 176, 194–5.

8 'Would have had', because in fact the case concerned the liability of guarantors, and not the buyers themselves; but one of the two grounds of decision clearly involved the holding that the buyers would have been liable if sued.

9 [1980] AC 367.

10 See above, p. 468.

11 [1980] AC 367, at 392.

Equally, it would seem to follow that the vendor cannot both claim to recover the entire purchase price, and at the same time insist that the whole contract is terminated because of the purchaser's breach. The problem is that the House seems to have been too formalistic in treating the various steps in a distinct chronological order in *Hyundai*: they seem to have thought that if the price (or instalment) is due before the contract is terminated, the obligation to pay the price or instalment cannot be affected by the subsequent termination of the contract. What this overlooks is the simple possibility that the duty to pay may be (and normally is) conditional on subsequent performance by the other party.[12]

There is little doubt that the *Hyundai* decision will return to haunt the courts because the potential injustice to which it may give rise is so gross, but for the present it is enough to note that the speeches in *Hyundai* contemplate that the decision may not apply to a *pure* contract of sale, as opposed to a contract for sale and manufacture. The reason for this distinction has been touched upon earlier: in a pure contract of sale, delivery of the goods is the whole consideration for the price, so it may well be inconsistent for the seller to claim the price and also the right to cancel or terminate. If the goods are never delivered in such a case there is a total failure of consideration, so the buyer cannot (it seems) be made to pay the price, or if he has paid it, must be entitled to recover it.[13] But where the contract involves manufacture as well as sale, the manufacture (and preliminary expenses of manufacture) may be part of the consideration, so the seller may not be acting inconsistently in first suing for instalments, and later cancelling the whole contract. Nevertheless, even this explanation is hardly satisfying given that it would extend to a situation in which substantially the entire price is payable in advance, and yet the seller may have incurred only minimal advance expenditure prior to cancellation.

Critique of present law

Obviously an action for the price is more favourable to the seller than a mere action for damages for non-acceptance. But where the goods have not been delivered, the law may in practice place the seller in a somewhat difficult situation. He may choose to take his stand on the argument that the property has passed to the buyer, disclaim all responsibility for the goods and sue for the price. But if he takes this course he runs the risk that the court may eventually decide that property had not passed to the buyer and that the seller's only remedy is for damages for non-acceptance. If the court takes this view, it follows that the seller will have been responsible for mitigating the damage by (for example) attempting to resell the goods. His failure to do so may then reduce the damages to which he would have been entitled. On the other hand, if the seller attempts to mitigate the loss by reselling the goods, or part of them, or by dealing with them in some way, a court may treat this as evidence of an acceptance by the seller of repudiation of the contract by the buyer. The result of this will be that even if the property had originally passed to the buyer it will now revest in the seller and

---

12 See Beatson (1981) 97 LQR 389.
13 See *Rover International Ltd* v *Cannon Film Sales* [1987] 1 WLR 1597, noted by Beatson (1989) 105 LQR 179.

an action for the price will no longer lie. If, therefore, the seller's efforts to resell the goods have failed, he will have made his own position worse by attempting to dispose of them.[14] And if his efforts to resell succeed, he may make his position worse in another respect. For by reselling these goods he may have lost an alternative sale and (at least in the case of second-hand goods) this will not be a recoverable item of damages.[15]

These difficulties largely stem from the fact that the seller is entitled to sue for the price of the goods where the property has passed but the buyer has refused to take delivery. It is doubtful whether in modern times this is the most sensible approach to the issues which arise. The most important practical problem in this situation is this: whose responsibility is it to resell or otherwise dispose of the goods and to hold them pending resale? If this responsibility should be the buyer's, then an action for the price is appropriate, but if it should rest on the seller, an action for damages for non-acceptance would be more appropriate. Which of the parties should bear this responsibility cannot, it is suggested, be answered simply by asking if the property has passed but should depend on a balance of convenience. For instance, if the seller is a dealer and the buyer is a private consumer (as has happened in several cases concerning the sale of motor vehicles) it seems more sensible that the seller should have the responsibility of reselling the goods, and should be confined to an action for damages. Conversely, there are situations – especially in export sales – where the responsibility for taking possession of the goods and trying to resell them should be on the buyer despite the fact that property has not passed. For instance, if the buyer refuses to accept shipping documents properly tendered in an f.o.b. or c.i.f. sale, it would be extremely inconvenient for the seller to make arrangements to land, store and dispose of the goods at the place of destination. In this case, it would seem more reasonable if the seller could sue for the price and leave the buyer with the responsibility of dealing with the goods. In practice if the price is payable by a banker's credit, the seller will probably be able to sue the bank if the documents are wrongly rejected, but there are some situations in which the seller should also have an action against the buyer for the price.

In this connection, it is interesting to note the provisions of Art. 2-709 of the Uniform Commercial Code which seem a considerable improvement on those of the Sale of Goods Act. Under Art. 2-709(1) the seller can sue for the price if the buyer has accepted the goods, or if the goods have been identified to the contract and 'the seller is unable after reasonable effort to resell them at a reasonable price, or the circumstances reasonably indicate that such effort will be unavailing'. Thus if the buyer refuses to take delivery of the goods, the seller is in the first instance obliged to try to resell the goods unless it is clear that this will be unavailing. The mere fact that property has passed, therefore, does not entitle the seller to sue for the price. Conversely, once the seller has made reasonable efforts to resell and these have proved unavailing he may sue for the price even though property has not passed. Moreover, once the seller is entitled to sue for the price under Art. 2-709(1), Art. 2-709(2) enables the seller to resell at any time prior to judgment if such resale becomes

---

14 See, e.g., *R V Ward Ltd* v *Bignall* [1967] 1 QB 534.
15 See *Lazenby Garages Ltd* v *Wright* [1976] 1 WLR 459, below, p. 495.

possible, without thereby forfeiting his right to sue for the price. He must, of course, give credit for the proceeds of the resale, but his claim will then be for the contract price less the resale price and does not become converted into an action for damages as it does under English law.

Claims for special damage

In addition to the seller's right to sue for the price, or for damages for non-acceptance, he may also have the right to claim special damages under s. 54 and the right to claim for any loss occasioned by the buyer's neglect to take delivery. In both cases, it seems immaterial whether or not the property has passed. A claim by a seller for special damages is likely to arise but rarely in practice,[16] and the principles governing such a claim may be more suitably dealt with when we come to examine the remedies of the buyer. A word needs to be said, however, on the possibility of a claim for loss occasioned by the buyer's failure to take delivery. Section 37 lays down:

(1) When the seller is ready and willing to deliver the goods, and requests the buyer to take delivery, and the buyer does not within a reasonable time after such request take delivery of the goods, he is liable to the seller for any loss occasioned by his neglect or refusal to take delivery, and also for a reasonable charge for the care and custody of the goods.

(2) Nothing in this section affects the rights of the seller when the neglect or refusal of the buyer to take delivery amounts to a repudiation of the contract.

Where, therefore, the property in the goods has passed to the buyer and he neglects to take delivery, the seller may either sue for damages or for the price and, in the latter case, he can add a claim under s. 37 for damages to cover the cost of care and custody, and any further loss he may have suffered, for example if the goods have gone bad and tainted other goods not sold to the buyer. If he sues for damages only, his claim will cover these items as a matter of course.

Price payable in foreign currency

Where the price is due in a foreign currency, but the action is brought in England and Wales, judgment can now be given in the foreign currency itself.[17] This is also the Scottish position.[18] There is, therefore, no need to convert the amount due into sterling, unless and until it becomes necessary to seek leave to enforce the judgment, when the conversion will be made at the rate of exchange prevailing at that date.[19] It is not yet clear whether the buyer can take advantage of these new rules, and demand that judgment be given in a foreign currency where that currency has depreciated against sterling.

---

16 For one example, see *Penarth Dock Engineering Co Ltd v Pounds* [1963] 1 Lloyd's Rep 359.
17 *Miliangos v George Frank (Textiles) Ltd* [1976] AC 443.
18 *Commerzbank Aktiengesellschaft v Large* 1977 SC 375.
19 *Miliangos v George Frank (Textiles) Ltd*, above n. 17. See *Practice Direction (Judgment: Foreign Currency)* [1976] 1 All ER 669; CPR 1998 Sch. 1, RSC Ord. 71 r. 3.

ACTION FOR DAMAGES[20]

We have already seen that the seller's only remedy where the property has not passed is an action for damages for non-acceptance, and that such an action is an alternative remedy where the property has passed but the buyer neglects to take delivery. It now becomes necessary to examine the principles on which these damages are calculable, leaving aside for the moment the question of special damages.

It may be convenient, first of all, to recall the general principle of contract law that the innocent party is bound to take reasonable steps to mitigate the damage. This principle applies to contracts of sale of goods as it applies to other contracts, and it applies equally whether the innocent party is buyer or seller. There is no need in a book of this nature to examine this principle at length, but it is mentioned here because the idea behind it underlies many of the detailed rules relating to damages in the law of sale of goods.

Moreover, in practice, breach of contract usually leads to some attempt at negotiating a settlement or finding some alternative way of performing the contract. Thus a seller who cannot supply the goods contracted for may offer alternatives, or may offer late delivery.[21] A seller who has broken an agreement to supply on credit may offer instead to sell for cash.[22] Generally speaking, at least in commercial contracts, reasonable offers of this kind should be accepted by the innocent party or he may be penalized in damages.

A second general principle of contract law is also worth noting at this point. In general, where a party has contracted for possible alternative performances, his liability is only to be assessed according to the least onerous or costly of those performances. For instance, in a contract for the sale of 5,000 tonnes, 5 per cent more or less at seller's option, the seller can only be liable for failing to deliver 4,750 tonnes; conversely, if the buyer has the option of choosing whether to take a larger or smaller quantity, he can only be liable for failing to take the minimum which he is obliged to take.[23] It has, however, been held that this principle only relates to the valuation of the defendant's promise; when the question is, 'What promises is he bound by?', it may well be that some term can be implied that the promise should be performed in a reasonable, not a minimal, way. So in *Paula Lee Ltd* v *Robert Zehil Ltd*,[24] where the buyer had agreed to buy at least 16,000 of the seller's dresses, it was held that it was an implied term that the buyer would take a reasonable selection of the dresses, and not 16,000 of the identical cheapest dress.

The general rule for the assessment of damages for the buyer's breach of contract is laid down by s. 50(2):

> The measure of damages is the estimated loss directly and naturally resulting, in the ordinary course of events, from the buyer's breach of contract.

And the general method of computing the loss directly and naturally arising from the buyer's breach is laid down by s. 50(3):

---

20 For a critique of these provisions and their equivalents in the Uniform Commercial Code see Adams [2002] JBL 553.
21 *The Solholt* [1983] 1 Lloyd's Rep 605.
22 *Payzu Ltd* v *Saunders* [1919] 2 KB 581.
23 See, e.g., *Laverack* v *Woods of Colchester* [1967] 1 QB 278.
24 [1983] 2 All ER 390.

Where there is an available market for the goods in question the measure of damages is prima facie to be ascertained by the difference between the contract price and the market or current price at the time or times when the goods ought to have been accepted or (if no time was fixed for acceptance) at the time of the refusal to accept.[25]

Meaning of 'available market'[26]

The first question to which this subsection gives rise is, what is meant by 'an available market'? It is surprising how scanty is the authority on this point. In *Dunkirk Colliery Co Ltd v Lever*[27] there is a dictum by James LJ which suggests that a market necessarily signifies some place where the goods can be sold. In *Marshall v Nicoll*,[28] an appeal to the House of Lords from Scotland, it was held, in a somewhat confusing and inconclusive discussion, that there might be a market within the meaning of s. 51(3) – the corresponding section dealing with non-delivery – although the goods were being specially made to order and the market for such goods was extremely limited. Next, in *W L Thompson Ltd v Robinson (Gunmakers) Ltd*,[29] the question was fully argued before Upjohn J who thought himself bound to follow the dictum of James LJ in *Dunkirk Colliery Co Ltd v Lever*,[30] although that case was decided before the Sale of Goods Act, and although the dictum was manifestly *obiter* and was not expressly concurred in by the other members of the Court.[31] But the learned judge gave his own opinion on the matter:[32]

> Had the matter been *res integra* I think that I should have found that an 'available market' merely means that the situation in the particular trade in the particular area was such that the particular goods could freely be sold, and that there was a demand sufficient to absorb readily all the goods that were thrust on it so that if a purchaser defaulted the goods in question could readily be disposed of.[33]

This opinion seems preferable to that of James LJ as becomes clear when the facts of *W L Thompson Ltd v Robinson (Gunmakers) Ltd*[34] are examined. In this case, the buyer contracted to buy a car from the plaintiffs, but failed to take delivery when the car was available. The sellers returned the car to the makers and claimed from the buyer damages for their loss of profit on the sale. It was found as a fact that the supply of cars exceeded the demand in that area when the contract was made. At that time, resale price maintenance was still rigidly enforced in relation to cars and other

---

25 This is not, as some suppose, a rule derived from the *Hadley v Baxendale* rule, the first limb of which appears in s. 50(2). It is an older rule – see *Dunlop v Higgins* (1848) 1 HLC 381, (1848) 6 Bell's App 195. It is regrettable, for the reasons which appear below, that Judge Chalmers chose to codify this rather than the *Hadley v Baxendale* principle.

26 See two interesting articles on this question in (1958) 36 Can Bar Rev 360, and (1969) 43 Aus LJ 52, 106.

27 (1878) 9 Ch D 20, 25.

28 1919 SC (HL) 129.

29 [1955] Ch 177.

30 (1878) 9 Ch D 20.

31 Moreover, two valuable dicta appear not to have been cited. In *The Arpad* [1934] P 189, 191, Bateson J said: 'Market means buyers and sellers'; and in *Heskell v Continental Express Ltd* [1950] 1 All ER 1033, 1050, Devlin J said: 'A market for this purpose means more than a particular place. It means also a particular level of trade.'

32 [1955] Ch 177, at 187.

33 This definition was in fact adopted by Sellers J in *ABD (Metals & Waste) Ltd v Anglo-Chemical & Ore Co Ltd* [1955] 2 Lloyd's Rep 456.

34 [1955] Ch 177.

consumer goods and, consequently, there was rarely any difference between the contract price and the market price in the sense of the fixed retail price. The buyer contended that there was a market and that there being no difference between the market price and the contract price, the sellers were only entitled to nominal damages. Had this contention succeeded, the plaintiffs would have been deprived of damages to which they were clearly entitled in the present state of the law.[35] For even if the sellers had not returned the car to the makers, but resold it to another buyer, they would still have lost one sale. For, with an excess of supply over demand, the sellers would still have been able to supply the second buyer with a car even had there been no breach, and thereby earned profit on both sales.[36] In the event, Upjohn J avoided this result by holding that, even if there were a market, yet s. 50(3) only laid down a prima facie rule and that this rule could not be applied in this particular case.

This conclusion received the approval of the Court of Appeal in *Charter* v *Sullivan*.[37] This case was the counterpart of *W L Thompson Ltd* v *Robinson (Gunmakers) Ltd* in that, on otherwise identical facts, the plaintiff was able to dispose of all the cars he could obtain, and he was accordingly held entitled only to nominal damages. The Court of Appeal agreed with Upjohn J that on such facts it was immaterial whether there was an available market or not, but Jenkins LJ disagreed (*obiter*) as to the meaning of the term 'available market'. He did not, however, offer his own definition, but rested content with saying that a market presupposes that prices are fixed by reference to supply and demand, and the goods are not sold at a fixed retail price.

Since the disappearance of resale price maintenance in the UK, this particular point has ceased to be of much importance. Both in retail and in commercial sales the 'market price' is now likely to be the average or mid-point of a number of different prices prevailing in the market in question.

It is clear that the onus is on the seller to prove that sales have been lost, and, as one commentator has noted, under the economic law of diminishing returns or increasing marginal costs[,] ... as a seller's volume increases, then a point will inevitably be reached where the cost of selling each additional item diminishes the incremental return to the seller and eventually makes it entirely unprofitable to conclude the next sale.[38]

If the meaning of the term 'available market' remains without firm judicial definition, the question whether there is an available market in any particular case seems now to be treated by the courts as a question of fact and, in some cases, even as a question of degree. There may, for instance, be evidence that sales occasionally take place of the commodity in question, but only rarely, or in small quantities.[39] Or there may be evidence that similar, though not identical, goods are readily available or disposable.[40] Or

---

35 Which, of course, is based on the assumption that a plaintiff should be entitled to damages for his lost expectations. For some doubts on this, see Atiyah, *Introduction to the Law of Contract*, pp. 456–64 (5th edn, Oxford, 1995).
36 Cf. *In re Vic Mill Ltd* [1913] 1 Ch 465, and see below, p. 496.
37 [1957] 2 QB 117. See also *Lazenby Garages Ltd* v *Wright* [1976] 1 WLR 459, below, p. 496.
38 Shanker 24 Case W Res 697, 699 (1973) – see *R E Davis Chemical Corp* v *Diasonics* 826 F 2d 678 (1987).
39 *Kwei Teh Chao* v *British Traders & Shippers Ltd* [1954] 2 QB 459, 498 (held: a market). Cf. *Garnac Grain Co* v *H M Faure & Fairclough* [1968] AC 1130, 1138 (held: evidence on which judge could find there was a market, although it was not possible to buy the contract quantity in one amount for immediate delivery).
40 *Hinde* v *Liddell* (1875) 10 QB 265.

again there may be evidence that it is possible to buy or sell the goods at a different place or in smaller quantities. In all these cases the courts take a fairly broad and commonsense view of the question. The question which is usually treated as decisive is whether or not it would be reasonable for the seller to dispose of the goods through such market as is in fact available. It has, in fact, been suggested that the market price rule is best seen as an illustration of the rule that the innocent party must mitigate his loss; accordingly, attempts to define 'market' in any narrow or technical sense are to be deplored. The important question is whether the seller can reasonably find a substitute purchaser, and not where or how this substitute sale is to be made.[41]

If something needs to be done to the goods to make them saleable on the market, and it would be uneconomic for the seller to carry out such work, it would appear that the contract/market measure would not be the appropriate measure.[42]

Effect of resale by seller on 'available market'

The market price rule is in principle based on the loss which the plaintiff (seller) would have suffered if, on non-acceptance by the buyer, the plaintiff had sold the goods in the market. It is thus concerned with a notional or hypothetical sale which might reasonably have been made by the seller. The rule then gives rise to problems where the seller actually has gone into the market and resold the goods. If this resale is actually at the market price there will, of course, be no difficulty; but if the resale is made at less than the market price, the seller may wish to claim as damages the difference between the original contract price and the resale price, rather than the market price. Equally, if the resale takes place at a price higher than the market price, the buyer may claim that the damages should only represent the difference between the contract and the resale price. The question then arises whether the actual resale price should be taken into account, or whether the damages must still be calculated by reference to the market price.

In attempting to answer these questions it is necessary to distinguish between the case where the seller finds a substitute buyer immediately on non-acceptance by the buyer, and the case where the seller chooses to retain the goods for some period before reselling them.[43] If he resells more or less forthwith on non-acceptance by the buyer at less than the market price, the seller will clearly have difficulty in claiming damages based on this resale price. For the obvious question will be why the seller should have resold at less than the market price. Prima facie, the requirement that he should mitigate his loss would have required him to sell at not less than the market price and, unless the seller can find some very convincing reason for what he has done, it is difficult to see why he should recover more than the difference between the contract and the market price. If, on the other hand, the seller succeeds in convincing the court that in the particular circumstances it was reasonable of him (despite the mitigation principle) to resell at the price which he in fact obtained, it

---

41 See Ogus, *Law of Damages*, pp. 326–7.

42 See *Tharros Shipping Co Ltd and another v Bias Shipping Ltd and another* [1994] 1 Lloyd's Rep 533 – this case involved a charterparty, but it would appear to support the point made in the text.

43 A third possibility is that the seller delays in reselling in the market because he is still trying to persuade the buyer to take the goods – see below, pp. 492–3.

seems improbable that the court would find that the resale price actually was lower than the market price. Such findings would be contradictory in the ordinary way, and a decision that the actual resale price was reasonable would normally connote a finding that there was no available market at which the seller could have disposed of the goods at a higher price.

If the seller resells promptly on breach by the buyer at *more* than the market price, it is not wholly clear whether the buyer can take advantage of this to reduce the damages he would otherwise have to pay. The seller will, of course, face the same evidentiary problem as in the converse situation discussed in the last paragraph. That is to say, the seller may have difficulty in convincing the court that there was an available market in which prices were lower than the price actually obtained, for this implies that the second buyer made a bad bargain. And although parties do, of course, make bad bargains from time to time, the situation envisaged here is one in which the seller has unexpectedly had the goods left on his hands by non-acceptance by the buyer and in which, therefore, one would have expected the seller to be in a poor bargaining situation. However, let it be assumed that the seller is able to establish that he has resold at more than the market price. As the seller cannot claim for the loss if he sells below the market price, it may seem only fair that he should be able to retain any profit he makes by selling at above the market price. But there does seem to be a modern trend to deny recovery for a 'loss' which is in fact counterbalanced by a profit and it seems probable that a court would today hold that the seller is only entitled to the difference between contract and resale price, as this is the true measure of his loss. There seems no clear authority on this point, but the present submission appears to be the correct inference from the decision of the Court of Appeal in *Campbell Mostyn (Provisions) Ltd* v *Barnett Trading Co*[44] where the seller *retained the goods after the breach and subsequently resold them* for more than the market price prevailing at the date of breach. It was held in these circumstances that the seller was entitled to recover the difference between contract and market price and did not have to account for the greater price at which he had in fact sold the goods. Somervell LJ quoted with approval the following passage from Lord Wrenbury's speech in *Jamal* v *Moolla Dawood*,[45] a Privy Council case dealing with shares:

> If the seller retains the shares after the breach the speculation as to the way the market will subsequently go is the speculation of the seller, not of the buyer; the seller cannot recover from the buyer the loss below the market price at the date of the breach if the market falls, nor is he liable to the purchaser for the profit if the market rises.

It seems a reasonable inference that the position is different where the seller resells immediately upon breach. This conclusion may also be supported by the decision of the Court of Appeal in *R Pagnan & Fratelli* v *Corbisa Industrial Agropacuaria Limitada*,[46] although here the circumstances were rather unusual. This case concerned a breach of contract by the seller, rather than the buyer, but in general the

---

44 [1954] 1 Lloyd's Rep 65.
45 [1916] 1 AC 175, 179. See *McGregor on Damages*, 17th edn, §24-009.
46 [1970] 1 WLR 1306. See also *Lazenby Garages Ltd* v *Wright* [1976] 1 WLR 459, below, p. 495, and *The Solholt* [1983] 1 Lloyd's Rep 605, below, p. 542.

same principles are applicable. In this case, the buyers rightly rejected the goods delivered but then, as part of a settlement of the dispute, agreed to buy the same goods at a substantially lower price. This price was lower even than the market price and the buyers consequently made a handsome overall profit which exceeded their loss on the original sale. It was held that the second contract was part of a continuous course of dealing between the parties and not a wholly new and independent event. Consequently, the profit made by the buyers on the second sale had to be set off against their loss on the first, and they were only entitled to nominal damages. While it is not wholly clear whether the result would have been the same if the second purchase had not been from the sellers, the case does illustrate a modern reluctance to award damages for a 'loss' which in one sense is purely notional.

In some cases, the court will lack evidence that the market price on the date when the goods should have been accepted was other than the price at which the seller eventually sold. In such a case it will necessarily have to be assumed that the relevant price for the purposes of s. 50(3) is the price at which the seller sold the goods.

Which market?

Where there is an available market in more than one place, the relevant place is prima facie the place at which the goods were to be delivered under the contract. So in *Hasell v Bagot, Shakes & Lewis Ltd*,[47] where Japanese superphosphate was sold for delivery at Adelaide, it was held by the Australian High Court that the question was whether there was a market at Adelaide and not in Japan. Had there been a market in both places, the market price at Adelaide would have been the relevant price. However, where goods are sold f.o.b. or c.i.f. for shipment to a particular market, then the relevant market would prima facie be that at the place of destination.[48] The point to remember in all cases is that if the buyer refuses to accept the goods the seller will ordinarily have to find a substitute purchaser, and the question is, where should the seller reasonably be expected to look for such a purchaser? Where the seller's business is limited to a particular local area, the availability of a market in that area and the market price in that area are the only relevant considerations.[49] In other cases the seller may reasonably be expected to look far afield for a substitute purchaser, for example where the seller is engaged in international trade.

Market price at what date?

The provisions of the Act dealing with the date at which the damages should be assessed by reference to the market price have given rise to a good deal of trouble, largely because the modern rules as to repudiation and mitigation were not settled when the 1893 Act was drafted. Some points are clear enough. Where the buyer's refusal to take the goods occurs at the time when they should have been accepted, the provisions of s. 50(3) are exactly in point, and the seller recovers the difference

---

47 (1911) 13 CLR 374.
48 *Aryeh v Lawrence Kostoris & Son Ltd* [1967] 1 Lloyd's Rep 63, 71 per Diplock LJ.
49 *W L Thompson Ltd v Robinson (Gunmakers) Ltd* [1955] Ch 177 – see above, p. 488.

between the contract price and the market price at that time. This rule, however, should not be too rigidly applied. It often happens that a breach by the buyer is not followed by the immediate resale of the goods in the market. Indeed, in practice the seller is much more likely to try to negotiate some alternative arrangement with the buyer, or to try to persuade him to take the goods after all. This is reasonable commercial behaviour which ought to be encouraged by the courts, and if as a result the goods are only resold after some delay, it now seems clear that the seller may be entitled to obtain damages based on the market price at this later date.[50] However, it has been recently stressed (in a case dealing with the sale of land) that the general rule remains that the damages ought to be assessed as at the date of breach, and that a seller cannot as a matter of course obtain damages based on the market price at the date when the contract is finally abandoned.[51]

Where no time for the delivery of the goods has been fixed by the contract, the tendency is for the courts to look to the market price at the time when the goods should have been accepted, and to ignore the last words of the section which state that the relevant time is the time when the buyer refuses to accept the goods.[52] In *Millett* v *Van Heeck*,[53] the Court of Appeal decided that the market price at the date at which the buyer refuses to take delivery is quite irrelevant where his refusal takes the form of an anticipatory breach. In such a case the seller has the choice of accepting the repudiation,[54] or of continuing to treat the contract as binding, but in either event the damages are prima facie assessable by reference to the market price at the date when delivery ought to have been accepted. So, for example, where the buyers failed to give 15 days' notice of readiness to load a vessel as required by the contract, the sellers were entitled to leave the contract open until the last date of the shipment period, and claim damages based on the market price as at that date.[55]

If the action comes on for trial before the date when the buyer was bound to accept the goods, the court must make the best estimate it can of the probable market price at this date. In either event, if the market rises between the date of repudiation and the date when delivery should have been accepted, the relevant market price appears to be that prevailing at the latter date. In other words, the seller is not entitled to receive a higher measure of damages merely because the buyer repudiates the contract at a time when the market is lower than it is on the delivery date.[56] Otherwise he would receive more as a result of the breach than he would have received if the contract had been performed. This result can be justified by suggesting that where the buyer repudiates before the date for delivery, it must be presumed that the seller will not be able to resell in the market before that date. Even if he accepts the repudiation he is entitled to wait until the contractual delivery date.

---

50 This is spelled out quite plainly in the dicta of Lord Wilberforce (speaking for the whole House of Lords) in *Johnson* v *Agnew* [1980] AC 367, 400–1, which were followed in *Suleiman* v *Shahsavari* [1989] 2 All ER 460.
51 *Janred Properties Ltd* v *Ente Nazionale Italiano per il Turismo* [1989] 2 All ER 444.
52 See *Tai Hing Cotton Mill Ltd* v *Kamsing Knitting Factory* [1979] AC 91, 104, a case on the equivalent provision dealing with damages for non-delivery, s. 51(3), discussed at p. 535 below.
53 [1921] 2 KB 369.
54 Reselling the goods following the buyer's repudiation can constitute acceptance of the repudiation – see *Vitol SA* v *Norelf Ltd* [1993] 2 Lloyd's Rep 301.
55 *Lusograin Comercio Internacional de Cereas Ltda* v *Bunge AG* [1986] 2 Lloyd's Rep 654.
56 *Melachrino* v *Nickoll & Knight* [1920] 1 KB 693.

On the other hand, where the market falls between the date of repudiation and the date when the goods ought to have been accepted, the result may be different. Here it has been held that if the seller does accept the repudiation, his duty to mitigate the damage means that he should resell at once in a falling market, and that if he fails to do this he cannot hold the buyer liable for a greater amount than the difference between the contract price and the market price at the date of the repudiation.[57] However, some justifiable scepticism has been expressed as to the idea that the innocent seller should be able to identify a 'falling market' before it has fallen,[58] and it must be said that it is difficult to justify an assessment of damages at the date of termination on this ground. Of course, it could be argued that once the seller accepts the buyer's repudiation, the contract is at an end, and the damages should be assessed as at the date when the seller should reasonably have resold the goods in the market. But that argument is equally applicable whether the market rises or falls after the termination of the contract; yet, as we have seen, where the market rises it is established that the damages must be assessed as at the contract delivery date and not when the contract is terminated.

Should the seller decline to accept the repudiation, however, as he is perfectly entitled to do,[59] he is under no obligation to mitigate his damage by reselling at once. He can stand by the contract and wait until the delivery date before reselling and, in this case, he is entitled to receive damages assessed in the normal way by reference to the market price at the date when the goods ought to have been accepted.[60]

The Court of Appeal's decision in *Millett* v *Van Heeck* was approved by the Privy Council in a case dealing with s. 51(3), the corresponding subsection concerning non-delivery.[61] In this case, the Privy Council accepted that the second limb of the subsection (that damages are to be assessed at the time of refusal to accept where no time is fixed for acceptance) may in fact have no application at all. First, they accepted the decision in *Millett* v *Van Heeck* that the subsection has no application to anticipatory breach, it being the clear assumption of the subsection that the breach has occurred after the date for delivery has passed. But it is also difficult to see how the subsection can apply even if the breach is not anticipatory. If no time for acceptance is fixed by the contract, it must nevertheless be the case that delivery must be made either in a reasonable time or on demand. But if delivery is to be made in a reasonable time, and at the expiry of such a period the buyer refuses to accept the goods, then the first limb of s. 50(3) would apply anyhow. In other words, in this situation, both limbs of the subsection give the same result. The relevant date for assessing the damages is the date when the goods ought to have been accepted, which in this case is also the date when the buyer has refused to accept them. If, on the other hand, the contract provides for delivery on demand, then, as soon as

---

57 *Roth* v *Tayson* (1896) 73 LT 628.
58 See *Lusograin Comercio Internacional de Cereas Ltda* v *Bunge AG* [1986] 2 Lloyd's Rep 654, 662–3 per Staughton J.
59 *Frost* v *Knight* (1872) LR 7 Ex 111. See also *Sudan Import & Export Co (Khartoum) Ltd* v *Société Générale de Compensation* [1958] 1 Lloyd's Rep 310, where the sellers at first refused to accept the repudiation but later agreed to do so.
60 *Tredegar Iron & Coal Co Ltd* v *Hawthorne* (1902) 18 TLR 716. These principles received the approval of the House of Lords in *Garnac Grain Co* v *H M Faure & Fairclough* [1968] AC 1130.
61 *Tai Hing Cotton Mill Ltd* v *Kamsing Knitting Factory* [1979] AC 91; see below, p. 535, for the facts.

demand is made, a time for the delivery of the goods has been fixed, so once again the subsection would seem to point to the date when the goods should have been accepted as the relevant date, and once again the date of refusal to accept would be irrelevant.

Cases where market price rule inapplicable

The rule laid down by s. 50(3) is only a prima facie method of calculating the damages, and if it would lead to an obviously incorrect assessment of the loss directly and naturally resulting from the breach, it must be discarded and some other method of assessment, based for example on the profit lost or expenses incurred (such as sums paid on the cancellation of a charterparty)[62], must be used. We have already seen that problems sometimes arise where specific goods are resold after the buyer has refused to accept them, and the question has arisen whether the seller has, in the result, suffered any loss at all.[63] In the case of new manufactured goods, the answer depends on whether the market situation is such that the seller has lost a sale. But this is not the rule with respect to unique goods. If the buyer refuses to accept goods in this category and the seller resells at (or at more than) the first contract price, he suffers no loss at all, for he could not have made more than one profit from a unique chattel. It has been held by the Court of Appeal that a second-hand car is a unique chattel for this purpose.[64]

Naturally, if there is no market at all the subsection is of no assistance. In these cases the amount recoverable must depend upon whether the seller has already procured or manufactured the goods for delivery or not. If he has done so, the prima facie measure of damages is the difference between the contract price and the value of the goods at the date of breach.[65] Since there is, on this supposition, no market, there will often be practical problems in assessing the value of the goods at the time of breach, but the court must do the best it can on the material available to it. Where the goods have been manufactured to some special order, it may even be that they have no value at all and the seller will then be able to sue for the full price. But his right to the whole of these damages will, of course, depend upon proof that the goods are useless and unsaleable, not only in their existing form, but even after reasonable alterations. For the seller must always mitigate his damage and, if he can make the goods saleable by small alterations, he should do so.[66] If, on the other hand, the seller has not yet procured or manufactured the goods, he will prima facie be entitled to recover the difference between the contract price and the cost to himself of so procuring or manufacturing the goods, that is to say, his profit.

The mere fact that the non-performance of the contract which has been broken has enabled the seller to make profits on other contracts does not of itself entitle the

---

62 *Bem Dis A Turk Ticaret S/A Tr* v *International Agri Trade Co Ltd* [1999] 1 Lloyd's Rep 729.
63 *W L Thompson Ltd* v *Robinson (Gunmakers) Ltd* [1955] Ch 177; *Charter* v *Sullivan* [1957] 2 QB 117; see above, p. 488.
64 *Lazenby Garages Ltd* v *Wright* [1976] 1 WLR 459.
65 *Harlow & Jones Ltd* v *Panex (International) Ltd* [1967] 2 Lloyd's Rep 509, 530.
66 It cannot be said as a general rule that the innocent party cannot be expected to lay out money to mitigate his damages, although this may be so where the suggested expenditure would be highly speculative: *Jewelowski* v *Propp* [1944] KB 510.

defaulting buyer to claim that the profits so made should be set off against those which have been lost as a result of his breach, because the seller might have been able to earn both lots of profit.[67] But in *Hill & Sons* v *Edwin Showell & Sons*,[68] the House of Lords held that a buyer is entitled to give evidence to show that in fact the seller would not have been able to earn both lots of profit, for example because his factory has been working to capacity the whole time. Although the burden of proof on the buyer in this respect is a heavy one, if he can succeed in establishing the point the seller will only be entitled to recover the difference between the profit he should have made and the profit he actually made.

Damages for non-acceptance can now be awarded in a foreign currency where appropriate.[69] For example, where overseas sellers sell goods to English buyers and the buyers wrongfully refuse to accept the goods, it will often be appropriate to award damages in the currency of the seller's business. The appropriate currency may be expressly or impliedly fixed by the contract (for example, it will often be the currency of the contract itself) or it may be fixed by the court as the currency which best expresses the loss. The rule, it has been said, must be sensibly and flexibly applied so as to produce a just and appropriate result. In some cases the immediate loss will indicate the appropriate currency; in others, there may be further factors indicating a different currency.

---

67 *In re Vic Mill Ltd* [1913] 1 Ch 465; *W L Thompson Ltd* v *Robinson (Gunmakers) Ltd* [1955] Ch 177.
68 (1918) 87 LJKB 1106.
69 *The Despina* [1979] AC 685; *Ozalid Group (Export)* v *African Continental Bank* [1979] 2 Lloyd's Rep 231.

Part VII

THE REMEDIES OF THE BUYER

27

REJECTION OF THE GOODS AND ADDITIONAL RIGHTS OF BUYER/TRANSFEREE OF GOODS IN CONSUMER CASES

BUYER'S RIGHT TO REJECT THE GOODS

The buyer's first and primary remedy for a breach of contract by the seller is to repudiate the contract of sale and reject the goods. As we have seen, the remedy of repudiation is available to the buyer only when the seller's breach of contract goes to the root of the agreement, either because it is a breach of condition or because of the nature and consequences of a breach of an innominate term.[1] The right to reject is separate from the right to repudiate the contract, and circumstances giving rise to a right of rejection do not, even if the right is exercised, necessarily put an end to the contract.[2] The seller can usually, until the time of performance has expired, therefore, tender a conforming delivery.[3]

The Sale and Supply of Goods Act 1994 makes significant changes to this area.[4] However, given that the former provisions apply to contracts made before the commencement date of that Act,[5] it is still necessary to deal with them.

Broadly, these provisions make no change to consumer sales, but in non-consumer sales the buyer will no longer have the right to reject for breach of the statutory requirements as to quality and quantity where the breach is so slight that it would be unreasonable to reject the goods. This change is implemented by a new s. 15A to the Act limiting the right to reject for a breach of ss. 13 to 15, where the buyer does not deal as a consumer,[6] and s. 30(2A)–(2E)(ss. 30(2A) and (2B) do not apply to Scotland, and s. 30(2D) applies to Scotland only), and where 'the breach is so slight that it would be unreasonable for [the buyer] to reject [the goods]'. In the case of a breach of s. 30, the new s. 30(2A) likewise limits the buyer's right to reject for a short-fall, or his right to reject all the goods for an excess, if the shortfall or the excess 'is so slight that it would be unreasonable for him to do so'. The right to reject an excess

---

1 See pp. 91 *et seq.* As to the loss of the right of rejection see p. 506.
2 See, however, the view expressed by Devlin J in *Kwei Tek Chao v British Traders & Shippers* [1954] 2 QB 459, 480. But since the HL decision in *Johnson v Agnew* [1980] AC 367 this view is surely incorrect. In [1966] CLJ 192, 194 Lord Devlin pointed out that what creates the breach is failure to tender conforming goods *within the contract time* – see below, n. 32. Furthermore, where rejection of the goods for breach of condition is a termination of the contract, it is not a rescission *ab initio*. Hence there is no inconsistency in rejecting some of the goods while keeping the rest – see p. 522 below.
3 See *Borrowman Phillips & Co v Free & Hollis* (1878) 4 QBD 500; *E E Brian Smith (1928) Ltd v Wheatsheaf Mills Ltd* [1939] 2 KB 302; and p. 505 below.
4 The Act is based on the proposals contained in the Law Commissions' Report *Sale and Supply of Goods*, paras 4.1–6.24.
5 3 January 1995.
6 As to 'dealing as consumer' see s. 61(5)(A), which adopts the definition of this term contained in the Unfair Contract Terms Act 1977 s. 12 at p. 236 above.

itself is unaffected by these proposals, and remains an absolute right. There are equivalent provisions relating to other contracts for the supply of goods.[7]

The Scottish approach is similar, but easier to state. The buyer may reject only if the breach, whether of an express or an implied term of the contract, is material. If the contract of sale is a consumer contract, breach by the seller of any term (express or implied) as to the quality or fitness for purpose of the goods, or correspondence with description, or with sample in quality, is deemed to be material, meaning that the consumer buyer is always entitled to reject for breach.[8] The right to reject for excess or shortfall of supply is likewise dependent upon the materiality of the excess or shortfall, as the case may be.[9] Again, there are equivalent provisions for other contracts relating to the supply of goods.[10]

As we have previously noted, a regrettable feature of the English provisions is that they only apply to breaches of the seller's statutory duties.[11] They therefore have no application to a breach of a stipulation as to time, or any other express term of the contract which is classifiable as a condition. Presentation of shipping documents one day too late, failure by the buyer to open a letter of credit by the stipulated date and similar breaches of contract will, therefore, continue to be governed by the existing law which permits rejection by the buyer (or repudiation by the seller) however reasonable or unreasonable it may be. Still less, of course, will these proposals have any effect on the general law of contract, as opposed to the law of sale of goods. It could well be desirable for the Law Commission to consider enlarging these recommendations to the general law of contract in England, because the unqualified right of repudiation which the law presently confers for a breach of condition is just as obnoxious in other kinds of contracts as it is in the law of sale.

Sections 13 to 15, including the new provisions, being subject to s. 55(1) of the 1979 Act,[12] are excludable by a contrary intention. It might be argued, however, that any contract term purporting to exclude the restrictions on the buyer's right to reject the goods would be subject to a test of reasonableness by virtue of the Unfair Contract Terms Act 1977. However, the application of ss. 3 and 17 is problematic, and the argument could only apply where the contract is made on the *buyer's* written standard terms, when it would have to be argued under s. 3(2)(b) or s. 17(1)(b) that the effect of the term is to allow the buyer to render a contractual performance substantially different from that which was expected of him, or no performance at all. Where the buyer deals as a consumer, the restrictions on the right of rejection do not, of course, apply. Moreover, s. 6 of the Act, as we have seen, prevents the exclusion of ss. 13–15 and any attempt by the *seller* to exclude the *buyer's* right of rejection would be ineffective by virtue of s. 6 read together with s. 13 or by s. 20 read together with s. 25(3).

---

7 Schedule 2 para. 6(5) and (9).
8 Sale of Goods Act 1979 s. 15B (added by Sale and Supply of Goods Act 1994 s. 5(1)).
9 Sale of Goods Act 1979 s. 30(2D) (added by Sale and Supply of Goods Act 1994 s. 5(2)).
10 Supply of Goods and Services Act 1982 Pt IA (added by Sale and Supply of Goods Act 1994 Sch. 1).
11 The Law Commission recognized that their draft Bill would not affect a breach of a stipulation as to time, but apparently thought that breach of an express term might be encompassed by their proposals (see para 4.22, n. 25) but the draft Bill in fact did not cover express terms, nor does the 1994 Act – and see above, p. 148. By contrast, the Scottish reform brings sale and supply of goods into line with the general law of contract and covers both express and implied terms.
12 See p. 106.

These changes are generally to be welcomed, because there is no doubt that the former law permitted rejection on capricious and technical grounds. In particular, rejection was often justified on the ground of a technical breach of the statutory implied terms, even though the buyer's real motive in rejecting the goods was that market prices had fallen since the contract was made. Of course, as the Law Commissions recognized, these changes in the law would introduce some element of uncertainty where previously the right of rejection was unqualified, but this may well be an acceptable price to pay for penalizing totally unreasonable commercial behaviour.

It is perhaps not entirely clear how far the personal position of the buyer will be relevant in examining the question of reasonableness in this context. Presumably if the buyer has his own good reasons for needing goods which are in precise conformity with the contract (even if this was not known to the seller) it will not be unreasonable of him to reject them for any slight nonconformity. On the other hand, whether or not the right of rejection arises at all will depend upon there being found a breach of one of the quality warranties, and in order to sue for breach of the fitness for purpose warranty the Act requires the buyer to have made known to the seller the particular purpose for which the goods are required. In consequence, whether or not this situation arises will almost certainly depend upon whether there is found to be a breach of the other quality warranties, and in particular the warranty that the goods are of satisfactory quality. It is also unclear whether other personal circumstances of the buyer (his market position, for instance) will be relevant in deciding whether rejection is reasonable.

Two further questions relating to the buyer's right of rejection remain to be discussed here.

Instalment sales

It is first necessary to consider the position which arises in a contract for the sale of goods by instalments, where the seller is guilty of a breach as to one or more instalments. Is the buyer entitled in such circumstances to reject the whole of the contract goods or is he entitled only to reject that part in respect of which there is a breach of contract, or again is he relegated to a claim for damages? The question is posed rather than answered by s. 31(2) as follows:

> Where there is a contract for the sale of goods to be delivered by stated instalments, which are to be separately paid for, and the seller makes defective deliveries in respect of one or more instalments, or the buyer neglects or refuses to take delivery of or pay for one or more instalments, it is a question in each case depending on the terms of the contract and the circumstances of the case, whether the breach of contract is a repudiation of the whole contract or whether it is a severable breach giving rise to a claim for compensation but not to a right to treat the whole contract as repudiated.

Non-severable contracts

Section 31(2), by its express terms, only applies where the goods are to be delivered by instalments and the instalments are to be separately paid for. But this is not an exhaustive statement of the circumstances in which a contract may be severable.[13] As will be seen later,[14] there are cases in which a contract is severable in law even though the goods are not to be delivered by separate instalments or the instalments are not to be separately paid for. But if the contract is not severable, then it is to be treated as an entire contract. Hence, in these cases a partial breach is to be treated in the same way as a total breach and the buyer is prima facie entitled to reject all the goods. In this situation the fact that the goods are delivered in instalments is immaterial once it is found that this does not make the contract severable.[15] The position under the former law was exactly the same as if the whole consignment were delivered at once and part of the goods were defective. In such a case, it was well established that the buyer could reject the whole.[16] In the case of contracts made after 2 January 1995 the provisions set out above will apply in such a situation.[17]

Severable contracts

Where the contract is severable because the goods are to be delivered in instalments and are to be separately paid for, the right of the buyer to reject the whole contract quantity depends, as stated by s. 31(2), on the terms of the contract and the circumstances of the case. If the contract is severable although the goods are not to be delivered in instalments, or the instalments are not to be separately paid for, the same rules probably apply as a matter of common law. If the contract is silent as to the events which have occurred:

> The main tests to be considered in applying the sub-section . . . are, first, the ratio quantitatively which the breach bears to the contract as a whole and secondly, the degree of probability or improbability that such a breach will be repeated.[18]

Two cases may be contrasted. In *Maple Flock Co Ltd* v *Universal Furniture Products (Wembley) Ltd*,[19] the plaintiffs contracted to sell 100 tons of rag flock to the defendants, delivery to be at the rate of three weekly instalments of one and a half tons each, as required, and the flock to conform to government standards. The first 15 loads were satisfactory, but a sample from the sixteenth load showed that it did not conform to government standards. In the meantime the defendants had taken delivery of four more loads, all of which were satisfactory. Applying the above test, the Court of Appeal held that the defendants were not entitled to repudiate the contract, as the breach only affected one and a half tons out of the flock already delivered

---

13 This is expressly stated by Atkin LJ in *Longbottom & Co Ltd* v *Bass Walker & Co Ltd* [1922] WN 245, but it is also implicit in many other cases.
14 See below, p. 521 *et seq.*
15 *Gill & Duffus SA* v *Berger & Co Inc* [1983] 1 Lloyd's Rep 622, reversed on different grounds [1984] AC 382, above, p. 139.
16 *Jackson* v *Rotax Motor & Cycle Co Ltd* [1910] 2 KB 937; *Re Moore & Co Ltd and Landauer & Co Ltd* [1921] 2 KB 519. Cf. the position where (in a case not falling within s. 31(2)) the buyer wrongfully refuses to accept part of the goods. This does not justify repudiation by the seller unless the part rejected is substantial: *Francis* v *Lyon* (1907) 4 CLR 1023.
17 See p. 499.
18 *Maple Flock Co Ltd* v *Universal Furniture Products (Wembley) Ltd* [1934] 1 KB 148, 157 per Lord Hewart CJ.
19 [1934] 1 KB 148.

and it was most improbable that it would recur. On the other hand, in *R A Munro & Co Ltd* v *Meyer*[20] A agreed to buy 1,500 tons of meat and bone meal, delivery at the rate of 125 tons a month, from B. After more than half of the total quantity had been delivered and discovered to be seriously defective, the buyer claimed to repudiate the contract. Wright J held that he was entitled to do so. 'Where the breach is substantial and so serious as the breach in this case and has continued so persistently, the buyer is entitled to say that he has the right to treat the whole contract as repudiated.'[21]

A more recent example which concerned an alleged repudiation by the buyers rather than sellers illustrates the delicate position in which commercial parties may find themselves when they claim that a breach in respect of one instalment amounts to a repudiation of the whole contract. In *Warinco A G* v *Samor SPA*[22] the contract was for the sale of crude rape seed oil in several instalments. The buyers rejected the first instalment, claiming that it was not of the colour required by the contract. The sellers disputed this and, in subsequent proceedings, they were held to be in the right on this point. But the sellers also told the buyers that the next instalment would be identical with the one which the buyers had rejected. The buyers replied, insisting that the instalment must conform to the contract, and the sellers eventually declined to deliver any further instalments, arguing that the buyer's action amounted to a repudiation. Evidently the sellers feared that, as the second instalment was going to be identical with the first and as the buyers had rejected that one, they would reject the second one as well. Donaldson J held that the sellers had acted wrongly in refusing to tender the second instalment but his decision was reversed on appeal. However, the disagreement related only to the application of the law, and no doubt was cast on Donaldson J's statement of the relevant principles as follows:[23]

> If a buyer under a contract calling for delivery by instalments commits a breach of that contract before all the deliveries have been made and that breach is so serious as to go to the root of the contract – in other words, to destroy the basis of the contract – common sense suggests that the seller should not be expected to go to the trouble and expense of tendering later instalments if he does not want to. The law so provides.
>
> Again, if it becomes clear that the buyer will be unable to accept or to pay for later instalments, common sense suggests that the seller should, if he wishes, be discharged from any obligation further to perform his part of the contract. The law so provides.
>
> Finally, if a buyer acts or speaks in a manner which declares in clear terms that he will not perform his part of the contract, the seller should, in common sense and fairness, have the option of being discharged from further obligation under the contract. And the law so provides. But common sense also suggests that there can be borderline cases in which it is not quite so clear what should happen. The law is at a disadvantage here in that it must draw a line. The line which it draws is indicated by the question: 'Has the buyer evinced an intention to abandon or refuse to perform the contract?' In answering this question, the law has regard to such factors as the degree to which the delivery of one instalment is linked with another, the proportion of the contract which has been affected by the allegedly repudiatory

---

20 [1930] 2 KB 312.
21 *R A Munro & Co Ltd* v *Meyer* [1930] 2 KB 312, 331.
22 [1977] 2 Lloyd's Rep 582; [1979] 1 Lloyd's Rep 450.
23 [1977] 2 Lloyd's Rep 582, at p. 588.

breach and the probability that the breach will be repeated. However, these are merely part of the raw material for answering the question. They cannot be conclusive in themselves.

A single contract, though severable, is not the same thing as a number of distinct and separate contracts. If parties enter into distinct contracts, breach of one would very rarely justify repudiation of the others. But a provision in a contract that each instalment or each delivery is to be treated as a separate contract does not mean that there are distinct contracts; it merely indicates that the contract is severable. Hence such a clause does not deprive a buyer of a right to throw up the whole contract if he would otherwise have such a right.[24]

It will be noticed that s. 31(2) appears to assume that the buyer has one of two possible remedies: repudiation of the whole contract or merely a claim for damages. The subsection does not appear to contemplate the third possibility of allowing the buyer to reject the defective instalments while retaining the rest of the goods. But there is no reason to suppose that the buyer cannot do this, subject to the somewhat complex rules governing the question of partial acceptance.[25] However, this possibility seems to have been overlooked in *Regent OHG Aisenstadt* v *Francesco of Jermyn Street*,[26] a case which nicely illustrates the importance of the distinction between a severable and a non-severable contract. In this case the contract was for the sale of 62 high-quality men's suits, to be delivered in instalments. The sellers delivered the suits in five instalments, the fourth of which was one suit short. If this had been a non-severable contract, under the law then applicable the buyer would have been entitled to reject the whole lot because a shortage of one suit was conceded not to be *de minimis* (it exceeded a one per cent shortage). But Mustill J held that the contract was severable and, applying s. 31(2), held that the breach, being unlikely to be repeated and affecting only one instalment, did not give the buyer the right to repudiate the whole contract. He did not, however, consider whether the buyer had the right to reject the whole of the fourth instalment which it would seem he ought to have had. If the goods had been defective in quality (rather than one suit short), it would seem clear that the buyer would have been able to reject the whole of that instalment. The question would then have arisen whether, in applying s. 31(2), the short delivery ought to have been regarded as a shortage of one suit only or of the whole of the fourth instalment. If the latter had been the correct approach, the result of the case would have been different.

There was one further puzzle about the right of rejection in instalment contracts which affected both severable and non-severable contracts, and which did not seem to have been expressly solved by the courts. The problem was this: if instalments were delivered and accepted – or anyhow not rejected – and a subsequent instalment was then delivered which was defective so that the buyer became entitled to repudiate the whole contract (either because it was non-severable, or because the breach was so serious that s. 31(2) justified the buyer in taking this step), what was to happen to the instalments already delivered and accepted, or not rejected? If the

---

24   *R A Munro & Co Ltd* v *Meyer*, above, n. 21.
25   See below, p. 521.
26   [1981] 3 All ER 327.

contract was genuinely non-severable, it was clear that the buyer could not accept part and reject part of the goods (see s. 11(4))[27] so his rejection of later instalments must have carried with it the right (and indeed the obligation) to reject the prior instalments as well; and this was presumably still the case even though he might already have accepted the prior instalments. His acceptance would have to be treated as conditional on the later instalments being satisfactory. Section 35A, inserted by the 1994 Act, confers a right of partial rejection, and s. 11(4) is expressly made subject to the new provision, so that for contracts made after 2 January 1994 the problem should not arise. This provision is discussed below.[28]

If, on the other hand, the contract is severable, but the defective instalment is sufficiently bad to justify the buyer in throwing up the whole contract under s. 31(2), the buyer does not *have to* reject the prior instalments, but is he entitled to do so? Section 31(2) does not necessarily exclude the possibility that the buyer may have this right, but by its terms, it deals with the future, so that the buyer can refuse to perform outstanding obligations, but usually his (severable) obligations to accept previous conforming instalments have already been fulfilled and cannot be undone.

It is somewhat surprising that these problems seem never to have been discussed in the cases,[29] though there is a hint of them in *Gill & Duffus SA v Berger & Co Inc*.[30] It seems to have been assumed by the Court of Appeal here that rejection of a second instalment retrospectively validated a wrongful original rejection of a prior instalment; but the authority of this case is weakened by the fact that the House of Lords held that the second rejection was wrongful, so that the point did not arise.

Consequences of rejection

Where the buyer repudiates the contract, having the right to do so, he can of course decline to pay the price or, if he has paid it, he can recover it. In addition, he may maintain an action for damages, for if the buyer acts within his rights in rejecting the goods tendered, he can normally hold the seller liable for non-delivery.[31] There may be some circumstances in which, after rejection by the buyer, the seller can tender delivery of a new lot of goods if he still has time to do this within the period allowed by the contract,[32] but in general it seems that the buyer is entitled to treat a wrongful delivery as itself a breach of contract which justifies repudiation by him.[33]

The assumption of the present law is that the right of rejection must be exercised in a fairly short period, so that, in practice, no question arises as to any use that the

---

27 See below, p. 506 *et seq.*
28 See p. 521 below.
29 Nor did the Law Commission's Report Cm. 137 propose solutions to them – see ibid. para. 6.15.
30 [1983] 1 Lloyd's Rep 622, reversed on other grounds [1984] AC 382.
31 *Millar's Machinery Co Ltd v David Way & Son* (1934) 40 Com Cas 204.
32 *Borrowman Phillips & Co v Free & Hollis* (1878) 4 QBD 500; *E E Brian Smith (1928) Ltd v Wheatsheaf Mills Ltd* [1939] 2 KB 302. Where the seller's breach consists of tendering faulty documents he will usually be able to correct the documents and retender them within the necessary time – see *Empresa Exportadora de Azucar v Industria Azucarera Nacional SA (The Playa Larga)* [1983] 2 Lloyd's Rep 171, 184.
33 Although on one reading, s. 11(3) and (4) may be taken to lay down that rejection of the goods involves repudiation of the contract (or more accurately, an acceptance of the seller's repudiation), the point made at the outset, that rejection and repudiation are separable, must be borne in mind – see above, p. 499.

buyer may have had from the goods.[33a] The buyer's right to recover the full price after rejecting the goods is based on the supposition that he has received no consideration at all when he rejects; in one sense this may not be completely accurate where the buyer may have used the goods before rejecting them. But as a matter of law it is probably generally correct to treat the rejection as demonstrating a total failure of consideration so that the seller is not entitled to any credit for any use that the buyer may have had from the goods.[34] However, the case may be different if the buyer claims damages in addition to seeking the recovery of his price. It would seem remarkable if the buyer did not have to set off the value of any use he may have had from the goods against a claim for damages.

Where the goods are so rejected, it is not the responsibility of the buyer to return the goods to the seller, for s. 36 states:

> Unless otherwise agreed, where goods are delivered to the buyer, and he refuses to accept them having the right to do so, he is not bound to return them to the seller, but it is sufficient if he intimates to the seller that he refuses to accept them.

As will be seen below,[35] this rule presents some problems where the buyer has redelivered the goods to a sub-buyer before they are discovered to be defective. In this situation, the normal solution is simply to deny the buyer's right to reject altogether.

The acceptance by the seller of the buyer's rejection revests the property in the former if it has passed to the buyer, and also restores to him the immediate right to possession. Consequently, as we have seen, the buyer has no lien on the goods for the repayment of the purchase price.[36] The seller, upon receipt of notice of rejection, is entitled to have the goods placed at his disposal so as to allow of his resuming possession forthwith.[37]

As we have already seen, it is not wholly clear whether the risk is to be treated as revesting in the seller on rejection, but the practical position seems to be that the risk does not pass at all where defective goods are delivered and then rejected by the buyer,[38] or even where a short quantity is delivered and the goods are rejected.[39]

LOSS OF THE RIGHT TO REJECT

Even though the seller may be guilty of a breach of condition and the buyer may prima facie be entitled to repudiate the contract and reject the goods, he may in certain circumstances lose this right, and have to accept the goods and be content with a claim for damages. It is now necessary to examine the circumstances in which this may occur and, first of all, s. 11(4) must be set out in full (although it is to be noted

---

33a Note however the Scottish sheriff court case of *Lamarra v Capital Bank plc* 2004 GWD 40-817, where the purchaser's rejection of a car in March 2001 was upheld, although he continued to use the vehicle until the following June.
34 See above, p. 114 *et seq*. Note that Scots law also reaches this position, but without reference to total failure of consideration.
35 See below, p. 513.
36 *J L Lyons & Co Ltd v May & Baker Ltd* [1923] 1 KB 685.
37 *Hardy & Co Ltd v Hillerns & Fowler* [1923] 2 KB 490, 496 per Bankes LJ. Cf. *Kwei Tek Chao v British Traders & Shippers Ltd* [1954] 2 QB 459, 488 per Devlin J.
38 See above, p. 356.
39 *Vitol SA v Esso Australia Ltd (The Wise)* [1989] 1 Lloyd's Rep 96.

that it does not apply in Scotland). In its present form this reads as follows:

> Subject to section 35A below, where a contract of sale is not severable, and the buyer has accepted the goods, or part of them, the breach of a condition to be fulfilled by the seller can only be treated as a breach of warranty, and not as a ground for rejecting the goods and treating the contract as repudiated, unless there is an express or implied term of the contract to that effect.

Loss of right to reject through passing of property

In its original form (as s. 11(1)(c) of the 1893 Act, which also had no application in Scotland[40]) this provision had a much wider effect. According to the original words of s. 11(1)(c), if the contract was for the sale of specific goods the buyer lost his right of rejection when the property passed to him.[41] Many writers had pointed out the difficulties which arose from this paragraph when read in conjunction with s. 18 Rule 1. This Rule is generally taken to mean that, in the absence of a contrary intention, in a sale of specific goods the property passes as soon as the contract is made, with the result that the right of rejection arose and was lost at the very same minute.

This was such an obviously unsatisfactory conclusion that methods of escape were sought. First, in a number of cases the courts attempted to avoid the whole difficulty by holding that in most (if not all) sales of specific goods the sale was not unconditional within the meaning of s. 18 Rule 1. In the second place, buyers sometimes rested their case on allegations of mistake and of innocent misrepresentation. Neither of these methods of evasion of s. 11(1)(c) proved very successful, although the possibilities of the latter remained, to some extent, unsettled. It was plain, however, that no satisfactory solution existed to these difficulties except the repeal of the words 'or where the contract is for specific goods the property in which has passed to the buyer' and this was eventually effected by s. 4(1) of the Misrepresentation Act 1967. Since then, the right to reject the goods has, in all cases of sales of specific and unascertained goods alike, been lost by acceptance and acceptance alone.

Loss of right to reject through acceptance

A few preliminary comments on the concept of acceptance and its relationship to other legal doctrines are necessary. First, the provisions of the Act concerning acceptance must be read against the general common law doctrines of affirmation, waiver and estoppel (*Scoticé*, homologation, waiver, personal bar). The concept of affirmation is in some respects a general common law principle parallel to the concept of acceptance, but there are important differences between them. In particular, it is generally held that an innocent party who wishes to terminate a contract because of

---

40 See, for the effect, *Nelson v Chalmers* 1913 SC 441.

41 Historically, the implied terms were conditions only in the case of unascertained goods: in the case of specific goods, they were mere warranties giving rise to an action for damages only, not a right of rejection. Having regard to this, the rule codified, that the right to reject was lost when the contract was made in the case of specific goods, is comprehensible. At all events, the passing of property had no effect on the right of rejection in sales of unascertained goods following the 1893 Act: *McDougall v Aeromarine of Emsworth Ltd* [1958] 1 WLR 1126. In *Perkins v Bell* [1893] 1 QB 193, buyers of unascertained goods lost their right of rejection on the passing of property, but it could equally have been said that they had accepted the goods.

a breach of condition (or a repudiatory breach) by the other party cannot be treated as having affirmed the contract unless he knew of the breach, and of his right to terminate.[42] On the other hand, a buyer can be held to have accepted the goods, and so lost his right of rejection under the Sale of Goods Act, even where he did not know of the seller's breach or of his rights. This means that termination for breach is in principle often possible long after the breach occurs, because the facts may only then come to light; but acceptance is usually something which happens very shortly after delivery in a contract of sale. It is not usually possible to reject goods long after delivery because some latent or hidden defect comes to light months or years after the goods are delivered.[43]

The Law Commissions discussed this question in their Report of 1987,[44] but recommended against any change in the law which would confer a long-term right of rejection on the buyer, where (for instance) serious defects come to light in the goods long after they are delivered. The chief reason for rejecting such a change seems to have been that it would introduce new complications regarding the use and benefit which the buyer may have had from the goods. At present, because rejection must take place within a relatively short period, it is possible for the law to insist that rejection of the goods produces a total failure of consideration, so that the buyer is entitled to the full repayment of his price. But if the law recognized a long-term right of rejection, it would hardly be possible to maintain this position, and the seller might well expect some credit for the use the buyer has had from the goods, even where the buyer does not seek damages. This would weaken the buyer's bargaining position where he rejects (or wants to reject) the goods, and introduce complications which the law currently avoids. Of course nothing said here detracts from the possibility of the buyer being able to pursue a claim for damages where hidden defects come to light long after delivery.[45]

In addition to the common law concept of affirmation, which is largely replaced for contracts of sale by the concept of acceptance, there are also other common law doctrines – such as waiver and estoppel (personal bar) – which are still frequently applied to contracts of sale, especially in commercial situations. Thus a buyer who makes clear and unequivocal representations (whether by express words, or by implication from conduct) that he will accept the goods, or that he will not reject them on the grounds of late delivery or some other ground of that kind, may lose his right to reject them under these common law doctrines.[46] So also a person cannot reject the goods if at the same time he acts in a way which is inconsistent with rejection,[47] whether this amounts to an acceptance or not.

---

42 See *Peyman* v *Lanjani* [1985] Ch 457. But, as also held in this case, the innocent party may lose his right to terminate even if he does not know the facts or his rights, if he represents (by words or conduct) that he is affirming the contract, and the other relies to his prejudice on that implied representation.

43 But see *Burrell* v *Harding's Exrs* 1931 SLT 76 (reredos rejected two years after sale after it was found not to be genuine); *MacGill* v *Talbot* 2002 GWD 12-382 (restoration of classic car found to be uneconomical 14 months after purchase); *Cruickshank* v *Specialist Cars (Aberdeen) Ltd* 2002 GWD 25-858 (reasonable for buyer not to test new car's caravan-towing capacity until he went on holiday four months after purchase).

44 See Law Commissions, *Sale and Supply of Goods*, paras 5.6–5.13.

45 As in the Scottish cases cited above, n. 43. See also *Lamarra* v *Capital Bank plc*, above, n. 33a.

46 Above, p. 134 *et seq.*

47 See *Vargas Pena Apezteguia y Cia Saic* v *Peter Cremer GmbH* [1987] 1 Lloyd's Rep 394.

A second preliminary comment is that there can be no acceptance of goods which the seller had no right to sell and, in such a case, the mere fact that the buyer has retained and used the goods does not prevent his rejecting them and recovering the full price as on a total failure of consideration.[48] It has been said, however, that 'Clearly the answer would not have been the same if the buyer, with knowledge of the true facts, had continued to use the [goods] for another twelve months or so, and had then found that the market had fallen and that he would like to hand [them] back again.'[49]

Third, a buyer who is entitled to reject goods for breach must, of course, mitigate his damage according to the ordinary rule. However, he cannot, it would seem, be required by this principle to accept goods when he wants to reject them (at all events when the goods are defective in quality),[50] nor to reject them when he wants to accept them.[51]

Fourthly, it should be observed that the buyer's right to reject defective goods may be, and very often is, qualified by express contractual provisions.[52] In some cases, restrictions on the right to reject may be imposed by making the right conditional on, for example, testing or sampling the goods. In others, there may be stringent time limits within which notice of rejection may be given, and so forth. In all such cases the provisions of the contract prevail, though subject, where appropriate, to the reasonableness requirements of the Unfair Contract Terms Act.

The meaning of 'acceptance' depends on the construction of ss. 34 to 35A(1), which are now as follows:

34. Unless otherwise agreed, when the seller tenders delivery of goods to the buyer, he is bound on request to afford the buyer a reasonable opportunity of examining the goods for the purpose of ascertaining whether they are in conformity with the contract, and in the case of a contract for sale by sample, of comparing the bulk with the sample.[53]

35. (1) The buyer is deemed to have accepted the goods subject to subsection (2) below—
   (a) when he intimates to the seller that he has accepted them, or
   (b) when the goods have been delivered to him and he does any act in relation to them which is inconsistent with the ownership of the seller.

   (2) Where goods are delivered to the buyer, and he has not previously examined them, he is not deemed to have accepted them under subsection (1) above until he has had a reasonable opportunity of examining them for the purpose—
   (a) of ascertaining whether they are in conformity with the contract and,
   (b) in the case of a contract for sale by sample, of comparing the bulk with the sample.

   (3) Where the buyer deals as consumer . . . the buyer cannot lose his right to rely on subsection (2) above by agreement, waiver or otherwise.

---

48 *Rowland* v *Divall* [1923] 2 KB 500 – see above, p. 114.
49 *Kwei Tek Chao* v *British Traders & Shippers Ltd* [1954] 2 WLR at 372, a passage omitted from the Report at [1954] 2 QB 459 – see above, p. 119, n. 34.
50 *Heaven & Kesterton Ltd* v *Etablissements François Albiac & Cie* [1956] 2 Lloyd's Rep 316. The position is different where there is no physical defect in the goods but the breach is, for example, late delivery: *The Solholt* [1983] 1 Lloyd's Rep 605. The reason for this distinction is that if the buyer proposes to buy in the market it would be reasonable to reject defective goods, but not necessarily reasonable to reject goods proffered by the seller a day or two late if they conform to the contract in quality.
51 *Kwei Tek Chao* v *British Traders & Shippers Ltd* [1954] 2 QB 459, 483.
52 For one example, see *W E Marshall & Co* v *Peat (Rubber) Ltd* [1963] 1 Lloyd's Rep 562.
53 The only change here made by the 1994 Act lies in the addition of the last few words relating to sales by sample, which are transferred from s. 15(2)(b). There is no change of substance otherwise.

(4) The buyer is also deemed to have accepted the goods when after the lapse of a reasonable time he retains the goods without intimating to the seller that he has rejected them.

(5) The questions that are material in determining for the purposes of subsection (4) above whether a reasonable time has elapsed include whether the buyer has had a reasonable opportunity of examining the goods for the purposes mentioned in subsection (2) above.

(6) The buyer is not by virtue of this section deemed to have accepted the goods merely because—

   (a) he asks for, or agrees to, their repair by or under arrangements with the seller, or

   (b) the goods are delivered to another under a sub-sale or other disposition.

(7) Where the contract is for the sale of goods making one or more commercial units, a buyer accepting any goods included in a unit is deemed to have accepted all the goods making the unit; and in this subsection, 'commercial unit' means a unit division of which would materially impair the value of the goods or the character of the unit.

[Subsection (8) which applies to contracts made before 22 April 1967[54] is omitted. The text of the new s. 35A which follows subsection (8) is set out at p. 521 where it is dealt with.]

It will be seen that under these sections there are in principle three ways in which the seller can accept the goods and so lose his right to reject them. First, he can expressly intimate that he accepts the goods; second, he can perform an act 'inconsistent with the ownership of the seller'; and third, he may simply retain the goods for a reasonable time, without rejecting them.

We proceed to examine these in turn.

Acceptance by express intimation

The first way in which the buyer can accept the goods appears simple enough, but the question was discussed by the Law Commission[55] whether a signed 'acceptance note' which a buyer simply signs without reading when the goods are delivered to him or her[56], and before he has examined them, or had an opportunity to examine them, can be treated as a true acceptance within the meaning of the sections. It must be appreciated that an express intimation of acceptance for the purposes of s. 35 has a rather special significance and must be interpreted accordingly. Such an acceptance amounts in substance and effect to a waiver of the right to reject the goods; it thus falls mid-way between a mere receipt or acknowledgment of delivery, on the one hand, and a complete waiver of all claims arising out of the sale, on the other hand. A person who simply signs a delivery note when goods are delivered in pursuance of a contract of sale plainly intends to do no more than to

---

54 This applies the provisions to be found in Sch. 1 para. 10 to such contracts.

55 Law Commissions, *Sale and Supply of Goods*, paras 5.20–5.25.

56 Where the buyer deals as consumer the buyer cannot lose his or her right of rejection in this way – see s. 35(3) dealt with below.

acknowledge receipt of the goods; it would be absurd to attribute to him the intention to waive his right to reject. The problem, of course, is that if he signs a printed form placed in front of him without reading it, and the form declares that the buyer accepts the goods within the meaning of s. 35 of the Act, there may be a tendency to treat this as binding on the buyer.[57] It seems unlikely that this in fact would have been held to be the case,[58] but the Law Commissions recommended that the law should anyhow be amended by making it clear that an intimation of acceptance is not in fact a binding acceptance if it occurs before the buyer has had a chance to examine the goods. This is the purpose of subsections (2) and (3) of the new provisions. A buyer who deals as consumer cannot lose his right to reject by agreement, waiver or otherwise until he has had a reasonable opportunity of examining them. It is also intended that a non-consumer buyer should not be deemed to have accepted the goods until he has had a reasonable opportunity of examining them, but in this case it will be possible (subject to the Unfair Contract Terms Act)[59] for the parties to agree otherwise.[60]

It is also possible that a buyer accepts the goods in such a manner as to waive, not merely the right to reject, but also any claim for damages which he may have. A buyer who actually examines some specific item and finds it defective in some minor respects, but accepts it without demur, may thus find that he has lost both the right to reject and the right to claim damages. This latter right, however, being more fundamental, is less easily lost. A real waiver or circumstances giving rise to a promissory estoppel may be necessary to deprive the buyer of the right to claim damages where defective goods are 'accepted' by him.[61]

Acceptance by an act inconsistent with the ownership of the seller

Much the most difficult questions concerning acceptance involve the second method mentioned in s. 35, and the difficulty was originally compounded because the 1893 Act did not expressly state whether s. 34 or s. 35 was the governing section. It therefore left open the position where the buyer had not had a reasonable opportunity of examining the goods within s. 34, but did something which brought him within s. 35. It is quite possible for the buyer to do some act inconsistent with the ownership of the seller before he has had a reasonable opportunity for examining the goods and, in this event, there was formerly a serious conflict between s. 34 and s. 35. The former said that in such circumstances the buyer was not deemed to have accepted the goods, and s. 35 said that in these circumstances the buyer was deemed to have accepted the goods.[62]

---

57 See *Mechans v Highland Marine Charters* 1964 SC 48.
58 Given the wide interpretation placed on s. 13 of the Unfair Contract Terms Act 1977 by the Court of Appeal in cases such as *Stewart Gill v Horatio Myer & Co Ltd* [1992] 2 All ER 257 and *Fastframe Ltd v Lohinski* 3 March 1993 (unreported) it might be that such acceptance notes would be held to be subject to that Act. See p. 229.
59 See p. 234 *et seq.*
60 See Law Commissions Report paras 5.23 and 5.24.
61 See *Ets Soules et Cie v International Trade Devpt Co Ltd* [1980] 1 Lloyd's Rep 129.
62 One is reminded of the famous dictum of Lord Mildew, 'There is too much of this damned deeming'; see *Travers v Travers*, in *Cod's Last Case*, p. 80, by Sir Alan Herbert.

In *Hardy & Co Ltd v Hillerns & Fowler*[63] the Court of Appeal held that s. 35 was the governing section. The facts of the case illustrate the hardship to the buyer which resulted from this interpretation of the Act. A contracted to sell to B wheat to be shipped from South America. The ship carrying the wheat arrived at Hull on 18 March. On 21 March, B resold a part of the cargo and dispatched it to the sub-buyers. On 23 March, B had his first opportunity to examine the goods and, on doing so, found them not to conform to the contract. It was held that by reselling the goods the buyers had done an act inconsistent with the ownership of the sellers within s. 35, and that they had therefore accepted the goods and lost their right of rejection.[64]

This decision was distinguished by a New Zealand court in *Hammer & Barrow v Coca-Cola*,[65] although the facts of the cases were very similar. In this case, the plaintiffs contracted to sell some goods to the defendants, it being a term of the contract that the goods would be delivered to the premises of a third party to whom the defendant had previously contracted to supply the same goods. Richmond J emphasized that under s. 35 two requirements must be satisfied before a buyer can be deemed to have accepted the goods in the second of the three ways mentioned in that section. First, the goods must have been delivered to him and, secondly, he must have done some act inconsistent with the seller's ownership. The learned judge held that, in dispatching the goods to the third party, the seller was acting as a seller delivering the goods to the buyer in accordance with the contract of sale. Nothing had been done thereafter which could be treated as inconsistent with the seller's ownership. In *E & S Ruben Ltd v Faire Bros & Co Ltd*,[66] on the other hand, Hilbery J held that, in delivering the goods to the carrier for transmission to the third party, the sellers were acting as agents for the buyer and that the goods must be treated as notionally delivered to the buyers before they were delivered to the carriers. The delivery to the carriers was, therefore, evidence of an act subsequent to delivery to the buyer which could be treated as inconsistent with the seller's ownership.

These cases left the law in an unsatisfactory state. It is common practice for goods to be bought and resold without examination until they are delivered to the sub-buyer. In these circumstances, the sub-buyer retained the right to reject the goods while the middle buyer was deemed to have 'accepted' them and so was deprived of his right to reject. The law was accordingly altered by s. 4(2) of the Misrepresentation Act 1967, which inserted in s. 35 of the Sale of Goods Act the words '(except where section 34 of the Act otherwise provides)', thereby making it clear that s. 34 was the governing section.[67] The position, therefore, was that the buyer was deemed to have accepted the goods: (a) when he intimated to the seller that he had accepted them, or (b) (except where section 34 of the Act otherwise provided) when the goods have been delivered to him, and (i) he did any act which is inconsistent with the ownership

---

63 [1923] 2 KB 490.

64 Cf. *Benaim & Co v L S Debono* [1924] AC 514 where all the goods were actually delivered to the sub-buyer. See also *Mechan v Bow McLachlan & Co* 1910 SC 758; *Morrison & Mason v Clarkson Bros* (1898) 25 R 427.

65 [1962] NZLR 723, noted in (1963) 26 Mod LR 194. See also *Pelhams (Materials) Ltd v Mercantile Commodities Syndicate* [1953] 2 Lloyd's Rep 281.

66 [1949] 1 KB 254. As pointed out by Richmond J it was not part of the original contract that the goods should be delivered to the third parties in that case.

67 This amendment also applied in Scotland.

of the seller, or (ii) when, after lapse of a reasonable time, he retained the goods without intimating to the seller that he had rejected them.[68]

There is no doubt that this was a considerable improvement in the law, but it became reasonably evident that it did not go far enough. Since the buyer cannot reject, in any event, unless he is in a position to restore the goods to the seller,[69] why should he lose the right to reject merely because he has done an act inconsistent with the ownership of the seller and has had an opportunity to examine the goods? Suppose the buyer failed to take the opportunity, or failed to discover the defect in question, and then resold and delivered to a sub-buyer. If the sub-buyer immediately discovered the defect and returned the goods to the buyer, the buyer would still be unable to reject the goods notwithstanding the new s. 35. Yet the fact that the buyer had done an act which might affect his ability to restore the goods to the seller was surely no reason for depriving him of his right to reject when in fact it did not affect his ability so to restore the goods.

The Law Commissions largely agreed with these criticisms of the law,[70] and the new s. 35(6)(b) provides that the buyer is not deemed to have accepted goods merely because the goods are delivered to another under a sub-sale or other disposition.

Unfortunately, the new provision leaves a consequential point somewhat unclear. This problem is that it will now be uncertain what is to happen where the sub-buyer rejects the goods without returning them to the buyer. Is the buyer then also to be entitled to reject the goods while they remain physically situated at the premises of the sub-buyer? It will be remembered that under s. 36 of the Act the buyer is not bound to return the goods to the seller when he rejects them; it is sufficient that he intimates to the seller that the goods are at his disposal. Similarly, if the buyer arranges for the retransport of the goods from the sub-buyer, can he charge the seller with the cost of this in addition to rejecting the goods? Prior to the passing of the Misrepresentation Act, the position on this point was somewhat obscure.[71] But since that Act the position seemed to depend on whether the buyer had had a reasonable opportunity to examine the goods and so lost his right to reject.

Under the law prior to 3 January 1995, the buyer still lost his right of rejection if he had had a reasonable opportunity to examine the goods and had resold and delivered the goods to a sub-buyer. In *Perkins* v *Bell*,[72] it was held that prima facie the place of delivery to the buyer was the place where he ought to examine the goods, and if he chose to redispatch the goods to the sub-buyer without examining them he would (it seemed) lose his right to reject. In this case the seller sold barley to the defendant for delivery at T railway station. The defendant could have examined the barley there but he sent it on to sub-buyers, who later rejected it. The buyer was held

---

68 This sub-division into paragraphs was not in the 1979 Act itself; and it was not entirely clear whether the words in brackets which were first inserted by the 1967 Act did control the third limb of the section, as they clearly would if the Act were set out as it is in the text. It is also to be noted that the words in brackets clearly did not control the first limb of the section (express intimation of acceptance), so, as mentioned above, p. 508, such an intimation would be effective even if the buyer had not had a chance to examine the goods. But the new provisions alter the law on this point – see above, p. 509 *et seq.*

69 See above, p. 505.

70 See Law Commissions, *Sale and Supply of Goods*, para. 5.38.

71 See *Perkins* v *Bell* [1893] 1 QB 193, decided just before the Sale of Goods Act was passed; *Molling & Co* v *Dean & Son Ltd* (1901) 18 TLR 217, which was adversely commented on in *Hardy & Co* v *Hillerns & Fowler* – see above – but became good law again following the 1967 amendments to the Sale of Goods Act.

72 See above.

to have lost his right to reject and the principal reason for this seems to have been the court's view that it would be unjust to compel the seller to collect the barley from the sub-buyer's premises. What the court did not consider was whether this injustice could not be avoided by a less drastic step than depriving the buyer of his right to reject. Justice would have been done and the seller's interest secured if the court had held that the buyer could reject, provided that he put the goods at the seller's disposal at the place where they were delivered to him. Unfortunately, the effect of s. 34 and s. 35 as they were in the 1979 Act was still to deprive the buyer of the right to reject in this situation.[73]

What is more, the effect of the new provisions on this point is obscure. Section 35(6)(b) makes it clear that the mere fact of delivery under a subcontract will not now be treated as an act inconsistent with the ownership of the seller; but will the buyer's refusal to recollect the goods from the sub-buyer make any difference? Given s. 36 of the Act, it seems that the answer will probably be 'no'; but the results may be somewhat drastic if the goods have (for instance) been shipped to a sub-buyer overseas, who ultimately rejects them on arrival, so that the buyer in turn then rejects them too. Presumably in this situation it will be the seller's responsibility to arrange for the handling of the goods at their overseas destination, even though the seller is a purely domestic producer who did not sell for export himself, and had no reason to know that the goods were going to be exported. Under the 1979 Act that result would be avoided, because the delivery under the sub-sale would be an act inconsistent with the ownership of the seller, so the buyer would not have the right at all to reject in this situation.[74]

There are some cases in which the courts are prepared to hold that the place of delivery to the buyer is not a reasonable place to examine the goods,[75] and, in this situation, the buyer does not lose his right to reject when the goods have been resold and delivered, even under the 1979 Act. Moreover, in this case the responsibility for retransporting the goods to the original place of delivery will be the seller's. For instance, in *Molling & Co v Dean & Son*,[76] the plaintiffs made 40,000 books to the defendants' order, knowing that they were intended for shipment and resale to an American sub-buyer. Indeed, the plaintiffs printed the books with the sub-buyer's imprint and packed them for shipment to him. They were delivered to the defendants, who consigned them to the sub-buyers without examination. The sub-buyers rejected and the defendants brought the goods back to England at their own cost. It was held that they were entitled to reject the goods and also to recover the cost of transport on the ground that the proper place for inspection was on delivery to the sub-buyers. Hence the buyers had not had a reasonable opportunity to examine the goods. Consequently, under the 1979 Act this decision is now clearly good law: the buyer would be deemed not to have accepted the goods under s. 34 because he

---

73 For the possibility of avoiding this result in appropriate cases by seeking rescission for misrepresentation, see below, p. 530.
74 *Saunt v Belcher* (1920) 26 Com Cas 115, 118–19.
75 This is especially true of f.o.b. contracts: see *Bragg v Villanova* (1923) 40 TLR 154; *Boks & Co v J H Rayner & Co* (1921) 37 TLR 800. But cf. *Commercial Fibres (Ireland) Ltd v Zabaida* [1975] 1 Lloyd's Rep 27.
76 See above, p. 513, n. 71.

had not had a reasonable opportunity to examine them under s. 35. The new provisions do not affect this sort of case, and the result anyhow seems perfectly reasonable.

'Act inconsistent with the ownership of the seller'

An unhappy feature still retained following the 1994 Act's amendments is the reference in s. 35 to an act 'inconsistent with the ownership of the seller'. This suggests that the ownership of the goods cannot pass until the buyer has accepted them, but of course this is not so. Furthermore, if the property has already passed to the buyer, how can he be said to do an act inconsistent with 'the ownership of the seller'? One possible answer is to be found in the judgment of Devlin J in *Kwei Tek Chao v British Traders & Shippers Ltd.*[77] If the property has passed in circumstances in which the buyer retains the right to reject, the passing is merely conditional:

> He [the buyer] gets only conditional property in the goods, the condition being a condition subsequent. All his dealings with the documents[78] are dealings only with that conditional property in the goods. It follows, therefore, that there can be no dealing which is inconsistent with the seller's ownership unless he deals with something more than the conditional property. If the property passes altogether, not being subject to any condition, there is no ownership left in the seller with which any inconsistent act under s. 35 could be committed. If the property passes conditionally the only ownership left in the seller is the reversionary interest in the property in the event of the condition subsequent operating to restore it to him. It is that reversionary interest with which the buyer must not, save with the penalty of accepting the goods, commit an inconsistent act.[79]

What this comes to can perhaps be put more simply. Although the property in the goods may have passed to the buyer, if he is still entitled to reject them and does reject them, the property will revest in the seller, and he will then become owner of the goods again.

But Devlin J's way of putting the law does not help to decide whether any other sort of act should be held inconsistent with the ownership of the seller. For example, in consumer sales where goods are bought for use, what kind of use would be inconsistent with the seller's ownership? If the seller's reversionary right is only to receive the goods in the state in which they are when the buyer rejects them, this formula simply gives no answer to the question, what sort of use by the buyer will prevent rejection? The truth is that the phrase 'an act inconsistent with the ownership of the seller' is one with no fixed meaning. The court is, in effect, empowered to decide whether it thinks that the buyer ought to be entitled to reject the goods according to the circumstances of the case. In order to ascertain what meaning the phrase has, therefore, it is necessary to examine the case law to see what acts the courts have in fact held to be inconsistent with the ownership of the seller.

It will be apparent from the above discussion that much the most common type of act 'inconsistent with the ownership of the seller' was a resale and delivery of the

---

77 [1954] 2 QB 459.
78 The case was concerned with a sale on c.i.f. terms, but the reasoning on this part of the case applies to all sales of goods.
79 [1954] 2 QB 459, 487.

goods.[80] The authorities did not go much beyond this. At all events, even under the former provisions, there seems to have been no case in which the mere fact of a sub-sale, without more, and in particular without delivery, was held to deprive the buyer of his right to reject.[81] It may well be that following the decision in *Kwei Tek Chao* v *British Traders & Shippers Ltd*[82] the courts would have held that nothing short of actual delivery would have this effect. Certainly it was said that a buyer was not deemed to have accepted the goods merely because he has made inquiries with a view to their resale, even after discovering them to be defective.[83] In Australia, it was also held that a claim by the buyer against the insurer in respect of damage to the goods was not inconsistent with the seller's ownership.[84] The effect of the new provisions is that the former of these decisions is confirmed by implication, because if resale and delivery to a sub-buyer is not by itself to be treated as an act inconsistent with the ownership of the seller, obviously preliminary steps on the way to this result cannot have this effect either.

Documentary sales

In the *British Traders & Shippers* case, Devlin J, after giving his explanation of the phrase 'an act inconsistent with the ownership of the seller', went on to hold that in documentary sales the buyer is not deprived of his right to reject merely by dealing with the documents:

> So long as he [the buyer] is merely dealing with the documents he is not purporting to do anything more than pledge the conditional property which he has. Similarly, if he sells the documents of title he sells the conditional property. But if, as was done in *Hardy & Co* v *Hillerns & Fowler*,[85] when the goods have been landed, he physically deals with the goods and delivers them to his sub-buyer, he is doing an act which is inconsistent with the seller's reversionary interest.[86]

The result of this case appeared to be that in a documentary sale the buyer had two distinct rights of rejection: a right to reject documents not conforming to the contract, and a right to reject the goods themselves if they failed to conform to the contract. A dealing with the documents might deprive the buyer of his right to reject the documents, but could not deprive him of his right to reject the goods. However, it now seems that this is not really a very satisfactory statement of the law. At least three qualifications need to be made to Devlin J's exposition. The first is that if (as sometimes happens) the goods arrive before the shipping documents, and the buyer physically takes delivery or otherwise deals in the goods, he will be held to have accepted them.[87] There will be no separate right of rejection of the documents when they arrive unless perhaps these disclose additional breaches of contract not previously known to the buyer.

---

80 *Hardy & Co* v *Hillerns & Fowler* [1923] 2 KB 490, which is still good law on this point.
81 Cf. *J & J Cunningham* v *R A Munro & Co Ltd* (1922) 28 Com Cas 42, 48.
82 [1954] 2 QB 459.
83 *Fisher Reeves & Co Ltd* v *Armour & Co Ltd* [1920] 3 KB 614, 624 per Scrutton LJ.
84 *J & S Robertson (Aust) Pty Ltd* v *Martin* (1955–6) 94 CLR 30. If the buyer rejects, he will of course have to pay over the insurance money to the seller (or credit him, if he has previously paid the price); ibid., p. 60.
85 [1923] 2 KB 490.
86 [1954] 2 QB 459, 487–8.
87 *Tradax International SA* v *Goldschmidt SA* [1977] 2 Lloyd's Rep 604.

The second qualification that needs to be made to Devlin J's statement of the law is that the buyer's acceptance of the documents may very well deprive him of his right to reject the goods where the breach of contract relating to the documents and the breach relating to the goods are in effect one breach only, and not two distinct breaches. Thus, if the goods are shipped late and this fact appears from the documents, the seller is, in principle, in breach of his obligations both as regards the documents and as regards the goods. Nevertheless, it is unreal to treat this as involving two separate breaches, and if the buyer accepts the documents he may well be treated as having waived the seller's breach and thus be bound to accept the goods.[88] Thus, even though acceptance of (or dealing with) the documents may not strictly amount to an act inconsistent with the seller's ownership, the buyer may be unable to reject the goods on other grounds in such circumstances, such as waiver or estoppel.

The third qualification that needs to be made to Devlin J's statement of the law in the *British Traders & Shippers* case is that whatever the law may say about dealing with the documents not amounting to a dealing with the goods, in practice such a dealing may affect the buyer's power to reject the goods. If he has resold the documents, for instance, he will hardly be able to reject the goods unless the sub-buyer himself rejects – but equally he is unlikely to want to reject except in this case. In the case of a pledge, however, the position may be more difficult because the buyer may be unable to reject the goods without the consent of the pledgee, who may insist on being paid off first. Certainly this appears to be the effect of the Uniform Customs.[89] Therefore, where the price has been paid to the seller by a banker's credit against documents, the buyer will in practice have to pay off the bank to obtain a release of the documents before he can return them to the seller and so reject the goods.

Goods bought for use

Where goods are bought for use, a somewhat different approach may be necessary in defining the meaning of an 'act inconsistent with the ownership of the seller', though there is little authority directly in point.[90] Probably any substantial or repeated or prolonged use would be held inconsistent with the seller's ownership if it prevented the buyer returning the goods in substantially the same condition as when purchased. In effect, this ground of the loss of the right of rejection merges (especially in consumer sales) into the next ground, namely that the buyer has allowed a reasonable time to elapse before rejecting the goods. It is therefore dealt with further under that heading, below.

---

88 *Panchaud Frères SA* v *Etablissements General Grain Co* [1970] 1 Lloyd's Rep 53; *Bremer* v *Vanden Avenne-Izegen* [1978] 2 Lloyd's Rep 109; *Bremer* v *C Mackprang* [1979] 2 Lloyd's Rep 220. It is controversial whether this is strictly a matter of waiver, or estoppel, or solely the effect of s. 35, but these differences of concept seem largely immaterial except for one point: under s. 35 absence of knowledge of the breach does not preclude a finding of 'acceptance', but it does seem to preclude a finding of waiver. As to estoppel, see above, p. 134.

89 See Art. 9.

90 See *Armaghdown Motors* v *Gray* [1963] NZLR 5 (registration of car in buyer's name held inconsistent with seller's ownership). Scottish authorities hold that if the buyer continues to use goods after intimating rejection of them, he cannot insist on his right to reject – *Electric Construction Co* v *Hurry and Young* (1897) 24 R 312; *Croom & Arthur* v *Stewart* (1905) 7 F 563. See also *Morrison & Mason* v *Clarkson Bros* (1898) 25 R 427; *Mechan* v *Bow McLachlan & Co* 1910 SC 750; *Cruickshank* v *Specialist Cars (Aberdeen) Ltd* 2002 GWD 25-858 (Sheriff A. L. MacFadyen); *Lamarra* v *Capital Bank plc* 2004 GWD 40-817 (Sh Prin J C McInnes).

Acceptance through lapse of reasonable time

The third way in which the buyer can accept the goods within the meaning of s. 35 is to retain them for more than a reasonable time before he informs the seller that he wants to reject them.[91] Section 35(5) now provides that the questions that are material in determining for the purposes of subsection (4) above whether a reasonable time has elapsed include whether the buyer has had a reasonable opportunity of examining the goods for the purpose mentioned in subsection (2), i.e. of ascertaining whether they are in conformity with the contract, and in the case of a contract for sale by sample, of comparing the bulk with the sample.

The question of what is a reasonable time in the case of goods bought for resale, was examined by Judge Jack QC in *Truk (UK) Ltd* v *Tokmakidis GmbH*[92] in which a vehicle chassis with a body specially fitted by the claimant was delivered on 14 June 1996. In December 1996 the defendant was informed by the sub-buyer that the body did not correspond to the chassis maker's guidelines. The judge found that the vehicle had been rejected in March 1997. He laid down a number of propositions as to what is a reasonable time to reject the goods: (1) it was necessary to look at the question by balancing the opposing interests of the buyer and the seller; (2) the reasonable time to exercise the right to reject could not be less than the time for the buyer to have a reasonable opportunity to examine the goods; (3) the reasonable time to exercise a right to reject might well be longer than is required to examine the goods; (4) the time could be extended by dealings between the buyer and the seller, in particular as regards the repair of the goods (as had been the situation in the present case);[93] and (5) there was only one reasonable time and not different times for different defects. What mattered in the present case was that the goods were to be resold. This consideration coupled with s. 35(6)(b) led to the conclusion that the reasonable time for rejection would normally be the time taken to resell the goods, together with an additional period in which they could be tested by the sub-buyer.

In the case of goods bought for use, and therefore in most consumer sales, this ground for treating the buyer as having accepted the goods tends to merge, as noted above, with the doctrine of the act 'inconsistent with the ownership of the seller'; because, clearly, the longer the buyer retains and continues to use the goods, the more difficult it will be for him to claim that his conduct is not inconsistent with the seller's reversionary rights – circular though that argument tends to be. In these cases, the question will nearly always be one of fact: what is a reasonable time? There has not been a great deal of litigation on the question in consumer sales, doubtless because if a seller refuses to receive the goods back, the consumer will in practice be in a very difficult position. If he continues to use the goods after the seller has refused to receive them back, the prospect of ever persuading a court that the right to reject is still alive becomes somewhat remote.[94] On the other hand, if the buyer abstains from using the goods while he tries to litigate the issue, he is also in a difficult practical position. What is he to do with the goods in the meantime? And if the goods are of some value – for instance, a motor vehicle – the

---

91 Section 35(4).
92 [2000] 2 All ER (Comm) 594.
93 See also *Rogers* v *Parish (Scarborough) Ltd* [1987] QB 933, p. 519 below.
94 On the other hand, if the buyer has no real alternative but to use the goods, e.g. a car required to get to and from work, the situation might be different – see, e.g., *Liarikos* v *Mello* 639 NE 2d 216 (Mass 1994) (a case on Art. 2-602 of the Uniform Commercial Code).

buyer may well have tied up so much capital that he cannot just store the goods pending litigation and go out and buy a replacement.[95] The result is that the case law on the consumer's right of rejection tends to be sparse, and is mostly confined to cases involving vehicles. There is no doubt that, in general, the tendency under the former provisions was to hold that the right of rejection is lost speedily where goods were in daily use, and this normally meant days, rather than weeks or months.[96]

Bernstein v *Pamson Motors (Golders Green) Ltd*[97] was something of a test case on this question in relation to the rejection of motor vehicles. Here the buyer sought to reject a new car for serious defects causing a major breakdown on a motorway after he had had the car for three weeks but only done some 140 miles. While holding that the buyer was undoubtedly entitled to damages, Rougier J held that he had lost the right to reject as a reasonable time for rejection had elapsed. In *Clegg* v *Olle Andersson*[98] the Court of Appeal held that *Bernstein* v *Pamson Motor* no longer represented the law since the Sale and Supply of Goods Act 1994. Moreover, in *Rogers* v *Parish (Scarborough) Ltd*[99] the vehicle had travelled over 5,500 miles when the plaintiffs rejected it after the lapse of a period of six months. Nevertheless, it seems not to have occurred to the defendants to argue that the right to reject had been lost.[100] In the most recent Scottish cases, the sellers' arguments that the buyers' right to reject had been lost through lapse of time were likewise unsuccessful.[101]

One or two earlier cases also indicate a slightly more favourable attitude to the buyer. In *Porter* v *General Guarantee Corpn*,[102] the plaintiff acquired a car at the end of January and by 4 March his solicitors were claiming the right to reject the vehicle; further attempts to put right the defects ensued, but on 20 March the plaintiff finally claimed the right to reject, and this was held not too late. This was, however, a hire-purchase rather than a sale, and there are certain distinctions in the legal position, first because the hire-purchase legislation contains nothing equivalent to s. 35 of the Sale of Goods Act, so that the loss of the right to reject is a common law matter; and, secondly, because the supplier in a hire-purchase contract remains owner and hence continues to have an interest in the condition of the goods after delivery. This means that it may be more reasonable to allow a longer time for rejection in a hire-purchase contract than in a sale. The same comments must apply to another hire-purchase case of a Daimler in which rejection seems to have been permitted several months after the car was first supplied.[103] Indeed, it could in theory be argued that since hire-purchase is a contract of hire (plus an option to buy) the supplier should supply goods which would remain fit to be used throughout the period of hire – assuming, of course, that the hirer used

---

95 See n. 94 above. Note also *Lamarra* v *Capital Bank plc* 2004 GWD 40-817 (Sh Prin J C McInnes).
96 See, e.g., *Long* v *Lloyd* [1958] 1 WLR 753 (strictly a case of misrepresentation); *Lee* v *York Coach & Marine* [1977] RTR 35; *Flynn* v *Scott* 1949 SC 442.
97 [1987] 2 All ER 220.
98 [2003] EWCA Civ 320.
99 [1987] QB 933.
100 Presumably, having regard to the circumstances of the case, the defendants' legal advisers took the view that such an argument was not worth running. It was only on appeal that they attempted to argue this point, and the Court of Appeal declined to deal with it because it had been put forward only at the appeal, having neither been pleaded nor argued at first instance.
101 *MacGill* v *Talbot* 2002 GWD 12-382 (Sheriff G. J. Evans); *Cruickshank* v *Specialist Cars (Aberdeen) Ltd* 2002 GWD 25-858 (Sheriff A.L. MacFadyen).
102 [1982] RTR 384.
103 *Laurelgates Ltd* v *Lombard North Central Ltd* (1983) 133 New LJ 720; See also *Lamarra* v *Capital Bank plc* above n. 95; cf. *Lutton* v *Saville Tractors (Belfast) Ltd* [1986] 12 NIJB 1.

them properly. However, the implied terms contained in the Supply of Goods (Implied Terms) Act 1973 (or strictly speaking the Consumer Credit Act 1974) are identical to those contained in the Sale of Goods Act and appear to require the goods to be of the required quality only at the time of supply. The same applies to the warranties implied in pure hire contracts by the Supply of Goods and Services Act 1982. In *UCB Leasing v Holtom*[104] the Court of Appeal held that in the case of a finance lease the issue is the fitness of the goods at the time of their delivery. But a finance lease and hire-purchase transactions are functional equivalents of sales of goods, and there may be an argument that, in hiring proper, the situation may be different.[105]

It used not to be clear what effect attempts to remedy defects might have on the buyer's right to reject in these consumer cases. It is, of course, the normal response of the parties where defective consumer goods are sold for the buyer to demand that they should be repaired. And in the case of vehicles, there is often a long history of such attempts before the buyer finally tries to reject. In one hire-purchase case the court seems to have treated the extra time taken up by such repeated attempts at repair as not counting against the buyer in deciding whether a reasonable time had elapsed since the sale,[106] but it is again unclear for the reasons given above whether this kind of reasoning would have been applicable in a contract of sale to which the former s. 35 applied. The new provisions, at all events, dispose of this point, because they contain the new s. 35(6)(a) which provides that the buyer is not deemed to have accepted the goods merely because he asks the seller for the goods to be repaired.[107] In the commercial case of *J & H Ritchie Ltd v Lloyd Ltd*,[107a] however, a purchaser of defective agricultural machinery who had accepted the seller's offer of repair was held unable later to reject the tender of repaired goods that on the evidence were con-form to contract. The purchaser's difficulty was its inability to obtain from the seller explanations as to what the original problem with the goods had been. For the majority of the court, so long as the contract remained un-terminated, the seller had a continuing opportunity to supply conforming goods, and once it had done so, any rejection would be too late. Section 35(6) did not preserve a right to reject even if the repair was satisfactory; the seller was not to be kept on the end of a string. Lord Marnoch, dissenting, argued that the original right to reject could not be lost simply through a retendering of repaired goods, since that was not performance according to the contract. On the whole, the majority view seems preferable; but s 35(6) probably needs clarification to confirm the point.

Where goods are not bought for use but for resale – as in the typical commercial contract – the question of the reasonableness of the time for rejection rarely arises; in practice, either the goods are passed on to sub-buyers who reject forthwith, or they are accepted by the sub-buyers so that the buyers themselves have no need to worry about rejection. But cases can occasionally arise (for instance, where some time elapses before the sub-buyers reject and return the goods to the buyer) in

---

104 [1987] RTR 362.

105 See Adams, *Commercial Hiring and Leasing*, 1989, para. 5.52 *et seq.*

106 *Farnworth Finance Facilities Ltd v Attryde* [1970] 1 WLR 1053.

107 And the remedies introduced into consumer sales by the Sale and Supply of Goods to Consumers Regulations 2002, SI 2002/3045, dealt with at p. 526 below, should be noted.

107a 2005 SLT 64.

which the reasonableness of the time for rejection can be in issue. In one case[108] it was held that, where the sellers were threatening the buyers that any rejection would be treated as a breach of contract, the buyers were entitled to take particular care to examine the goods, and consult with sub-buyers, before committing themselves to rejection. A seller who insists all along that the goods are in accordance with the contract cannot complain if the buyer takes some extra time to satisfy himself beyond question that the goods are defective before he rejects them.

Acceptance of part of the goods

The question whether the buyer is entitled to accept part and reject part of the goods delivered is one of some difficulty. The opening words of s. 11(4), it will be recalled,[109] are now as follows:

> Subject to section 35A below, where a contract of sale is not severable, and the buyer has accepted the goods or part of them, etc.
> 35A. (1) If the buyer—
>   (a) has the right to reject the goods by reason of a breach on the part of the seller that affects some or all of them, but
>   (b) accepts some of the goods, including, where there are any goods unaffected by the breach, all such goods
>   he does not by accepting them lose his right to reject the rest.
> (2) In the case of a buyer having the right to reject an instalment of goods, subsection (1) above applies as if references to the goods were references to the goods comprised in the instalment.
> (3) For the purposes of subsection (1) above, goods are affected by a breach if by reason of the breach they are not in conformity with the contract.
> (4) This section applies unless a contrary intention appears in, or is to be implied from, the contract.

Read literally, s. 11(4) only applies to a contract of sale which is not severable; but severability is only relevant where the buyer purports to accept part of the goods, so the paragraph should probably be read as meaning:

> Where the buyer has accepted the goods, or where the contract of sale is not severable and the buyer has accepted part of the goods, etc.

Assuming that this is the correct construction, it seems clear that if the contract is severable the buyer is entitled to reject goods not conforming to the contract and to accept the balance of the goods if he chooses to do so. (He may also be entitled to throw up the entire contract in the circumstances referred to in s. 31(2), as previously discussed.)[110] Even this proposition may seem open to theoretical objections if the right to reject the goods is merely a species of the right to rescind,[111] and it would seem inconsistent for the buyer to rescind the contract while retaining part of the goods. However, this objection is purely academic; as a matter of practical convenience, it is plainly right that the buyer should be entitled to accept part and

---

108 *Manifatture Tessile Laniera* v *J B Ashley Ltd* [1979] 2 Lloyd's Rep 28.
109 See pp. 506–7. Section 11(4) does not apply in Scotland, but s. 35A does.
110 See above, p. 501 *et seq.*
111 A view which is almost certainly wrong – see p. 483 *et seq* above.

reject part of the goods in the case of severable contracts. (The position under the new provisions in the case of severable contracts is dealt with below.)

A further question arises in relation to the above discussion: what contracts are severable?

What contracts are severable?

This is not a question which has been the subject of much judicial discussion. It will be recalled that under s. 31(2), a contract is severable if the goods are to be delivered in instalments and the instalments are to be separately paid for. But it is clear that a contract may be severable in many other situations also. For instance, a contract for the sale of a quantity of cloth was held to be severable where the cloth was to be delivered in instalments although the price was to be paid by monthly account and not separately for each instalment.[112] And a contract for the sale of some motor accessories was held to be severable purely on the ground that the contract specified 'deliveries as required'.[113] This was interpreted to mean that the goods would necessarily be delivered in instalments and it was assumed that this was enough to render the contract severable. In other cases, a buyer has been held entitled to accept part and reject part of the goods though it has not always been clear whether this was on the ground that the contract was severable.[114]

Export contracts often provide that the seller is entitled to ship the goods in separate loads and that in this event each shipment is to be considered a distinct contract. Such a clause gives the seller the option to treat the contract as an entire contract by shipping the goods in one load, or to treat it as severable and ship different loads.[115] If he ships the goods in different lots it may be important for the buyer's right to reject that the contract be treated as severable because different loads involve different shipping documents; hence one load may be resold to X, who may reject the goods, and another load to Y, who does not reject. In this situation, the middle buyer will wish to have the right to reject part and accept part of the total quantity sold to him.

Buyer's right to accept part and reject part of goods in non-severable contracts

Prima facie the former s. 11(4) would seem to have prevented a buyer from accepting part and rejecting part of the goods if the contract was not severable. But the position was much complicated by s. 30(4) of the Act (now repealed), which was set out above[116] and which provided that if the seller delivered 'the goods he contracted to sell mixed with goods of a different description' the buyer might accept the conforming goods and reject the rest. Section 11(4) was treated by the courts as subject to this provision[117] so that, even if the contract was non-severable, the buyer might, in the circumstances specified in s. 30(4), accept part and reject part of the goods. For example, in *Ebrahim Dawood Ltd* v *Heath Ltd*[118] sellers contracted to sell 50 tons

112 *Longbottom & Co Ltd* v *Bass Walker & Co Ltd* [1922] WN 245.
113 *Jackson* v *Rotax Motor & Cycle Co Ltd* [1910] 2 KB 937; see also *Regent OHG Aisendstadt* v *Francesco of Jermyn Street* [1981] 3 All ER 327.
114 See, e.g., *Molling & Co* v *Dean & Son Ltd* (1901) 18 TLR 217 (sale of 40,000 books printed by plaintiff to defendant's order).
115 For an unusual case in which the goods were shipped on one ship, but as two lots, with separate shipping documents, see *Esmail* v *J Rosenthal & Sons Ltd* [1965] 2 All ER 860.
116 See above, p. 143.
117 *London Plywood & Timber Co Ltd* v *Nasic Oak Extract Factory Co Ltd* [1939] 2 KB 343.
118 [1961] 2 Lloyd's Rep 512.

of steel sheet in varying lengths. In fact, they delivered the whole quantity in 6 foot lengths. This was plainly a non-severable contract, yet the buyer was held entitled, under s. 30(4), to accept part of the goods and reject the rest.

But the buyer could only do this where the case fell within the precise wording of s. 30(4) (now repealed); therefore the buyer had to show that the seller had delivered 'the goods that he contracted to sell mixed with goods of a different description'. We have already seen that[119] the courts construed the words 'the goods he contracted to sell' as including the case where the seller did not deliver the correct total quantity of contract goods. Thus if the seller contracted to sell 100 tons of wheat and he delivered 50 tons of wheat and 50 tons of barley, he had delivered 'the goods he contracted to sell mixed with goods of a different description'.

However, s. 30(4) did not apply where the goods delivered by the seller were *all* of the contract description, but some part of them were of unmerchantable quality.[120] In this situation, the buyer could not reject part and accept part of the goods under s. 30(4) and would therefore only be able to do this under s. 11(4) if the contract was severable. Nor did s. 30(4) apply where all the goods were unmerchantable or failed to conform to the contract. Such a case also had to be governed solely by s. 11(4).

Some hypothetical examples may make the point clearer. Suppose, for example, that a person bought 700 bags of nuts from a seller. Prima facie that was (and still is) a non-severable contract, that is it is a contract for the sale of a quantity of nuts, the fact that they were in 700 bags being immaterial. If the seller delivered 700 bags and 600 were satisfactory, but the remaining 100 bags contained nuts which were unmerchantable, the buyer could not accept the 600 and reject the remainder, since 'the contract of sale was not severable and the buyer has accepted the goods or part of them'. On the other hand, if the remaining 100 bags contained nuts of a different description, the buyer could reject those bags while retaining the other 600 under s. 30(4).

If the contract was a severable contract (for example, because the nuts were to be delivered in instalments which were to be separately paid for) the position would be different. For instance, if the 700 bags were delivered in seven instalments of 100 bags and the first six instalments appeared satisfactory and were accepted, but the seventh contained nuts which were unmerchantable or were of a different description, then the buyer could reject the last bags, while retaining the other 600.

But if all the bags contained unmerchantable nuts or those of a different description, the buyer could not accept part and reject part of the bags unless the contract was severable. The somewhat illogical result was that, where the contract was not severable, if the seller was in partial breach in delivering goods, some of which were non-contract, the buyer was better off than if the seller delivered goods all of which were non-contract. In the former case, acceptance of the part did not preclude rejection of the non-conforming remainder, while in the latter case it did. This strange result seemed to stem from the fact that if all the goods were non-contract goods it was not possible to rely on s. 30(4), which was more favourable to the buyer than s. 11.[121]

---

119 See above, p. 143.
120 See *Aitken Campbell & Co Ltd* v *Boullen and Gatenby* 1908 SC 490.
121 This was accepted as settled law by Roskill J in *Esmail* v *J Rosenthal & Sons Ltd* [1964] 2 Lloyd's Rep 447 at 454. The point was not argued in the CA and the HL avoided pronouncing on it: [1965] 2 All ER 860.

The explanation for this somewhat paradoxical state of the law may well be that suggested by Salter J in *W Barker & Co Ltd v E T Agius*,[122] namely that s. 30(4) was never intended to apply to such a case, but was only intended to apply where the seller delivered not only the whole of the contract goods but also other goods of the same or a different description. If this construction were put on s. 30(4) it would follow that a buyer could never accept part and reject part of the goods covered by the contract except in the case implicitly covered by s. 11(4), namely where the contract was severable. But as a matter of policy it would have been a retrograde step to move in that direction. The truth was that the concept of 'severability' was far too narrow in this context. There seemed to be no sound reason of commercial policy for refusing to allow the buyer to accept part and reject part of the goods delivered, whether or not the contract is severable in the technical sense, provided only that the goods constituted different 'commercial units'.[123] In the hypothetical examples discussed above, for instance, it was absurd that a buyer of 700 bags of nuts could not accept 600 bags and reject the remainder merely because they were all of the same description if they were in fact unmerchantable. It was perhaps possible that the meaning to be attached to the word 'severable' in s. 11(4) of the Act was not so conclusively determined as to be beyond the reach of the House of Lords. If the word could be given a very wide meaning so as to bring it into line with the approach of the UCC, it would have been unnecessary to rely on the haphazard use of s. 30(4) to mitigate the results of applying s. 11(4).

The Law Commissions largely adopted the above proposal.[124] The 1994 Act, as we have seen, provides that the buyer should always be entitled to reject part of the goods, even though he has accepted part, so long only as the goods constitute 'different commercial units'.[125] This made it possible to repeal s. 30(4) which seemed to have no other utility, except that, as we have seen, it dealt with the case where the correct contract quantity (and quality) was delivered but was mixed with other goods.[126] This possibility is now to be left to be dealt with by the courts as a matter of common law, since it might be excessively rigid to allow the buyer to reject in all such cases. The provisions of s. 11(4) remain, though these are now declared to be subject to the new right of partial rejection conferred by the new s. 35A. This means that in severable contracts the law remains unaltered, but the new right of partial rejection will in practice probably tend to supersede the provisions about severable contracts.

This new remedy is grafted onto the existing structure of the Act, so that it does not prejudge the question whether the buyer has a right of rejection at all. That question must still, subject to the changes made to s. 14, be answered as under the previous law. But if there is such a right of rejection, then under the 1994 Act, the buyer will only lose it by accepting all the goods, or by accepting goods included in the same 'commercial unit', or (in the case of severable contracts) as at present, by accepting the non-conforming goods which he could otherwise have rejected.

All this will simplify the law in a number of respects. In general it means that the question of acceptance will only arise with respect to the very goods accepted, other

122 (1927) 33 Com Cas 120.
123 This is the test employed by Art. 2-601 of the UCC.
124 See *Sale and Supply of Goods*, paras 6.6–6.16.
125 For definition of this term, see s. 35(7) of the 1994 Act above, p. 510.
126 See p. 143.

goods under the same contract not being affected – except in the one, rather obvious, case where the goods are all part of one commercial unit. Obviously, if a buyer buys one commercial unit, he cannot accept part and reject part.

ADDITIONAL RIGHTS OF BUYER/TRANSFEREE IN CONSUMER CASES

Sales of goods

The remedies set out in the previous sections of this chapter apply to commercial *and* consumer sales (subject to the particular rules applicable to consumer sales noted therein). However, the Sale and Supply of Goods to Consumers Regulations[127] add an entirely new part to the Sale of Goods Act 1979, to be inserted after s. 48. These new provisions considerably strengthen the consumer buyer's remedies.

The trigger for these provisions is that the buyer 'deals as consumer' or in Scotland 'there is a consumer contract'.[128] Section 61 (1) defines these terms by reference to the equivalent terms in the Unfair Contract Terms Act 1977.[129] In both the English and Scottish definitions there was a requirement that the goods in question were of a type ordinarily supplied for private use or consumption.[130] This requirement is not present in the definition of 'consumer' in Art. 1(1)(a) of the Directive:

> Consumer: shall mean any natural person who, in the contracts covered by this Directive, is acting for purposes which are not related to his trade or profession.

Accordingly, s. 12 of the Unfair Contract Terms Act has been amended so that if a party is an individual, the requirement that the goods be of a type ordinarily supplied for private use or consumption is ignored. Otherwise, the concept of 'dealing as consumer' in the Unfair Contract Terms Act is somewhat broader than that contained in the Directive because the purchase in the course of a business of goods merely incidental to that business will not prevent the purchaser being held to deal as consumer.[131] Regulation 14(2) further amends the Unfair Contract Terms Act 1977, s. 12(2):

> But the buyer is not in any circumstances to be regarded as dealing as consumer –
> (a) if he is an individual and the goods are second hand goods sold at public auction at which individuals have the opportunity of attending the sale in person;
> (b) if he is not an individual and the goods are sold by auction or by competitive tender.[132]

Article 2(3) of the Directive provides –

> There shall be deemed not to be a lack of conformity for the purposes of this Article if, at the time the contract was concluded, the consumer was aware, or could not reasonably be unaware of, the lack of conformity, or if the lack of conformity has its origins in materials supplied by the consumer.

---

127 SI 2002/3045 implementing the Sale of Consumer Goods and Associated Guarantees Directive 99/44/EC, OJ 1999 L177/12.
128 Section 48A.
129 Respectively Part I and s. 25(1) of that Act.
130 Sections 12(1) and 25(1)(b).
131 *R & B Customs Brokers* v *United Dominion Trust* [1988] 1 All ER 847.
132 Directive, Art. 1(3).

Thus, if a consumer supplies a tailor with cloth to make a suit, and the suit turns out to be defective due to a fault in the cloth, the tailor would not be liable under the terms of the Directive. This provision has not been implemented at all, but it is very doubtful if such a transaction would be treated as a sale of goods.[133] The requirement of domestic law that the tailor exercise reasonable care and skill could, however, lead to a different result from that required by Art. 2(3) in that it does not seem that it is required under the Directive that the consumer should have been aware of the fault. If the tailor should have been aware of it, it would seem that there could be liability under the Supply of Goods and Services Act.

In consequence of these amendments, in the case of breaches of ss. 13, 14 or 15, or of an express term of the contract,[134] it has been argued that Art. 2(a) is broader than the Sale of Goods Act in that it is not limited to essential commercial characteristics and does not require the sale to be by sample,[135] but in practice any description likely to induce reliance is likely to be held part of the contract description;[136] and arguably s. 15 is redundant anyway – the Uniform Commercial Code manages perfectly well to achieve a similar effect without an equivalent provision. Consumer buyers acquire the right to demand repair or replacement of the goods[137] within a reasonable time at the seller's expense, price reduction or rescission of the contract.[138] However, if the buyer requires repair or replacement, the consumer buyer's right to rescind the contract is suspended until the seller has had a reasonable opportunity to repair or replace.[139] The expenses the seller must bear in repair or replacement include labour, materials and postage.[140] The only excuses for a seller are that repair or replacement is: (a) impossible; (b) disproportionate to other remedies; or (c) disproportionate to a reduction in the purchase price or rescission.[141] In judging whether the remedy of repair or replacement is disproportionate, regard is to be had to the value of the goods had they conformed, the significance of the lack of conformity, and whether any other remedy could be effected without significant inconvenience to the buyer.[142] The

---

133   See p. 27. In which case, s. 14(2C)(b) of the Sale of Goods Act would not be applicable. This provides that the 'satisfactory quality' warranty does not extend to any matter making the quality of goods unsatisfactory, where the buyer examines the goods before the contract is made and which that examination ought to have revealed.

134   Section 48F. This is not exactly the same as Art. 2 of the Directive, but presumably the drafters thought that the effect would be the same. The Directive, Art. 2 requires the seller to deliver goods that are in conformity with the contract of sale.
   Goods are presumed to be in conformity with the contract if they:
   (a) comply with the description given by the seller and possess the qualities of the goods which the seller has held out to the consumer as a sample or model;
   (b) are fit for any particular purpose for which the consumer requires them and which he made known to the seller at the time of conclusion of the contract and which the seller has accepted;
   (c) are fit for the purposes for which goods of the same type are normally used;
   (d) show the quality and performance which are normal in goods of the same type and which the consumer can reasonably expect, given the nature of the goods and taking into account any public statements on the specific characteristics of the goods made about them by the seller, the producer or his representative, particularly in advertising or on labelling.

135   Twigg-Flesner [2003] *European Community Private Law Review* 12, 14.

136   See Chapter 13.

137   Ibid. s. 48A.

138   Ibid. ss. 48B and 48C.

139   Ibid. s. 48C.

140   Ibid. s. 48B(2)(b).

141   Ibid. s. 48B(3).

142   Ibid. s. 48B(4). It has been pointed out that in effect the consumer in Scotland now has two rights to rescind: an unrestricted one under s. 15B and the one described here (Hogg 2003 SLT (News) 277). See also Davidson & Macgregor *Commercial Law in Scotland* (2003), pp. 33–35; and Ervine 2003 SLT (News) 67.

proportionality test discussed set out in s. 48B(3) is an extension of Art. 3 of the Directive in that under s. 48B(3)(c) repair or replacement may not be available where these are disproportionate to a price reduction or rescission.[143] To this extent it appears that the Directive is incorrectly implemented. In determining what is a reasonable time under these provisions, or what is significant inconvenience, regard is to be had to the nature of the goods and the purpose for which they were acquired.[144]

It is unclear how the price reduction under s. 48C will work in relation to goods commonly bought in sets. Section 48(1)(a) provides that the buyer has the right to require the seller to reduce the purchase price of 'the goods in question'. Presumably this means the commercial unit, because otherwise the result would be absurd. For example, if in a newly purchased chess set only the black king is broken, it would scarcely be reasonable to offer an allowance off the part of the price attributable to the black king. A chess set without a black king is essentially worthless. The same would apply to a 'Scrabble'® set with missing letters. On the other hand, a consumer purchasing a standard 'Staunton' pattern chess set, or a 'Scrabble' set which matched one already in his or her possession with different pieces or letters missing might be prepared to accept a substantial reduction in price. The starting point for negotiations in these cases would be that replacement is the appropriate remedy, but the consumer might gain advantage from a significant price reduction instead. In the case of goods which can be bought separately, or as a package, such as audio equipment and computers, the situation is more problematic. It is presumably simply a question of fact whether 'the goods in question' refers to the individual items (as it well might), even though bought in a package, or to the goods as an entity.

As an exception to the usual rule in England, Wales and Scotland that specific performance or implement is not generally awarded in actions involving the sale of goods, the court is given a clear power to order specific performance or implement of the buyer's repair or replacement remedy.[145] However, for reasons explained previously, there are problems in enforcing these remedies against defendants outside the jurisdiction.[146]

We will give some illustrations as to how these provisions will work. We will recall *Millars of Falkirk* v *Turpie*[147] where an oil leak was noticed in the steering box of a new car, shortly after the buyer had taken delivery of it. The court denied the buyer a right to reject the goods, on the ground that minor defects of this sort were not uncommon in new cars, i.e. it held the goods were merchantable. The effect of this, strictly, would have been to deny the buyer any remedy at all. Yet it seems a strange conclusion that a car with a leak in the steering box is, in present terminology, of

---

143 Article 3(3) of the Directive provides:
     In the first place, the consumer may require the seller to repair the goods or he may require the seller to replace them, in either case free of charge, unless this is impossible or disproportionate.
     A remedy shall be deemed to be disproportionate if it imposes costs on the seller which, in comparison with the alternative remedy, are unreasonable, taking into account:
     1. the value the goods would have had if there were no lack of conformity,
     2. the significance of the lack of conformity, and
     3. whether the alternative remedy could be completed without significant inconvenience to the consumer.
     Thus, price reduction or rescission are not a part of the Directive's scheme of things.
144 Section 48B(5).
145 Section 48E(2). This is, however, consistent with principle in Scotland.
146 See p. 63.
147 1976 SLT (Notes) 66 – see p. 186.

'satisfactory quality'. With the changes to the Act effected by the Regulations, the court will not have to strain to reach what it considers a proportionate result. The buyer's right to reject the goods is suspended, but the seller must effect repair within a reasonable time.

In *Bernstein* v *Pamson Motors (Golders Green) Ltd*[148] a very minor fault, the presence of a piece of sealant in the lubricating system, led to engine seizure and could have had even more serious consequences had the plaintiff not stopped in time. The repairs to this vehicle took several days, and cost over £700. In the event, it was held that the car was unmerchantable, but the buyer, who had had the vehicle for three weeks and driven it 140 miles, had lost the right to reject it. This aspect of the case is not likely to be followed were the same facts to occur today. From the Court of Appeal decision in *Clegg* v *Anderson*[149] it would appear that the nature and complexity of the goods are relevant factors in deciding whether the consumer had had a reasonable opportunity to examine the goods.[150] Under the new regime if the buyer wishes to reject, he should do so within a reasonable time of the fault developing, i.e. of the engine seizure (as the buyer in *Berstein* had in fact done[151]). After timely notice of rejection, the seller could (as it had done), go ahead and repair the vehicle, but the buyer would not be bound to accept it. If the buyer took the option to require repair, the position under the new provisions would be as follows. In the first place, a vehicle in this condition is clearly not of satisfactory quality, so that the buyer has the right to require repair under s. 48B above. The vehicle had in fact been repaired, and the makers claimed that it was as good as new again. The cost of the repairs was presumably not disproportionate to the value of the goods, or the makers would not have carried out the repairs. Consequently, s. 48B(3) would not be applicable and, having repaired the vehicle within a reasonable time, the seller would not be in breach of the obligation to repair under s. 48B(2)(a). Accordingly, the right to rescind under s. 48C would not arise.

The third in this trio of well-known cases is *Rogers* v *Parish (Scarborough) Ltd*[152] where a fairly expensive new car, a Land Rover, was delivered with a number of minor defects in the engine and bodywork,[153] which remained notwithstanding the efforts on the part of the dealer to remedy them. In the event the buyer was held entitled to reject. Under the Regulations, the seller's failure to repair would bring into play s. 48C. The buyer has required the seller to repair, and the seller has failed to do so within a reasonable time – consequently, the condition for rescission set out in s. 48C(2)(b) is satisfied, and the buyer can rescind under s. 48C(1)(b).

The result in the first and third of these cases, then, is not different from the results reached by the courts without the assistance of the Regulations, but the Regulations enable the result to be reached without fudging. The result in the second case would now almost certainly be that the buyer would be held to have made an effective rejection, but that is a result of case law developments, not legislative amendment.

---

148 [1987] 2 All ER 220 – see p. 187.
149 [2003] EWCA 320.
150 As required by s. 34 – see p. 171. Article 2 of the Uniform Commercial Code has been interpreted similarly – see, e.g., *Zabriskie Chevrolet Inc* v *Smith* 240 A 2d 195 (1968); *Harney-Morgan Chevrolet* v *Morgan* 455 NE 2d 130 (1983).
151 He advised the sellers that he was rejecting the goods the following day.
152 [1987] QB 933 – see p. 186.
153 The full facts are given at p. 186.

Contracts for the transfer of goods

As we have seen, the Supply of Goods and Services Act 1982 implies a similar set of quality warranties into contracts for the transfer of the property in goods, which are not sales of goods as defined by the 1979 Act.[154] The Sale and Supply of Goods to Consumers Regulations[155] imply a similar set of provisions to those dealt with above in relation to sales of goods, into contracts for the transfer of the property in goods.[156] What was said above in relation to the application of these provisions to contracts for the sale of goods, applies *mutatis mutandis* to contracts for the transfer of the property in goods.

However, installation is another area where implementation of the Directive is problematic. Article 2(5) treats incorrect installation of consumer goods by the seller, and by the consumer which is the result of shortcomings in the installation instructions, as a lack of conformity. The Regulations amend the Supply of Goods and Services Act 1982, and insert a new s. 11S(1)(b) as follows:

> Goods do not conform to a contract for the supply or transfer of goods if ... (b) installation of the goods forms part of the contract for the transfer of goods and the goods were installed by the transferor, or under his responsibility, in breach of the term implied by section 13 below.

Section 13, it will be recalled, requires the exercise of reasonable care and skill on the part of the transferor. The Directive does not seem to require negligence on the part of the seller, however, and to this extent this appears to be another example of incorrect implementation. Moreover, any exclusion of liability for negligence on the part of the transferor will be subject only to the test of reasonableness set out in the Unfair Contract Terms Act 1977, s. 2(2). However, it should be noted that s. 16(3) of the Supply of Goods and Services Act 1982 preserves the possibility of imposing a stricter duty than the reasonable care and skill standard imposed by s. 13,[157] and in order to achieve consistency with the Directive a court might in such cases impose strict liability on the supplier, though the explicit reference to s. 13 might make this argument difficult. However, a careful reading of s. 13 does not suggest that it seeks to impose a ceiling on liability, but rather a minimum liability, and accordingly it is arguably open to a court to impose a stricter liability.[158] The same thing applies in the case of consumer goods to be manufactured or produced, which Art. 1(4) expressly makes subject to the Directive. As we saw in Chapter 2, generally English law has treated such contracts as sale of goods and thus subject to the strict liability imposed by the Sale of Goods Act, but, in those cases where it has not, the Directive might require the imposition of strict liability.

---

154 See p. 23 *et seq.*
155 SI 2002/3045.
156 Regulation 9, inserting Part 1B into the 1982 Act to follow s. 11.
157 See, e.g., *Greaves & Co (Contractors) Ltd* v *Baynham Meikle and Partners* [1975] 1 WLR 1095 – imposition of stricter obligations in a building contract.
158 Certainly in other contexts both negligence liability and strict liability can co-exist. Thus leaving aside the terms of the contract of carriage, the liability of the carrier to the cargo owner is in negligence only, but if the carrier is held to be a common carrier, its liability is strict.

28

RESCISSION FOR MISREPRESENTATION

RESCISSION OF THE CONTRACT

It is an astonishing fact that the relationship in English law[1] between the right to reject goods for breach of condition and the right to rescind for misrepresentation has not yet been fully explored by the courts.[2] It was at one time thought that 'a right to reject is merely a particular form of the right to rescind'[3] but it is clear since *Johnson* v *Agnew*[4] that this is no longer correct. Rescission of the contract *ab initio* differs from mere termination of the contract, because the former is in principle retrospective, while the latter is not. Termination is the appropriate remedy where one of the parties is guilty of a breach of contract. The circumstances in which a rejection of defective goods can amount to termination was discussed above. Nevertheless, the practical distinction between rescission and a termination arising from the rejection of defective goods (or faulty documents) is not nearly so great as the conceptual divide between rescission and termination may suggest. In particular, where the buyer rejects the goods or documents, having the right to do so, the effect is very much the same as where the contract is rescinded. The termination of the contract does here have some retrospective results – for instance, if the property has passed to the buyer, it revests in the seller, and if the buyer has paid the price he is entitled to recover it. So the relationship between the right to rescind and the right to reject is very close.

The first question which must be answered is whether the remedy of rescission of a contract of sale of goods for misrepresentation has survived the Sale of Goods Act. The point seems never to have been argued in England and the answer depends upon whether the rules of common law saved by s. 62 include the rules of equity. In *Riddiford* v *Warren*[5] the New Zealand Court of Appeal held, on the construction of

---

1 In Scots law, strictly speaking, rescission is the remedy by which a contract is terminated for breach, while reduction is the remedy with which a contract may be invalidated on the grounds of error, fraud and others. Again, strictly speaking, Scots law does not treat misrepresentation as such as a ground for the invalidation of a contract. If a misrepresentation is intentional then a resultant contract may be struck down on the ground of fraud; a non-intentional misrepresentation will go to support a plea of error, typically in motive (see Chapter 13, above). There seems to be no doubt that a contract of sale of goods can be reduced on the grounds of fraud or error induced by a misrepresentation but for which the misrepresentee would have declined to contract. The misrepresentee may homologate the contract rather than reduce it, but it is unclear how this relates to the doctrine of acceptance barring rejection. On the other issues raised in this chapter, Scots law is best regarded as undeveloped.
2 This problem arises in relation to Art. 2 of the Uniform Commercial Code because Art. 1-103 preserves the principles of common law and equity. However, there are cases where the effect of a unilateral mistake arising out of an innocent misrepresentation has been discussed – see, e.g., *Harney-Morgan Chevrolet Olds Co* v *Rabin* 37 UCC Rep Serv 50 (1983).
3 *Kwei Tek Chao* v *British Traders & Shippers Ltd* [1954] 2 QB 459, 480 per Devlin J.
4 [1980] AC 367.
5 (1901) 20 NZLR 572; followed in *Watt* v *Westhoven* [1933] VLR 458. Howard (1963) 26 MLR 272, 282–5.

an identical statute, that they did not and that the right to rescind for innocent mis-representation could no longer be applied to contracts for the sale of goods. The judgment of Atkin LJ in *Re Wait*,[6] an extract from which is quoted above, is also very much in point. Atkin LJ there pointed out that a code which only set out the common law rules, and left equitable rights inconsistent with them, would have been futile.

On the other hand, it never seems to have been doubted that the Act leaves the general law relating to fraud unaffected, and the rules concerning fraud include the right to rescind for fraudulent misrepresentation. Then there are a number of cases in which it has been assumed that a contract of sale of goods may be rescinded for innocent misrepresentation in an appropriate case. In *Abram Steamship Co Ltd* v *Westville Shipping Co Ltd*[7] the House of Lords, in a Scots appeal, upheld the rescission of a contract for the assignment of the benefit of a shipbuilding contract. The contract rescinded in this case was treated as a mere assignment of the shipbuilding contract, but since the ship was already under construction it seems that it also involved the sale of the ship itself. More recently, the Court of Appeal has several times assumed that rescission is available for contracts of sale of goods. In particular, in *Leaf* v *International Galleries*[8] the Court of Appeal clearly thought that the remedy was available in a suitable case, although they denied it there because of unreasonable delay. And again in *Long* v *Lloyd*,[9] the Court of Appeal seems to have had no doubt that the remedy was available. Finally, in *Goldsmith* v *Rodger*,[10] the Court of Appeal actually rescinded a contract of sale of goods. In this case the misrepresentor was the buyer, but the court held that the remedy of rescission is equally open to either party.

It seems certain, therefore, that an English court would not now follow the New Zealand Court of Appeal.

Assuming, then, that this remedy is still available, it becomes a matter of some importance to decide when exactly it can be invoked, what is the relationship between the right of rejection and the right of rescission, and what is the effect of the Misrepresentation Act 1967. The first two of these problems were considered at some length in *Leaf* v *International Galleries*[11] and *Long* v *Lloyd*,[12] although neither case can be regarded as wholly satisfactory owing to the many difficult points which were glossed over. But as a result of the provisions of the Misrepresentation Act, these cases can now be dealt with quite shortly.

In *Leaf* v *International Galleries*, the plaintiff bought a picture from the defendants which was stated by them to be a Constable. Some five years later the plaintiff sought rescission of the contract on the ground that this was an innocent misrepresentation (fraud was not alleged) for which the normal equitable remedy should be available. The Court of Appeal decided that, assuming the plaintiff to have this right, he was in any case too late to rescind since five years was far more than a reasonable time. Similarly, in *Long* v *Lloyd*, the plaintiff bought a second-hand lorry

---

6 [1927] Ch 606 – see above, p. 352.
7 [1923] AC 773, 1923 SC (HL) 68.
8 [1950] 2 KB 86.
9 [1958] 1 WLR 753.
10 [1962] 2 Lloyd's Rep 249.
11 [1950] 2 KB 86.
12 [1958] 1 WLR 753. See further on this case a note by Grunfeld (1958) 21 MLR 550 and another by Professor Atiyah in (1959) 22 MLR 76.

from the defendant on the faith of certain statements made by the latter as to its condition. Despite repeated complaints by the plaintiff to the defendant – which the defendant made some attempt to meet – the plaintiff continued to use the lorry until it broke down more or less completely, though only a few days after he had bought it. Again the plaintiff claimed rescission for misrepresentation, and again the court decided that he was too late, apparently on the ground that the buyer had accepted the lorry.

Two questions which gave rise to difficulties in these cases have been set at rest by the Misrepresentation Act. First, it is not now material to inquire whether a statement in this kind of case becomes incorporated into the contract as a contractual term. For by s. 1(a) of the Misrepresentation Act, the fact that a pre-contractual representation has become a term of the contract does not in itself deprive the innocent party of the right to rescind. Secondly, the rule in *Seddon* v *North East Salt Co*[13] (sometimes also called the rule in *Angel* v *Jay*[14]) barring rescission of an executed contract for innocent misrepresentation was abolished by s. 1(b) of the Act. Therefore the vexed question whether this rule applied to contracts of sale of goods cannot now arise, at least in England.[15] This means that rescission of such a contract will only be barred on one of the other grounds on which rescission may be barred, that is by affirmation, lapse of time, inability to make *restitutio in integrum*, or the acquisition of rights by an innocent third party. It seems probable that, so far as concerns the right of a buyer to rescind, the effect of the Act will be to put rejection for breach of condition and rescission for innocent misrepresentation largely on the same footing. An act which constitutes an acceptance within the meaning of s. 35 will presumably amount to an affirmation of the contract within normal equitable principles.

But there appear to be at least two situations in which the rules governing acceptance in s. 35 differ from the equitable principles governing rescission for misrepresentation. First, we have seen that under s. 35, if the goods are delivered to the buyer and he does not within a reasonable time intimate that he rejects the goods, he is deemed to have accepted them.[16] But in equity it seems that lapse of time by itself does not prevent rescission: it will only do so if it is evidence of affirmation or if the representor is thereby prejudiced.[17] Since it is possible that a reasonable time for rejection may elapse without the seller being prejudiced by the delay, it seems that equity might allow rescission in a case where rejection would be barred under s. 35.

Another possible divergence concerns the buyer who has had a reasonable opportunity to examine the goods and has resold and delivered them to a sub-buyer. As we have seen,[18] under the 1979 Act, and subject to the amendments made by the new s. 35(6) inserted by the 1994 Act, this remains a case in which the buyer loses his right of rejection under ss. 34 and 35 of the Act, even though the buyer is willing and able to place the goods at the seller's disposal at the original place of delivery. It seems

---

13 [1905] 1 Ch 326.
14 [1911] 1 KB 666.
15 With the exception of the modifications to s. 35 effected by s. 4(2), the Misrepresentation Act 1967 does not extend to Scotland.
16 See above, p. 518.
17 *Allen* v *Robles* [1969] 1 WLR 1193; *Fenton* v *Kenny* [1969] NZLR 552. It is not clear how this can be reconciled with *Leaf* v *International Galleries*, above.
18 See above, p. 513.

that a right to rescind for misrepresentation would not be lost in this situation. The buyer would (it seems) only lose his right to rescind if he could not make *restitutio in integrum*. For example, if he cannot get the goods back from the sub-buyer, he plainly cannot rescind his own purchase of the goods. But where he is in fact in a position to restore the goods to the seller, it does not seem that previous dealings by the buyer will deprive him of the right to rescind.[19]

The further question which now arises is the effect of this divergence between the statutory and the equitable principles. In *Leaf* v *International Galleries*[20] Denning LJ expressed the view that a right to rescind for misrepresentation cannot survive beyond the point when a right to reject for breach of condition is lost because a misrepresentation is 'much less potent' than a breach of condition. But it seems that this reasoning cannot survive s. 1(a) of the Misrepresentation Act, which clearly permits rescission for a misrepresentation even where the misrepresentation has become a term of the contract. This being so, it would be very anomalous if the right to rescind is lost at an earlier date when the misrepresentation does not become a term of the contract.

The conclusion is that, whenever a buyer wishes to reject goods and the seller may wish to contend that the buyer has lost the right to reject, the buyer will be well advised to seek, in the alternative, rescission for misrepresentation. This will not, of course, be possible where the breach complained of was non-performance of a promise and not a misstatement of fact; nor will it always be advantageous to the buyer, particularly as the court may in its discretion refuse rescission under s. 2(2) of the Misrepresentation Act and award damages in lieu. The court has no discretion to deprive a buyer of the right to reject under the Sale of Goods Act and it is unlikely that the Misrepresentation Act affects the position in this respect.

It is unfortunate that the Law Commissions' 1987 report, *Sale and Supply of Goods*, on remedies for breach of contracts of sale, and in particular on the buyer's right of rejection, made no reference to the parallel problems of rescission for misrepresentation. It seems absurd that where a false representation of fact is made by a seller, the question whether the buyer can reject the goods or rescind the contract will continue to depend on two completely different sets of legal principles, even though they are designed to serve the identical purpose.

---

19 See, e.g., *Abram Steamship Co Ltd* v *Westville Shipping Co* [1923] AC 773.
20 [1950] 2 KB 86, 90–1.

29

ACTION FOR DAMAGES

DAMAGES FOR NON-DELIVERY[1]

The buyer's action for damages for breach of contract may take one of two forms. It may be an action for damages for non-delivery[2] or it may be an action for damages for breach of a term in respect of goods which have been delivered.[3] A borderline case is where part of the goods which are part of a global whole has not been delivered. In *Sealace Shipping Co Ltd* v *Oceanvoice*[4] it was held that the appropriate measure in such a case was damages for non-delivery. First, we shall deal with damages for non-delivery.

Unlike the seller's remedy, the nature of which depends upon whether the property has passed or not, the buyer's action for damages for non-delivery is the same and the damages are assessed in the same way, whether or not the property has passed. In both cases, his essential complaint is the same, namely that the seller has failed to deliver goods which he ought to have delivered, and the buyer claims damages accordingly. The only difference is that where the property has passed the buyer may have a claim in conversion as well as, or as an alternative to, his action for damages for non-delivery, but, as will be seen, in practice the result is the same in either case.

The main rules for the assessment of damages are laid down by s. 51:

(1) Where the seller wrongfully neglects or refuses to deliver the goods to the buyer, the buyer may maintain an action against the seller for damages for non-delivery.
(2) The measure of damages is the estimated loss directly and naturally resulting, in the ordinary course of events, from the seller's breach of contract.
(3) Where there is an available market for the goods in question the measure of damages is prima facie to be ascertained by the difference between the contract price and the market or current price of the goods at the time or times when they ought to have been delivered or (if no time was fixed) then at the time of the refusal to deliver.

The market price rule

If, then, there is a market the prima facie rule is the same as in an action by the seller, that is to say the damages are to be assessed by reference to the market price of the goods at the time when they ought to have been delivered, and by giving the buyer

---

1 For a critique of these provisions and their equivalents in the Uniform Commercial Code see Adams [2002] JBL 553.
2 Under s. 51.
3 Under s. 53.
4 [1991] 1 Lloyd's Rep 120.

the difference between the market price and the contract price the court puts him in the position he would have been in had the goods been delivered.[5] If the market price is lower than the contract price it follows, of course, that the buyer is only entitled to nominal damages because he can go into the market and buy replacement goods without extra cost.

The general rule is not displaced merely because the buyer has already contracted to resell the goods to a third party at a price higher or lower than the market price at the date when delivery should be made. This principle was laid down by the Court of Appeal in *Rodocanachi* v *Milburn*[6] and was affirmed by the House of Lords in *Williams* v *Agius*.[7] The resale price is treated as irrelevant because the buyer must, in order to fulfil his sub-sales, buy in the market if the seller fails to deliver. Damages for the non-delivery are intended to compensate for the additional cost of buying in the market.

In option contracts, it would appear that the appropriate measure is a sum which will compensate the buyer for the loss of the opportunity to buy, and in assessing this account must be taken of the fact that the buyer might not have exercised the option.[8]

Market price at what date?

We have already seen in dealing with the action for non-acceptance that the concluding words of s. 51(3) have no relevance where there is an anticipatory breach of contract.[9] Should the seller repudiate the contract before the date for delivery arrives,[10] the market price to be taken in the assessment of the damages is not that prevailing at the date of the repudiation but that at the time when delivery might have been expected to be made.[11] In *Tai Hing Cotton Mill Ltd* v *Kamsing Knitting Factory*[12] the sellers failed to deliver 424 bales of yarn to buyers under a contract without a fixed delivery date. On 31 July 1973, the sellers wrote repudiating the contract. The buyers did not accept this and continued to press for delivery, as they were entitled to do. But eventually they recognized that the sellers would not deliver and on 28 November 1973 the buyers issued a writ claiming damages. It was held by the Privy Council that right up to that date the buyers could have demanded delivery on reasonable notice. They went on to hold that one month would have been sufficient notice and that, accordingly, they could have demanded delivery up to 28 December, one month after they issued their writ. That, then, was the date when the goods ought to have been delivered within the meaning of the section and the date by reference to which the damages were to be assessed.

---

5 See, e.g., *Allen* v *W Burns (Tractors) Ltd* 1985 SLT 252. The buyer also recovered extra financing charges caused by the seller's breach.

6 (1886) 18 QBD 67.

7 [1914] AC 510.

8 See *Geogas SA* v *Tramono Gas Ltd* [1993] 1 Lloyd's Rep 215.

9 *Millett* v *Van Heeck* [1921] 2 KB 369 – see p. 493.

10 An inability to perform can amount to a repudiation by the seller, but the buyer must be able to establish this fact on the balance of probabilities – see *Alfred C Toepfer Int* v *Itex Italgrani Export* [1993] 1 Lloyd's Rep 361, and see pp. 454–5 above for the related point in relation to repudiation by a buyer.

11 *Melachrino* v *Nickoll & Knight* [1920] 1 KB 693; *Attorney-General of Ghana* v *Texas Overseas Tank Ships Ltd* [1993] 1 Lloyd's Rep 471 – action against a carrier for non-delivery.

12 [1979] AC 91.

It will be observed that the buyer is not bound to accept the seller's repudiation when it is first made. In accordance with the general principles of the law of contract, as affirmed by the House of Lords in *White & Carter (Councils) Ltd* v *McGregor*,[13] the buyer can keep the seller's obligations alive by refusing to accept the repudiation. However, if this principle is combined with that laid down by the Privy Council in the *Tai Hing Cotton Mill* case, it would seem that the buyer could prolong the seller's duty to deliver more or less indefinitely in a contract without a fixed delivery date. If he simply tells the seller that he does not accept the repudiation and then waits five years before issuing his writ, are the damages to be assessed by reference to the market price at that date? This result presumably could be avoided by holding that the intention of the parties was that the goods would be delivered within a reasonable time after the contract was made, and then finding an appropriate date for that purpose.

Of course, the whole situation is changed if the buyer accepts the seller's repudiation,[14] for he must then mitigate his damage, as a reasonable man.[15] And if the market is rising, it seems that the buyer must then buy in the market without delay, although we have also seen that some scepticism has been expressed about the possibility of identifying rising and falling markets in advance.[16] But in any event, according to the *White & Carter* case, the buyer is under no obligation to accept a wrongful repudiation, and the duty to mitigate does not arise until and unless he does so accept it, and brings the primary contractual duties of the seller to an end.

Where a contract expressly provides for a period of time during which delivery is to be made – as is very common in commercial sales – the seller is not in breach until the end of the last day of the permitted period. That is the time when the goods ought to have been delivered within the meaning of the subsection, and it is by reference to the market price at that time that the damages must be assessed.[17] In a c.i.f. contract, the time when the goods ought to have been delivered within s. 51(3) is the time when the documents ought to have been delivered[18] and, therefore, if a period of time is allowed, as is usual, it is the last day of the period which fixes the day by reference to which the damages must be assessed.

Although the market price rule is now firmly established in English and Scots law, it may be observed that there are cases in which it would lead to injustice if the rule were rigidly applied. In particular, it is unrealistic to suppose that a buyer will in practice be able to buy goods in the market on the very day on which the seller fails to deliver. The buyer will often wish to consider his position, or to negotiate with the

---

13 [1962] AC 413, 1962 SC (HL) 1. But see also *The Alaskan Trader* [1984] 1 All ER 129. Note that the Scottish Law Commission, *Remedies for Breach of Contract* (Scots Law Com. No. 174, 1999) has recommended that the decision in *White & Carter* be reversed by legislation imposing a requirement of reasonableness.

14 Presumably, on the analogy of *Vitol SA* v *Norelf Ltd* [1993] 2 Lloyd's Rep 301, buying on the market on the basis of the seller's repudiation would be sufficient act of acceptance.

15 As to what amounts to such acceptance see *Vitol SA* v *Norelf Ltd* [1993] 2 Lloyd's Rep 301 – acceptance by conduct as well as words.

16 *Roth* v *Tayson* (1896) 73 LT 628. On the doubts about identifying rising markets in advance, see *Lusograin Comercio Internacional de Cereas Ltda* v *Bunge AG* [1986] 2 Lloyd's Rep 654, 662–3, per Staughton LJ, and on the whole question, see p. 492 *et seq*, above.

17 *Toepfer* v *Cremer* [1975] 2 Lloyd's Rep 118, following *Brown* v *Muller* (1872) LR 7 Ex 319; *Roper* v *Johnson* (1873) LR 8 CP 167.

18 *C Sharpe & Co Ltd* v *Nosawa & Co Ltd* [1917] 2 KB 814; *Garnac Grain Co* v *H M Faure & Fairclough* [1966] 1 QB 650, affirmed [1968] AC 1130.

seller on breach and some delay before he buys substitute goods is likely to be the rule rather than the exception. In this situation, although it has been stressed that assessment of damages as at the date of breach remains the prima facie rule,[19] there are some circumstances in which the relevant market price will be that prevailing on the date when the buyer finally accepts (or perhaps ought reasonably to accept) that the seller is not going to deliver, so that the buyer will have to go into the market and buy substitute goods.[20] Indeed, once this is established as the right approach there seems no real reason why the courts should not adopt the rule of the Uniform Commercial Code[21] – at least as prima facie evidence of the buyer's loss – that the price of the substitute goods should be taken as the basis for the assessment of the damages. Of course, care must be taken not to permit the buyer to prejudice the seller's position by delaying for too long his decision to buy in the market, though there is once again some difficulty in reconciling this with the *White & Carter* decision which seems to rule out any duty to mitigate unless and until the repudiation is accepted. Certainly the buyer will have difficulty in making out a case for higher damages where he has, after the seller's failure to deliver, bought in the market at higher than market prices. There is, perhaps, more likelihood that the damages will be reduced if the buyer has bought at lower than market prices.[22]

Market price at what place?

The relevant market for the purposes of the rule is generally that at the place of delivery, because that will usually be the market on which the buyer will buy. Any principle requiring the buyer to go into another available market in order to mitigate his loss is of limited applicability, because it is the value of the goods at the port of destination for which the buyer is being compensated.[23]

Cases where the market price rule is inapplicable

It is now necessary to examine those cases in which the damages are assessed by some other yardstick than that of market price. In the first place, even where there is a market for the goods in question[24] the buyer may in some exceptional cases be able to claim damages representing the loss he has suffered on sub-sales which he has been unable to fulfil. For example, a buyer may contract to buy goods at £10 per tonne and may contract to resell the same goods at £12 per tonne. If the market price at the date of non-delivery to the first buyer is £11 per tonne, the question is whether the first buyer should recover as damages £1 per tonne (the difference between market price and contract price) or £2 per tonne (the difference between market price and resale

---

19 *Janred Properties Ltd* v *Ente Nazionale Italiano per il Turismo* [1989] 2 All ER 444.

20 *Johnson* v *Agnew* [1980] AC 367, 400–1; *Suleiman* v *Shahsavari* [1989] 2 All ER 460; see also *Asamera Oil Corp* v *Sea Oil & General Corp* (1978) 98 DLR (3d) 1.

21 Art. 2-712.

22 See *R Pagnan & Fratelli* v *Corbisa Industrial Agropacuaria Limitada* [1970] 1 WLR 1306, though the facts here were rather special – see above, p. 492.

23 *Attorney-General Rep of Ghana* v *Texaco Overseas Tank Ships Ltd* [1993] 1 Lloyd's Rep 471.

24 On the meaning of 'market', see above, p. 488.

price). As we have seen, the normal rule is that sub-sales must be ignored in assessing the damages, but this rule only applies to damages arising directly and naturally from the breach under s. 51. The buyer may, in addition, be able to claim special damages, the right to which is reserved by s. 54, and which are based on loss not directly or naturally following from the breach, but on loss arising from special circumstances of which the parties were aware. These two different types of damages correspond to the first and second rules in *Hadley* v *Baxendale*,[25] which were authoritatively restated by the House of Lords in *Koufos* v *Czarnikow Ltd (The Heron II)*.[26] According to this decision, the question in every case is whether on the information available to him at the time the contract was made, the seller should, or a reasonable man in his position would, have realized that such loss was sufficiently likely to result from the breach of contract to make it proper to hold that the loss flowed naturally from the breach, or that loss of that kind should have been within his contemplation.[27]

A simple example of special damage which may be alleged by the buyer is for freight which he has had to pay despite non-delivery of the goods,[28] or sums paid for the cancellation of a charterparty.[29]

But it is one thing to recognize in principle that damages may be given in respect of a resale price. It is another thing to define the precise circumstances in which a buyer is entitled to claim damages in respect of sub-sales. The leading case is the decision of the House of Lords in *Re R & H Hall Ltd and W H Pim (Junior) & Co's Arbitration*,[30] which 'astonished the Temple and surprised St Mary Axe'.[31] In this case, the sellers sold a specific cargo of corn in a specific ship to the buyers at fifty-one shillings and ninepence per quarter. The buyers resold at fifty-six shillings and ninepence per quarter, but when the vessel arrived the market price had fallen to fifty-three shillings and ninepence per quarter. The sellers failed to deliver and the question was whether the measure of damages was the difference between the contract price and the resale price, on the one hand, or the contract price and the market price, at the date when the goods should have been delivered, on the other. It was held that the former was the appropriate measure of damages but the precise *ratio decidendi* is not easy to state. It seems that there were two critical factors in the case which displaced the general principle: first, the sale was for a specific cargo on a specific ship, and it was this same specific cargo which had been resold, and, secondly, the contract of sale by its terms actually provided for resale by the buyer in the sense that various provisions of the contract dealt with this eventuality.

It has been suggested that the reason why the buyer can claim a higher measure of damages where these two conditions are satisfied is that the buyer cannot fulfil his sub-sales by buying in the market. If the buyer has contracted to resell the specific goods which he has agreed to buy under the first contract, he will necessarily be

---

25 (1854) 9 Ex 341.

26 [1969] 1 AC 350.

27 Per Lord Reid, p. 386.

28 *E Braude (London) Ltd* v *Porter* [1959] 2 Lloyd's Rep 161.

29 *Bem Dis A Turk Ticaret S/A Tr* v *International Agri Trade Co Ltd* [1999] 1 Lloyd's Rep 729 – this case involved a seller suing for these expenses, but the principle is the same.

30 (1928) 139 LT 50; [1928] All ER Rep 763.

31 See *James Finlay & Co* v *NV Kwik Hoo Tong Handel Maatschappij* [1929] 1 KB 400, 417. Indeed, the decision seems to have been found so distasteful by some that it was not even reported in the Appeal Cases!

unable to fulfil the second contract if the goods are not delivered. Substituted goods bought in the market will not do, and accordingly the market price is irrelevant.[32] The only alternative is to assess the damages by reference to the resale price provided (and this is the second requirement) that it was known or foreseen that the goods were to be resold. It was suggested in the eighth and earlier editions that the difficulty with this solution was that, although the buyer would not be able to fulfil his sub-sales by buying in the market where he had contracted to resell the specific goods bought, the damages payable to his sub-buyer would be nil if equally good substitutes were in fact available in the market at equal prices. This of course is the case, but nevertheless the buyer's expectation loss is surely the difference between the contract price and the resale price. The right of the buyer to recover the higher measure of damages on a sub-sale is surely simply an application of the second limb in *Hadley* v *Baxendale*, and it is clear that the seller must have been aware, or ought to have been aware, of the buyer's intention to resell.[33]

It seems clear that both requirements must be satisfied because the mere fact that sub-sales may be contemplated as a reasonable probability is not enough to displace the general principle. For as Maugham LJ said in *The Arpad*:[34]

> I suppose most vendors of goods and most carriers might be taken to know that if the purchaser or consignee is a trader the goods will probably be sold, or be bought for sub-sale; but the authorities seem to show conclusively that something more than that is necessary to enable the damages to be assessed by reference to a contract of sub-sale entered into before the date of delivery.[35]

But it has been said that the position may differ where 'the seller knows that the buyer is buying the goods in order to fulfil an already existing special contract, and knows that if he fails to deliver the goods the buyer will come under a specific liability to his sub-buyer'.[36]

Where the two conditions are satisfied but the buyer has contracted to resell the goods at *less* than the market price the question arises whether the seller is to be given the benefit of this. All the cases which have arisen so far in which sub-sales have been taken into account have been cases in which the buyer *increased* his damages by proving that this loss was more than the difference between the contract and the market price. A possible reason for this is apparent from the facts of *Williams* v *Agius*. In that case Agius sold a quantity of goods to Williams at sixteen shillings and threepence per unit. Williams sold to a third party X at nineteen shillings. X sold to Agius at twenty shillings. Agius failed to deliver to Williams, no doubt because the market price had now risen to twenty-three shillings and sixpence. The question to be decided by the court was whether Williams should recover the contract/market difference at the time of non-delivery (seven shillings and threepence), or be limited by the amount of the sub-sale to X to two shillings and ninepence. It was held that Williams should recover the full contract/market difference. After all,

---

32 See, e.g., Ogus on *Damages*, pp. 333–5.

33 *Seven Seas Properties* v *Al-Esso* [1993] 3 All ER 577.

34 [1934] P 189, 230.

35 Cf. *James Finlay & Co* v *NV Kwick Hoo Tong Handel Maatschappij* [1929] 1 KB 400, 411–12 per Scrutton LJ, and 417–18 per Sankey LJ. Cf. also *Horne* v *Midland Rly Co* (1873) LR 8 CP 131.

36 *Aryeh* v *Lawrence Kostoris & Son Ltd* [1967] 1 Lloyd's Rep 63, 68 per Willmer LJ.

in order to fulfil his contract with X, he would have had to pay twenty-three and sixpence on the market. If he did not fulfil his contract with X, or was unable to because this was a specific cargo on a specific vessel as in *Hall & Pim's Arbitration*, he would have had to pay X the difference between X's contract price of nineteen shillings and the market price, i.e. four shillings and sixpence, to which there would have to be added his own gain of two shillings and ninepence. Either way the damages suffered by Williams work out at seven shillings and threepence.

If the buyer can bring himself within the principle of *Hall & Pim's Arbitration*, he may be entitled to recover not only his loss of profit on sub-sales (for that is what it comes to), but also any damages which he may have had to pay his sub-buyer in respect of his loss of profit and, indeed, that of other sub-buyers in the string. Moreover, if the buyer has been sued by his sub-buyer and has had to pay damages and costs, he is entitled to claim from the seller the total sum he has had to pay as well as a sum in respect of his own costs.[37] The only qualification on this rule is that the buyer must have acted reasonably in defending the action. In string contracts, it may well be easier for the buyer to claim loss of profit than in other sales because, in such a case, if the seller knows that the buyer 'is not buying merely for resale generally but upon a string contract where he will resell those specific goods and where he can only honour his contract by delivering those goods and no others, the measure of profit on resale is the right measure'.[38]

Where there is no market for the goods in question, the buyer's damages clearly cannot be assessed in the usual way in terms of the market price. In such a case, the method to be adopted for assessing the damages depends partly on whether the buyer is a trader buying for resale or whether he is buying for use, and partly on what measures the buyer actually adopts to meet the seller's failure to deliver. Where he is a trader, the buyer is entitled to recover the difference between the value of the goods at the time they should have been delivered and the contract price. The value of the goods is prima facie to be assessed at the price at which the buyer may have contracted to resell them. Putting it briefly, the buyer is able to recover his loss of profit.[39] And, again, if the buyer can prove special knowledge on the part of the seller, he may also be able to recover in respect of damages which he has to pay to his sub-buyer.[40] Alternatively, the buyer may choose to buy substitutes with which to fulfil his contracts, and, should these cost more than the contract goods, he can prima facie recover this excess cost and is not bound to account for the better quality of the goods so bought.[41] In the case of goods bought for use, the buyer may be able to recover damages to meet the additional

37 *Hammond & Co Ltd v Bussey* (1887) 20 QBD 79.
38 *Kwei Tek Chao v British Traders & Shippers Ltd* [1954] 2 QB 459, 489–90 per Devlin J. In *Aryeh v Lawrence Kostoris & Son Ltd* (see n. 36) at p. 72, Diplock LJ suggested that these remarks must be confined to string sales in standard form entered into by dealers on a commodity market where it is contemplated that the buyer may resell on the same terms.
39 *J Leavey & Co v Hirst & Co* [1944] KB 24; *Patrick v Russo-British Export Co Ltd* [1927] 2 KB 535; *Household Machines Ltd v Cosmos Exports Ltd* [1947] 1 KB 217.
40 In a suitable case the court may grant a declaration that the buyer is entitled to an indemnity in respect of damages and costs he may have to pay his sub-buyer: *Household Machines Ltd v Cosmos Exports Ltd* (see n. 39). But this remedy is sparingly used – see, e.g., *Trans Trust v Danubian Trading Co Ltd* [1952] 2 QB 297.
41 *Hinde v Liddell* (1875) LR 10 QB 265.

cost of buying reasonable alternative goods, or of adapting or modifying alternative goods for his purposes.

It should be observed that a sub-sale price cannot be taken as conclusive evidence of the value of the goods. In particular, where it is proved that the contract of sub-sale was entered into long before the date at which delivery should have been made and that the price of similar goods has fallen heavily in the meantime, some other mode of assessing the value of the goods must be chosen.[42] So also, where the sub-sale was made on very unusual terms, the buyer cannot claim loss of profit based on the sub-sale price, though it may be possible to adjust the price notionally by eliminating the unusual features, and asking what the sub-sale price would then have been.[43]

Another situation where the market price rule may be inapplicable arises where, even if the seller had delivered the goods, the buyer would not in fact have been able to dispose of the goods in the market. So where goods were sold c.i.f. Beirut, and the sellers failed to deliver, it was held that the damages must be assessed by reference to the value of the goods in the vessel, and not the landed value, because the port was closed and the buyer would not have been able to land the goods even if they had been delivered.[44] A similar situation might occur where a buyer orders goods for resale in a particular market into which they cannot be imported due to the existence of a third party's intellectual property rights. Assuming that the seller did not warrant the saleability of the goods in the particular market,[45] it would appear that the value of the goods would have to be assessed by some other criteria such as the price at which the buyer could have disposed of the goods in another market (assuming the buyer used reasonable endeavours to get the best price possible).

DAMAGES FOR BREACH OF CONDITION OR WARRANTY

In English law, the seller may deliver the goods to the buyer, but may still be guilty of a breach of a contractual term entitling the buyer to damages, that is to say a breach of warranty, or a breach of condition or of an innominate term which the buyer chooses, or is compelled, to treat as a breach of warranty. In this event, s. 53 applies:[46]

---

42 *The Arpad* [1934] P 230; *Heskell* v *Continental Express Ltd* [1950] 1 All ER 1033.

43 *Coastal International Trading Ltd* v *Maroil AG* [1988] 1 Lloyd's Rep 92.

44 *R Pagnan & Filli* v *Lorico* (1981) Com LR 152. But there are puzzling features to this decision. Usually the market price is taken as the yardstick because if the seller fails to deliver, the buyer will have to buy in the market in lieu. Here it seems to have been assumed that the reason why the market price is the yardstick is because, on delivery, the buyer can resell in the market. Perhaps this case would have been better decided on the ground that in a c.i.f. contract the seller fulfils his duty by delivering documents; inability to unload is the buyer's problem, not the seller's – so long at least as the seller has made a proper contract of carriage and supplied proper documents. See also *Sealace Shipping Co Ltd* v *Oceanvoice* [1991] 1 Lloyd's Rep 120 referred to in n. 4 above. In that case the seller failed to deliver a spare propeller with a vessel. There was no available market in spare propellers, and accordingly the measure of damages fell to be assessed under s. 51(3). In the event, the arbitrator held that the damages suffered by the buyer assessed under that subsection were to be fixed by reference to the scrap value of the spare propeller.

45 See p. 202 *et seq.*

46 The section does not mention innominate terms which were of course not invented when the Act was first passed. But it can be assumed that the measure of damages for breach of such a term is exactly the same as the measure of damages for breach of warranty.

(1) Where there is a breach of warranty by the seller, or where the buyer elects (or is compelled) to treat any breach of a condition on the part of the seller as a breach of
warranty, the buyer is not by reason only of such breach of warranty entitled to reject
the goods; but he may—
   (a) set up against the seller the breach of warranty in diminution or extinction of the
   price; or
   (b) maintain an action against the seller for damages for the breach of warranty.
(2) The measure of damages for breach of warranty is the estimated loss directly and naturally resulting, in the ordinary course of events, from the breach of warranty.

Since Scots law does not know the technical distinctions between conditions, warranties
and innominate terms, it has its own provision on damages, s. 53A(1):

The measure of damages for the seller's breach of contract is the estimated loss directly and
naturally resulting, in the ordinary course of events, from the breach.

Late delivery

Late delivery may, of course, justify the buyer in refusing to take the goods at all.
Whether it has this effect depends upon whether time is of the essence so that late
delivery is treated as a breach of condition; in cases where time is not of the essence,
late delivery may still be so inordinate that eventually the buyer is justified in refusing to take delivery, though he may sometimes have to give notice before he does so.[47]
If the buyer does refuse to take the goods, his claim for damages will be a claim for
non-delivery rather than, strictly, a claim for late delivery, and the applicable rules
will be those relating to non-delivery, considered above. The only additional point to
note here is that the mitigation rule may operate in a somewhat strange way in the
case of late delivery, in effect undercutting the buyer's claim for non-delivery altogether. In *The Solholt*,[48] for instance, sellers had contracted to sell a ship for $5m,
delivery not later than 31 August; in fact, they only tendered the ship on 3 September
and the buyers refused to accept it, as they were entitled to do. The market price had
actually risen by this time to $5.5m so that prima facie it would seem the buyers might
have expected to recover half a million dollars in damages. In fact they recovered nothing, because their refusal to accept the ship amounted to a termination of the original
contract, as a result of which their duty to mitigate came into operation. Reasonable
mitigation demanded that they should have sought some arrangement after the
breach, it being found as a fact that they could have negotiated a settlement with the
sellers after the breach under which the ship would still have been delivered, albeit a
few days late. This was, of course, a case dealing with a rather special type of goods –
a ship; in other cases, late delivery will usually result in the buyer going into the
market to buy replacements, and once this has been done it will obviously be too late
for the seller to tender delivery and claim that the buyer can best mitigate the damage
by taking the goods late. But the case does suggest that a late delivery is worth tendering, because if the buyer has not yet made other arrangements his failure to accept
even a late delivery may well cut his damages significantly, even perhaps to nil.

---

47 Above, p. 137.
48 [1983] 1 Lloyd's Rep 605. The case is severely criticized by Bridge (1989) 105 LQR 398 at 417–23.

If, however, the goods are delivered late and are accepted, the method of assessing the damages may depend on whether the buyer is a trader buying for resale or whether he is buying for use. If he is buying for use, the appropriate damages may be calculated by considering how much it would have cost the buyer to hire substitute goods during the delay, or what additional costs may have been incurred by the buyer as a result of having to make do without the goods during the delay. Much will depend here on what the buyer has actually done to mitigate his loss arising out of the delay and whether his conduct has been reasonable.

Where, on the other hand, the buyer is a trader buying for resale, it seems that the normal rule is that the buyer is entitled to recover as damages the difference between the market price at the time the goods should have been delivered and the market price at the time they were in fact delivered. Oddly enough, there appears to be no clear authority to this effect in the law of sale, but this was the measure of damages awarded by the House of Lords for delayed delivery in a contract of carriage in *Koufos v Czarnikow*,[49] and it seems to be generally accepted that the same measure applies in a sale.[50]

Under this measure of damages it will be observed that the contract price is irrelevant. The rule is based on the assumption that the buyer resells the goods as soon as they are delivered to him; on this assumption, the loss to the buyer which is caused by the delay is the fall in the market between the contract delivery date and the actual delivery date.

A difficult and controversial case is *Wertheim v Chicoutimi Pulp Co Ltd*,[51] where A contracted to sell goods to B at twenty-five shillings a ton. With the costs and expenses of transport, the total cost to the buyer was thirty-eight shillings a ton. A was late in delivering the goods. The market price at the date when the goods ought to have been delivered was seventy shillings a ton, but the market price at the date when the goods were in fact delivered was forty-two shillings and sixpence a ton. The buyer, however, resold the goods at sixty-five shillings a ton. It was held by the Privy Council that the buyer was only entitled to the difference between seventy shillings and sixty-five shillings the ton, i.e. five shillings, not the difference between seventy shillings and forty-two shillings and sixpence, i.e. twenty-seven shillings and sixpence a ton. Although this case was accepted as good law in *Williams v Agius*[52] by Lord Dunedin and by Lord Atkinson,[53] it has given rise to a certain amount of criticism[54] on the ground that it conflicts with the general principle that subcontracts are to be ignored unless they were especially contemplated. What seems to have weighed with the Privy Council was that, had the goods been delivered as promised, the plaintiff would have made a gain of thirty-two shillings had he resold at seventy shillings. He had in fact resold at sixty-five shillings, and so got back twenty-seven shillings of the potential gain of thirty-two shillings. Thus giving him five shillings gives him his expectation of gain. If he were

49 [1969] 1 AC 350 (*The Heron II*).
50 McGregor on *Damages*, 17th edn, §20-037 *et seq* (2003).
51 [1911] AC 301.
52 [1914] AC 510.
53 Who delivered the judgment of the Privy Council in *Wertheim*.
54 See *Slater v Hoyle & Smith* [1920] 2 KB 11, especially at p. 24 per Scrutton LJ. See also McGregor on *Damages*, 17th edn, §7-141 *et seq*, and 20-039 (2003) and Ogus on *Damages*, p. 345.

allowed to recover twenty-seven shillings and sixpence a ton he would have gained fifty-nine shillings and sixpence (twenty-seven shillings and sixpence plus thirty-two shillings), which is more than he would have got had the goods been delivered timeously, and would be contrary to the principle that damages should be compensatory only. The Privy Council had evidence to support the above analysis, but in many cases the court will not have any such evidence. Thus in other cases the fact that the buyer did not suffer the full loss which might have resulted from the seller's breach would, in a sense, be due to his own business success in selling goods for sixty-five shillings a ton when the market price was only forty-two shillings and sixpence. The buyer might, if the goods had been delivered on time, have resold those goods at their market price of seventy shillings per ton and bought other goods to fulfil his contract. In this way he would have made a large profit of which he would have been deprived by the breach of contract.

A number of difficult cases have raised questions as to the buyer's damages where shipping documents have been antedated to conceal a late shipment, and market prices have fallen by the time the goods are delivered. In this situation the buyer can still find himself compelled to accept the goods before he is fully aware of the breach which has occurred. As we have already seen, this remains possible even though it is now less likely to occur since the amendment of ss. 34 and 35 of the Sale of Goods Act.[55] In this event, the buyer may feel that it is unreasonable to confine him to the measure of damages prescribed by s. 53(3), because he will have lost the opportunity of rejecting the goods and buying replacements in the market at the now lower market price. He may therefore claim damages based on the fall in the market price of the goods, that is he may claim damages representing the difference between the contract price and the market price of the goods at the date when they were delivered. This is different from the normal measure of damages for late delivery, because that measure would only give the buyer the difference between the market price at the date when the goods should have been delivered, and the market price at the date when they were delivered.

Although it is by no means obvious why any sympathy should be shown to a buyer who has thus lost the opportunity for escaping from a bad bargain, the courts have in fact come to the assistance of the buyer in two cases of this nature. Both cases concerned late shipment under c.i.f. contracts in which the bills of lading were wrongly antedated to make it appear that the goods had been shipped during the contract period. In the first case,[56] it was held that the buyers, who had lost their right to reject before being aware of the late shipment, could recover damages representing the difference between the contract and the market price at the date of delivery. This decision was, it seems, partly based on the argument that the buyers were claiming damages, not merely for the late shipment of the goods, but for the separate breach involved in tendering false bills of lading. It was because of this falsity that the buyers did not discover until too late that the goods had been shipped late and, in a sense, it was therefore true to say that it was the falsity of the bills of lading which caused the buyers' loss; had the bills of lading been accurate, the buyers would probably have rejected the documents (owing to the fall in the market price) on the ground of late shipment and thus escaped their bad bargain.

---

55 See above, p. 511 *et seq.*
56 *James Finlay v NV Kwik Hoo Tong Handel Maatschappij* [1929] 1 KB 400.

In the second case,[57] the buyers were again deceived by false bills of lading, but in this case they knew of the late shipment by the time the goods themselves arrived. Although it was too late for them to reject the documents they could (it was held) have still rejected the goods when they arrived, and the case had to be decided on the supposition that they had accepted the goods with knowledge of facts from which the right to reject arose. Even in this situation it was held by Devlin J that the buyers could recover the difference between the contract price and the market price at the date of delivery and thus throw onto the sellers the loss caused by the drop in the market. This case seems to push this principle as far as it can be taken, and it was based on Devlin J's view that a buyer who has accepted documents under a c.i.f. contract may have practical difficulties about rejecting the goods, and that his choice to accept them is therefore not a wholly free and unconstrained one. Subsequently, some doubts were expressed in the Court of Appeal about the validity of the argument that there are two rights of rejection, one for the documents and one for the goods, in a c.i.f. contract.[58] Certainly it would seem wrong to allow a buyer quite freely and voluntarily to accept goods which he is entitled to reject and then try to place himself in the same financial position that he would have been in if he had rejected. A buyer who wants to do this should reject the goods first and then try to negotiate a new price with the seller based on the fall in the market. However, the two decisions referred to above may be justified because of the seriousness of the practice of antedating bills of lading to conceal a late shipment and the desirability of ensuring that the seller should not be able to retain any advantage as a result.

The above cases were distinguished by the Court of Appeal in *Procter & Gamble Philippine Manufacturing Corp* v *Kurt A Becher GmbH*[59] where the sellers tendered bills of lading falsely dated 31 January, though the goods were shipped in February, which was in fact still during the contractual shipment period. The buyers accepted the documents, not then being aware of the false date, and they also accepted the goods when they arrived, by which time the market price had fallen. They then tried to recover damages in respect of this fall in the market for breach of the contractual duty to tender correctly dated documents, but their claim was rejected. Although the buyers could have rejected the documents if they had known that they were falsely dated (and then they could of course have renegotiated the price to take account of the fall in the market), their acceptance of the goods was not the result of the mis-dating of the documents. If the documents had been correctly dated, the buyers could not have rejected either the documents or the goods, so that the mis-dating of the bill of lading caused the buyers no loss. The earlier cases were different because in both of them the mis-dating of the documents was the cause of the buyers accepting the goods and thus losing their opportunity to reject them and take advantage of the fall in the market. In the result, therefore, the mis-dating of the documents here caused the buyers no loss.

---

57 *Kwei Tek Chao v British Traders & Shippers Ltd* [1954] 2 QB 459.
58 *Panchaud Frères v Etablissements General Grain Co* [1970] 1 Lloyd's Rep 53; *Vargas Pena Apezteguia y Cia Saic v Peter Cremer GmbH* [1987] 1 Lloyd's Rep 394.
59 [1988] 2 Lloyd's Rep 21.

Breach of warranty of quality

Different considerations arise again where goods defective in quality are delivered. To such a case, s. 53(3) applies in English law:

> In the case of breach of warranty[60] of quality such loss is prima facie the difference between the value of the goods at the time of delivery to the buyer and the value they would have had if they had fulfilled the warranty.

In Scots law, s. 53A(2) applies:

> Where the seller's breach consists of the delivery of goods which are not of the quality required by the contract and the buyer retains the goods, such loss as aforesaid [under s. 53A(1) – see pp. 541–2 above] is prima facie the difference between the value of the goods at the time of delivery to the buyer and the value they would have had if they had fulfilled the contract.[61]

The prima facie rule is thus that the buyer is entitled to the difference between the value of the goods actually delivered and the value which the goods would have had if they had conformed to the contract. Of course this means that if the goods are so seriously defective as to have no value at all, the buyer is entitled to recover the full value which the goods should have had.[62] The market price of the goods is in principle irrelevant to an action for damages of this kind, although in some cases (especially in consumer sales) the market price of the goods as warranted may be some evidence of the value of the goods as warranted. So in a simple consumer sale where, say, a defective car is delivered, the buyer is prima facie entitled as damages to the difference between the value which the car ought to have had – which is likely to be taken to be (at any rate if the car is new) the contract price – and the value which the car in fact had.[63] To assess this latter value, it must be asked what would the market value of the defective car have been if buyers and sellers had known of the defects.[64] In fact claims by consumers in cases of this kind are often complicated by additional claims for consequential losses, which are readily allowable.[65]

The normal rule here, as elsewhere, is that sub-sales by the buyer are irrelevant to the buyer's claim for damages. In *Slater* v *Hoyle & Smith*[66] the buyers contracted for the purchase of 3,000 pieces of unbleached cloth of specified quality. Some 1,625 pieces of

60 It is curious that this section refers to a breach of warranty of quality, when all the terms as to quality implied by ss. 13–15 are conditions. This suggests that the draftsman may have thought that a condition becomes a warranty if the buyer claims damages in respect of it, but it has been held that this is not so: *Wallis Son & Wells* v *Pratt & Haynes* [1911] AC 394. Presumably, as already suggested, breach of an innominate term would be treated in the same way as a breach of warranty for this purpose.
61 Note that this provides in effect for an *actio quanti minoris*, rejected at Scots common law before 1893 (*McCormick* v *Rittmeyer* (1869) 7 M 854), but now allowed generally in contract law by virtue of the Contract (Scotland) Act 1997 s. 1.
62 See *Argos Distributors* v *Advertising Advice Bureau*, 15 February 1996 (unreported), where, as well as extinguishing the price, the court ordered the seller to compensate the buyer for lost profits on an existing sale and lost profits on expected repeat orders.
63 As to the additional remedies given to consumer buyers under the Sale and Supply of Goods to Consumers Regulations 2002, SI 2002/3045, see p. 525 *et seq*.
64 *Jackson* v *Chrysler Acceptances Ltd* [1978] RTR 474, 481. Thus a seller of a defective car cannot claim that the market value of the car was the same as the contract price merely because the defects were latent, and most buyers would have been willing to pay the contract price which this buyer paid. In this context, the market value means the value assuming the market knows of the defects.
65 See below, p. 551.
66 [1920] 2 KB 11.

lower quality than specified were delivered, but the buyer delivered 691 of them under a subcontract he had made for the higher grade material, and obtained payment from his sub-buyer at the full rate. The Court of Appeal held that these facts must be ignored in assessing the damages, and that the buyer was entitled to the difference between the value of the contract goods and the value of the goods actually delivered.

Although it is stated that the relevant date for valuing the goods actually delivered is the time of delivery to the buyer, this does not always work well in practice. It may, for instance, be some time after delivery that the breach of warranty is first discovered. Or the goods may be consigned and delivered to sub-buyers before the defect is discovered. In this last situation the courts have held that the goods should be valued at the time and place of delivery to the sub-buyer provided that the seller knew or could have foreseen that the goods might be redelivered without examination.[67]

It will be seen that the prima facie rule laid down by the two sections treats the market price as irrelevant except insofar as the market price may be taken to be the value which the goods should have had. It is the defects in the goods for which the buyer is to be compensated, and the damages are thus based on the deficiency in their value arising from the defects. If, however, the market price of the goods has fallen significantly since the contract was made, the buyer is likely to reject defective goods, as he is often entitled to do. In this event, the buyer is able to take advantage of the seller's breach to throw onto him the loss flowing from the fall in the market; there is in law no general principle of good faith which prevents the buyer from rejecting for any reason he chooses, so long only as there is a right to reject.[68] Likewise, in Scots law the only control is the requirement that the breach be material. But where the buyer, with full knowledge of the defective nature of the goods, chooses to keep them and merely to claim damages for the breach, the normal rule must be applied and the buyer will be able to recover only the difference between the value of the goods and their value as warranted.[69] The buyer cannot accept the goods with full knowledge of the seller's breach, and then claim the damages for the loss he might have avoided by rejecting the goods.[70] But by analogy with the cases discussed above concerning wrongly dated shipping documents, it may be that the buyer would be permitted to obtain damages covering the fall in the market price of the goods if he does not know of the defects when he accepts the goods, particularly if he has in some way been deceived by misrepresentations by the seller, or by the concealment of defects in the goods. This may happen, for instance, where a clean bill of lading is wrongly issued for goods whose apparent condition is manifestly unsatisfactory.

Goods bought for use

Sections 53(3) and 53A do not differentiate between goods bought for use and goods bought for resale, and the same measure of damages is thus prima facie applicable in

---

67 *Van den Hurk v Martens & Co Ltd* [1920] 1 KB 850. *Saunt v Belcher* (1920) 26 Com Cas 115. Much the same result is arrived at by the UCC, Art. 2-714, which substitutes the place of acceptance for the place of delivery.
68 As to which, see p. 499 *et seq.*
69 *Vargas Pena Apezteguia y Cia Saic v Peter Cremer GmbH* [1987] 1 Lloyd's Rep 394.
70 Ibid.

the two cases. The buyer can thus recover the difference between the actual value of the goods and their value as warranted, even where he buys for use. In practice, however, the damages in this case are likely to take a different form, or at least to be calculated in a different manner. One possibility is that the buyer will simply have the goods modified or repaired so as to bring them up to the requisite standard. Clearly, in this event the cost of such work is likely to be treated as equal to the difference in value between the goods delivered and their value as warranted.[71] But what happens if there is no difference in value, but a considerable one in having the goods modified or repaired? In the case of *Ruxley Electronics and Construction Co v Forsyth*[72] the plaintiffs had built a swimming pool in the defendant's garden which was shallower than the depth specified. The trial judge found that the shortfall had not decreased the value of the pool and awarded £2,500 general damages for loss of amenity.[73] The Court of Appeal pointed out that there were two methods of assessing the buyer's loss, namely to assess the difference in value, or, alternatively, to assess the costs of modification or repair. The difference in value method was appropriate when the chattel which was damaged[74] or was not up to specification was of a kind commonly available. But this method was inadequate where the buyer's chattel had some unique quality and could not be replaced. Although it would be unreasonable for a buyer to claim an expensive remedy when a cheaper one would make good his loss, on the facts, it was not unreasonable to award as damages the costs of replacing the swimming pool. The House of Lords, however, unanimously restored the trial judge's decision.[75] The House of Lords took the view that to award the cost of reinstatement was wholly unreasonable.

Peculiarly difficult problems attend the calculation of damages for breach of warranty of quality in respect of profit-earning chattels. This is partly because of the need to avoid duplicating the damages by including the same item as a capital loss and an income loss, and partly because there is a large number of ways in which loss of profits may be calculated. Difficulties of this nature led to a divided Court of Appeal in *Cullinane v British 'Rema' Manufacturing Co Ltd*,[76] but it is doubtful if any general principle can be extracted from this troublesome case.[77] The case was considered in *A C Daniels & Co Ltd v Jungwoo Logic*[78] which involved a contract for the supply of injection moulding machinery for making plastic bins. It was held that since the buyer had properly rejected the goods, the claim was one for non-delivery under s. 51, and the buyer was entitled to damages which would place it as far as possible in the position it would have been in had the contract been performed. *Cullinane* properly understood, was not authority for the proposition that damages for breach of contract

---

71 See *Keely v Guy McDonald* (1984) 134 NLJ 522 (Rolls-Royce found unmerchantable; held: seller liable for repair costs); see also *Bernstein v Pamson Motors (Golders Green) Ltd* [1987] 2 All ER 220.
72 [1996] AC 344 (HL); [1994] 3 All ER 801 – on appeal from a decision of Judge Diamond QC in the Central London County Court.
73 It should be noted that the pool as constructed was perfectly safe for diving.
74 [1996] AC 344. The swimming pool was not, of course, a chattel, but the Court of Appeal treated this distinction as immaterial. This decision was applied by the House of Lords in *Farley v Skinner* [2001] UKHL 49.
75 [1996] AC 344.
76 [1954] 1 QB 292.
77 See Macleod [1970] Journal Bus Law 19; see also *TC Industrial Plant Pty Ltd v Roberts Queensland Pty Ltd* (1964) ALR 1083.
78 14 April 2000 (unreported).

could be recovered on the basis of restoration of the claimant to the position it would have been in if there had been no contract. The claimant was allowed the return of the price paid to the seller, plus the claimant's wasted expenditure. The court did not allow an alternative claim of loss of profit because, on the evidence, it could not quantify this in a satisfactory way. In *Beoco Ltd* v *Alfa Laval*[79] a heat exchanger supplied by the first defendant was found to be cracked. It was negligently repaired by the second defendant, as a result of which an explosion occurred causing damage to equipment and loss of production. The plaintiffs were found to be negligent in failing to check the repair before switching the machine back on. It was held, applying the same principles as in tort, that the plaintiffs' damages should be limited to the repair costs and losses incurred due to loss of production on the day the repair was effected.

Where the damage caused by the breach requires the buyer to replace plant or machinery, he will not necessarily be compelled to give credit for the fact that he is replacing worn or partly used plant or machinery with new plant or machinery. But he probably would if the old plant or machinery were so worn that it had little life and would have had to be replaced soon anyhow.[80]

Where the buyer buys goods for the use of members of his family, it seems that he can recover damages in respect of (at least some of) their losses, as well as his own.[81] But it does not seem likely that the buyer could recover in respect of personal injuries suffered by members of his family through defective goods bought by him.

Consequential loss

Claims for damages for consequential loss are more commonly associated with breaches of warranty of quality and the like than with claims for non-delivery. Obviously the main reason for this is that defective goods can cause damage or injury in use, and this type of claim for consequential loss is therefore more frequently made when the goods have been bought for use. Where personal injury or physical damage to property is caused by defective goods in this way, the damages are assessed in much the same way as in the tort/delict of negligence. In such circumstances the damages may run into thousands of pounds, although the inherent value of the goods may be only a few shillings, as where a child was blinded by use of a defective catapult,[82] or where a man contracted dermatitis from wearing underpants containing an excess of harmful chemicals.[83]

The general principle remains, of course, that the loss must have been in the contemplation of the parties at the time the contract was made, in accordance with the decision in *Hadley* v *Baxendale*.[84] In recent times, claims for consequential losses in contracts of sale of goods have multiplied, both in commercial and consumer sales. Generally speaking, the courts appear to treat such claims very favourably

---

79 [1994] 4 All ER 464.
80 *Bacon* v *Cooper (Metals) Ltd* [1982] 1 All ER 397.
81 *Jackson* v *Horizon Holidays Ltd* [1975] 1 WLR 1468. As to the possibility of persons for whom goods are bought suing directly under the Contracts (Rights of Third Parties) Act 1999, see p. 270 *et seq.*
82 *Godley* v *Perry* [1960] 1 WLR 9.
83 *Grant* v *Australian Knitting Mills* [1936] AC 85.
84 (1854) 9 Ex 341. This is also the leading case in Scots law, although the principles were established in Scotland long before 1854 – see MacQueen, 1996 JR 295, 296.

from the buyer's point of view. In *Parsons (Livestock) Ltd v Uttley, Ingham & Co Ltd*[85] the defendants sold a large feeding hopper to the plaintiffs, who were pig farmers. In installing the hopper, the defendants failed to open a ventilator at the top (which was not visible from the ground) with somewhat disastrous consequences. The nuts stored in the hopper became mouldy and some of the pigs became ill; later, this triggered off an attack of a much more serious pig disease and many of the pigs died. The value of these pigs amounted to some £10,000 and, in addition, the plaintiffs claimed for substantial losses of profits. It was held that the former losses were recoverable, but not the latter. Although the gravity of the consequences could not have been foreseen in this case, it was held that the parties could reasonably have contemplated that some of the contents of the hopper would become mouldy from the ventilator being closed and that this might have caused some illness of the pigs. In effect, the court here applied the tort/delict decision in *Hughes v Lord Advocate*,[86] that the general *kind* of damage must be foreseeable, but it is not necessary to show that the precise *extent* could have been foreseen. On the facts the decision is somewhat remarkable and must stand as a warning against taking the foreseeability test too seriously. It seems absurd to suppose that any person would have foreseen anything remotely resembling what happened here as a result of leaving the ventilator closed. The House of Lords passed up an opportunity to consider *Parsons* in the Scottish case of *Balfour Beatty v Scottish Power plc*.[87] Balfour Beatty were building an aqueduct, using a 'continuous pour' of concrete for the purpose. A power failure constituting breach of contract by Scottish Power interrupted the pour and led ultimately to the demolition of the work done and its later reconstruction at considerable expense. The Court of Session held the loss recoverable, on the basis that it was of a foreseeable kind, even if the amount was greater than might have been foreseen. The House of Lords held that the loss was too remote under the first leg of *Hadley*, saying that while business people were to be taken as having knowledge of the ordinary course of each other's business, that did not extend to specialist technical aspects such as concrete pours. On the other hand, the test is sometimes used to limit recovery of losses which an ordinary person might think are foreseeable, such as losses consequent on a damaged reputation. In *Amstrad plc v Seagate Technology Inc*,[88] the defendants supplied defective hard disk drives for the plaintiff's new range of computers. It was held that the plaintiff was entitled to damages for lost and delayed sales and costs under s. 53(2), but not for lost sales on the plaintiff's successor range as this was not within the contemplation of the parties at the time of the contract.

On the other hand, in a later case (which was not a sale of goods case) where the plaintiff claimed damages falling within the second limb in *Hadley v Baxendale*, the

---

85 [1978] QB 791.

86 [1963] AC 837, 1963 SC (HL) 31.

87 1994 SC (HL) 20.

88 (1997) 86 BLR 34. On the other hand, in *Argos Distributors v Advertising Advice Bureau* (p. 546) damages were awarded for loss of profits on repeated orders. The crucial difference is probably that in that case the supplier knew that the goods were for resale to third parties, whereas the launch of a new product range, although within the buyer's contemplation, is unlikely to be within the seller's.

Court of Appeal took a markedly more realistic, if less sympathetic stance.[89] Here the plaintiff had booked a holiday through the defendants, and it had been mentioned that he needed medical insurance because he was liable to attacks of asthma. A breach of contract by the defendants triggered off a serious attack of asthma but the defendants were held not liable for the additional consequences of this, on the ground that the information about the plaintiff's medical condition had been volunteered conversationally, and was not part of the contractual terms. So far as contracts of sale of goods are concerned, damages under the second limb of *Hadley* v *Baxendale* are usually regarded simply as 'special damages' which are recognized by s. 54, though that section merely preserves the common law rule.

A failure by the buyer himself to take normal or reasonable precautions may be a *novus actus interveniens* which prevents the seller being responsible for the ultimate consequences of his breach. For instance, in *Lambert* v *Lewis*[90] a farmer bought a towing coupling from a retail seller. The coupling was defective so that the seller was guilty of a breach of the implied terms under the Sale of Goods Act. But the farmer continued to use the coupling even though he was or should have been aware that it was defective. When the coupling gave way, causing an accident in which the plaintiff was injured, it was held that the farmer could not claim an indemnity from the seller in respect of his own liability to the plaintiff. If, however, the seller warrants the quality or fitness of the goods in such terms as to indicate that there is no need for the buyer to examine or check upon the continued safety of the goods, and the buyer is (despite this warranty) held liable to a third party for injury caused by the goods so warranted, then the buyer could expect to recover a complete indemnity from the seller.[91]

Again, where a seller delivered some yarn to the buyer at the docks in damaged cartons, it was held that the seller was not responsible for the very much greater damage done to the goods as a result of being shipped in the damaged cartons.[92] The buyer's agents had handled the goods and should have appreciated that the cartons were not fit for shipment. Thus the buyer's damages were limited to the difference between the value of the damaged cartons and the value of undamaged cartons. He was unable to recover for the damage done to the goods while at sea as a result of being shipped in those cartons. But again, if the seller had warranted the cartons in such terms as to lead the buyer to suppose that there was no need for him to have the cartons further examined or inspected, it would seem clear that the seller would have been responsible for all the ultimate damage.

In consumer cases, where goods are bought for use, there is now no difficulty in obtaining damages for inconvenience and even disappointment and distress in appropriate cases. In *Jackson* v *Chrysler Acceptances Ltd*[93] the plaintiff bought a new car from the defendants, informing them that he specifically wanted to take it abroad for his holiday. Owing to repeated breakdowns as a result of defects in the car, the plaintiff's holiday was ruined. It was held that he was entitled to damages for this, in

---

89 *Kemp* v *Intasun Holidays Ltd* [1987] 2 FTLR 234.
90 [1982] AC 225.
91 *Lambert* v *Lewis*, see last note.
92 *Commercial Fibres (Ireland) Ltd* v *Zabaida* [1975] 1 Lloyd's Rep 27.
93 [1978] RTR 474.

addition to normal damages for the defects in the car. In *Bernstein* v *Pamson Motors (Golders Green) Ltd*,[94] where a new car broke down on a motorway, and the plaintiff and his wife had to summon emergency assistance, he recovered as damages (1) the cost of wasted petrol; (2) the cost of the plaintiff and his wife getting home by alternative transport; (3) damages for vexation and distress for the ruined day's outing; and (4) loss of the use of the car while it was being repaired. He would also have been entitled to the cost of the repairs and the emergency services, if these had not already been borne by the defendants.[95]

Although the Court of Appeal denied that damages for breach of contract can ever include an item for 'mental distress',[96] damages for vexation and disappointment and distress continued to be regularly awarded in minor consumer cases, often in the County Courts, or before County Court District Judges sitting as arbitrators. (Many such cases are reported every year in *Current Law*.) Moreover, in *Farley* v *Skinner*[97] where a surveyor was specifically asked to advise whether a holiday property the claimant was proposing to buy could be affected by aircraft noise, the House of Lords held that the claimant was entitled to non-pecuniary damages when it turned out after the claimant had bought the property that it was indeed affected by aircraft noise.[98]

A different type of consequential loss is encountered where the goods are bought for resale, and that is where the buyer has resold and delivered the goods to a sub-buyer who later has claimed damages against him for the defects in the goods. We have already seen that, in the usual course of events, sub-sales are ignored in claims under ss. 53(3) and 53A and claims of this kind therefore are normally treated as claims for 'special damages' under the second limb of *Hadley* v *Baxendale*, which requires proof of special knowledge of the probability of resale. But the buyer's burden of proof here is lighter than where he claims similar damages in an action for non-delivery, because he need only show that sub-sales were contemplated as a reasonable probability and need not go on to show (as it seems he must in the non-delivery cases) that he had contracted to resell the specific goods to sub-buyers. Once it is shown that the seller should have contemplated that the goods were bought for resale, any damages and costs paid to the sub-buyer as a result of defects of quality can be properly regarded as special damage recoverable under the second limb of *Hadley* v *Baxendale*.[99] But it has been stressed that in order that the buyer should be able to claim such damages and costs it is an overriding requirement that the subcontracts should have been made on the same terms and conditions as the first contract. For, clearly, if the buyer chooses to resell the goods on more onerous terms or with more extensive warranties, he cannot fix liability on his seller for damages he

---

94 [1987] 2 All ER 220.
95 Note also that if the buyer is entitled to reject the car, he can recover his full price and damages in addition, see p. 505 *et seq*, above.
96 *Bliss* v *South East Thames Regional Health Authority* [1987] ICR 700.
97 [2001] UKHL 49.
98 Note that in Scotland damages may be awarded for 'trouble and inconvenience', including in commercial cases – see *Webster & Co* v *Cramond Iron Co* (1875) 2 R 752; *Smith* v *Park* 1980 SLT (Sh Ct) 62; *Gunn* v *NCB* 1982 SLT 526.
99 But a buyer claiming damages for breach of condition as to quality cannot of course tender as evidence of his loss the amount paid by him to his sub-buyers as damages for non-delivery: *Aryeh* v *Lawrence Kostoris & Son Ltd* [1967] 1 Lloyd's Rep 63; *Danecroft Jersey Mills* v *Criegee, The Times*, 14 April 1987.

has had to pay in respect of these more onerous terms or more extensive warranties. The law on this topic was well summed up by Branson J in *Kasler & Cohen* v *Slavouski*:[100]

> If a man has sold goods to another in such circumstances as to fix him with special knowledge of the purpose for which those goods are being bought, and that other sells them on the same terms and conditions and then is subjected to an action because the goods do not come up to the contract quality, or for any other reason entitling him to claim damages upon such contract, the first purchaser is entitled, if he has acted reasonably in defending the action and has yet been cast in damages and costs, to claim from his seller not only the damages but also the costs he has had to pay.[101]

And if the buyer reasonably settles a claim made against him by the sub-buyer, the amount paid under such a settlement is prima facie the measure of damages recoverable from the seller, and is in any event the upper limit. But it is open to the seller to contest the amount and to show that the sum paid was excessive, for he is of course not bound by the settlement to which he was not party.[102] Moreover, the buyer still has to show that there was a breach of contract by the seller; the settlement is only admissible to show the prima facie level of damages once liability is proved or established.[103]

Another type of case in which sub-sales may be taken into account, at least indirectly, is illustrated by *GKN Centrax Gears Ltd* v *Matbro Ltd*.[104] Here it was held that the buyers could recover damages in respect of the loss of repeat orders from customers to whom they had resold defective goods supplied by the sellers. So long as such losses are within the contemplation of the parties, no question of principle is raised by a claim of this nature.

DAMAGES IN TORT

In English law, where the property and the immediate right to possession have passed to the buyer he may have, in addition to his remedies in contract, an action in tort for conversion. As between the parties to the contract, the action in tort has no advantages and is rarely used. The buyer cannot get higher damages by suing in tort than in contract, even where the measure of damages in the former case would normally be the higher,[105] nor can he obtain a decree of specific restitution except in cases where he could obtain a decree of specific performance.[106] The only advantage to the buyer of the action in tort is that it avails against third parties who have meddled with, or

---

100 [1928] 1 KB 78, 85.
101 Cf. *Bostock & Co Ltd* v *Nicholsons & Co Ltd* [1904] 1 KB 725; *Dexters* v *Hill Crest Oil Co Ltd* [1926] 1 KB 348, 359 per Scrutton LJ. If the sub-sales are not on exactly the same terms, it is uncertain if the buyer can claim damages paid to the sub-buyer in respect of defects for which the seller would have been liable. According to Devlin J in *Biggin & Co* v *Permanite Ltd* [1951] 1 KB 422 the answer is 'Yes', but with qualifications.
102 *Biggin & Co Ltd* v *Permanite Ltd* [1951] 2 KB 314.
103 *Fletcher & Stewart Ltd* v *Peter Jay & Partners* (1976) 17 Build LR 38.
104 [1976] 2 Lloyd's Rep 555.
105 *The Arpad* [1934] P 189. In Australia a buyer has been held entitled to exemplary damages for wrongful seizure of goods delivered to him (*Healing Sales Pty Ltd* v *Inglis Electrix Pty Ltd* (1968) 121 CLR 584), but it is doubtful if such damages could be awarded in England under *Rookes* v *Barnard* [1964] AC 1129. And note that (in a different context) the Court of Appeal has indicated that the amount of damages recoverable does not depend on whether the claimant's (pursuer's) course of action is in contract or tort – see *Parsons Ltd* v *Uttley Ingham*, p. 550.
106 *Cohen* v *Roche* [1927] 1 KB 169.

caused damage to, the goods at a time when the buyer had the property in the goods.

A buyer of goods which are imported from overseas is usually entitled to sue the carrier for damage done to the goods at sea, subject to the restrictions on liability contained in the Hague-Visby Rules as laid down in the Carriage of Goods by Sea Act 1971. Even in these cases, however, the buyer will rarely need to rely on his property in the goods as a basis for his claim. The reason for this is that by virtue of the Carriage of Goods by Sea Act 1992, the contract of carriage is actually transferred to the buyer when the bills of lading are transferred to him. This gives the buyer in most cases a right to sue for damage done from the time of the original shipment of the goods, since they would have been covered by the contract of carriage from that time. The buyer will, of course, have his recovery limited to the amount permitted under the Hague-Visby Rules.[107] It has been held by the House of Lords that the buyer cannot sue the carrier in tort in respect of damage done at a time before he became owner of the goods.[108] Nor, presumably, can he avoid the limitations of liability imposed by the Hague-Visby Rules by suing in tort *after* he becomes owner.[109]

It remains unsettled whether a buyer who does have the property at the relevant time, and sues the carrier for damages in tort, will always find his tort action subject to the limitations on contractual liability imposed by the Carriage of Goods by Sea Act 1971. No doubt, where the contract of carriage is transferred to the buyer – as it usually is – the tort action will become subject to the terms of the contract, including the statutory regime in the 1971 Act. But if there should be some rare case in which the contract of carriage is not transferred although the buyer has acquired the property, it may be that the 1971 Act will not restrict the buyer's action in tort. In this event, there would be very clear advantages in suing in tort; but it is certain that a sequence of successful actions of that nature would rapidly lead to legislative amendment of the 1971 Act.

DAMAGES FOR MISREPRESENTATION

In a work of this nature it is unnecessary to make more than a brief reference to the possibility of an action for damages for misrepresentation. In English law, such an action lay at common law for fraud, but under s. 2(1) of the Misrepresentation Act, damages may be obtained also for a misrepresentation unless the representor proves he had reasonable grounds to believe, and did believe up to the time the contract was made, that the acts represented were true. Moreover, under s. 2(2) of the Act, the court may award damages even for innocent misrepresentation, in lieu of rescinding the contract. There are advantages in making a claim for damages for misrepresentation in the alternative to a claim for breach of express warranty. The remedy created by the Act is tortious, and the damages are to be calculated according to the rules for tort.[110] The claimant can recover the loss (including consequential loss) he incurred by entering the contract.[111] He cannot recover loss

---

107 See Carriage of Goods by Sea Act 1971.
108 *Leigh & Sillivan Ltd* v *Aliakmon Shipping Co Ltd (The Aliakmon)* [1986] AC 785.
109 See [1986] AC 785, 801.
110 *Sharneyford Supplies Ltd* v *Edge* [1986] Ch 128, 169; *Royscot Trust Ltd* v *Rogerson* [1991] 2 QB 297; *Pankhania* v *London Borough of Hackney* 22 January 2004 (unreported).
111 *Davis & Co (Wines) Ltd* v *Afa-Minerva (EMI) Ltd* [1976] 2 Lloyd's Rep 27; a curious decision – see Taylor (1982) 45 MLR 139.

of profits, but he can recover the difference between the purchase price and the value the goods should have had if the representation had been true,[112] and he can recover profits which would have been made had the misrepresentation not been made, and the plaintiff entered into an alternative contract.[113] Moreover, the remoteness rules applicable are those of the tort of deceit, and are thus not limited by foreseeability.[114]

In Scots law, delictual damages may be recovered for fraud and negligent misrepresentation, including pre-contractual negligent misrepresentation, under s. 10 of the Law Reform (Miscellaneous Provisions) (Scotland) Act 1985.

REMEDIES AVAILABLE TO A BUYER IN BREACH

English law

Obviously a buyer who is himself in breach of contract has no right to sue for damages; but buyers sometimes pay, or agree to pay, part or all of the price of the goods in advance; and important and difficult questions may arise with regard to such advance payments if the buyer subsequently fails to fulfil his contract and the seller accepts this as a discharge of the whole contract.

If the price, or part of it, has actually been paid in advance and the contract is then abandoned because of the buyer's breach the seller may, of course, claim damages for non-acceptance from the buyer. But the amount paid by the buyer may greatly exceed any damages recoverable by the seller. In *Dies* v *British International Mining etc Corp*[115] the buyers contracted to buy goods to a total value of £270,000 and paid £100,000 before the agreed delivery date. The buyers then failed to take the goods or pay the balance of the price, and the sellers treated this as discharging the whole contract. The buyers sued to recover their advance payments, and this claim was upheld by Stable, J, though the buyers did not dispute that the sellers were entitled to damages which were set-off against the £100,000.

On the other hand, it has always been held that payments by way of earnest only, that is by way of forfeitable deposit, are not recoverable by the party in breach. The distinction between a part-payment which is thus recoverable by the buyer, and a deposit which is not, is said to depend on the intention of the parties. Was it the intention that the amount paid in advance should be forfeited if the buyer refused or failed to complete the purchase? In practice, contracts often fail to indicate whether such advance payments are forfeitable or not, so the question has to be answered by looking to the customs of the trade, and also to the amount of the part-payment. Forfeitable deposits of up to 10 per cent of the price are not uncommon (indeed, almost invariable in the case of contracts for the sale of land and houses); and it is well established that prima facie deposits of this amount are not recoverable by the buyer if he is in breach, even if the seller resells without loss after the buyer's

---

112 *Naughton and another* v *O'Callaghan* [1990] 3 All ER 191 – it will be necessary to show, however, that the fall in market value is not simply due to a market trend.
113 *East* v *Maurer* [1991] 2 All ER 733.
114 *Royscot Trust Ltd* v *Rogerson* [1991] 2 QB 297.
115 [1939] 1 KB 724.

breach.[116] The law relating to penalties, it has been insisted, has no application to this situation.[117]

But in the *Dies* case the amount was not only very large in itself but was also about 37 per cent of the total price. It seems, therefore, that such very large part-payments will not be regarded as forfeitable deposits, but will prima facie be recoverable according to the true construction of the contract, if the buyer fails to complete.

Unfortunately, the position as set out above is greatly complicated by three further problems which often cause great difficulty. The first of these difficulties concerns the question whether the above rules also apply where the sum payable in advance is not in fact paid. If the buyer was required by the contract to pay a deposit which would have been forfeited on breach, but he failed to pay it, can the seller sue for the deposit, irrespective of the amount of damage which he has suffered? Although the point is by no means free from doubt, the general view seems to be that nothing turns on the accidental fact of the time of the actual payment: if the money should have been paid before breach, it can be sued for after breach.[118] The result gives cause for unease since an action to recover more than the plaintiff has lost through the breach of contract must inevitably look penal. The present rules are usually justified by saying that the buyer should not be advantaged by the fact that he has broken his contract and failed to pay the deposit when he should have paid it, but this often happens when the buyer fails to pay the price, because prima facie the seller's remedy is only an action for non-delivery, and not for the price itself. It must also be remembered that a contract of sale of goods is different from other contracts in that rejection of the goods does to some degree work a retrospective rescission of the contract – the goods revest in the seller, and his duty to deliver conforming goods can no longer be enforced by the buyer. It is also disturbing that the seller is able to recover damages for a totally non-existent 'loss' in this situation, without any regard to the law relating to penalties. Since there is no real loss, the damages must inevitably be penal – the purpose of the action is to punish the buyer for his breach in not paying the deposit, and the denial of the relevance of the rules as to penalties rests simply on reiteration rather than on any rational justification.

The current rules were pressed even further in *Damon Cia Naviera* v *Hapag-Lloyd (The Blankenstein)*.[119] In this case the buyers had agreed to sign a contract for the purchase of three ships for $2.36m. The written contract, if signed, would have required the buyers to pay a deposit of 10 per cent of the price ($236,000) which was expressly stated to be forfeitable in the event of non-completion by the buyers. The buyers failed to sign the written contract, or to pay the deposit, and the sellers sued for damages. The sellers had resold the ships for $2.295m, and thus suffered a loss on resale of $65,000 which was plainly recoverable once it had been decided that the buyers were guilty of a breach of contract. But the sellers argued that they were entitled to much more than this; they sought damages representing the amount of the unpaid deposit, on the ground that if the buyers had signed the written contract they would have had to pay the deposit, which would have been irrecoverable. Because

---

116 *Howe* v *Smith* (1884) 27 Ch D 89.
117 *Linggi Plantations Ltd* v *Jagatheesan* [1972] 1 MLJ 89 (PC).
118 *Dewar* v *Mintoft* [1912] 2 KB 373.
119 [1985] 1 All ER 475. Leave to appeal to the HL was given, but no appeal was pursued.

the written contract here had never been signed, the sellers did not sue for the deposit itself; their claim was for damages for non-payment of the deposit. A majority of the Court of Appeal upheld this claim on the ground that the sellers were entitled to be put in the position they would have been in if the contract had been performed, but Goff LJ dissented on the ground that if the whole contract had been performed the sellers would not have obtained more than the total purchase price. Effectively, the sellers were claiming, not to be put in the position they would have been in if the whole contract had been performed, but in the position they would have been in if the buyers had first signed the written contract, and then defaulted. Whatever the merits of these somewhat refined arguments, the net result seems indefensible. The sellers were, in effect, awarded damages far above their loss.

The converse case concerning this point raises no problem. If the amount in question is a genuine part-payment rather than a forfeitable deposit – so that if, as in *Dies*, the money had actually been paid in advance, it would have been recoverable by the buyer – then it must follow *a fortiori* that if the buyer has failed to pay it, the seller cannot sue for it.

The second major difficulty concerning the above rules arises from the possibility of equitable relief. Where a seller sues to recover an agreed penalty payable for breach by the buyer, the buyer may try to set up by way of defence the standard equitable doctrines restricting the enforcement of penalty clauses. Under these rules, which apply, of course, irrespective of the parties' actual intention, and therefore override the freedom of contract of the parties, a clause designed to operate *in terrorem*, rather than to provide for a genuine pre-estimate of the damages, is a penalty clause rather than a liquidated damages clause;[120] and penalty clauses are unenforceable. But as we have already seen, it has several times been insisted that the doctrine of penalties has no application to these clauses for the forfeiture of deposits.[121] Moreover, the House of Lords has shown a strong disinclination to extend the principles of equitable relief to forfeitures in commercial contracts.[122] But there have been suggestions that a different form of equitable relief may be available – that is, relief to enable the buyer to complete the contract late, if he is able to pay in full all the sums due plus any costs incurred by the seller.[123] It is also well established that a forfeiture of a property right is challengeable under the penalty rules,[124] and it seems the barest technicality to insist that a deposit is a contractual right and not a property right.

A third problem arising from the rules about deposits and part payments has been touched on earlier,[125] and it stems from the decision of the House of Lords in *Johnson* v *Agnew*[126] which for the first time laid down a much more clear and precise demarcation line between *termination* of a contract for breach and rescission *ab initio* for

---

120 The leading case is *Dunlop* v *New Garage* [1915] AC 79.
121 See *Linggi Plantations Ltd* v *Jagatheesan*, above, n. 117, but cf. *Public Works Commission* v *Hills* [1906] AC 368.
122 See, e.g., *Scandinavian Trading Tanker Co* v *Flota Petrolera* [1983] 2 AC 694; *Sport International Bussum* v *Inter-Footwear* [1984] 1 WLR 776.
123 See *Stockloser* v *Johnson* [1954] 1 QB 476; *Barton, Thompson & Co Ltd* v *Stapling Machines Co* [1966] Ch 499.
124 *BICC* v *Burndy Ltd* [1985] Ch 232.
125 See above, pp. 22 and 486.
126 [1980] AC 367.

fraud or other invalidating cause. A termination does not operate retrospectively in the same way that rescission *ab initio* does. So it may seem that if the buyer pays part of the price in advance, or is bound to do so and fails, his obligation to do this remains binding on him, despite the subsequent termination of the contract. But if that were the law, then the decision in *Dies* would be wrong, and a buyer who paid part of the price in advance – no matter how large a part, or indeed, even if he paid the whole price in advance – would be unable to recover it if he were subsequently guilty of non-acceptance of the goods.[127]

This, indeed, seems to have been the conclusion which the House of Lords were inclining towards in *Hyundai Heavy Industries Co Ltd* v *Papadopoulos*,[128] which has been discussed earlier. It was here held that instalments payable by the buyer of a ship while the ship was under construction remained payable, despite the seller's subsequent decision to treat the non-payment as a repudiation and to terminate the whole contract.[129] Doubt was cast on the decision in *Dies* though in the end it was distinguished rather than overruled. It was said that if *Dies* was correct, it only applied to a pure contract of sale and not to a contract to *manufacture* and sell goods on grounds which have been given earlier.[130] Since then, the Court of Appeal has suggested that the difference between *Hyundai* and *Dies* lies in the fact that there was a total failure of consideration in the second case but not in the first.[131] On this view, a prepayment (not being a forfeitable deposit) will be recoverable by the buyer – or not payable – where there is a total failure of consideration, and in an ordinary contract of sale there will be such a total failure of consideration whenever the goods are not delivered or accepted, from whatever cause, even if the seller is also the manufacturer.[132]

Scots law

In Scots law, the principle of mutuality of contract will disable a party in breach from claiming performance of the contract from the other party.[133] But the contract-breaker may have other remedies in respect of part-performance under the contract.[134] Whether there is also a claim for restitution of advance payments was left unclear by *Zemhunt Holdings Ltd* v *Control Securities plc*.[135] At first instance, the

---

127 If the whole price is paid in advance, it may be arguable that a non-acceptance by the buyer could never be sufficiently serious to justify treating the contract as repudiated; but though this is improbable, it cannot be said that such a result could never be justified.
128 [1980] 1 WLR 1129. But another difficulty which did not actually arise in the *Hyundai* case is that the mere fact that the obligation to pay the price is binding on the buyer does not mean he can be sued for the price. The seller's remedy for a breach of the buyer's duty to pay the price is not in general an action for the price, but an action for damages; see s. 49(1), above, p. 481, which was not mentioned in the *Hyundai* case, presumably because in that case each instalment was payable on 'a day certain' within the meaning of s. 49.
129 Of course, on any view, instalments only payable after the date on which the contract was terminated ceased to be payable as a result of termination, or rather, never became payable.
130 Above, p. 22.
131 *Rover International Ltd* v *Cannon Film Sales Ltd* [1987] 1 WLR 1597; see the very helpful article by Beatson, in (1981) 97 LQR 389 and his note in (1989) 105 LQR 179.
132 As in the *Fibrosa* case [1943] AC 32 where there was a total failure of consideration even though the contract was for the sale of machinery to be manufactured by the seller.
133 McBryde, *Contract*, 2nd edn, 2001, paras 20.44–20.61.
134 See MacQueen, 1994 JR 137, 149–66.
135 1992 SC 58.

Lord Ordinary (Marnoch) held that the *condictio causa data causa non secuta* could not be invoked by a contract-breaker; but in the Second Division the advance payment was held to be a deposit which was forfeited as a result of the breach, making the enrichment question irrelevant. However, an obiter dictum by Lord Morison favoured the contract-breaker's claim in principle, and it is submitted that this was correct. That claim will of course have to be set off against the other party's damages in respect of the breach. *Zemhunt* is also illustrative of the absence in Scots law of any control over forfeiture clauses, although the Scottish Law Commission has proposed reform in this area.[136] Finally, in *Lloyds Bank* v *Bamberger*,[137] the Second Division rejected the extreme interpretation of the *Hyundai* case to the effect that rights arising before termination of a contract are unaffected because termination is only prospective in its effects. The Division preferred the view of Lord Fraser in *Hyundai*, that the payments in that case were not truly advances but were rather to maintain cash flow against work being done, and also affirmed that genuine advances fell to be returned after termination.

---

136 *Penalty Clauses* (Scot Law Com. No. 171, 1999).
137 1993 SC 570.

SPECIFIC PERFORMANCE OR IMPLEMENT

The buyer, but not the seller,[1] may invoke the discretion of the court and ask for a decree that the contract be specifically performed. This remedy of specific performance is separate from that conferred by s. 48E(2)[2] dealt with above.[3] The right with which we are concerned here is regulated by s. 52 which says:

(1) In any action for breach of contract to deliver specific or ascertained goods the court may, if it thinks fit, on the plaintiff's application, by its judgment or decree direct that the contract shall be performed specifically, without giving the defendant the option of retaining the goods on payment of damages.
(2) The plaintiff's application may be made at any time before judgment or decree.
(3) The judgment or decree may be unconditional, or on such terms and conditions as to damages, payment of the price, and otherwise, as seems just to the court.

Section 52(4) goes on to say that these provisions are to be deemed supplementary to, and not in derogation of, the right of specific implement in Scotland. The significance of this is that, as a number of cases have affirmed recently, the basis of specific implement is distinct from that of specific performance. In Scotland, implement is a right and, although this is subject to the equitable control of the court, the exercise of that control is coloured by the different starting point. Thus the Scottish courts have specifically enforced 'keep open' clauses in leases[4] and have not followed the judgment of the House of Lords in *Co-operative Insurance Society Ltd* v *Argyll Stores (Holdings) Ltd*.[5] In theory, therefore, there might be enforcement of a contract for unascertained goods, although the courts have generally held against this on the basis that the buyer cannot show any reason for preferring to obtain his goods by this route (*pretium affectionis*) rather than buying replacements on the market at the seller's expense.[6]

Specific goods, as we have seen, are defined by s. 62 as being goods 'identified and agreed upon at the time the contract is made', and it has been said that 'ascertained

---

1 Although the seller has not in name a right to a decree of specific performance, he does of course sometimes have a right to sue for the price, which is much the same thing. If the seller sues for and obtains payment of the price, the title to the goods and the right to possession will vest in the buyer by satisfaction, if they have not yet vested in him already.
2 Added by the Sale and Supply of Goods to Consumers Regulations 2002, SI 2002/3045.
3 See p. 525 *et seq.*
4 *Retail Park Investments Ltd* v *Royal Bank of Scotland* 1996 SC 227; *Highland & Universal Properties Ltd* v *Safeway Properties Ltd* 2000 SC 297.
5 [1998] AC 1.
6 See, e.g., *Union Electric Co* v *Holman* 1913 SC 954.

goods' in this context probably means goods 'identified in accordance with the agreement after the time a contract of sale is made'.[7]

Section 52 applies whether or not the property has passed to the buyer,[8] although if the property has passed the buyer has the option of claiming in the alternative a decree of specific restitution in an action of conversion. But even here he cannot ask for such a decree as of right. This was formerly so as a matter of common law[9] and is now expressly provided for in s. 3 of the Torts (Interference with Goods) Act 1977. In other words, the remedy rests entirely within the discretion of the court and will not be granted in respect of chattels of no special importance, where damages would be an adequate remedy. But where a chattel is of peculiar importance and of practically unique value to the plaintiff, the court will grant the necessary decree.[10]

The English courts still seem most unwilling to use this jurisdiction, still less to extend it. In one case,[11] for example, the Court of Appeal refused to order specific delivery of a machine manufactured by the defendants, although it was over 220 tons in weight, cost some £270,000 and could only be bought in the market with a nine to twelve months' delivery date. It was formerly thought that a contract for the sale of a ship would be specifically enforceable almost as a matter of course, because a ship is a pretty unique chattel, but even this proposition was rejected in *CN Marine Inc v Stena Line*.[12] According to Parker J in this case, a buyer of a ship is not even prima facie entitled to a decree of specific performance, nor does mere inconvenience to the buyer or the possibility of remote loss justify such a decree. It must be shown that the ship was of peculiar importance to the plaintiff, in that the design was especially suited to his needs, or something of that kind.

Although the statutory provisions referred to above seem to make it immaterial whether the property has passed to the buyer or not, it seems that the courts are still more inclined to protect a property owner than someone with a bare contractual right. So where goods were sold and property had clearly passed, but the sellers – though claiming no contractual or proprietary rights over the goods – wanted to use them to satisfy other clients and pay damages to the buyer, the court granted an interim injunction to restrain the sellers from delivering the goods to the other clients.[13] In this case it was held that it was no defence for the sellers to show that damages would be an adequate remedy, an approach which seems very different from that adopted where the buyer actually seeks a decree of specific performance. Yet the result of this case must surely have been that the sellers actually delivered the goods to the buyer.

Where the property has not passed to the buyer, there can be no question of conversion and the only claim which can be made is on the contract. Until recently it was generally thought that the court had no power to grant specific performance of a contract for the sale of goods as yet unidentified, and that a contract for the sale of an

---

7 *Re Wait* [1927] 1 Ch 606, 630 per Atkin LJ; *In Re London Wine Co (Shippers) Ltd* (1986) PCC 121.
8 *Re Wait* [1927] 1 Ch 606, 617 per Lord Hanworth MR.
9 *Cohen v Roche* [1927] 1 KB 169, 180–1 per McCardie J.
10 *Behnke v Bede Shipping Co Ltd* [1927] 1 KB 649.
11 *Société des Industries Metallurgiques SA v Bronx Engineering Co Ltd* [1975] 1 Lloyd's Rep 465.
12 [1982] 2 Lloyd's Rep 336.
13 *Redler Grain Silos Ltd v BICC Ltd* [1982] 1 Lloyd's Rep 435.

unidentified part of a specific whole was not a contract for the sale of specific or ascertained goods, of which specific performance could be ordered under s. 52.[14]

But some doubt is thrown on these traditional ideas by *Sky Petroleum Ltd* v *VIP Petroleum Ltd*,[15] where the plaintiffs obtained an interlocutory injunction to restrain the defendants from breaking a contract to supply the plaintiffs with all their petroleum requirements for ten years. Goulding J treated the injunction as in effect a decree of specific performance, but went on to hold that the general rule was inapplicable where damages would clearly not be an adequate remedy. In the case before him there was a real danger that the plaintiffs would be forced out of business if the defendants broke their contract in the very peculiar circumstances then holding. This decision may suggest that a buyer can sometimes obtain a decree of specific performance outside the circumstances contemplated by s. 52, by invoking the residuary equity jurisdiction of the court, but the point remains unsettled.[16]

A buyer who gives the seller reason to believe that he will only claim damages and not specific performance may be estopped from changing his mind if the seller has changed his position by acting to his detriment in reliance on this belief.[17]

In addition to s. 52, under the Sale and Supply of Goods to Consumers Regulations[18] a consumer has a right to demand repair or replacement.[19] It remains to be seen how this will work in practice, but in principle, a consumer could have a right specifically to enforce this right.

---

14 *Re Wait* [1927] 1 Ch 606; *In Re London Wine Co (Shippers) Ltd* (1986) PCC 121. See above, pp. 345 and 351.
15 [1974] 1 All ER 954.
16 In *In Re London Wine (Shippers) Co Ltd*, above, n. 14, Oliver J was inclined to think that the contract in the *Sky Petroleum* case was not strictly a contract of sale of goods, but 'a long-term supply contract under which successive sales would arise if orders were placed and accepted' (see PCC 121, 149), but he went on to hold that even if *Sky Petroleum* was evidence of a jurisdiction to grant specific performance outside s. 52, it was still not possible to grant a decree where the goods were not ascertained, and the buyer had no proprietary interest in the goods.
17 *Meng Leong Development Pte* v *Jip Hong Trading Co Pte* [1985] AC 511.
18 SI 2002/3045.
19 See p. 525 *et seq.*

INDEX

Gift, contract of sale distinguished, 7, 11–12
Good title, duty to pass
  Rowland v *Divall*, rule in, 114–15,
    116–17, 119
  seller's right to sell the goods *see* Seller's
    right to sell the goods
  warranty, freedom from encumbrances
    and quiet possession, 19–122
    implied statutory term, 119
    scope, uncertain, 120–1
Goods
  existing, 84
  future, 84
  meaning of, 77
  sources of law, covering, 3–6
  specific goods, meaning, 108
  unascertained, 85–6
    meaning of, 332
Goods, existence of
  construction of the contract and, 103–4
  implied condition precedent and, 104
  no implied condition as to, 103–11
  perish–meaning of, 109–11, 360
  perishing of goods, 108–9, 361–2
  risk, of buyer, 104
  specific goods, meaning of, 108
  warranty by seller, 104–8
Guarantees
  extended, 301–4
    Competition Commission report and
      recommendations, 302–4
    risks covered, 301
  manufacturers' guarantee, 297–304
    definition, 297
    ownership of goods, 298–9
    Sale of Consumer Goods and Associated
      Guaranteess Directive, 299–301
    Sale and Supply of Goods to
      Consumers Regulations, 299–301
  persons liable under, 299
  retailers', 298
  use of term, 297
  see also Directive on Certain Aspects of
    the Sale of Goods and Associated
    Guarantees

Hire-purchase
  buyer in possession and transfer by
    non-owner, 400–1
  Consumer Credit Act and, 17–18

historical development of, 14–17
  motor vehicles, transfer by non-owner,
    410–13
  sale, contract of sale distinguished from,
    7, 13–18
Hire-purchase agreements, 224

Import licences *see* Export and import
  licences
Innominate terms *see under* Obligations,
  types created
Insolvencey
  reservation of title clause and, 476–7
  unpaid seller's lien, 454–5
Instalments
  buyer's right to reject goods, 501
  delivery of goods by, 140
  rejection of defective, 503–5
  unpaid seller's lien on contract for, 453
Intellectual property, e-commerce, 72–4

Jus quaesitum tertio doctrine, 76

Law Reform Committee, transfer of title by
  non-owner, recommendations for
  reform, 414–15
Lien, 452–9
  buyer obtaining possession, 456, 457
  of carrier, 465
  credit, goods sold on, 453–4
  delivery of goods to carrier or other
    bailee, 455, 456–7
  insolvency of buyer, 454–5
  instalment contracts, 453
  loss of, 456–9
  possession of goods, essential, 455, 457,
    459
  price paid or tendered, 456
  of seller, problems of, 407
  storage charges, 455–6
  waiver of, 456, 458
Loan on security
  contract of sale distinguished, 7, 19–21
  substance considered not form of, 19–20
Lock-out agreement, 32–3

Mail order, 53–4
  see also E-commerce
Manufacturers' guarantee, ownership of
  goods, 298–9